American Medical Schools
and the Practice of Medicine

About the Author

William Rothstein is Associate Professor of Sociology at the University of Maryland Baltimore County. He is the author of *American Physicians in the Nineteenth Century: From Sects to Science* and other publications in medical history, the sociology of professions, and the sociology of work.

American Medical Schools and the Practice of Medicine

A HISTORY

William G. Rothstein

New York   Oxford
OXFORD UNIVERSITY PRESS
1987

Oxford University Press

Oxford   New York   Toronto
Delhi   Bombay   Calcutta   Madras   Karachi
Petaling Jaya   Singapore   Hong Kong   Tokyo
Nairobi   Dar es Salaam   Cape Town
Melbourne   Auckland

and associated companies in
Beirut   Berlin   Ibadan   Nicosia

Published by Oxford University Press, Inc.,
200 Madison Avenue, New York, New York 10016

Oxford is a registered trademark of Oxford University Press

Library of Congress Cataloging-in-Publication Data

Rothstein, William G.
American medical schools and the practice of medicine.

Includes bibliographical references and index.
1. Medical education—United States—History.
2. Medicine—United States—History. I. Title.
[DNLM: 1. Education, Medical—history—United States.
2. History of Medicine, Modern—United States.
3. Schools, Medical—history—United States. W 19 R847a]
R745.R68   1987   610'.7'1173   86-23667
ISBN 0-19-504186-0

2 4 6 8 9 7 5 3 1

Printed in the United States of America
on acid-free paper

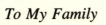

To My Family

Preface

The ability of medical schools to prepare students for the type of medical practice needed in the community has become a central issue in American medicine. This concern has arisen because of the emphasis of contemporary medical schools on research, the training of specialists, and the care of seriously ill patients who are unlike those seen in community practice.

One useful way to study how medical schools have prepared students for the practice of medicine is to examine it historically. A historical analysis can show when and how changes occurred in medical schools and examine their consequences. It can suggest reasons for the changes by relating the activities of medical schools to external factors like the practice of medicine, higher education, and government policies. That is the objective of this study.

This book continues my previous research published in *American Physicians in the Nineteenth Century* (Baltimore: Johns Hopkins University Press, 1972). Since that book was published, much valuable research in medical history has been made available in books, journal articles, and unpublished Ph.D. dissertations. That research and my research for this book have caused me to alter some of my previous conclusions. I believe this to be an inevitable and beneficial consequence of research.

No study of a subject as broad as the history of medical education can be comprehensive. This study does not deal with the founding or history of individual medical schools, the development of individual disciplines, or the contributions made at medical schools to clinical medicine and medical science. Nor has it fully analyzed the great differences that have always existed among medical schools.

In order to reduce the size of the manuscript, compromises were made in the use of notes. Many references not directly related to the topic under discussion were omitted. Frequently only one of several useful references was cited. In recognition of this problem, I have tried to cite references that would assist the reader seeking additional information.

I would like to express my gratitude to the National Endowment for the Humanities, whose fellowship enabled me to pursue this research beyond my original intentions. Research grants from the University of Maryland Baltimore County permitted a number of important analyses to be made. The UMBC library's Interlibrary Loan Services provided invaluable assistance in obtaining necessary materials. Dr. James Mohr, my colleague at UMBC, and Dr. Daniel Fox of the State University of New York at Stony Brook each read a substantial part of the manuscript and made many valuable suggestions. Brian Humble, Sue Volk, and John Schlimm provided diligent assistance in the quantitative and bibliographic aspects of the study. Interviews with Harry F. Dowling, John Mather of the Veteran's Administration, and John Dennis, Dean of the medical school at the University of Maryland, proved valuable. I would also like to express my appreciation to my family, friends, and colleagues for their patience, encouragement, and support.

Catonsville, Md.   W. G. R.
October, 1986

Contents

List of Tables

American Medical Schools
and the Practice of Medicine

The fact that each individual has a body and mind of his own, which give him uniqueness in structure and function and individuality in character and personality, has not yet been realized adequately. . . . The doctor must treat people, not diseases, and use every means possible at his disposal in order to attain his results. . . .

When a person consults a doctor, he does so because he thinks he has some disease. He expects the doctor to identify this enemy to his well-being and then to fight and destroy the intruder. The patient assumes that he has turned over to the doctor the onus of disposing of this opponent to him or, in other words, that the doctor has now taken on the fight with the disease as a substitute for him. . . .

This attitude of the public, of the doctor fighting the disease, is so frequently present that steps must be taken to correct it. It is not the doctor who fights the disease, it is the patient, the person in whom the disease occurs, who has to overcome its effects. The doctor is the auxiliary force who is brought in to help the person win the battle. He gives his services to the patient to the best of his ability, but he can never substitute for him. . . . In order to [best assist the patient], the doctor must know the human being both from a scientific standpoint and from personal experience. . . .

If the study of man is so essential for the doctor, and if the doctor treats the patient and not the disease, is our present system of medical education the best that can be devised to fulfill this purpose?

E. STANLEY RYERSON (1938)

I

METHOD OF ANALYSIS AND MEDICAL EDUCATION, 1750–1825

The beginnings of intellectual, religious and political movements are always difficult to discover. But the part played . . . by individual thought and action is always large and often predominant. Here and there events, men and books act as landmarks in the continuous stream of events. Economic movements are more confused. Their progress is like the slow growth of seeds scattered over a vast area. Endless obscure facts, in themselves almost insignificant, form great, confused wholes and mutually modify one another indefinitely. No one can hope to grasp them all, and when we pick out a few for description it is obvious that we must give up, together with some of the truth, the rather vain ambition of arriving at rigorous definitions and final explanations.

PAUL MANTOUX (1928)

1

Policy Making in Medical Schools

Medical schools today are being closely scrutinized. Questions have been raised about their educational policies, the activities of their faculty members, and the quality of care provided in their clinical facilities. The concern is due in part to the activities of the medical schools themselves, in part to their accountability for use of government funds, and in part to changes in the American health care system.

It is thus appropriate to examine the history of American medical schools to understand how the central issues in medical education have changed and how medical schools have responded to the changes. In this study, medical schools in each period have been placed in the context of that period. Their educational policies have been analyzed in terms of the state of medical practice of the time. Their educational standards have been compared to those of other institutions of higher education.

This chapter will develop a framework for the analysis by examining the major issues and groups involved in medical education. The casual reader may wish to know that this framework is not essential for understanding the historical narrative, and that each part of the narrative can be read independently.

Practical and Theoretical Approaches to Medical Education

Because medical education is designed to prepare students for employment as physicians after graduation, a fundamental pedagogical issue concerns how to balance the need to teach students the basic concepts of medical science with the need to train them in the practical skills needed to practice medicine. This becomes particularly difficult when the two bodies of knowledge are as intellectually demanding and as different as they are in medicine.

The science and practice of medicine, in their broadest sense, are concerned with the structure and functions of the human organism in health and disease, the causes of change from one to the other, the prevention of disease, and the means of restoring health when disease occurs. Medical science is concerned primarily with the first two of these, medical practice with the last three.

The epigraph preceding Part I is from E. Stanley Ryerson, "Health and Medical Education," *Journal of the Association of American Medical Colleges* 13 (1938): 1–3.

The epigraph for Part I is from Paul Mantoux, *The Industrial Revolution in the Eighteenth Century* (1928; reprint ed., New York: Harper, 1961), p. 42.

Medical practice also involves a social and economic relationship between a patient and a physician. The patient agrees to compensate the physician, either directly or through a third party. The physician agrees not only to treat the patient's disease, but also to understand how the disease and the treatments affect the patient's life. Thus, the practice of medicine goes beyond the application of scientific principles and includes judgments about the patient as a human being, judgments that constitute part of the "art of medicine."[1]

The great intellectual demands of each of the two aspects of medicine have posed a fundamental problem for medical education. William Pusey, a leading educator and clinician early in the twentieth century, observed: "It is not possible to give equal devotion to both and attain one's highest potential success with either. Both are too exacting; their demands are too large for a man to satisfy fully either one without failing somewhat to satisfy the other." Given the limited time available in the medical school curriculum, the only reasonable compromise is to reduce the time spent on one in order to provide adequate time for the other.[2]

A practical medical education would emphasize those aspects of medicine relevant to the prevailing illnesses in the community. It would be concerned with the sociology and psychology of patient and physician behavior, the economics of medical care, and the social organization of health care. Clinical training would emphasis ambulatory care and the most important kinds of hospital treatment.

A theoretically oriented medical education would emphasize the basic medical sciences and the basic concepts of the clinical specialties, including appropriate laboratory skills. The concepts of each discipline would be taught separately, emphasizing their distinctive features. Clinical training would consider the patient's medical problems abstracted from his personal situation. For example, a surgical patient would be used in teaching with little concern for his other health problems or the effect of the surgery on his daily life. In this case, the patient would be used in a manner analogous to a laboratory animal.

There are several advantages to a practical approach to medical education:

1. Students learn practical medicine in a systematic curriculum rather than by trial and error after graduation. They learn their skills under the close supervision of skilled faculty members, they can be drilled in the routines of practice, and their mastery of the material can be tested and, if deficient, corrected before they enter practice.

2. Medical students are highly motivated to learn practical medicine; they aspire to careers as physicians and want to learn to practice medicine correctly. They respond to the teaching of practical medicine enthusiastically and conscientiously. If they learn practical skills after graduation, they may use shortcuts and inappropriate techniques to save time and effort and may never learn thoroughness in clinical technique.

3. Patients are at risk when exposed to unskilled medical students or physicians. This risk can be minimized in medical schools by careful supervision of medical students by faculty members. If students graduate without a thorough training in practical medicine, the health and safety of their patients may be endangered.

A number of disadvantages also follow from the practical approach to medical education.

1. The practical aspects of medicine change rapidly and some of the students' education will become obsolete soon after they begin practice. They then will be left without the ability to educate themselves to maintain their skills.

2. Medicine involves a conceptual as well as a practical body of knowledge. Students need to learn why they are using certain techniques as well as how to use them properly. A practical education tends to deteriorate into the memorization of a number of techniques without understanding the rationale behind them.

3. Professionals need to know more than the techniques of their trade. They should be educated to understand the role of their profession in society and the nature and significance of health and medicine generally. These subjects can be relegated to a minor role in practical education.

A theoretical education is considered to have the following advantages to the student:

1. Students learn how clinical practice is based on the structure and functions of the human organism using the concepts and methods of the basic medical sciences.

2. An understanding of the basic medical sciences can be used by physicians to evaluate new developments in practical medicine after graduation.

3. Students learn a methodology of scientific research that teaches a systematic approach to the study of disease in human beings.

The theoretical approach also has a number of disadvantages:

1. Concepts in the basic sciences often change as frequently as practical techniques. An education based on the basic sciences may be no more durable than one based on more practical aspects of medicine.

2. The teaching of the basic concepts may become so abstracted from their practical applications that students fail to see the relationship between the two. This often occurs when those who teach the concepts are not familiar with their practical applications.

3. The goal of the basic medical sciences is to explain the structure and function of the human organism using concepts that are in turn physiological, biochemical, and ultimately molecular. This reductionism is often irrelevant and impractical from the perspective of medical practice. Physicians are not interested in the molecular changes that accompany disease; their interests remain at the level at which medical intervention operates.[3]

4. The methodologies of medical science and medical practice are fundamentally different. The goal of basic science research is explanatory: researchers wish to find the cause of a phenomenon which they are investigating. The goal of practical medicine is predictive: clinicians want to predict the future course of the patient's disease to decide on the need for medical management and the beneficial and undesirable effects of the possible treatments. Prediction and explanation are quite different and the skills appropriate for one may be inadequate for the other.[4]

The subjects of medical research and medical practice differ. Basic science researchers use laboratory animals or other organisms whose past histories and current status are carefully controlled and known to them. Clinicians deal with patients who vary greatly in their past histories, degree of sickness, and outside environments, much of which may be unknown to the physicians.

The type of data gathered by researchers and clinicians differ significantly. Researchers use standardized and sophisticated apparatus that lead to a concern with precision of measurement and complexity of technology. Clinicians use measures which are often crude, poorly standardized, and characterized by a large amount of observer variability. Their methods produce a highly probabilistic mode of thinking that draws inferences from a variety of data gathered in different ways and with varying levels of accuracy.

5. The concepts used in the basic sciences and practical medicine differ. Laboratory researchers describe disease in terms of structural changes observed in tissues and organs and usually disregard environmental influences. Clinicians supplement their use of structural changes with the signs and symptoms visible when examining a patient. They use environmental and social factors like the patient's occupation, family life, habits, and social class in diagnosis and treatment. Practitioners also often find structural descriptions of illness to be too limited for clinical purposes. Some patients with a particular disease may lead almost normal lives, while others are seriously disabled. Different patients with the same illness vary in their rates of recovery or deterioration. These differences are an essential part of clinical medicine that are not revealed by the concepts of the basic medical sciences.[5]

This analysis of the differences between the techniques used in the basic medical sciences and in clinical practice has shown that no single "scientific method" is applicable to all of medicine. The specific scientific method used depends on the nature of the data being studied. The education of medical students should therefore involve training in the techniques that they will use in their ultimate professional activities.

Other issues are also involved in choosing between an emphasis on a practical or theoretical education. The subjects included within each approach have changed repeatedly over time. Highly theoretical subjects in one era have become practical ones in another as a result of new developments in medicine. Practical subjects in one era have sometimes turned into theoretical ones, such as the study of a disease whose incidence has declined but which has remained of theoretical significance.

Physicians have disagreed over the practical or theoretical nature of particular aspects of medicine. Controversies have occurred over the practical significance and place in the medical school curriculum of specialties like psychiatry, rehabilitation medicine, preventive medicine, genetics, and public health.

Within the medical sciences, the demarcation between basic and applied science has been a long-standing source of controversy. Dowling has observed that the distinction between the two is an arbitrary one: "research occupies a continuous spectrum from the most basic to the most applied, and investigators often move from one point on the spectrum to another as the answers begin to come in." Furthermore, according to Seldin, basic medical science can only be defined in terms of the "frame of reference from which the problems emerge. In this light, what is 'basic' for biochemistry may be crude or even irrelevant when the problems are posed by issues arising from a clinical context." Blissett has suggested that the distinction between basic and applied science has been created by scientists to enable them to control the choice of research topics, rather than let business or government choose them.[6]

This discussion has endeavored to show that the strengths and weaknesses of the practical and theoretical approaches to medical education are evenly balanced. Consequently, the emphasis on one or the other approach at any period in the history of medical education cannot be justified by the claim that it was educationally more valuable. Instead, it is necessary to examine organizational decision making in medical schools to ascertain who makes such decisions and how they are made.

Organizational Decision Making in Medical Schools

Medical schools are formal organizations in that they have a division of labor and a hierarchy of organization roles with graded responsibility and authority. Two major theories of organizational decision making, among others, have been proposed for formal organizations.[7]

The traditional theory of decision making holds that the power to make decisions resides in the administrative hierarchy of the organization. Administrators are given formal authority to make decisions, and their decisions can be satisfactorily explained by an analysis of their goals and behavior. This approach has been ineffective in understanding educational policies in academic institutions. Cohen and March found that college administrators engaged in little planning, and that academic policy making was highly fragmented. They concluded: "Academic 'policy' is the accretion of hundreds of largely autonomous actions taken for different reasons, at different times, under different conditions, by different people in the college." They also found that the top administrators, college presidents, did not see "their interests as being heavily involved" in educational policy making and often avoided it.[8]

The hierarchical theory of decision making fails to consider the influence of the environment on the organization. All organizations survive by obtaining resources from the external environment. To obtain these resources, they must negotiate with outsiders in the marketplace in which they operate. A focus on individual decision makers in the organizational hierarchy fails to consider the power of those outside the organization to affect internal decisions.[9]

The hierarchical theory also fails to recognize that organizational structures are themselves policy decisions that result from the same forces that produce other organizational decisions. Medical schools have been organized in many different ways over their history. A particular organizational structure reflects the distribution of power within the medical school as much as any other decision. Academic hierarchies are a consequence of the decision-making process, not the cause of it.[10]

The approach to organizational decision making to be used in this study is based on the organization's need for outside resources. A medical school requires funding, students, highly trained personnel with widely different skills, certification of the school's training programs, extensive physical facilities, and patients for teaching purposes. Medical schools have needed these resources continuously, and the relative importance of each has varied widely from one school to another and from time to time.[11]

The groups involved in medical education that have provided the needed resources have been able to influence medical school decisions. The relative influence of each group has depended on the resources that it has provided, the issues involved, the needs of the medical school, and specific situational factors. Each group has rarely been interested in all decisions, which has limited the number of groups seeking to influence any particular policy.

Despite the great changes in medical schools over their history, the frames of reference of the various groups involved in medical education have remained quite stable. Each group will be examined in turn.

Groups Involved in Decision Making at Medical Schools

The most important administrator involved in medical school decision making has been the medical school dean, whose position has steadily grown in stature during the twentieth century. The dean has been in a position to influence medical school policies because he deals with many groups in the medical school's environment and controls some organizational resources.

In practice, the dean has had relatively little influence over much medical school decision making. Most financial resources have been earmarked for individual units within the medical school and have not been subject to reallocation by the dean. Much funding has come from research grants and patients cared for by individual faculty members, who influence its disbursement. In this regard, medical school deans have been similar to the college presidents studied by Cohen and March, who had little power in institutions with a strong research emphasis and substantial public funding, both of which have characterized most medical schools. In response to this situation, medical school deans, like college presidents, have often concentrated their efforts on institution building, where they can be more influential. This has further removed them from the day-to-day decisions that make up medical school education policies.[12]

The universities with which medical schools are affiliated have commanded significant resources needed by medical schools, including the ability to grant degrees, the ownership of the buildings and property, and control over some parts of the operating budget. However, parent universities have always had little influence over medical school policies. Before the twentieth century, those medical schools that were nominally affiliated with universities were actually owned or controlled by the faculty. Today, medical schools continue to be largely autonomous, primarily because most of their funding has not been controlled by the university and many of their outside relationships have not been mediated through the university.[13]

Medical school students have always influenced medical school educational policies. Before this century, admission standards were low, class size was virtually unlimited, competition among schools for students was severe, and student fees accounted for most or all of the income of the school. Under those conditions, student preferences greatly influenced medical school policies. In recent decades, twice as many students have applied to medical schools as have been admitted, student tuition and fees have accounted for a minor portion of medical school income, and the cost of educating students has far exceeded the direct funds they have provided. For these reasons their direct influence on medical school policies has diminished significantly.[14]

Nevertheless, students have remained potentially influential in medical schools. Medical schools have placed a high value on enrolling outstanding students, because such students have attracted other excellent students, motivated the faculty, and have been responsible for some kinds of outside funding. Medical schools have encouraged outstanding students to enroll by demonstrating at least some concern with student desires. Although this concern has often been limited, it has been significant at times.

Medical students have always preferred a practical education. Students were largely responsible for the highly practical curriculum in all medical schools during most of the nineteenth century. Their continuing strong preference for a practical medical education has been demonstrated in recent studies. A study at one medical school in the late 1950s found that the perspective of medical students had "an intensely practical and short-run character. Students . . . tend to reject . . . the acquisition of scientific knowledge for its own sake, intellectual curiosity, and similarly less practically oriented descriptions." Another study a decade later reached similar conclusions and found that students judged worst those courses that taught "'straight hard-core science' without providing clinical applications." Students have preferred a practical education because they have believed that they will soon enter the practice of medicine and must be prepared to treat patients and their illnesses.[15]

Medical school faculty members, who have monopolized the professional skills needed to operate their institutions, have often been considered to be the dominant force in medical school decision making. In fact, the power of the faculty has waxed and waned throughout the history of medical schools as the schools have altered their structure, sources of income, personnel, and functions.

Medical school faculty members can be divided into three major groups, each of which has had significantly different interests. One group has consisted of the paid part-time faculty and the unpaid volunteer faculty. This group comprised practically the entire medical school faculty during the nineteenth century, and constituted the majority of clinical faculty members until the 1950s. In recent years, most part-time and volunteer faculty members have been physicians who have taught clinical courses partly for the prestige of the faculty appointments (which enhance their private practices), partly for the hospital privileges involved, partly for the patients referred from the medical school, and partly for the enjoyment of teaching. The second group, the full-time basic science faculty, has taught the basic medical sciences in most medical schools since the beginning of the twentieth century. The third group, the full-time M.D. clinical faculty, has been the dominant element of the clinical faculty since the 1950s.

Considered collectively, medical school faculty members have favored the theoretical approach to medical education to a greater extent than have medical students. They have always emphasized the basic sciences and other subjects not directly related to medical practice. They have regarded professional education as continuing throughout the physician's career, and have been more aware than the students of the high rate of obsolescence of many aspects of medical education.[16]

The differences between faculty members and students were shown in a survey of 1,795 faculty and 2,606 students at 15 medical schools in the mid-1950s. When both groups were asked to rank 10 possible "motivations" of students for professional training using a rank of 1 as most important, the students ranked more highly than did the faculty "desire to be economically secure" (student mean ranking of 5.2 as compared to a faculty mean ranking of 6.7). The faculty ranked more highly than did the students "desire to contribute to the welfare of society" (faculty mean of 2.9, student mean of 3.7), "desire to be technically proficient" (faculty mean of 4.2, student mean of 5.4), "desire to acquire knowledge for its own sake" (faculty mean of 4.5, student mean of 5.9), and "desire to make original contributions to science" (faculty mean of 4.9, student mean of 6.9). When asked to rank 10 possible "objectives" of medical education, the faculty ranked "acquire habits of continuing self-education" first with a mean ranking of 2.5, while students ranked it fourth with a mean ranking of 4.3.[17]

Full-time basic science faculty members have always been more strongly in favor of a theoretical approach than have clinical faculty members. One 1965 survey of 795 medical school faculty members asked them "which phase of medical education will be most important for the students' later careers in medicine." The first two years of medical school (when the basic medical sciences are taught) were preferred by 28 percent of the basic science faculty and only 11 percent of the clinical full-time, part-time, and volunteer faculty.[18]

Many full-time faculty members in both the basic sciences and clinical fields have preferred a theoretical approach largely because of the emphasis on research in medical schools. A survey of about 2,000 faculty members in the late 1970s found that 76 percent said that research "strongly contributes" to the "system of rewards (e.g., promotions, raises)" at their school, while only 18 percent said that teaching strongly contributed to it (responses were not mutually exclusive). A ranking of the reputations of medical schools by 583 medical school faculty members about the same time found that the best correlates of the rankings were research activities in the schools.[19]

The faculty group most strongly in favor of a practical education has been the part-time and volunteer faculty. In the survey of 1,795 faculty members cited above, the opinions of the part-time clinical faculty were almost always closer to those of the students than were the opinions of the full-time faculty, although the differences between the faculty groups were small. The part-time faculty have felt, according to Kendall, that their role in medical education has been to provide students with a "picture of what practice is like and a notion about some of the practical aspects of medicine which they do not now receive from their research-oriented instructors."[20]

Thus there have been substantial and deep-rooted disagreements among the three faculty groups with regard to their preferences for a practical or theoretical education. These differences have divided the faculty and weakened its influence over medical school policies.

University and closely affiliated teaching hospitals have influenced medical school policy making during the twentieth century because medical schools have needed them to provide patients for teaching and research. Teaching hospitals have preferred a practical approach to medical education, partly because teaching and research costs have made them more expensive to operate than non-teaching hospitals. Teaching hospital income can be significantly increased if clinical faculty members have extensive practices and hospitalize their patients in the hospitals. Their preference has also been due to their desire for high quality patient care, which has required the presence of clinical faculty members with a significant interest in the treatment of hospitalized patients.

Community physicians have historically been a major factor in medical school decision making. They have influenced opinion about medical schools in the community, the state legislature, and the medical licensing boards. They have served as part-time faculty members in the medical schools and hospitalized their private patients in medical school hospitals. In recent decades these activities have become less important as full-time faculty members have replaced part-time ones. Community physicians have favored a practical approach to medical education because it is in harmony with their professional activities and would increase their influence in medical schools.[21]

The American Medical Association (AMA) has influenced medical school educational policies since the beginning of this century. Its influence has been largely due to the reliance of state licensing boards on its evaluations of medical schools, although in recent decades the evaluations have been carried on jointly with several other organizations. The AMA has also been an influential lobbyist before Congress. Its major concern has been the impact of the number of medical school graduates on the supply of physicians. It has been concerned with the quality of medical education primarily at the level of minimum standards for medical schools.

The AMA has taken the position that medical education should be fundamentally practical, but with a significant component of the basic medical sciences. For many years it opposed a strong research emphasis in medical schools as part of its opposition to large-scale federal funding for medical schools. The AMA first favored federal funding of basic medical research in the late 1960s.[22]

Governments have shown greater interest in the number of medical school graduates than the content of medical education. They have usually become concerned with medical school educational policies when public opinion held that medical education had become either too practical or too theoretical.

State governments first became concerned with the content of medical education at the turn of the twentieth century when they enacted licensing laws specifying the length and content of medical education required of applicants for licenses to practice medicine. At that time many of them also undertook to assure a steady supply of medical school graduates in their states by taking ownership of private medical schools. After mid-century, when a shortage of physicians developed, states established many new public medical schools, assumed closer control of existing ones, and provided financial assistance to many private schools.

Historically, state governments have supported the educational policies espoused by medical educators. They favored a significant theoretical component in medical education for most of the twentieth century until a shortage of physicians, particularly family physicians, developed in the 1960s. At that time, many states required medical schools that received state funding to create departments of family medicine or otherwise alter their educational programs in a more practical direction.[23]

The federal government first became significantly involved in medical education when it provided large sums for medical research in medical schools in the 1950s. This greatly increased the number of research oriented faculty members, who preferred a theoretical approach to medical education. In response to public concern over the shortage of physicians in the 1960s and 1970s, the federal government tied some of its funding to the development of medical school programs intended to increase the number of physicians generally and family physicians in particular.[24]

Many philanthropic foundations have supported medical education and medical research. Some have provided general support while others have supported research on specific diseases, such as cancer or polio. Both types of foundations have advocated federal aid to medical schools for biomedical research. The strong interest of foundations in medical research has tended to increase the theoretical emphasis in the medical schools that they have supported.[25]

Conclusion

This analysis has sought to show that decision making in medical schools has involved many different groups within and outside medical schools and that the relative influence of the various groups has changed over time. The remainder of this study will seek to apply this framework to the history of American medical schools.

2

Medical Care and
Medical Education, 1750–1825

Medical care at the end of the eighteenth century, like that in any period, was determined by the state of medical knowledge and the available types of treatment. Some useful knowledge existed, but most of medical practice was characterized by scientific ignorance and ineffective or harmful treatments based largely on tradition. The empirical nature of medical practice made apprenticeship the dominant form of medical education. Toward the end of the century medical schools were established to provide the theoretical part of the student's education, while apprenticeship continued to provide the practical part.[1]

Medical Care

Medical Science

The scientifically valid aspects of medical science in the late eighteenth century comprised gross anatomy, physiology, pathology, and the materia medica. Gross anatomy, the study of those parts of the human organism visible to the naked eye, had benefitted from the long history of dissection to become the best developed of the medical sciences. This enabled surgeons to undertake a larger variety of operations with greater expertise.

Physiology, the study of how anatomical structures function in life, had developed at a far slower pace. The greatest physiological discovery up to that time, the circulation of the blood, had been made at the beginning of the seventeenth century and was still considered novel almost two centuries later. Physiology was a popular area for theorizing, and the numerous physiologically based theories of disease were, as a physician wrote in 1836, "mere assumptions of unproved, and as time has demonstrated, unprovable facts, or downright imaginations." [2]

Pathology at that time was concerned with pathological or morbid anatomy, the study of the changes in gross anatomical structures due to disease and their relationship to clinical symptoms. The field was in its infancy and contributed little to medicine and medical practice.

Materia medica was the study of drugs and drug preparation and use. Late eighteenth century American physicians had available to them a substantial armamentarium of drugs. Estes studied the ledgers of one New Hampshire physician from 1751 to 1787 (3,701 patient visits), and another from 1785 to 1791

(1,161 patient visits), one Boston physician from 1782 to 1795 (1,454 patient visits), and another from 1784 to 1791 (779 patient visits). The two New Hampshire physicians resided in towns with slightly under 1,000 persons each, and Boston's population was 18,000 in 1790. He found that the four physicians used a total of 225 different drugs, with each one using at least 40 percent of the total.[3]

The range of action of these drugs was very limited. The largest group consisted of evacuants: about 25 percent of the drugs prescribed by the four physicians were cathartics, another 4 percent were emetics, and 2 percent were diuretics. Another group consisted of narcotics: about 14 percent of the drugs prescribed were sleep-inducing narcotics and another 5 percent were antispasmodics to reduce pain. Tonics, used to improve appetite, skin tone, and circulation, constituted 14 percent of the prescriptions, and astringents, used to reduce discharges from diarrhea or excessive sweating, comprised another 10 percent.[4] The evacuants and opium were the most medically effective of the drugs.

The Diagnosis and Treatment of Disease

Physicians of the time, who had little knowledge of the causes of disease or the internal changes produced by disease, based diagnosis and treatment on the signs and symptoms of disease observable to the naked eye. This approach led them to believe that most diseases were simply the sum of their symptoms and that fever was the most common disease. Because thermometers were not available to measure body temperature, fever was diagnosed in terms of the warmth of the patient's skin to the touch, the florid color of the skin, or the patient's subjective feeling of feverishness. Fevers were usually subdivided into classes based on different symptoms, such as general fevers, fevers with eruptions (e.g., smallpox), intermittent fevers (e.g., malaria), and local inflammations (e.g., the swelling of a limb). This method of subdividing diseases invariably caused confusion and controversy.

Treatment was designed to relieve the most important symptoms, and physicians favored prompt and vigorous medical intervention. Drugging was so common that physicians' case records often listed only the drug prescribed, not the patient's illness. Estes found that virtually every patient of the four physicians he studied received some kind of treatment. Over 90 percent received drugs, with purgatives, emetics, and narcotics being the most common.[5] Much of the prescribing was also due to the fact that physicians were often the only sources of drugs in their communities.

Physicians varied widely in their choices of drugs. Estes found that only 14 percent of the 225 drugs used by the four physicians he studied were prescribed by all four of them, despite the fact that they lived less than 200 miles apart. Furthermore, the four physicians used many different drugs with the same properties, often having no particular favorites. While this may have been partly due to variations in the availability of individual drugs, it also indicates the highly idiosyncratic nature of medical practice of the period.[6]

Surgery, Smallpox Vaccination, and Cinchona Bark

Physicians did have available several medically valid treatments. Primary among them were many aspects of surgery, which was distinguished from medicine. Medicine was concerned with the patient's general therapeutic regimen, which included his drugs, diet, bed rest, travel, housing, work, and environment. Surgery was concerned with external treatments like setting fractures, prescribing trusses and artificial limbs, correcting defective vision, bandaging, administering ointments, bloodletting, treating boils and abscesses, and extracting teeth. Operative surgery was a very small part of the surgery of the period.

The most common surgical treatments performed by the physicians in Estes' sample were bloodletting, extracting teeth, and opening abscesses. Bloodletting had been found centuries earlier to reduce fever and relax the patient temporarily and had become a popular treatment in many serious diseases, despite its harmful effects. Patients were bled through a vein in the arm either a specified quantity of blood or until they fainted. Bloodletting was also administered by cupping or the use of leeches. It was administered to about 5 percent of the patients in Estes' sample.[7]

Cantharides, or skin irritants, were another group of surgical treatments of no medical benefit. The pus produced by the irritant was believed to contain harmful matter that was being removed from the body. The major irritant was the blister, applied over the affected area, such as the abdomen in abdominal illnesses and the head in the case of the mental illness. Drugs also were used topically to produce irritation, and about 5 percent of the drugs in Estes' sample were of this class.[8]

While advances in anatomy enabled physicians to perform some major operations, most physicians were sufficiently deterred by their own ignorance and the risks involved to limit their surgery to elementary procedures. About 20 percent of the procedures of the two rural physicians in Estes' sample and 10 percent of those of the two urban physicians were surgical. None of the four performed any major surgical operations.[9]

A few physicians were willing to undertake the dangerous and difficult major operations known at the time, such as amputating limbs, removing some kinds of tumors, and operating for cataract. These master surgeons traveled regularly throughout a wide region around their home communities to perform operations on individuals who had waited, often for months, for their visits. They also operated in their own communities on local residents and visitors who came to them for surgery. Major operative surgery became a medical specialty practiced by a small number of courageous master surgeons who took risks (sometimes needless risks) that other physicians avoided. It remained that kind of specialty until the end of the nineteenth century.

The most famous of this generation of surgeons was Valentine Mott (1785–1865), who lived in New York City. Mott performed almost 1,000 amputations and 165 lithotomies during his career, and pioneered many difficult operations. A biographer wrote that, like other master surgeons, Mott had the skills needed in an era when surgeons performed practically unassisted without anesthesia in poorly lighted homes: "undisturbable coolness and self-reliance, iron nerves, phenomenal muscular strength, and wonderfully keen eyesight, and he was able to operate equally well with either hand.'' Another master surgeon was Alden March (1795–1869), who lived in Albany, New York. March performed 7,124 operations in his career, not including a full decade for which records were lost. A third, Nathan Smith (1762–1829), traveled regularly throughout New England performing operations. All three were faculty members of medical schools and regularly operated before their classes.[10]

Operative surgery was severely limited by the absence of both satisfactory anesthetics and methods for preventing infection in the surgical wound. The available methods for deadening pain were opium, whiskey, and similar drugs, and, in amputations, tightly binding the part involved. The pain of surgery discouraged its widespread use and the high risk of infection greatly limited the range of permissible surgical procedures. Any operation on the head, thorax, or abdomen was almost always fatal and was avoided by all surgeons. Nevertheless, surgical operations could, when properly used, produce great benefit to suffering patients.

A second form of medically valid treatment was vaccination to immunize against smallpox, one of the great scourges of the time. Vaccination was discovered in the 1790s and was quickly promulgated throughout Europe and America. Its discovery was immediately recognized as one of the few great existing contributions of medicine.

The last form of treatment of demonstrable benefit to patients was the use of cinchona bark for the treatment of malaria, another major disease of the period. The use of the bark, which did not cure malaria, relieved the symptoms and enabled the victim to live a more normal life. Cinchona bark was widely used after its importation to Europe from South America in the seventeenth century, despite significant problems with its preparation and administration.

These three useful forms of therapy were applicable to a relatively small number of conditions, although important ones. The only drug of value in a wide range of illnesses was opium. Apart from these few treatments, the limitations of medical knowledge made the physician of little value in most medical care.

Illness

The major health problems at the end of the eighteenth century were infectious diseases brought about by harsh living conditions and urbanization. Malaria and respiratory diseases like influenza, pneumonia, and tuberculosis afflicted much of the population. Dysentery and diarrhea, caused by the lack of pure food and water, were major problems in settled areas and leading causes of infant mortality. Typhoid, caused by improper sewage treatment, was just becoming a major urban health hazard. These endemic diseases were supplemented by periodic epidemics of other infectious diseases, especially yellow fever, smallpox, and cholera. The drastic impact and high death rates of the epidemic diseases made them particularly terrifying.

Mortality statistics are available for three New Hampshire towns in the second half of the eighteenth century, for Portsmouth, New Hampshire from 1801 to 1820, and for Boston, Massachusetts from 1811 to 1820. There were 1,784 recorded deaths in the three New Hampshire towns, 1,654 in Portsmouth, and 8,491 in Boston. The proportion of deaths from infectious diseases in the five communities combined was 41.1 percent and varied among them from 34 to 78 percent. Information on 9,883 patients treated at the Philadelphia Dispensary from December, 1786, to November, 1792, showed that 65 percent of all diagnoses were infectious diseases. Although the death rate from infectious diseases was only 5.5 percent, they accounted for 79 percent of all deaths.[11]

The Providers of Medical Care

The sick of the period, like those today, had access to many kinds of medical treatment. Self-medication was the first line of defense in cases of illness. Drug recipes were printed in newspapers, almanacs, and books on domestic medicine, and many were passed down in family records from generation to generation. Families grew medical botanicals in their gardens, gathered them wild, and purchased them from merchants. The herbs were dried or prepared according to the recipes and stored for future use. Proprietary medicines were not widely available until the nineteenth century.

When outside help was desired, the patient and his family chose among physicians, Indian doctors, botanical healers, midwives (who often provided other types of care as well), nostrum dealers, and others who claimed to have healing powers acquired through experience, heredity, or divine guidance. As evidence of the importance of other kinds of healers, Estes found that obstetrical cases constituted only 2 percent of the cases treated by the two urban physicians and none of the cases treated by the two rural physicians that he studied.[12]

The availability of physicians varied widely among communities. In Massachusetts, a study found 1 physician, broadly defined, for every 1,000 inhabitants in 1700. This increased to 1 for every 417 inhabitants by 1780. Boston directories listed 14 Boston physicians for 12,000 inhabitants in 1780 and 31 for 25,000 inhabitants in 1798. In Philadelphia, a study found 80 physicians for 68,000 inhabitants in 1800. The Philadelphia physicians catered to the middle and upper classes, suggesting that the lower class patients resorted to other kinds of healers.[13]

Physicians treated many patients in their homes, having been summoned there at the onset of illness. They returned several times during an illness, sometimes daily or even more often. Rural physicians spent many hours on horseback riding along crude trails to visit their patients. Home visits served several important functions. The physician brought drugs for the patient, provided some nursing care, and observed changes in the patient's condition, which was often essential to a diagnosis. The two New Hampshire physicians studied by Estes saw about 40 and 60 percent of their patients respectively in the patients' homes.[14]

In their offices, physicians treated patients, performed minor surgery, and sold drugs. Drugs, which were dispensed as part of the treatment, were a major part of the physician's activities and income. Physicians' records of the period show large purchases of drug ingredients, pill boxes, bottles, corks, mortars, and pestles.[15] Physicians' apprentices spent much of their time preparing drugs for sale and use.

Many late eighteenth century physicians were unable to earn a living solely by the practice of medicine. One study found that two rural Massachusetts physicians each saw about 10 patients a week, compared to a Salem, Massachusetts physician who saw about 10 patients a day in 1756. Estes found that one of the two New Hampshire physicians he studied saw an average of 4.4 patients per day and the other 2.9 per day.[16] Rural physicians often engaged in farming to support themselves.

Care of the Sick in Almshouses

Adequate medical care was most difficult for three classes of patients: those who lived alone or lacked others to care for them when they were ill; the homeless, visitors, and those in the community temporarily; and the poor who were unable to afford adequate housing or who had no income to purchase food and fuel while they were sick. All three groups were objects of social concern.

Early in the colonial period, each case of need was handled individually. Those who could not care for themselves were boarded with others, receiving nursing care in their homes at public expense, or were placed in a lodging house if they could afford it. The sick poor were sometimes given food and fuel. Many communities hired a physician to treat the poor on a case by case basis. The larger towns appointed a "town physician" on a contract to treat all the poor in the community for a fixed annual fee.[17]

Eventually, larger communities accumulated enough dependents of all kinds to construct a building, called an almshouse, to provide shelter for them. Almshouses housed orphans, the chronically ill, the aged and infirm, the insane, the retarded, the disabled, expectant mothers, and sick strangers. The groups were commingled because too few persons were in each group to warrant separate care. By 1750, the almshouse was well established as an institution in urban areas throughout the colonies.[18]

Almshouses were also used as temporary shelters for the sick and needy. One study found that half of the 174 men admitted to the Boston asylum between 1764 and 1769 were strangers, and most spent little time there. Another study found that many almshouse inmates were recuperating from illnesses or were there because of unemployment and destitution. Almshouses organized infirmaries and appointed salaried physicians to their staffs to provide medical care for their inmates. An appointment as almshouse physician became sufficiently prestigious that communities were able to select leading physicians for the positions.[19]

As communities grew, they placed each class of dependents in separate facilities. Asylums were constructed for the insane, workhouses for the able-bodied, and the sick were distinguished as a separate category with problems different from those of other groups.[20]

The first of the sick to be separated were those needing isolation because of contagious diseases such as smallpox. They were housed in temporary "pest-houses" established during epidemics in the seventeenth and early eighteenth centuries. The pest-houses were primarily for the protection of the healthy and only secondarily concerned with the care of the sick.[21]

The next major development was the establishment of almshouse hospitals to care for both the almshouse's sick inmates and the sick inmates of workhouses and prisons, which were often located in the same or nearby buildings. Almshouse hospitals intermingled an extraordinary variety of patients. A 1775 petition to the legislature by the Philadelphia Almshouse reported that the almshouse served as a lying-in hospital for "upwards of 30 poor destitute women in a year," as a foundling hospital for "more than 50 poor helpless infants on an average," and as "a Hospital for Curables and Incurables of all ages and sexes, and in every Disease and Malady, even to Lunacy and Idiotism."[22]

The care of the sick in almshouses left much to be desired, even by the standards of the time. Food, heat, and housing were inadequate. Patients were usually cared for by other residents of the almshouse, overseen by regular visits from a local physician. Given the poor facilities and the extraordinary variety of acute and chronic diseases, almshouse hospitals soon gained a reputation as a place to be avoided at all costs.

Hospitals

Popular dissatisfaction with the almshouse led to the building of independent hospitals in major cities. The major rationale for their construction was the need for a facility to care for needy patients who refused almshouse care. A letter circulated in 1810 by two Boston physicians to promote the construction of the Massachusetts General Hospital observed that the local almshouse had become "disreputable" and "those who are the most deserving objects of charity cannot be induced to enter it." The deserving persons, the industrious workman afflicted with a "long-protracted disease," the widow or wife of a profligate husband, or the servant of a family, would greatly benefit by a "well-regulated hospital." There "the poor man's chance for relief would be equal perhaps to that of the most affluent, when affected by the same disease."[23]

The belief that a suitable hospital would enable more patients to recover was based as much on better shelter and diet for the patient as on medical care. An article in the *Pennsylvania Gazette* in 1751 that promoted the founding of the Pennsylvania Hospital in Philadelphia claimed:

> [In a hospital a patient] will be treated according to the best rules of art, by men of experience and known abilities in their profession. His lodgings will be commodious, clean and neat, in a healthy and open situation, his diet will be well chosen, and properly administered. . . . In short, a beggar, in a well regulated hospital, stands an equal chance with a prince in his palace for a comfortable substance, and an expeditious and effectual cure of his diseases.[24]

Several types of patients were singled out as particular beneficiaries of hospital care. One group was sick residents of rural communities who could not afford to come to cities for treatment because of the high cost of lodging, nursing, and medical care. A petition to the Pennsylvania House of Representatives in 1751 observed that these residents "languish out their lives, tortured perhaps with the stone, devoured by the cancer, deprived of sight by cataracts, or gradually decaying by loathsome distempers." A hospital would enable many of them to "be made in a few weeks useful members of the community, able to provide for themselves and families."[25]

A second group was the insane. The Pennsylvania petition noted that the number of insane in the colony had "greatly increased" as a result of population growth and that some of them at large were "a terror to their neighbors" and others were "continually wasting their substance . . . , ill-disposed persons wickedly taking advantage of their unhappy condition, and drawing them into unreasonable bargains, etc." If they could be provided proper care, it was believed that "some might be cured."[26]

The self-supporting members of the laboring classes who fell ill comprised a third group of potential patients. Sickness deprived them of their earnings and thus of proper food, fuel, and often shelter. Sickness could lead to death or long-term or permanent disability, with consequent economic hardship to the family as well as a financial burden on the community. The founders of hospitals stressed the importance of maintaining the health and productivity of the laboring classes and keeping them off the poor rolls, where they would be a burden to their fellow citizens.[27]

When voluntary hospitals opened in Philadelphia (the Pennsylvania Hospital), New York (the New York Hospital), and Boston (the Massachusetts General Hospital), they fell far short of their goals. They operated as supplements to, rather than replacements for, the almshouse. No patients with contagious or incurable diseases (except the insane) were admitted. Residents of other communities were usually admitted only if they or their town's overseers paid for their care. Charity patients were often required to have a letter of recommendation from an influential person as a character reference. The hospitals also accepted paying patients, primarily the servants and insane relatives of the wealthy as well as paupers paid for by the overseers of the poor.[28]

All three hospitals developed identical problems that significantly altered their character. The insane failed to recover as rapidly or in as large numbers as expected and occupied an increasing proportion of hospital beds. To deal with this problem, separate asylums primarily for those insane whose families could pay for their care were opened by the Massachusetts General Hospital in 1818, the New York Hospital in 1821, and the Pennsylvania Hospital in 1841.[29]

The treatment of the sick also turned out to be less successful than anticipated. The three hospitals were soon burdened with many long-term patients who needed only nursing care and adequate shelter. This caused numerous problems. Many patients left the hospital during the day, sometimes to earn money, sometimes for other reasons. Both the New York and Pennsylvania Hospitals prohibited their patients from begging in their respective cities, and the Pennsylvania Hospital forbade its patients from gambling in the hospital and getting drunk. The visiting committee of the New York Hospital complained in 1808 that "many of the Pauper Patients are in the practice of going over the Wall, & by means of the excesses they run into during their absence from the House, their cure is render'd tedious & expensive." Of the 1,094 patients discharged from there in 1806, 58 were "disorderly" and 64 "eloped."[30]

Long stays were common in the hospitals. At the Pennsylvania Hospital, the median length of stay of 41 women admitted as obstetrical patients from 1801 to 1840 was more than 42 days. The average length of stay from 1826 to 1850 for 99 cured or relieved fever patients was about 15 days, and for 111 cured or relieved patients with fractures, about 40 days. The Massachusetts General Hospital decided shortly after it opened that a patient would be declared incurable and removed after 3 months in the hospital unless he could pay for further care.[31]

Charity patients were expected to work if possible to defray their cost to the hospitals. The rules of the Pennsylvania Hospital required patients well enough to do so to "assist in nursing others; washing and ironing the linen, washing and cleaning the rooms, and such other services as the matron shall require." The same was required of patients at the New York Hospital.[32]

The financial problems created by the long stays of many charity patients led the hospitals to admit more paying patients. At the Pennsylvania Hospital, fewer than 20 percent of the patients were paying patients during its first two decades. Financial exigencies then forced it to accept more paying patients, most of whom were the insane relatives of the wealthy. By the 1780s the hospital had become largely an insane asylum. The number of paying patients continued to equal or exceed the number of charity patients until the 1830s. All hospitals during this time had mostly middle and upper class patients in the insane department and poor patients in the rest of the hospital.[33]

After 1800, the federal government became a major source of financial support for voluntary hospitals in seaport towns and cities. Many of the strangers needing health care were merchant seamen who lacked friends or funds. Because the local communities were unwilling to provide for their care, Congress enacted legislation in 1798 taxing the wages of merchant seamen and using the funds to care for "sick and disabled seamen." Although the legislation permitted the construction or purchase of federal hospitals, and one was built near Boston, the government preferred to contract with local hospitals, if available, or with boarding houses or individual physicians for the care of seamen. In the second quarter of the century, the federal government established a policy of building marine hospitals, and 27 were constructed by 1861, most in the South and West.[34]

The major beneficiaries of this federal program were the voluntary hospitals in the major eastern seaports. The Pennsylvania Hospital contracted to care for seamen in 1800, and from 1826 to 1850 30 percent of all patients treated in the hospital were seamen. At the New York Hospital, a similar arrangement was effected, and in 1866, 48 percent of the patients were seamen (this figure may have been abnormally high).[35]

Other sources of hospital income were grants from legislatures, room and board fees from paying patients, per diem payments from local governments for the care of charity patients, and contributions by citizens (which usually entitled them to admit charity patients, such as their servants, to the hospital). Private contributions were forthcoming because hospitals served as a major source of care for the servants, slaves, and insane relatives of the wealthy. Their interest in the hospitals probably maintained the quality of care at a level above what it otherwise would have been.[36]

Dispensaries

Dispensaries were more important than hospitals in providing medical care for the poor because they cared for the sick both in the dispensaries and in the patients' homes. Dispensaries were a response to the need for medical care by the rapidly increasing urban working classes. The voluntary hospitals cared for only a few patients, excluded those with contagious and chronic diseases, and operated at a high cost to the public. Dispensaries continued a practice that had existed since the seventeenth century of providing outdoor relief for the poor, and were an expeditious and inexpensive way to provide medical care.[37]

Dispensaries were established in Philadelphia, New York, Boston, and Baltimore between 1786 and 1801, occasionally in hospitals but more often as independent organizations. Like the voluntary hospitals, dispensaries were designed to serve the needs of the deserving poor. The proposal for the Philadelphia Dispensary stated that there were "many poor persons afflicted by disease, whose former circumstances and habits of independence will not permit them to expose themselves as patients in a public [charity] hospital." Others to be helped included those who could not easily be moved to a hospital or who had diseases "of such a nature that the air of a hospital, crowded with patients, is injurious to them." A dispensary would enable patients to be "attended and relieved in their own houses without the pain and inconvenience of being separated from their families." The public also benefitted because "the sick may be relieved at much less expense to the public than in a hospital, where provisions, bedding, firewood, and nurses must be provided for their accommodation."[38]

Dispensaries were organized by philanthropic groups which established the facilities and hired the physicians. Each dispensary physician was assigned a geographic territory where he visited patients in their homes, and one or more of the physicians held daily office hours at the dispensary for ambulatory patients. Medicines were provided without cost, dispensed at first by the physician and later by a hired pharmacist. Dispensaries were able to recruit many young physicians, who often had difficulty establishing their practices. The Baltimore General Dispensary paid its physicians a surprisingly high $300 per year from 1803 to 1825, when it reduced the salary to $100 per year if funds were available.[39]

The dispensary became an extraordinarily successful institution, in contrast to the tribulations experienced by the voluntary hospitals. The New York City Dispensary treated more than 2,000 patients in the first five years after it opened in 1791, 2,866 in 1816, 8,000 in 1821, and 26,744 patients in 1836 (in combination with two other dispensaries) at a cost of less than 20 cents per patient. The Philadelphia Dispensary treated 2,196 patients in 1805, and the Baltimore General Dispensary treated over 1,000 each year from 1801 to 1810 and over 2,000 each year from 1811 to 1820.[40]

Because dispensaries served specific geographic areas, the growth of cities led philanthropic groups and municipal governments to establish additional dispensaries in different parts of the city. By 1850 large cities had a network of dispensaries, each providing home and outpatient care to residents of its part of the city.

Medical Education

The Education of Physicians Before the Establishment of Medical Schools

During the seventeenth and most of the eighteenth centuries, students seeking medical education had three alternatives: (1) travel to Europe to study in a medical school or hospital there; (2) become formally apprenticed to a physician willing to train students, call a preceptor; or (3) learn the profession in some less formal way. Because no effective legal restrictions on the right to practice medicine existed until the late nineteenth century, an aspiring physician could choose whatever method of training he desired or could afford.

Medical training in Europe was generally possible only for the sons of wealthy colonists. Several hundred Americans studied in Europe before the revolution, most of them either at the University of Edinburgh or at a hospital in London. Many of them visited continental hospitals as well.[41]

A larger group of American physicians were trained as apprentices to other physicians. One study of almost 1,600 Massachusetts physicians from 1630 to 1800 found that about one-third had at least one year's apprenticeship training, compared to a few that were European trained and the majority who had no formal training of at least a year's duration. Forty-four percent of the apprentice-trained physicians were sons of physicians, suggesting that they were simply learning their father's trade and that apprenticeship training was not common during most of this period.[42]

The great majority of physicians had no formal training and probably entered medicine from other occupations. They may have sold drugs, "cured" or nursed some sick individual back to health and thus established a reputation as a healer, or performed simple surgical procedures like extracting teeth or lancing boils. The Massachusetts study found that many of the untrained physicians were highly mobile, suggesting an inability to establish a stable practice in a community. They probably delivered less medical care than their numbers would indicate.[43]

The apprenticeship system became more popular after 1750. One study found that the proportion of apprentice-trained physicians in Massachusetts increased substantially at that time, and another study found that the number of Boston physicians with apprenticeship training increased from 14 in 1780 to 31 in 1798.[44] This was undoubtedly due both to the growing number of trained physicians who could serve as preceptors and the greater wealth of the population, which motivated students to undertake systematic study for the profession.

As the apprenticeship system developed, its form and content became standardized. The term of apprenticeship was three years, at a cost to the apprentice of $100 a year. The apprentice performed much routine work for the physician, including preparing drugs, acting as a nurse, cleaning the office and stables, and making himself useful around the physician's office and house.[45]

The apprentice's education consisted of two parts. One involved the theoretical aspects of medicine. The apprentice read the preceptor's medical books and was regularly quizzed on the material by him. Given the few medical books published at the time, the preceptor's library usually consisted of a book on anatomy and perhaps a book on medical theory and treatment. The apprentice also received training in drug preparation in the most practical manner possible. He spent many hours grinding the raw ingredients, preparing the drugs, and putting up prescriptions for the preceptor's patients.

The apprentice and his preceptor sometimes dissected a human cadaver in order to study gross anatomy and operative surgery. Cadavers were usually exhumed from the local cemetery, a practice not viewed favorably by the local population. Dissection or operative surgery using domestic animals was often substituted for practical anatomy.

The second part of the course involved participating in the preceptor's treatment of patients. The student assisted the preceptor as a nurse in his office, sometimes treated patients when the preceptor was out, and traveled with him on house calls. The preceptor discussed the cases and his management of them with the apprentice during their travels.

In his education, the apprentice learned medicine as it was practiced in the community. He watched patients from the beginning to the end of their medical treatment. He observed the natural history of their illnesses, mostly infectious diseases, in the environment in which they occurred. He learned about the doctor's relationship with the patient and his family. He saw the family life and economic and social situation of the patient and learned what could and could not be done in that environment. Although the state of medical knowledge limited what he could learn about treatment, an observant apprentice could learn a great deal about illness.

The apprentice also learned about the professional role of the physician in the community. He benefitted or suffered from his preceptor's reputation. He became acquainted with other physicians in the region when they met with his preceptor on consultations or social occasions. He learned about the professional community of physicians and about differences in medical practices among physicians.

When the student completed his apprenticeship, he had earned a reputation for himself among the residents of the community. Sometimes he was invited by his preceptor or another physician to become his partner or associate, and many apprentice-trained physicians began their careers in this way. Sometimes he settled in a nearby community where he thought there was a shortage of physicians.

The new physician's network of professional relationships played an important role if he decided to practice in or near the community. A new physician did not practice every aspect of medicine when he opened his office; he recognized many of his limitations and concentrated on those aspects of medicine he felt competent to treat. When he encountered a case that was beyond his capabilities, he either consulted with more experienced physicians or turned the case over to them. Substantial social pressure was placed on the young physician to do this. A grossly mishandled case produced enough public disapproval in a small town to affect a physician's career for years. Older physicians and patients frequently reminded apprentices and young physicians of the failed careers of physicians who mishandled cases.

The apprenticeship system had some major flaws. Any physician could serve as a preceptor, and many were motivated to do so by the prospect of the apprenticeship fee and the free labor of the apprentice. Even if the preceptor was a competent physician, the apprentice could easily spend his days preparing drugs, running errands, or engaging in other menial tasks. Popular preceptors often had many patients and of necessity placed their patients' needs above those of their apprentices.

The number of incompetent preceptors was reduced by the mode of selecting preceptors. Most apprentices either selected preceptors whom they knew previously, such as family physicians, or ones who were highly regarded as physicians and preceptors. The more successful and experienced physicians in a community tended to be the most popular preceptors. Although students sometimes misjudged the abilities of their preceptors (and often changed preceptors as a result), the selection process did reduce the number of gross abuses of the system.

The content of the apprenticeship was most inadequate in its coverage of the theoretical material. Few preceptors were competent to teach gross anatomy or theories of disease to their apprentices. Even the best of them only quizzed students about the textbooks, which were usually outdated. Most preceptors were not educators and were not concerned with the best way to teach medicine to students. They taught the material as they had learned it decades earlier.

The apprenticeship was also limited in that the apprentice learned only the preceptor's way of practicing medicine. Even though he heard discussions among physicians about different treatments or methods of diagnosis, the advantages and disadvantages of each were never clearly explained to him. Consequently, the apprenticeship system contributed to a highly idiosyncratic system of medical practice where each student used the techniques of his preceptor.

Despite these weaknesses, the apprenticeship system appears to have been as good as apprenticeship training in the Congregational ministry, where the recent college graduate served as an assistant to a local minister and participated in the daily activities of the local congregation. It also appears to have been considerably better than apprenticeship training for lawyers. The legal apprentice, as an 1846 law journal observed, was often little more than a scribe who was "instructively occupied in copying over a thousand times the same cabalistic forms, 'running errands,' and swearing to affidavits." He usually received little or no formal instruction from his preceptor and was expected to obtain his education by reading the law library in the lawyer's office.[46]

Formal Instruction in Medicine

Two developments in medical education occurred in response to the limitations of the apprenticeship system. Late in the eighteenth century some preceptors began to devote special attention to teaching apprentices. They organized the material much like courses. They used skeletons, models, illustrations, and other teaching aids, especially in teaching anatomy and pathology. They obtained and used the recent medical literature in a systematic way. If they had enough apprentices at the same time, they organized them into classes. They gradually replaced the casual relationship of apprentice and preceptor with the more formal relationship of student and teacher. This development reached its zenith in the middle of the nineteenth century and will be described in a subsequent chapter.[47]

The more important and more seminal development was the teaching of anatomy as one of the many private courses offered in colonial cities. In the eighteenth century, private instructors offered a wide variety of courses not available in the colleges and academies (secondary schools). They were open to men and women, young and old, poorly educated and well educated, vocationally inclined and academically inclined. Mathematics courses ranged from bookkeeping, surveying, and navigation to astronomy, calculus, and analytical geometry. Modern foreign languages, history, geography, and English grammar were frequently offered. The remarkable range and depth of private courses in almost all of the new and important areas of knowledge stood in dramatic contrast to the drab parochialism of the colonial colleges, which taught only the classical languages, mathematics, and a smattering of science. The availability of instruction to all who wanted it contrasted with the education of adolescent boys in the colleges and academies.[48]

The instructors were usually well trained, professionally competent, and experienced. Teachers of modern languages were native speakers of the language. The mathematics instructors included some of the nation's leading mathematicians. Competition forced the instructors to keep pace with current educational needs and to improve their methods of teaching.

Many of the courses provided theoretical training for workers and apprentices. Surveyors learned algebra, geometry, trigonometry, and mensuration; clerks learned the Italian method of double entry bookkeeping; workers in mercantile establishments trading with Europe learned modern foreign languages; and seamen learned astronomy and navigation.

Private courses were soon used to improve medical education. Courses in anatomy were advertised or offered in the 1750s and 1760s in Philadelphia, New York, Boston, and Newport, Rhode Island, and in other cities soon afterward. Anatomy was selected because it was a subject which the average preceptor could not teach well. It was also the most important and best developed medical science, in demand by students, practitioners, and interested laymen, all of whom attended the courses.[49] Private courses were the true beginning of formal medical education in America, and they established a distinction between the theoretical parts of medicine, which were taught in courses, and the practical parts, which were taught by the apprenticeship system.

Private courses in anatomy were the basis of every medical school established in the eighteenth and early nineteenth centuries, except for schools organized by dissident faculty members from existing medical schools.[50] Private courses became even more important in medical education during the second quarter of the nineteenth century and their development will be analyzed in a subsequent chapter.

The First Medical Schools

Whatever their virtues, private courses were not the same as a medical school. Medical schools offered degrees, had a physical presence in the community that enhanced the professional reputations of their faculty, and had stability. For these reasons ambitious young physicians, many with European training, began to approach colleges about organizing medical schools after the middle of the eighteenth century.

The colonial colleges were enthusiastic about adding medical schools. The physicians agreed to provide instruction at no cost to the colleges, which were only asked to award the degrees. The colleges would have their reputations enhanced by the medical schools and expand their curriculum to include medical lectures which their students could attend. For these reasons, medical schools were organized in New York City at what later became Columbia University in 1767, in Philadelphia at the University of Pennsylvania in 1769 (although the first faculty appointment was made in 1765), and in Cambridge, Massachusetts, at Harvard University in 1783. In all three cases, the colleges organized the medical schools with appropriate ceremonies and considered the addition of a medical school to be highly significant.[51]

Later developments were quite different. A one-man medical school was established at Dartmouth College in 1797, but the college was not disturbed by the fact that it was just a well-organized apprenticeship. A group of physicians organized an independent medical school in Baltimore in 1807, because the city had no college. The medical school at Harvard University moved to Boston in 1810 because the faculty lived there and found the trip to Cambridge to be too time consuming. Medical schools were established at Yale in 1812, at Brown about 1815, and at Bowdoin in 1821. They had little relationship with their colleges except the awarding of degrees, as did all the previously established medical schools by this time.[52]

The attempt to organize medical schools as true academic departments in colleges had failed. Colleges and medical schools maintained an affiliation only because the medical school needed to use the college's authority to award degrees and the college was willing to accept a school that cost it nothing and gave the appearance of broadening its curriculum. To understand why a closer relationship failed to develop, it is necessary to examine the colleges of the period.

The Eighteenth Century College

Colleges were enthusiastic about adding medical schools because they were in the process of broadening their educational functions beyond those of training clergymen. The many new religious denominations and the development of new occupations had reduced interest in their programs. Although their curriculum continued to emphasize preparation for the ministry, most students entered other occupations and professions. Only 35 percent of Yale graduates from its founding in 1701 to 1792 became ministers, as did 26 percent of the graduates of Brown from 1770 to 1800, and 34 percent of graduates of Dartmouth from 1780 to 1800. In the three schools, 15 to 30 percent of the students became lawyers and about 10 percent became physicians.[53]

In order to satisfy the increasingly varied interests of their students, the colonial colleges expanded their curriculum beyond the traditional emphasis on Greek and Latin grammar. After mid-century, arithmetic was added to Greek and Latin as an entrance requirement and mathematics courses were added to the final three years of the curriculum. Astronomy and natural philosophy (general science) were also taught. In practice, the additional entrance requirements were often not implemented and the other changes had little impact. The mathematics courses were taught primarily by tutors who had little knowledge of advanced mathematics. The range of topics in the sciences and mathematics was so broad that the coverage was superficial. The status of the new faculty members was marginal and they were often poorly qualified for their positions. Few of the leading scientists of the period taught at the colleges.[54]

The expansion of the curriculum was also hindered by the small college enrollments. The typical graduating class in the eighteenth century consisted of fewer than 20 students, not enough to make elective courses feasible. Individual students could study other subjects with the faculty, although not for academic credit.[55]

More basically, a college education at that time was not truly higher education. Entrance examinations were low and a bright student could prepare for college in a couple of years. Most teaching was done by recitation. Few examinations were given and, as John Trumbull complained about Yale in the 1760s, "after four years dozing there, no one is ever refused the honors of a degree, on account of dullness and insufficiency." An English visitor to Princeton about 1800 noted that the college was "held in much repute," and then commented, "like all the other American colleges I ever saw, it better deserves the title of a grammar-school than of a college."[56]

Colleges and medical schools had virtually nothing in common with regard to their students, faculty, or curriculum. The joint attempt by colleges to move out of their narrow intellectual world and by medical schools to gain academic respectability was soon abandoned.

The Growth of Medical Schools

Medical schools had several advantages over apprenticeship training and private courses. Students liked them because they awarded a degree, at first, Bachelor of Medicine, but after the Revolutionary War, Doctor of Medicine. The degree impressed patients more than the preceptor's certificate given after apprenticeship training because the medical school was widely known, while a preceptor was known only in one community. Preceptors supported medical schools because they did not like to teach the time-consuming theoretical subjects. Both preceptors and students knew that medical school faculty members were up-to-date in their knowledge of the material and interested in teaching it. In addition, significant economies of scale were possible in medical schools that taught the theoretical material in lectures to many students at a time.

Faculty members also benefitted from medical schools, although earnings from teaching were small in the early years. A medical school appointment had considerable prestige among patients, and the names of the faculty were popularized by the advertisements of the school. Graduates of the school consulted with faculty members on difficult cases and medical students sought out faculty members as preceptors.

For these reasons, the number of medical schools soon increased. The 2 schools in operation on a degree granting basis in 1780 increased to 4 in 1800 and 13 in 1820, with 10 of the 13 in New England, New York, or Philadelphia. Other medical schools operated briefly and failed. The larger number of schools turned out more graduates. The estimated 221 graduates of medical schools prior to 1800 increased to an estimated 1,375 in the decade from 1810 to 1819 (the figures are not precise because medical schools sometimes exaggerated the number of their graduates). An even larger number of students attended lectures without graduating.[57]

Many of the early nineteenth-century medical schools were located in towns or villages in rural areas and were established by one or two successful local preceptors seeking to organize their students into classes for greater efficiency of teaching. The local physicians made arrangements to have degrees awarded by a nearby college and recruited other faculty members, most of whom were urban physicians who came to the colleges only for the medical school term.[58]

Rural medical schools were successful for the same reasons that the growing number of rural colleges were: they appealed to students who could not afford the expenses of urban schools and who often delayed their educations in order to earn money to pay for it. A study of many of the graduates of two rural medical schools in Vermont operating during this period found that the average age at graduation from a two-year course in medical schools that had a modest admission requirement was almost 26 years. It has been estimated that one-third of all students attending medical school before the Civil War attended rural medical schools.[59]

The Administration of Medical Schools

All medical schools before the Civil War were jointly owned and operated as commercial ventures by four to seven faculty members. Each faculty member took an active interest in the joint enterprise.

The faculty of a medical school consisted of the professors, a demonstrator of anatomy, and sometimes one or two clinical professors. The professors taught the lecture courses and the demonstrator of anatomy ran the dissection laboratory. The clinical professor, who was employed only if there was a local hospital, was on the hospital staff and gave the students clinical instruction there.

The professors owned and operated the medical school and ran it as partners. Any professor could individually examine and admit or reject an applicant for admission. Each professor personally collected the fee for his course (usually $15 to $20) from the students, giving each student a ticket of admission in exchange. Graduation examinations consisted of the professors assembling in a room, each giving a brief oral examination to the student, and then voting, with a majority vote in favor usually being sufficient for graduation.

The major administrative issues decided by the professors included teaching assignments, the hiring of faculty members, the management of the school property, and the division among themselves of surplus medical school income, which was usually small. The only direct income received by the medical school itself was usually the graduation fee, which was about equal to the fee for a single course.

The most time-consuming administrative activity was the highly speculative management of the property. Medical schools were constantly selling their existing land and buildings to buy larger lots and erect larger buildings, thereby both demonstrating the school's prosperity and increasing the faculty's equity in the institution. Medical schools were able to borrow money freely because they were considered a solid investment and a community asset that attracted students who spent money in the communities. The indebtedness often led to financial crises, sometimes severe enough to cause the demise of the schools.

One faculty member assumed responsibility for catalogue preparation and routine administrative matters, and was occasionally called the dean. His role was more secretarial than administrative. Overall, the early nineteenth century medical school was an egalitarian organization of colleague-entrepreneurs.

Entrance and Graduation Requirements

Entrance requirements posed a major problem for medical schools. A college education was of little value as a prerequisite for medical education and its expense posed an intolerable financial burden for most students. An education in an academy was also of little value because it prepared students for college and consisted largely of Latin and Greek grammar.

Consequently, medical schools adopted specific knowledge requirements for entrance. The standard requirements in 1800 were a knowledge of Latin and some natural philosophy, but not mathematics. Latin was considered desirable for reading the classical medical literature but its presence was also used as evidence of general education. Natural philosophy was taught only in the colleges until the nineteenth century, so that a student would either have to attend college or study the subject with a tutor. However, medical schools made their admission requirements appropriately vague and gave themselves wide latitude in selecting students. They erred more on the liberal than the strict side in order to increase enrollments.[60]

Medical school graduation requirements were based both on the role of the schools in medical education and the existing licensing situation. Medical schools provided only the theoretical part of a student's medical education. The practical education was provided in the apprenticeship, which the schools did not control. Furthermore, the absence of effective licensing laws meant that anyone could practice medicine when and where he chose. The schools therefore held that their degree was evidence of achievement in certain aspects of medicine, not a certificate of competence to practice medicine in the community.

In order to graduate from a medical school, a student was required to be 21 years of age, to certify that he spent three years as an apprentice with a preceptor, to complete two courses of medical school lectures (usually taken during the last two years of the apprenticeship), to pass an oral examination, and, in the eighteenth century, to prepare and defend a thesis. Some students had practiced medicine before entering medical school and were treated accordingly. The two most important requirements were the apprenticeship and the two courses of lectures.[61]

The three-year apprenticeship requirement was based on the faculty's belief that clinical medicine could only be learned in the patient's home or the physician's office. Clinical medicine could not be taught successfully in a medical school, which consisted of a lecture hall, a room for dissection, and possibly a museum of anatomical specimens. Most of the student's clinical education was left to his preceptor.

Medical schools also required an apprenticeship because most students began their medical education with a preceptor. The schools cultivated the support of preceptors to encourage them to send apprentices to their schools. They listed the preceptors' names prominently in the catalogues next to the names of the students, awarded some local preceptors honorary degrees (sometimes for a fee), and made others "fellows" of the college. Honorary degrees became so common that about 1850 the American Medical Association recommended that their use be restricted.[62]

The second major graduation requirement was attendance at two courses of lectures, each between 16 and 20 weeks long. The most remarkable aspect of this requirement was that there was no graded curriculum: the student attended all lectures offered at the school twice to qualify for the M.D. degree.

One reason for the lack of a graded curriculum was that the faculty offered lectures, not courses. The material was not presented in a sequence from more elementary to more advanced material. The faculty member's responsibility was to present his views on aspects of the subjects assigned to him. Material included the first time the student attended the lectures might well be omitted the second time. However, faculty members often settled into a routine in which they delivered the same lectures year after year, sometimes for decades. Another reason for the repetitive curriculum was the lack of available medical textbooks. The student had no other way to obtain the information, so that attendance at two courses of lectures was not unreasonable. Of course, the requirement also maximized faculty earnings.

Medical School Teaching

Medical schools agreed that the curriculum consisted of seven subjects, usually but not always anatomy, physiology, chemistry, materia medica, medicine, surgery, and midwifery. Diseases of women and children were added to the curriculum early in the nineteenth century. Few medical schools had as many faculty members as subjects in the curriculum. In 1827, 2 of 20 medical schools had 7 faculty members, 6 schools had 6 faculty, and the rest had fewer than 6, with at least 2 having only 3 faculty members each. Faculty members often taught two or more subjects jointly in a single course of lectures.[63]

Course preference was usually decided by seniority, with the older professors choosing the clinical courses and leaving the basic science courses to their junior colleagues. The clinical subjects provided more prestige among laymen, attracted consultations from former students and other physicians, and were more interesting to the faculty, who were primarily practitioners. Faculty members frequently switched subjects, and the only subjects taught by specialists were surgery and chemistry.[64]

The lectures consisted primarily of faculty members reading from hand-written manuscripts. The students sometimes saw a few demonstrations in chemistry and pharmacy and witnessed the treatment of ambulatory patients and minor operations in the clinical courses. Practical ideas on how to practice medicine, such as useful prescriptions and descriptions of natural histories of diseases, pervaded all the courses.

Medical schools located in cities with hospitals also taught a small amount of clinical medicine. As an optional part of the curriculum, medical students were brought into the wards of a local hospital where they heard lectures by the attending physicians and walked the wards with them to listen to their descriptions of cases. When the professors did not have hospital appointments, teaching was done by a clinical professor who was appointed to the faculty because he had a hospital appointment.[65]

Hospital teaching had major pedagogical limitations. The student only listened and had no contact with the patient. Also, most hospital patients were convalescing from illnesses and offered little of interest to medical students. The few cases of interest did not warrant regular hospital visits by students. Medical school faculty members realized that hospital training was clearly inferior to apprenticeship training and did not make it a required part of medical education.

The Curriculum

The medical school curriculum was divided into scientific and clinical subjects. The scientific subjects included anatomy, physiology, chemistry, and, early in the period, natural philosophy, which covered physics, chemistry, botany, mineralogy, and zoology. The clinical subjects included medicine, surgery, obstetrics, and diseases of women and children. Hospital instruction was an optional clinical course. Materia media had both scientific and clinical aspects. Other courses were sometimes offered on an optional basis.[66]

The keystone of the curriculum was anatomy, the most popular and important course in the medical school. Anatomy was the only medical science with demonstrable value in the practice of medicine. It could be taught effectively only in the medical school, which had the necessary skilled teachers and equipment. The teaching of anatomy was divided into two courses. Lectures on anatomy described the human skeleton and organs, illustrated by cadavers when possible and by skeletons, drawings, models made of wax, plaster, wood, or papier-mâché, and both dry and wet specimens. The use of models had just been developed in Europe, indicating that American medical education was abreast of European medical education in this regard. The lectures also included morbid or pathological anatomy, the anatomical changes that occurred in disease. The significance of anatomy for surgery was a frequent topic of discussion.[67]

The second part of the teaching of anatomy was "practical anatomy" or the dissection of cadavers. Most medical schools in the early nineteenth century offered practical anatomy as an optional course, unwilling to require it because of the difficulty of obtaining cadavers and unsympathetic public opinion. By 1848, 25 schools required a course in practical anatomy, although many of them permitted students to take it elsewhere and some did not even teach the course. Practical anatomy provided actual experience in dissection under the supervision of a demonstrator and was the only laboratory course in the medical school curriculum.

Many cadavers had been preserved in barrels and were in poor condition, which reduced their educational value. Nevertheless, most students regarded practical anatomy, as one recalled, "the chief event of the course."[68]

The other basic medical science courses were chemistry and physiology. Chemistry covered inorganic chemistry, with perhaps some animal chemistry. Nonphysicians usually taught the course, which indicates the faculty's opinion of its professional utility. Physiology was taught partly in the course on the theory and practice of medicine and partly in anatomy. It covered the "vital" properties of the body, like motion and irritability, and the functions of the human organs, including respiration, locomotion, excretion, and circulation of the blood. Scientific knowledge of these subjects was limited, and physiology provided the student with little of value for medical practice.[69]

Materia medica straddled the medical sciences and clinical medicine. Because botanical and mineral drugs were dispensed in their crude states (usually ground into powders or put in solution with water or alcohol), much of the course involved describing, identifying, and preparing the ingredients. So long as physicians prepared their own drugs, the course was very useful. Unfortunately, the content was not altered when commercial drugs became readily available. Materia medica was usually taught in conjunction with therapeutics.[70]

The clinical courses included medicine, surgery, obstetrics, and diseases of women and children. All were taught as lecture courses, designed to supplement the clinical training in the apprenticeship. Medicine was called "institutes of medicine" or "theory and practice of medicine" and consisted of descriptions of the effects of disease on the human organism and the changes produced in the blood, circulation, respiration, digestion, and secretions. The descriptions were based on contemporary theories rather than actual observation, so that the course was of little practical value. Surgery was far more practical. Minor operations were often performed before the class, but most students were too distant from the patient to see much. Obstetrics (which usually included diseases of women) was taught with the use of plaster or other models because it was considered indecent to expose a parturient woman to the class. It was also a highly practical course, although its value was obviously limited.[71]

The advantage of medical school education was that students received a systematic, thorough, and up-to-date account of material that was rarely provided by preceptors or textbooks. Whatever its deficiencies, formal medical education was undeniably superior in its coverage of the scientific and theoretical aspects of medicine to anything available to the medical student elsewhere.

Conclusion

The development of the medical school curriculum was the result of a variety of forces. Student demand led to the teaching of anatomy and dissection and a few of the clinical courses, but it was not responsible for the theoretical courses that comprised most of the curriculum. These courses were taught because the faculty felt they should be part of a medical school curriculum.

Students accepted faculty determination of the content of medical education for several reasons. Most cities only had one medical school and students had to accept the education that the faculty provided unless they were willing to travel. Students also viewed attendance at medical school with great anticipation because of their unsatisfactory experiences with their preceptors. Even though the lectures failed to live up to the students' expectations, they were more systematic and up-to-date than their preceptors' coverage of the material.

An equally important reason was that the faculty subsidized the students' education. Enrollments in most schools were small, and faculty members earned little from their lectures. They were willing to subsidize medical education because of the professional advantages described above. In addition, those faculty members who were preceptors were able to spend more time on their practices because they no longer had to do all of the teaching of their apprentices. Many faculty members also found teaching more stimulating than medical practice alone. Their hectic lives indicate that they were willing to make real sacrifices to be teachers.

No other parties interested in medical education were willing or able to influence the medical schools. The medical profession was poorly organized. State and local governments frequently subsidized medical education directly or indirectly, but they supported the policies of the faculty. Their only conditions for government aid were usually the free admission of a number of local students.[72]

By the second quarter of the nineteenth century, enrollments in medical schools had increased so much that student fees provided rich rewards for faculty members. Many new medical schools were established, leading to competition for students and a corresponding increase in student influence over the content of medical education.

II

MEDICAL EDUCATION
1825–1860

Those who contend for longer [medical school] sessions appear to make too high an estimate of the value of lectures as one of the means of imparting medical knowledge. Lectures . . . are of less utility than a judicious course of reading, or than the experience gained in a Hospital; and they should not be allowed to engross too large a part of the student's time to the prejudice of other modes of study.

SAMUEL CHEW (1864)

3

Medical Care and
Medical Education, 1825–1860

During the early nineteenth century, medical practice became professionalized and medical treatment standardized as medical school training became more popular and medical societies and journals were organized. Dispensary and hospital care increased with the growth in urban populations. Medical students became dissatisfied with the theoretical training in medical schools and turned to private courses from individual physicians and clinical instruction at hospitals and dispensaries. By mid-century, private instruction had become almost as important as medical school training.

Medical Care

The Nature of Medical Practice

Because little progress occurred in medical knowledge during the first half of the nineteenth century, the quality of medical care remained low, although it became more standardized due to the greater popularity of medical school training.[1]

Diagnosis continued to be unsystematic and superficial. The physical examination consisted of observing the patient's pulse, skin color, manner of breathing, and the appearance of the urine. Physicians attributed many diseases to heredity and often attached as much credence to the patient's emotions and surmises as the natural history of the illness. Although the invention of the stethoscope in France in 1819 led to the use of auscultation and percussion, the new diagnostic tools contributed little to medical care in the short run because more accurate diagnoses did not lead to better treatment.[2]

Few useful drugs existed in the materia medica and they were often misused. According to Dowling, the *United States Pharmacopoeia* of 1820 contained only 20 active drugs, including 3 specifics: quinine for malaria, mercury for syphilis, and ipecac for amebic dysentery. Alkaloid chemistry led to the isolation of morphine from opium in 1817 and quinine from cinchona bark in 1820. Morphine was prescribed with a casual indifference to its addictive properties and quinine was widely used in nonmalarial fevers, where it was ineffective and produced dangerous side effects. Strychnine, a poisonous alkaloid isolated in 1818, was popular as a

The epigraph for Part II is from Samuel Chew, *Lectures on Medical Education* (Philadelphia: Lindsay and Blakiston, 1864), pp. 140–41.

39

tonic for decades, and colchine, another alkaloid discovered in 1819, was widely used for gout despite its harmful side effects.[3]

Purgatives and emetics remained the most widely used drugs, although mineral drugs replaced botanical ones among physicians trained in medical schools because their actions were more drastic and immediate. The most popular purgative was calomel, a salt of mercury. Frequent use of calomel caused salivation and soreness of the gums and prolonged use produced ulceration of the mouth, loss of teeth, and destruction of facial bones. A popular emetic was tartar emetic, compounded of antimony, another poisonous mineral. Most of the mineral drugs that became popular at this time were dangerous poisons.

Surgery continued to involve many routine activities and little operative surgery. A private course on the "daily duties of the surgeon" offered in 1842 in Philadelphia covered "bleeding, cupping, leeching, enemata and other injections, the stomach-pump; bandaging . . . ; the construction . . . of ligatures; sutures and dressings; the treatment of certain wounds and deformities; fractures and luxations, with the construction of splints." Operations remained hazardous because of the lack of anesthetics and ignorance of the causes of infection.[4]

The physician's treatment of simple ailments was little different from that of centuries past or decades to come. He lanced boils, extracted teeth, and performed most of the surgical procedures described above. He dispensed drugs to relieve pain, constipation, and a few other common symptoms. He also used placebos, as indicated by one physician's treatment of a patient who had been bitten by a snake:

> In all that region whiskey was a popular remedy for snake bites, and of course I prescribed whiskey. The old fellows gathered from the entire neighborhood, and those who were familiar with that article heartily endorsed the prescription, and agreed that the young doctor was up to date on snakes. But it occurred to me that something more must be done, since I had come twenty miles, and the neighbors could have prescribed whiskey without any help from me. So I ransacked my brain to select from my saddle bags something a little above their comprehension. It was purely a matter of accident that I hit upon a bottle containing aqua ammonia and sweet oil. Its repeated application would give the people something to do, and the fumes of the ammonia would convince them that it was something "mighty powerful." That snake bite gave me the business of that neighborhood.[5]

Patients shared their physicians' beliefs in the benefits of the treatments of the period. Bloodletting, for example, was considered of preventive as well as therapeutic value. Samuel Gross, the eminent surgeon, observed that "bleeding in the spring and autumn was then very common, as a means, as was believed, of purifying the blood and relieving congestion. . . . The quantity of blood lost for these and other purposes generally varied from sixteen to twenty-four ounces. Unless the loss was considerable the patient did not consider that he had received an equivalent for his money."[6]

The treatment of serious illnesses, particularly infectious diseases, posed a greater challenge to the physician. It became standardized into a pattern known as "heroic therapy" by the teachings of medical schools, articles in medical journals, and discussions in medical society meetings. Heroic therapy was characterized by bloodlettings, purgative doses of calomel, emetics, and blisters, all designed to reduce the patient's fever, inflammation, and related symptoms. A starvation diet was also prescribed. Jacob Bigelow wrote that "so great [was] the ascending of heroic teachers and writers, that few medical men had the courage to incur the responsibility of omitting the active modes of treatment which were deemed indispensable to the safety of the patient."[7]

Heroic therapy was obviously a great danger to a seriously ill patient. Frequent bloodlettings, purgatives, and emetics weakened the patient, delayed recuperation, and sometimes caused or hastened death. Physicians rarely withheld treatment to allow the recuperative powers of nature to operate. The physicians in a small town in Pennsylvania where Samuel Gross practiced medicine in the 1830s were typical. He wrote that they "all bled, all gave emetics, all purged, all starved their patients. They were all real Sangrados, mowing down alike the infant, the youth, the adult, and the old man."[8]

The use of heroic therapy reached its zenith in the periodic terrifying epidemics of cholera and yellow fever. These epidemics created havoc in cities as the wealthier residents fled to rural areas and the remaining healthy residents spent their time nursing the sick and burying the dead. Physicians knew neither how to prevent the diseases nor how to treat the sick. Gross visited New York City hospitals and physicians during the cholera epidemic of 1832 and reported: "No one seemed to have definite notions upon any of these points. Empiricism reigned with unlimited sway. Every hospital had its peculiar formulae; every physician his peculiar views." The result was that heroic treatment was carried to even greater excesses, with even greater loss of life.[9]

The prevalence of heroic therapy is indicated by available hospital records. One study of all 187 cases of acute lobar pneumonia treated at the Massachusetts General Hospital before 1850 found that almost two-thirds of the patients were bled, often in large quantities, and "almost every case was vomited and purged, given mercury to salivation and sore gums [and] blistered with cantharides." Many were given no food except small amounts of liquids. A study of the Baltimore Almshouse in the first 10 months of 1848, when about 1,700 patients were treated for a wide range of major and minor illnesses, found a total of 220 blisterings and 4,300 drug prescriptions. Mercury and antimony (calomel and tartar emetic) were the most common mineral drugs. There were 13 bleedings, 67 cuppings and 3 applications of leeches, usually administered to patients with fever.[10]

Public opposition to heroic therapy developed in the second quarter of the century and led many patients to turn to homeopathic and botanical physicians, who opposed its use. By mid-century, heroic therapy was also under attack within the regular medical profession.

The Professionalization of Medical Practice

The number of trained physicians increased substantially during the first half of the nineteenth century. The earliest U.S. census data listed 40,755 physicians in 1850 and 55,055 in 1860, a rate of growth over the decade matching that of the total population. Trained physicians crowded into urban areas, which increased competition for patients and lowered earnings. Fees in New England increased from 25¢

to 40¢ in 1790 to 35¢ to 75¢ in 1840. In Rochester, New York, the proportion of physicians who were property owners decreased from two-thirds in 1836 to one-third in 1860. Among those who were property owners, the value of the property owned dropped from $2,400 to less than $1,500, while the average property value of all voters increased from $1,420 to $1,500. Many physicians survived on other sources of income, the liberal use of credit, and, in rural areas, barter.[11]

A few physicians became wealthy by catering to middle and upper class families. Gross reported that in one community where he practiced physicians charged $5 for deliveries among the poorer classes and $10 to $25 if they practiced among the wealthy. Gross, who developed a large surgical practice with many referrals, made as much as $9,000 a year. This may be compared to O'Hara's estimate of $2,000 a year earned by conscientious physicians in Philadelphia in 1860. Even that was well above the earnings of most physicians.[12]

Throughout the first half of the century, local medical societies were organized to reduce competition by means of fee bills and codes of professional etiquette. Many state medical societies were established and the American Medical Association was founded in 1847. One study of membership in medical societies early in the century found that 20 percent of the physicians in a New Hampshire county, 42 percent of those in a Connecticut county, and 82 percent of those in a Massachusetts county belonged to one or more medical societies. O'Hara found that fewer than one-third of the physicians in Philadelphia around 1860 were members of the county medical society, but that many physicians joined other local medical societies.[13]

A large number of medical journals contributed to the growing professionalism of medicine. Between 1797 and 1857, 178 medical journals were founded, 135 of them after 1832. Most had 400 to 700 subscribers and were short-lived, since only 30 of the 178 survived to 1857. The majority were connected in some way with a medical school or its faculty members. The journals published a few original articles, many articles taken from European or other American journals, and book reviews. Most did little to advance or promulgate medical knowledge, but a few achieved a reasonable level of quality by mid-century. Medical journals also contributed to the profession by publishing notices and reports of medical societies, medical schools, hospitals, and dispensaries.[14]

Changes in the Need for Medical Care

The need for medical care increased significantly in the second quarter of the nineteenth century because of the effects of immigration on urban housing and poverty. During the first quarter of the century, American cities had a reasonably low population density and satisfactory housing. Houses were separated by yards that provided space for family gardens; pure water was generally available; outdoor privies were in watertight vaults that were emptied regularly; fresh unadulterated milk was provided by family cows or reliable vendors; stables, slaughterhouses, and other disease-producing industries were separated from residential areas; and refuse did not create a health hazard.[15]

During the second quarter of the century, foreign immigration reached its highest level in relation to the existing population in the history of the nation, swelling the populations of large cities. The combined population of 21 major cities in 1860 was 1,127,000 in 1830, 3,544,000 in 1850, and 6,217,000 in 1860.[16]

Housing construction did not keep pace with the growth of the cities. At first, the exodus of the middle and upper classes from the center of the cities enabled large homes and mansions to be converted into apartments. As the demand for housing continued to grow, warehouses, cellars, and attics also were also converted into apartments. Shanties were constructed in the yards, gardens, and courts of the houses, producing crazy-quilts of ramshackle dwellings in previously quiet residential neighborhoods. The population densities in some neighborhoods in New York City doubled or tripled in the second quarter of the century, often with little increase in the number of houses.[17]

Toward mid-century a new form of housing developed, especially in New York City: the multi-story, multi-apartment tenant house or tenement. The tenement was designed to provide individual apartments at reasonable rents to families as a solution to the housing problem. However, in order to meet the incessantly growing demand for housing, additional tenements were often built in the back yards of the lots, resulting in substantial overcrowding.

Tenements created serious health problems. Only one or two rooms of each apartment had windows, and the bedrooms were placed in unventilated rooms in the interior of each apartment. Heat was the responsibility of the tenants, who usually could not afford the coal or wood necessary to keep their apartments warm. The outdoor privies built behind the tenements frequently overflowed and the sewage ran down the streets to the nearest stream. Garbage was placed in the unpaved streets and rarely cleaned up. Water was available only from pumps or wells in the streets, and was often contaminated by sewage leaking into cracks in the wooden pipes or into the water supplies for the wells. Most tenement residents bathed in the rivers, which was only possible in warm weather.

Substandard housing had a significant effect on mortality, as data from Boston indicate. Infant death rates, always a good measure of public health, increased significantly. In 1820–1829, 8.7 percent of all deaths occurred among those under one year of age; in 1850–1859 the proportion had risen to 23.8 percent. Tuberculosis became a major health problem. Even deaths from a preventable disease like smallpox increased from 6 in 1811–1815 to 331 in 1851–1855 as unvaccinated immigrants brought the disease with them. The death rate in one slum neighborhood in 1850 was 56.5 per thousand, compared to 13.0 per thousand in the most exclusive neighborhood. The death rate in New York City increased from about 21 per thousand in 1810 to 37 per thousand in 1857.[18]

The burden of this increasing mortality and morbidity ultimately fell on the community, which needed to care for the sick, their dependents, the widows, and the orphans. Poor relief expenditures in Boston increased from $28,000 around 1820 to $168,000 in 1860, doubling in cost per capita. In Philadelphia, total public expenditures for the poor increased from about $100,000 around 1820 to close to 200,000 by the early 1850s. Most of the poor and paupers were immigrants:

80 percent of those admitted to the New York City almshouse from 1849 to 1858 were immigrants.[19]

Dispensaries and Hospitals

The health problems of the poor led to the increased use of dispensaries and hospitals. Dispensaries continued to serve as the first line of defense in the institutional care of the sick, treating ambulatory patients at the dispensaries and the bedridden in their homes. Neighborhood dispensaries were established throughout cities in response to population growth. Where 1 dispensary in New York City had treated almost 15,000 patients in 1830, 10 treated over 150,000 patients in 1866. Medical specialization also developed within dispensaries. In 1825, the New York City Dispensary had separate clinics for surgical diseases, head and chest diseases, abdominal and female diseases, eye and ear diseases, and skin diseases.[20]

Dispensaries had no difficulty recruiting medical staffs, even with their low pay ($50 a year in New York City in the 1830s and $240 a year around 1850). They were attractive to young physicians because they were an excellent source of clinical training. In 1837, Oliver Wendell Holmes wrote that "a consulting-room well attended is one of the most valuable schools for students as well as practitioners of medicine, since many cases of disease may be seen within a very limited time; and being thus collected, may be compared with and illustrate each other." Turnover among the staff was high, however, as physicians used the experience as a stepping-stone to private practice.[21]

Hospitals remained far behind dispensaries as providers of health care because of their high costs and low incomes. The bedridden sick who could afford to pay for their care preferred to be treated at home, and the poor who used the hospitals had to be treated for free. The hospitals' only regular paying patients were seamen and some of the insane. Almshouses continued to provide most hospital care for the poor, thereby reducing the need for voluntary hospitals. In 1845, the United States had only 12 voluntary and public general hospitals located in 9 cities, plus a few specialized mental and marine hospitals.[22]

Hospitals did change their roles in some ways. They began to receive nearby cases of accidents or sudden illness. Voluntary hospitals attracted paying patients from communities without suitable facilities for treatment. Almshouse hospitals expanded into full-fledged public hospitals. Both voluntary and public hospitals admitted many immigrants. Irish immigrants comprised 38 percent of the patients admitted in 1840 to the Pennsylvania Hospital, a voluntary hospital in Philadelphia. Bellevue Hospital, a public hospital in New York, admitted 10,766 American-born and 57,310 foreign-born patients between 1846 and 1858. Boston established two hospitals in 1847 to care almost exclusively for immigrant Irish paupers.[23]

Hospitals remained limited in their range of services and types of patients. The most common diseases of hospital patients continued to be infectious diseases like typhoid, tuberculosis, influenza, syphilis, and various gastrointestinal disorders. Downie analyzed admissions to the Pennsylvania Hospital for all years ending in zero or five from 1755 to 1850, with 73 percent of all admissions occurring after 1810. Fevers and inflammations accounted for 45 percent of all medical and surgical admissions. In public hospitals, drunkenness and alcoholism were also common reasons for admission.[24]

Although many hospital cases were surgical, few operations were performed. At the Baltimore Almshouse, 60 to 80 beds were used for surgical patients, with most patients suffering from wounds, fractures, lacerations, ulcers, and similar conditions. However, only 104 of 2,571 patients admitted in the 12 months beginning May, 1834, were operated on, including 7 amputations. The Pennsylvania Hospital study cited above found that 26 percent of the medical and surgical admissions were for trauma like that at the Baltimore Almshouse, but that few of the patients underwent operations. Hospitals did not have operating rooms until the end of the century, and operations were performed in the hospital amphitheater. The distinction between medical and surgical wards in hospitals was often a casual one. The Pennsylvania Hospital did not bother to distinguish between them until 1821.[25]

Obstetrical cases were also uncommon in hospitals. The Baltimore Almshouse had only 224 births and 25 stillbirths among 16,500 cases treated between 1832 and 1841. In the Pennsylvania Hospital study, only 3 percent of all admissions studied between 1755 and 1850 were obstetrical. Deliveries posed major problems for hospitals because of the danger of puerperal fever. Many obstetrical departments were closed periodically and sometimes permanently because of outbreaks of the disease.[26]

Psychiatric patients continued to cause difficulties for hospitals. The Pennsylvania Hospital study found that the insane, who were mostly paying patients, comprised about one-half of the patients at the year-end census from the late eighteenth century until the asylum department opened in 1841. Public hospitals, which did not accept paying patients, had fewer psychiatric patients. The Philadelphia Hospital had only 188 insane patients among its 1,400 patients in 1841, plus 23 epileptics and 24 idiots. The high cost of incarcerating the insane in hospitals forced both private hospitals and governments to construct separate asylums. The small private asylums cared for 50 to 100 patients, practically all of whom were paying patients. The large public asylums provided care for the great majority of the insane, whose families could not afford to pay for their care. By 1860, most states had at least one public insane asylum.[27]

Public hospitals assumed responsibility for the care of the sick with contagious diseases. Cities like New York and Philadelphia established separate hospitals for contagious diseases to free their municipal hospitals of the burden, while other cities provided for them in separate sections of municipal hospitals.[28]

Hospitals provided more nursing care than medical treatment. Most patients were recuperating from infectious diseases or injuries, and few needed frequent medical treatment or close attention. The quality of nursing care left much to be desired because most hospitals, particularly the public hospitals, could only afford to recruit nurses from patients, ex-patients, and almshouse residents. Few nurses had any interest in or aptitude for nursing, although some nurses in private hospitals were skilled and dedicated. One physician in a private hospital observed: "The nurses, . . . were, as to the women, usually faithful, and sober and clean, up to their light. The men usually faithful, not always sober, and never clean, as we now consider cleanliness. But the nurses knew as much about cleanliness as did the surgeons."[29]

The immediate medical needs of patients were met by several house officers who were medical students or, less often, recent graduates of medical schools. Because the number of students desiring hospital experience exceeded the number of hospitals, students paid hospitals for the privilege. The Baltimore Almshouse charged its house officers $50 in 1818 and $225 in the 1830s for a one-year term of service, which included room and board. Fees at the Philadelphia Hospital were quite similar. Some hospitals did not provide room and board and the house officers lived outside the hospital.[30]

The duties of the house officers varied from hospital to hospital. In a graded arrangement, such as at the New York Hospital, the student started as a "junior walker" who took orders, dressed and bandaged wounds, administered bloodlettings, and copied the cases into the medical records. He was later promoted to a "senior walker" who dressed fractures and dictated the case histories. The highest level, the house physician or surgeon, was the only one who resided in the hospital and was responsible for the care of the patients in the absence of the attending staff. At other hospitals house officers also served as hospital pharmacists.[31]

House officers were frequently accused of assuming too much responsibility for the care of the patients. A report of a committee at the Philadelphia General Hospital stated in 1845:

> [The house officers] were supposed to be under the direction of the Visiting Staff, and under the rules they were not allowed to prescribe, unless in a case of emergency. It was said that the rules were not complied with, and that the residents, recently from school and anxious to practice, often rather unduly elated with the first honors of the Doctorate, are placed at once, and while totally inexperienced, in situations of the highest responsibility, in charge of a Hospital often containing 500 patients, subject only to such limited control as the attending physicians see fit to exercise; or rather such as the residents themselves are willing to submit to.[32]

Hospitals also provided house officers with opportunities for dissection, regardless of the hospital regulations. The Baltimore Almshouse hospital had between 150 and 300 deaths a year in the 1830s, almost all of which could be autopsied. At the Philadelphia General Hospital, there were "rules of the most stringent character," according to the committee referred to above, "for the safe keeping of the bodies and to preserve them unmutilated in cases where the friends of the deceased can be found." However, the committee found "little heed given to the first injunction and the utter disregard to the second."[33]

Relations between the house staff and the lay boards of the hospitals were marked by repeated conflict. The boards felt free to oversee every aspect of hospital management, including the performance of the house staff. Thomas Emmet observed: "I have never known an instance of where [the house officers] have been . . . treated with the proper respect. . . . The members of the medical profession are generally regarded by those in authority as a necessary nuisance and treated as such."[34]

The medical leadership of hospitals was in the hands of 6 to 12 community physicians called the attending staff. Each attending physician was responsible for a ward or group of wards and visited the hospital for a few hours daily to oversee the care of his patients. In order to reduce the impact of the hospital appointment on the attending physician's private practice, he served one three-month term annually. At the end of the term, his patients were turned over to his successor. The attending staff received no pay from the hospital or the patients, but the advantages of a hospital appointment were more than adequate compensation.

The quality of hospital attending physicians left much to be desired. Even as late as 1870, when the staffs had improved greatly, J. Collins Warren observed about the Pennsylvania Hospital: "An appointment to the visiting staff of this hospital was the goal of every Philadelphia doctor, but curiously enough the most prominent surgeons of the day were not to be found there." The great majority of attending physicians served for a few years and left; a few remained for years or decades and comprised about one-half of the staff at any given time. Hospitals sorely missed the fresh talent and leadership that greater turnover would have provided.[35]

The most significant consequence of the hospitals' failure to attract high quality physicians was the establishment of separate specialty hospitals. Urban physicians interested in a particular aspect of medicine organized specialty hospitals to attract enough patients with appropriate diseases to permit them to learn more about the field. Eye and ear hospitals were opened in New York, Philadelphia, and Boston between 1821 and 1830. An infirmary for diseases of the lungs was opened in New York City in 1823, a children's hospital was opened in Philadelphia in 1855, and a lying-in hospital was opened in Boston in 1832.[36]

Many, but not all, specialty hospitals were successful. The New York Eye Infirmary received state aid after 1824, and a committee of the state legislature spoke of "this excellent charity" in 1848. It treated 6,000 patients in 1866. The eye infirmary was so successful that the New York Ophthalmic Hospital was opened in 1852. The lying-in hospital in Boston, on the other hand, had only 650 deliveries in its first 22 years, and closed from 1856 to 1872.[37]

Specialty hospitals could easily have used the facilities of general voluntary hospitals, which were not overcrowded. However, the lay boards and medical staffs of voluntary hospitals were not interested in using their hospitals for specialty care. Thus the few attempts to provide specialty care in general hospitals failed. For example, the New York Hospital made its facilities available for the lying-in hospital in 1801, but the latter left in 1827. The eye infirmary used the same hospital's facilities from 1824 to 1826, but it also left. The specialty hospitals constructed their own facilities, depriving the general hospitals of the services of some of the leading physicians of the period.[38]

Overall, hospitals were less successful than dispensaries in recruiting physicians, even though the work was less demanding. Physicians preferred dispensaries because there they learned how to treat patients of all ages and with many kinds of illnesses under conditions similar to those of private practice, while hospital physicians and house officers saw the same convalescing patients day after day. In addition, many dispensary patients had jobs and could become paying patients in the physician's private practice, while hospital patients were usually charity patients.

Hospital staff members actively used hospitals for educational purposes. They regularly brought their apprentices on hospital rounds with them, a practice which had begun in the eighteenth century. Apprentices of physicians without hospital appointments also sought admission to hospitals in order to participate in these activities. Hospital appointments became increasingly valuable because educational activities enabled staff members to attract apprentices as well as consultations and referrals from practicing physicians who had gone on hospital rounds with them as students.

In order to expand their educational activities, hospitals built amphitheaters that served a variety of educational functions. The few hospital operations were held there as a means of teaching surgery (and enhancing the reputation of the surgeons). Autopsies were carried out in them. Amphitheater clinics enabled the attending staff to present cases of interest to medical students and local physicians. One of the first hospital amphitheaters was used for clinical lectures in the Pennsylvania Hospital beginning in 1804. Some time later the Philadelphia General Hospital built an amphitheater accommodating up to 800 persons. In New York at mid-century, the New York Hospital had two amphitheaters, the smaller of which held 250 persons.[39]

Ward rounds and amphitheater operations and clinics were turning hospitals into educational centers that offered students instruction in a range of clinical subjects. In fact, medical education was moving out of the medical schools in several ways, a development that was actively supported by the medical schools.

Medical Education

The Growth of Medical Schools

The number and enrollments of medical schools increased significantly during the first half of the nineteenth century, as did all institutions of higher education (Table 3.1). The number of medical schools offering instruction on a degree-granting basis increased from 4 in 1800 to 47 in 1860, with many others in operation during part of the period. The number of graduates of medical schools increased from 343 in 1800–1809 to 17,213 in 1850–1859. Thousands of additional students attended medical school but did not graduate.

Medical schools, like colleges generally, were established first in the Northeast and expanded to the South and West. The proportion of medical schools that were located in New England, New York State, and Philadelphia decreased from 10 of 13 in 1820 to 16 of 47 in 1860. Medical schools and colleges in the Northeast had higher admission requirements and academic standards than those elsewhere because of the larger number of secondary schools in that part of the country.[40]

Medical schools, like colleges, provided many benefits to their communities. They educated local students and held public lectures and other cultural events. Their faculties were professional and social assets. They attracted students and dollars to the community. In 1842 one observer described the influence of medical schools in Philadelphia, which, along with New York City, was the leading medical center in the nation:

> Consider that there are three flourishing medical colleges in the very heart of the city, and near each other, either of which would stand high in any part of the country. About

the first of November from seven hundred to one thousand medical students and strangers are, all at once, to be seen traversing the streets and inquiring for the various medical offices. This noticeable influx . . . is a matter of commercial and social interest. These students scatter into many families, and medical men and medical subjects become legitimate matters of discourse. They spend the winter, and leave to the boarding-houses, lecturers, book-sellers, merchants, private teachers, &c., &c., many thousand dollars. Even strangers can see that medicine is a subject of general interest in Philadelphia. When comparing these flourishing medical schools with literary colleges, law schools and theological schools, the difference often appears marvelous. What other distinction has this city achieved except in medical science? But, here, all is enthusiasm—all spirit.[41]

Medical schools, like colleges, received substantial aid from their communities and states. Communities provided contributions, loans, and paying students. Many states permitted medical schools to hold lotteries and receive taxes on sales at auctions or other transactions. Direct state appropriations to medical schools between 1804 and 1861 exceeded $750,000, with New York State, Maryland, and Louisiana providing over $130,000 each. Only Pennsylvania, Rhode Island and Vermont did not appropriate funds for medical schools during this period.[42]

The proportion of physicians of the period with medical school training varied with the personal characteristics of the physicians. Hudson analyzed the eminent physicians listed in the 1928 edition of the *American Medical Biography*. He found that 69 percent of the physicians trained between 1801 and 1810 and 85 percent of those trained between 1811 and 1820 held medical school degrees, with the proportion increasing thereafter. O'Hara studied physicians listed in an 1860 Philadelphia directory and found that 70 percent of the 834 physicians who could be traced attended three years of medical school. The majority of physicians, who lived in small towns and rural areas, were less likely to have degrees. Waite estimated that

TABLE 3.1. Medical Schools and Institutions of Higher Education, 1800–1860

Year	Medical Schools[a]	Medical School Graduates[b]	All Institutions of Higher Education	
			Schools[c]	Enrollments[b]
1800	4	343	32	1,237
1810	6	1,375	37	2,562
1820	13	4,338	67	3,872
1830	22	6,849	106	7,822
1840	30	11,828	142	12,964
1850	42	17,213	217	17,556
1860	47	16,717	—	32,364

[a]Medical schools are those in operation on a degree-granting basis.
[b]Medical school graduates are for decade beginning in year listed; higher education enrollments are for year listed only.
[c]Dates for institutions of higher education vary slightly.

Sources: William G. Rothstein, *American Physicians in the Nineteenth Century* (Baltimore: Johns Hopkins University Press, 1972), pp. 93, 98; Colin B. Burke, *American Collegiate Populations* (New York: New York University Press, 1982), p. 18; Colin B. Burke, "The Expansion of American Higher Education," in *The Transformation of Higher Learning, 1860–1930*, ed. Konrad H. Jarausch (Stuttgart, West Germany: Klett-Cotta, 1982), p. 111.

only about 20 percent of the physicians in Ohio about 1835 had medical degrees, although many others attended medical school without graduating.[43]

Medical Students

Most medical students entered medical school without having obtained a college education. Waite studied the preliminary education of students who attended two rural medical colleges in Vermont and found that 7 and 4 percent of the students of the two schools, respectively, had received a Bachelor of Arts degree prior to entering the school. Another 10 percent of the students at one of the schools had some college education prior to matriculation. Allowing for students who could not be traced, probably 15 to 20 percent had received some college education before entering medical school. The lack of college training was not for want of opportunity, because a college education was readily available to the 84 percent of the students who came from New England or New York State. Hudson found in his study of eminent physicians that about 35 percent of those who completed their medical education from 1801 to the 1830s had college degrees and that the proportion increased gradually to about 50 percent in the 1870s.[44]

The practice of medicine was not a popular career among college graduates. An 1850 study of 12,400 graduates of eight northeastern colleges found that one-half became lawyers or clergymen, and only 8 percent became physicians. Burke's study of thousands of pre-Civil War college graduates found that medicine was less popular than the ministry, law, and some other occupations. He estimated that about 20 percent of the college graduates with known occupations chose medicine, a proportion that would have been much lower if the graduates with unknown occupations were included. Burke also found that graduates in medicine and the ministry tended to be older than those in law and business, probably because they delayed their educations to raise the needed money.[45]

Most students who attended medical school never received degrees. This is indicated by the ratio of graduates to all students in the two-year medical school course. If all students graduated, the graduates should have constituted 50 percent of the enrollment. However, records of the Harvard Medical School and the Berkshire Medical Institution from 1823 to 1838 show that the ratio of graduates to students remained fairly constant at 23 percent at Harvard and 28 percent at Berkshire. At the University of Pennsylvania from 1830 to 1859 the ratio was 37 percent. Because students often transferred between medical schools, some students may have left to obtain degrees at other schools. However, Waite found that the number of students who left a Vermont medical school to obtain their degrees elsewhere just about equalled the number who came there from other schools to obtain their degrees. He concluded that only about one-half of the students actually received degrees from any medical school. [46]

Characteristics of Medical Schools

The typical medical school before the Civil War was housed in one main building with two lecture halls. The lecture hall on the lower floor was used for chemistry, materia medica, and theory and practice of medicine. The upper lecture hall, which had a skylight, was used for anatomy, physiology, and surgery. The same or another building held facilities for dissection, a chemistry laboratory, offices for the faculty, and a museum of anatomical specimens and materia medica. Libraries were usually the personal possession of faculty members.[47]

Medical schools differed among themselves in many respects. In 1825, the average enrollment of 14 schools was 147 students, but 1 school had 480 students, while 4 schools had 60 or fewer students. With regard to the length of the sessions, about 1850, 2 schools had sessions of 5 or more months, 26 had sessions of 16 to 18 weeks, and 5 had sessions of less than 16 weeks. Shorter sessions were common in the rural schools, which often employed faculty members of urban schools and arranged their sessions to avoid overlapping terms. Some schools with shorter sessions offered optional sessions that covered material taught in the regular sessions of other schools.[48]

Student fees varied between urban and rural schools. In the second quarter of the century, urban schools charged from $15 to $20 per course and rural schools from $10 to $15, with both types of schools requiring 5 to 7 courses. A few decades later the fees were put into a single payment of $200 to $285 at the urban schools and $150 at the rural ones. Room and board was about $1.50 to $2.50 per week in rural areas and $3.00 per week in urban areas.[49]

Medical Schools and the Sciences

Medical schools were foremost among American institutions of higher education before the Civil War in their commitment to education in the sciences. They were the first to introduce laboratory courses into the curriculum through their courses in practical anatomy and chemistry. They were among the first to teach the use of the microscope, as medical school faculty members returned from Europe with training in its use. They frequently introduced science courses into the curriculum of their affiliated and other nearby liberal arts colleges.[50]

Medical schools were the major academic employers of the leading scientists of the period, according to an analysis carried out for this study. The analysis was based on 56 scientists whom Daniels found had contributed more than half of the material in the leading American scientific and medical journals published between 1815 and 1845, excluding popularizing articles and articles on nonscientific subjects like the art of medicine and pharmaceuticals. Of the 22 scientists who had M.D. degrees, 20 taught in medical schools, 15 for at least five years. Of the 34 who did not receive M.D. degrees, 11 taught in medical schools, 7 for at least five years. The 31 who taught in medical schools taught in 20 different medical schools. These data indicate that a large number of medical schools employed the best scientists available. The 25 scientists who did not teach in medical schools almost always had research interests unrelated to medical education, such as astronomy, mathematics, geology, and archaeology. Many of them never taught in any institution of higher education.[51]

Scientists were employed by medical schools because of their scientific skills, not because of their interest in medicine. For example, Robert Hare, the eminent chemist, taught chemistry at the University of Pennsylvania medical school for many years, even though, according to a student, he "did not pretend to teach medical chemistry, but confined himself only to general chemistry as taught in scientific schools."[52]

Medical schools also trained many science teachers and scientists. Guralnick fround that many of the chemists and other scientists who taught at liberal arts colleges toward mid-century received their training in a medical school. Elliott studied scientists who wrote three or more scientific articles in American journals that were indexed in the *Catalogue of Scientific Papers* of the Royal Society between 1800 and 1863. Of 474 who were traced, 20.7 percent had studied medicine, and medicine was the second most common occupation of the scientists in the sample. Kohlstedt analyzed members of the American Association for the Advancement of Science from 1848 to 1860. Of the 337 whom she considered "leaders" of the society, 84 had received some medical school training. Of the 1,109 members she was able to trace, 23.2 percent were physicians, more than those in any other occupation.[53]

In contrast to the emphasis on the sciences in medical schools, liberal arts colleges added the sciences to their curriculum warily and reluctantly. The average number of faculty members per college in mathematics and the sciences increased from about one in 1800 to two in 1830 and four in 1860.[54]

The unwillingness of colleges to teach the sciences is exemplified by the scientific schools of the leading colleges. Colleges established scientific schools as separate departments using the donations of wealthy manufacturers after whom the schools were named. They included the Sheffield school at Yale, the Lawrence school at Harvard, the Greene school at Princeton, and the Chandler school at Dartmouth. The colleges accepted the donations willingly, but established the schools grudgingly. Sheffield gave more than $100,000 to Yale, but Yale refused to pay the scientific school's faculty for some years, forcing them to work for virtually nothing. At Harvard, teachers in the Lawrence Scientific School, including eminent scientists like Louis Agassiz, Wolcott Gibbs, Jeffries Wyman, and Asa Gray, were not considered faculty members of the university so long as the school was separated from Harvard College.[55]

The scientific schools were carefully differentiated from the colleges and short-changed in every conceivable way. Their full-time faculty, if any were employed, were paid less or otherwise differentiated from the faculty in the college. Their admission standards, if any, were lower than those in the college, so that their students were younger and had less education. The curricula consisted of personal study with faculty members or individual courses so diffuse that they did not comprise an academic program. The total course of study, if any existed, was usually three rather than four years. The students either did not receive any academic degrees or received degrees that were carefully differentiated from the degrees awarded to students in the college. Despite this treatment, most scientific schools succeeded. The colleges thereupon isolated the scientific students by denying them the right to take courses in the college, to participate in extracurricular activities in the college, and to live in college dormitories.[56]

Many smaller colleges created parallel courses in the sciences that emulated the scientific schools, but the parallel courses did not have the same standards, the same degrees, or the same level of faculty and financial support as the classical courses. As late as 1871, a commission of the Province of Ontario visited eight major scientific schools in the United States to gather ideas on a scientific school for the province. It concluded: "On no point was the testimony at the Institutions we visited more clear, distinct, and uniform than that the proposed School of Practical Science should, in its teaching and management and government, be kept entirely distinct from any other Institution. The more efficient the Institution to which it might be attached, the more certain would be the failure of the School."[57]

Clinical Teaching in Medical Schools

Student pressure for better clinical teaching was the greatest problem confronting medical schools. The schools lacked the resources, faculty, and patients to add more clinical training to the curriculum. They vacillated between avoiding clinical teaching altogether and providing it with a minimum of faculty time and resources. Despite that problem, the quality of clinical teaching improved considerably over the first half of the century.

Evidence of student pressure is found in the claims of medical school catalogues about their "practical" clinical instruction. An 1840 New Orleans medical school catalogue was typical when it described the course on theory and practice of medicine as "avoiding useless dissertations on Nosology, Contagions, Miasms, etc.; it is devoted to the history, causes, character, nature and treatment of particular diseases." In the course on obstetrics and diseases of women and children, it claimed that "care is taken to touch lightly upon all that is not useful, and to bring forward everything of practical importance."[58]

Nevertheless, the lecture method forced medical school teaching to be didactic and theoretical. No other form of instruction was feasible given the high ratio of students to faculty members. The students sat in the lecture rooms for five or six hours a day while each faculty member in turn gave a one-hour lecture. This continued for five days a week. The students sometimes attended a local hospital once or twice a week where they either sat in the amphitheater or walked the wards. In both cases their only activity was to listen to the attending physicians. Laboratory training occurred in dissection and sometimes in chemistry.

Examinations for graduation reflected the didactic nature of the instruction. Each faculty member administered a brief oral examination and a student graduated if he passed a majority of the examinations. James C. White said that his oral examination in surgery at Harvard medical school in the 1850s consisted of one question: "Well, White, what would you do for a wart?"[59]

The most significant improvement in clinical teaching in the first half of the nineteenth century was the publication of medical textbooks. It greatly reduced the student's dependence on lectures, which varied according to the lecturer's clinical and teaching skills and the student's note-taking ability. Textbooks contained up-to-date information about clinical medicine to which students could refer regularly. The first textbooks used in American medical schools were written by English physicians or were English or American translations of French texts. From

1800 to 1849, 777 reprints and translations of foreign medical books were published in the United States, compared to only 543 American books. The first American textbooks were published in the 1820s and 1830s, and, despite their limitations, they revolutionized clinical education.[60]

Medical colleges did make significant efforts to improve clinical teaching. Museums of anatomical and pathological specimens were the pride of most medical colleges, and were used extensively to illustrate lectures. Models of body parts were widely used after papier-mâché models were manufactured in Europe in the 1820s. Obstetrical models of chamois or leather were also used in teaching. Although personal instruction was impractical on a regular basis because of the large amount of faculty time required, it was provided occasionally. The 1845 catalogue of the University of Maryland announced:

> In order to facilitate the acquisition of the practical knowledge of the physical signs of disease—so essential to accurate and positive diagnosis—[the professor] will meet the members of his class in small clubs near the commencement of the term, and in this way endeavor to give to each of them individually such demonstrative instruction as may be necessary in order to enable them subsequently to prepare themselves for the profitable use of auscultation and percussion.[61]

A more common development in clinical education was to have a patient present in the room while the lecturer described his illness and treatment. This kind of instruction occurred in the clinics in hospitals and dispensaries, where patients were available. By mid-century, medical schools used hospitals for teaching in Philadelphia, New York, New Orleans, Baltimore, Boston, St. Louis, and other cities.[62]

A few medical schools built their own hospitals. Probably the first was at the University of Maryland, where several members of the faculty built a hospital in 1823 that was taken over by the medical school in 1830. Medical school hospitals were no more widely used for instruction than were other hospitals. At the University of Maryland hospital, clinical lectures were given twice a week in medicine and twice a week in surgery, which was the practice in many non-university hospitals. Ward rounds consisted of an invitation to students to accompany the surgery professor on his early morning daily rounds.[63]

The most frequent proposal to improve medical school instruction was to lengthen the 18-week medical school term. Most faculty members opposed this, claiming that improvement was needed most in the rest of the three-year period of medical education. John Ware, Jacob Bigelow, and Oliver Wendell Holmes of the Harvard Medical School observed in 1849:

> The whole proposition proceeds from what seems to us an exaggerated view of the importance of teaching by lectures, as compared with the other means of medical instruction. It is virtually assumed that they constitute the principal and most valuable part of this instruction; it seems to the committee, on the contrary, that they constitute a subordinate and subsidiary part. . . .
> The great purpose of lectures should be, to teach the student how to learn for himself. They are not to take the place of private, individual study, but to inform the

pupil how that study may be pursued to advantage. . . . Learning is a thing which no one man can do for another; the weight of education must fall upon the learner.[64]

Ware, Bigelow, and Holmes called for "a system of personal private study in the interval between courses of lectures, under the direction of competent instructors. This system should embrace examinations, recitations from books, and, in the demonstrative branches, demonstrations on the part of the student, instead of the instructor, but still under his direction and superintendence."[65] Instruction of this kind had existed outside medical schools for some time.

Medical Education Outside the Medical School

Student dissatisfaction with medical school instruction led them to attend three types of private medical education outside the medical school: systematic apprenticeship training, private courses, and teaching in hospitals and dispensaries. All played a major role in medical education.

Most medical schools continued to require a three-year apprenticeship for graduation. An analysis for this study of the annual catalogues of the Harvard medical school for all years ending in zero or five from 1830 to 1870 found that over the whole period only 6 percent of the students had no preceptors. In the mid-century period from 1840 to 1860, 10 percent had no preceptor. Many students chose faculty members as preceptors partly in the hope of receiving better instruction and partly in the hope of improving their chances of graduating. At the University of Maryland medical school in 1850–1851, an analysis for this study found that of the 182 students listed in the catalogue, 51 had faculty preceptors, 72 had nonfaculty preceptors, 35 had institutional preceptors, 18 had no preceptors but had licenses to practice medicine, and 6 others had no preceptors. The most common institutional preceptor was the University of Maryland hospital, which was equivalent to a faculty preceptor. Thus about one-half of the students had faculty preceptors.[66]

While many faculty preceptors were no better than community preceptors, some provided excellent educations for their students. In the late 1840s George B. Wood of the University of Pennsylvania required his apprentices to attend: (1) the normal two courses of lectures at the medical school; (2) daily recitations throughout the term on the material taught in the medical school using different textbooks selected by Wood; (3) a course on demonstrative and clinical midwifery from a private teacher chosen by Wood; (4) a summer session taught at the medical school; and (5) daily clinics and twice weekly clinical lectures at the Pennsylvania Hospital. Wood's fee of $100 included the fees for the private course, the summer session, and the hospital clinics. The daily recitation consisted of Wood quizzing each of the 25 students in the class in turn about an assigned reading from a textbook. A former student recalled: "The recitation continued without regard to time until the assigned lesson had been completed. He never made the agreeable mistake of assigning a short lesson."[67]

Samuel Gross was another faculty member who served as a preceptor. He wrote that his "practice was to examine [the apprentices] at a certain hour regularly . . . thrice a week, as long as they were under my charge, not with book in hand, . . . but extemporaneously, often explaining matters in the form of familiar lectures, interspersed with apt questions. . . . One and a half to two hours were generally consumed in this exercise. The teaching was always conducted in the most systematic manner; the pupils were obliged to be punctual in their attendance; and whenever it was in my power, I showed them cases and illustrated the application of bandages and apparatus.'' Gross also charged $100 per year but complained that "although I had altogether a considerable number of private pupils, I am sure I never made three thousand dollars in this way, as there were many who never paid me anything. . . . Now and then I was decidedly a loser, as some of them borrowed money of me which they never returned."[68]

Some community physicians developed highly organized apprenticeship programs to attract medical students. An 1857 description of private instruction in Philadelphia observed:

> we have in this city numerous clubs of two or more physicians, who take office students for one, two or three years, examining them at intervals upon the subjects they are studying, advising them in regard to the apportionment of their time, directing them into what channels to turn their minds during the intervals between the regular courses of instruction, and performing the double service of teachers and friends to those who in the crowd and whirl of the great medical class are so much in need of guidance and counsel.[69]

Some groups of preceptors in cities organized students into classes. In Boston, a group of Harvard medical school faculty members established the Boston Private Medical School in 1825. They added other highly qualified physicians to their teaching staff and provided year-round instruction in all branches of medicine and hospital teaching at the Massachusetts General Hospital. A second private school followed in 1830 and a third in 1836. The total enrollment of these private schools between 1825 and 1840 was 20 percent of Harvard's enrollment during this period, although not all students in the private schools attended Harvard.[70]

The most important private school in Boston was the Tremont Street School, organized in 1838. During the medical school term, the school held evening classes to review the material covered in the medical school lectures. When the term was over, daily recitations continued and instructors taught courses covering all of the medical school subjects as well as diseases of the eye and ear, diseases of the skin, auscultation and percussion, embryology, and microscopic anatomy. Clinical instruction was given at local hospitals. The fee was $100 per year, the standard fee for a preceptorship. From 1838 to 1858, an average of 23 percent of the Harvard medical school class attended the Tremont Street School. Other private schools also operated in Boston at this time. One, the Boylston Street School, organized in 1847, was authorized to award medical degrees, but it never did.[71]

Some of the teachers in the private schools were or later became eminent educators. Oliver Wendell Holmes and Jacob Bigelow were among the teachers at the Tremont Street School who were appointed to the faculty of the Harvard medical school. Their appointments led Harvard to make the Tremont Street School its official summer school and later to merge it into the medical school. Louis Agassiz and Jeffries Wyman, who also taught at the Tremont Street School, subsequently taught in the Lawrence Scientific School at Harvard.[72]

Private instruction in Philadelphia was even more extensive, in that the private schools were supplemented by private courses on individual subjects. Students were encouraged by the medical schools to attend the private courses, many of which were taught by faculty members. The University of Pennsylvania medical school notified its students around 1840 of the:

> numerous and skilful private teachers, whose aid may be advantageously sought by the Students, and Dispensaries, which afford the most valuable opportunities for obtaining practical familiarity with the phenomena and treatment of disease. A peculiar feature . . . of medical tuition in this city, is the great extent and variety of private instruction . . . serving as a highly useful auxiliary to the schools.[73]

The early impetus for private instruction in Philadelphia was the teaching of anatomy. The University of Pennsylvania lacked the facilities to teach dissection to all of its students and permitted them to take the course with private instructors. The first private anatomy school was established in 1817 by some of the school's faculty members. It soon expanded its curriculum to cover all branches of medicine. Between 1825 and 1835 it averaged over 100 students a year, after which it slowly declined. A second school, the Philadelphia School of Anatomy, was founded in 1820 and taught dissection with great distinction for about four decades. Many of its instructors were appointed to faculty positions at medical schools, and some were instrumental in establishing two new medical schools in the city. Another private school founded in 1821 by private physicians became the second medical school in the city, the Jefferson Medical College.[74]

Still another Philadelphia school, the Obstetrical Institute organized in 1837, taught obstetrics to groups of 12 second-year medical students. Nursing students were admitted later and trained side by side with the medical students. During the course, which consisted of about 60 class periods over 11 weeks, each medical student was required to use models to become familiar with every aspect of deliveries. At the end of the course, the medical student was assigned to a case of labor. He visited the pregnant woman late in her pregnancy, delivered the child (with the help of assistants at the institute), visited the mother and child after the delivery, and wrote a report of the case. By 1857, this course had trained over 430 physicians and 100 nurses, and offered four sessions a year.[75]

Individual physicians taught many private courses. In the late 1850s these included: pathological anatomy and the clinical use of the microscope (taught by J. J. Woodward); auscultation and percussion (taught by W. Gerhard); physical diagnosis; diseases of the lungs and heart (taught by J. DaCosta); medicine and surgery of the eye and ear, with instruction on the use of the ophthalmoscope and otoscope; a number of courses on operative surgery where students performed operations on cadavers (taught by Samuel Gross and others); and medical chemistry and its relation to toxicology and therapeutics.[76]

Quiz sessions were especially popular private courses that reviewed the lecture material systematically in daily or weekly sessions. A description of one such course in Philadelphia noted: "This Quiz, as it is called, is an old and well established institution, and despite the idea of some that it is adapted to cram the student with answers to test questions, and thus to fit him for graduation rather than for practice, it will always be popular."[77]

Private medical instruction developed in other cities as well. The New York Medical Institute was established in 1841 and was followed by others in the succeeding decades. Private courses were also taught at rural medical schools. In the 1850s, some faculty members of the University of Vermont College of Medicine remained after the regular term and offered three-month summer terms covering dissection and microscopy.[78]

Medical schools were strong supporters of private medical education. The private schools did not compete with the medical schools for students because they could not award degrees. Private instruction saved the schools the time and expense of teaching additional courses and building new facilities. Medical school faculty members taught many of the private courses, which were both remunerative and sources of referrals and consultations from former students. Private courses benefited medical students by enabling them to pace their education, taking the courses when their resources and previous training permitted. Even the few private schools that received charters and awarded degrees, like those in Philadelphia, benefited the medical schools by attracting more medical students to the city and thereby increasing enrollments in all of the schools.

The quality of private teaching was highly impressive. In contrast to the theoretical emphasis of the increasingly obsolete medical school curriculum, the private courses taught the newest discoveries and most important developments in medicine, as well as essential practical skills. The teachers included many outstanding physicians, which enabled students to study with eminent clinicians whom they otherwise never would have known.

The enthusiasm of students for private instruction was equally impressive. Even though the courses were not required for degrees (with the exception of anatomy), large numbers of students attended them because they wanted to become better physicians. Students showed a remarkable ability to choose courses that covered what was new and important in medicine. Private courses became so central to medical education that one observer commented: "The student who enters upon the study of medicine at this day cannot afford to confine himself to the oral instructions from Professorial Chairs. . . . [I]f he would qualify himself for his practical duties, . . . he must avail himself also of the services of the young, the active, the enthusiastic teachers of what the French call *les écoles de perfectionment.*"[79]

The third form of private instruction was hospital and dispensary instruction. By the second quarter of the century, most hospitals were open to all medical students, who were allowed to attend ward rounds for a fee of about $10 a year. The fees were often used for a medical library that was open to the students. As the number of students seeking hospital instruction increased, the hospital staff replaced ward rounds with regularly scheduled formal lectures. Operations were performed before students in the amphitheater. Students were permitted to attend obstetrical cases. The hospitals gave students diplomas or certificates of attendance. Hospital teaching gradually turned into a formal system of medical education, supplementing both the medical school and the private teachers.[80]

Although hospital teaching was clinical, students were not directly involved in the care of patients. James C. White described the ward rounds at the Massachusetts General Hospital in the early 1850s in this way:

> [The attending physicians] pass from bed to bed in the large wards, the students following. The house [officer] narrates any incidents in each patient's condition during the previous twenty-four hours; the physician asks questions, makes the necessary explanations, and directs treatment. Over new and interesting questions much time is spent. . . . Students have nothing to do with the investigation of cases; they have only to look and listen.[81]

Instruction in the amphitheater also provided little direct contact with patients. An observer wrote in 1842 of the Philadelphia General Hospital, whose amphitheater was constructed to enable patients to be brought from the wards in their beds:

> [The hospital staff], half on Wednesday and half on Saturday, select from their respective wards such groups of diseases as are most interesting, and exhibit them to their classes with the accompanying prescriptions and operations. . . . While sitting at their seats, after the patients are carried out, the specimens of morbid anatomy, the result of recent dissections, are passed round to the students, who can examine them thoroughly without the hindrance of the dissection, and contrast them with what they previously saw and heard of the disease. At each session about three hours are spent; one half devoted to the surgical and one half to the medical clinique.[82]

The popularity of hospital teaching led medical school faculty members to seek appointments to hospital staffs in order to give hospital lectures to their students. Because faculty members were among the leading physicians in their communities, they were often given appointments. When more than one medical school existed in a community, the faculty members at different schools spent considerable time and effort jockeying for hospital appointments.

Hospital teaching was less public than medical school lectures, which enabled sensitive subjects to be raised there more easily. For example, the use of live deliveries to teach obstetrics was considered socially unacceptable in medical schools. In 1850 a faculty member at the Buffalo Medical College allowed his students to observe the delivery of a woman in labor, which led to an extensive debate in both the medical and lay press. The next year, a committee of the American Medical Association rejected the need for this kind of teaching.[83] Yet in the more private surroundings of hospitals and private courses students had participated in deliveries for decades without arousing complaint.

Hospital teaching was the most attractive part of an appointment to a hospital staff. It was often a stepping stone to a medical school appointment, especially if the medical school needed a faculty member with a hospital affiliation. Hospital surgeons were able to publicize their skills by performing operations in the amphitheater before an audience of students and physicians. Clinicians used ward rounds and clinics to impress medical students with their skills, which might lead to referrals and consultations when the students began to practice.

The popularity of hospital instruction among medical students varied from city to city. In Philadelphia about 1828, 185 medical students purchased tickets to the Philadelphia General Hospital. According to the hospital board, only 30 to 50 made ward rounds when the medical schools were not in session. When the medical schools were in session, the board reported that "the most interesting cases being brought into the lecture room, attendance in the wards is not usual." Clinics in the amphitheater were more popular, and were attended by about 170 students. At the Massachusetts General Hospital in Boston in the 1850s, on the other hand, White stated that "the hospital wards were so overfilled by students that little was to be learned by attending the clinical visits."[84]

Hospital administrators and boards of directors were critical of hospital teaching, and not only because it disrupted the hospital routine. The board of the New York Hospital complained that medical education was too often the cause of "the vicious policy that has expended efforts rather in multiplying patients within their wards, than in making Hospitals instruments of treatment, that has studied facilities of access rather than facilities of cure, and has invested the administration of medicines, and brilliant or ingenious operations with more attraction than the provision of good nursing, of pure air, and free ventilation."[85]

The board of the Philadelphia General Hospital also questioned the educational value of ward rounds, claiming that "the number of persons who can be really benefited by attending the practice of the house is limited . . . to a much smaller number than do attend, for it is only those who can approach the patient and observe by personal inspection and observation the symptoms on which treatment is predicated who can derive any material advantage from it." It also disputed the benefits of amphitheater clinics where the patient was displayed to the students: "except that the lecture is made more imposing by the subject of it being present, and possibly the student's attention to the case being fastened by the display, we know of no benefit which can accrue from it which would not equally result from the case being lectured, in the absence of the patient, on the notes of the physician, which, in reality, form the basis of the lecture. . . . An image of the patient would be just as efficient."[86]

Some medical educators also were ambivalent about the value of hospital instruction. W. W. Gerhard considered among the advantages that the patients were gathered together in a single location, that "different diseases [were] presented at the same time, so that the symptoms which characterize them may be compared together," that the patients could be carefully examined, and that the progress of the patient could be observed by regular visits. On the other hand, he observed:

> The patients admitted into [the hospitals] are rarely seen in those early periods when therapeutic agents are most efficient; most of them are labouring under the effects of diseases of such long standing, that the structure of the organs has become altered by deposits of new products into the tissues. [Previous treatments sometimes mask] the real symptoms of disease, . . . confounding them with the effects of different medicinal agents. It is . . . generally known, that the . . . most severe examples of disease are met with in hospitals, so that the physician who has studied chiefly in these large institutions is agreeably disappointed, at his entrance upon practice, at the milder aspect which disease presents.[87]

More thorough hospital training was available to students who served as house officers, because they participated directly in the care of patients. However, few such positions were available. Hudson's study of the physicians listed in the 1928 edition of *American Medical Biography* found that fewer than 10 percent of those educated before 1850 had hospital training, despite the fact that they were much better trained than most physicians.[88]

Hospital training was complemented by dispensary training, where medical students attended dispensaries and heard lectures very similar to those at the hospitals. Dispensary teaching had several advantages over hospital teaching. The larger number of dispensaries permitted classes to be smaller and made instruction more personal. Students saw more typical diseases and more cases of the same disease because dispensaries treated large numbers of ambulatory patients. Dispensaries were more likely to have specialty clinics. Medical students at dispensaries also saw something of home practice when they visited patients in their homes. These advantages of dispensary teaching would make it the major form of clinical training later in the century.

The Role of the Medical School Faculty Member

By 1850 medical school faculty members had become leaders of the medical profession. They edited most of the journals, wrote most of the books and journal articles, served on the medical staffs of the hospitals, and were the leading consultants in their communities. There were several types of medical educators with different careers and interests.

One type of medical educator in the early nineteenth century was the peripatetic lecturer. Medical schools had terms of four or five months, with the rural schools staggering their terms to avoid overlap with the urban schools. A faculty member could thus teach at two or even three different medical schools in a year. Waite found that 19 of the 31 faculty members at one rural medical school were peripatetic faculty, including one instructor who gave 49 courses in 17 years.[89]

The peripatetic lecturers were experienced and popular teachers who raised the standards of medical education wherever they taught. They were especially useful at the rural schools, where they strengthened the teaching and brought new ideas about both pedagogy and medicine from the urban schools. Some peripatetic faculty members were renowned teachers. Victor Vaughn wrote of the anatomist, Corydon Ford:

> He never practiced medicine and was a full time teacher throughout his life. His services as a teacher were in great demand, and until within a few years of his death he gave two courses annually, one at Michigan and one in some other school. He . . . taught [anatomy] in a way that held the individual attention of every student. . . . Professors and students from other departments [of the University of Michigan] crowded the upper seats in his lecture room, and how many young men he attracted to medicine I can not say.

Ford's renown was truly remarkable. E. C. Dudley wrote:

> Through the mists of fifty years I can see him with deft hand and delicate touch making a dissection, the beauty of which I have never observed before nor since and then revolve the table on its swivel and . . . drive home the lesson in words that

sounded like the tinkling of a silver bell; and clinch the idea as he looked up to the benches with his winning smile—"Now gentlemen, forget that if you can."[90]

Another type of faculty member was the entrepreneur, who moved from school to school as he advanced his professional career. Daniel Drake and Samuel Gross exemplified this type of educator. Drake spent much of his career founding medical schools and then leaving them to found other medical schools, sometimes in the same communities. He was a prolific author and editor and a popular consulting physician wherever he lived. He earned around $7,000 a year about 1817. Samuel Gross, considered the foremost surgeon of his time, was also mobile. He estimated that between about 1840 and 1870, he earned about $110,000 from professorships in several medical schools, another $18,000 from his books, and "repeatedly" earned $500 for surgical operations in his large practice. Although these men were among the earliest medical school entrepreneurs, they were far from the last.[91]

The typical faculty member was a community physician who occupied two roles. During the medical school term, he spent most of his time on his medical school activities. During the rest of the year, he maintained a busy practice that was enhanced by his reputation as a faculty member. As a practitioner and teacher, he was a generalist. Every faculty member was expected be able to teach any medical subject except surgery and chemistry, and many did. A very few faculty members did not engage in private practice, but taught private classes and apprentices when the medical school was not in session.

A faculty member's earnings from teaching depended on the type of medical school. In the 1840s and early 1850s, faculty members at two large urban schools, the University of Pennsylvania and the University of Maryland, earned over $5,000 and $4,000 annually, respectively, from professorships. Faculty members at a small medical school in Philadelphia and at Western Reserve medical school in Cleveland, Ohio, received from $1,500 to $2,000 around 1850. Earnings at two rural medical schools were $1,200 and $500, respectively, plus fees resulting from consultations with local physicians. Faculty members at some rural medical schools often subsidized their schools by paying some expenses out of their own pockets. The faculty at all medical schools shared in the equity of the buildings and property. Earnings varied greatly from year to year with variations in enrollments.[92]

Medical school faculties, like physicians generally, were well known for their contentiousness. The division of the profits was always a source of disagreement. Faculty members who referred cases to nonfaculty members were viewed with open hostility by their colleagues. Faculty members sometimes formed cliques to eliminate the chairs of uncooperative colleagues or remove them from the faculty.[93]

Faculty members had considerable independence from the local medical profession. Most of their earnings came from their teaching, from referrals and consultations with former students, and from patients attracted by the reputation of the medical school. This made them were more willing than other physicians to criticize the profession in both public and professional forums.

Faculty members were the major critics of heroic therapy at a time when such criticism was sure to damage a physician's career. When laymen, botanics, and homeopaths attacked heroic treatment in the second quarter of the century, regular physicians pressured their colleagues to defend it. A few medical school faculty members were the only regular physicians who spoke out in medical society meetings and journal articles against the excesses of heroic therapy.

Faculty members also fought with the medical societies over the number of medical school graduates. The American Medical Association was organized in 1847 largely as a reaction to the increased number of physicians educated by the medical schools. The AMA and other medical societies wanted to restrict the number of medical school graduates, while the medical schools wanted the profession to be open to anyone with suitable training. The societies lacked any mechanism to force their views on the medical schools and were unable to influence medical school policies during the nineteenth century.

This analysis has shown that medical schools became stronger and more important during the first half of the nineteenth century as they displaced the apprenticeship system. At the same time, a new form of competition for students developed from private schools and classes that offered more useful and up-to-date training. Only the medical schools' monopoly of the M.D. degree prevented them from losing control of medical education to these new types of training. The popularity of private instruction indicated that the power to determine medical school policies had shifted from faculty members to students. The growing power of medical students, together with changes in the nature of medicine, forced a significant alteration in medical school policies in the last decades of the nineteenth century.

III

MEDICAL EDUCATION
1860–1900

4

Medical Care, 1860–1900

During the latter part of the nineteenth century, few changes occurred in drug therapy and the treatment of nonsurgical disorders, which comprised the bulk of medical practice. Major improvements occurred in the diagnosis and prevention of infectious diseases and in surgery, which was revolutionized by the discovery of anesthetics and antiseptic techniques. Dispensaries and hospitals continued to expand as providers of health care in urban areas, with dispensaries playing the larger role. Hospitals assumed a significant educational role.

Medical Care

The Role of the Physician

The number of physicians increased at a rate comparable to the growth in population in the latter part of the nineteenth century. The 55,055 physicians enumerated by the census in 1860 increased to 132,002 in 1900, about 175 physicians per 100,000 population at both dates.[1] Medical schools graduated enough students to assure a reasonable supply of physicians in almost all towns and villages in the country, although urban areas continued to have more physicians per capita.

The physician who began practice in a large city entered a highly competitive profession. He usually started by caring for the tenement population, perhaps augmenting his income by working as a dispensary or railroad physician or assisting another practitioner. His earnings were low and he had few regular patients. Eventually he found a neighborhood where he was able to attract enough patients to establish himself. Competition from other physicians and from pharmacists and dispensaries remained a problem throughout his career.

A physician who chose a small town or rural area, where most of the population lived, had a different type of career. Rural families were poor and the physician's services were low on their list of priorities. Professional relations reflected this fact. Established physicians often greeted the newcomer by sending him their nonpaying patients. Once the rural physician established a clientele, he had less difficulty keeping it than an urban physician. The stability of rural populations enabled him to retain the patronage of families from one generation to another. The rural physician worked longer hours than his urban counterpart and had to be more self-reliant because of the absence of specialists and hospitals. He maintained an office in town, usually in his home, where his wife served as receptionist, bookkeeper, secretary, and nurse. His trips to patients involved many hours of travel in a horse and buggy on bad roads often made worse by harsh weather.[2]

The limited clinical training provided by medical schools made physicians approach their first patients with trepidation. One said that when he was called to his first delivery, he "was as lame on the practice side as can well be imagined," and got through the case only by relying on an experienced physician who was called in. Other physicians participating in their first deliveries benefited from the previous births of both the patient and her friends.[3]

Somehow, physicians of the period seemed to practice reasonably well even with their limited clinical training. Hertzler suggested that the system of medical education was a contributing factor: "If one knows thoroughly the facts about a disease through the simple act of memory, he has gone a long way toward recognizing it when he sees it in practice, though he never saw such a condition during his school course. . . . [O]f common diseases we had more fundamental facts ground into us than the student of today."[4]

Probably a more important factor was the state of medical knowledge. Hertzler wrote:

> As I look back over the old casebooks I wonder now just how much real good I did. Certainly the medicines I dispensed were merely symbols of good intentions. The friends of the patient felt better when I called but the muttering patients were often oblivious to the presence of the doctor. . . .
>
> No reproach attaches to the practice of masterly inactivity, for in most cases the disease was self-limited and all that could be done was to make the patient comfortable until the disease ran its course. . . .
>
> [T]he country doctor's activities had less to do with the saving of life than with relieving a patient's pain and the mental suffering of the family. . . . However, the picture must not be painted unduly drab. The patient's sufferings were relieved and in occasional cases the measures employed were unquestionably life-saving.[5]

Many European physicians felt that American physicians were the equal of their European counterparts, who were trained in more elaborate and better supported medical schools. Arpad Gerster, a surgeon trained in Vienna, described his early impressions in this way when he settled in the United States about 1880:

> When I had my first insight of the imperfect methods of medical education prevailing in New York . . . , I was amazed by the general efficiency of the medical profession. . . . [T]he lower ranks possessed three fundamental qualities. First, a wonderful amount of "horse sense" in meeting emergencies; secondly, the ability quickly to adopt a new thing, which was good—this of course occasionally included the uncritical acceptance of novelties of questionable value; and thirdly, an imperturbable phlegm and self-possession—one of the most important qualities of the ideal physician.

A British observer wrote in 1891:

> It is generally agreed, by unbiassed and unprejudiced observers, that American practitioners are wonderfully good practical men. . . . The average American is a well-educated empiric. He may not be thoroughly acquainted with the pathological anatomy of disease, but he is brimful of the various remedies for it. He may not know

the pathology, he may not know the exact action of the drug, but he can diagnose, he knows the treatment to use, and . . . he generally "gets there."[6]

Gerster believed that the major difference between American and European medical practice was the greater social equality between American physicians and patients. He wrote that in Europe the "medical degree per se invested the physician with a social standing and authority unknown in America." In America the general education of physicians was "little, if any, above the level of their clientele. And the clientele . . . knew it. Hence the medical man had to be . . . circumspect, even deferential, in facing ignorance, absurd pretensions, and ill manners—especially" among the newly rich. According to Gerster:

> [T]his precariousness of position had its useful side; it compelled close observation, diligence, and attention to detail. It was the mother of invention, and the cause of the well deserved reputation of the American practitioner for cleverness in the face of emergency. . . . [T]he American physician of those days wielded less authority over his patients than did his European colleagues; he had to endure too much quizzing, and had to waste time in arguing patients into acquiescence. This misdirection of energy made practice unduly burdensome. . . . However, the absence in America of the brusqueness of some continental practitioners was gratifying to me.[7]

The most common ailments treated by physicians were, as Hertzler observed, "trivial and obvious conditions," such as sore throats, bronchitis, and rheumatism. "If there was an injury involving the skin one sewed it up without ceremony." However, there were also "many serious and arduous problems to meet such as try the souls of even experienced men." These were infectious diseases like tuberculosis, pneumonia, typhoid, and diphtheria. In Massachusetts, which kept the best mortality statistics in the nineteenth century, death rates from tuberculosis remained at more than 300 per 100,000 from 1860 to 1885, those from typhoid averaged over 90 per 100,000 from 1860 to 1875, and those from diphtheria varied between 50 and 100 per 100,000 from 1860 to 1897.[8]

Typhoid fever produced its highest death rates in the cities, but it was also a problem in many smaller communities. One small town physician recalled: "The great prevalence of typhoid fever in pioneer days was a source of considerable income to the general practitioner. A case of typhoid some miles in the country called for daily or almost daily visits on the part of the attending physician for from several weeks to a month. . . . There was then no method of prevention, except that of boiling the drinking water, and this people would not do."[9]

Many infectious diseases were difficult to diagnose. Typhoid, for example, was often confused with malaria. According to one physician:

> When finally the case, after dragging along, plainly became [typhoid rather than malaria], it was the custom of some doctors to explain to the friends that the case had "changed into typhoid," an explanation that in many cases "made good." . . . Others, too proud to adopt such means for getting out of the difficulty, either frankly confessed their confusion, or else held their tongues, "looked wise" and breasted the storm as best they could. It was the seemingly simple, yet really confusing cases that often gave the young man his first "black eye" from a professional standpoint.[10]

Infants and children suffered especially from infectious diseases. In Massachusetts, the death rate for those under one year of age remained at about 200 per 1,000 from 1865 to 1900, and for those one to four years of age at over 60 per 1,000. Thus one out of every four children died before the age of five. Gastrointestinal diseases like diarrhea and dysentry were major killers, especially in the summer in urban slums, where milk was adulterated, full of bacteria, and unrefrigerated by either distributor or consumer. One early pediatrician observed that "the doctor himself probably did nothing helpful. Generally he prescribed the usual calomel and castor oil; and if the baby was not already suffering from diarrhea, this medication produced it and the subsequent dehydration. His food was then restricted to rice-water and barley-water, on which he slowly starved."[11]

Therapy changed in some ways after mid-century, although the principle of vigorously attacking the disease remained unaltered. Bloodletting, blistering, and other aspects of heroic therapy were abandoned, but mercury, arsenic, strychnine, antimony, opium, ipecac, quinine, and others remained the physician's main resources. New synthetic drugs that reduced pain and fever and induced sleep were obtained from coal tars, but they also produced serious side effects. Beverage alcohol became popular as a tonic. All were used to excess.[12]

Pharmaceuticals were still manufactured in the druggist's office from raw materials. Pharmacists usually ground roots and herbs by hand and prepared them by boiling and filtering them or adding alcohol in a percolator. Physicians sometimes called for prescriptions composed of incompatible drugs, and the ceilings of pharmacies were pock-marked with the effects of the resulting explosions. The pharmacist, as one physician observed, "was not averse to prescribing for his customers himself and, whenever he had a chance, made up mixtures containing a little of everything commonly used for the supposed ailment."[13]

Most drugs, like morphine or calomel, were dispensed casually as powders. According to one physician: "The doctor called for a piece of newspaper, cut it into the size wanted for powder papers and with his pocket knife dished out the powder into as nearly equal portions as possible and folded the paper over the powder." Pocket spatulas improved the physician's accuracy when they were introduced late in the century.[14]

Developments in Clinical Medical Science

Diagnosis was revolutionized in the second half of the century by instruments that systematized it and permitted quantification of the patient's condition. The first major innovation, the stethoscope, had been developed in the second quarter of the century. It was followed by the ophthalmoscope, the laryngoscope, a variety of specula, the achromatic microscope, the medical thermometer, the X-ray, and other devices.[15]

These instruments made it possible to observe signs and symptoms precisely and make detailed case histories and records. S. Weir Mitchell wrote: "The instrument trains the man; it exacts accuracy and teaches care. . . . Thinking over the number of instruments of precision, a single case may require, it is clearly to be seen that no matter how expert we may be, the diagnostic study of an obscure case must today exact an amount of time, far beyond that which Sydenham may have found need to employ." The first American text on the use of instruments to make systematic diagnoses was published in 1864 and was soon followed by others.[16]

The use of instruments in medicine was promoted by the growing number of organizations that employed physicians. By the end of the century, physicians were employed to treat patients and administer physical examinations to clients and workers by life insurance companies, railroads, businesses, the military, and government agencies. These organizations trained physicians to use many of the new instruments.[17]

Life insurance companies were particularly important in this regard. By 1901 they spent over $5 million a year on medical examinations, and in 1911 they employed 80,000 physicians in the United States and Canada. Life insurance companies correlated data from physical examinations with the incidence of mortality and morbidity among their policyholders. Based on these analyses, they selected tests for physicians to perform on applicants, often paying physicians extra for X-rays or other special procedures. In order to insure accurate results, life insurance companies trained tens of thousands of physicians in the use of medical instruments, physical examinations, and case records.[18]

Other organizational employers also educated their physician-employees about new developments in medicine. Railroads employed 5,466 part-time railroad surgeons in the United States and Canada in 1894. At first, they trained their physicians in closing wounds, setting broken bones, and amputating limbs, but by 1900 they added instruction in the care of neurological and other injuries. Some years later, the U.S. armed forces drafted thousands of physicians to serve in World War I, where many of them had their first training in clinical pathology and related aspects of hospital medicine.[19]

Thus the education of physicians did not end with graduation from medical school in the late nineteenth century. Many thousands of physicians received detailed training in new developments in medicine from organizations that employed them. Practically all of this training was useful for their private patients as well, leading to higher standards of medical practice.

Cellular Pathology and Bacteriology

The instrument that had the greatest effect on the relationship between basic medical science and clinical medicine was the microscope. By mid-century, compound microscopes that showed undistorted images at high levels of magnification were available at reasonable prices, which led to a virtual explosion of microscopic research in Europe. Microscopic changes in tissues were discovered to be much more useful in understanding disease than changes in organs observed with the unaided eye. This led to the development of cellular pathology and the correlation of clinical symptoms with cellular changes in organs. Soon thereafter the role of bacteria in causing disease was discovered, and specific bacteria were identified as the etiological agents in many infectious diseases. These discoveries complemented those in cellular pathology by confirming the value of microscopic analysis.

Cellular pathology and bacteriology had a major impact on medicine. They led to new kinds of specialists who did not treat patients. Clinical pathologists made laboratory diagnoses of the diseases of patients and public health officials diagnosed and prevented infectious diseases in populations, but neither worked with individual patients. Pathology and bacteriology established standards for medical practice that affected the professional conduct of physicians. Public health officials required physicians to report incidents of contagious diseases to them. The laboratory findings of pathologists contributed to an increase in the number of malpractice suits at the beginning of the twentieth century.[20]

Bacteriology had an especially profound impact on public opinion. Many of its contributions involved highly visible public health measures like the filtration and chlorination of water supplies, better methods of sewage disposal, pasteurization of milk, and the quarantine of patients with contagious diseases. In 1894, bacteriology also produced diphtheria antitoxin, the first therapy to come from the new medical sciences, which successfully combatted one of the most dreaded of all children's diseases. The public was more receptive to bacteriology than were many physicians, who distrusted microscopic analysis and the emphasis on social rather than personal health measures.[21]

Specialization in Medicine

Specialization was another consequence of medical instrumentation. Many new instruments or techniques required extensive study and practice if physicians were to become proficient in their use. This was a major reason for specialization.[22]

In order to observe patients with conditions involving the specialty, physicians established specialty dispensaries and hospitals where patients were treated for free. Specialists also organized medical journals to promote the advancement of knowledge and medical societies to recognize physicians whom they considered qualified in the specialty. At least 14 national specialty societies and many more local and regional ones were established in the nineteenth century. These new institutions formed the basis around which specialty practice developed.[23]

Many general practitioners were skeptical of the value of specialization. They were unwilling to refer patients to specialists, and the medical staffs of hospitals and dispensaries often refused to establish separate departments for the patients of specialists. Some of the skepticism existed because many specialists were self-designated and had little or no special training, but much of it was due to the fear that specialists would leave general practitioners with nothing to treat. The general public was more willing to accept the concept of the specialist.[24]

Specialties varied in the degree of resistance they encountered from physicians. Those specialties most removed from general practice experienced the least resistance. Ophthalmology and some fields of surgery developed quite early, although Gerster stated that the early specialists "were more or less in general practice." Pediatrics and obstetrics experienced considerable resistance. Cone has estimated that in 1889 there were only 30 to 40 pediatricians in the whole country, and practically all of them also treated adult patients. One obstetrician stated that the desire of women for better medical care was more important than referrals by general practitioners in developing that specialty.[25]

Most physicians entered specialty practice cautiously. The usual route was for a physician to begin practice as a general practitioner, distinguish himself in a field, and then gradually limit his practice to that field. A less common method was to become a full-time specialist unequivocally in order to convince general practitioners that their patients would be returned to them after treatment. Either way, the specialist had to make both the public and his colleagues aware of his specialty. When the American Medical Association recognized specialists in 1869, it established codes of ethics that forbade them from advertising.[26] The ban on advertising greatly increased the publicity value of medical school and hospital appointments for specialists.

Specialization first developed on a large scale at the end of the nineteenth century. Hudson's study of eminent physicians listed in the *Dictionary of American Medical Biography* classified about 70 percent of those who began practice in the 1880–1900 period as specialists, compared to about 30 percent of those who began practice in the 1830–1850 period. Atwater found that specialization became common among the physicians in Rochester, New York, only in the 1890s.[27]

The Development of Surgery

The most important specialties were those in surgery, which changed much more than medicine during this period. The first developments in surgery were due to the discovery of anesthetics, including nitrous oxide, ether, and chloroform, in the late 1840s. Anesthesia enabled the surgeon to pay greater attention to detail in operations, because he did not have to race through them to minimize the patient's pain and suffering. The ensuing refinement of operative technique led to a substantial increase in the number of operations.[28]

Surgery still had to contend with the problem of wound infection, the causes of which were unknown. Hence few surgeons were concerned with cleanliness. Sometimes they washed their hands, instruments, and sponges before the operation, sometimes not; sometimes they wore clean clothes, sometimes not. In the hospital surgical wards, wounds were washed with sponges that were rinsed in the same bowl of water between patients, carrying germs from patient to patient and producing horrifying and often fatal epidemics in the wards. Weir observed:

> [In] the surgical wards erysipelas was always rife and . . . that strange and fearful disease called hospital gangrene appeared as a thick, grayish mould over the wounds with an intense burning pain accompanied by high fever and rapid loss of strength. . . . [P]yaemia was characterized by chills indicating infection which had passed into his system and was setting up abscesses in his lungs, liver and other organs. The issue in most cases was fatal. In 700 amputations that I had in the military hospital under my charge, 1861–65, in only one case did I have what was called primary union of the stump, that is to say, a stump entirely free from infection of a mild or severe form.[29]

The greater amount of surgery after the discovery of anesthetics increased the incidence of wound infection and made postoperative care a major part of all hospital care. Patients spent weeks or months recuperating from surgery. Practically all wounds suppurated and were dressed daily by house officers. Bandaging became an important skill and a significant part of their training.[30]

Less than three decades after the discovery of anesthesia, Joseph Lister discovered that germs entering wounds from the environment were the cause of infection. However, this discovery did not explain where the germs came from and how they could be prevented from entering the wound. Surgeons seeking to apply Lister's principle were, as Franklin Martin observed, "pioneers, enmeshed in the mysteries of new and befogging theories. . . . In those early operations, if the surgeon was not entirely sure of himself he would ask members of the audience for advisory comments, which were usually freely given." In the 1890s, David Edsall recalled that his professors of surgery operated under what they thought were antiseptic conditions, but wore regular cloth jackets and touched bacteria-laden objects after scrubbing their hands thoroughly.[31]

For several decades Lister and others believed that germs entered the wound from the air. To neutralize the germs during operations, atomizers were used to spray the operating field with carbolic acid vapor. Postoperative dressings were soaked in carbolic acid to kill any germs that entered the wound from the air. Changes of dressings and removals of stitches and drainage tubes became complex rituals that were viewed skeptically by surgical critics of antisepsis.[32]

By the turn of the century, over thirty years after Lister's original discovery, it was recognized that objects which came into physical contact with the wound, such as the instruments and hands of the surgeon, were the major cause of infection. This led to new procedures, called aseptic rather than antiseptic, that abandoned disinfecting agents and relied on heat sterilization of instruments and the use of clothing, masks, dressings, and gloves that could be boiled after each use.[33]

Antiseptic surgery was adopted gradually in the United States. In the early 1880s, a debate on the use of Lister's system at the American Surgical Association revealed that it had many critics. However, the author of a paper supporting Lister argued that "the present system of surgical practice has been modified to a very great extent by the introduction of the Lister treatment. . . . The great care and attention that is paid to cleanliness was not thought of until Mr. Lister came forward with his system of practice."[34]

During most of the century, few operations were performed in hospitals, although hospital surgery increased among the poor after the discovery of anesthesia. Even that limited increase made hospital infections so common that operating rooms and surgical wards were periodically closed. Hospitals discouraged operations with a high likelihood of infection, such as those in the abdomen or thorax. At the Massachusetts General Hospital, a surgeon who had performed many ovariotomies was appointed to the staff in 1876, but told not to bring any of his ovariotomy patients to the hospital. The two first successful abdominal operations connected with the hospital, in 1874 and 1875, were performed on hospital patients by attending physicians, but in a neighboring house. Abdominal surgery was not performed in the Massachusetts General Hospital until 1884.[35]

Most surgery in the nineteenth century took place in patients' homes, or, if the patients were away from home, in boarding houses or hotels. By the end of the century, home surgery was so common that it was standardized. The surgeon carefully prepared trunks or large cases filled with everything required for surgery, all sterilized and carefully wrapped. If possible, the surgeon's assistants went to the house, hotel, or boarding house the day before the operation and prepared two rooms, one for the operation and one to serve as a recovery room and bedroom. The furniture in the operating room was removed and the room was thoroughly cleaned. If the physician had to travel to another community, as often occurred, a nurse might be sent ahead to prepare the patient and the facilities. Surgery was usually performed on a kitchen table.[36]

One problem with home surgery was that surgeons had an audience of interested spectators. The windows were soaped or covered with sheets to keep neighbors from viewing the operation. Another problem, according to one surgeon, was that the "surgeon, as advocate, sometimes had to face a jury of twelve people ranging in ages from nine to ninety carrying opinions . . . all of which must be brought to a single focus of agreement. This did not occur where a family had full trust and confidence in some capable family physician who had sent for the surgeon."[37]

Surgery in the home, as well as hospital surgery, maintained the dominance of master surgeons, who continued to perform most of the difficult operations. The availability of railroad travel enabled them to cover large territories. One surgeon observed that he had "an out-of-town surgical practice which rapidly extended to a territory within a radius of 400 miles from Chicago. In going to surgical cases . . . I was often on sleeping cars three or four nights a week." He cited the case of an ophthalmologist "who had a deservedly large practice . . . in Minnesota and the states west to the Rocky Mountains." Many master surgeons were well known to the railroad crews, who often made special stops for them.[38]

Surgery in the home was the great testing ground for many innovations. Hertzler observed: "Kitchen surgery made it necessary to learn the essentials of technique. The surgeon found that only the wound matters." The danger of excessive damage to tissues was first recognized by surgeons in home surgery. Many ritualistic aspects of antiseptic and aseptic surgery were cast aside in surgery in the home where surgeons learned that they were unnecessary. Research during World War I supported the home surgeons when it was shown that many antiseptics widely used in hospital surgery neither penetrated very far into the wound nor diffused throughout the wound to kill bacteria.[39]

Opinions about the effectiveness of home surgery varied widely. One physician observed in 1911 that "with trained nurses and a moderate outlay it is possible to give every advantage in a private house." Certainly the patient was far less likely to experience wound infection in a home. Others, like Franklin Martin, felt that "it was impossible to treat serious conditions, especially surgical cases, outside of a hospital." Still others, thinking of emergency surgery in homes in small towns far removed from the physician's office, complained about the fatigue of travel, the poor operating conditions, the inept assistants, and the lack of previous knowledge of the patient or his doctor. Hertzler reflected around 1940 that "in retrospect kitchen surgery does not seem so bad. Many of my best operations, figured in end results, were done under the most adverse conditions." He added, however, "I would not consider tackling such things under those conditions now."[40]

Surgery in the home, and indeed all medical care in the home, made physicians realize that the practice of medicine was no longer an individual activity. Surgeons needed assistants to help with operations. They needed other physicians and

nurses to help with postoperative care when wound infection often made the difference between life and death for the patient. All physicians recognized the deficiencies of nursing by, as one observed, "relatives who may have no aptitude or
experience, . . . the average 'handy' neighborhood woman whose knowledge may
be utterly inadequate, or the 'domestic' nurse who is far too frequently inefficient
in many ways, owing to lack of systematic training." The practice of medicine now
involved a number of different occupations that had to work together effectively. The
organization in which this was increasingly done was the hospital.[41]

Dispensaries and Hospitals

Dispensaries

Dispensary care increased dramatically with the growth in urban populations and the
urban poor. In 1871, 26 New York City dispensaries treated 216,000 patients when
the city had about one million residents. In 1893, the 9 most important of the 63
dispensaries treated 217,000 patients at the dispensaries and another 26,000 at their
homes. In 1915, 92 of New York City's 106 dispensaries and hospital outpatient
departments treated 2.2 million patients and recorded 4.1 million visits in a city with
5.5 million residents. In 1880 in Boston, 6 of 20 dispensaries and outpatient
departments had 83,000 visits in a city of 360,000. In Baltimore, the largest of the
18 dispensaries treated 4,000 patients annually in the 1870s, 9,000 annually in the
1880s, and over 10,000 annually for the next three decades. In Philadelphia, the 10
dispensaries with 30,000 consultations in 1858 increased to 61 in 1902, with 42 of
them providing 305,980 consultations.[42]

Dispensary care ranged from routine treatments in the dispensaries to deliveries
and major operations in patients' homes. One physician said of the New York
Dispensary: "Operations of all kinds had to be done in tenement houses of the
poorest kind . . . in rooms illuminated with tallow candles or in some more favored
places with a kerosene lamp, with untrained assistants and with few or no antiseptic
precautions." The quality of care provided by dispensaries enabled them to have a
major impact on the medical care provided to the poor. Savage observed at the time:

> The "poor man's doctor" is too often either inexperienced or incompetent or worse,
> a scheming quack from whom the poor should be protected. To neither does the
> community owe a living or "protection." Through the dispensaries, with their
> carefully selected physicians, the poor classes have the benefit of the best
> service. . . . It is this knowledge that nerves the more fastidious among the poor to
> submit themselves to the ordeal of the free clinic.[43]

By the end of the century, dispensaries attracted middle class patients who
sought specialty care that they could not afford to pay for. Davis found that specialty
clinics (that is, not general medical, surgical, or pediatric) accounted for over
one-half of the attendance at a number of dispensaries in New York City and
Boston. Lambert's 1915 study of New York City dispensaries and hospital
outpatient departments found that only 20 percent of the visits were at general
medical, 19 percent at general surgical, and 7 percent at general pediatric clinics.
He concluded: "The majority of care . . . desired by the people coming to these
dispensaries is something which the general practitioner does not give."[44]

Physicians sought dispensary appointments to obtain clinical experience. A dispensary official observed: "Dispensaries are not primary schools for the instruction of students, but post-graduate educators in advanced and original studies and preparation for instruction in hospitals and medical schools, or for higher skill in private practice, with its larger compensation as a reward." In 1915, 3,031 of the 8,000 physicians in New York City worked in a dispensary or outpatient department, in most cases without compensation. This was many times the number serving in hospitals.[45]

By the end of the century, hospitals added outpatient departments, which functioned like dispensaries except that patients were sent into the hospitals for inpatient care instead of being treated at their homes. In New York City, Mount Sinai Hospital treated 40,000 outpatients in 1885 and Bellevue Hospital and its two branches treated almost 90,000 outpatients about 1893. The Boston City Hospital treated 12,000 outpatients in 1884, 60,000 in 1903 at the hospital, and over 30,000 in 1905–1906 at a relief station in downtown Boston.[46]

Many hospitals added specialty outpatient clinics instead of specialty inpatient wards for specialists on their staffs. In 1877 there were five different specialty outpatient clinics in the Boston City Hospital and four in the Massachusetts General Hospital; in 1890 there were nine in the Mount Sinai Hospital in New York City. All too often these clinics reflected the self-interests of the specialists rather than the needs of the patients. Clinic hours were usually scheduled in the morning, instead of the afternoons, evenings, or weekends when working patients could attend, largely because the staff members refused to add more physicians to work during those hours.[47]

Dispensaries and outpatient departments had little support from the medical profession or hospitals. Medical societies insisted that dispensaries took paying patients away from physicians, despite the fact that the allegation was repeatedly shown to be false. The American Medical Association had a committee on "Dispensary Abuse" but, as Michael Davis observed, none to do constructive work on dispensaries. Hospitals took little interest in outpatient departments because they did not treat paying patients. About 1910 Davis surveyed 49 hospitals and found that practically none of them had an administrator responsible for the outpatient department. The American Hospital Association also had no significant committee on outpatient departments.[48]

Teaching in dispensaries continued to be popular and became more formalized with the development of specialty clinics. The major criticism of dispensary teaching was that patients failed to keep their follow-up appointments to permit students to observe their progress. Davis and Warner found that by differentiating those who needed continued treatment and carefully reminding them, a very high proportion returned when requested.[49]

Hospitals

Hospitals were avoided by all who could afford to do so for most of the nineteenth century. The reasons are exemplified by hospital treatment for infants and children. Children needed careful attention from trained nurses, who were seldom available.

They needed pure milk and other foods to prevent diarrhea, which were rarely provided. They needed facilities for contagious diseases, which few hospitals had. Abt wrote about one experience at Cook County Hospital in Chicago:

> In summer, when the diarrheal diseases were at their worst, many little patients came to us in a desperate condition. Those who were admitted because of other ailments soon developed diarrhea. When I visited the ward one Friday during a heat wave, I found seven or eight infants suffering from the disease. That afternoon I was called away and did not get back to the hospital until Monday. It was a sweltering day, and I expected to find more patients than ever, but, on the contrary, the mezzanine was empty.
>
>   I looked at the head nurse in astonishment. "Where are all of our babies?" I asked.
>
>   "Doctor," she replied, "while you were out of town the weather was very hot. It was too much for the babies. Every one of them has died."[50]

Most hospital patients continued to suffer from infectious diseases or injuries that required general nursing care and long periods of recuperation, but not much medical treatment. At a Milwaukee hospital about 1880, the majority of patients suffered from tuberculosis, typhoid, pleurisy, or "debility." By 1900, almost two-thirds of the patients were in the surgical wards, but most were accident cases. At the Pennsylvania Hospital in Philadelphia, 65 percent of the patients were surgical patients from mid-century to the 1890s. An analysis of 5,580 surgical patients treated there from 1873 to 1878 found that 30 percent suffered from fractures, 23 percent from wounds, 8 percent from sprains, burns, railroad accidents, or frostbite, with the remainder divided among many different categories.[51]

Patients suffering from accidents and infectious diseases required lengthy hospital stays to recuperate. In Boston, patients at the Boston City Hospital and the Massachusetts General Hospital had average stays of about 4 weeks in the 1870s and 3 weeks in the 1890s. At a private hospital in Milwaukee, the average stay was 24 days until late in the century. At a Brooklyn hospital from 1885 to 1895, the average stay was about 30 days. Convalescent nonpaying patients were often well enough to act as orderlies.[52]

Many new hospitals were constructed in the late nineteenth century, both in cities and in communities that previously had no hospitals. Kingsdale has estimated that from 1873 to 1889 the number of community hospitals (excluding federal and proprietary institutions) increased from 35 public and 137 private to 115 public and 593 private. The number of beds increased from 11,767 to 24,806 in the public hospitals and from 15,248 to 43,111 in the private hospitals. The 35 percent decrease in the average number of beds per hospital indicates that most of the new hospitals were quite small.[53]

Many of the new hospitals were sponsored by ethnic and religious groups, who were undeterred by the lack of need for additional hospitals in most cities. Their hospitals competed not only with those of other groups, but sometimes with other hospitals built by members of the same group. The hospitals were often started in converted homes. If successful, a moderate sized building was constructed. Ultimately an edifice was built that exhibited, in unmistakable Victorian architecture, the importance of the particular group. Although the hospitals prided themselves on their denominational affiliations, they never restricted their care to members of that group. The group members were sufficiently prosperous that they rarely used hospitals.[54]

Hospital architecture changed significantly in the last quarter of the century. The Crimean War and the American Civil War demonstrated that fewer wound infections occurred in hospital tents than in traditional buildings. This was joined to the theory that most diseases were transmitted by foul air, leading to the belief that circulation of the air was the most desirable feature in a hospital. One- or two-story hospital pavilions were constructed with windows and fireplaces that functioned like wind tunnels. In order to avoid the passage of air between buildings, everyone, patients included, went in the open air from one building to another. One army surgeon wrote of the concept: "The cry of the hospital builders . . . is air, air!, ventilation, ventilation! If such people had seen as much of great hospitals as they have of books, the cry would be water, water!, cleanliness, cleanliness!"[55]

Private and public hospitals continued to care for different kinds of patients. Private hospitals selected respectable patients needing short-term care for acute illnesses. In 1878 Rideing described the patients at the New York Hospital by saying that "many of them are mechanics or small tradesmen; an impoverished actor or journalist may be found amongst them; and a few are prosperous and even wealthy." Public hospital patients were quite different. Rideing described the patients at Bellevue Hospital as "the poorest of the poor, the dregs of society, the semi-criminal starving, unwelcome class, who suffer and die unrecognized . . . with no tenderer hand to clasp at the parting than that of the strange nurse, who has grown callous through long familiarity with such experiences. . . . There is no luxury here; not much gentleness."[56]

In the hope of achieving financial solvency, private hospitals constructed expensive accommodations for wealthy travelers who normally stayed in hotels or boarding houses while ill. In the 1870s the Massachusetts General Hospital maintained what it described as "some very elegant and luxurious private apartments" for any sick visitor "without relatives or intimate friends . . . who wished to enjoy all the care and luxuries to which an easy lot may have accustomed him." The Presbyterian Hospital in New York City, in order to obtain its fair share of the affluent victims of misfortune, devoted its first floor to private rooms at rates of $30 to $50 a week, enormous sums at the time.[57]

The accommodations and care in private rooms were appropriate to the cost. The rooms were luxuriously furnished and included adjoining servants' quarters. The quality of care and nursing was exemplary. One physician who was a house officer at the Presbyterian Hospital in New York in the 1870s wrote: "Expensive drugs, surgical equipment and nursing supplies were willingly furnished when it was shown that they would afford better results. Everything was provided for the patient that would be given to one in easy circumstances, being cared for at home." However, Rideing expressed the views of most people at the time when he observed: "[W]e wonder how many there are in the city, rich or poor, who would not choose the sympathy of a plain home in preference to such formal splendors as these in an institution?"[58]

Hospitals obtained other paying patients by contracting with firms for the care of their injured workers. Railroads especially contracted for the medical care of their employees, who were often far from home when injured. In Pennsylvania, public and private hospitals were constructed in mining and industrial regions specifically to care for injured workers. They received state aid as well as payments from firms.[59]

Despite these efforts, paying patients provided little income to general hospitals. Rosner found that for 10 private hospitals in New York, New England, and Detroit in 1889–1890, patient payments accounted for only 16 percent of total revenues. A survey of 17 hospitals in 13 cities in the same years found that patient payments provided less than one-third of operating revenues. Between 1873 and 1894 at the Pennsylvania Hospital, only 12 percent of all patients admitted were paying patients.[60]

A much more important source of income was public funds from cities and states. In 1903, governments provided over $2.2 million in annual subsidies to private hospitals, which amounted to 8 percent of the total cost of maintenance of all public and private hospitals combined. Private hospitals also benefitted from being tax-exempt. States and cities often gave private hospitals block grants unrelated to the care provided or number of patients treated. At the end of the century, governments adopted reimbursement systems tied to the amount of hospital patient care.[61]

Philanthropy was a source of income in private hospitals. The contributions of religious and ethnic groups to the hospitals that they sponsored were often the only real connection between them. Local social, financial, and industrial elites often supported one or more hospitals and served on their boards. Board memberships were sometimes handed down from one generation of a family to another.[62]

A few private hospitals were able to construct physical plants that greatly impressed European visitors. Their size, kitchens, laundries, heating, gas light, and cleanliness were far superior to those of the many antiquated European hospitals. The operating rooms, laboratories, and autopsy rooms were also impressive, as were the accommodations for house officers. European visitors were often not as impressed with the quality of the medical staffs, however.[63]

The quality of hospital staffs was uneven because appointments were in great demand and became politicized. A position as a staff member provided free publicity and often led to a faculty appointment in a medical school that wanted to use the hospital for clinical teaching. Staff physicians formed cliques to control staff appointments. In Philadelphia in 1900, O'Hara has calculated that 70 of 1,941 physicians in the city held 309 senior consulting or attending hospital positions, 55 percent of all available positions.[64]

After 1900, when hospitals began to attract paying patients, they opened their staffs to more physicians whom they hoped would send them paying patients. In Brooklyn, 24 percent of the physicians had hospital appointments in 1890, 16 percent in 1900, but over 40 percent after 1910. In Providence, Rhode Island, the percentage of physicians with some hospital connection increased from 25 percent in 1868 to 35 percent in 1890 and 50 percent in 1914.[65]

Hospital staffs were weak also because they refused to create specialty services until the 1890s. Dowling has observed: "In addition to new knowledge, specialty services brought to . . . hospitals a fresh, vigorous group of doctors, whose enthusiasm for new, rapidly developing fields of medicine was contagious." Until specialty hospitals merged with general hospitals in the twentieth century, much of this energy and enthusiasm went into separate specialty hospitals.[66]

Specialists established their own hospitals because general hospitals could not provide specialized nursing and postoperative care. Children's hospitals needed intensive nursing care unavailable in general hospitals. Orthopedic hospitals carried out protracted postoperative mechanical treatment of deformities, mostly in children, that could neither be provided by general hospitals nor carried on successfully at home. Before orthopedic hospitals were established, the field was neglected because operations were unsuccessful without extensive postoperative care. The only type of specialty hospital that did not require specialized skills was the lying-in hospital, which was established by laymen primarily to meet the social needs of unmarried and impoverished women.[67]

Restrictions on the number of staff positions in voluntary private hospitals led to the establishment of proprietary hospitals. Many surgeons were unable to obtain hospital staff appointments or were not permitted by hospitals to accept professional fees from hospital patients. This led some surgeons and businessmen in large cities to establish proprietary hospitals solely for paying patients. These hospitals were open to all physicians and placed no restrictions on professional fees. In the Boston area, a 1911 survey found 37 strictly private hospitals with 797 beds, all of which had inadequate facilities. In Kansas City, Missouri, 8 proprietary hospitals were established between 1895 and 1913, with none surviving more than a decade. Some were turned over to nonprofit groups.[68]

Proprietary hospitals were also built by physicians in rural areas to increase their practices. Most of them were established in physicians' homes or converted boarding houses. If that succeeded, the physician constructed a wood frame building. Rural proprietary hospitals increased rapidly in the South and West in the twentieth century because they were the only hospitals in their communities. In 1890, Kingsdale estimated that 62 of 732 community hospitals were proprietary. In 1928, 1,877 of 4,306 community hospitals were proprietary, with an average of only 31 beds. Most successful rural proprietary hospitals were taken over by religious or nonprofit groups. By 1941, Hertzler considered them "a thing of the past."[69]

Hospitals and Education

Hospitals greatly expanded their educational activities during the late nineteenth century. They gave medical students more opportunities to see patients, hired more house officers, and began training large numbers of nurses. Educational programs in hospitals were rarely successful because they conflicted with the hospital's primary service responsibilities.

Ward rounds continued to be a popular form of medical education. Medical schools in all cities did not hold classes on Saturdays to permit students to attend the hospitals, and in some cities they also did not hold classes on one weekday morning. Hospital physicians who wanted to teach but could not obtain faculty appointments held regular ward rounds for medical students at these times. One physician recalled the advantages and disadvantages of ward teaching:

> The visiting physician or surgeon was usually given the right of way by courtesy, but with the students it was every one for himself. They crowded about the beds as best they could, that they might see and hear what was said and done. Often the less energetic or the indifferent ones on the outside of the circle, unable to see or hear much of anything, would stroll about the ward until corralled by the nurse and directed to their proper place. The more earnest students were not long in finding out the most interesting cases, and would take especial pains to get in the front row at those beds and ignore the others. . . .
>
> Hospital attendance was left entirely to the caprice or judgment of the student. It formed no stated part of the curriculum, and yet most students "walked the hospitals," as it afforded a welcome relief to the mental anxiety of scores of didactic lectures.[70]

Ward teaching often interfered with the other goals of the hospitals. Patients were sometimes admitted because of their teaching value and not because they needed the charity care that the hospital provided. The chiefs of service often spent their time with the few patients they used for teaching and placed the others in the hands of the inexperienced house officers. One physician observed that "the chiefs of service in our large city hospitals could do much to improve hospital treatment if they only would consider their position more as one of duty and less one of opportunity."[71]

By the end of the century, ward rounds fell into disfavor with students. Too many students crowded around the beds and too many surgical patients were hidden behind elaborate bandages. To replace ward rounds, some hospitals organized clinics for small groups of students, sometimes in the hospital but more often in the outpatient departments. At the Boston City Hospital, small groups of 3 or 4 students examined patients in dispensaries and performed the necessary laboratory work to arrive at a diagnosis. In 1893, Bellevue Hospital in New York City had a weekly schedule of 19 classes of 20 students each in the wards, 8 clinics of 12 students each in the operating rooms, and 12 clinics in the amphitheater, each attended by 150 to 200 students.[72]

The real glory of hospital teaching was surgery performed in the amphitheater before hundreds of students and physicians. Students were eager to attend because the surgeons were the leaders in their field. Surgeons competed to perform amphitheater surgery because it publicized them and their medical schools. Amphitheater surgery was performed on Saturdays, when no classes were held. Each hospital sought to provide the most interesting operations in order to attract the most students. One observer described the situation in the Philadelphia General Hospital around 1880:

> In the great amphitheater, the circling rows of seats were crowded with students, tier above tier. . . . The patient lay on a high, revolving, wooden table in the centre of the arena, and was clearly displayed in the light which streamed from the skylight in the lofty roof. Close by stood Dr. P., knife in hand, lecturing to the students in his rather stagey manner. On either side . . . were grouped the resident assistants. . . . Everything is calm, systematic, almost druidical. There is a breathless hush and the

light, sweet, sickening odor of ether fills the air. "Gentlemen, the next case which we now bring before you," says Dr. P., "I have explained already, and the operation will now proceed."[73]

From the end of the century to the 1920s, amphitheater surgery reached circuslike proportions. At the Massachusetts General Hospital, each surgeon sought to outdo the others in the operations performed. In order to accommodate them all, according to Churchill:

> [A]n operation would be started in a small room and then the entire outfit trundled like a troupe of gypsies into the pit of the amphitheater, where the crucial phase of the procedure was demonstrated to visiting doctors, students, and nurses. The surgeon would be allotted, say, fifteen minutes. Whether or not the operation had been completed, at the expiration of the allotted time the tents were folded, the troupe moved off stage to complete the operation elsewhere, and a new act took over. . . . Tensions mounted when some prima donna showed reluctance to withdraw from the spotlight and overstayed his time to hold the audience spellbound in an ad-lib recounting of his surgical prowess.

In smaller hospitals, one or two surgeons would perform operation after operation, often for hours at a time.[74]

The health of the patient was often secondary to the showmanship. Weir recounted this incident from the days before antiseptic surgery:

> Dr. Wood . . . loved the limelights. If he could do an operation rapidly he enjoyed the applause that followed. . . . [H]e used to fill the big amphitheater at Bellevue, holding nearly a thousand students, and do a number of operations. . . . Once . . . he invited a distinguished English surgeon to operate before the class and to do an amputation of the thigh for a tubercular knee joint. The surgeon guest made a few concise remarks and did his work carefully, tying the vessels, and ended by closing the stump with suture and applying the necessary bandage, all this occupying over half an hour. Then a similar case was brought for Dr. Wood to perform a similar operation. Flash! Flash! went the amputating knife. "Saw," said the surgeon, and rasp, rasp, the leg was off, two or three big vessels tied, a towel put over the stump and the patient rolled out; Dr. Wood beamed. The next week I asked one of the house surgeons how the patients got along. He said, the Englishman's is doing nicely—Dr. Wood's died the same night from hemorrhage![75]

Conscientious surgeons brought patients back to show their progress after surgery and lectured on the pathological and physiological changes involved. They invited students to examine the patients. Yet even they conceded that students could not see very much, that the surgeons were often too busy to explain what they were doing, and that assistants obstructed the view.[76]

Amphitheater medical clinics were used to present and describe nonsurgical patients to large numbers of students. The patient was brought in and the case history and test results were described either by the physician or a house officer. Frequently, the patient would be examined by a few students or other physicians, and then all participated in general discussion and a diagnosis. The patients were usually brought back afterwards to confirm the diagnosis and show the results of treatment.[77]

The redeeming features of amphitheater teaching were the eminence of the teachers and the importance of the cases. Students saw how medicine was practiced by highly skilled surgeons or physicians who made every effort to teach well to attract students to their clinics. However, even that advantage was weakened by the lack of relationship between the subjects covered in the amphitheater and those in the medical school. Until the two were coordinated, both would suffer.

As hospitals grew, their manpower needs grew correspondingly. One major source of cheap labor was the house officer, who by this time was a recent graduate of a medical school. He was given an appointment of a year or two in the hospital, generally with room and board and a nominal salary. Graduates sought the positions because they were becoming increasingly important for a successful career. Hudson found in his survey of 1,513 physicians listed in the *Dictionary of American Biography* that fewer than 10 percent of those trained before 1850 had served as house officers. The proportion reached 20 percent in the 1860s, 32 percent in the 1870s, and over 42 percent in the 1880s and 1890s.[78]

Competition for the few available house officer positions was severe. Medical school and family connections were often essential. At the Massachusetts General Hospital, house officers were chosen almost exclusively from the Harvard medical school and occasionally from those students with family connections to the attending staff. In Philadelphia, where some hospitals used competitive examinations, hospital staff members sometimes discussed unusual topics in their medical school classes and then placed questions about them on the examinations, knowing that applicants from other schools would probably not know the answers.[79]

In New York City, rigorous competitive examinations were held every spring after about 1880. Students often prepared by hiring teachers and organizing quiz sessions in the preceding fall. One student wrote that he paid $200 for a quiz session taught by Joseph W. Howe, "because Howe had the reputation of getting men into hospitals." He joined a class of 10 or 12 students who had been preparing for six months. "Howe, in a staccato voice, would give first one student and then another some comprehensive question that perhaps required a minute to answer, and the response would come back at him as if shot out of a machine gun."[80]

House officers assisted the attending physicians on rounds, carried out their treatment regimen, and did anything else that the physicians wanted. The more senior house officers admitted patients, took case histories, assisted at operations, and prescribed. They also served in the outpatient departments and cared for accident and emergency patients. The growing amount of surgery added yet another set of responsibilities. One former house officer recalled:

> The technical, long, tedious preparation for a major operation also fell to the interne. The sterilization of instruments, sponges, dressings, silk, catgut, and linen sutures and ligatures and the boiling of gallons of water to be used in the operation was a work often of two or three days. . . . Even when the operation was finished our responsibilities continued. There was no trained nurse who could report important variations in the patient's condition. It fell to the interne to watch the pulse, respirations, temperature and general conditions. . . . A stormy post-operative convalescence was expected; an uneventful recovery was remarkable.[81]

House officers attended to their own needs as well as those of the patients. When admitting patients, one physician who served as a house officer at the Philadelphia General Hospital observed that "the young medical man was too often disposed to be sarcastic, cynical, suspicious, and anxious to drive away every applicant who did not bear in his or her body the symptoms of being an interesting medical or surgical case." Lay officials who supervised the admission process at the hospital "not infrequently" reversed these decisions.[82]

House officers received little training from the attending staff. The staff members, who were busy physicians and surgeons, gave them brief instructions and few explanations. Occasionally, a house officer would be invited to assist a surgeon at an operation in a private home. J. M. T. Finney observed: "These were great occasions. They gave us the opportunity to note the vast difference between surgery as done in a hospital and as done in a home," where it was commonly performed on paying patients.[83]

A position as a house officer provided much clinical experience but little clinical education. Henry Hurd described interns as "energetic and well-intending, but inexperienced, young men, who, during their first year of service, have usually learned their duties at the expense of their patients, and at considerable ultimate cost to the hospital." House officers spent most of their time on hospital medicine, which was increasingly surgical and atypical of community practice. They performed a great many routine tasks later delegated to nurses. Nevertheless, they considered their experiences to be valuable. Because house officers were generally unsupervised and unevaluated, it is difficult to determine how much they actually learned.[84]

Nursing

Hospitals also made efforts to improve the poor quality of their nursing. The only nurses in most hospitals were convalescing patients, maids, and house officers. A few private hospitals that could afford to do so hired and trained nurses, but no hospital had a nursing staff. Each nurse was responsible to the attending physicians on her ward. Some nurses ran their wards efficiently and were admired and respected, but most did not.[85]

In order to improve nursing, its functions had to be defined systematically, nurses had to be trained to perform those functions, and they had to be placed in an organizational hierarchy where they could be supervised and evaluated by other nurses. These needs were first recognized by Florence Nightingale. Nightingale gained her opportunity and fame when she was sent to the Crimea at age 34 to deal with the horrifying mortality rates in British hospitals during the Crimean War. There she developed and introduced an organizational hierarchy of nurses based on strict discipline and businesslike administration. She was able to reduce the mortality rate in the hospitals she supervised from 42 percent to 2.2 percent. This achievement earned her a worldwide audience for her system of nursing.[86]

Nightingale defined nursing quite specifically. Nurses were responsible for the discipline and condition of the wards, for the administration of food, medicine, minor dressings, and other treatments to patients, for insuring that patients obeyed the orders of physicians, and for the care of hospital supplies and the patients' clothing. She wrote that an administrative hierarchy of the nursing staff was essential because without it "discipline becomes impossible. In this hierarchy the higher grade ought always to know the duties of the lower better than the lower grade does itself."[87]

The major opposition to a nursing hierarchy came from physicians who believed that nurses had to obey them, not their nursing supervisors. Nightingale replied that it was a matter of "placing the Nurses in all matters regarding management of the sick absolutely under the orders of the medical men, and in all disciplinary matters absolutely under the female superintendent." She insisted that physicians should never discipline nurses, but rather report all need for changes to the head nurse. When it was claimed that this would lead to conflict between physicians and nurses, she observed: "A patient is much better cared for in an institution where there is the perpetual rub between doctors and nurses" because "any neglect of the sick is far less likely to pass unnoticed."[88]

In order to prepare nurses for these functions, training schools were established in hospitals. Students received both formal instruction and on-the-job training, plus room and board and a small salary. The first American nursing school was established in 1872 at Bellevue Hospital, the largest public hospital in New York, after a committee of socially prominent women inspected the hospital and were appalled by the conditions. Using their social position and the support of a few of the attending physicians, they forced the proposal through a hostile medical staff and raised money to support the school. The school was a great success and served as a model for others.[89]

The development of nursing benefitted from the growing number of working women, who increased from 1.9 million in 1870 to 7.4 million in 1901, from 15 to 20 percent of all workers. Nursing was an occupation that, as the proposal for the Bellevue Hospital school announced in 1872, could be recommended to women "whose education and early associations would lead them to aspire to some higher and more thoughtful labor than household service or work in shops." Mottus found that the majority of the early nursing students at Bellevue and the New York hospitals came from "respectable families living in small communities throughout the United States." Many of the families had suffered financial reverses, forcing the students to support themselves. The personal independence of the women is indicated by a median age at graduation in the late 20s and the requirement of the schools that students be unmarried. Their desire to avoid a working-class occupation is shown by an early incident. When the board of managers of the Bellevue school suggested that students wear a uniform, according to a member of the board, "to our surprise, great opposition was expressed by the pupils; they objected to a 'livery.' " When an attractive dress was designed by a student from a socially prominent family, opposition vanished.[90]

Nursing rapidly became a popular occupation. The number of nursing schools increased from 15 in 1880 to 432 in 1900, and the number of graduates increased from 157 to 3,456. The number of women employed as trained nurses increased from 1,154 in the 1880 census to 11,046 in the 1900 census, 76,505 in the 1910 census, and 143,664 in the 1920 census.[91]

Nursing schools were either independent schools (which Nightingale advocated) or hospital schools. The Bellevue school was an independent school organized and maintained by a board of managers unconnected with the hospital. The board hired the head of the school, approved the program, and contracted with Bellevue Hospital to provide nursing services. The hospital school was organized by the hospital management. The head of the school was a hospital employee who was responsible to the hospital board or the hospital superintendent. Practically all nursing schools were hospital schools and the few independent schools were forced into the same mold. Unfortunately, hospital schools sacrificed educational programs to meet service needs. Isabel Stewart wrote:

> The hospitals . . . were calling for more scientific and expert service from nurses, but they wanted it at the lowest possible cost and it was hard to convince them that proper scientific and technical preparation could not be acquired as a by-product of full-time nursing service in the wards. The conflict between economic and educational interests became sharper as scientific medicine advanced. . . .
>
> [I]nstead of welcoming [education] as the greatest ally of service, hospital officials too often regarded it jealously as a rival whose appeal to the attention and interest of students was to be opposed rather than encouraged. The tendency was to belittle educational interests and activities.[92]

Nursing schools often became recruiting programs for unskilled workers. The first schools were able to maintain fairly high standards because they had many applicants for each position. As the number of schools and available positions increased, admission standards declined. A supply of potential students was always assured by the hospital's practice of providing them with room, board, clothing, and usually a small monthly salary.[93]

The hopes for a thorough education for nurses in the medical sciences were destroyed by the hospital's service needs. Nursing schools had no endowments and virtually no educational funds, and hospitals never sought them. Lectures in most schools were given solely by members of the attending staff without compensation. For years the only lectures were on medical subjects, mostly descriptions of diseases. Topics were usually chosen by the instructor, with no sequencing or integration of topics. As late as 1912, a survey of 692 schools showed that only 10 had any full-time instructors and nearly half had no paid instructors at all. Teaching was conducted in the evenings, after the students had worked 10 or more hours. Students on the night shift were unable to attend. Classrooms, libraries, and teaching materials often did not exist. One businessman observed that if the hospital "were in the business instead of the philanthropic world [it] would run serious risk of being put out of business for conducting its school under false pretenses."[94]

In the first few decades, a student was put to work before receiving any training. According to Stewart:

> [She was] plunged headlong into the ward, taking her full share of the day's work and learning chiefly by imitation or by trial and error. . . . [M]uch of the instruction came from fellow students or even from ward maids. . . . Much of what they learned through experience was invaluable but costly for patients and for themselves. While some became skilled and competent nurses in spite of such haphazard teachings, others acquired slipshod or slap-dash methods or became routine rule-of-thumb workers.[95]

Hospitals did not skimp on practical experience for their nursing students. An 1896 survey of 111 training schools found that nearly two-thirds of them required their students to work 10 hours or more a day. After a student had worked a few months, she was assigned to night duty as well, where she was virtually unsupervised. According to the same study, 70 percent of the schools had 12-hour shifts for night duty and the rest had shifts longer than 12 hours. The standard program was two years, usually involving work on all seven days of the week, with two weeks of vacation each year. By 1900, the leading schools had increased their programs to three years, but the third-year students were simply put to work on the wards or used as teachers or supervisors.[96]

Perhaps the most flagrant abuse of students was the practice of sending them out on 24-hour duty to care for private patients in their homes, with the fees going to the hospital. Students might spend weeks or months in their second year in these profit-making ventures, in which they received no instruction, no supervision, and no education. The practice declined in the twentieth century because of the hospital's growing need for nursing labor, but as late as 1912, 248 of 692 nursing schools surveyed engaged in it.[97]

Because hospitals used their nursing students as their total nursing labor force (except for a few administrators), the graduates had to become private duty nurses. This was the occupation of close to three-fourths of the employed graduates of the nursing schools at Bellevue and New York Hospitals before 1900 and 87 percent of those graduating from the Boston City Hospital nursing school between 1879 and 1906.[98]

Nursing developed in a period when the public health and settlement movements were thriving. Despite the close relationship of nursing to these two other fields, nursing's contribution to both grew slowly, largely because of its hospital ties. Only 400 nurses were in public health as late as 1905. This number increased to 8,770 by 1919. Nurses were also employed as visiting nurses, where they were paid by public or private agencies to provide nursing to families. The number of organizations providing visiting nursing care increased from 21 in 1890 to 589 in 1910.[99]

All physicians agreed that good nursing care made a major difference in hospitals. Antiseptic and aseptic surgery required skilled pre- and postoperative care, which was increasingly provided by nurses. Nursing was also recognized as essential in nonsurgical care. William Osler wrote in his standard textbook on internal medicine that in typhoid, "careful nursing and a regulated diet are the essentials in a majority of the cases." Pneumonia could also best be managed "under the favoring circumstances of good nursing and careful diet."[100]

Student nursing never reached this level. By the time student nurses had achieved a reasonable level of skill, they graduated and left the hospitals. Few hospitals employed experienced staff nurses to provide leadership and guidance to the students. In public hospitals, student nurses were an improvement over the convalescing patients and others used previously. In private hospitals, a hospital historian observed in 1926: "[I]t is an open question whether the present undergraduate is as satisfactory an attendant as was the good, old-fashioned experienced nurse of fifty years ago."[101]

Three types of education in hospitals have been examined in this chapter: the education of undergraduate medical students in ward rounds and amphitheater clinics, the education of house officers, and the education of nurses. All three groups were poorly educated in hospitals. Hospitals were primarily service organizations, and service needs took precedence over education whenever they had to choose between the two.

5

Medical Schools, 1860–1900

During the last half of the nineteenth century, medical schools grew significantly in number and enrollments, as did all institutions of higher education. Many medical schools added optional fall and spring sessions to compete with the private courses and provide additional training for their students. Faculty members were appointed in the clinical specialties, which led to the expansion of the curriculum to include courses in the specialties and the replacement of the repetitive course with a graded one.

The Expansion of General Higher Education

After the Civil War, enrollments in higher education grew significantly, especially in professional schools. The number of students enrolled in all institutions of higher education increased from 32,000 in 1860 to 256,000 in 1900. The 1860 enrollments, which consisted almost entirely of men, comprised 3.1 percent of the white male population between 18 and 21 years of age. The 1900 enrollments, which included many women in colleges and normal schools, comprised 5.0 percent of the white male and female population between 18 and 21 years of age. In 1860, 51 percent of the students were enrolled in colleges and universities, 44 percent in medical, law, and theological schools, and 6 percent in normal schools. In 1900, 41 percent were enrolled in colleges, 33 percent in professional schools, and 27 percent in normal schools.[1]

A higher standard of living and greater access to education led many students to enter college directly from secondary school, according to a study of 20,000 graduates of 11 well-established colleges. The study found that the median age at graduation, between 22 and 23 years, changed very little between the late eighteenth century and 1900, but that the range of ages became smaller over the period. This indicated that students had more preliminary education and were less likely to delay attending college.[2]

The admission standards of the colleges remained low. Most did not require a high school diploma. Entrance requirements included Latin and mathematics, plus Greek for admission to the classical course. Equivalents were widely accepted. Most students did not meet even these requirements. In 1889, 335 of about 400 colleges and universities had preparatory departments for students unable to enter the college, and many preparatory departments had as many students as did the colleges. In 1908, the majority of students in the entering classes at Harvard, Yale, Columbia, and Princeton were admitted with deficiencies.[3]

The college curriculum became more diverse during this period. The classical course still attracted many students who, as Charles Francis Adams, Jr., observed in the 1850s, devoted "the best part of [their] school lives to acquiring a confessedly superficial knowledge of two dead languages." The wealthy colleges appointed additional faculty members and created new degree programs like bachelor of science, bachelor of philosophy, and engineer in their scientific schools or parallel courses. The new programs differed from the classical course in that they substituted modern languages, English, and the social and natural sciences for the classics. At Pennsylvania, Michigan, Cornell, Columbia, Wisconsin, and California between 1883 and 1897, from 49 to 89 percent of the graduates received degrees other than bachelor of arts. At Harvard, Princeton, Brown, and Yale, the proportion varied from 4 to 35 percent. At the end of the century, large colleges changed their curriculum further by adopting an elective system. Most small colleges could afford neither the nonclassical courses nor the elective system.[4]

The traditional classical curriculum retained its preeminence in the leading colleges during this period. The scientific schools were still considered inferior, although less so as they grew in popularity. The professional schools, except for theology, were staffed by part-time teachers with busy private practices. The classical curriculum had the virtue of stability at a time when the other programs changed with every innovation. Of course, some thought that the classical curriculum was more antiquated than stable. Henry Seidel Canby wrote about Yale in 1900, when it was widely considered to be the leading undergraduate college:

> I went to college at a time when . . . an old curriculum was still tottering like a rotted house about to fall and in parts already fallen. The curriculum . . . consisted of the classics . . . , of mathematics, of rhetoric, and of some philosophy, literature, and history. . . .
>
> How many classrooms do I remember where instruction consisted in a calling up of one man after another to translate from a heavily cribbed text of Latin, Greek, or French. How many an English recitation where in sleepy routine the questions went round:—"What does our author say about Lucifer's ambitions?" . . . Never in business, in law, even in religion, has there been more sham, bunk, and perfunctoriness than in the common education of the American college in that easy-going time. It seemed to me incredible that [faculty members] should be willing to earn a living . . . by asking trivial questions day after day of young men who had either memorized the answers . . . or constructed a system of bluff.[5]

Instruction in most subjects in the classical course consisted of recitations taught by recent college graduates. The few faculty members in the sciences felt compelled to water down their material, as one graduate reminisced about his education at Yale in the 1880s:

> [The instructor] evidently felt that science must be presented with caution and kindness to those whose scholastic experience had been almost wholly limited to contacts with the language and ideology of the Greeks and Romans. There is a tradition in the Class that the course which he offered us was in Physics. It may have been, or it may quite as well have been Chemistry. There was, of course, no laboratory. That just wasn't done. Such truck belonged over in [Sheffield]. He held

up before us . . . certain vials and other apparatus and told us what would happen if certain things were done or certain combinations made. We took his word for it.[6]

The major problem of the classical curriculum was that it failed to recognize the development of the sciences, social sciences, arts, and humanities. Daniel Coit Gilman wrote: "There was a time when to be merely a good Latin and Greek scholar was to be well educated; now, such a one is only a specialist, and may be a narrow-minded pedant, as really deficient in true discipline as if he knew nothing but mathematics, or chemistry, or zoology." Scholarly societies and journals were formed at this time in many academic disciplines, and the number of graduate students increased from 219 in 1872–1873 to 4,919 in 1896–1897. The natural sciences grew most rapidly. Between 1863 and 1910, 2,513 doctorates were awarded in the sciences, and by 1903, there were 3,000 college and university science teachers.[7]

The formalization of academic disciplines led to a system of faculty appointments based on scholarly training and achievements. At Harvard, the rank of assistant professor was created in 1857 and was used for initial appointments. The rank of professor became restricted to experienced scholars. The proportion of full professors at Harvard with 4 or more years of academic experience at the time of their appointment increased from 12 to 80 percent between 1845 and 1892. The proportion of full professors appointed at the age of 35 years or younger decreased from 77 percent in 1845 to 43 percent in 1892.[8]

Professional education expanded both in the number of professions using formal education and in overall enrollments. Between 1878 and 1899, the number of schools of dentistry, law, medicine, pharmacy, theology, and veterinary medicine increased from about 293 to 532 and the number of students from about 16,726 to 55,669 (Table 5.1). The professional schools affiliated with universities often enrolled a substantial proportion of all students in the university. Between 1900 and 1905, medical and law students comprised 22 percent of the total enrollment at five major private universities—Columbia, Cornell, Harvard, Yale, and Pennsylvania— and 23 percent of the total enrollment at four major public universities—California, Illinois, Michigan, and Minnesota. Most of these universities had other professional schools as well.[9]

Professional school admission requirements progressed toward a secondary school education in the 1880s and 1890s. This was often equivalent to a college education. F. A. P. Barnard observed in 1871 that some secondary schools in New York State were "immensely superior to many" colleges, differing only in that they admitted both sexes, provided a more flexible and broader education, and awarded degrees that did "not carry with them a prestige like that which accompanies a degree in Arts." He also claimed that they attracted many students away from colleges. In 1900, William Rainey Harper said that the better high schools, "the people's college," had a course of study that was "stronger and more effective in the results produced than is the course of study provided in many of the smaller colleges of today." A college was legally defined by the states of New York and Pennsylvania around 1910 as having at least six full-time faculty members.[10]

TABLE 5.1. Professional Education in the United States, 1878–1899

Profession	Number of Schools		Enrollment	
	1878	*1899*	*1878*	*1899*
Dentistry	12	56	701	7,633
Law	50	86	3,012	11,883
Medicine	100[a]	156	11,826[a]	24,119
Pharmacy	13	52	1,187	3,563
Theology	118[a]	165	n.a.	8,093
Veterinary medicine	n.a.[b]	17	n.a.[b]	378

[a]1880
[b]Very few veterinary schools existed at this time.
Sources: James Russell Parsons, Jr., "Professional Education," in *Monographs on Education in the United States* (Albany, N.Y.: Lyon, 1900), 2:468, 490–549; William G. Rothstein, *American Physicians in the Nineteenth Century* (Baltimore: Johns Hopkins University Press, 1972), p. 287.

Medical Schools and Medical Students

Medical schools shared in the growth of higher education. The 65 medical schools in 1860 increased to 75 in 1870, with fewer than 2,000 graduates per year. In 1880, the 100 medical schools had 3,241 graduates and 11,826 students, and in 1900, the 160 medical schools had 5,214 graduates and 25,171 students. Between 1880 and 1900, the number of medical schools increased by 60 percent and the average number of students per school increased by 33 percent, from 118.3 to 157.3. Some medical schools were commercial enterprises that appealed to poorly prepared low-income students. A few were well-endowed schools that provided a thorough education in excellent facilities to well-educated students who could afford that level of training. The majority tried to provide a good education on a limited budget to students between these two extremes.[11]

Medical students at the largest schools came from a wide range of backgrounds. One physician said of his class at Rush Medical College in Chicago around 1885:

> The students were men of all types. The refined, well-educated, neatly dressed, well-to-do student, twenty-one to twenty-three years of age, who had high ideals concerning his chosen career, might sit next to a poorly dressed, thirty-year-old man who, likewise with high ideals, was working his way through college. Or his neighbor might be a rougher specimen who, after twenty or thirty as a teacher, druggist, traveling salesman, or western farmer, had given up his former occupation because he believed he could make more money as a doctor. In my class of 1888, there were only seven men out of the one hundred and thirty-five who could show diplomas from colleges of literature, science, and arts.[12]

Medical schools maintained entrance requirements designed to meet the needs of their students. A college education was not required, not only because its educational value was limited, but also because most students could not afford to obtain both college and medical school degrees. A medical school education in New York City in 1890 cost about $450 annually for a two-year program, half for tuition and fees and half for room and board. Costs were lower in small cities, but were probably at least $375 a year. The financial problems of many medical students are indicated by their continuing high ages at graduation. A study of 5,719 licensed practitioners in Illinois about 1891 found a median age at graduation from medical school of 26 years.[13]

Medical students had less preliminary education than theology or law students, even though the three types of schools had similar entrance requirements. In 1890, just under 25 percent of 6,500 theology students and 21 percent of the students at 50 law schools had college degrees, compared to less than 8 percent of 16,000 medical students. A few medical schools did attract better educated and wealthier students. At Harvard medical school, the proportion of students with bachelors degrees varied irregularly from about one-fourth to one-half between 1880 and 1900.[14]

In the 1880s, medical schools first adopted a formal entrance requirement of a high school diploma or the equivalent by examination. This was due to newly enacted state medical licensing laws that required applicants for licenses to have degrees from medical schools with that admission requirement. The entrance requirements adopted at Columbia University medical school in 1888 were evidence of a "fair proficiency in the English and Latin languages, arithmetic, algebra and geometry; such as is usually demanded for graduates in academies or for entrance in advanced literary colleges." High school graduates who had studied these subjects were considered to have fulfilled the requirement. The weaker medical schools, like many colleges, rarely enforced their entrance requirements.[15]

Recruiting students was a major activity of medical schools, which depended on student fees for all of their income. Many medical schools advertised extensively. The Chicago Medical College mailed out 28,000 pamphlets in 1884, 700 copies for each new student enrolled. Two years later, they also spent $255 for advertising in medical journals and $260 more in other publications.[16]

Many students chose a medical school by coming to a city shortly before the beginning of the school term, visiting the schools, and selecting one to attend. When Franklin Martin and a friend visited Chicago in 1877 to choose a medical school, they first went to Rush Medical College, where they saw an "impressive" building and "were received with extreme cordiality by officials and a large group of prospective students." They then visited the Chicago Medical College (affiliated with Northwestern University) and saw an "old and battered" building. Two instructors greeted them:

> They soon reasured us in our doubts. . . . "Rush is all new building; it has no exclusive hospital, and the large number of students all attend the same classes." They contrasted this uninviting picture with: "Our College has Mercy Hospital right here in the same block. We have quality in students rather than numbers. We advocate a three-year course, and our students are divided into classes—junior, middle, and senior. Look at our faculty. . . . Come over and on Friday and see Andrews amputate a leg." etc., etc. They were real propagandists, and fortunately for us in our indecision, good salesmen.[17]

Martin and his friend returned for the amputation, which was a typical recruiting device. He described it as follows:

Three days before the formal opening of school, we saw Professor Edmund Andrews amputate a leg. This was field day at the clinic and all of the junior students and many from the the middle and senior classes were crowded into the old amphitheater at Mercy Hospital. . . .

When Professor Andrews shuffled in, big and bustling, there was uproarious applause which indicated to us "new ones" that he was a great favorite. . . .

A wretched individual was brought in, and his useless ankle joint demonstrated. The professor explained how bravely the patient had cooperated in an effort to save the leg, and that now he had courageously volunteered to sacrifice his limb to save his life. We duly applauded the hero, who showed his appreciation by turning his face to us and attempting a smile of thanks. Some of us, I am sure, felt sorry for the poor devil, although it was not good form to admit it to one's self or to one's neighbor. . . . [It] was with bated breath that we awaited the first bloodshed that we were to witness of our own volition.

[After the amputation,] the students, old and new, filed out of the ether-saturated room, with its sordid operating field and splotches of blood, pieces of soiled cotton, and the tin receptacle beneath the table with the severed end of a man's leg peering out at us. . . . It was our baptism of blood.[18]

Medical students worked quite hard, according to European observers. Their mornings and early afternoons were occupied with lectures and their late afternoons and evenings with dissection and laboratories. Most students attended hospital or dispensary clinics several times a week. Gerster, who received his medical education in Vienna, observed that American students worked "much harder than in Vienna or . . . anywhere else abroad." He attributed this to the poor preliminary education of American students, including the college graduates.[19]

Students often formed quiz sections to review the course material and asked local physicians to serve as teachers. One physician recalled: "The term was not far advanced when two or three members of the class drifted into my office for informal talks about Surgical Gynecology; then others followed until a considerable part of the class came." Many young physicians were eager to teach quiz sessions because they sometimes led to faculty appointments. This informal teaching could be quite stimulating. David Linn Edsall wrote that it was "beyond all question the most valuable thing to me in the whole undergraduate medical period, because of the point of view of independent thought, reading, etc. which it gave." However, many quiz sessions were merely drill sessions designed to enable students to pass the examinations.[20]

Written final examinations gradually replaced the oral examinations in the 1870s and 1880s. At Columbia University, the first written examinations in 1879 covered only the lecture courses: anatomy, physiology, chemistry, materia medica, obstetrics, surgery, and practical medicine. Written examinations in the clinical specialties were added in 1888. The examinations were sufficiently rigorous at many schools that one physician claimed that "intensive cramming or . . . cribbing and cheating . . . were common occurrences."[21]

In order to examine the differences among medical schools, students were studied at six private medical schools in Baltimore, Maryland. Baltimore was a major middle Atlantic center of medical education whose medical schools varied from among the best to the worst. Three schools that provided quality educations on

TABLE 5.2. Status of Students in Selected Medical Schools, Baltimore, Maryland

Medical School	Years	Number of Students	Percentage of Students from Maryland	Percentage of Students Who Graduated		
				All Students	Maryland Students	Others
U. of Maryland	1876–1900	5392	43.8	78.6	79.4	78.1
Maryland Medical College	1893–1913	1121	15.5	61.6	34.9	62.4
Baltimore U.	1885–1905	961	20.3	72.1	51.0	74.0

Note: Information on the number of students and the percentage graduating was obtained from the listing of all students in the annual catalogues. Information on the students' residences was obtained from a sample of every fourth name in the same listings.

Sources: University of Maryland: annual catalogues; Maryland Medical College and Baltimore University: Harold Abrahams, *The Extinct Medical Colleges of Baltimore, Maryland* (Baltimore: Maryland Historical Society, 1969).

limited budgets were the University of Maryland, established in 1807; the College of Physicians and Surgeons, established in 1872; and the Baltimore Medical College, established in 1881. Two commercial schools of low repute were the Baltimore University School of Medicine (1884–1907) and the Maryland Medical College (1898–1913). The sixth school was the Johns Hopkins University medical school, which opened in 1893. It represented a new kind of medical school that had the resources, the faculty, and the entrance and graduation requirements that enabled it to provide the highest level of medical training.[22]

Baltimore, like other centers of medical education, attracted students from a large geographic region (Table 5.2). At the University of Maryland between 1876 and 1900, 43.8 percent of the students came from Maryland, 12.0 percent from Virginia, and 22.9 percent from North Carolina, West Virginia, and South Carolina. Many of the out-of-state students may have been attracted by the opportunity to attend a large urban medical school. At the Maryland Medical College and Baltimore University, only 15.5 percent and 20.3 percent of the students, respectively, were from Maryland. Another 32.9 percent of the former school's students and 46.8 percent of the latter's came from New York, New Jersey, Pennsylvania, Ohio, Massachusetts, and Connecticut. These out-of-state students may have been attracted by the low standards of the schools, because they could have attended urban medical schools closer to home.

The three schools also differed in the proportion of students who graduated. The University of Maryland had the highest graduation rate, 78.6 percent, while the Maryland Medical College and Baltimore University had graduation rates of 61.6 and 72.1 percent, respectively. At the University of Maryland, in-state and out-of-state students had equal chances of graduation. At the other two schools Maryland residents had lower rates of graduation than nonresidents, suggesting that their low standards might have attracted local students with only a casual interest in medicine. Some students who did not receive degrees from these schools may have received them later from other medical schools. There is no reason to believe that this proportion was higher at one school than another.

TABLE 5.3. Medical Practitioners in 1906 among Graduates of Medical Schools
in Baltimore, Maryland

School	Years of Graduation	Number in Sample	Percentage Who Were Practicing Medicine
Johns Hopkins U.	1897–1901	166	80.1
U. of Maryland	1891–1901	661	79.6
College of Physicians and Surgeons	1891–1901	909	71.5
Baltimore Medical College	1891–1901	999	70.9
Maryland Medical College	1896–1901	91	61.5
Baltimore U.	1891–1901	489	56.9

Notes: Findings based on study of every fourth graduate for University of Maryland, Maryland Medical College, and Baltimore University, and every graduate for College of Physicians and Surgeons, Baltimore Medical College, and Johns Hopkins University. In approximately 10 percent of the cases, the listing of the graduate could not be confirmed and a judgment was made.

Sources: University of Maryland, Baltimore Medical College, College of Physicians and Surgeons: annual catalogues; Maryland Medical College and Baltimore University: Harold Abrahams, *The Extinct Medical Colleges of Baltimore, Maryland* (Baltimore: Maryland Historical Society, 1969); Johns Hopkins University: W. Norman Brown, *Johns Hopkins Half-Century Directory* (Baltimore: Johns Hopkins University, 1926).

In order to ascertain how many graduates entered medical practice, the graduates of all six schools from 1891 to 1901 were analyzed to ascertain whether they were included in the 1906 *American Medical Directory,* a listing of all practicing physicians in the United States published by the American Medical Association. A minimum of 5 years between graduation and practice was chosen because some graduates did not enter medicine immediately after graduation and others probably left the profession after practicing briefly. A maximum of 15 years after graduation was chosen to include the largest possible number of graduates who practiced medicine with any regularity.

Table 5.3 shows a strong relationship between the quality of the school and the proportion of graduates who practiced medicine in 1906. About 80 percent of the graduates of the two best schools, Johns Hopkins University and the University of Maryland, were in practice, compared with less than 60 percent of the graduates of the two worst schools, the Maryland Medical College and Baltimore University. About 70 percent of the graduates of the two medium grade colleges were in practice.

Using these data, it is possible to estimate the percentage of matriculants at three schools who both graduated from the medical school and practiced medicine in the time periods specified. Approximately 63 percent of all students who matriculated at the University of Maryland practiced medicine, compared to 38 percent of the students at the Maryland Medical College and 41 percent of those at Baltimore University. These data indicate that students at the better schools were much more likely to practice medicine than those at the poorer schools.

Medical students used fewer community preceptors during the late nineteenth

TABLE 5.4. Preceptors of Medical Students in Selected Medical Schools, 1830–1913

School	Years	Students in Sample	Medical School[a]	Institution	Private Physician	None
				Type of Preceptor		
Harvard U.	1830	95	27.4%	—	72.6	0
	1840–41	88	26.1	—	65.9	8.0
	1850–51	116	0	37.8	48.4	13.8
	1860–61	205	25.4	—	64.8	9.8
	1869–70	311	34.4	10.0	52.7	2.9
U. of Maryland	1876–79	557	7.4	6.3	66.2	20.1
	1880–89	2,241	14.6	4.9	68.3	12.1
	1890–1900	2,564	17.9	7.9	53.8	20.4
Maryland Medical College	1893–1913	277	21.3	0	37.5	41.1
Baltimore U.	1885–1905	241	35.3	4.6	59.3	0.8

[a]Includes both the medical school and individual faculty members.

Notes: Data obtained from listing of all students at Harvard medical school and the University of Maryland and from a sample of every fourth name in listings at other schools.

Sources: Harvard University and University of Maryland: annual catalogues; Maryland Medical College and Baltimore University: Harold J. Abrahams, *The Extinct Medical Colleges of Baltimore, Maryland* (Baltimore: Maryland Historical Society, 1969).

century. Analyses were made of the preceptors listed in medical school catalogues for Harvard medical school at mid-century and three Baltimore medical schools at the end of the century (Table 5.4). The data show a trend away from the use of community preceptors toward a greater use of preceptors affiliated with the medical school or no preceptors at all. One of the two inferior schools, the Maryland Medical College, did not appear to enforce a preceptorship requirement, since 41 percent of its students had no preceptors.

The Medical School Faculty

Medical schools added many faculty members toward the end of the century, partly because new subjects were added to the curriculum, partly because faculty members wanted to spend more time on their private practices. At Harvard University medical school, the 7 faculty members and 1 clinical instructor who taught 10 subjects to 127 students using 1 laboratory in 1853 increased to 301 faculty members and 16 clinical instructors who taught 27 subjects to 310 students using 15 laboratories in 1913, a change in the student–faculty ratio from 18 : 1 to 1 : 1. The 11 faculty members at Northwestern University in 1859 increased to 115 in 1906. The 50 at 6 Philadelphia medical schools in 1860 increased to 372 in 1900. Even at a small rural school like the University of Vermont, the number of faculty members increased from 6 in 1853 to 22 in 1898. These figures do not include instructors who taught exclusively in hospitals or dispensaries, who numbered 445 at the 6 medical schools in Philadelphia in 1900. Altogether in Philadelphia, almost one-third of the physicians in the city were involved in medical education.[23]

Large numbers of other types of faculty members were hired at this time. Assistants to the professors comprised such a group. Traditionally, medical schools, like all institutions of higher education, had only one faculty member for each subject. Gradually, faculty members, who were busy with their private practices and other responsibilities, selected unpaid personal assistants to provide support, conduct recitations, and give lectures in their absence. Assistants took the positions in order to gain experience and become candidates for future professorships. Assistants gradually came to be appointed in the same manner as professors, although their duties remained the same.[24]

Medical school clinical faculty members (often called lecturers) taught only in the hospital or dispensary clinics and had a status subordinate to that of the professors. As the number of clinical faculty members increased, they sought additional privileges, often without success. A lengthy struggle over this issue occurred at the University of Pennsylvania in the 1870s and 1880s. The Johns Hopkins University medical school, which opened in 1893, refused for years either to permit its dispensary teachers to admit patients to the hospital wards without permission of the chief of service (that is, to treat them as faculty) or to pay them (that is, to treat them as employees). Both schools professed a greater commitment to clinical teaching than existed in most schools.[25]

By the end of the century, the number of faculty members increased sufficiently to necessitate the creation of academic departments. Once there were several faculty members in a department, appropriate titles were adopted, including department head, professor, clinical professor, associate professor, assistant professor, and instructor.[26]

Faculty earnings, which now usually took the form of salaries, decreased significantly because of the rising costs of operating the medical schools, including the greater number of faculty members. At the University of Maryland, faculty members earned less than $1,000 from their teaching in 1900, compared to about $2,500 in 1870. At the University of Pennsylvania, the full professors received $2,000 in salaries in the early 1890s, well under their earnings two decades earlier. They also received bonuses if the school earned a surplus for the year. By the end of the century, faculty salaries and income from preceptorships hardly compensated for the teaching time involved. The only remaining economic benefit was the value of a faculty position in obtaining patients, consultations, and referrals. Consequently, faculty members spent more time on their practices and less time at the medical school.[27]

Changes in the Medical School Curriculum

Toward the end of the century, medical schools assumed greater responsibility for the clinical education of medical students. They realized that they could attract more students to the school by adding material covered in the private courses and dispensary and hospital clinics to their own curriculum, thereby saving students the time and expense of obtaining it elsewhere. However, if the new material were added to the regular term, the longer terms would have deterred many low-income students from attending medical school. The solution adopted by medical schools as early as the 1840s was to add optional fall courses before the regular term and/or optional spring courses after the term. The students who desired the additional education would benefit from the continuity and convenience. The students who did not attend would still be able to obtain a degree.

Medical schools used a variety of organizational devices to operate their optional sessions. Harvard medical school simply absorbed the Tremont Street School. The University of Pennsylvania medical school opened an Auxiliary Department of Medicine in 1865 with a separate faculty of five professors and its own dean, with each professor receiving $500 a term. Its courses were taught in the spring after the regular session had ended. The university's medical students were encouraged to attend and charged a fee of $10. Those who completed the course received a "certificate of proficiency." After 33 years the department was merged into the medical school. Most schools simply added two optional sessions to the regular sessions. A preliminary session of several weeks before the regular term was taught by the medical school faculty and designed to encourage students to attend the medical school. A longer session following the term was more formally organized and taught by a different group of instructors.[28]

Many optional sessions operated successfully for decades. The students were urged to attend by the medical schools and charged low fees. The classes had fewer students and provided more clinical teaching than regular medical school courses. Medical schools had no difficulty finding instructors to teach the courses, which, according to one physician, served as "a training school for instructors who might become Professors in the Faculty chairs." An appointment of this kind was a major opportunity for a young physicians.[29]

The optional sessions taught the most advanced medical knowledge, but did it as a hodge-podge of courses with no integration, very much like the private schools. Some courses were scientific, such as medical botany and comparative osteology. A few were in the basic medical sciences, such as pathological anatomy, poisons, and reproduction. Most were in the clinical specialties, including courses on operative surgery, pediatrics, orthopedic surgery, and diseases of various organs, such as the eye and ear, thorax and chest, uterus, and kidneys. Many of these courses later became part of the regular curriculum.[30]

Medical schools with no formal extra sessions often provided informal instruction. One student traveled to St. Louis in 1868 hoping to attend a summer session at the St. Louis Medical College. There, he recalled, a faculty member told him that "while there would be no regular lectures given, yet if I saw fit to remain, he felt sure I would find enough to keep me busy and interested." The student dissected a cadaver, visited patients with the faculty member, and assisted him in operations. Other students were also interested in receiving instruction and the group was formed into a class. The student reported that "certain members of the faculty . . . gave us every opportunity in their power. We had medical and surgical clinics at the City hospital and at a Catholic hospital . . . where Dr. Gregory operated before us and gave clinical lectures. Here also we had clinical instruction from [an] oculist. . . . At the college we were favored with anatomical instruction from the Demonstrator of Anatomy" and other clinical instruction and didactic lectures.[31]

Thus, most large medical schools engaged in significant amounts of supplementary teaching in order to attract students. Formal lectures became only one part of an expanding medical school curriculum.

The European Influence on Clinical Education

During the second half of the nineteenth century, central European physicians established many new clinical specialties as a result of their work in urban public hospitals that provided free care for the poor. The hospital staffs consisted of medical school professors appointed by the government, although no formal relationship existed between the hospitals and the medical schools. The staff members had access to thousands of patients and hundreds of cadavers for study, and were given government support for research. Using these resources, individual staff members studied particular medical problems and became specialists in their fields. Their achievements were so great that physicians from throughout the world came to study with them.

Vienna was the mecca for aspiring American specialists. Its great hospital, with 3,000 beds, was actually a collection of specialty hospitals in one location. Here, as one American wrote, "one can attend a medical lecture from 8 to 9 o'clock, a laboratory course from 9 to 11, a skin clinic from 11 to 12, a surgical operation from 1 to 3, and so on until the day is ended." Berlin was the other leading clinical center, but its facilities were scattered inconveniently throughout the city. The remaining medical schools in Austria, Germany, and Czechoslovakia lacked clinical facilities and were visited by Americans only for study with individual specialists. France and England lacked the specialists to make them major clinical teaching centers.[32]

Thousands of American physicians traveled to Europe for specialty training. Between 1870 and 1914, Bonner estimated that 10,000 Americans studied in Vienna, 3,000 in Berlin, and perhaps 1,000 to 2,000 elsewhere. Hudson found that more than one-third of the eminent physicians listed in the *Dictionary of American Medical Biography* who received their medical educations between 1871 and 1900 studied in a European university. European study was not limited to the wealthy. Hun estimated at the time that the cost of a year's study in the 1880s was about $1,000, which many physicians could afford after several years of medical practice.[33]

American physicians in Europe did not attend lectures at the local medical schools. They had already graduated from medical school and most had several years of medical practice. Instruction in European medical schools was too elementary, insufficiently practical, and was taught in German, which few Americans understood.[34]

Most Americans took postgraduate courses in the clinical specialties that were taught to classes of about a dozen physicians for one hour daily for four to eight weeks. Many courses were arranged specifically for visiting Americans by the American Medical Association of Vienna (no relation to its American namesake). The instructors were low-level faculty members, assistants to the great professors, or private teachers, all of whom were poorly paid and eager to earn the extra money.

The eminent professors, who were well paid, were seldom available. Most Americans took only courses taught in English. One American wrote that in most specialties, "a knowledge of German is absolutely necessary to obtain the best. Many Americans fool themselves into attending second rate men who talk second rate English."[35]

The educational value of these courses lay in the large number of patients available for study. The Vienna hospital teemed with patients from all over Austria, who were carefully placed in the appropriate specialty clinics. Physicians could study a wide variety of diseases in any specialty under the most convenient circumstances. The major disadvantage of the courses was that the physicians were observers who did not assume responsibility for the care of patients. Maverick observed that "one going to Vienna expecting to learn surgery or therapeutic technic of any kind will be disappointed. For pathology and diagnosis go to Austria or Germany, but for treatment, surgical or medical, continue your journey east until you strike America."[36]

American physicians also discovered that Vienna had fine cafes and restaurants, delightful music and entertainment, female companionship, and more than enough to keep an American physician busy if he found the courses boring. Many American physicians learned more about Viennese life and customs than about Viennese medicine. Once they set foot in Vienna, they achieved all that they wanted: the ability to return to the United States saying that they had studied in Vienna.[37]

Observant American physicians returned with a better understanding of central European medical education and medical practice. European medical schools were not as well organized and offered less guidance to students than those in America. The schools had few low income students. Clinical instruction was often no better in Europe than in America. American physicians also learned that the quality of medicine practiced by European specialists was far superior to American medicine, with the possible exception of operative surgery. They also learned that specialty medicine was much more profitable than general medicine, and that they wanted to be specialists.[38]

The Teaching of Clinical Specialties
in American Medical Schools

In order to practice a specialty, specialists needed to inform the profession and the public about their availability and qualifications. As H. C. Wood wrote in 1875, a faculty appointment was ideal for this:

> [I]n the great majority of cases, the professor's chair becomes very valuable as a road to practice. The college announcements in the daily press, the catalogues and circulars scattered broadcast by the thousands, the exercises and eclat of commencement day, all keep before the public the fact that Dr. —— is a great authority on this or that class of diseases. Moreover, what is more legitimate and natural, the graduates of the school when they meet with difficulties in practice are very prone to call in consultation their old teachers.[39]

The existing medical school professors, who were generalists, were not eager to share their positions with specialists. For example, at the University of Pennsylva-

TABLE 5.5. First Medical School Faculty in Selected Specialities in Three Medical Schools

| | Harvard U. | | U. of Maryland | | Western Reserve U. | |
| | First | First | First | First | First | First |
Specialty	Faculty	Professor	Faculty	Professor	Faculty	Professor
Ophthalmology[a]	1871	1871	1869	1873	1865	1865
Dermatology	1871	1871	1880	b	1880	b
Genitourinary	1881	b	b	b	1872	1890
Otology[c]	1872	1888	1869	b	1871	1871
Neurology	1875	1893	1869	b	1892	1893

[a]Either alone or combined with otology.
[b]No appointment made at this level before 1900.
[c]Either alone or combined with ophthalmology or rhinology and/or laryngology.

Sources: Thomas F. Harrington, The Harvard Medical School (New York: Lewis, 1905), 3:1361-66; Eugene F. Cordell, Historical Sketch of the University of Maryland School of Medicine (Baltimore, 1891); Eugene F. Cordell, University of Maryland 1807–1907 (New York: Lewis, 1907), Vol. I; Frederick C. Waite, Western Reserve University Centennial History of the School of Medicine (Cleveland: Western Reserve University Press, 1946), pp. 140–41, 181, 407.

nia in the 1870s, the faculty refused to create new faculty positions in ophthalmology, otolaryngology, or the other emerging clinical specialties because it would detract from the existing professorships.[40] Similar conflicts occurred at most medical schools. Consequently, the first formal instruction in the medical specialties occurred in private courses and in the optional sessions of the medical schools. These courses were responsible for much of the success of private courses and optional sessions, because specialists wanted the opportunity to teach them and students were eager to take them.

Medical schools gradually appointed instructors in the specialties. Unlike the generalist professors, who expected to be paid handsomely and were willing to work hard for it, specialists sought no pay and as little work as possible. They wanted the positions as evidence of their clinical skills. Medical schools therefore hired specialists at junior levels with little or no salary. Professorships in the specialties were usually created later.

Evidence for this process is shown in an analysis of the first appointments at any rank and the first appointments at the rank of professor in five newly developed specialties at three of the better medical schools: Harvard University, the University of Maryland, and Western Reserve University. The specialties were ophthalmology, neurology, dermatology, genitourinary diseases, and otology. Faculty appointments were made in the five specialties before 1900 in 14 of the 15 possible cases (Table 5.5). The initial appointments were made at the level of professor in only 4 of the cases; in the other 10 cases a lower level appointment like instructor or clinical professor was made first. The lower level appointments did not lead to senior level appointments for at least 15 years in 8 of the 10 cases.

The teaching of specialty courses varied greatly from school to school. Many schools taught them but did not include them in the graduation examinations. Schools differed in the number of hours alloted to the specialties. For example, an examination of the catalogues of 13 medical schools in 1900 found that some required four or five times as many hours in diseases of the eye, ear, nose, and throat as others. Schools also differed in the qualifications of their faculty members in the specialties. One physician surveyed 120 medical schools in 1912 and received replies from 43 professors of obstetrics. Only 26 were full-time obstetricians, and 8 conceded that they were unable to ''care for some of the complications of deliveries.''[41]

Specialties were taught at the rural medical schools as well as the urban ones. From 1875 until at least 1911 at the University of Vermont, specialists were brought to the school for periods of two or three weeks to teach short courses in their specialties and hold clinics. The teachers were not paid, but their presence at the school was announced in advance and many patients appeared for treatment and were shown at the clinics.[42]

The value of teaching the specialties to medical students was widely debated at this time. One advocate claimed that ''specialism in medical teaching must make up all the integral parts of the course, and a medical education which does not embrace absolutely everything relating to treatment of disease and injury cannot be counted complete, or even satisfactory. . . . Whenever the nature of the work is either so difficult of performance as to require special training, or so extensive as to require all one's time in the practice, it at once becomes a specialty, and must be taught by the expert specialist in the regular course of a general medical education.'' Critics observed that few graduates became specialists and that the more important courses were being sacrificed to the specialties. These physicians felt that training for the specialties should come after medical school, preferably in the hospitals.[43]

Regardless of the merits of their case, specialists soon obtained a major role in the curriculum. In many medical colleges, specialties were given two lectures a week, and general medicine and surgery only three.[44] Medical schools willingly added specialty courses to the curriculum because junior faculty specialists taught them at minimal cost, treated patients at the school dispensary or hospital, and attracted students to the medical school.

Expanding the Medical School Course

By the 1870s, the major medical schools were involved in an expanding array of poorly coordinated educational activities. They taught a course of two repetitive terms involving a steadily increasing amount of scientific and clinical knowledge. They taught optional sessions before and after the regular term to provide students with additional information. Their faculty members served as preceptors to a growing proportion of medical students. Clearly, it was necessary to integrate these activities in some more meaningful way.

Two major alternatives existed. One was to continue to lengthen the term, as medical schools had been doing since the 1840s. The four-month term in use at that time had been periodically extended so that by 1882 about half of the medical schools had a six-month term. The terms became longer when medical schools incorporated their optional courses into the regular term. The Columbia University medical school adopted a seven-month term in 1880 for that reason. The other alternative was to replace the repetitive curriculum with a three-year graded course, which most schools believed would lead to an unacceptable loss of students and tuition revenues.[45]

Medical schools compromised by adding an optional three-year graded course. It was first offered by the Chicago Medical College (later Northwestern University) in 1868, although students taking the graded course had the same curriculum as those taking the repetitive course. Other medical schools soon offered their own optional graded courses. During the 1870s medical school catalogues, according to Waite, "'offered,' 'suggested,' 'recommended,' 'advised,' and finally 'urged' [students] to enroll in the optional graded course." Some schools even charged no lecture fees for the third year. Students, however, showed little enthusiasm for the three-year course. Only 11 of 47 students entering the Chicago Medical College in 1871 chose the graded course. In the late 1880s, only half of the students at Western Reserve University and the University of Maryland enrolled in the graded course.[46]

Gradually, a few schools that could afford to do so adopted a compulsory graded course. The first was Harvard University, which in 1871 adopted a three-year graded course of nine-month terms. Harvard also incorporated its summer course into the regular medical course at that time. This was equally significant because it added new specialty courses to the curriculum. The first professors in ophthalmology and dermatology were appointed in that year, and in otology in the next. By 1880, 10 medical schools adopted a required three-year graded curriculum, and 26 adopted it by 1890.[47]

Changes were more rapid thereafter due to external pressures. In 1891 the National Conference of State Medical Examining and Licensing Boards required applicants for licenses to have degrees from medical schools with three-year graded courses, and several years later extended the requirement to four years. By the turn of the century, practically all medical schools had adopted a four-year graded course of instruction.[48]

The major beneficiaries of the graded course were the clinical specialties. The third year was used for both the medical sciences and the specialties, but the fourth year was used almost completely for the specialties. At Harvard, 14 elective courses were offered in the fourth year, practically all in the clinical specialties. In 1895, the Association of American Colleges, which had recently been reorganized after an unsuccessful beginning, required its member schools to have at least 25 hours of instruction in each of the following specialties: ophthalmology and otology, mental and nervous diseases, dermatology, orthopedics, genitourinary diseases, pediatrics, and laryngology. Most of these fields were in their infancy and did not merit special attention in medical school. A visiting British physician said in 1891 that the number of specialty lectures was "enormous" and that "the time must come off the more elementary subjects, which are the only true foundation of a good education."[49]

These changes demonstrated the growing power of faculty specialists and the declining influence of students and faculty generalists. The graded course and longer terms raised the cost of attending medical school and deprived many students of a medical education. Lower enrollments reduced medical school incomes, which the faculty generalists had always tried to increase. The specialists were not disturbed by either development because they used their faculty appointments to obtain referrals and consultations. Nevertheless, the resulting financial deficits soon created major problems which even the specialists could not avoid.

Instruction in the Basic Medical Sciences

The influence of European medicine affected the basic medical sciences as well as the clinical specialties. The preeminent country in the basic medical sciences was Germany, which established and funded 173 separate institutes in the basic medical sciences and clinical medicine between 1860 and 1914. The institutes were headed by university professors but were unconnected with German universities. Students were admitted for institute study, and scholarships were given to attract the best students. Many institutes welcomed students and scientists from all over the world.[50]

The research institutes created a cleavage between medical science and medical practice in Germany. German medical scientists became removed from those aspects of the medical sciences most concerned with practical medicine. For example, despite the greater institutional development of the medical sciences in Germany, the fundamental discoveries in bacteriology and its medical applications were made in France (by Louis Pasteur and his coworkers) and England (by Joseph Lister). Much of the early work on bacteriology in Germany, with some exceptions, was carried out by private practitioners like Robert Koch.[51]

The German system of institutes and their relationship to medical school professorships led to the proliferation of new disciplines in the basic medical sciences. Once a number of institutes and associated chairs in the medical schools had been established in a discipline, few positions were available for younger scholars, especially given the conservatism of the institute directors. The younger scholars therefore developed new disciplines in which new professorships and institutes could be established. In this way, anatomy led to physiology and pathology, and later to bacteriology and other medical sciences.[52]

Many American physicians interested in the basic medical sciences studied in central European research institutes between 1870 and 1914. Unlike American clinicians, the Americans studying the basic medical sciences often went to smaller cities where an eminent scientist had an institute in a discipline of interest to them. They settled there for a year or two and pursued their studies in some detail. Consequently, they were less knowledgeable about European medical education than the American clinicians who studied in Europe.[53]

When the first basic medical scientists returned to America, they discovered that American medical schools had little interest in full-time faculty appointments in their disciplines. Medical schools continued to regard the basic medical sciences as secondary and used part-time younger physicians as teachers. The part-time teachers were rarely interested in the medical sciences for their own sake but used their positions as stepping stones to appointments to the clinical chairs.[54]

The part-time teachers taught the basic medical sciences with an emphasis on their practical implications. This occurred even in dissection, the only true laboratory course, according to Hertzler:

Here we learned chiefly those things which would be needed in practice, because the young surgeons who taught us knew what structures were of practical importance and stressed them. . . . we learned only the practical things, but we learned them well. We came out of school with a pretty clear idea of where not to cut. On the whole, anatomy was better taught then than now [1941], at least in so far as it relates to the practice of medicine.[55]

Laboratory courses in the medical sciences taught by full-time medical scientists were added slowly at the end of the century. A few leading medical schools established laboratory courses in physiology in the 1870s in the premature hope that knowledge of the functions of the healthy organism would provide a useful basis for the study of pathology. In the 1880s some American medical schools offered laboratory courses in biochemistry, but this was also premature. Even in Europe only one-third of the German-speaking medical schools had chairs in biochemistry as late as 1900.[56]

The most significant new basic medical science for medical students and the public was bacteriology, which produced the most dramatic developments in the history of medicine up to that time. Lewellys Barker wrote that "with the advent of Pasteur's discoveries and Koch's researches, bacteriology sprang suddenly into favor; and laboratories fitted out with thermostats, culture tubes, and oil-immersion lenses were everywhere demanded." A survey of 28 major medical schools in 1888 found that 11 of them offered a significant amount of bacteriology, involving either a special instructor or a special laboratory. This was an impressive number given the newness of the field and the small number of qualified instructors.[57]

It was not until the 1890s, after medical schools had adopted a three-year graded curriculum and after the state licensing boards demanded improvements, that medical schools instituted laboratory courses in pathology, bacteriology, chemistry, and physiology. Waite examined the catalogues of all medical schools in Ohio from 1870 to 1910 and found that laboratory courses were first required in most of the schools in the 1890s.[58]

To teach the laboratory courses, the medical schools turned to the young European-trained medical scientists, who were the only ones trained in microscopy and laboratory methods. Many medical schools turned over the entire basic science curriculum to one or two individuals. Hertzler wrote that he taught "histology, bacteriology, pathology, experimental surgery, gynecology, and ran the dissecting room for two years" at a Kansas City, Missouri, medical school beginning in 1901.[59] The significant shortage of qualified teachers enabled many medical scientists to obtain full-time appointments and facilities for research as well as teaching.

The salaries paid the basic scientists were sometimes satisfactory, but basic medical scientists were not important enough to be paid well. At the University of Pennsylvania and the Johns Hopkins University in the 1890s, basic scientists were paid annual salaries of between $3,000 and $4,000. By 1894 at the University of Pennsylvania, preclinical department heads earned over $6,000. Clinical professors at the same school, in contrast, earned $4,000 in 1894 from the medical school in addition to their lucrative private practices. The less well-endowed schools paid much lower salaries. Hertzler earned $50 a month for his full-time position, the same salary as the janitor.[60]

Expanded teaching in the basic medical sciences reduced student enrollments and revenues, especially at the leading schools that taught the most demanding courses. Fewer students were willing to enroll in the schools and some of them left after the first year because of the difficulty of the courses. When the schools realized that the more poorly prepared students were not enrolling or were dropping out, they raised their entrance requirements, which at least reduced their drop-out rates. In the first decade of the century, the leading schools began to require some college education as a prerequisite for admission.[61]

Clinical Teaching in the Medical School

Medical school faculty members after the Civil War continued to combine teaching, hospital appointments, and private practice. James C. White wrote: "My work has been with two classes of patients, widely separated, and evenly divided between the two,—the poor in hospital and dispensary practice from whom I have received nothing; the rich from whom I have obtained my means of living; and in the duties of teaching, in which remuneration is small."[62]

Medical schools proliferated so rapidly at the end of the century that it has been suggested that their faculties consisted of community physicians who were poorly qualified to teach clinical medicine. To examine the qualifications of clinical faculty members, a study was made of the teaching activities of the members of the two leading organizations of clinicians at the time, the Association of American Physicians (AAP) and the American Surgical Association (ASA), as well as the presidents of the American Medical Association (AMA) from 1847 to 1920, who were among the country's leading physicians. The AAP membership list was that of its founding year, 1886; the ASA membership list was the first published list of members in 1883, although the association was founded in 1881.[63]

A very high proportion of the traceable members of all three organizations were members of medical school faculties for some length of time: 83.3 percent of all 72 AMA presidents, 90.0 percent of the 60 AAP members who could be traced, and 80.0 percent of the 85 ASA members who could be traced (Table 5.6). Furthermore, they taught in medical schools for a major part of their careers: 113 of the 217 physicians who could be traced taught for more than 20 years in medical schools. Even making the most conservative estimate by including untraceable members among those who did not teach, over 60 percent of those from each organization taught at a medical school for some length of time and over 40 percent of them taught for at least 10 years. These eminent physicians taught at many different medical schools: the AMA presidents taught at about 53 different medical schools, the AAP members at about 35, and the ASA members at about 48. The schools included practically all of the major medical schools of the period.

Thus, medical schools were not parochial institutions established by a few local physicians for personal profit. Many of their faculties included the nation's most prominent clinicians, who spent a large part of their careers as medical educators. Furthermore, because these eminent physicians taught in the largest medical schools that graduated a significant proportion of all practicing physicians, their influence was greater than their numbers would indicate.

TABLE 5.6 Medical School Teaching of Leading Physicians in the Late Nineteenth Century

Number of Years Teaching	AMA Presidents 1847–1920	AAP Members 1886	ASA Members 1883
0	16.7%	10.0	20.0
1–9	12.5	18.3	8.2
10–19	9.7	13.3	9.4
20 or more	61.1	48.3	47.1
Taught, but number of years unknown	0	10.0	15.3
Total	100.0	99.9	100.0
Number of cases identified	72	60	85
Number of cases not identified	0	22	22

Sources of cases: Morris Fishbein, *A History of the American Medical Association 1847–1947* (Philadelphia: Saunders, 1947); *Transactions of the American Surgical Association* 1 (1883): v–xi; *Transactions of the Association of American Physicians*, 1 (1886). *Sources of biographies*: Howard A. Kelly and Walter L. Burrage, *American Medical Biographies* (Baltimore, 1920); Martin Kaufman, Stuart Gallishoff, and Todd L. Savitt, eds., *Dictionary of American Medical Biography* (Westport, Conn.: Greenwood Press, 1984); Richard F. Stone, ed., *Biography of Eminent American Physicians and Surgeons* (Indianapolis, 1894).

Methods of clinical teaching underwent major changes during this period. The use of the lecture came under attack in the 1880s by the young European-trained clinical faculty members. This led to what Herrick called an "epidemic of unrest that swept the country and resulted in an upheaval in methods of medical education." The critics compared the passive role of students in clinical lectures to their active participation in basic science laboratories. William Osler asked: "How can we make the work of the student in the third and fourth year as practical as it is in his first and second? . . . [T]ake him from the lecture-room, take him from the amphitheater,—put him in the out-patient department—put him in the wards." Here the student would receive an education that "begins with the patient, continues with the patient, and ends . . . with the patient, using books and lectures as tools, as means to an end."[64]

This new method of teaching was based on two developments in medical education. One was the small enrollments in a few well-funded medical schools. Even Osler conceded: "With a small class I have been satisfied with the results, but the plan would be difficult to carry out with a large body of students." A second was the availability of excellent clinical textbooks that reduced the need for lectures and served as reference books for students. Osler's 1892 text in internal medicine became the standard text in that field for some decades. Outstanding texts were also published about the same time in pediatrics, dermatology, and other fields.[65]

Many educators argued that lectures were useful and should be retained. Textbooks were never completely up-to-date and excluded much material of regional, local, or temporary significance that could be provided only by lecture. Furthermore, students needed to be told what to expect when they saw patients. The number of possible symptoms is virtually infinite and the student's time can be put to best use if he knows what to look for when he examines the patient. W. Gilman Thompson observed:

> There is some danger of bedside teaching becoming too pictorial and hence superficial. The student is presented with a picture-book without adequate text. Moreover, such clinical pictures as he really needs at first should be well-defined composites, not a collection of exceptions to the average (as so many clinical cases are . . .). . . . [H]e should have certain composite standards of comparison clearly established for him, and not be trusted always to form them himself.[66]

Another difficulty with a total dependence on bedside teaching was that many important diseases could not be shown to students because patients were not available at all or when the material was to be covered in class. Thompson reported that of 42 infectious diseases in a standard textbook of medicine, only 13 could be shown regularly from patients at the Bellevue Hospital in New York City, one of the largest general hospitals in the country.[67]

Hospital or dispensary teaching was also inherently unsystematic. A sufficient number of patients with a particular disease were rarely available when the instructor wished to use them. Furthermore, a systematic approach to the study of diseases should describe their etiologies, their relationship to other illnesses and conditions, their prognosis and general treatment, and the significance of factors like heredity and environment. This kind of analytical approach was not possible with the inductive methods that characterized bedside teaching.[68]

The necessity for systematic instruction was such that even the most well-known advocates of bedside teaching used it. The Johns Hopkins University medical school, where Osler taught, was supposed to have had no clinical lectures. However, Herrick described how "William H. Welch . . . had with an apologetic air admitted to me that once a week he 'gave a talk'—he didn't like to call it a lecture—on 'immunity and kindred topics that have not yet gotten into the schoolbooks.'" William Osler held a regular weekly amphitheater clinic where, as he observed, "I like the clinical clerk and the patient to do the teaching, adding comments here and there, or asking the former questions, sometimes giving ten or fifteen minutes talk on some special feature or on a group of cases." It was easier to do away with the lecture in theory than in practice.[69]

Given that the lecture had an essential role in the teaching of clinical subjects, why should it have been so denigrated? The answer lay in the long tradition of ward rounds preferred by medical educators. Thompson observed:

> "Bedside teaching" . . . is most seductive from the teacher's standpoint. . . . [H]ow much more interesting it is for ourselves to spend an hour at the bedside than to stand up and "lecture" for a similar time. There is more opportunity for finding something new and instructive for oneself, and hence it is easier to put enthusiasm into the work. Bedside teaching never acquires the monotony for the teacher that lectures too often do when repeated for thirty years.[70]

Hospital and Dispensary Teaching

Medical schools had two possible sites for clinical teaching: hospitals and dispensaries. Hospitals were unsuitable until the end of the century because they housed a small number of convalescing patients with a limited variety of illnesses. Dispensary patients, on the other hand, had illnesses and problems very much like that of patients seen in ordinary practice. Medical schools could easily establish their own dispensaries or take over existing ones and organize them in conformity with their educational needs. For these reasons, medical schools preferred dispensaries for clinical instruction during most of the nineteenth century.

Although dispensaries were established at both urban and rural medical schools, they flourished at the urban schools. The first one was organized in 1825 at the Jefferson Medical College in Philadelphia, and in 1850 it treated about 2,000 cases, equally divided between medical and surgical. A room or two was used for postoperative recoveries, but most patients were taken to their homes after operations. By 1872–1873, 3,000 cases were treated, although J. Collins Warren found the facilities to be very limited. These arrangements were typical of many medical school dispensaries.[71]

By 1900 medical school dispensaries dominated the dispensary movement. Davis estimated that about 100 of the approximately 150 dispensaries and outpatient departments either were owned by medical schools or were independent dispensaries that were staffed and partially supported by medical schools. He wrote that the influence of medical schools "was primarily toward an intensive or qualitative development of out-patient service." Community physicians often referred difficult cases to medical school dispensaries for care.[72]

In the earliest medical school dispensaries, patients were brought to amphitheater clinics for diagnosis and treatment. As more patients attended the dispensaries, physicians were appointed or hired to treat them and provide clinical instruction to small groups of students. The quality of the early teaching often left much to be desired. Abt recalled about his medical education around 1890:

> [C]linical instruction [was given] in the dispensary, which was located in the basement of the school. Here some men tried to make accurate diagnoses, but the old-time Doctor in Charge, for the most part, followed the honored custom of asking the patient a few questions, feeling his pulse, looking at his tongue, and, if he happened to be quite advanced, making a superficial examination with the stethoscope. Usually, he found that the patient was bilious or had a torpid liver, for which he was told to take at least three compound cathartic pills at night and a teaspoonful of medicine after meals.[73]

As a younger generation of clinicians became faculty members, dispensary conditions improved. At Abt's dispensary, Frank Billings, who had studied in Europe, was brought in and "examined a patient from the crown of his head to the tips of his toes, and made a carefully considered diagnosis." The new clinicians also established specialty clinics in the dispensaries. Columbia University medical school had 10 separate specialty dispensary clinics in 1876, with 8 clinical professors and 30 assistants staffing them in 1883.[74]

The major problem of the medical school dispensary was that it had no sources of income. Patients paid nothing and the general public was not willing to contribute to proprietary medical schools. The Rush Medical College in Chicago tried to attract donations by putting its dispensary under a separate board of trustees about 1870, but with no success. Medical schools were not considered objects of philanthropy.[75]

At this point, a pathbreaking event in the history of medical education occurred. The Vanderbilt family made a series of lavish gifts to improve the College of Physicians and Surgeons of New York, which was then nominally affiliated with Columbia University. Over a period of 15 years beginning in 1884, the children and grandchildren of Cornelius Vanderbilt gave $2,250,000 for a new campus and buildings, a new teaching dispensary to be called the Vanderbilt Clinic, and the Sloan Maternity Hospital. William Pusey observed about the gifts:

> At that time it was a unique experience for medical education and, indeed, a very unusual one for medicine at all. . . . [O]ur first comic paper, *Puck*, had a front page cartoon in which it represented Mr. Vanderbilt going up the steps of the medical school with his bags of money and a college president pulling at his coat tails and telling him: "You are going into the wrong place; nobody ever gives money there."[76]

The new Vanderbilt Clinic was designed to provide individual and small group dispensary teaching. Separate facilities with the most up-to-date equipment were provided for each specialty. Consulting rooms were constructed with small stalls, where patients could be examined by individual students under the supervision of faculty members. An amphitheater was available for lectures. Every effort was made to construct the best possible ambulatory care clinic, with student education as a major purpose.[77]

Well staffed and equipped dispensaries had great value for teaching. Osler wrote: "The student must first be taught to observe and can not do better than begin his acquaintance with disease among out-patients. A man with typhoid fever in bed, scoured and cleaned, looks very different from the poor fellow who totters into the dispensary." In the outpatient department of the Johns Hopkins Hospital, groups of 10 students each met for two hours a day, three days a week. There, according to Osler, they received "practical instruction . . . in seeing the cases in a routine way, in receiving instructions how to take histories, and in becoming familiar with the ordinary aspect of disease as seen in a medical out-clinic." In the surgical outpatient clinics, the students saw minor surgery, learned bandaging, gave ether and helped "in all the interesting work in the surgical dispensary." Students also went to the wards in the hospital if the patients were sent there, or were "encouraged to make a visit at least once a week" if the patient went home.[78]

Osler used the dispensary to teach the fundamentals of medical care. He wrote that the instructors drilled "the class systematically in the use of the stethoscope and methods of examining the heart, lungs and abdomenal organs. . . . Plenty of time, oft-repeated opportunities and intelligent supervision of patient and student are the essentials in teaching physical diagnosis." He added: "I am not particular [as to disease]; anything will do, so long as it has an educational value. . . . [T]he primary importance . . . is to give the student a practical, objective, first-hand acquaintance with disease."[79]

This emphasis on the teaching of routine medical care was characteristic of a previous generation of medical generalists whose lifework had been in office practice and the dispensary. It was not the view of the new generation of specialists. This is shown by the failure of the Vanderbilt Clinic to achieve its objectives. A

British physician observed when he visited it in 1891 that "it was a very long way behind the Wiener Polyclinic, which it takes as its model. The more famous men give clinical lectures, but they do not do the work as the Viennese professors do, examining and explaining each case to the students. That work in the Vanderbilt is done by a number of young practitioners, and only picked cases go before the professors."[80]

The new generation of specialists did not like dispensaries because most dispensary patients did not need specialized care. The specialists wanted to study patients with problems involving their own fields, even though the teaching of routine care was more important to medical students. Patients with specialized problems could most effectively be treated and kept under observation in hospitals, which was where specialists preferred to teach.

Medical School-Hospital Affiliations

Hospital teaching posed significant problems for medical schools. The schools had to convince skeptical hospital boards to admit faculty members to their staffs and permit students to care for their patients, all the while looking out for other schools that sought to replace them. Medical schools devoted considerable effort to establishing good relationships with hospitals. For example, about 1900 the Northwestern University medical school paid 90 percent of the $25,000 cost of the construction of a 500-seat amphitheater at a local hospital, which it then used for its teaching.[81]

Competition among medical schools in soliciting the favor of hospitals was widespread. Gerster wrote about hospitals in New York City:

> [T]he practice of politics was simply a matter of self-preservation. Hospital positions were the stakes of the game, in which a blow below the belt was not always considered reprehensible. . . .
>
> The favorite procedure was to gain the backing of the few men who dominated the board of directors of any given hospital. The advantages of such "inside positions" . . . were shamelessly exploited. Suddenly, without apparent rhyme or reason, a "reorganization" of the medical board was decreed by the [directors] and all positions were declared vacant. Most of the men were promptly reappointed, except those whose places were wanted for the favored aspirant of one or another college. . . .
>
> All this will appear less reprehensible . . . if we consider how precarious was the life of most medical colleges. . . . They performed an arduous and time-devouring task with funds supplied from their own resources, without any aid from the Government, and, considering the circumstances, performed it marvelously well.[82]

Small hospitals often permitted a medical school to control all staff positions, but large hospitals maintained their independence. In Boston, although the Massachusetts General Hospital appointed many Harvard medical school faculty members to its staff, it firmly resisted Harvard's efforts to control all staff appointments concerned with medical education. A hospital superintendent wrote:

> The Trustees have always maintained their independence, not forgetting that the functions of the hospital are the kindly care of the patient, research into the cause of

disease, and the advancement of the public health, as well as medical education. It has not been lost upon them that in some hospitals dominated by medical schools, zeal for medical education outweighs the well-being of the patients. . . . May the Trustees always remember that there should be co-operation with, not domination by, the Medical School.[83]

Multiple relationships between hospitals and medical schools often developed. Several medical schools divided services in the largest hospitals among themselves. At the Bellevue Hospital in New York City, faculty members from several large medical schools gradually assumed responsibility for patient care during the 1860s and completely controlled hospital staffing by 1900. Conversely, leading medical schools maximized their options by affiliating with a number of hospitals. In 1900, Columbia University medical school used four different hospitals, in addition to its own maternity hospital and the Vanderbilt Clinic.[84]

Many medical schools located near hospitals. Sometimes they were in nearby buildings, as occurred when the Harvard University medical school moved next to the Massachusetts General Hospital in 1846. At one time in the late nineteenth century, five medical schools were located in the vicinity of the Cook County Hospital in Chicago and three near the Bellevue Hospital in New York City. On a few occasions medical schools moved into hospitals. An Ohio medical school occupied a building jointly with a hospital in the late 1880s and a New York medical school was located in the New York Hospital for several years after its building had been destroyed by fire.[85]

Medical schools sometimes constructed their own hospitals, whose quality of care varied with the available funding. A few medical school hospitals received substantial funding from state governments. In Pennsylvania, three medical school hospitals received between $890,000 and $1.4 million each from the state between the 1870s and 1911. At the other extreme, a medical school in Kansas City, Missouri, opened a hospital in 1892 with no outside funding. The hospital admitted only private patients who were not used for teaching. Some medical school hospitals were turned over to a lay board to encourage contributions.[86]

At least two medical schools were established as hospital schools, a common practice in England but rarely used in the United States. In 1858, the Long Island College Hospital was founded with a specific emphasis on clinical instruction, but it was not particularly successful. Three years later a private school that had taught classes of 300 students at Bellevue Hospital obtained a charter as the Bellevue Hospital Medical College. It soon became one of the city's leading medical schools.[87]

Hospital Teaching

The theory behind hospital instruction was that the patient was in a hospital bed where he could be observed continuously by the student. The problem was to make the patient educationally useful to the student. When hospitals admitted small numbers of patients and kept them for weeks while they recuperated, the patients were of little educational value. Nevertheless, in the 1870s and 1880s medical students at Harvard and Iowa, among others, were periodically assigned hospital patients to care for.[88]

In the 1890s, hospital admissions increased and medical schools were able to give students more responsibility for patient care. A faculty member at the University of Michigan reported in 1895:

> It is the custom during the senior year to assign patients in the hospital to the members of the class, making them responsible for carrying out the treatment advised. This plan results in each student having charge of several patients in each clinic during the entire nine months of his senior year. . . . A careful record of all cases is required to be kept by the student during the time he has charge of them. These records are kept on file, both for the purpose of perfecting the history of the patient, and as evidence of the faithfulness of the student in the discharge of his duties.

Students also made presentations before the class, where they described the patient's history and physical signs, made a diagnosis, and suggested treatment. The professor in charge then led a class discussion of the case.[89]

Students were assigned obstetrical cases as early as 1880 at Harvard and Northwestern University. The student or pair of students cared for the woman during her confinement and then participated in the delivery, usually at the hospital. One Harvard student in the 1870s participated in six hospital deliveries before graduation. Deliveries in the hospital were not necessarily good preparation for the more typical deliveries in the home.[90]

The use of students to care for hospital patients, which became known as a clinical clerkship, was refined by William Osler at the Johns Hopkins Hospital. Each student was assigned six beds for several months, and was responsible for taking the histories and performing any laboratory tests required on the patients in those beds. The student was supervised by a faculty member and participated in any treatments given to the patient. Osler visited the wards three mornings a week, where, he wrote, "the histories of the new cases are read, the patient examined, questions asked, and in general a Socratic method of instruction is followed." Osler felt that this system made the student familiar with the natural history of disease and the day-to-day care of the patient. He wanted the students to take "their share in the work in the hospital, just as much as the attending physician, the interne or the nurse."[91]

The clinical clerkship required the clerk to perform many routine tasks of no educational value. Osler wrote that the clerk learned "all the minutiae in practice that are so important—the supervision of the tub-bath, the preparation and giving of enemata, the mode of giving medicines, and the study of their action."[92] While detailed long-term study of the actions of medicines was invaluable, the study of tub-baths for several months was not, yet it probably occupied more of the clerk's time than the study of drug actions. The clerkship failed to separate the educationally useful from the educationally trivial.

Furthermore, the clinical clerkship did not correlate teaching and ward work. The student may not have received instruction in the medical problems of cases assigned to him in the wards. He then had to learn about the patient's illness on his own, for which he was ill-prepared. Contrast this with the well-organized and sequential didactic teaching used at the Boston City Hospital:

> [A] lecture is given at the Medical School on appendicitis, on Monday; on Tuesday the students are shown five to fifteen cases, illustrating various stages of the disease; on Wednesday another didactic lecture is given, finishing the subject . . . ; on Thursday again clinical material is shown, and operations on appendicitis are done. The following week a recitation on the subject is held. This concentration of teaching on a given subject is found to be of great value.[93]

Despite the problems involved in clerkships, students spent a steadily increasing amount of time on them as the need for cheap hospital labor grew in the twentieth century.

Other Types of Medical Schools

Medical education for women developed slowly in the nineteenth century, largely because many regular medical schools refused to admit them. This led to the founding of several medical schools specifically for women, and by 1882 five were in operation in Baltimore, Philadelphia, Chicago, and New York City, which had two of them. Women's medical schools were characterized by a dedicated and self-sacrificing faculty of male physicians, reasonably good students, a clean and well-organized physical plant, and abject poverty. Many medical schools admitted women because they needed the tuition income, so it is not surprising that the wealthiest medical schools held out the longest. The University of Pennsylvania first admitted women students in 1914, Yale and Columbia in 1917, and Harvard in 1945. Johns Hopkins University medical school became coeducational earlier because a woman gave a substantial donation to the school with that condition attached. Northwestern University medical school first admitted women shortly after a woman gave a large gift to the school.[94]

During the late nineteenth century, schools for the postgraduate education of physicians, called polyclinics, developed. At least a dozen such schools were founded, although most were short-lived. The most successful ones, two in New York City and one in Philadelphia, attracted over 13,000 students between 1882 and 1889. Similar postgraduate courses were established by the Jefferson medical school in 1883, and later at other medical schools as well. The courses were originally six weeks long, but gradually were extended to several months. Postgraduate instruction was also offered by hospitals. The Lying-In Hospital of New York provided short courses and experience in deliveries to over 5,800 physicians between 1902 and 1932.[95]

The polyclinics provided practical training in the specialties. This was the major interest of both the young physicians who were the students and the young specialists who were the teachers. The courses usually followed the amphitheater clinic model, with dispensary patients shown to the class by the instructor. The emphasis was on therapeutics, practical medicine, and the gadgetry of practice. Gerster, who taught at one, wrote that all of the students "were keen on therapy, but few manifested deep interest in pathology and diagnosis." The polyclinic, which was later replaced by residency training in the specialties, exhibited what would become the dominant pattern of medical education in the twentieth century: a preoccupation with specialization, a lack of concern with thorough training in the fundamentals, and the disjuncture of the basic medical sciences from clinical medicine.[96]

By the end of the century, clinical faculty members had become the most influential of the groups that determined the content of medical education. They subsidized clinical education in several ways. They taught courses for practically nothing, they treated the hospital and dispensary patients who were used in teaching, and they supervised the clinical clerks and assumed responsibility for the care of their patients. Without the participation of the clinical faculty in the clerkships, medical students would have had no experience in patient care. Hence, if students wanted clinical training, they had to accept the kind of clinical training that faculty members wanted to provide.

IV

MEDICAL EDUCATION
1900–1950

The whole problem of premedical and medical education would be simplified if there were any agreement as to the real aims of medical education. Should the student be trained in general principles, or instructed in many specialties? Should he acquire technical training and facility, an impressive collection of facts, or that which is vaguely referred to as "culture?" Or is the aim the development of attitudes, methods, ideas, ideals, and a broad sociological viewpoint? All these conflicting aims are reflected in the writings of those concerned with medical education and in various premedical schedules; yet there has been little or no attempt to reconcile them or to achieve unanimity of opinion as to the goal to be sought.

FRANKLIN G. EBAUGH AND CHARLES A. RYMER (1942)

6

Medical Care, 1900–1950

During the first half of the twentieth century, both mortality rates and the incidence of infectious diseases declined, due primarily to public health measures and a higher standard of living. Developments in surgery and drug therapy improved medical care and increased the amount of specialization among physicians. On the other hand, fewer physicians were available to care for the sick because of a decline in the per capita number of medical school graduates. The urban poor continued to receive most of their care from outpatient departments in public and private hospitals, while a growing number of the middle classes became paying inpatients in private hospitals. Hospitals expanded their educational activities to include internships and residency programs.

Changes in the Medical Profession

In the first half of the century, physicians became less accessible to much of the population. The number of physicians per capita decreased substantially from 1900 to 1930 and remained at that level until 1950 (Table 6.1). The greatest impact of this decline occurred in rural areas: between 1906 and 1923, communities of under 5,000 population experienced about a 25 percent reduction in the physician–population ratio, while cities of 50,000 or more experienced a decline of less than 8 percent. Young physicians especially preferred the cities. In 1906 in communities of fewer than 1,000 persons, the proportion of graduates from 1901 to 1905 who practiced in those communities exceeded the proportion of all physicians who practiced in those communities by a ratio of 1.17 to 1. By 1923 in the same size communities, the proportion of graduates of the classes of 1916 to 1920 who practiced there compared to the proportion of all physicians who practiced there dropped to a ratio of 0.58 to 1. Thus rural communities changed from locations preferred by younger physicians to locations avoided by them. The same ratio in cities of over 100,000 population increased from 0.99 to 1 in 1906 to 1.36 to 1 in 1923, which indicated the growing popularity of large cities for young physicians.[1]

Several factors accounted for the preference of physicians for towns and cities. Urban physicians earned more than rural ones and had greater opportunities to specialize. Physicians in towns near rural areas now had automobiles and telephones

The epigraph for Part IV is from Franklin G. Ebaugh and Charles A. Rymer, *Psychiatry in Medical Education* (New York: Commonwealth Fund, 1942), p. 44.

TABLE 6.1. Enumerations of Physicians, 1900–1950

	Census Tabulations		AMA Tabulations	
Year	Total (000s)	Per 100,000 Population	Total (000s)	Per 100,000 Population
1900	132.0	173	119.7	157
1910	151.1	164	135.0	146
1920	145.0	137	145.4[a]	134[a]
1930	153.8	125	156.4[a]	126[a]
1940	166.0	126	175.2	133
1950	191.9	128	203.4	134

[a]Data for the year after that listed.

Source: U.S. Bureau of the Census, *Historical Statistics of the United States* (Washington, D.C.: U.S. G.P.O. 1975), 1:76.

that enabled them to travel quickly to rural patients, which permitted them to serve rural areas without living there. Automobiles also enabled rural patients to travel to nearby towns, which led to the construction of town hospitals that offered admitting privileges only to urban physicians. The growing disadvantages of rural practice were aggravated by the steady decline in rural populations and the deteriorating economic situation of the remaining population.[2]

Specialization also increased among physicians, as shown by a longitudinal study of the graduates of the University of Buffalo medical school for every fifth year from 1915 to 1935. One pattern that persisted over the whole period was for graduates to become full-time specialists as they grew older. As an example, only 4 percent of the class of 1915 specialized 6 years after graduation, but 27 percent specialized 16 years after graduation, and 54 percent specialized 35 years after graduation. The other trend was for the graduates of each succeeding class to be more likely to specialize at any time after graduation than the graduates of preceding classes. For example, 15 years after graduation, full-time specialists accounted for 25 percent of the class of 1915, 27 percent of the class of 1925, 35 percent of the class of 1930, and 46 percent of the class of 1935. Data on all U.S. physicians showed that in 1923, 10.6 percent of physicians listed themselves as full-time specialists and 12.7 percent listed themselves as part-time specialists. In 1938, the proportions had increased to 19.8 percent and 14.5 percent, respectively.[3]

Specialists were more likely than other physicians to locate in urban areas. In 1940, 42.9 percent of all board-certified specialists were located in cities of 500,000 or more population, which had only 17.0 percent of the total U.S. population. Cities with fewer than 10,000 persons, which had 16.1 percent of the U.S. population, had only 5.0 percent of the board-certified specialists.[4]

Many specialists earned more than general practitioners, but not all specialties were equally remunerative. Lewellys Barker estimated that surgery was the "most liberally rewarded," but that this was true primarily for older surgeons. Barker considered other specialties, such as obstetrics and internal medicine, to be "as yet under-compensated as compared with surgery."[5]

An equally significant change in medical practice was the growth in opportunities for young physicians. In the nineteenth century, new physicians underwent a long and arduous competitive struggle to establish themselves. New physicians in the twentieth century had better prospects because of a lower physician–population ratio and a wealthier population. James C. White wrote in 1914:

> There is more immediate confidence in the ability of the young physician, both on the part of the public and the profession. He is made office assistant by the over-busy practitioner, helper and dresser by the surgeon in his private work, takes on the practice of his elders during their annual vacations . . . , or establishes a summer clientele at the innumerable country and seaside resorts, which cleaves to him in part throughout the year. None of these opportunities were open to the beginner of my time.[6]

Physicians also worked for many organizations. Railroads and manufacturing firms employed physicians to treat injured workers. Insurance companies employed physicians to examine clients. Contract practice was common in many cities, especially among immigrants. Hospital outpatient departments, dispensaries, and municipal health departments were major employers of physicians. Fox has estimated that in 1900 the New York City Department of Health employed from one-third to one-half of the regular physicians in the city on a part-time basis in public organizations like schools, hospitals, and clinics. The demand for physicians' services was increasing much faster than the supply.[7]

The organizations that employed physicians continued to train them. One physician wrote about World War I, when many of the nation's physicians were drafted into the armed forces: "They . . . sent us to medical officers' training camps, and there the best scientific minds in the profession put us to our lessons again. Everything that was newest was learned. Every latest and best invention, contrivance and discovery for the diagnosis, relief and prevention of disease was at our command. . . . The average midle-aged country doctor got more training out of three months in camp than he had out of his whole college course."[8]

Disease

During the first half of the twentieth century, death rates declined significantly, as shown by data from Massachusetts. The crude death rate in Massachusetts remained at over 19 deaths per 1,000 persons from 1860 through the 1890s. In 1910 it dropped to 16.1, in 1920 to 13.8, and in 1930 to 11.6, where it generally remained until after World War II. Infant mortality rates from 1870 to 1900 exceeded 150 deaths in the first year of life per 1,000 live births. The infant mortality rate dropped to 116.7 in 1910–1914, 78.7 in 1920–1924, 53.9 in 1930–1934, and 34.3 in 1940–1944.[9]

Public health measures were one major cause of this decline. Water purification reduced typhoid fever death rates nationally from 31.3 per 100,000 population in 1900 to 4.8 in 1930. Pasteurized milk and other measures reduced deaths from selected gastric disorders, which occurred primarily in infants, from 142.7 per 100,000 population in 1900 to 53.7 in 1920 and 10.3 in 1940. Deaths from diphtheria declined from 40.3 per 100,000 population in 1900 to 21.1 in 1910 and 4.9 in 1930, due partly to the work of health departments in diagnosing the disease, manufacturing antitoxin, and distributing it to physicians.[10]

Death rates were also reduced by improvements in the standard of living, as shown by the decreasing mortality rates from infectious diseases. Pulmonary tuberculosis death rates declined from over 350 per 100,000 persons in Massachusetts in the third quarter of the nineteenth century to about 190 per 100,000 by 1900, 96.8 in 1920, and 34.6 in 1940. A similar nationwide trend occurred in the major infectious diseases taken as a group (typhoid fever, scarlet fever, whooping cough, diphtheria, tuberculosis, dysentery, malaria, syphilis, measles, pneumonia, influenza, diarrhea, and enteritis). Their national death rates per 100,000 population declined from 676.2 in 1900 to 446.8 in 1920, 148.9 in 1940, and 78.7 in 1949. Most of this decline can be attributed to better housing and general health levels of the public.[11]

As life expectancy increased, diseases that afflicted older persons became more important as causes of mortality. Death rates from cardiovascular and renal diseases increased from 345.2 per 100,000 population in 1900 to 485.7 in 1940. Cancer death rates increased from 64.0 per 100,000 population in 1900 to 120.3 in 1940. Death rates from diabetes increased from 11.0 per 100,000 population in 1900 to 26.6 in 1940.[12]

Medical Practice

Many aspects of medical practice did not change much from the late nineteenth century. Office and home visits continued to predominate. A survey of more than 500 general practitioners in 26 states from 1915 to 1922 found that 55 percent of 20,000 patient visits occurred in the office, 35 percent occurred in the home, and 10 percent in the hospital. Most patient complaints continued to require primary care. The same survey found that 75 percent of office visits were for "minor surgery, upper respiratory infections, and general medical and venereal disease." Ninety percent of the home calls were for "respiratory infections, general medical and contagious diseases, obstetrics and minor surgery." The poor continued to receive less medical care than the rich. A 1928–1931 survey of 8,406 families found that 20.2 percent of those with incomes of under $1,200 did not visit a physician during the year, compared to only 7.2 percent of those with incomes over $10,000.[13] Many of the poor used outpatient facilities.

Drug therapy changed little in the first decades of the twentieth century. Violent purgation remained popular for some time, as did Fowler's solution (a compound of arsenic), strychnine, and potassium iodide. An analysis of the recommended treatments of 362 medical problems in a 1927 textbook of medicine found that 60 percent of the treatments are now considered ineffective or harmful. Only about 30 of the drugs mentioned were still in use a half century later.[14]

For the first three decades of the century, research to develop new drugs generally failed to achieve very much. Medicinal chemistry had appeared very promising when Ehrlich discovered a compound of arsenic as a treatment for syphilis in 1909. However, with the exception of pamaquine naphthoate in 1924 for malaria, the chemicals used to kill microorganisms were excessively toxic to human organs. Another approach was the use of biological serums like diphtheria antitoxin, which was developed in 1894. Although a few other serums were developed, most notably for pneumonia, adverse patient reactions rendered them generally unsatisfactory.[15]

A more useful approach was the discovery in the 1920s of treatments to replace deficiencies in metabolism. Probably the most important was the production of insulin, but thyroxine, vitamin B_{12}, adrenal extracts, and hormones were major contributions in the following decades.[16] These drugs created a new role for the general practitioner and internist: that of treating a chronically ill ambulatory patient with drugs over a long period of time while caring for the patient's general health to create an optimum level of social functioning.

The discovery in the 1930s of the sulfa drugs for the treatment of bacterial diseases was even more revolutionary. These drugs operated on an entirely new principle, which was not discovered until some time after the drugs had been developed. Instead of killing the bacteria, as earlier drugs had done with extremely harmful side effects for the patient, the sulfa drugs (and the antibiotics that followed) interfered with the growth and reproduction cycle of the microbes, thereby rendering them harmless.[17]

The sulfa drugs had a major impact on the general practice of medicine, even though their effectiveness was limited. They reduced the mortality from bacterial diseases, shortened the duration of many illnesses, prevented individual cases of diseases, and stopped epidemics. They gave physicians the first drugs that were effective in treating a range of common diseases. However, drugs of equal benefit were unavailable for viral infections or most other kinds of medical problems. In these conditions, drug therapy changed little from that used in the late nineteenth century, although new synthetic drugs replaced some older ones.[18]

Medical care was also changing the physician–patient relationship from a sporadic to a continuing one. This is indicated by the popularization of the periodic health examination in the 1920s. The periodic health examination was based on the premise that asymptomatic individuals harbored diseases which could be arrested, cured, or reversed if diagnosed and treated early enough. Detection was improved by a number of new medical technologies such as the X-ray for tuberculosis, chemical tests of blood, urine, and other body fluids, electrocardiograms, and sphygmomanometers. The periodic health examination was first widely used by life insurance companies, employers, and the U.S. armed forces in World War I, when three million inductees were examined. Physical examinations for the armed forces uncovered many health problems unknown to the examinees, which led to the belief that more frequent general medical examinations would be of even greater value to patients.[19]

Periodic health examinations soon became an accepted part of medical care, despite a lack of evidence as to their usefulness.[20] They helped establish the belief that the physician should be consulted regularly by a healthy patient as well as a sick one. The physician, on his part, assumed a new responsibility for maintaining longitudinal medical records on his patients so that he could recognize changes in their state of health. Here, as in the care of the growing number of chronically ill, the physician was developing a new kind of long-term relationship with his patients.

Surgery

Although aseptic techniques in surgery developed at a rapid pace early in the century, other problems remained, especially blood loss during operations. A good number of patients died from hemorrhage and others spent weeks recovering from shock and other effects of the loss of blood. Matters improved in the second decade of the century with the discovery of blood types and the use of transfusions, but postoperative care remained highly empirical. One surgeon recalled: "The generally accepted supporting measures consisted of subcutaneous infusions of normal salt solution preferably into the axilla, coffee and salt solution per rectum, elevation of the foot of the bed, morphine and cardiac stimulants hypodermically as indicated, and conservation of body heat by means of hot water bags and blankets."[21]

Surgery was changing so rapidly that many surgeons failed to adopt important new techniques or used poor judgment in the techniques that they did adopt. A British visitor in 1904 found numerous instances of poor aseptic practices in leading American hospitals, despite the newness of the operating rooms and the high quality of their equipment. As operative techniques continued to develop, the short incisions and brief operations of the nineteenth century gave way to long incisions and longer operations. This led to greater blood loss, incidence of shock, and damage to tissues. The overuse of technique occurred most frequently in the leading medical schools where new surgical procedures were being developed.[22]

Surgery continued to benefit from new instruments and discoveries. The invention of the X-ray in the late nineteenth century enabled physicians to improve the accuracy of their diagnoses before operating. The discovery of blood types permitted the use of blood transfusions to replace lost blood and prevent shock. The technique of intravenous replenishment of salts, fluids, and nourishment was developed. However, wound infection continued to be a major problem. Even the sulfa drugs of the 1930s were unable to deal with the many different organisms present in wounds.[23]

As surgery expanded from a specialty practiced by a few master surgeons to one carried out by many physicians, there occurred a significant decline in clinical acumen and judgment. The 1920s witnessed the proliferation of faddish operations that provided no demonstrable benefit to the patient. Many operations removed organs in order to eliminate "focal infections," a concept that is wholly discredited today. It was also alleged that operations were sometimes performed primarily for the economic benefit of the surgeon.[24]

One major cause of improper surgery was the ease with which physicians became surgeons. Many surgeons had little formal training or were part-time surgeons. The latter was especially common in general surgery, the specialty practiced by over one-fourth of all surgeons in the 1920s and 1930s. In 1923, 20.9 percent of all full-time specialists were general surgeons, but 37.5 percent of all part-time specialists were general surgeons. In 1938, the proportions were 16.0 and 39.1 percent, respectively.[25]

The poor quality of much surgery was also caused by the unwillingness of hospitals to regulate the appointment of surgeons to their staffs. The American College of Surgeons, which began accrediting hospitals in 1919, concluded in 1929 that the greatest hospital problem was the granting of staff privileges to surgeons without any minimum standard of qualifications. Hospitals were reluctant to limit their surgical privileges because surgery provided a major part of their income. The survey of 500 general practitioners referred to above found that 55 percent of 2,000 hospital visits involved surgery, 30 percent medical care, and 15 percent obstetrical care.[26]

Two developments gradually improved the quality of surgery. One was the establishment of hospital and medical school residency programs to train surgeons, which will be described below. The other was the creation of specialty boards to evaluate and certify physicians as competent in the specialty. Previously, a physician's expertise was demonstrated by an appointment as a medical school professor or a membership in an exclusive medical society. So few physicians obtained these positions that they were of little use to hospitals that wanted to evaluate their physicians' competence. Specialty boards, on the other hand, approved all qualified applicants, and therefore became a useful guide to assessing the skills of physicians in most communities. The first boards were established in ophthalmology in 1917 and otolaryngology in 1924. From 1930 to 1940, seven boards were established in surgical specialties, and one each in the related fields of radiology and anesthesiology. The specialty boards led to subspecialization within surgery, which had the effect of limiting general surgery to abdominal surgery. In 1940, 28.7 percent of 9,446 full-time specialists in surgery and surgical subspecialties were board-certified.[27]

Dispensary and Outpatient Care

The use of outpatient facilities continued to increase during the first half of the twentieth century. A report based on a 1927 survey of 5.4 million clinic visits in 14 large cities and on studies of 264 clinics reporting to the New York State Board of Health concluded that "between 10 to 15 percent of the population of the larger cities were receiving all or part of their ambulatory attention in the outpatient department. This represents between 25 and 30 percent of the sick." The American Medical Association estimated in 1922 that there were 30 million outpatient visits annually in the United States, and Davis and Rorem claimed that this had grown to over 40 million by 1932.[28]

The providers of outpatient care changed from independent dispensaries to the outpatient clinics of hospitals. A survey estimated that in 1916 there were 255 general dispensaries and 645 hospital outpatient departments, the latter located in about one-fourth of all general hospitals. The shift occurred for several reasons. Hospitals were more likely to have X-ray machines, clinical pathology laboratories, and other equipment that had become important in medical care. The governments that subsidized ambulatory care preferred the larger and better financed hospital outpatient departments. Physicians also preferred appointments to hospital outpatient departments, which might lead to appointments to the inpatient staff. Finally, medical schools often closed their independent dispensaries once they obtained hospital facilities.[29]

Hospitals and their staffs continued to consider their outpatient departments as secondary to their inpatient care. Davis wrote that the leading physicians took the inpatient appointments in order to hospitalize their private patients and left the charity patients in the outpatient departments to "the young men or the second-raters." Hospitals regarded the outpatient department either as a "medical soup kitchen," providing emergency short-term care, or a "medical feeder" for "interesting" cases. Interesting cases were patients who had unusual or rare diseases, required hospitalization, or were of value for medical teaching. The American College of Surgeons, which first accredited aspects of hospital care in 1919, did not establish standards for outpatient and social service facilities until at least a decade later.[30]

The treatment of patients in outpatient departments was inferior to the care of inpatients. Ambulatory patients had long waits, regardless of their jobs or family responsibilities, and those with little understanding of English were seldom given language assistance. The overburdened and unpaid physicians tended to ask a few questions, prescribe a drug or two, and dismiss the patient. Patients with chronic diseases were treated no differently than those with short-term acute conditions. Few inquiries were made into the patient's social and personal condition. Richard Cabot wrote:

> To order for one patient a diet which he cannot possibly procure; for the next, a vacation which he is too poor to take; to forbid the third to worry when the necessary cause of worry remains unchanged; to give the fourth directions for an outdoor life which you are morally certain he won't carry out; to try to teach the fifth . . . how to modify milk for her baby when she understands perhaps half of what you say and forgets most of that half—this makes a morning's work not very satisfactory in the retrospect to anybody, and hardly more useful than the old-fashioned wholesale drugging.[31]

To alleviate these problems at the Massachusetts General Hospital where Cabot worked, a social service department was established in 1906. Similar departments were soon established elsewhere. However, they had neither the resources nor the staff to care for the large number of patients who used the outpatient facilities.[32]

Despite the indifference of hospitals and physicians, the outpatient department contributed far more to meeting the medical needs of the community than the inpatient facility. Its value extended far beyond caring for the sick, as Cabot observed in 1912 when he described its advantages: "1. It roots out foci of disease in families or neighborhoods, following home the clues presented in the person of the dispensary patient and so preventing disease. 2. It checks disease in its incipiency. 3. It deals with chronic cases and keeps the patient from relapsing in a discouraged and vegetative existence."[33]

Some hospitals demonstrated that dispensary care could be improved. In 1911 the Presbyterian Hospital in New York City had the typical dispensary problems: no patient records of any medical value; lax attendance and work habits of the physicians; poor relations between the inpatient and outpatient services; patients for whom hospital admission had been arranged not showing up at the hospital; and little or no follow-up of patients. Better record keeping was established, patient follow-up was improved, and the number of outpatients was limited to those whom

TABLE 6.2. General Hospitals, 1909–1940

Year	General Hospitals	Beds per Hospital	Beds per 1,000 Population	Admissions per 1,000 Population
1909	4,359[a]	96.6[a]	4.7[a]	n.a.
1920	4,013	77.5	2.9	n.a.
1931	4,309	89.2	3.1	51.0
1940	4,432	104.3	3.5	69.9
1950	4,713	124.7	3.9	104.7

[a]All hospitals, including mental hospitals, tuberculosis hospitals, etc.

Source: U.S. Bureau of the Census, *Historical Statistics of the United States* (Washington, D.C.: U.S. G.P.O. 1975), 1:8, 78, 80.

the hospital could care for satisfactorily. This led to almost complete patient compliance in such matters as follow-ups and inpatient referrals.[34] The problem with the outpatient department was not the patients; it was the system that emphasized the care of inpatients.

Hospital Growth

During the twentieth century, hospital facilities and hospital care increased significantly (Table 6.2). Between 1920 and 1950, the number of general hospitals increased by 17.4 percent, the number of beds per hospital increased by 60.9 percent, and the number of hospital beds per capita increased by 34.5 percent. These changes indicated both a significant movement toward larger hospitals and a rate of hospital growth that exceeded population growth. The number of admissions per 1,000 population doubled between 1931 and 1950, which showed that people became more willing to use hospitals for health care. Some of this increase was due to the construction of hospitals in communities that previously had none. For example, of the 69 counties in Wisconsin, the number with no hospital declined from 32 in 1910 to 16 in 1930 and 9 in 1940.[35]

By the 1920s, the primary function of hospitals had changed from nursing care to active medical treatment. Surgery moved from the home to the hospital: surveys in the 1930s found that 69 percent of all hospital admissions were surgical and another 6 percent were obstetrical. Deliveries in hospitals increased from less than 5 percent of all deliveries nationally in 1900 to 50 percent of all deliveries nationally and 75 percent of urban deliveries in 1939. Many of the new users of hospitals were well-to-do. In 1928–1931, upper income groups had hospital admission rates nearly twice as high as lower income groups, although the latter comprised the majority of all hospital patients because of their predominance in the population.[36]

Public Hospitals

Public hospitals continued to accept patients that private hospitals refused to take or discharged, who were usually the poor suffering from problems of aging, chronic diseases, mental diseases, drug addiction, and alcoholism. For these reasons, public hospital patients remained in the hospital much longer than private hospital patients. The average length of stay in 1935 in New York City's municipal hospitals was 23 days, compared to 14 days at the city's private general hospitals. By 1945, the lengths of stay were 17 and 10 days, respectively. In the Baltimore City Hospital in 1925, only 43 percent of the patients were discharged. The remainder either died in the hospital or were transferred to long-term care units of the hospital.[37]

Public hospitals lacked an influential constituency because most physicians and well-to-do patients used private hospitals. Consequently public hospitals were over-crowded, underfunded, and often poorly managed. In 1925, six major public hospitals in Boston, Chicago, and New York had costs per patient-day that were about one-half of those of eight private hospitals in the same cities. Management of public hospitals was hampered by excessive political interference and public indifference.[38]

On the other hand, public hospitals attracted outstanding house officers. Their large numbers of patients and variety of illnesses made them as appealing to medical students of the early twentieth century as the great European public hospitals had been to students in an earlier era. While the house officers had extensive opportunities for clinical experience, the shortage of attending physicians and other workers detracted from their education and required them to perform many routine tasks that were carried out in private hospitals by less skilled workers.[39]

By the 1930s, public hospitals, as the refuge of the poor and unwanted, were at the bottom of a three-tier system of hospitals. In the middle were the voluntary hospitals, which were staffed by leading community physicians and accepted primarily paying patients. At the top were a small number of medical school hospitals and medical centers that provided highly specialized care.[40]

Voluntary Hospitals

During this period voluntary hospitals became centers for acute care, especially surgery. About 1930, Davis and Rorem estimated that surgical cases constituted 60 to 75 percent of the patients in the smaller general hospitals, and 50 percent of those in the larger ones. At the Presbyterian Hospital in New York, the number of operations increased from 402 in 1889, with a mortality rate of 16.5 percent, to 3,259 in 1939, with a mortality rate of 2.1 percent. Appendectomies, thyroidectomies, and operations for hernia, intestinal cancer, and gallbladder, all once considered prohibitively dangerous, increased from 12 to 1,173.[41]

Greater use of laboratory tests accompanied the increase in surgery. A French visitor wrote in 1912:

> I was simply thunderstruck with the number of Wassermann tests I saw being made; blood-cultures and Widal tests seemed to me, like the Lord's rain, to descend from Heaven on the just and on the unjust in the most impartial fashion; while as for blood-counts, simple or differential, they were as common as temperature or pulse-taking and analysis of urine. . . . The final impression left on me by all this was that the diagnosis and treatment of a given patient depended more on the result of these various tests than on the symptoms present in the case.[42]

This observer saw only the beginning of a flood of tests and testing instruments in both private and public hospitals. At the Philadelphia General Hospital, the number of laboratory tests increased from 38,323 in 1915 to 172,694 in 1927, while the number of autopsies increased from 300 to 1,248 over the same period. One of the first electrocardiographs in the United States, at the Massachusetts General Hospital, wrote 21,160 electrocardiograms from 1913 to 1930, despite being extremely cumbersome and difficult to use. The unit which replaced it in 1931 wrote 17,118 in its first five years of use.[43]

By the 1920s many large hospitals had fully equipped laboratories headed by resident physicians and staffed by technicians and professionals. Hospital laboratories usually had four or five divisions: clinical pathology, bacteriology, serology and immunology, biochemistry, and radiology. Most of the tests performed in them had been developed since 1910, indicating the rapid movement of hospitals to take advantage of their ability to provide services not available from private practitioners.[44]

The changing functions of voluntary hospitals led to significant increases in costs. At the Brooklyn Hospital, the average cost of care per day rose from $0.89 in 1890 to $2.78 in 1915. At a gynecological and obstetrical hospital in New York City, per diem costs rose from $1 in 1867 to $2 in 1887, $3.20 in 1897, $4.60 in 1907, $8.65 in 1927, and $9.15 in 1937. The increase in costs in the latter hospital between 1897 and 1937 exceeded the increase in the cost of living by 66 percent.[45]

These cost increases occurred at the same time that governments reduced their funding to hospitals. Instead of continuing to make flat grants to hospitals, governments paid for specific hospital services for the poor and other groups on a per diem or per case basis. Statewide programs like workman's compensation paid for patient care on a contractual basis.[46]

Confronted with rising costs and lower government subsidies, private hospitals sought to increase the number of their paying patients. Many hospitals began to cater to well-to-do patients, who were now using hospitals for routine surgery and obstetrics. The Children's Hospital in Boston, for example, which was founded to care for sick children of the poor, turned to the treatment of deformities by means of orthopedic surgery. As a result, the hospital's patients now included children of the middle classes and the wealthy. Hospitals also constructed new facilities that catered to the tastes of paying patients. Surveys of architects belonging to the American Hospital Association found that in 1928, 71 percent of the beds designed for new hospitals and additions to existing ones were in private and semiprivate rooms, compared to 49 percent in 1908. These changes in goals did not go uncriticized, as a medical journal observed about one hospital: "Here is a great . . . hospital, endowed richly, consecrated to philanthropy and benevolence, using the funds left in charity's name to equip private rooms . . . for those able to pay the price."[47]

Hospitals also began to charge their working class ward patients. At the Brooklyn Hospital between 1892 and 1917, the number of patients using private rooms increased the least, paying ward patients the most, and free ward patients somewhere in between. By 1905, 40 percent of the hospital's income was coming from paying patients, primarily working class ward patients of the same income groups as those who had been treated for free a decade or so earlier. Ward patients were able to pay for some of the costs of their care because of shorter hospital stays.

At the Brooklyn Hospital, the average length of stay decreased from 29.4 days in 1895 to 15.6 days in 1915.[48]

In the 1920s, hospitals started to look for ways to attract middle class paying patients. They already had wards for the poor and working classes and expensive private rooms for the rich. Middle class patients did not want to stay in the wards and could not afford the costs associated with private rooms, which also included charges for laboratory services and the use of operating rooms. Hospitals therefore constructed special facilities for middle class patients, usually with semiprivate rooms or small private rooms, and worked out informal agreements with physicians to lower their fees and to bill patients only after the hospital bill had been paid.[49]

The most important of these projects was the Baker Memorial Building at the Massachusetts General Hospital, which opened in 1930 and was completely designed for middle class patients. It was large (up to 330 beds) to distribute overhead costs broadly. Staffing was carefully designed to relieve nurses of the less skilled secretarial and janitorial duties. Operating room and laboratory services were provided to patients at reduced charges. The hospital's physicians agreed to a maximum fee of $150 for their private patients, regardless of the length of stay, which the hospital enforced by collecting the physicians' bills for them. Patients were required to state their income before admission, and no private nurses were allowed without hospital approval.[50]

Other hospitals emulated the basic principles of the Baker Memorial plan, although few integrated them so carefully. The Johns Hopkins Hospital expected their physicians to charge patients in semiprivate rooms no more than $100 per stay. In 1931, the Mount Sinai Hospital in New York opened a 120-bed semiprivate pavilion with weekly fees of $35, compared with $56 to $105 in the private rooms. In 1929, a Baltimore hospital opened a 106-bed building for middle income patients and the donor also gave $1 million to six other hospitals in the city to subsidize moderately priced private and semiprivate rooms.[51]

By means such as these, voluntary hospitals increased their income from paying patients. At the Massachusetts General Hospital, the proportion of expenses met by patient receipts increased from 36.4 percent in 1900 to 68.6 percent in 1935. Data from 2,469 nonprofit hospitals with 250,000 beds showed that 79 percent of their income in 1935 came from patients.[52]

A spate of hospital construction occurred as hospitals sought to attract paying patients with the newest buildings, the latest and most elaborate equipment, the most recent remodeling, the largest staff of nurses, and the best food. In Baltimore, the acute care capacity of private hospitals increased by 24 percent between 1921 and 1927. The inevitable overbuilding created a glut of hospital beds in many communities, especially during the depression. The occupancy rates in 12 Baltimore voluntary hospitals declined from 80 percent in 1920 to 66 percent in 1935–1936. Operating deficits were substantial.[53]

The victims of the hospital's emphasis on paying patients were the charity patients. The endowment used to support charity patients dwindled as hospital fund-raising campaigns were used to add new facilities for paying patients, which were built on the premise that paying patients would support the charity patients. Instead, expenses rose and less money was available for the care of charity patients.

Beds intended for the use of charity patients were converted to use by private patients. Convalescent patients were discharged as soon as possible to avoid their becoming charity patients, "many of them," one hospital superintendent wrote, "in no condition to care for themselves and with no place to which to go where they can receive proper attention." Only the public hospitals and some university hospitals addressed themselves to the needs of the poor.[54]

A few voluntary hospitals began to provide diagnostic services in direct competition with private physicians. In 1915 a committee at the Massachusetts General Hospital reported that the diagnosis of "obscure cases of disease" could be "ruinously expensive when the patient goes to each of a group of specialists at his office. The hospital offers the only opportunity for the reasonably accurate diagnosis of obscure cases in persons of moderate means." A Diagnostic Clinic, as it was later called, was established in the following year. Several years later another one was established at Cornell University's hospital in New York City.[55]

The helter-skelter growth of hospitals led to a concern with the quality of hospital care. A survey of 929 case records in 32 New York City hospitals about 1924 found that only one-third were satisfactory. The study also found many other deficiencies throughout the New York City hospital system, which included some of the nation's finest hospitals. A few years earlier, in 1918–1919, the American College of Surgeons undertook a preliminary study of 692 hospitals to assess the need for hospital accreditation and found only 89 that completely met some rather simple requirements. The college established a formal set of minimum standards in 1919 which it used to accredit hospitals on a voluntary basis. The most common source of failure to meet the standards was the performance of the medical staff, especially in such matters as clinical records, qualifications for staff appointments, the right to perform operations, and physician review procedures.[56] This situation indicated the importance of the medical staff and the growing need for its regulation.

Hospital Staffing

Hospital staffing needs increased not only because of more admissions, but also because of new hospital technologies. Surgery required the services of physicians and other health personnel before, during, and after the operation. The increased use of specialized units like clinical laboratories required new kinds of trained workers. At the Massachusetts General Hospital, the hospital medical staff increased from 15 visiting inpatient physicians, 15 outpatient physicians, 21 assistants, and 20 house officers in 1900, to 282 physicians and 67 house officers in 1935. The 17 graduate and 71 student nurses in 1902 increased to 221 graduate and 323 student nurses in 1935, plus about 150 special duty nurses.[57]

The increase in medical staff was also due to greater specialization of physicians. This is indicated by the composition of the medical staff at Mount Sinai Hospital in New York as early as 1912. The active staff of 65 included 13 pathologists, 3 pediatricians, 6 gynecologists, 4 ophthalmic surgeons, 3 aural surgeons, 3 genitourinary surgeons, 3 neurologists, 3 dermatologists, an orthopedist, 2 laryngologists, and 2 district physicians for home visiting. They were supported by 5 anesthesiologists, a radiologist, and 2 dentists. The outpatient department had 195 physicians in 12 specialty departments, including all of the above and others.[58]

The role of the medical staff in the hospital was greatly altered by the admission of large numbers of middle and upper income paying patients. Up to this time, hospital medical staffs had three major characteristics: they were unpaid, in that they received neither a salary from the hospital nor professional fees from hospital patients; they were "closed," in that the hospital staff was limited to a small number of physicians; and they were rotating, in that each physician on the staff served for a period of three consecutive months each year.

The first characteristic to be altered was patient fees. Hospital staff members wanted to place their paying patients in the hospital and collect professional fees from them for services performed in the hospital. This issue was important to physicians because hospitals were a remarkably efficient way to practice medicine. In a given amount of time, a physician could see many more patients in a hospital than in private homes. A surgeon could easily do as much surgery in a day at a hospital as he could in a week in private homes. Hospitals also saved physicians much time and effort by performing medical tests and providing routine and emergency medical care when the physicians were elsewhere.

Hospitals had reservations about this proposal. If hospital physicians were to be paid by patients, what about nurses, house officers, and others? In addition, the intermixing of paying and charity patients would lead to a double standard of patient care. Henry J. Bigelow, an eminent surgeon, wrote that "a public hospital is a trust; originally set apart as a charity for the sick, and not for the pecuniary benefit of their attendants. . . . Once allow fees and perquisites within a hospital, the institution would be legitimately worked for all it is worth, and patients who paid their attendants would be not the worst cared for."[59]

Other arguments were presented as well. Hospital appointments were already so valuable to physicians that additional inducements were not needed. Bigelow wrote: "To be associated medically, and especially surgically, with a hospital in high repute, to share in the experience it affords, to stand as its representative at once before the medical world and the never-ceasing current of patients who are often attracted mainly by its traditional reputation, is to be largely in debt to it. . . . [T]hese hospital offices would command a considerable premium in money from the best class of practitioners were they annually put up at auction." Bigelow also argued that the hospital is a charity: "Whatever diverts the property, the resources or the conveniences of a charity trust, or even the patients who apply there, to the private advantage of its officers, is a form of the spoils system." If some patients felt so grateful to their physicians that they wished to show their gratitude financially, they could make contributions to the hospital.[60]

Whatever the ethical issues, economic imperatives favored the physicians. Hospitals recognized that paying patients were much more likely to enter hospitals if their physicians recommended that they do so. Permitting staff physicians to collect fees from their hospitalized patients was the hospital's way of encouraging business. Consequently, despite their initial reluctance, practically all hospitals permitted their staff physicians to collect fees from private patients by the second decade of the century.[61]

The issue of opening of hospital staff privileges to more physicians was resolved by hospitals in a way opposed by their staffs. Hospitals wanted to add more physicians to their staffs to obtain more paying patients. Physicians already on the staffs resisted this, because it meant that more physicians would use the beds and personnel. One hospital physician expressed his opinion in no uncertain terms:

> In 1900, the question of "open or closed" hospitals arose. The increase in the number of hospitals brought about increased pressure for men occupying responsible staff positions, and an inevitable conflict between the "ins" and "outs" appeared. The best hospitals were carefully organized and "closed" with a select staff. Equally good men having no such hospital connections became the "outs." . . .
>
> Doctors who are still complaining about the injustice of a closed hospital system . . . are quite at liberty to . . . secure the erection of . . . open hospitals.[62]

Hospitals disregarded the views of their staffs and developed several mechanisms for adding more physicians. Some hospitals added more staff members with the same responsibilities as existing ones, that is, to work in the charity wards as well as care for their own private patients. Others created an additional "courtesy" staff that could only admit and care for their private patients in the hospital. Some hospitals opened their beds to the private patients of all reputable physicians. All hospitals eliminated rotating terms of service and replaced them with year-round terms. Hospitals were able to do this because they were not responsible for their staffs' treatment of patients. Until the 1960s, most state courts held that hospitals were not legally liable for the care provided to patients by hospital physicians, regardless of whether the patients were charity or paying patients.[63]

When some major hospitals refused to expand their staffs, the excluded physicians turned to proprietary hospitals and small voluntary hospitals. In Baltimore, part-time faculty members of the Johns Hopkins University medical school were denied admitting privileges at the university hospital. They thereupon convinced the trustees of local voluntary hospitals to modernize and expand, and personally raised some of the funds. The need of physicians for hospital beds was responsible for the establishment and survival of many small hospitals. In the 1920s, over 37 percent of the hospitals in New York City had fewer than 100 beds.[64]

Because many physicians served on the staffs of two or more hospitals, the hospitals were forced to compete for their private patients. Some physicians took advantage of the situation to pressure hospitals to give preferential admissions to their patients or to discharge patients early to free beds for their patients. They imposed excessively upon the use of operating rooms and the services of nurses, interns, and other employees.[65]

The role of the hospital board of directors changed from one of practically unlimited authority to that of a counterbalance to the medical staff. During the nineteenth century, board members had great power because they were either major donors to the hospitals or personally responsible for contributions from major donors. Thus they had no hesitation about making policy without consulting the medical staff. Trustees in the twentieth century were community businessmen and other economic leaders who provided little income directly to the hospital. Power was therefore transferred to the staff physicians who admitted paying patients. The new trustees tried to restrain the medical staff by hiring administrators to improve hospital efficiency. When the American College of Surgeons began to accredit hospitals, they required the medical staff to maintain adequate case histories and the hospital administrators to see that this was done. The AMA criticized this policy as instituting lay control over physicians.[66]

Hospital Interns

Until the twentieth century, the interns who comprised the house staff were a small part of the hospital labor force. In New York City, the number of internships increased from 3 in 1792 to 53 in 1862 and 273 in 1895. Internships were often awarded as personal favors by the trustees. In describing his own experiences in Philadelphia early in the century, G. Canby Robinson wrote that, although the system of personal appointments by the trustees "had the disadvantage of seeming to favor Philadelphians, it worked well toward the selection of men of superior cultural and educational backgrounds and tended to keep up the line of some of the famous families of physicians on the hospital staff."[67]

Members of the house staff served terms of one to two years, lived in the hospital and were given room, board, uniforms, and laundry. In Robinson's hospital the house officer "had charge of about thirty-five [ward] patients. . . . The visiting physicians spent only an hour or two a day on each ward, and the chief [house officer] came to see patients only when called. The [house officer was responsible for] taking their histories, making all examinations, and directing their treatment, the diagnosis and treatment of each case being checked by the experienced visiting physician."[68]

Service as a house officer in the nineteenth century could provide valuable clinical experience, but it was not a form of medical education, which interns and physicians of the time clearly recognized. Internships lacked teachers, formal instruction, and an educational program.

Interns became much more useful to hospitals with the increase in surgery. They carried out most of the pre- and postoperative care, administered anesthetics, served as operating room assistants, and performed many laboratory tests. Hospitals therefore increased the number of internships that they offered. The proportion of medical gradutes with hospital training grew from an estimated 50 percent in 1904 to 75 percent in 1914. In 1926, the number of available internships exceeded the number of medical graduates for the first time. By 1940, 7,998 internships were available in 732 hospitals, but only 5,097 graduates were available to take them.[69] This did not necessarily indicate a substantial shortage of interns, because hospitals did not offer internship based on a careful assessments of their manpower needs. Interns, like student nurses, were cheap labor and hospitals hired as many as they could house.

As competition for interns increased, hospitals offered inducements to attract them. The major inducement was greater personal responsibility, such as opportunities to perform major surgery. Only a few major teaching hospitals used a better educational program as an inducement to prospective interns. One physician wrote in 1921: "In the average hospital the intern or resident is left too much to his own devices, to pick up what he can as an underling dancing attendance on his busy chiefs, who hurry through the hospital with little thought of any responsibility for giving any time to directing along proper lines the training of these young men."[70]

During the first two decades of the twentieth century, the internship came to be perceived as part of a student's medical education rather than a form of postgraduate clinical experience. In 1905, the Council on Medical Education of the American Medical Association first proposed that students take an internship after their medical education, and in 1914 it issued its first list of hospitals approved for internships. State licensing boards began to require applicants for licenses to have completed an internship, and 17 states had this requirement in 1932. By 1932, 14 medical schools required internships for the M.D. degree, but most medical schools never adopted the requirement because they could not control off-campus internships.[71]

The redefinition of the internship as a form of medical education occurred despite little increase in its educational content. The AMA did not establish educational standards for internship programs until 1919. The number of hospitals that offered internships was large and increased from 508 in 1914 to 732 in 1940. The AMA could not monitor them all effectively and only a few had the staff or facilities to provide worthwhile educational experiences for their interns.[72]

The AMA standards were also of limited value because they permitted so many variations in internships. Three major types of AMA-approved internships existed: straight, rotating, and mixed. The traditional straight internships, which dated from the nineteenth century, were limited to one specialty, either medicine or surgery. Rotating internships were developed in the twentieth century because the new specialty services were too small to have their own full-time interns. In a rotating internship, the student spent part of his time in general medicine, surgery, and obstetrics, plus a few weeks in each of the various specialty services. Rotating internships, which were taken by 75 percent of all interns in the mid-1930s, varied greatly because each hospital had a different mix of specialties. One survey of 60 New York hospitals about 1940 found that no two had identical rotating internship programs. The mixed internship was like the rotating internship, except that it involved only a few specialty services. The AMA also permitted approved internships to vary in length. In the middle 1930s, about two-thirds were 12 months, one-fourth were 24 months, and a few were as long as 36 months.[73]

Available evidence indicates that most internships failed to provide even a minimally satisfactory education. A 1927 survey of over 500 general practitioners of the medical school classes of 1915–1922 reported: "There is a great deal of criticism against the intern period, to the effect that the student is not receiving instruction, and is not getting what he ought to get out of it." Studies of graduate medical education in 1934–1938 by the New York Committee on the Study of Hospital Internships and in 1940 by the Advisory Board of Medical Specialties criticized most aspects of the internship: the large number of routine chores of no educational value performed by interns; the lack of systematic education provided by the medical staff; the emphasis on acute care and the lack of any training in the care of the chronically ill; and training in the specialties at the expense of general medicine. Most of all, they criticized the absence of any training in the care of the patient as an individual. The 1940 report observed:

> During the entire intern period, stress should be laid upon the patient as an entity rather than exclusively upon his pathological conditions. His mental as well as his physical condition should be given careful consideration. . . .
>
> The intern tends to concentrate his attention on [the patient's] particular condition, which frequently is in an advanced stage. Often he does not view the patient as an individual or see him when the disease is in its early stages. To overcome these potential weaknesses in his training and to give him experience that will more nearly resemble the problems he will face in practice, he should have considerable experience in a well-rounded outpatient department. During this period, stress should be laid on the early recognition of departures from normal and on methods of arresting their advance and, if possible, of eliminating their causes. . . . Emphasis should be laid upon follow-up work so that the intern may see the end results of treatment and the extent to which the individual is able to adapt himself to normal life.[74]

Interns did not get much experience in outpatient departments because outpatients were charity patients who were being cared for by the free labor of practicing physicians who sought appointments to the inpatient staff. Hospitals saw little reason to use interns to assist in the care of patients who provided no income. Interns were put to work in the wards where their labor was most valuable to the medical staff.

The training that house officers did receive was often unrelated to their subsequent practices. Reznikoff wrote in 1939:

> In one New England city, . . . a recent survey showed that only one-third of all the physicians who received surgical training as interns and residents were practicing surgery. The remainder were practicing general medicine without adequate preliminary hospital training. The reason for this is obvious. Modern surgical practice requires many house officers as aides, but offers opportunities for relatively few visiting surgeons [in private practice]. . . . The most practical solution . . . is to afford all interns a good basic training in general medicine *in addition* to any specialty service.[75]

Thus the internship remained a form of practical experience that often bore little relationship to the intern's future career. Although the AMA and the licensing boards endorsed the internship as education, this redefinition of its role had little impact on its content. Interns remained hospital employees.

Residencies

Two forms of postgraduate training in a medical specialty existed at the beginning of the twentieth century. Some students took formal or informal apprenticeships with eminent specialists. Others took short courses on the specialties offered by postgraduate schools and some medical schools. Neither type of training was satisfactory. The apprenticeship lacked diversity of perspective and the postgraduate courses lacked opportunities for clinical experience.

The first residencies in hospitals were developed as extended internships in a specialty. Municipal hospitals in particular had large caseloads and offered further training to experienced house officers to obtain more skilled staff members. Some medical schools, beginning with the Johns Hopkins University, offered residencies to house officers who sought specialty training. Before World War I, residencies were available only in the leading hospitals and admission to them was highly competitive.[76]

The residency system became more formal and grew rapidly in the 1920s. The AMA established principles for residency programs in 1923, including a requirement that residency training be limited to graduates of medical schools who had completed at least a one-year internship. The length of the residency was two to three years, depending on the specialty, although short courses were also permitted. Residency programs grew rapidly thereafter. In 1930 the AMA Council on Medical Education listed 338 hospitals that offered 2,208 residencies, and in 1939, 518 hospitals that offered 4,556 residencies.[77]

The problems of residency training were much the same as those of the internship, with two major exceptions. While most hospitals had staff physicians who were qualified to teach interns, few had staff specialists with the time and ability to teach residents. The original idea of the residency had been intensive study with an outstanding specialist and teacher; this had degenerated into clinical experience in a hospital with occasional advice provided by a few average specialists. In addition, few hospitals could provide the necessary training in the relevant basic medical sciences and in related specialties.[78]

Residency programs were also criticized because they occurred directly after the internship. Many physicians believed that residency programs narrowed the interests of physicians too early in their careers and that physicians should specialize only after experience in general practice. On the other hand, experienced physicians who applied for highly competitive residencies at good hospitals were at a disadvantage compared to new graduates. Many practicing physicians also could not afford the financial sacrifices involved in a residency.[79]

The residency system was responsible for the development of much clinical research, especially at the leading medical schools. Residents did not have private practices and were able to devote their time to the detailed study of the specialty. When they were given guidance by qualified faculty members, this often led to significant achievements. In 1940 the president of the American College of Surgeons said that "graduate training in surgery . . . has done more to stimulate original scientific work in surgery in this country than any other force."[80]

Thus, in the first half of the twentieth century, the hospital internship and residency displaced all other forms of extramural medical education: private schools, private courses, informal study, and dispensary training. The internship and the residency had the great advantage of involving the student in direct patient care. They had the disadvantages of providing little formal training, of limiting the student to patients who were atypical of private medical practice, and of requiring the student to spend most of his time on routine tasks of little educational value. Hospital training was not the panacea that its advocates had claimed.

Nursing

The number of nurses increased rapidly during the first half of the century. The 11,804 graduate nurses in 1900, 15 per 100,000 population, increased to 103,878 nurses in 1920 and 284,159 in 1940, when the ratio reached 215 nurses per 100,000 population. The number of practical nurses and midwives increased from 101,511 in 1900 to 109,287 in 1940, which demonstrated a growing preference for trained nurses.[81]

Student nurses, like interns and residents, continued to be financially remunerative to hospitals. A study at the Massachusetts General Hospital in 1932 showed a "substantial net income derived from student nursing service" over the cost of housing, feeding, clothing, and educating the nursing students. Because the Massachusetts General Hospital spent much more on its nursing program than all but a few hospitals, the net income from nursing education at most hospitals must have been quite impressive.[82]

Although educational programs at hospital nursing schools improved during the century, the clinical experiences of most nurses were geared to the service needs of the hospital. Hospitals with large surgical services gave their students a great deal of surgical training; muncipal hospitals with many chronic patients emphasized that kind of care. In practically all hospitals, students spent as much as 20 percent of their time making bandages, mending rubber gloves, dusting, sweeping, cleaning lavatories, putting away linen, and sterilizing equipment. Student nurses rarely received clinical training that was unprofitable to the hospital. No training occurred in dispensaries, where students would see a different kind of medicine that emphasized the early stages of illness and the needs of the patient's family. Staff-level graduate nurses were rarely available to teach nurses in the wards. Student nurses were the only nonsupervisory nurses in many hospitals.[83]

The goals of many nursing schools were reflected in their admissions and educational policies. One study reported that the strict supervision practiced in hospitals made it "possible for the school to admit as students many young women who will be useful hands and feet in hospital wards, but who are not at all safe prospects" as graduate nurses. Most nursing schools were too small to provide a satisfactory education. A 1929 survey of 1,458 of the 2,205 nursing schools found that one-third had 22 or fewer students and three-fourths had fewer than 63. These schools could not afford full-time teachers, libraries, or other educational facilities.[84]

Nursing educators continually bemoaned these practices and their unfortunate effect on nursing. They always returned to the same theme: "The student nurse is worth money! . . . The amazing growth of schools of nursing . . . has come about not because the public wanted more nurses, but because the hospitals wanted more students."[85] Nurses, like interns and residents, were accepted for the value of the services they provided, and given a meager education in return.

At the same time that nursing schools were preparing students for careers as private duty nurses, the demand for private duty nursing was decreasing due to changes in illness and medical care. According to one 1934 study, "When patients are ill, there are fewer prolonged cases. The typhoid cases, for example, which of old kept many nurses busy for weeks on end during the summer and fall, are becoming rare." A study of 118 nurses found that one-fourth of their time was spent on patients who did not need trained nurses. Physicians also sent more patients to hospitals, where they were cared for by student nurses.[86]

The major alternative to private duty home nursing as a source of employment was hospital nursing. Specialists in particular recognized the value of trained nurses in hospitals. One survey of about 4,000 physicians found that 77 percent of specialists "often" needed private duty graduate nurses in the hospital, compared to only 42 percent who "often" needed them in the home. Among general practitioners, the corresponding figures were 66 percent and 80 percent.[87]

Large numbers of graduate nurses were first used in hospitals during the depression. Fewer families could afford private duty nurses, which forced nurses to seek jobs elsewhere. Lower hospital occupancy rates led to the closing of many nursing schools, which declined from a high of 1,885 in 1929 to 1,311 in 1940. Hospitals replaced their student nurses with graduate nurses, usually under conditions of understaffing and low pay. By 1941, more than 47 percent of active nurses were involved in institutional nursing and only 27 percent were in private duty nursing. Hospitals also employed graduate nurses to supplement student nurses. The proportion of hospitals with nursing schools that employed graduate nurses increased from an estimated 27 percent in 1927 to 90 percent in 1937. Despite the low pay, hospital nursing had major benefits. The work was more varied and interesting, equipment was superior, assistance was available, the pay was assured, and there was less of the "personal maid work" common in private homes.[88]

Thus, hospital education for interns, residents, and nurses continued to expand in the twentieth century. However, hospital training did not follow the same pattern of development that had occurred in the nineteenth century hospital and dispensary clinics and private courses. The earlier pattern was toward greater formalization and improvement of teaching. While hospital education improved during the century, it never became an important activity that merited the infusion of significant resources.

7

Medical Education, 1900–1950: General Trends and Basic Medical Sciences

During the first half of the twentieth century, American medical education underwent drastic changes. Greater costs of operation and the requirements of licensing agencies forced many medical schools to close and most of the others to affiliate with universities. The surviving medical schools were able to raise their admission and graduation requirements, which was also made possible by the rise in the general educational level of the population. The growth of the basic medical sciences led to the development of a new kind of faculty member whose career was confined to the medical school.

Changes in General Higher Education

During the first half of the twentieth century, the educational level of the population rose significantly. The proportion of the 17-year-old population with high school educations increased from 6.3 percent in 1900 to 16.3 percent in 1920, 28.8 percent in 1930, and 49.0 percent in 1940. The number of bachelors' degrees conferred per 100 persons 23 years old increased from 1.9 in 1900 to 2.6 in 1920, 5.7 in 1930, and 8.1 in 1940. Between 1910 and 1940, the number of college undergraduates more than tripled. Because the number of medical students did not increase, medical schools were able to raise their admission standards.[1]

At the same time, many new professions competed with medicine for students. Between 1900 and 1940, dentistry, engineering, chemistry, accounting, and college teaching, among others, grew significantly faster than the traditional professions of medicine, law, and the clergy (Table 7.1). Graduate education also became an alternative to professional training. Between 1900 and 1940, the number of masters' and doctors' degrees awarded, excluding medicine and other first professional degrees, increased from 1,965 to 30,021, or from 6.7 to 13.9 percent of all degrees awarded.[2]

Colleges and universities decentralized their organizational structure to deal with the increasingly technical and specialized content of academic disciplines. They established academic departments that consisted of faculty members who shared a common body of knowledge and taught the same or related courses. Departments were given the responsibility of supervising their faculty members,

TABLE 7.1. Increases in Selected Professions, 1900–1940

Profession (000s)	1900	1910	1920	1930	1940	Percentage Increase 1900–1940
Clergymen	114	118	127	149	141	23.7
Physicians	131	152	146	157	168	28.2
Lawyers	108	115	123	161	182	68.5
Dentists	30	40	56	71	71	136.7
Chemists	9	16	28	45	57	533.3
Engineers	38	77	134	217	297	681.6
Accountants	23	39	118	192	238	934.8
College faculty	7	16	33	62	77	1000.0
U.S. population (000,000s)	76	92	106	123	132	73.7

Source: U.S. Bureau of the Census, *Historical Statistics of the United States* (Washington, D.C.: U.S. G.P.O., 1975), 1:8, 140.

recruiting new faculty, and operating the department's academic program. By 1950, departments existed in most of the sciences, social sciences, and humanities.[3]

Departmentalization affected all aspects of university life. Each department sought to make its courses available to all students, which led to the elective system. Departments duplicated courses offered by other departments as a result of disagreements over departmental boundaries. Criteria for hiring faculty members were changed from personal characteristics, like teaching ability, work experience, administrative skills, and social background, to formal training and demonstrated competence in the department's body of knowledge. The refusal of departments to expand their bodies of knowledge sometimes led to the creation of new departments. Journalism and public speaking developed out of the unwillingness of English departments to teach those subjects, and statistics courses proliferated throughout universities because of the indifference of departments of mathematics to that subject.[4]

Most new departments were established in response to economic and political forces. Student demand was the most important and frequent determining factor. Competition for faculty members and the desire to teach new and prestigious fields led to the earliest departmental structures, which were created in private universities seeking national eminence. Pressures from community groups for various types of training were important factors in the establishment of many departments in public universities. The resulting growth in courses was extraordinary: the University of Minnesota taught 3,500 courses in 1941, double the number offered two decades earlier.[5]

The expansion of the curriculum occurred primarily in public universities. They had the resources needed to establish new departments and thus became the dominant institutions of higher education everywhere except the Northeast, which had many large private universities. Public universities also led in the establishment of new types of professional education. Examples are engineering and agriculture, which were the first professions after the ministry to develop within universities rather than in independent or autonomous professional schools. Both fields developed significant bodies of knowledge after the Civil War, had more support among the public than among academicians, and required expensive equipment and facilities. State universities established separate colleges for them modeled after other professional schools and became the educational leaders in the two fields. In 1915–1916, 62.7 percent of all engineering students were enrolled in state universities, which have remained the determining influence in the profession. In agriculture, state universities had practically all of the students and programs.[6]

College admission requirements varied widely during much of this period. Public universities, which enrolled the largest number of students, had the lowest standards. The leading private universities tried to become national institutions by organizing the College Entrance Examination Board to provide entrance examinations for students all over the nation. The examinations were first offered in 1901, and in 1916 Harvard, Yale, and Princeton gave up their own entrance examinations and required most of their applicants to take the College Board's Scholastic Aptitude Test. Even these schools varied widely in their admission standards: around 1934, Harvard accepted about 80 percent of approximately 1,400 applicants, while Princeton accepted only 43 percent of an equal number of applicants.[7]

The growth of colleges and universities significantly affected medical schools. By the second quarter of the century, almost all entering medical students had obtained some college education. They had taken courses in the sciences on which medicine was increasingly based. They had performed reasonably well in institutions of higher education. Medical schools could become true professional schools instead of institutions providing both general and professional education.

Changes in the Number of Medical Schools

Around the turn of the twentieth century, medical schools experienced a period of major growth (Table 7.2). Between 1880 and 1906, the number of medical schools increased from 100 to 162, and the number of medical students from 11,826 to 25,204. The average enrollment per school increased by more than 30 percent. The growth in the number of medical students matched the growth in all higher education, because the ratio of medical students to students in all institutions of higher education remained unchanged. A much smaller increase occurred in the number of medical school graduates, from 3,241 to 5,747, due to the change from a two-year to a four-year course. The increase in the number of medical school graduates barely exceeded the growth in population.

Between 1906 and 1920, the number of medical schools and medical students declined rapidly. In 1920, the ratio of medical students to all students in institutions of higher education was only one-fifth of its 1900 level and the ratio of medical school graduates to the U.S. population was the lowest that it had been in over 40 years. After 1920, the number of medical schools continued to decline, but their average enrollments and numbers of graduates increased by two-thirds by the late 1930s.

TABLE 7.2. Medical Schools and Medical Students, 1880–1940

Year	Medical Schools	Medical Students	Students/ Medical School	Medical Students/ All Higher Education Students[a]	Medical Graduates	Medical Graduates/ 1,000 Population
1880	100	11,826	118.3	.10	3241	.064
1890	133	15,404	115.8	.10	4454	.071
1900	160	25,171	157.3	.11	5214	.069
1904	160	28,142	175.9	.11[b]	5747	.070
1906	162	25,204	155.6	.09[b]	5364	.063
1910	131	21,526	164.3	.06	4440	.048
1915	96	14,891	155.1	.04	3536	.035
1920	85	13,798	162.3	.02	3047	.029
1925	80	18,200	227.5	.02[b]	3974	.034
1930	76	21,597	284.2	.02	4565	.037
1935	77	22,888	297.2	.02[b]	5101	.040
1940	77	21,271	276.2	.01	5097	.039

[a]Includes professional schools.
[b]Estimated.
Source: U.S. Bureau of the Census, *Historical Statistics of the United States* (Washington, D.C.: U.S. G.P.O., 1975), 1:8, 76, 383.

Certification of Medical Schools

The increase in the number of medical school graduates in the late nineteenth century led many physicians to conclude that the profession was becoming overcrowded, despite the fact that the ratio of physicians to population decreased slightly between 1880 and 1900. Medical societies first tried to reduce the number of physicians by convincing medical schools to raise their entrance requirements and reduce their enrollments. This was contrary to the interests of the schools and was unsuccessful. They then lobbied successfully for state licensing of physicians. By 1900, 48 states and other jurisdictions had licensing laws, most of which required that applicants for licenses have degrees from approved medical schools. In 1910, written examinations for licensure were also required in 44 states. State licensing laws were often ineffective from the AMA's perspective because of lack of enforcement and variations in requirements that permitted students denied a license in one state to obtain one elsewhere.[8]

In its search for a more effective vehicle to control medical schools, the AMA realized that state licensing agencies lacked the skilled personnel and resources needed to evaluate the medical schools that awarded degrees to applicants for licensure. The AMA therefore organized its Council on Medical Education in 1904 as a source of information and expertise on medical schools. In 1905 the council established standards for medical schools, including a minimum preparatory education of four years of high school, a four-year course, and satisfactory performance by the school's graduates on licensing examinations. In 1906–1907, the council undertook an inspection of all medical schools, using these criteria and additional standards for the physical plant and curriculum. Medical schools were ranked as "acceptable," "doubtful," or "nonacceptable," signified by a ranking of A, B, or C. The council ranked 82 schools as class A, 46 as class B, and 32 as class C. Each medical school was notified of its own evaluation, but the rankings were never made public.[9]

The AMA began to publish annual reports on medical education in its journal about this time. The reports provided descriptions of each school and results of the licensing examinations in each state and for each medical school. In 1905, 20.8 percent of 7,173 graduates taking the state licensing examinations failed to qualify, as did 18.4 percent of 7,004 graduates taking the examinations in 1910.[10]

Meanwhile, many proprietary medical schools were experiencing overwhelming financial problems. Students demanded a scientific medical education and, according to the secretary of the Association of American Medical Colleges in 1907, were "willing to pay for it." The local physicians who served as part-time basic science instructors were unable to teach the new material, and many schools could not afford salaried instructors and the necessary equipment. Another problem was the expansion of the curriculum beyond the skills of the faculty. The faculty of one medical school that closed voluntarily in 1909 observed that "subjects . . . that once belonged to the 'mere mention' hour in the course of study, have developed into great fields with divisions and subdivisions, each demanding a special training for its comprehension and most certainly for its proper teaching." More hospital facilities were also needed, which often were unavailable to weak medical schools and those in small towns or cities. Finally, some medical schools could not attract enough students after they raised their admission requirements to conform with state licensing laws.[11]

Medical schools reacted to these changes by merging with other medical schools, affiliating with universities in the hope of obtaining additional funds, and by closing their doors. Between 1900 and 1910, 43 medical schools were involved in mergers and 27 ceased operation. The number of medical students declined even more precipitously, from a high of 28,142 in 1904 to 21,526 in 1910.[12]

The Flexner Report

In order to obtain impartial evidence of the inadequacies of many medical schools, in 1908 the AMA Council on Medical Education convinced the Carnegie Foundation for the Advancement of Teaching to undertake its own study of medical schools. According to the minutes of a meeting of the council, the foundation agreed not to make any more mention "in the report of the Council than any other source of information" in order to give the report "the weight of an independent report of a disinterested body." The study was undertaken by Abraham Flexner, a secondary school educator with no previous knowledge of medicine or medical education.[13]

Flexner prepared for his study by meeting with the faculty at the Johns Hopkins University medical school, from whom he adopted his ideas about medical education. In 1909–1910 he carried out his field work by accompanying the secretary of the Council on Medical Education on most of the site visits involved in its second inspection of medical schools. According to the president of the Carnegie Foundation, Flexner and the foundation worked "hand in glove" with the Council on Medical Education. In 1910, the Carnegie Foundation published Flexner's report as *Medical Education in the United States and Canada,* which immediately became a major and controversial document.[14]

Flexner's report emphasized the facilities and physical plant of the medical schools. Each school was described in terms of its entrance requirements, enrollments, number of teachers, resources, and laboratory and clinical facilities. No reference was made to the quality of the faculty, the nature of the teaching, or the relationship between students and faculty. Flexner apparently believed that good facilities, high entrance requirements, and a sufficient number of qualified faculty members automatically produced quality education. In this regard, Flexner followed the standards of the AMA Council on Medical Education, which had also disregarded teaching in its two evaluations.

Most medical schools were highly critical of the report, in some cases based on their personal experiences with Flexner. As an example, a faculty member at the Albany Medical College reported that Flexner telephoned the school to request a site visit and a meeting with the registrar. He wrote:

> The school had never applied to the Foundation for advice or assistance; was in no way answerable to it, and the Foundation had no jurisdiction in the premises. Nevertheless . . . everything was exhibited to him, and even the college books were put at his disposal. He was given every opportunity to make a proper inspection of the school, the Bender Laboratory, the hospitals, dispensaries and other institutions used by the college . . . but he contented himself with a hasty glance here and there and hurried back to New York by a mid-day train. . . . The faculty was assured that a proof of the report would be submitted to them for suggestions before printing but this was done at such a time and in such a manner that no revision was possible. . . .
> It is filled with flippant and unwarranted judgments and is based upon hastily formed opinions resting upon careless observation and preconceived opinions and prejudices.[15]

The reaction of the medical profession to Flexner's report was mixed. The *New York Medical Journal* and the *Medical Record,* the two leading medical journals of the period, were critical of Flexner's attack on the independent medical schools and dubious about his whole approach. Physicians in many communities defended their local medical schools against Flexner's criticisms. On the other hand, the *Journal of the American Medical Association* was enthusiastic. It claimed: "Emphasis is laid on the fact that the social order is best served when the number of men entering a given profession reaches and does not exceed a limited ratio and that the present condition of the medical profession, overcrowded by ill-trained physicians, is very unsatisfactory."[16]

Over the years, the perception has developed that the Flexner report was a major cause of the reform of medical education during this period. Its specific contributions are claimed to be: (1) it convinced medical schools to increase the amount of laboratory training in the basic medical sciences and to use hospitals for clinical training; and (2) it exposed many poor quality medical schools that allegedly flooded the profession with incompetent physicians.

Flexner believed that the scientific method used in the basic medical sciences was the true foundation of both medical research and medical practice. This method was best taught through laboratory instruction, the "didactic lecture [being] pedagogically sound only at a relatively late stage of the student's discipline." He held that the basic medical sciences should be taught without regard to their medical applications or the student's career goals, and that research, "untrammeled by near reference to practical ends," should play a major role in the medical school. Clinical teaching was to occur almost entirely by means of clinical clerkships in the dispensary and especially the hospital, which was the clinical equivalent of the basic science laboratory. Flexner believed that only university-owned hospitals could properly support education and research.[17]

Flexner acknowledged that considerable improvement along these lines had been made prior to his report. He wrote: "in the last fifteen years, substantial progress has been made. . . . [T]he course has . . . been generally graded, and extended to four years. . . . Didactic teaching has been much mitigated. Almost without exception the schools furnish some clinical teaching. . . . Relatively quicker and greater progress has been made on the laboratory side." It was shown in an earlier chapter that most schools introduced laboratory teaching and extended their course to four years in the 1890s and that many improvements occurred in clinical teaching at that time. These reforms in medical education occurred in the decades before the Flexner report, not as a result of it.[18]

The Flexner report was also supposed to have caused the closing of many inferior medical schools by exposing their inadequacies. Certainly Flexner emphasized the impact of these schools on medical education. He described in detail the "wretched" facilities, the "foul" dissecting rooms, the "meager" equipment, and the "shockingly bad" dispensaries of the weaker medical schools.

However, as was shown above, 43 medical schools had merged and 27 had ceased operating between 1900 and 1910. Flexner noted in his report that "the number of medical schools has latterly declined" and that many were "gasping for breath." He claimed that this was caused by the rising costs of medical education: "Nothing has perhaps done more to complete the discredit of commercialism than the fact that it has ceased to pay. It is but a short step from an annual deficit to the conclusion that the whole thing is wrong anyway."[19] There is no reason to believe that these trends, which resulted from fundamental changes in the economics of medical education, would have ceased without the Flexner report.

Another claim for the Flexner report has been that it was responsible for closing many weak medical schools that were flooding the profession with thousands of ill-trained physicians. Flexner complained about a "century of reckless overproduction of cheap doctors" by schools whose "advertising costs more than laboratories." However, these schools, although relatively large in number, produced few graduates and even fewer practicing physicians. To demonstrate this, a study was made of the licensing statistics for 1909. Although Flexner did not rank the medical schools based on his joint evaluations with the AMA Council on Medical Education, the council published its own rankings in 1910. It ranked 70 medical schools as "acceptable" (class A), 29 as "needing certain improvements

TABLE 7.3. Characteristics of Medical Schools by Class, 1909

Characteristic	Class A	Class B	Class C	Total
Enumerations				
Schools	61	31	31	123
Students	14,422	3,923	1,975	20,320
Graduates	2,943	757	408	4,108
Averages per school				
Students	236.4	126.5	63.7	165.2
Graduates	48.2	24.4	13.2	33.4
Percentages				
Schools	49.6	25.2	25.2	100.0
Students	71.0	19.3	9.7	100.0
Graduates	71.6	18.4	9.9	99.9

Sources: Hubert Work, "Report of the Reference Committee on Medical Education," *Journal of the American Medical Association* 54 (1910): 2061–62; "Statistics of Medical Colleges in the United States," *Journal of the American Medical Association* 53 (1909): 546–49.

to make them acceptable" (class B), and 27 as requiring "a complete reorganization to make them acceptable" (class C).[20]

Table 7.3 shows the insignificant role of the class C or unacceptable medical schools in medical education in 1909. Although they comprised one-fourth of all medical schools, they taught fewer than 10 percent of the students and graduates. The class C schools individually were also quite small, averaging only one-fourth of the number of students and graduates of the class A medical schools.

Table 7.4 shows the performance of the graduates of the three classes of medical schools on the 1909 licensing examinations. The class C schools accounted for only 11.0 percent of those taking the examinations and 8.4 percent of those passing them. They also accounted for 24.6 percent of all those who failed, with only 63.8 percent of their graduates passing the examinations. The class A schools accounted for 71.3 percent of those taking the examinations and 75.4 percent of those passing them. Almost 90 percent of their students passed the examinations.

These data demonstrate that the class C medical schools played an unimportant role in educating physicians at the time of the Flexner report. The small number of their graduates who entered practice had no real impact on the overall quality of medical care and very little effect on competition among physicians. Given the historical tendency of poorly prepared physicians to practice in communities avoided by other physicians, they probably provided medical manpower where none was otherwise available.

Flexner's approach to medical education emphasized research and academic education rather than professional training. He relegated to a secondary consideration the need for medical schools to provide the nation with an adequate number of physicians and scarcely mentioned the problems confronting low income medical students. This is shown by Flexner's proposal in the report that only 30 or 31 four-year medical schools, enrolling 300 students each, were needed in the entire

TABLE 7.4. Licensing Statistics for Medical Schools by Class, 1909 Graduates

Licensing Examination Results	Class A	Class B	Class C	Total
Enumerations				
Passed	3,837	826	425	5,088
Failed	490	250	241	981
Examined	4,327	1,076	666	6,069
Percentages				
Passed	75.4	16.2	8.4	100.0
Failed	49.9	25.5	24.6	100.0
Examined	71.3	17.7	11.0	100.0
Percentage passing	88.7	76.8	63.8	83.8

Sources: Hubert Work, "Report of the Reference Committee on Medical Education," *Journal of the American Medical Association* 54 (1910): 2061–62; "State Board Statistics for 1909," *Journal of the American Medical Association* 54 (1910): 1733–55.

nation in 1910. Perkin has called him a "prize academic snob . . . who endlessly belittled the greatest academic achievement of his countrymen, the democratization of higher education."[21]

The Council on Medical Education undertook a third evaluation of medical schools in 1911–1912 and a fourth one in 1913–1914. A fifth inspection was scheduled for 1914, but abandoned. In the next several years, the council and the Association of American Medical Colleges (AAMC) agreed on two years of college as the minimum admission requirements for grade A schools. In 1918 the Federation of State Medical Boards agreed to accept for licensure all schools that were listed as "acceptable" by the AMA and that were members of the AAMC, thus making the AMA's evaluations public policy in most states.[22]

In succeeding years, the Council on Medical Education stopped trying to control medical education by mass inspections of medical schools. Instead, it evaluated individual schools in difficulty. These confidential studies resulted in private reports to the schools involved, with recommendations for improvements. The council gradually became a source of advice to medical schools rather than a publicizer of their faults.[23]

Only two major studies of medical education were carried out between 1914 and World War II. The first was undertaken in the mid-1920s and published in 1932 by the Commission on Medical Education, an organization created by the AAMC with contributions from individual medical schools, the AMA, and several foundations. Its report was a general analysis of medical education that neither evaluated nor compared individual medical schools. The Council on Medical Education undertook its fifth full-fledged inspection of all medical schools in 1934–1936 (the Weiskotten report) in order to assess the effects of the depression on medical education. This report also did not rank individual medical schools and stated that "individual comment was deemed unworthy." Instead, it provided a detailed analysis of the overall state of medical education in order that "faculties and administrative officers may learn what other schools are doing, emulating that which is good and avoiding that which experience has shown to be unprofitable."[24]

The changing role of the Council on Medical Education was most clearly indicated in 1930 when the Federation of State Medical Boards recognized the AAMC rather than the council as the "standardizing agency" for "all matters of premedical education, course of study, and educational requirements for the degree of Doctor of Medicine." The federation limited its own role to the "determination of fitness to practice" and "the enforcement of regulatory resources." This policy acknowledged that inferior medical schools no longer needed to be eliminated and that the Council on Medical Education's rigid standards for medical schools were undesirable. Shortly thereafter, the council made its standards more flexible and eliminated a number of requirements.[25]

During the depression of the 1930s, the AMA again urged the medical schools to reduce their enrollments,[26] but medical schools instead added students to obtain additional revenue. The average enrollment per medical school rose from 227.5 per school in 1925 to 284.2 per school in 1930 and 297.2 in 1935. It then dipped slightly to 276.2 in 1940 (Table 7.2). Despite the ineffectiveness of its exhortations, the AMA did not use its most powerful weapon: another mass inspection and public ranking of medical schools. The association had good reason to avoid another direct attack on medical schools.

The AMA changed its tactics because of public dissatisfaction with the lower physician–population ratio brought about by reduced medical school enrollments. The ratio declined from over 150 physicians per 100,000 population in 1900 to fewer than 130 per 100,000 population from most of the 1920s to about 1940. The AMA was widely blamed by physicians and laymen alike for creating this situation. To appease its critics, in the early 1920s the AMA House of Delegates supported the expansion of the existing high-grade schools, greater financial aid for the poorer schools, and the establishment of new schools in a few large states. In 1928, the chairman of the Council on Medical Education observed that since 1919 "there has been a steady healthy increase in the number of students and the number of graduates." He conceded that physicians, like other people, were moving "from the country to the cities" and that some small towns could not "attract or support a physician."[27]

During this period, the licensing boards took steps toward a national licensing examination with the establishment of the National Board of Medical Examiners in 1916. The board prepared and administered standardized examinations as a service to state licensing boards, although it was not affiliated with the boards. After 1922, the examinations were divided into three parts, one covering the basic medical sciences, a second covering the clinical subjects taught in the last two years of medical school, and the third consisting of a practical examination given at the bedside. By 1936, all but five states recognized the board's examination for licensure, but as late as 1940, only 1,200 students, less than one-fourth of all medical school graduates, took the examination.[28]

Medical School Affiliations with Universities

Proprietary medical schools developed overwhelming financial problems when they upgraded their facilities and appointed full-time faculty members. For example, two outstanding proprietary medical schools in 1880, the Jefferson Medical College of Philadelphia and the University of Maryland medical school of Baltimore, by 1900 had fallen far behind their respective neighbors, the medical schools of the University of Pennsylvania and the Johns Hopkins University. Proprietary schools had few resources and their faculty ownership made donors unwilling to give them funds, as the Jefferson and Maryland medical schools discovered when they sought philanthropic assistance. To obtain support, the Jefferson Medical College reorganized in 1895 under a lay board of trustees and put the faculty members on salary. Most proprietary schools affiliated with colleges or universities, especially public universities. In 1920 the University of Maryland became a public institution and was linked with the state agricultural college located 25 miles away to create a state university.[29] Medical schools affiliated with public universities more often than with private universities because state governments were concerned about maintaining an adequate supply of physicians in their states.

The affiliation of medical schools with universities was strongly advocated by the new leaders of medical education. William H. Welch of the Johns Hopkins University medical school argued that endowments would grow as philanthropists made donations to university medical schools. Research would prosper as medical school faculty members were appointed based on their research skills, made their careers in universities, and adopted the values of university educators. The basic medical scientists would establish close ties with their counterparts in the university science departments. Laboratories would be used for both university and medical school students and thereby lower costs.[30]

Despite these expectations, the affiliations of universities and medical schools were unsuccessful. The Weiskotten report of 1940 found that "some schools of medicine have adopted a policy of complete isolation with reference to participation in the university's financial burdens, have not readily undertaken additional responsibilities to fulfil the university's legitimate demands, and have ignored all claims to attention on the part of the university." The universities, on their part, sometimes diverted medical school funds or surpluses to other purposes and curtailed the budgets of medical schools. The report noted "that the opinion was quite common that . . . medical schools had been governed best by being governed least" and advocated limited involvement by the university in the medical school's affairs. This is what actually occurred in most medical schools during this period.[31]

Medical School Costs and Incomes

During the first part of the twentieth century, the costs of medical education climbed sharply, especially compared to the costs of other types of professional education. The Weiskotten report found that per student per credit hour, medical schools cost $26.96, dentistry $15.87, law $11.05, engineering $10.52, and commerce and education less than $6.00. Most of the costs were due to the basic medical sciences, which were responsible for 50.4 percent of the total instructional budget. The costs that were rising most rapidly were those of clinical education, especially after clinical faculty members were paid salaries.[32]

Most medical school expenses went toward facilities and faculty. In the first quarter of the century, medical schools spent an estimated $100 million on new buildings and equipment, and full-time faculty members required $10 million in salaries annually by 1925. Forty-two percent of medical school expenses in 1926–1927 went to salaries for the full-time faculty, a group which had not even existed a few decades before. A few leading schools spent five to ten times as much in the 1920s as they had two decades earlier, which raised their cost per student to more than $2,000 per year. The average cost per student in all medical schools in 1930 was $1,163. The Weiskotten report observed that "some schools were able to make remarkable progress. . . . Magnificent buildings, extensive equipment, generous support for research, good facilities, liberal budgets based on large endowments, have placed not a few of our institutions in a position second to none."[33]

These expenditures were the result of substantial increases in medical school incomes. Tuition remained the largest single source of income, although it was much less important than in the previous century. The Commission on Medical Education found in its survey of 63 medical schools in 1926–1927 that student fees accounted for 34 percent of medical school income. About a decade later, the Weiskotten report found that the median proportion of income obtained from student fees was 39.5 percent, varying from 10 to 96 percent at different medical schools. Tuition accounted for one-third of the income at both public and private medical schools. It was sufficiently important that medical schools increased enrollments during the 1920s and 1930s to augment their incomes, sometimes to the point of straining their resources. Ray Wilbur complained in the forward to the Weiskotten report of an "abnormal growth in the size of the student bodies in institutions without sufficient clinical, laboratory, or financial resources for their proper instruction."[34]

The Commission on Medical Education found that the other major sources of income in 1926–1927 were state and city funds, which provided 22 percent of total income and went primarily to public schools, and endowment income, which provided 23 percent of total income and went primarily to private ones. By 1941, 50 percent of the funds of public schools came from states, cities, or their affiliated public universities, while endowments accounted for about 32 percent of the funds of private schools. A few private schools accumulated impressive endowments. Between 1910 and 1924, the endowment of the Johns Hopkins University medical school increased from $437,000 to $7.5 million, that of Harvard from $3.2 million to $7.3 million, that of Yale from $278,000 to $4.2 million, and that of Washington University in St. Louis from none to $4.9 million. At Harvard in 1932, 78 percent of medical school funds came from investments.[35]

Another major source of medical school income was the free labor provided by volunteer clinical faculty members. The Weiskotten report found that "if schools of medicine were forced to forego these services and to compensate adequately all instructors, the present budgets of the schools would be entirely insufficient."

Volunteer clinical faculty members enabled medical schools to devote more of their income to the salaries and equipment required to teach the basic medical sciences.[36]

Medical School Administration

As medical schools became large organizations with substantial budgets, they developed a more formal administrative structure. The medical school dean had more autonomy than the heads of the other major units of the university. Lippard has written that "the deanship was a comparatively comfortable position to which many faculty members aspired. The problems encountered were relatively uncomplicated and external pressures were minimal. Funds, although limited, were derived from internal sources." Deans even had time for teaching and research or clinical activities.[37]

A more important administrative development was the emergence of the department chairmanship. The chairman of a basic medical science department functioned much like a liberal arts department chairman, but the chairman of a clinical department was responsible for its clinical activities as well as its teaching and research. According to one faculty member, he had "to supervise the work of a hundred or more doctors and provide for the care of large numbers of bed patients, as well as a huge clientele in the outpatient department. He must manage the difficult task of running his part of the hospital efficiently and economically."[38]

The complexity of the department chairmanship led to major debates over the skills required. Francis Peabody wrote that a suitable chairman "has had an intensive scientific training, has done important research, is a good administrator, is a competent teacher, and finally has had clinical experience." He added: "Such a man is, of course, almost impossible to find." Consequently in the leading medical schools, Peabody wrote, " 'clinical experience' is apt to be put last among the specifications . . . because some . . . think that clinical medicine can be 'picked up' very easily [and that] someone else can tell the students how to take care of patients." The primary qualification in the leading schools was research, which Peabody criticized: "If the general ward is the backbone of the clinic, then the head of the department must be close to it" and both have clinical skills and be willing to spend time there.[39]

Medical Students

During this period, the preliminary education of medical students outpaced medical school admission requirements. In 1915, 85 of 96 medical schools required one or sometimes two years of college as an admission requirement. This increased in all schools during the 1930s to two years of college. Only a few medical schools required a bachelor's degree. Nevertheless, the proportion of medical students with bachelors' degrees reached 50 percent in the mid-1930s. As in the nineteenth century, actual admission standards depended more on the educational level of the population than the formal requirements of the schools.[40]

Many medical students, whatever their educational level, continued to be poorly qualified. The dean of the University of Minnesota medical school said in 1944 that "most medical schools accept the last 20 to 25 percent of students with distinct reservations as to their qualifications, intellectual or personal, for the study or practice of medicine." As late as 1945, the failure rates in licensing examinations were 25 percent in New York and 11 percent in Massachusetts, although they were lower in less demanding states.[41]

The failure of medical schools to attract enough qualified students had several causes. One was the cost of tuition and fees and the lack of financial aid. In 1935–1936, only 14 of 87 medical schools studied (including two-year schools) had tuition and fees of $200 or less, while 21 charged between $400 and $500, and 11 over $500. Medical education was becoming less available to the poor, especially in states without public medical schools. This was clearly indicated by the high proportion of medical students with college degrees. Another reason was the policy in some schools, including some of the leading schools, of discriminating against first- and second-generation immigrants, women, Jews, Catholics, and blacks.[42]

The Medical School Curriculum

After a century of courses determined by the idiosyncrasies of diverse faculty interests, a standardized curriculum emerged in the twentieth century. The first two years were devoted to the basic sciences, and the last two to clinical medicine. The first year included the traditional courses of anatomy, physiology, and biochemistry (which had replaced medical chemistry). The second covered pathology and the newer disciplines of bacteriology, clinical pathology, and pharmacology. Clinical medicine was introduced to the student in the second year in physical diagnosis and sometimes in other courses as well. The third and fourth years were spent primarily in lectures and clinical clerkships in general medicine and the specialties.[43]

By 1925, most medical schools were exceeding the hours specified by the AAMC in almost every required course. In many schools the curriculum was almost totally prescribed. One survey found that fewer than half a dozen schools had a definite number of elective hours in their programs. Around 1930, the state licensing boards agreed to allow greater flexibility in the curriculum. Many schools, especially the better ones, responded by introducing more electives courses and experimenting with requirements.[44]

Most schools increasingly focused on biological aspects of disease at the expense of psychological, social, and environmental factors. In 1914, William Graves wrote:

> In this age of specialism and short cuts to diagnoses the whole individual is often lost to view. Indeed, he is nowhere more completely buried than in the clinical years in our medical schools. During the fundamental years he is a commanding figure; he awakens interest in the student body; he dominates it. During the clinical years he shrinks into darkness and for many is lost beyond recall—crushed by the weight of specialism, crammed into the tired brain of the student body. The general advance in medical knowledge should render the appreciation of the concept of the patient as a

whole individual more thorough, more complete than ever before. That such appreciation is actually less must be due in part to the dominance of specialized branches in teaching during the clinical years.[45]

One example of the emphasis on organic disease was the teaching of neurology and psychiatry, the only specialties concerned with nonorganic factors in disease. In 1914, according to an analysis of the teaching in 85 medical schools by Graves, both were "unfortunately considered by curriculum makers and the profession generally as belonging to the narrowest and least important of specialties." Medical schools averaged many fewer hours in the two fields than the amount called for by AAMC standards. In 1932 a survey of 66 medical schools in the U.S. and 2 in Canada found that only 21 of them had departments of psychiatry and 15 had departments in which psychiatry was joined with neurology. In the remaining 32 schools, psychiatry was taught in the department of medicine. Teachers of psychiatry generally were part-time, poorly trained, and, according to a 1940 study, "bound by ideas of the general hopelessness of mental disease, . . . uninterested in improving their teaching, and . . . lacking in a forward-looking and investigative attitude." Although a few medical schools established psychiatric clinics or hospitals, most lacked relations with psychiatric hospitals and did little clinical teaching using psychiatric patients.[46]

The organic emphasis was also reported in a 1941 survey of a group of American and Canadian medical schools that found little interest in social and environmental factors in disease. Students rarely investigated the home environment of patients by being involved in home deliveries, the home care of patients, or research in public health. In the teaching of history taking, according to the study, "the students' attention has been directed toward the physical aspects of the patient's illness. The social and environmental factors have not been related to the present illness or the past history as a rule. The Family History has been usually interpreted narrowly to cover only hereditary, familial, and communicable diseases."[47]

Few schools devoted much attention to preventive medicine or other aspects of public health. The Weiskotten report found that only 18 medical schools had full-time departments of public health in the mid-1930s, and 25 others combined the subject with bacteriology, where the scientific aspects often overwhelmed the practical ones. The study also found that "considerable confusion existed as to terminology and course content in hygiene, public health and preventive medicine."[48]

The new schools of public health also contributed to the biological emphasis in medical schools. For example, an Industrial Disease Clinic was established at the Massachusetts General Hospital about 1915 by a Harvard medical school faculty member to study occupational and industrial factors in illness. It was transferred a decade later to the newly established Harvard school of public health, thus removing it from use in medical school teaching. Schools of public health focused on the diminishing problems of sanitation and infection instead of new health issues. They avoided even hospital administration, which was first taught in 1934 in conjunction with a school of business administration.[49]

The Basic Medical Sciences

Basic science departments grew in importance during the early twentieth century, as shown by the construction of many new laboratories and other physical facilities. The Weiskotten report examined facilities in anatomy, biochemistry, physiology, pharmacology, bacteriology, and pathology in 66 medical schools in the 1930s and found that about two-thirds of the facilities in each science were satisfactory.[50]

Although most basic science departments employed one or more full-time Ph.D. faculty members, physicians continued to play an important role. The Weiskotten study found the following number of department heads with M.D. degrees in 66 medical schools in the mid-1930s: biochemistry, 17; physiology, 42; anatomy, 46; bacteriology, 49; pharmacology, 50; and pathology, 65.[51]

A major issue confronting basic science departments involved the balance between the teaching of laboratory techniques and the basic concepts in the disciplines. William Welch expressed the view of most full-time basic medical scientists when he observed in 1893 that laboratory techniques not only had produced the great discoveries of the recent past, but also instilled in the student "the quality of mind, the methods of work, the disciplined habit of correct reasoning, the way of looking at medical problems" essential for a physician.[52]

Many clinicians strongly opposed this emphasis. A survey of over 500 general practitioners who graduated between 1915 and 1922 reported criticism of the "redundant laboratory work" and lack of emphasis on the fundamental concepts "that would give them understanding of the sciences themselves." The Commission on Medical Education and the Weiskotten report reserved some of their harshest language for the teaching of the medical sciences. The commission felt that "an unreasonable amount of time is consumed in meaningless laboratory work as a method of education," that there was too much presentation of "temporary, miscellaneous, and inconsequential [details], the overemphasis on the technical procedures of laboratory work, and the artificial segregation of the subjects." Topics were "presented too frequently from the standpoint of the special interest of the teacher and from the aspect of technical details." The Weiskotten report expressed the same views and added that there was a need for a closer relationship between the basic medical sciences and clinical medicine:

> In too many instances the preclinical courses were merely a mimicry of nonmedical university courses practically devoid of any medical and clinical implications. Without wishing to in any way minimize the importance of pure science, it is important to point out that the primary objectives involve the laying of a foundation for the future practice of medicine and that such a program calls for preparation of the student for his introduction to clinical medicine in the third year.[53]

A few basic medical scientists conceded that laboratory techniques were sometimes overemphasized. In 1894, Welch observed that "the student whose knowledge of a subject is derived exclusively from laboratory courses is likely to lose his perspective in details, or acquire only fragmentary knowledge of a subject, to fail to comprehend the general bearing of observed facts, and not to acquire the general principles and systematic concepts which are essential." He recommended that "laboratory work should be accompanied and supplemented by the reading of text-books and by lectures."[54]

Clinicians, however, did not want laboratory work to be supplemented by anything; they wanted formal instruction in the basic concepts to be supplemented by laboratory training. Thus the nub of the issue was that basic scientists saw the laboratory as the key element in their teaching because it would engender the scientific spirit; the clinicians saw it as a set of tedious and detailed techniques often unrelated to the concepts involved and inapplicable to clinical problems. The outcome was a compromise that satisfied no one. The basic medical sciences were taught with a greater emphasis on applications in the United States than in Europe, but the applied elements and the experimental techniques were not integrated into a meaningful whole.[55]

Another issue was the role of basic science research in the medical school. Welch observed in 1893 that in order to teach the scientific method "there is no one thing so essential as that the teacher should also be an investigator and should be capable of imparting something of the spirit of investigation to the student. The medical school should . . . do its part to advance medical science and art by encouraging original work, and by selecting as its teachers those who have the training and capacity for such work."[56]

Research in the basic medical sciences was seriously hampered by lack of funding. A few private foundations provide some research funds, but they could support only a few faculty members. The Weiskotten report carefully analyzed the research activities, which it defined quite liberally, in the basic science departments in the 1930s. They found that some degree of research was carried on in practically all of the higher ranking departments, but little or none occurred in the remainder. However, the growing number of American researchers made major contributions. Ben-David found that between 1850 and 1899, German scientists accounted for 46 percent of a list of medical discoveries compiled by Fielding Garrison, French scientists accounted for 14 percent, Americans 13 percent, and the English 10 percent. From 1900 to 1926, American scientists were responsible for 33 percent, Germans 30 percent, and the English and French 12 and 8 percent, respectively.[57]

Another major problem of the basic science departments concerned operating costs. Most of them employed at least one full-time faculty member and all of them used expensive laboratories. The clinical departments kept their costs low with volunteer and part-time teachers, and thereby subsidized the basic sciences. Each basic science department approached this economic dependency somewhat differently.

Anatomy. The movement of anatomists away from problems related to medicine during this period is shown by developments in the American Association of Anatomists, which was organized in 1888. The proportion of members with the M.D. degree declined from 88 percent of the 118 members in 1900 to 66 percent of the 440 members in 1924. The proportion of members teaching in medical schools who had M.D. degrees declined from 95 percent to 67 percent. Similar changes occurred in the content of papers presented at the annual meetings of the association. The papers on gross anatomy declined from 10 of a total of 12 in 1900 to 41 of a total of 112 in 1924. Papers on experimental topics became more popular, constituting 48 of the papers in 1924. Many anatomists found greater kinship with zoology and human biology than with medicine.[58]

For these reasons, surgeons felt that anatomists were no longer qualified to teach surgical anatomy. This led to decreased time for anatomy in the curriculum and general impoverishment for anatomy departments. The Weiskotten report said that the use of "young, part time practicing physicians as teachers is more common in the department of anatomy than in any of the other preclinical departments." Anatomy moved away from medical anatomy but paid a heavy price for it.[59]

Physiology. Physiology was one of the first basic medical sciences to offer laboratory teaching. The field grew slowly, as shown by the membership of the American Physiological Society. Organized in 1887, it took 25 years to reach 205 members. The development of electrocardiograms and basal metabolism tests in the 1920s demonstrated the clinical relevance of physiology and provided it with a limited service role in medical schools. However, the leading physiologists were more interested in scientific research than medical applications. Consequently, like anatomy, physiology suffered from low budgets, inadequate facilities, and many part-time faculty.[60]

Biochemistry. During the nineteenth century, chemistry courses in medical schools combined general chemistry and what was later called biochemistry. The discipline was unique among medical school subjects in its dependence on nonphysicians as instructors: in 1900, 29 percent of the faculty were not M.D.s, and 12 percent of the remainder held the Ph.D. degree as well as the M.D. degree. Many leading academic chemists were on medical school faculties.[61]

Once most medical students had previous college training in chemistry, medical school chemistry became limited to biochemistry. In 1909 at least 60 of 97 medical schools surveyed by the American Medical Association taught biochemistry, and textbooks and laboratory manuals were written shortly thereafter. The American Society of Biological Chemists was organized in 1906–1907, which indicated the growing academic perspective of the field. The proportion of members of the Society who also belonged to the AMA decreased from about 28 percent at its founding to less than 10 percent only a few years later. The Weiskotten study found that 39 of 66 biochemistry departments did not even have an M.D. at professorial rank in the mid-1930s.[62]

Biochemistry assumed a major service role in medical school hospitals. The clinical use of laboratory tests increased rapidly after 1910, and biochemists were responsible for urinalyses, toxicological examinations, and blood, digestive, respiratory, and other tests. By 1925, a review of the field expressed concern about the "tendency to subordinate the field to its practical applications and to teach not the fundamental principles illustrated by specific applications, but only the immediate applications themselves."[63]

The service role of biochemistry provided laboratory facilities and manpower that were also used for research. In the 1930s, the Weiskotten study found that 48 of 66 biochemistry departments had graduate students, and that "biochemical laboratories have been more productive, as evidenced by the number of publications, than those of other preclinical sciences." Only 9 departments had little or no research activity. Thus resources provided by service activities enabled biochemists to engage in research despite their heavy teaching and service responsibilities, something which other basic science departments felt could not be done.[64]

Pathology. Pathology was the only basic medical science to remain dominated by physicians, largely because the autopsy was refined to include bacteriological and serological findings that were of greater medical than academic significance. Pathology gradually became a medical specialty engaged in undertaking autopsies and histopathological examinations, primarily for cancer. Many pathology laboratories in medical schools and affiliated hospitals were used for service, teaching, and research. Research in pathology developed slowly. The American Society for Experimental Pathology increased from the initial 40 members in 1913 to only 400 as late as 1955.[65]

The teaching of pathology emphasized histopathology and the autopsy. The clinical-pathological conference was added about this time as a teaching technique in which pathologists verified or disproved the diagnoses of clinicians. A review of the field characterized the conference "as a very important feature of instruction [that] has done much to enable the student to visualize pathological lesions and to think in terms of pathological anatomy at the bedside." Courses in experimental pathology were also developed, but were not very popular.[66]

The service role of pathology reached overwhelming proportions after 1926, when the American College of Surgeons required accredited hospitals to hire qualified pathologists and to perform diagnostic tests and autopsies. The Weiskotten report observed a decade later that the hospital service responsibilities of pathology departments were often excessive: "Too many departments function essentially as diagnostic laboratories with members of the department carrying an almost impossible load imposed by responsibilities to a large group of hospitals." The result often was "inadequate opportunity to devote the necessary amount of time to teaching and research."[67]

Pharmacology. The traditional nineteenth century course on materia medica provided a taxonomy and description of drugs, their uses, and their methods of compounding. By the end of the century, synthetic drugs and experimental methods for examining their effects led to a new science, pharmacology. Many medical schools revised their teaching accordingly. However, pharmacology had virtually no service role and the primitive state of drug knowledge attracted the attention of few students. As a result, it was among the less influential basic science departments.[68]

Bacteriology. Bacteriology was the newest basic medical science and was making great strides in the diagnosis, prevention, and treatment of infectious diseases. A reviewer of the field wrote in 1925 that "even the public enjoys considerable familiarity with and great respect for bacteria." Bacteriology departments assumed a moderate service role in university hospitals, with seven of them serving as city or state bacteriology laboratories in the mid-1930s. For these reasons, bacteriology enjoyed a reasonable status in medical schools. Eighteen bacteriology departments also taught public health, preventive medicine, or hygiene, making bacteriology the only preclinical science to expand its teaching responsibility so broadly.[69]

This review has shown that the basic medical science departments improved their position in the medical school in the early twentieth century. However, their status remained insecure because they were subsidized by the clinical departments. Those basic science departments that generated their own revenues though service activities had the most power in the medical school and sometimes did the most research. Consequently, service activities became the highest priority activities of most basic science departments.

The basic medical sciences became increasingly subspecialized during this period. The early programs of the American Physiological Society, according to a historian, "covered the whole range of the medical sciences, experimental physiology, physiological chemistry, histology, pharmacology, and pathology." Gradually, each of these fields established independent societies. In 1912, they formed the Federation of American Societies for Experimental Biology (later renamed the Union of Biological Societies). It was composed of the American Physiological Society, the American Society of Biological Chemists, the American Society for Pharmacology and Experimental Therapeutics, and, shortly thereafter, the American Society for Experimental Pathology.[70]

Relations between the basic medical sciences and clinical medicine grew more distant. The American Physiological Society held its early meetings jointly with the Congress of American Physicians and Surgeons, a federation of specialty medical societies. As the interests of the two groups diverged, they abandoned joint meetings. Clinicians complained that the basic medical sciences were losing interest in medicine. Harvey Cushing wrote in 1930:

> More and more the preclinical chairs in most of our schools have come to be occupied by men whose scientific interests may be quite unrelated to anything that obviously has to do with Medicine, some of whom, indeed, confess to a feeling that by engaging in problems that have an evident bearing on the healing art they lose caste among their fellows. They have come to have their own societies, separate journals of publication, a scientific lingo foreign to other ears, and are rarely seen in meetings of medical practitioners with whom they have wholly lost contact.[71]

Thus, the power structure of medical schools was changed because of new sources of funding. Increased support from government and endowments enabled basic science faculty members to pursue their own interests rather than those of medical students. The interests of basic science faculty members also increasingly diverged from those of the clinical faculty. Because clinical faculty members made a larger contribution to the medical school, their views were more influential.

8

Medical Education, 1900–1950: Clinical Teaching

The professionalization of academic medicine occurred in the clinical as well as the basic science curriculum. Full-time clinical faculty members replaced part-time faculty members in the wealthier schools. Medical specialties, many of which were rare outside the medical school, dominated the clinical courses. Clinical teaching, which was improved by more student contact with patients, occurred primarily in hospitals, whose patients were atypical of those seen in community practice. The growing importance of hospitals in medical education led to the construction of university hospitals.

Full-Time Clinical Teaching and German Medical Education

Early in the century, some leading basic medical scientists called for full-time faculty members in the clinical fields. They noted that full-time faculty members in the basic sciences had produced great scientific discoveries in Europe and had improved American basic science departments. In 1907, William Welch proposed that "the heads of the principal clinical departments, particularly the medical and the surgical, should devote their main energies and time to their hospital work and to teaching and investigating without the necessity of seeking their livelihood in a busy outside practice." Few clinicians endorsed this proposal. They found the costs prohibitive and disliked the German system of medical research and education on which it was based.[1]

Medical research in Germany was carried on, not in medical schools, but in government research institutes headed by medical school professors and staffed by researchers without faculty appointments. All of the researchers were basic medical scientists who were interested in basic research, not practical problems like bacteriology. Although the institutes monopolized the available laboratory and hospital facilities, they were not affiliated with medical schools, had no educational programs, and did not formally train students, although much informal training occurred. For these reasons, their research findings were seldom integrated into the medical school curriculum, and German medical students were not trained to do research.[2]

German medical schools had three faculty ranks. Each discipline was headed by one professor, who was a salaried employee of the state and also earned substantial amounts from student fees. Most professors had no institute appointments and did little or no research. Professors of the clinical subjects were permitted to have private practices, and, according to an American medical educator, the "leading" ones did not have "a particle of sympathy with the American full-time plan." The middle level faculty were the equivalent of American associate professors, and were also salaried full-time employees. At the bottom were the rapidly growing number of privatdozents, unsalaried instructors who taught private courses to medical students for fees and usually aspired to full-time faculty appointments. Some privatdozents were physicians with private practices, but others had positions in research institutes with neither job security nor the right to publish the results of their research without the approval of the head of the institute.[3]

The German medical school was marred by several factors. One was the autocratic control of the professors, especially over the privatdozents. Another was the professors' practice of teaching large lecture classes to obtain more student fees, which eliminated personal contact with students and reduced teaching by the other salaried faculty members. Faculty appointments were often based on factors other than ability. An American physician, James Herrick, wrote: "That promotions in Germany and Austria were often dependent on political partisanship, personal favoritism, wire-pulling, or racial prejudices I knew from my observations at Prague. It is clearly revealed to one who read the memoirs of Billroth, Strumpell, or Von Leyden." A last impediment was the limited power of the faculty, which had to present up to three names to the government for each faculty appointment. Ringer found that between 1817 and 1900, 322 of the 1,355 faculty appointments in theology, law, and medicine were made by the government against or without the faculties' recommendations.[4]

Medical students in Germany came largely from the propertied classes, unlike the United States, where medical schools prided themselves on admitting students from a wide range of social classes. All German higher education had a high degree of class consciousness and limited opportunities for the poor. In 1885, there were only 27,000 university students compared to 7.5 million children in German primary schools.[5]

American basic medical scientists studying in Germany were more ignorant of German medical education than American clinicians studying there. The former studied in research institutes, often in small towns, while the latter went to the large cities where the major German medical schools were located. The scientists came to Germany with postdoctoral educational goals well suited to the institutes' programs. They were often given favored treatment and were unconcerned with the institutes' lack of educational programs, intellectual narrowness, absence of applied research, weak relationships with the medical schools, and the professional insecurities of the privatdozents.[6] American clinicians, on the other hand, had more contact with medical students and the clinical faculty, and therefore could make a more realistic appraisal of German medical education. They found much there to dislike and little that could be adopted by American medical schools. Most of them reacted negatively to the idea of transplanting any aspect of German medical education to America.

Abraham Flexner, The Foundations, and the Full-Time Plan

Abraham Flexner, who was greatly influenced by William Welch, recommended in his report that clinical professors should be full-time faculty members without private practices. He made several suggestions to deal with the increased costs, one of which was that clinical faculty members accept lower incomes: "[T]heir salaries will be inadequate, i.e., less than they can earn outside—all academic salaries paid to the right men are. But there is no inherent reason why a professor of medicine should not make something of the financial sacrifice that the professor of physics makes: both give up something . . . in order to teach and to investigate." Another was to reduce the number of medical schools to 31, which no one took seriously. A last recommendation was "abundant benefaction" from private philanthropy.[7]

Flexner's appeal to philanthropy came at a time when the interests of philanthropists were changing. During the nineteenth century, wealthy donors made many contributions for local medical care, especially the construction of hospitals and dispensaries. However, the only major contribution to medical education was the Vanderbilt donation to the Columbia University medical school in the 1880s. The largest gift to the Harvard University medical school in the nineteenth century was a $400,000 bequest from a deceased faculty member.[8]

Philanthropists began to make major contributions for medical education and research early in the twentieth century. J. Pierpont Morgan and John D. Rockefeller contributed about $1 million each for a new campus for the Harvard University medical school. Rockefeller also established the Rockefeller Institute in New York, which opened in 1903, and contributed $6 million to it by 1910. In 1902, Andrew Carnegie incorporated the Carnegie Institution of Washington with a $10 million gift. The Rockefeller Institute was primarily concerned with medical research, the Carnegie Institution with biological research. A number of other independent medical research institutes named after their donors were also established, including the Phipps Institute in Philadelphia, the Hooper Institute in San Francisco, the Cushing Institute in Cleveland, and the Sprague Memorial Institute in Chicago. Most of them had insufficient researchers, graduate students, and other resources. Donors soon realized that their contributions were used more effectively in medical schools.[9]

Gifts to medical schools grew rapidly as additional philanthropic foundations were established. By 1919, at least 26 foundations were providing funds primarily for medical research, often for specific diseases. Seventeen of them were associated with individual universities. In the 1930s they were joined by the citizen-supported foundations, such as the National Foundation for Infantile Paralysis and the American Cancer Society. Foundations contributed an estimated $154 million directly to medical schools up to 1938.[10]

Most of this aid did not improve the problem areas in medical education. Little concern was shown for the medical needs of different geographic areas, because few western or southern medical schools received any funds. Little aid was given to medical schools that emphasized the training of general practitioners and physicians for rural and other underserved areas. The disease-oriented foundations had highly focused research interests and little concern with medical education. The great bulk of foundation assistance went to a small number of wealthy urban medical schools that trained specialists. The major exception was the General Education Board, which aided several public medical schools outside of the northeastern states.[11]

The foundations favored the elite medical schools largely because the foundation staffs wanted to enhance the good name of the foundation as well as to promote research. They recognized the value of making awards to famous scientists at prestigious medical schools. In 1927 William Pusey, a leading physician and medical educator, called these scientists "an ultrascientific group" for whom "research and scholarship [were] the ends of medicine:"

> Back of this ultrascientific group whose influence I am now considering—largely responsible for it, in fact—is a certain sort of influence in the great philanthropic foundations. . . . [T]his influence will have it that medicine must be all science, and it is using its enormous weight to bring this about. It has been able to get overemphasis on this point even outside strictly academic circles in medicine. . . . [T]here has been too much insistence on one policy in medicine; on one pattern in the organization of medical education and research; on one sort of man, on one sort of training. . . .
>
> Men may properly have as much pride and pleasure in an intellectual technical vocation as in one primarily scientific. The technical pursuit may require just as interesting and just as high intellectual exercises as the scientific one.[12]

The most influential foundation supporting medical education was the General Education Board, organized in 1902 by John D. Rockefeller. The board contributed over $61 million to 24 medical schools up to 1928, and another $33 million to the same medical schools from then until its termination in 1960. Over one-half of the $90 million expended up to 1936 went to only 5 medical schools—Cornell, Chicago, Johns Hopkins, Vanderbilt, and Washington University. During its first years, the General Education Board had no specific goals for medical education. However, in 1912 Flexner joined its staff. In 1919 he persuaded Rockefeller to set aside $50 million to implement the proposals in his report, especially those concerning full-time clinical faculty members.[13]

Meanwhile, William H. Welch was also working toward the appointment of full-time clinical faculty members. As a member of the Board of Scientific Directors of the Rockefeller Institute, he advised the Board in 1907 to recommend that Rockefeller aid those medical schools that had approximately the same standards as the Johns Jopkins University medical school. In 1911, after years of effort, he successfully urged the trustees of the Johns Hopkins University to support full-time clinical faculty, subject to the consent of the medical school faculty.[14]

The Johns Hopkins University medical school was an unlikely choice for a plan to forbid clinical faculty members from having private practices. The school had opened in 1893 with the highest admission requirements and the most advanced curriculum in the nation. Its faculty consisted of some of the country's leading clinicians and medical scientists. The clinical faculty, including the professors of medicine (William Osler), surgery (William S. Halsted), and gynecology (Howard A. Kelly), were in great demand as private practitioners. Osler reminisced that Halsted's fees for private patients "were enormous. . . . The natives were simply aghast at them. . . . He really had not much conscience in [the] matter of charges, but he had the feeling of a high class artist about the value of his work.'' Kelly ''had probably the largest professional income of any surgeon in the United States. He charged very large fees, $10,000 and $12,000 for some of his more important operations. He seemed conscienceless in the matter.'' Osler was not far behind his colleagues in his own earnings.[15]

The first generation of clinicians trained by these men, who included Lewellys F. Barker, Francis W. Peabody, J. M. T. Finney, William S. Thayer, Harvey Cushing, and Hugh Young, were in great demand as private practitioners and were excellent teachers. Osler once observed that the achievements of the Johns Hopkins University medical school made ''a splendid record, but much more brilliant from the clinical than from the laboratory side.''[16]

By 1911, Osler had left Hopkins and Kelly and Halsted were nearing the end of their careers. Some of the younger clinicians favored a full-time plan, and the remainder were no match for Welch, who was now the preeminent medical educator in the United States. Welch had been preparing to implement a full-time plan since 1905, when Osler stepped down as professor of medicine and physician-in-chief of the hospital. As his replacement, Lewellys Barker was hired from the University of Chicago, where he had been professor of anatomy since 1900. Barker acknowledged that his major qualification for the job was his support for the full-time plan for clinical faculty. Certainly his record at Chicago did not qualify him for the position. Barker did not have a license to practice medicine in Illinois from his arrival there in 1900 until November, 1904. Thus Osler, the most eminent professor of medicine in the nation, was replaced by someone who had not practiced medicine for the previous five years.[17]

In 1911 Flexner wrote a private report to the General Education Board urging them to support a full-time clinical faculty plan at the Johns Hopkins University medical school. He criticized the school's clinical faculty for their ''lucrative private practices'' at the expense of teaching and research:

> The clinicians have with very few exceptions proved too easy victims to the encroachments of profitable practice. Not only has productive work been sacrificed to private professional engagements—routine teaching and hospital work go by the board when a large fee is in prospect. Classes are turned over to subordinates in order that the chief may leave town to see patients, not because they were scientifically interesting, but because they are pecuniarily worth while.[18]

In 1913, Welch, as acting president of Johns Hopkins University, announced the implementation of a full-time plan for clinical faculty in some departments. In response, the General Education Board agreed to contribute $1.5 million to defray the costs of the change. According to Barker, both Flexner and Welch (as well as Simon Flexner, Abraham's brother and head of the Rockefeller Institute) ''had much to do with the securing of funds from the Rockefeller Foundation'' for the plan.[19]

Edward Richardson, a part-time faculty member, has written that the plan was ''bitterly opposed, almost unanimously'' by the clinical faculty and alumni and ''enthusiastically endorsed by the entire preclinical faculty.'' The major issue was not the hiring of full-time faculty members, but the dismissal of the part-time faculty members. "If instead, the part time faculty had been permitted to continue their brilliant careers unmolested, and a research faculty of equal achievement and promise had been added, we would have voiced no objection, since [the school] would have been immeasurably strengthened."[20]

Replacing part-time faculty members with full-time faculty proved to be a long and arduous process. The first full-time professorship, in medicine, was offered in turn to Barker and Thayer, both of whom rejected it. It was then accepted by a distinguished clinician and teacher, Theodore Janeway, who resigned after three years because of dissatisfaction with his low earnings and lack of clinical opportunities. After a long and difficult hiatus, Warfield Longcope accepted the position in 1922 and served for many years. In 1918 the professor of surgery, William Halsted, died, and the position was offered to an eminent local surgeon, J. M. T. Finney, who refused it but served as interim professor for three years until someone else was found. Full-time department heads were appointed in obstetrics in 1919, psychiatry in 1923, ophthalmology in 1925, and others after 1945. A substantial number of other full-time appointments at lower leveles were also made during this period.[21]

The full-time plan exacerbated relations between the full-time and the part-time faculty. Richardson wrote: "[T]he former congenial and cordial atmosphere that always had pervaded the Hospital became rapidly altered into one of uninviting formality, if not thinly veiled hostility. The 'holier than thou' attitude became plainly discernible on all sides." According to Turner, a later dean of the medical school, the part-time faculty were "relegated to a secondary role in teaching, assigned the less attractive clinical tasks, and were often the forgotten men at promotion time." As late as 1946, a physician declined an appointment as head of the urology department because of the "spirit of antagonism and resistance" of the part-time faculty.[22]

The full-time plan also created difficulties for the university hospital. The hospital was sympathetic to the part-time faculty members because they cared for the thousands of dispensary patients and admitted practically all of the paying inpatients. However, under the full-time plan, the medical school denied many part-time faculty members who had served for years the right to admit their patients to the hospital. Part-time faculty also could not teach medical students on the wards, but only in the outpatient clinics. Mary part-time faculty members who held senior titles in the hospital were given medical school appointments at the lowest levels.[23]

The full-time plan adversely affected fund raising at the medical school. The part-time faculty, who were among the leading physicians in Baltimore, were often not only personally wealthy but had considerable influence over the contributions of wealthy residents. In the 1920s, when four private Baltimore hospitals raised $2.8 million, the Johns Hopkins medical school and hospital were able to raise only $458,000 of a campaign seeking $1.5 million, and $250,000 of that was given by a New York philanthropist.[24]

The medical school justified its policies by claiming that the emphasis had to be on research at all costs because the school was training researchers. In fact, it was training clinicians. A 1916 student of 456 graduates of the classes of 1897–1906 found that 80 percent were in practice, 9 percent were in teaching or research, and the remainder were in other occupations or had died.[25] There is no reason to believe that these proportions changed significantly in later years.

The full-time plan never achieved its goal of replacing clinicians with outstanding researchers. Recruiting committees frequently had to choose between skilled researchers who were mediocre clinicians and able clinicians who did little research. They did not always choose the researchers. Furthermore, the appointment of full-time faculty members did not assure eminence in research. Hopkins lost its position as the leading research-oriented medical school to Harvard during the 1920s. This was partly due to Harvard's greater resources, but Harvard never adopted a full-time plan like that at Hopkins.

Early in 1914, the General Education Board (GEB) decided to devote all of its medical education funds to installing full-time clinical plans at medical schools. Flexner was put in charge, and over $8 million was spent in the next few years on full-time plans at Washington University in St. Louis, Yale University, the University of Chicago, and Vanderbilt University. The grants were awarded on the condition that the funds would be returned if the full-time plan was altered. These medical schools all had several characteristics in common. All were at prestigious private universities of the kind favored by foundations. All had poorly endowed medical schools, and were easily enticed into accepting the full-time plans by the lure of funds. Two of them, the University of Chicago and Vanderbilt University, overreached themselves and were forced to abandon the plan.[26]

When the GEB approached the Harvard and Columbia medical schools to fund full-time plans there, it received a very different reception. Both schools were well endowed and not in desperate need. Harvard refused an offer of $1.5 million to adopt the plan in 1913. Columbia refused a proposal to install a full-time plan in 1918, but later accepted $2 million for a compromise plan which began in 1921 and quickly turned out to be unworkable. It was significantly altered the next year.[27]

In order to demonstrate the value of a full-time plan, Flexner convinced George Eastman to join the GEB in establishing a medical school at the University of Rochester that would use the plan. It is difficult to understand why Flexner, who wanted to reduce the number of medical schools, would promote one in Rochester when others were already located in nearby Albany, Syracuse, and Buffalo. The full-time plan at Rochester turned out to be unsatisfactory to all concerned and was modified in 1931.[28]

The heavy-handed tactics of the GEB created much resentment. Charles Eliot, president of Harvard University, attacked their methods when he retired in 1917. In 1919, the president of the foundation that sponsored the Flexner report criticized the GEB's policy of binding the schools with contractual agreements. Arthur Bevan of the AMA called the plan a "grotesque proposition" for permitting fees from paying patients "not to go to the individual who renders the service but to the institution," and for placing medical schools in competition with community physicians for the care of the "well-to-do and rich." Newspapers faulted it for depriving the public of outstanding clinicians.[29]

The full-time plan was also attacked by medical educators. The most common criticism (with which Welch agreed) was that the plan could be afforded only by the so-called "foundation schools." Medical schools that agreed to the GEB's conditions complained that could not hire many outstanding clinicians and teachers who refused to work under a strict full-time arrangement. Both proponents and opponents agreed on the need for full-time department chairmen, but more to compensate them for their administrative responsibilities than to avoid private practice and encourage research.[30]

Full-time faculty members were often accused of having inferior clinical skills. One physician observed that "there has been a tendency to accept for clinical heads, especially in schools of medicine 'subsidized by the foundations,' laboratory trained men who have had little or no clinical experience except from a limited hospital residency." Some clinicians with full-time appointments complained that they had insufficient opportunity to improve or retain their clinical skills. Theodore Janeway, who resigned as the first full-time professor of medicine at Johns Hopkins over this issue, wrote:

> The physician . . . must be a skilful diagnostician, and command . . . the technic of modern treatment. . . . The surgeon must be a dexterous and resourceful operator, the obstetrician an accomplished midwife. Only long practical training can make them masters, and only constant application of their knowledge can keep them such. They must be men of sound judgment based on long personal experience. . . . These qualities are not acquired in the laboratory but at bedside and operating table and in the postmortem room.[31]

The clinical activities of full-time faculty members took place entirely in the hospitals used by the medical schools. David Edsall, the dean of the Harvard University medical school, criticized this in a letter to Flexner in 1919:

> [W]e can not grow successive crops of good clinical teachers and investigators without actually seeing to it that they . . . get contact with the differing types of disorders and the methods of therapeutics that are used with the nonhospital class of the community. . . . [F]ine hospital interns and young instructors who have had only hospital experience with ward cases have so very distorted an idea of what good medical service to the community is that were I to choose between continuing the present conditions . . . or . . . having medical education entirely dominated by a group of men who had been brought up strictly in hospital wards . . . I should feel the [former] was right for the public.[32]

Edsall believed that the relationship between the physician and ward patients in a large bureaucratic hospital was different from that between a physician and his private patients. He observed that "skill in practice . . . is retained not by practice alone, but by undivided and keen responsibility in practice." Reginald Fitz wrote that "A doctor with too much hospital experience is always narrow. He handles but a relatively limited type of clinical material. . . . In order to keep up his skill and vision, and to make his teaching as broad and inclusive as possible, he must find a certain amount of time in which to peg away at taking case histories, making physical examinations and deciding medical problems for his own patients, both in and outside the hospitals."[33]

Another criticism of the full-time plan was the possible exploitation of the full-time faculty by the medical school. If the fees of private patients went to the hospital or the medical school, the faculty might be presumed to care for large numbers of private patients in order to increase the income of the hospital or the school, thereby distorting the plan's purpose.

The full-time plan also deprived the local community of a close relationship with the medical school and medical students. Clinical faculty members and the university hospital were not longer resources available to most residents and local physicians. Medical students no longer learned about community medical practices from part-time faculty members or worked in local medical institutions, which was important to those who planned to practice there. The medical school was also deprived of the stability provided by the part-time faculty at a time when many full-time faculty members were geographically mobile.[34]

Alternatives to the Full-Time Plan

An alternative to the strict full-time plan, later called the "geographic full-time" plan, was adopted about this time by the Harvard University medical school and quickly spread to other medical schools. As described by Arthur Bevan in 1915, the plan specified that "all the man's work in medicine is to be done under one roof. He is not to have any consultations outside of the hospital. He has an office in the hospital . . . [A] limited number of private beds are set aside, and the clinician takes care of a certain number of private patients in these beds, with the same team of assistants and laboratory workers and all that he employs in taking care of his charity [and teaching] cases."[35]

The geographic full-time plan had several consequences. Its impact on surgeons was small, because their patients were hospitalized anyway. Its most significant effect was on internists and general practitioners, who could no longer visit patients in their homes. It had the advantage of making all private patients available for teaching, unlike the private patients treated by faculty members outside the medical school.

Arrangements similar to the geographical full-time plan were often adopted as a convenience for the faculty. In 1913, the Massachusetts General Hospital constructed the Phillips House largely for the private patients of the hospital's full-time medical staff, many of whom were also on the faculty of the Harvard medical school. When the Columbia University medical school moved its campus about 1925, it constructed offices to enable part-time faculty members to see private patients at the new campus. The offices turned out to be popular with the faculty and profitable to the medical school.[36]

After 1919 the General Education Board changed its position on the full-time plan. Its 1919 annual report questioned whether the plan was worth the "very great" cost and observed that many other aspects of medical schools were more in need of improvement, including "well-equipped, well-supported and well-manned laboratories, modern hospitals owned by or properly affiliated with the university, and a strengthening of the educational as against the professional motive on the clinical side." In 1920 the GEB aided the University of Cincinnati and Flexner personally hired a geographic full-time surgeon for the school. In 1924 an agreement was reached with Harvard medical school that permitted geographic full-time appointments. In 1925, the GEB modified its plan with Columbia medical school to permit the faculty to choose among strict full-time (with supplemental salaries from GEB), geographic full-time, or part-time appointments. In 1927, the board relieved those schools who had signed binding agreements with it of their strict full-time obligations. Unrestricted funding was also given to other medical schools.[37]

The strict full-time plan spread slowly during this period. The Weiskotten report in the mid-1930s found that all of the 20 highest ranking departments of medicine had at least one strict full-time faculty member, compared to only 1 of the 10 lowest ranking departments. Full-time faculty members were also found in many surgery, pediatrics, radiology, and obstetrics and gynecology departments, 17 neurology and psychiatry departments, and 8 to 10 of about 66 ophthalmology, dermatology, and otolaryngology departments. Meanwhile, medical schools with strict full-time plans often moved away from them. At the Johns Hopkins University medical school, the department of surgery permitted geographic full-time appointments in the 1940s and took other liberties with the full-time plan.[38]

Medical schools continued to increase the use of their facilities for patient care by faculty members. Some of them established private pay clinics, partly to provide additional income to faculty members through higher salaries or separate fees. While the clinics were originally designed to serve patients unable to pay high fees to specialists, they sometimes proved to be profit-making enterprises for the faculty and medical school.[39]

Although Flexner became more liberal about clinical faculty appointments, he continued to be critical of the earnings of clinical faculty members. He wrote in 1925: "[T]he clinical sciences cannot be prosecuted in the spirit of the university unless clinical teachers practically identify themselves in respect to income and scale of living with the university rather than with the medical profession. . . . It remains to be seen whether medicine can be generally converted into a university discipline, or whether proximity to a prosperous practicing profession will result in professional rather than academic standards of living." Most clinical faculty members took a dubious view of academic standards of living.[40]

Clinical Departments

Significant disparities existed among the clinical faculties of medical schools. At most schools, departments tended to be small, poorly organized, and composed largely of part-time faculty members. In the wealthy schools, the large departments with full-time faculty members became, according to Harvey Cushing in 1930, "miniature medical schools complete in themselves, each striving for its separate institute, its own several laboratories for experimentation or diagnosis, its own library, separate organs of publication, and so on." They were restrained only by the "capacity of the university purse."[41]

Research activities of clinical departments varied widely. The Weiskotten report found that the highest ranked departments in medicine, surgery, pediatrics, and obstetrics and gynecology, were actively engaged in research, but that most of the others were not. A 1935 review of clinical research publications concluded that "the volume . . . has been large, the quality uneven, but some of it well up to the standards of the pre-clinical departments." One problem was finding clinicians qualified to do research. The shortage of available researchers rapidly pushed up salaries, so that by 1929, full-time clinical professors were earning over $15,000 at the leading schools.[42]

Clinical Teaching and the Clerkship

The teaching of clinical subjects was marked by significant variations among schools. A study of the teaching of surgery in the 1930s found widespread agreement about the basic topics, but a bewildering variety of surgical courses. Some schools introduced the subject in the second year while most began teaching it in the third year. The use of didactic instruction varied widely. At the University of Vermont, as at most of the less affluent schools, it was heavily used in the third year and still important in the fourth. At Harvard in the 1920s, lectures and drill sessions in clinical subjects occurred in the third year. At Johns Hopkins, crowded ward walks were used in the 1920s until their unwieldiness forced their replacement by traditional amphitheater clinics.[43]

Medical schools also differed in their implementation of the clinical clerkship, largely because many of them did not have access to enough hospital beds. In 1925, a reviewer reported that it was implemented in the "higher grade schools." The Weiskotten report found a decade later that medical schools "varied greatly in the duration, extent and character of the assignments, responsibilities and supervision given the students during their clerkships." Another study about the same time found that three-fourths of the medical schools placed the third-year students in the outpatient department and the fourth-year students in the inpatient wards, with the remaining schools reversing the procedure. In the ward clerkship at the higher ranking schools, according to the Weiskotten report, "students were on call at all times and were assigned patients on their admission to the hospital. They were held accountable for the medical literature relating to their cases, were required to present and discuss their patients on rounds or at clinics and were responsible for following their progress during their stay in the hospital.[44]

One major limitation of the clerkship was the practice of assigning clerks according to the hospital's service needs rather than the student's educational needs. Clerks spent much of their time, according to Atwater, doing " 'scut'—the simpler diagnostic and therapeutic procedures such as phlebotomies, blood counts, urinalysis, stool examinations, lumbar punctures, thoracenteses, paracenteses, and, later, electrocardiograms." Most of these procedures could be learned in a short time, yet students did them for months on end.[45]

The clerkship raised major questions about the care of patients by medical students that were rarely addressed by medical schools. A history and physical examination performed by a student might include serious errors or omissions. Repeated examinations of the same patient by different students could fatigue the patient and aggravate his condition. The student might perform unnecessary tests on the patient that could be painful or dangerous. A student's treatment of a patient might not be carried out optimally or safely.[46] Despite these risks, few medical schools had formal orientation programs for clerks, systematic mechanisms to monitor the performance of clerks, or close faculty supervision of clerks.

As the clerkship developed, questions arose about its overlap with the basically similar internship. Medical schools could not design their clerkships to minimize redundancies with internships, because the latter occurred primarily at nonmedical school hospitals and varied greatly among themselves in content. Part of the problem was the unwillingness of medical schools to assume greater responsibility for internships. Most refused to become involved in the training of interns at nonmedical school hospitals, which left a gap that was filled by the AMA Council on Medical Education.[47]

A last problem was the distorted view of medicine that students learned in the hospital. Hospital medicine, with its large staff, extensive equipment, and elaborate tests, differed greatly from the type of medicine practiced in the patient's home or the physician's office. The student learned little about the hospital patient's home life, financial situation, occupation, and other factors that affected the cause, treatment, and possible recurrence of his condition. Furthermore, hospital illnesses were atypical of community medicine. David Edsall wrote about the clerkship in 1924: "I do not believe that present conditions are satisfactory. The undefined and the mild conditions, early chronic disease, and the like, will constitute [the physician's] chief work always, and especially in his early practise. They are the most difficult of all to achieve real skill in. . . . I do not think that he now gets as much training in the milder things as he should have."[48]

Outpatient Teaching

Most observers shared Edsall's view that the best corrective for ward teaching was the outpatient department, where clinical teaching had occurred in the nineteenth century. The Commission on Medical Education maintained that the "outpatient services provide the best opportunities for presenting the health needs of the community and the demands of practice under the most satisfactory supervision." A medical school dean observed that in the outpatient department the student "learns what the care costs in the time and effort of the physician and nurse. He learns something of the accessory costs of medical care, including nursing services, drugs, laboratory procedures, and hospitalization. . . . He learns that . . . serious illness [of] the person in moderate circumstances may mean financial ruin or the acceptance of charity." Another dean wrote that in the outpatient department the student

> sees the beginings of disease, not the end results, and he learns to recognize subjective symptoms. . . . He learns the management of patients; the friends and relatives, and the control of the unruly child or the frightened mother. He is face to face with the human side of medicine—with the responsibility. . . . Instead of feeling helpless because of lack of hospital facilities, he must acquire a definite and clear-cut idea of the wide possibilities of office and ambulatory management.[49]

Outpatient departments were seldom used in an effective manner. The teachers were part-time junior-level faculty members who were not permitted to provide hospital care for those of their outpatients who were admitted to the hospital. The facilities were unsatisfactory. One critic observed that "too often the outpatient clinic has been allowed to carry on in surroundings and with an equipment which at best is a very poor makeshift and which would not be tolerated in the hospital." For example, the outpatient department at the Johns Hopkins hospital opened in 1889, grew slowly for its first 25 years, and rapidly thereafter. The head of the social service department described the facility in 1909 as a "small one-story dispensary building, with its foul odors, rooms dark and badly ventilated, used by one clinic in the morning and by another in the afternoon, with only one nurse in the whole General Dispensary." Outpatient instruction was provided in physical diagnosis, surgery, and nervous diseases. Most clinics kept separate records of their patients, so that a physician in one clinic did not know what was being done to the patients in another.[50]

Many medical schools continued to be major providers of outpatient care. In 1930, the Johns Hopkins Hospital handled 36 percent of 633,029 outpatient visits in the city of Baltimore (population 804,878), and another 16 percent were treated at the University of Maryland hospital. The annual cost of the Hopkins outpatient department was $206,600, while income from patients amounted to $116,400.[51]

Outpatient departments were often treated as the stepchildren of their hospitals. The Johns Hopkins hospital outpatient department was organized into the same departments as the inpatient services, the major ones being medicine, surgery, gynecology, obstetrics, psychiatry, and pediatrics. Each was further subdivided into as many as six specialty clinics. Every department was formally headed by the chief of service of the same inpatient department, but part-time faculty members carried out the actual work. An internal study in 1931 found a "surprising lack of contact" between the outpatient staff and their counterparts in the inpatient service in the same specialty and recommended that more full-time faculty members be assigned to the outpatient services. During the 1930s, according to Turner, "the hurried scramble of the outpatient clinics, the hopeless social situation that mediated the health care of so many outpatients, and the less than satisfactory educational operation mounted for third year medical students in this setting gave the outpatient department a low priority" for the department chairmen.[52]

These problems, which occurred in all medical schools, were the direct result of medical school organizational policies. Instead of a mix of full-time and part-time faculty on both the inpatient and outpatient services, rotated to assure the participation of everyone in both services, practically all of the part-time faculty were relegated to the outpatient clinics and denied access to the hospital wards, even to treat their outpatients. Although patients treated in outpatient departments were carefully selected for hospitalization for use in inpatient teaching, few schools selected outpatients for use in outpatient teaching and organized the outpatient educational program around those patients.

The differences between inpatient and outpatient teaching exemplified the new power structure in medical schools. At schools subsidized by the foundations, the full-time faculty had become the major force in the medical school and established its policies. In 1930, the Johns Hopkins University medical school had 60 full-time and 70 part-time clinical faculty. There, and at other schools, according to Edsall, "the department heads and other men of advanced positions usually throw off [outpatient] work almost completely as soon as they can."[53] Part-time faculty members were now relegated to doing what the full-time faculty did not want to do—teach in the outpatient department.

A few medical schools, primarily public institutions in states with large rural populations, developed programs that enabled students to care for more typical kinds of patients. At the University of Wisconsin beginning in 1926, students were assigned to work with a community physician in his community for 12 weeks in their senior year. Off-campus teaching occurred in several centers around the state. In the 1920s, the University of Georgia medical school operated a public program in its community to provide home care for the sick poor. A faculty member first visited each new patient, after which a fourth-year student was sent to the patient's home to take a history, perform a complete physical examination, and obtain and later analyze specimens of blood and urine. The student, under the supervision of the faculty member, visited the patient daily for the duration of the illness and had at least five patients under his care at all times.[54] These and other programs indicated that medical schools could develop useful and innovative forms of clinical teaching.

The Medical Specialities and Medical Education

The growth of clinical specialities after World War I raised many questions about the objectives of medical education. Some suggested that the medical school could no longer teach everything that was known about medicine and should restrict its teaching to fundamental concepts. The Commission on Medical Education proposed in its report:

> The medical course cannot produce a physician. It can only provide the opportunities for a student to secure an elementary knowledge of the medical sciences and their application to health problems, a training in the methods and spirit of scientific inquiry, and the inspiration and point of view which come from association with those who are devoting themselves to education, research, and practice.[55]

Others proposed that medical schools should train physicians for general practice. A committee of the Association of American Medical Colleges observed in 1910:

> The function of the medical schools is to train general practitioners for the proper care of the sick public. In its undergraduate department it should aim first to teach with sufficient thoroughness a knowledge of the common things every doctor must be able to do to meet the every-day demands of the public. Beyond this as much may be taught as time permits and the capacity and preparation of the individual student warrants. It follows that some things now included in "required" courses should be made post-graduate or optional. . . . The too early limitation to one field of study by those who think they want to become "specialists" is especially to be decried.[56]

A third perspective was that of the specialists who now dominated the medical school clinical faculties. They wanted the curriculum to be composed largely of courses in the specialties. Their approach prevailed because they had the most influence over the decision. In the well-endowed schools, specialists comprised the full-time clinical faculty. In schools employing part-time clinical faculty, the specialists provided beds for teaching in affiliated hospitals and brought badly needed paying patients into the university hospital. As a result, the number of hours devoted to the specialties increased significantly, partly by extending the school year and partly by cutting down on the hours devoted to courses like anatomy.[57]

Teaching in the specialties varied widely among medical schools. Most medical schools gave short introductory courses of lectures in each specialty in the third year and rotated the student through specialty clinics in the fourth year. Others used only one of those methods, and a few taught the specialties in elective courses. A common criticism was the lack of integration of the material. Ebaugh and Rymer observed:

> Too much detail is presented as each department tries to teach its whole field to every student; each instructor is so engrossed with his own specialty that he loses perspective and attempts to crowd all of his subject into his course. Subjects become important; forgotten is their relation to the whole curriculum, their part in painting a unified picture of patients. This tendency is an inevitable outgrowth of the great increase in knowledge in all fields of medicine and of the growing specialization among medical practitioners.[58]

Specialization also led to an emphasis on the details of the specialty. The Commission on Medical Education found that recent graduates believed that "too much of the clinical teaching is from the standpoint of the specialist and on rare diseases. Insufficient attention is given to the ordinary needs of most patients." Highly technical procedures used by specialists were emphasized instead of the basic techniques of clinical medicine. The commission concluded: "Students should be made to realize from the beginning of their clinical studies that the diagnosis in a large majority of illnesses can be made on the basis of a searching history, a thorough physical examination, relatively simple laboratory determinations, and the thoughtful consideration of the problem presented. The needs of a majority of patients can be solved by well recognized, relatively simple clinical methods."[59]

Specialists were rarely interested in research. Most were part-time faculty members with private practices who found that a medical school appointment was an effective way to attract paying patients. Even those with research interests, as one educator observed, were "lured into lucrative practice."[60]

Specialists pressed for close affiliations between medical schools and hospitals because they were highly dependent on hospitals. They used hospitals to treat their patients, do research, and obtain patients for teaching. Affiliations between medical schools and hospitals thus became a major issue during this period, overshadowing even the full-time plan.

Medical Schools and Affiliated Hospitals

Early in the century few medical schools had formal affiliations with hospitals. When the AMA carried out its inspection of medical schools in 1906–1907, only 6 medical schools had hospital privileges where medical students could examine patients and write histories (i.e., clerkships) and 5 other schools could engage in ward walks at hospitals. Another 88 had clinics in hospital amphitheaters either regularly or occasionally, and 55 had no hospital connections. These figures do not include the many hospital staff appointments of individual faculty members, which was the standard means of providing hospital instruction.[61]

During the next two decades, medical schools greatly increased the number of their hospital affiliations. In 1927, 317 hospitals were affiliated in varying degrees with medical schools, and 82 of them were located within three blocks of the medical school. Forty-nine of the hospitals were owned and operated by medical schools, and 77 others gave medical schools total or substantial authority to use patients for educational purposes. A study of 548 New York City hospitals in 1928 found that affiliation was more common among wealthier hospitals: 16 of the 31 New York City hospitals with endowments of $2 million or more were affiliated closely with medical schools as teaching hospitals. Leading medical schools often had multiple hospital affiliations, while many lower ranking medical schools did not have access to enough hospital beds for proper teaching. The Weiskotten report found that the 10 lowest ranked schools averaged only 2 beds per student in the mid-1930s.[62]

Affiliations between hospitals and medical schools usually involved financial considerations. The Weiskotten report found that some medical schools paid hospitals for teaching, while other hospitals reimbursed medical schools for the patient care provided by full- or part-time faculty members. Affiliation could produce significant economies for hospitals with salaried staff members, because the medical school usually paid part of the salaries of those staff members who taught students.[63]

Public hospitals, which were understaffed and underfunded, were more likely than private hospitals to affiliate with medical schools. The Weiskotten report found that in the mid-1930s 40 of 63 medical schools studied used public hospitals for teaching. By 1940, 49 of 67 medical schools (14 of 27 public schools and 35 of 40 private schools) reporting to a survey were associated with a city hospital or other government hospital that functioned as a city hospital.[64] Private hospitals tended to have fewer staffing problems, so that they were less willing to accept the medical schools' conditions for affiliation. These often included appointing the chiefs of every hospital service as well as all of the attending physicians and house officers.

A major problem for medical schools was that no single hospital had patients in all of the different specialties. The Johns Hopkins hospital dealt with this problem in the 1920s by establishing clinics within the hospital in pediatrics, psychiatry, urology, obstetrics and gynecology, and ophthalmology. By 1928 only 100 of the hospital's 740 beds were in general medicine and surgery, which was insufficient for teaching. The hospital was forced to exclude patients with some common illnesses, like fractures, because they occupied beds for too long a time. The specialty clinics were also inadequately endowed and underfunded. Beds in some of them remained unoccupied for years after their construction for lack of funds. During the depression the hospital virtually closed its social service department as an alternative to reducing the number of beds.[65] For these reasons, the Hopkins approach was rarely used elsewhere.

The more common approach among the leading medical schools was to develop a close affiliation with a number of private hospitals, with the combined facility known as an academic medical center. In the 1920s, Edward Harkness, a major philanthropist of medical schools, provided funding for the relocation of the Columbia University medical school to a site in New York City which also included space for the Presbyterian Hospital, the Vanderbilt Clinic, and the Sloan Maternity Hospital. They were later joined by the Neurological Institute, Babies Hospital, the New York Orthopedic Hospital, and the Municipal Board of Health building. The second academic medical center was established in New York City in 1929 when Cornell University medical school and the New York Hospital built a similar complex with joint resources of $60 million. Both centers were delayed and hospital-medical school relationships marred for years by distrust engendered by Flexner's efforts to get the schools to adopt a full-time plan.[66]

Academic medical centers enabled clinical teaching of medical students to be concentrated in a limited geographic area and reduced the affiliation arrangements involved. They also attracted outstanding physicians. According to Lepore, the Columbia-Presbyterian medical center in the 1930s was "one of the finest if not the best center for clinical medicine in the world." It had available a large pool of strict full-time, geographic full-time, part-time, and volunteer faculty who worked without the rigid distinctions that existed at Johns Hopkins.[67]

On the other hand, academic medical centers had many problems, Even the Columbia-Presbyterian center did not have enough patients to teach all the specialties to undergraduates, and the medical school was required to use at least six other affiliated hospitals. Another problem, according to S. S. Goldwater, was that medical centers, "by their stupendous size and the very terms of their organization," made efficient operation impossible. They intensified the problems of medical specialization, separated clinical departments from each other, and greatly reduced cooperation among physicians.[68]

The major problems of affiliated hospitals for medical schools concerned the hospital staff. Early in the century, staff members were unpaid and served terms of three consecutive months, after which they were off duty for the remainder of the year to pursue their private practices. As late as the 1920s, this was the dominant system of staffing in New York City hospitals.[69] The rotating staff system adversely affected teaching because instructors were replaced in the middle of the course. It created problems for research because physicians could not study their patients over any length of time. Patient care suffered because responsibility for patients changed when the new staff took over. These problems were eventually solved by the use of faculty members as year-round staff members.

A source of friction that was never fully resolved was the medical school's role in making hospital staff appointments and policies. In order to use a hospital for teaching, medical schools had to give faculty appointments to the existing staff physicians or convince the hospital to appoint medical school faculty members to the staff. Medical schools disliked the first alternative because it did not provide hospital appointments for their faculty members. The second alternative had the disadvantage of discouraging hospital staff members from participating in teaching activities. Medical schools also encountered resistance from voluntary hospitals when they tried to use the private patients of staff members for teaching.

Full-time faculty members had greater difficulty in obtaining hospital staff appointments than part-time faculty members. Many part-time faculty members were highly regarded local physicians with large private practices who could obtain hospital appointments on favorable terms. Full-time faculty members lacked the private practices that would give them leverage in hospital appointments. Consequently, the proponents of the full-time system became advocates of university-owned hospitals.

University Hospitals

Many medical schools were able to construct their own hospitals at this time. By the mid-1930s, 35 of 66 four-year medical schools studied by the Weiskotten commission had hospitals owned by the university or a closely related corporation. Sixteen of the hospitals were government owned. The rationale for university hospitals and faculty control was explained by James C. White:

> Hospitals should be conducted . . . not on such narrow interpretation of their highest objects as to how many sick persons have been relieved in the year alone, but how far through them has medical knowledge been so advanced that there shall be fewer sick and larger percentages of recoveries hereafter. Both the immediate practical success and the grander development of the hospital in the future rest accordingly with the physician alone. To him belongs the credit, to him should be given the untrammelled guidance of the hospital toward such humane ends.[70]

These arguments failed to recognize the economic realities of hospital care. In order to obtain patients for teaching, university hospitals became major providers of hospital care to the indigent. For example, in 1932, 752,710 days of free inpatient care were provided to the poor in Baltimore. Forty-nine percent of the days were provided in the municipal hospitals, 13 percent in the Johns Hopkins hospital, and 5 percent in the University of Maryland hospital. Forty-four percent of the patients admitted to the Johns Hopkins hospital and 42 percent of those admitted to the University of Maryland hospital were free patients.[71]

The prevalence of charity patients in university hospitals produced enormous financial burdens that were dealt with in a variety of ways. Governments owned almost one-half of the university hospitals and subsidized the care of those patients. Some states also aided private medical school hospitals. Pennsylvania, one of the most munificent, provided between 30 and 47 percent of the funding for the University of Pennsylvania, Jefferson, and Hahnemann medical school hospitals in 1910, and between 11 and 26 percent of their funding in 1924. In 1931, the city of Baltimore and the state of Maryland provided about 3 percent of the income of Johns Hopkins hospital and 30 percent of the income of the University of Maryland hospital to pay for the treatment of indigent patients. Another source of income was private patients, who provided two-thirds of the funding in the three Philadelphia medical school hospitals in 1924 and the two Baltimore medical school hospitals in

1930. Endowments, gifts, and university funds were vital to the survival of some private medical school hospitals. In the 1920s, the Johns Hopkins hospital received almost $12 million from the General Education Board, the Carnegie Foundation, and E. S. Harkness for hospital construction and charity care.[72]

The financial problems might have been worthwhile had university hospitals actually provided the patients needed for training students and carrying out research. They did not. Financial exigencies forced many university hospitals to admit paying patients regardless of their educational and research value. Control of the hospitals was often taken out of the hands of the medical school and vested in independent boards to obtain funding. The Weiskotten report found that in the mid-1930s only 23 of the 35 medical schools with their own hospitals had adequate control of them and that many of the hospitals were "relatively small institutions." Even the large Johns Hopkins hospital was inadequate. In 1910 the medical school began to use the city hospital for teaching undergraduates, and regularly expanded its use of that hospital thereafter.[73]

The absence of a university hospital was not detrimental to many medical schools that lacked one. Harvard medical school did not own its own hospital, because, according to its dean, David Edsall, "we have such hearty cooperation in medical education and research from nine hospitals that there would be little academic advantage to the University even if it did actually own and administer them." The nine hospitals provided Harvard with many more patients from different backgrounds and with different illnesses than could ever be obtained in a single university hospital. They also freed the medical school from the need to administer a hospital and assume financial responsibility for the care of patients.[74]

This analysis has shown that the growth of university hospitals cannot be explained by their contribution to teaching and research. They grew because they provided important benefits to the faculty. They were conveniently located next to the medical school. Patients were admitted solely because the faculty members wanted them to be admitted. Faculty research activities were rarely subjected to questions of cost, utility, or ethicality. Faculty members had available the free labor of many residents and interns. Hospital administrators and boards of directors gave priority to faculty interests and were more subservient than administrators and boards in affiliated hospitals.

Thus by mid-century a revolution had occurred in the power structure of the medical school. Students, once a major source of power, now had to compete for admission and provided a minor part of the funding. Full-time clinical faculty members wrested control away from the part-time faculty in the better medical schools. They used that control to allocate the medical school's resources and endowment, appoint the staffs to the affiliated hospitals, and influence outside philanthropists, governments, and other sources of funding. Most of the remaining part-time faculty, who were specialists, shared the interests of the full-time faculty in such matters as hospital ownership and affiliations, hospital-based clinical teaching, and the emphasis on the specialties. Consequently, medical school faculty members increasingly viewed the world of medicine as totally encompassed by the medical school and its adjoining hospital.

V

MEDICAL SCHOOLS AFTER 1950

1953: It is increasingly the opinion of all medical educators that the financial support of our medical schools is inadequate, particularly if the needs of the nation for health and medical services are to be met in a manner consistent with our expanding body of scientific knowledge and the demands of our people.

WARD DARLEY (1953)

1980: What used to be a medical school, pure, simple, one color, and functional, like a Model T, . . . is now a complex, top-of-the-line, eight-cylinder, airconditioned, automatic transmission, six-miles-to-the-gallon academic medical center.

WARREN H. PEARSE (1980)

1980: There is little doubt that containing costs is the most serious current problem for academic health centers and their parent universities.

ASSOCIATION OF ACADEMIC HEALTH CENTERS (1980)

9

Medical Care After 1950

In the years after mid-century, declining mortality rates from infectious and other diseases increased both life expectancy and the proportion of older persons in the population. These changes, the development of third-party payment systems, and new methods of treatment have led to more use of health-care services and greater demands on physicians for quality medical care. Practically all physicians have become specialists, mostly in fields other than primary care. The shortage of family physicians has led many specialists to provide primary care, for which their training has not prepared them.

Changes in Mortality and Morbidity

The major demographic change in the population after mid-century has been the increased proportion of older people. Between 1950 and 1982, the population of the United States increased from 152.2 million to 232.1 million. The proportion of the population ages 55 and over increased from 17.0 percent in 1950 to 21.1 percent in 1982, with those 65 years of age and older increasing from 12.4 million to 26.8 million, and those ages 55 to 64 increasing from 13.4 million to 22.1 million. The number under 5 years of age, by comparison, increased by only 1 million, from 16.4 million to 17.4 million.[1]

The greater proportion of the elderly in the population has resulted from lower mortality rates and increased life expectancy. The nation's crude death rate declined from 9.6 per 1,000 population in 1950 to 8.6 per 1,000 population in 1982, even with a larger proportion of older people. The death rate for those under 1 year of age declined the most over the period, from 33.0 per thousand to 11.4 per thousand. This produced an increase in life expectancy at birth from 68.2 years in 1950 to 74.1 years in 1982. The life expectancy of those 65 years of age increased from 13.9 to 16.8 years over the same period.[2]

Lower mortality rates from infectious diseases were responsible for much of the overall decline in mortality rates. For example, the age-adjusted death rates from

The epigraphs for Part V are from Ward Darley, "The Financial Status of Medical Education," in *Medical Education Today,* ed. Dean F. Smiley (Chicago: Association of American Medical Colleges, 1953), p. 50; Warren H. Pearse, "The American College of Obstetricians and Gynecologists," in *The Current Status and Future of Academic Obstetrics,* ed. John Z. Bowers and Elizabeth F. Purcell (New York: Josiah Macy, Jr. Foundation, 1980), p. 101; and Association of Academic Health Centers, *The Organization and Governance of Academic Health Centers* (Washington, D.C.: Association of Academic Health Centers, 1980), 2:83.

tuberculosis and the combination of influenza and pneumonia, the two most serious infectious diseases at mid-century, declined from 21.7 and 26.2 per 100,000, respectively, in 1950, to 1.0 and 11.3 per 100,000, respectively, in 1982. Improved standards of living and new treatments like antibiotics and vaccines have had a greater impact on infectious diseases than any other kind of disease.[3]

While mortality rates from infectious diseases have declined, their incidence and that of other acute medical problems remained high. At some time during 1981, 55.7 percent of the population suffered from upper respiratory ailments and 56.2 percent from other kinds of respiratory illnesses, 23.6 percent had infective and/or parasitic diseases, 9.7 percent experienced disorders of the digestive system, and 33.2 percent received injuries. All of these conditions were more common among the young than among the elderly.[4]

Death rates from most chronic and degenerative diseases also declined during this period. The age-adjusted death rate from diseases of the heart declined from 307.6 per 100,000 population in 1950 to 190.8 per 100,000 population in 1982; that from cerebrovascular diseases declined from 88.8 to 36.1; and that from cancer increased slightly from 125.4 to 133.3. However, because of the increased proportion of older people in the population, the crude death rate from diseases of the heart decreased only slightly (from 355.5 to 327.8 per 100,000), that from cancer increased substantially (from 139.8 to 188.1), and that from cerebrovascular diseases decreased from 104.0 to 68.9.[5]

As life expectancy increased, the prevalence of chronic and degenerative conditions in the population did also. In 1981, for every 1,000 persons, 113.4 were hypertensive, 76.4 had heart conditions, and 24.4 had diabetes. For every 1,000 persons 65 years of age and older, 378.6 were hypertensive, 277.0 had heart conditions, and 83.4 had diabetes. In 1981, persons 65 and older reported an average of 39.9 restricted activity days and 14.0 bed disability days a year, compared to 16.5 and 6.0 days, respectively, for those under 65 years of age.[6]

The increase in chronic and degenerative diseases has produced new diagnostic and therapeutic problems for physicians. Many of these diseases are characterized by a slow and erratic onset, unexpected and unexplainable episodes of acute illness, a wide variety of sometimes bewildering complications, and a natural history that rarely proceeds in a predictable pattern. These characteristics make it more difficult to diagnose them using the traditional taxonomy based on a close relationship between a specific etiological agent (such as a virus or bacteria) and the patient's symptoms. Patients with chronic and degenerative diseases often develop other illnesses because of their conditions. Many of them are poor risks for surgery and cannot tolerate some kinds of drugs. Proper treatment of chronic and degenerative diseases is essential because they are not self-limiting and will eventually worsen. More than ever before, physicians must consider all aspects of the patient's health in their diagnosis and plan of treatment. A continuing, long-term relationship between physicians and patients is essential for optimum health care.

The Use of Medical Care Facilities

Physician visits are an important measure of the state of health care. Between 1964 and 1981 the age-adjusted number of physician visits per person remained unchanged at 4.6 annually. In 1981 persons 17 to 44 years of age averaged 4.2 visits, those 45 to 64 years of age averaged 5.1 visits, and those 65 years of age and over averaged 6.3 visits. Differences in physician visits by income have been eliminated by Medicare and Medicaid. In 1964, the year before the programs were enacted, those families whose annual income was less than $7,000 in 1981 dollars averaged 3.9 physician visits per year, while those whose family income was $25,000 or more in 1981 dollars averaged 5.2 physician visits per year. By 1981 the lowest income group had 5.6 visits per year, while the highest income group had 4.4. Urban-rural differences in physician visits have remained, however. In 1981 residents of Standard Metropolitan Statistical Areas, the major urban areas in the nation, averaged 4.7 physician visits per person, but those living elsewhere averaged only 4.4 physician visits per person. The residents of nonmetropolitan areas traveled farther for physician visits and had longer waits while there.[7]

Social class and urban-rural differences remain important in other aspects of the delivery of medical care. Lower income and rural groups are less likely to have health insurance coverage, which affects hospital use. Lower income persons are more likely to receive care at health-care centers, whose costs per person averaged $69 in 1980, compared to average expenditures of $198 per person for physician's services for the total population. Health-care centers also spent less than 40 percent as much per person as did the total population for laboratory, X-ray, and pharmacy services in 1980.[8]

The site of physicians' visits remained generally unchanged between 1964 and 1981. About two-thirds of the visits took place in a physician's office, about one-eighth in a hospital outpatient department, another one-eighth by telephone, and the remainder in other settings. Hospital outpatient visits in 1981 accounted for one-fifth of the visits of those with incomes under $7,000 and about one-tenth of the visits of those with incomes of $15,000 or more.[9]

The use of short-term general hospitals expanded significantly during this period, especially among the elderly. The number of nonfederal short-term hospital beds per 1,000 population increased from 3.6 in 1960 to 4.4 in 1981, and the number of admissions per 1,000 population from 128 to 159. In 1975, 10.6 percent of the total population had at least one hospital episode, compared to 17.4 percent of those ages 65 and over. The average length of stay in short-term hospitals in 1981 was 6.5 days for patients 17 to 44 years of age, but 10.0 days for those 65 years of age and over. In 1981 the population aged 17 to 44 experienced 648 days of hospital care per 1,000 persons, compared to 4,155 days per 1,000 persons for those aged 65 and over.[10]

The long-term health problems of older persons have led to a significant increase in the use of nursing home facilities. Between 1963 and 1980, the number of resident patients in nursing homes increased from 491,000 to 1,396,000.[11] Nursing homes also replaced many long-term general and specialty hospitals.

The care of psychiatric patients has shown more complex patterns. Between 1953 and 1963, the number of nonfederal psychiatric hospitals declined from 541 to 499, but their total average daily census changed little from 662,000 to 657,000. The subsequent development of new forms of drug therapy reduced the average daily census of the 564 psychiatric hospitals in 1983 to only 160,000 patients. The prevailing pattern of care has become one of short hospital stays for diagnosis and the initiation of drug therapy. This is shown by the increase in the number of psychiatric admissions to these hospitals from 290,000 in 1953 to 551,000 in 1983. The brief periods of hospitalization of many psychiatric patients have led to inpatient psychiatric services in about two-thirds of all short-term general hospitals with at least 300 beds in 1983.[12]

Health-Care Expenditures

There has been a significant acceleration of health-care costs since 1950. From 1929 to 1950, national health expenditures rose from $29 to $82 per capita, and from 3.5 percent to 4.4 percent of the gross national product. In 1982, national health-care expenditures were $1,365 per capita and 10.5 percent of the gross national product. The proportion of national health expenditures going for hospital care increased from 30.4 percent in 1950 to 42.0 percent in 1982, while that for physicians' services declined slightly from 21.7 percent to 19.2 percent. The remainder was divided among many other types of expenditures.[13]

Health-care expenditures have been significantly higher for older than for younger users. In 1964, personal health-care expenditures for those 65 years of age and over averaged $472, compared to $215 for those 19 to 64 years of age. In 1978, the corresponding amounts were $2,026 and $764. In 1977, those 65 years of age and older accounted for 10.8 percent of the population, but were responsible for 29.0 percent of all health-care costs.[14]

The source of health-care expenditures has continued to shift from private to public funds. The proportion of all national health expenditures obtained from public funds increased from 13.6 percent in 1929, to 27.2 percent in 1950, and 42.4 percent in 1982. Most of the increase in government funds came from the federal government. In 1929, the federal government provided 2.7 percent of all health care funds. This increased to 10.4 percent in 1950 and 29.2 percent in 1982.[15]

Another major change in the source of health-care expenditures has been the use of health insurance instead of personal funds. Direct payments by individuals declined from 88.4 percent of all health-care expenditures in 1929, to 65.5 percent in 1950, and 31.5 percent in 1982. Private health insurance was the source of none of the expenditures in 1929, but 9.1 percent in 1950, and 26.7 percent in 1982. The proportion of the population covered for hospitalization by private health insurance increased from 9.3 percent in 1940 to 50.7 percent in 1950. In 1979, 79.5 percent of those under 65 years of age and 64.1 percent of those 65 and over were covered for hospitalization. Health insurance also covered a wide range of medical care. In 1979, 79 percent of those under 65 years of age and 43 percent of those over 65 were insured for surgical services, X-rays, and laboratory examinations, and 65 and 27 percent of the two groups, respectively, for office and home physicians visits.[16]

The remaining costs were assumed by government programs, especially Medicare and Medicaid, which were enacted in 1965. Between 1967 and 1983, Medicare expenditures increased from $4.5 billion to $57.4 billion and Medicaid expenditures increased from $2.9 billion to $34.0 billion. These programs have become the major sources of payment for health care of the elderly. In 1984,

Medicare provided 44.1 percent and Medicaid 13.9 percent of all payments for the health care of those 65 and over, compared to a total of 30.0 percent of all payments for the population generally in 1982.[17]

The increases in health-care expenditures per capita since mid-century can be divided into three components: (1) increases in the price of care, such as labor costs and the cost of medical facilities and equipment; (2) changes in the nature of medical care, such as new methods of diagnosis and treatment; and (3) increases in the use of health services by the population.[18] Each of these will be examined in turn.

Rising prices for health care, especially in hospitals, have been the major cause of the increase in medical care costs. Most hospitals constructed new buildings and other facilities paid for through debt financing rather than philanthropy, which has increased their interest costs. Specialized facilities that were once limited to a few large hospitals, like intensive and coronary care units, spread to many hospitals, requiring additional labor and equipment. As a result, the number of hospital employees per 100 average daily patients increased from 226 in 1960 to 402 in 1981. Higher wages of hospital employees, which rose to parity with those of workers in other industries in the 1960s, have also raised costs. Largely because of hospital cost increases, rising prices accounted for just under one-half of the total increase in personal health-care expenditures from 1965 to 1973 and about two-thirds of the total increase from 1973 to 1982.[19]

Hospital costs have also risen because of third-party payment systems like Blue Cross and Medicare. These insurors have paid for many hospital services, such as extensive laboratory tests, that patients previously could not afford and did not use. Insurors have paid hospitals on a cost-plus basis, thereby eliminating the hospital's incentives to economize.[20] Recent changes have been made in federal programs to motivate hospitals to reduce costs.

Insurors have also raised the price of physicians' services. Blue Shield, the largest private insuror, has accepted physicians' fees on the basis of "usual, customary, and reasonable" (UCR) charges. This policy approved any fee that did not exceed the highest 10 percent (or some similar percentage) of the fees charged for that service by other physicians in the same area. The UCR system assumed the existence of some standard fee for a medical procedure in a community that would serve as a basis of comparison. Instead, as Roe has observed, "many physicians submitted as their usual charges fees that they would like to be collecting or that they collected once in a while from their affluent patients." The UCR system is so expensive to monitor that insurors can challenge only the most excessive charges. It has also failed to reduce charges for procedures that merited high fees when they were new and difficult but not when they became routine. Supplemental payments for technical problems that may be the fault of the physician have had the effect of rewarding inept physicians and punishing proficient ones.[21]

Blue Shield plans have had little motivation to reduce costs because they have been controlled by physicians rather than those paying for the insurance. In 1979, 31 of 69 Blue Shield plans had a majority of physicians on their governing boards, and 11 more had a combined majority of physicians and hospital representatives. Physician majorities existed in between 51 and 63 of the 69 plans in the composition of board committees responsible for fee schedule modifications, determination of criteria for reasonable charges, adjudication of fee claims, and utilization reviews. In a number of plans, any modifications that would affect physicians' fees had to be approved by majority vote of the physicians participating in the plan.[22]

A second component of the increase in health-care costs has been changes in diagnosis and treatment. A study of one large group practice in 1951 and 1971 found that the average number of laboratory tests for perforated appendicitis increased from 5.3 to 31.0, for maternity care from 4.8 to 13.5, and for breast cancer from 5.9 to 27.4. New operations, like organ transplants and coronary artery bypass surgery, have led to an increase in the number of persons undergoing at least one surgical operation from a rate of 48.9 per 1,000 population in 1963–1965 to 59.5 per 1,000 population in 1976–1978. The comparable figures for those 65 and older, who had the greatest increase, were 64.1 and 104.7. Operations experiencing the greatest increases have been those on the cardiovascular system for men and gynecological and obstetrical operations for women, especially Cesarean sections. New nonsurgical procedures, like renal dialysis, therapeutic radiology, and nuclear medicine, have also raised the cost of medical care. A trend toward lower costs has been demonstrated by the steady reduction in the diagnosis-specific length of hospital stay of patients. However, this may be due to the admission of patients with less serious conditions as well as to earlier patient discharges.[23]

The third factor affecting health-care costs has been the increased utilization of health-care services by the population. As was shown above, the number of physicans' visits has increased among the poor and those in rural areas, and hospitalization rates have increased among all groups. Increased utilization has occurred largely because of the larger number of elderly in the population, government programs, and the expansion of private health insurance coverage.[24]

The Supply and Specialty Distribution of Physicians

The shortage of physicians that developed in the 1920s continued until the 1970s. In 1950 there were 14.1 physicians (M.D.s and D.O.s) per 10,000 persons in the United States. This declined slightly to 13.6 in 1960, and rose to 15.6 in 1970. It then increased to 17.4 in 1975 and 19.7 in 1980. The proportion of physicians who were engaged in patient care declined from 83.3 percent in 1970 to 80.5 percent in 1980.[25]

Recent increases in the supply of physicians have not eliminated disparities in their geographic distribution. In 1970, the number of physicians per 10,000 persons varied from a high of 18.5 in the Northeast to a low of 11.5 in the South. In 1980, the Northeast had 23.4 physicians per 10,000 population, while the South had 16.4. Within each region, physicians were concentrated in populous areas. According to a 1973 study, the major population centers (the Standard Metropolitan Statistical Areas—SMSAs) had 17.4 physicians per 10,000 persons, but the areas outside the SMSAs had only 7.4 physicians per 10,000 persons.[26]

Excessive numbers of physicians in urban areas have led some physicians to settle in smaller communities, according to a study of a sample of 23 states. The proportion of towns between 5,000 and 10,000 population with board-certified specialists in internal medicine increased from 11 percent in 1960 to 23 percent in 1977. The proportion with board-certified specialists in surgery increased from 19 percent in 1960 to 38 percent in 1977, and the proportion with board-certified specialists in pediatrics increased from 6 percent in 1960 to 14 percent in 1977. By 1978, 98 percent of cities of 30,000 or more had board-certified specialists in the above fields and urology, obstetrics/gynecology, and radiology.[27]

The other major change in the supply of physicians has been an increase in the proportion of physicians who are full-time specialists. A full-time specialist has been defined by the medical profession as a physician who limits his practice to a recognized field within medicine. The field may involve a set of techniques, as in surgery or radiology; a particular organ or a set of organs, as in dermatology or ear, nose, and throat; a specific class of patients, as in pediatrics or occupational medicine; or some combination of them, as in orthopedic surgery or child psychiatry.

Medical specialties have developed and declined because of changes in the demand for particular kinds of medical care, not because of the development of a body of medical knowledge that merits special attention. Most specialties, like ophthalmology and obstetrics, were created because patients wanted better quality care and encouraged physicians to devote special attention to the fields. The body of medical knowledge that developed in those fields was the result of specialization, not the cause of it. Other specialties, like pathology, arose because of an increased demand for skills that had been available for decades before the specialty existed. Specialties have disappeared or declined because of diminished demand for their services. A lower incidence of polio and tuberculosis has led to the demise of specialists in those fields. New modes of treatment have adversely affected specialists in venereal diseases and ear, nose, and throat disorders. The use of technicians or other less skilled workers to replace physicians has had a major impact on clinical pathology. Medical specialties are part of the marketplace of medical services, not intellectual movements concerned with bodies of knowledge.[28]

One major issue in specialization has been the designation of qualified specialists. In response to concern about self-designated specialists, 16 specialty boards were organized between 1917 and 1940. The boards established criteria for and granted formal certification in individual specialties, usually based on graduate training, practical experience, and examinations. In 1940, only 23.5 percent of the 157,000 physicians in active practice were full-time specialists, and only 42.3 percent of those were board-certified specialists.[29]

During World War II, the armed forces gave major privileges to board-certified specialists. This led many physicians to believe that similar practices would develop later in civilian hospitals. After the war, GI educational benefits for residency training enabled many physicians who were veterans to enter residency programs and become specialists. The number of hospital residencies rose from about 9,000 in 1946 to 15,000 in 1948, with no vacancies.[30]

A more important factor encouraging specialization was the use of board certification as evidence of physician competence by hospitals, health insurors, government agencies, and medical schools. Hospitals limited the use of operating rooms and other privileges to board-certified specialists. Health insurors paid higher fees to board-certified specialists and established payment systems geared to specific medical procedures used by specialists, such as operations, X-rays, and clinical tests. Physicians soon realized that specialization could be highly profitable in a system of medicine where payment was based on the performance of procedures rather than the treatment of patients.

The idea soon developed that every physician should have a specialty. After the establishment of the American Board of Family Practice in 1969, practically all American-educated physicians have obtained some specialty training. Specialty boards and specialty certificates proliferated. Between 1949 and 1984, the number of specialty boards increased from 19 to 23, with some offering two or more general certificates. Many boards created additional special certificates. Altogether in 1984, specialty boards offered a total of 31 general certificates and 41 special certificates. The American Board of Internal Medicine had 11 special certificates and the American Board of Pathology 9.[31]

The number of certificates awarded to physicians by the specialty boards grew at a moderate pace up to about 1970 and rapidly thereafter. During the early 1950s, about 4,000 certificates were issued annually. This figure rose gradually to about 6,500 by the end of the 1960s. In 1975 the rotating, or nonspecialized, internship was abolished and all internships were incorporated into residency programs. As a result, from 1974 to 1983 specialty boards issued an average of 16,166 general certificates and 3,0877 special certificates annually.[32]

A study during the 1960s found the continuation of two long-term trends with regard to specialization. One was that graduates of each succeeding medical school class were more likely to specialize at any time during their career than the graduates of earlier classes. Twelve years after graduation, 62 percent of the graduates of the medical school class of 1960, but 71 percent of the graduates of the class of 1964, were board-certified specialists. Eight years after graduation, 47 percent of the graduates of the class of 1964, but 60 percent of the graduates of the class of 1968, were board-certified specialists. The second trend was for more physicians to obtain board certification as they grew older. For graduates of the medical school class of 1960, 62 percent were board-certified 12 years after graduation and 71 percent were board-certified 16 years after graduation. For graduates of the class of 1964, 42 percent were board-certified 8 years after graduation and 71 percent were board-certified 12 years after graduation.[33]

The Structure of Medical Practice

The places where physicians provided medical care changed significantly after mid-century. Throughout history, physicians had delivered a considerable amount of medical care in the patient's home. As late as 1931, 40 percent of patient visits occurred in the homes and in 1940, 44 percent of all deliveries occurred at home. After mid-century, urbanization and automobiles gave patients greater access to physicians' offices and hospitals. Hospital equipment and facilities became vital for much medical care. As a result, home visits declined to only 2 percent of all patient visits in 1966 and 1 percent of all deliveries in 1965. Physicians' work activities have moved instead to the hospital. In 1982, specialists in internal medicine spent an average of 52.7 hours per week on patient-care activities, including 26.2 in office hours and 15.2 on hospital rounds. Surgeons spent 22.8 of their 51.4 patient-care hours per week in surgery and on hospital rounds.[34] Physicians also located their offices in or near hospitals. The result has been a significant diminution of the physician's understanding of the patient's personal and social situation.

Group practice, usually defined as three or more physicians who pool their incomes, has also become more popular. The proportion of nonfederal physicians in group practices increased from 0.9 percent in 1932, to 5.2 percent in 1959, and 18.5 percent in 1975. Two-thirds of the group practices in 1975 involved three to five physicians, and another 15 percent involved six or seven physicians. The most common type of group practice consists of physicians in the same specialty, who can substitute for each other and share the costs of specialized labor and equipment. In 1975, 54 percent of group practices were single-specialty practices. The other type of group practice is organized so as to provide patients with a broad range of care. This was carried to its ultimate limit in health maintenance organizations (HMOs), which charged patients a fixed annual fee for comprehensive care and contracted with a group of physicians for professional services. In 1975, 35 percent of the group practices were multi-specialty practices, and 11 percent were family practices.[35]

Physicians' earnings have increased dramatically in recent years due to third-party payments. Before World War II, physicians' earnings fluctuated greatly with changes in economic conditions. In 1929, physicians' net earnings averaged $5,224, compared to an average of $1,543 for all manufacturing workers. Physicians' earnings dropped to $2,948 in 1933 during the depression (compared to $1,086 for all manufacturing workers) and rose to $4,441 in 1940 (compared to $1,432 for all manufacturing workers). By 1949, when manufacturing workers averaged $3,095, physicians earned an average of $11,744, with one-third earning less than $7,000, one-third earning between $7,000 and $12,999, and one-third earning $13,000 or more. General practitioners averaged $8,835 while specialists averaged $15,014. Physicians in communities with fewer than 2,500 residents and those on the entire East Coast earned less than their counterparts elsewhere.[36]

In recent years physicians' earnings have grown far beyond those of other occupations (Table 9.1). Between 1959 and 1982, physicians' median earnings have remained at about 4.3 times the level of federal civilian employees, who are primarily white collar and service workers. The dollar difference in earnings between the two groups has grown from $17,000 to $76,000. Since 1970, physicians' annual earnings have remained at about 5.4 times those of all wage and salary workers.

Patient Care

The hours devoted to patient care by physicians have declined between 1949 and 1982 (Table 9.2). The number of total hours spent in professional activities declined

TABLE 9.1. Average Earnings of Physicians and Other Workers, 1951–1982

Year	Physicians	Federal Civilian Employees	All Wage and Salary Employees
1951	$13,432	3,481	——
1959	22,100[a]	5,165	——
1965	29,000	6,868	——
1970	41,800	9,234	7,750
1975	56,400	13,529	10,836
1982	99,500	22,839	18,506

[a]Median earnings.

Sources: U.S. Bureau of the Census, *Historical Statistics of the United States: Colonial Times to 1970* (Washington, D.C.: U.S. G.P.O., 1975), 1:175, 2:1103; U.S. Bureau of the Census, *Statistical Abstract of the United States, 1980* (Washington, D.C.: U.S. G.P.O., 1980), pp. 112–13; Roger A Reynolds and Jonathan B. Abram, eds., *Socioeconomic Characteristics of Medical Practice 1983* (Chicago: American Medical Association, 1983), p. 116; U.S. Bureau of the Census, *Statistical Abstract of the United States, 1984* (Washington, D.C.: U.S. G.P.O., 1983), pp. 335, 431.

about 5 percent and the number of patient visits per week declined about 10 percent. There has also been a diminution in the number of weeks worked annually. In 1982 physicians averaged 46.7 weeks of work per year, which was down from 47.2 in 1973 and from considerably more in 1949. About 90 percent of total work hours were spent in patient care in 1982. This has probably increased since mid-century due to the elimination of home visits and the increased number of telephone and hospital patient contacts.[37]

Patient visits to physicians have usually been part of a pattern of continuing medical care. A 1974 study of patient visits found that the physician had seen the patient previously for the same problem in 62.1 percent of the visits and for another problem in 23.0 percent. Among patients 65 and over, 92.5 percent had been seen

TABLE 9.2. Work Practices of Physicians by Selected Specialties, 1949–1982

Specialty	Hours/Week All Activities 1949	Hours/Week All Activities 1982	Hours/Week Patient Care Activities 1982	Patient Contacts/Week 1952[a]	Patient Contacts/Week 1982
General and family practice	60.6	57.4	53.4	165	160.6
Internal medicine	59.0	58.9	52.7	136	118.9
Obstetrics/gynecology	61.1	58.4	53.5	167	128.2
Pediatrics	62.2	57.2	51.3	144	134.9
Surgery[b]	59.5	57.0	51.4	155	118.8

[a]Estimate based on the average number of minutes per patient visit.
[b]Includes different surgical specialties in 1949 and 1982.

Sources: U.S. President's Commission on the Health Needs of the Nation, *Building America's Health* (Washington, D.C.: U.S. G.P.O., 1953), 3:147, 150; Roger A. Reynolds and Jonathan B. Abrams, eds., *Socioeconomic Characteristics of Medical Practice 1983* (Chicago: American Medical Association, 1983), pp. 48, 50, 66.

by the physician previously. Patients were seen for a very wide variety of conditions, with the physicians rating 80.7 percent of the principal problems as "slightly serious" or "not serious," as opposed to "serious" or "very serious." For those 65 years of age and older, only 69.0 percent of their principal problems were rated slightly or not serious. The most common procedures used by the physician during these visits were medical examinations and laboratory tests. A general history or examination was carried out in 33.1 percent of the cases, laboratory procedures in 19.4 percent, and X-rays in 7.0 percent.[38]

The outcome of most patient visits in this study was usually one or more therapeutic procedures and a request for a return visit. The physician prescribed a drug in 50.4 percent of the visits, administered an injection or immunization in 17.9 percent, and performed office surgery in 8.4 percent. Counseling or psychotherapy was provided in 24.7 percent of the cases. The patient was instructed to return at a specified time in 59.7 percent of the cases, referred to another physician in 3.7 percent of the cases, and sent to the hospital in 2.2 percent. He was told to return if needed in 21.7 percent of the cases. Older patients were more likely to have follow-up visits than younger ones: 93.9 percent of those 65 and over had a definite or possible follow-up planned, compared to just over 80 percent of those under age 25.[39]

The years after mid-century saw dramatic changes in both surgery and drug therapy. The development of many new operations contributed to the increased incidence of surgery among the adult population. In a study carried out in 1963–1965, 5.1 percent of those ages 15 to 44 and 6.5 percent of those 65 and over had an operation in the year preceding the interview. In a similar study in 1976–1978, 5.7 percent of those 15 to 44 and 7.8 percent of those 65 and over had an operation in the comparable year, increases of 12 percent and 20 percent, respectively, in less than 15 years.[40]

Many pharmaceuticals have been developed to prevent and treat disease. Vaccines have greatly reduced the incidence of diseases like polio, measles, rubella, and mumps. Antibiotics provide an effective method of treatment for many infectious diseases. They have also reduced the need for some operations, like tonsillectomies, and made possible others that require careful control of postoperative infections, like heart surgery. Other drugs that have improved treatment include antihistamines, diuretics, psychotherapeutic drugs, antifungal agents, and steroids, which are used to treat inflammations and skin disorders, as well as for birth control pills. In a comparison of the treatment of 362 conditions described in the 1927 and 1975 editions of a textbook of internal medicine, Beeson found that the proportion of conditions where effective treatment or prevention existed increased from 3 percent to 22 percent, and the proportion where symptomatic relief was available increased from 3 percent to 28 percent. Viral diseases and cancers are the major areas where progress has been limited.[41]

Drug consumption has greatly increased as a result of the many new types of drugs. Between 1962 and 1978, the value of all prescription and nonprescription drugs shipped by manufacturers, excluding vitamins, nutrients, and veterinary drugs, increased from $2.4 billion to $8.3 billion. This is especially impressive because drug prices have increased much less than the general cost of living.

Increases in the value of some major categories of drugs shipped include: drugs acting on the central nervous system (including tranquilizers) and the sense organs, from $0.7 to $2.4 billion; drugs for parasitic and infectious disease (including antibiotics), from $0.5 to $1.3 billion; drugs affecting neoplasms and endocrine diseases, from $0.3 to $1.0 billion; and drugs affecting the cardiovascular system, from $0.1 to $0.8 billion.[42]

The Quality of Medical Care Delivered by Physicians

The many new treatments have increased the demands on physicians to provide quality medical care. However, their widely varying benefits and side effects have made it more difficult to choose the appropriate treatment for the condition. In addition, the greater number of chronic and degenerative diseases has increased the importance of choosing the correct treatment. In those diseases, unlike infectious diseases, the physician is not aided by the healing powers of nature. Without proper treatment, the patient's condition will never improve and will eventually worsen. Inaction by the physician can therefore be as dangerous as incorrect action, a situation which rarely occurred in the past in internal medicine. Some indication of the quality of medical care can be ascertained by an analysis of studies of prescribing practices, decisions to operate, and malpractice claims.

Prescribing Practices

Physicians' prescribing practices have come under scrutiny because most new drugs have serious side effects or cause other problems. In order to use these drugs properly, physicians must know what adverse reactions to look for, the conditions under which the drugs should be used, how best to measure their results, and when to stop treatment. This information is not as widely promulgated as descriptions of the more favorable aspects of the drugs. It has therefore been suggested that physicians too often prescribe drugs without adequate awareness of their benefits and limitations.[43]

Antibiotics are one major prescribing problem. Their excessive use has genetically altered some pathogenic bacteria so that they are antibiotic resistant, which has forced physicians to use other treatments that are less effective, more expensive, or more dangerous. Patients can also develop allergic reactions to antibiotics because of excessive or unnecessary use, which can create grave risks for them in future illnesses. Despite these dangers, physicians often use antibiotics inappropriately. One study of physicians' treatment of the common cold in 1972 found that broad- or medium-spectrum antibiotics were prescribed in 28 percent of the cases and penicillin was prescribed in 21 percent, even though neither are of any value in viral diseases. Studies of the widespread use of antibiotics in hospitals (it was estimated that 27 percent of patients in general hospitals in 1972 received them) have found no clear-cut evidence of bacterial infections in 30 to 60 percent of the patients who received the antibiotics.[44]

Evidence that much of this use was quite casual was found in a study comparing prescribing patterns before and after a hospital committee placed restrictions on the use of certain antibiotics. Despite the fact that physicians could readily administer the restricted drugs after verbal consultation with a member of the hospital committee, the prescribing of drugs dropped drastically while they were on the restricted list compared to their use before and after being placed on the list.[45]

Another major issue has been the prescribing of psychotherapeutic drugs by physicians. The newly developed major and minor tranquilizers, antidepressants, and stimulants can be used in many more conditions than older drugs like morphine, cocaine, and the barbiturates, because they have less serious side effects. Valium, introduced in 1963, and Librium, introduced in 1960, produced combined sales of 4 billion tablets in 1974. In 1970, tranquilizers stimulants, antidepressants, sedatives, and hypnotics accounted for one-sixth of all prescriptions filled or refilled in drug stores.[46]

Studies of psychotherapeutic drug use among U.S. and Canadian adults in the 1970s found that during the year about one-fourth of all adults used a prescription psychotherapeutic drug for some time. Only one-sixth of the prescriptions were written by psychiatrists or neurologists, which indicated that this class of drugs is used in many specialties in medicine. One study found that minor tranquilizers were often prescribed for patients with physical disorders, where the value of the drugs is highly problematic.[47]

The widespread use of minor tranquilizers has provoked considerable debate about inappropriate prescribing. They are used in many unrelated disorders and their therapeutic effectiveness compared to placebos has not been conclusively demonstrated. In many cases there seems to be no clear-cut relationship between their use and the condition of the patient. In an era when drugs are increasingly designed to be used for specific conditions, the ill-defined role of minor tranquilizers is considered highly unsatisfactory.[48]

Several explanations have been offered for the unnecessary prescribing of drugs of all kinds by physicians. One, according to an editorial in *JAMA,* is "patient pressure:"

[M]any patients (seen in the office of the general practitioner or internist) need little (sometimes no) medication. . . . [A] major dimension of our problem has been created by our inability to resist the pressures of patients and the constrictions of time. How time-consuming is it to teach a patient the difference between bacterial and viral illnesses—to explain that an antibiotic is not indicated—that it possibly could cause harm—that just because he "always got a shot" it is still not indicated? How does this compare to the time and effort expended in writing a prescription for an oral antibiotic or telling your nurse to give a "shot"? Which is more immediately "satisfying" to the patient? . . .

[M]any patients remain unsatisfied unless they are given some talisman of good faith. Perhaps the "prescription" should consist of written instructions: "Rest in bed 24 hours"; "drink two quarts of fluid daily." But, it is a fact of life that many patients will not settle for your earnest, well intentioned words and investment of time. *They expect "medication."*

It is unrealistic to believe that any physician wishes to use drugs that are not indicated. "Patient pressure," on the other hand, is a formidable force. . . .

As scientists we are obliged to practice scientific medicine. In the real world it is not easy, for many times patients are their own worst enemies.[49]

Certainly the public engages in widespread drug use. One survey of two Canadian communities found that within a 48-hour period, some medicine, pill, or ointment had been used by about 60 percent of the respondents. Another survey of 1,633 respondents in the southeastern United States found that 53.3 percent of the sample were taking one or more drugs at the time of the interview. The most common drugs were vitamins, aspirin, psychotherapeutic drugs, hormones, and birth control pills. At least 21 percent of the sample were taking prescription drugs at the time of the survey.[50]

Drugs can also be used as a substitute for diagnostic judgment. Instead of making the sometimes laborious efforts to reach an accurate diagnosis, the physician may prescribe a drug as a prophylactic. This raises the cost of medical care and risks exposing the patient to unnecessary and sometimes dangerous side effects. Physicians often use drugs prophylactically that they believe have few or no side effects. This belief may result from the overly favorable description of the drugs by pharmaceutical firms and their salesmen. There are few objective analyses available to physicians of the benefits and side effects of new drugs.[51]

Physicians vary widely in their prescribing patterns. One survey found that 37 primary care physicians in a community prescribed an average of 270 different drugs in their practices, with individual physicians varying from about 100 to 500 different drugs. The latter number is considered sufficient for the total inpatient and outpatient practice of an entire hospital. The survey obtained expert evaluations of the physicians' responses to questions about their prescribing practices concerning five common complaints, five common illnesses, and five drugs. The experts rated more highly the prescribing patterns of younger physicians, physicians with more patients, physicians in group practice, physicians who used medical journal articles to learn about new drugs, and physicians who were more critical of the pharmaceutical industry. Analyses were not performed to see if the characteristics were interrelated. No statistically significant relationships were found between prescribing patterns and the age, education, race, income, or religion of the physician's patients.[52]

Prescribing practices seem to be linked to other behaviors, according to a study that found a relationship between drug prescribing and the use of diagnostic tests. A study of the treatment of carefully selected comparable patients by 33 faculty internists found a median annual prescription cost per patient of almost $88, which varied from $33 to $145 among the physicians. The median annual laboratory cost per patient was $64, and varied from $10 to $169 for each physician. Physicians with high prescription costs tended to have high laboratory costs. This study found no significant relationship between laboratory or drug costs and the physician's age or selected measures of his background.[53]

Widespread evidence of inappropriate drug prescribing raises serious questions about the quality of medical care. Research on this issue has found no consistent relationship between personal characteristics of physicians and their prescribing practices. This suggests that one cause of the problem may be deficiencies in the medical education of physicians.

Inappropriate Surgery

Another issue in the quality of medical care is the appropriateness of surgical operations. A surgical operation may be inappropriate for several reasons: the surgeon involved may not be qualified to perform it; new therapies or new kinds of operations may have made the particular operation obsolete; or the patient's condition may not have warranted surgery at all or surgery at the time when it was performed.[54]

The standard measure of physicians' qualifications to perform surgery is board certification in a surgical specialty. One major study of surgical operations in four regions of the United States in 1970 found that board-certified surgeons performed only 58.1 percent of the operations studied and carried out only 64.9 percent of the operative work weighted by the California Relative Value (CRV) scale of weighting operations according to their complexity. Another 24.2 percent of all operations and 23.3 percent of the CRV-weighted operative work were performed by full-time surgeons who were not board-certified. The remaining operations were performed by general practitioners, medical specialists, interns, and residents.[55]

Surgeons may also be unqualified because they do not perform enough surgery to maintain and improve their skills. The same study examined the four operations most frequently performed in each surgical specialty and concluded that "even the commonplace operations were not frequent events on average for the individual surgeon." Another study found that operative surgery and preoperative and postoperative care occupied only 54.8 percent of the time of general surgeons, 41.8 percent of the time of orthopedic surgeons, and less than 15 percent of the time of obstetrician/gynecologists and ear, nose, and throat specialists. The first-mentioned study found that surgeons in prepaid group plans spent more time in these activities than other surgeons, which the study attributed to the plans' keeping their surgeons "fully occupied in surgical care." Using the workloads of prepaid group surgeons as a baseline, the study concluded "that there are too many physicians in surgical practice in the United States. The low operative work loads per surgeon are the prime evidence."[56]

A more complex issue is whether surgeons perform operations that are inappropriate for the disease or the patient for financial gain. Surgeons claim that this is difficult to assess because indications for surgery are imprecise. This was found in a study of 411 surgeons in general surgery and four surgical specialties who evaluated the appropriateness of surgery in several hypothetical case studies specific to their specialties. In those cases designed by the researchers "to represent a pathological process in definite need of surgical intervention," at least 95 percent of the surgeons in the specialty agreed in their evaluations. On the other hand, 80 percent or more of the surgeons in a specialty agreed in only 8 of 19 more ambiguous cases and in none of those cases did more than 91 percent of the surgeons agree. The disagreements were not due to the surgeons' education, their salaried or fee-for-service compensation for surgery, their solo or group practice, or the type of hospital where they operated. The authors concluded that "surgical decision-making is a semi-exact scientific process, and it is unreasonable to expect exact answers to clinical problems."[57]

Studies of second opinions, where the decisions of surgeons are confirmed or rejected by other surgeons, have produced similar findings. One study of mandatory second opinions concerning surgery for 1,591 Massachusetts Medicaid recipients in 1977 found that 88.7 percent of the consultants supported the original recommendations for surgery. The researchers concluded that lack of support by consultants indicated "honest disagreements about indications for surgery."[58]

The lack of agreement among surgeons raises questions as significant as those of inappropriate surgery. If surgeons cannot agree whether or not a patient's clinical condition justifies surgery, many surgeons will decide to operate on grounds that are idiosyncratic and unscientific. The problem of unnecessary surgery is replaced by the far more serious one of unwise and unscientific surgery.[59] This problem places a much greater burden on the surgeon's education as a factor in improving medical care.

Surgery rates are also affected by the availability of surgeons and hospital beds. Research has consistently shown that geographic areas with higher rates of surgeons to population and with higher rates of hospital beds to population tend to have higher rates of surgical operations. However, more surgery does not necessarily mean more inappropriate surgery. One study found that geographic areas of Manitoba with high tonsillectomy and adenoidectomy rates did not have a higher proportion of inappropriate operations (based on a number of criteria) than areas with low tonsillectomy and adenoidectomy rates. The study also found that only one-fourth to one-third of the operations in all geographic areas met their most liberal criteria of appropriateness, supporting the position that much surgery is idiosyncratic.[60]

Fee-for-service reimbursement systems produce higher surgery rates than systems with salaried surgeons. This has been found both in comparisons within the United States and among nations with different payment systems. However, the studies have not systematically measured the proportion of inappropriate operations under the different systems.[61]

Hospital surveillance and feedback also affect surgery rates. One study found a 46 percent reduction in tonsillectomy rates in Vermont hospitals between 1969 and 1973 (compared to a 14 percent reduction for the entire United States) after the hospitals were informed of a 13-fold difference in age-adjusted rates among them. Another study, which resulted from a concern with a rising rate of hysterectomies, established a list of indications for their use after reviewing five Saskatchewan hospitals in 1970 and two more in 1973. Follow-up studies in 1974 found a decline of 32.8 percent in the total number of hysterectomies and a reduction in the proportion considered inappropriate from 23.7 percent to 7.8 percent.[62]

Independent decisions by patients also affect surgery rates. One study found that 25.4 percent of 696 patients whose need for surgery was confirmed by consultation with a second surgeon had not had surgery one year after the confirming opinion. Of the 710 patients whose need for surgery was not confirmed by the second surgeon, 77.9 percent accepted the recommendation of the consultant. This raises questions about the relationship between patients and the first surgeons, in whom they would be expected to have more confidence. At the same time, patient decisions do not seem to be affected by the extent of their knowledge of surgery. A study of physicians, lawyers, ministers, and businessmen in California found that male and female physicians and their spouses had rates for selected operations that were as high as or higher than those for the other groups.[63]

Overall, these data indicate that surgeons have not developed satisfactory criteria to indicate the need for many kinds of surgery, despite the tremendous increase in surgical research in medical schools since 1950. The decision to operate still depends too much on the idiosyncratic judgment of the surgeon performing the operation and too little on scientific criteria established by the collective judgment of surgeons.[64] Once again, this suggests an important role for medical education in improving medical care.

Malpractice

One inevitable problem of patient care is iatrogenic disorders, illnesses caused by physicians, other health workers, or by medical-care institutions. In 1975, it was estimated that about 700,000 medical injuries involved negligence of some kind. A more limited study of 821 cases in two general hospitals about the same time found an iatrogenic injury rate of 7.6 percent, which the study felt to be very conservative. The most common injuries were postoperative complications and adverse drug reactions. About 70 percent of the known sources of the injuries were physicians. Last, a major study of 500 medical records at each of 338 hosiptals in 1970 and 1976 found that 5 percent of all hospital patients acquired infections during their stay and that the rate of infections increased by 18 percent between 1970 and 1976. The study estimated that 33 percent of all infections were preventable but that only 7 percent were actually being prevented, based on comparisons with hospitals that had good infection-control programs.[65]

Only a very small proportion of iatrogenic injuries have produced claims of legal malpractice. The study of 821 cases at the two hospitals referred to above estimated that 6 percent of the iatrogenic injuries involving negligence led to malpractice suits. The overall estimate of 700,000 annual iatrogenic injuries can also be compared to the 20,000 malpractice claims filed annually, a rate of less than 3 percent.[66]

The incidence of malpractice suits against physicians has been steadily rising. A recent survey of physicians found 6.2 liability claims per 100 physicians annually in the 1976–1981 period, compared with 2.9 claims annually for some unspecified period prior to 1976. The surgical specialties had claim rates in both periods about twice as high as those for family practice and internal medicine.[67]

Several reasons have been advanced for the small proportion of patients with iatrogenic illnesses who file malpractice claims. Most patients consider their chances of success to be very low: one public opinion survey found that the median estimate was that 10 percent of the claimants collect money in a malpractice suit. Many patients may not know enough to file claims. Older persons and persons of upper socioeconomic status have been the most frequent claimants. Lawyers also reduce the incidence of malpractice claims. A survey found that 88 percent of lawyers have rejected malpractice cases brought to them, primarily because the potential awards were too small or the case had no adequate basis for liability.

Ninety-nine percent of the lawyers said that they would not proceed with a case unless the patient's claim was supported by a consulted physician.[68]

Malpractice claims have not been a major legal issue. Somers observed in 1977 that "the bulk of malpractice compensation remains a small claims business." One study found that most claims were settled out of court and only 10 percent reached trial. Payment to the plaintiff occurred in about 45 percent of all claims filed but in only about 20 percent of the cases that went to trial. Of the awards settled in 1974, 43 percent were for less than $5,000 and only 1 percent exceeded $500,000. The amount of the awards increased steadily during the 1970s, but the increases were comparable to cost increases in the health sector generally.[69]

Physicians have differed in their likelihood of being sued for malpractice. Those in surgical specialties, especially obstetrics, have been more likely to have claims against them than those in medical specialties. Physicians with more experience in practice have higher claim rates than those with less experience. A history of previous malpractice claims also predisposes physicians to future claims, even taking specialty and experience into account. Only a minority of physicians have been sued for malpractice and an even smaller number have been subjected to multiple malpractice suits. A sutdy of Maryland physicians from 1960 to 1970 found that only one-sixth of the physicians surveyed had ever been sued for malpractice during their whole careers. A four-year study of 8,000 physicians in California found that 46 physicians account for 10 percent of all claims and 30 percent of all payments from the malpractice insurance plans.[70]

Increases in the incidence of malpractice suits have been attributed to changes in the physician-patient relationship. The shortage of physicians has permitted many of them to be less concerned with satisfying their patients. Third-party payment systems have virtually guaranteed payment of physicians' bills and have also reduced concern with satisfying patients. This reduction of patient leverage, according to Magraw, has affected the behavior of physicians:

> [P]ersonal care of patients . . . ([often involving] disagreeable endeavor with an unlovely or complaining person) is actively avoided by most human beings including doctors unless "there is something in it for them." . . .
>
> There must be some incentive for the doctor to provide that extra and somewhat hard-to-see part of the care which is implicit in the skillful management of the doctor-patient relationship. Otherwise he will be inclined to settle for a technically competent job of cutting and stitching which may have little relevance to getting the patient back to health. . . . [He] may not try to ascertain whether the patient remains sick or disabled or is fully rehabilitated. He may even feel that such concerns are the patient's problem, or at least a problem for someone other than himself.[71]

Physician Discipline

The purpose of malpractice law is to punish and deter unprofessional or incompetent physicians, not to compensate victims, who would be better served by insurance systems. According to a 1970 study, most malpractice claims are appropriate for this objective: 86 percent of them involved improper treatment, but only 21 percent involved emergency situations where improper treatment would be most defensible. Death was a result in 18 percent of the claims. Surgery was the subject of 57 percent of the claims, internal medicine 21 percent, and the rest were divided among other specialties. Many claims do not serve a deterrent function because they do not affect a physician's malpractice insurance rates. All physicians in a given specialty in the same geographic area pay the same premiums. The physician who assiduously avoids the kind of behavior that produces malpractice claims pays no less than other physicians in his specialty and geographic area who are regularly sued by patients.[72]

In the absence of deterrence through the malpractice system, medical licensing agencies are the primary source of professional discipline. Derbyshire located 938 disciplinary actions taken by state licensing boards between 1963 and 1967, 47.2 percent of which led to probation or reprimands, 35.6 percent revocation of license, and 17.2 percent suspension of license. Less than 1 percent of all disciplinary action resulted from malpractice. Addiction, alcoholism, and mental incompetence accounted for 41.9 percent of disciplinary actions and 42.5 percent involved narcotics violations (mostly illegal prescribing or sales), felonies (including abortions), and fraud or deceit in practice. Derbyshire found that professional incompetence of any kind was rarely used as a basis for disciplining physicians, and was often not listed in the relevant statutes of the states. Other studies have reached the same conclusions.[73]

Physicians have also been subject to regulation by Peer Review Organizations that have been established in connection with Medicare and Medicaid and have been given the power to set standards of professional conduct. These organizations lack the legal authority to discipline physicians that has been given to state licensing boards and have not yet played a significant role in physician discipline.

Public Health and Preventive Medicine

Public health has undergone a major change in orientation in recent decades. Before mid-century, public health measures were directed toward the prevention of infectious diseases. Public works projects provided pure water and disposed safely of sewage and human excrement. State and federal laws regulated the production of milk and foods to prevent contamination by pathogenic and other organisms. Vaccines were developed (and continue to be developed) to prevent bacterial and viral illnesses. After mid-century, public health was revolutionized by the discovery of the effect of cigarette smoking on illness, the most important and seminal medical discovery in the last 50 years. This and other discoveries have shown that consumption patterns and exercise directly affect health and that exposure to chemicals and minerals in the environment increases the incidence of cancer and other diseases.

These findings have created a "second epidemiological revolution" concerned with host susceptibility and resistance to illness. One area of concern includes personal behaviors such as smoking, alcohol, drug and food consumption, body weight, exposure to hazards at work, exercise, and stress. A second involves the presence in the individual's environment of carcinogens and other disease-causing elements. A third concern is genetic determinants of disease.[74]

The significance of the new epidemiology for medical practice lies in the identification of asymptomatic individuals with high likelihoods of contracting chronic and degenerative diseases. Concern for asymptomatic hypertensive and diabetic patients has long existed in medicine. Equal concern can now be shown for persons who are, among other things, obese, smokers, employed in certain occupations, or who have a certain genetic makeup. Physicians can no longer concentrate primarily on finding specific etiological agents as causes of disease in patients with certain symptoms. They need to be equally concerned with eliminating or reducing predisposing causes of disease that may not produce illness for years or decades. Many physicians have fallen behind patients in their recognition of this approach. It has often been suggested that their medical education has failed to prepare them for it.

Changing Distribution of Medical Specialties

Before mid-century, the trend toward specialization moved at a fairly slow pace. The proportion of physicians who were general practitioners gradually declined from 89.4 percent of all physicians in 1923 to 77.7 percent in 1940 (Table 9.3). Full-time specialists in internal medicine and its subspecialities and in pediatrics increased from 2.6 percent to 5.4 percent of all physicians. Full-time general and specialty surgeons and obstetricians and/or gynecologists increased from 6.7 percent of all physicians to 12.8 percent.

After mid-century, the movement toward specialization accelerated dramatically. General practitioners and family physicians declined from 67.3 percent of all physicians in 1949, to 38.4 percent in 1961, and 13.9 percent in 1976. General internists and pediatricians, who provide some primary care, increased from 8.3 percent of all physicians in 1949 to 24.8 percent in 1983. Thus providers of primary care—general practitioners, family physicians, general internists, and pediatricians—declined from 75.6 percent of all physicians in 1949 to 38.7 percent of all physicians in 1983. The number of providers of primary care per 10,000 persons in the population decreased from 12 in 1923 to 10 in 1940 to 7 in 1983.

Primary care physicians were replaced by clinical specialists and specialists not engaged in patient care. General and specialty surgeons and obstetricians and/or gynecologists increased from 15.4 percent to 26.5 percent of all physicians between 1949 and 1983. Medical subspecialists, including cardiologists and gastroenterologists, increased from 1.9 to 6.4 percent of all physicians. Psychiatrists and neurologists increased from 2.5 percent to 8.9 percent of all physicians. Pathologists, radiologists, and anesthesiologists, who are not engaged in direct patient care, increased from 3.0 percent of all physicians in 1949 to 12.5 percent in 1983. Altogether, close to 20 percent of active physicians in 1983 (including those in public health and other specialties) were not treating patients, compared to 5 percent in 1949, 3 percent in 1940, and 1 percent in 1923.

Several reasons have been suggested for the movement to full-time specialization. The single most important factor has been the sustained shortage of physicians. Physicians could choose practically any specialty they desired and feel confident that they could obtain enough patients to earn a substantial livelihood. Had more physicians been available, physicians would have had to adjust their specialty choices much more closely to the nature of patient demand.

TABLE 9.3. Physicians in Active Practice by Full-Time Specialty, 1923–1983

Percentage of Physicians	1923[a]	1931	1940	1949	1961	1970	1976	1983
General and family[b]	89.4	83.5	77.7	67.3	38.4	18.6	15.9	13.9
Internal medicine	1.3	2.7	3.9	6.0	12.2	13.5	16.6	17.8
Pediatrics	.5	1.0	1.5	2.3	4.8	5.8	6.5	7.0
Other Medical specialties[c]	.5	.7	1.0	1.9	2.6	5.6	5.4	6.4
General surgery	2.2	2.9	4.0	5.2	9.3	9.6	9.3	8.0
Obstetrics/gynecology[d]	.5	.9	1.5	2.6	5.6	6.1	6.4	6.3
Other surgical specialties[e]	4.0	5.7	6.3	7.6	10.8	12.0	12.7	12.2
Psychology/neurology[d]	.6	.9	1.5	2.5	6.0	8.5	9.0	8.9
Pathology, radiology and anesthesiology	.7	1.1	1.7	3.0	7.9	11.2	12.1	12.5
Public health	.2	.5	.9	.8	.9	1.2	1.0	.5
Other specialties	.0	.0	.0	.8	1.4	8.0	5.2	6.7
Total	100.0	100.0	100.0	100.0	100.0	100.0	100.0	100.0

[a]Includes physicians not in active practice.

[b]Interns and residents included with general and family practitioners before 1961.

[c]Includes allergy, cardiovascular, dermatology, gastroenterology, pulmonary disease.

[d]Includes physicians in either and/or both specialties.

[e]Includes ophthalmology, otolaryngology, urology, orthopedic, colon and rectal, neurological, plastic, and thoracic surgery.

Sources: Willard C. Rappleye et al., *Graduate Medical Education* (Chicago: University of Chicago Press, 1940), p. 261; Paul Q. Peterson and Maryland Y. Pennell, *Health Manpower Source Book: 14. Medical Specialists* (Washington, D.C.: U.S. G.P.O., 1962), pp. 9, 18. Jack W. Cole, *Graduate Medical Education Present and Prospective* (New York: Josiah Macy, Jr., Foundation, 1980), pp. 94–95; *Physician Characteristics and Distribution in the U.S.* (Chicago: American Medical Association, 1983).

Another factor has been the higher median net earnings of specialists: general practitioners and family physicians earned $40,000 in 1973 and $63,000 in 1982, internists earned $45,000 and $75,000 in the same two years and general and subspecialty surgeons $54,000 and $112,000. Pathologists, radiologsts, and anesthesiologists all averaged $100,000 or more in 1982.[75] Specialists' greater earnings were due to the policies of insurors of paying larger fees for procedures than for the office visits characteristic of primary care.

Specialists have enjoyed smaller workloads. The Mendenhall survey of 1975–1977, which was based on log diaries of 10,372 physicians, found that general practitioners averaged 190.6 ambulatory, hospital and telephone patient encounters per week and family physicians average 175.1, compared to averages of 129.3 in internal medicine and 131.9 in general surgery. Encounters of primary care physicians were more rushed, averaging only 10.4 minutes for general practitioners and 11.2 minutes for family physicians, compared to 18.5 minutes in internal medicine and 12.5 minutes in general surgery. Most other specialties had even fewer encounters, with those encounters being of longer duration.[76]

Specialization has also resulted from the fear of many physicians that nonspecialists would lose their hospital and insurance privileges. It has often been claimed that ultimately only board-certified specialists will be permitted to care for hospital patients with appropriate illnesses or receive third-party payment for treatment.

Primary Care Physicians

Primary, secondary, and tertiary care have been distinguished as three aspects of medical care. Primary care provides an initial and accessible source of care for the patient, assumes responsibility for most of the patient's less serious health problems, provides continuity of care over time, and coordinates and evaluates the delivery of other kinds of health care to the patient. Secondary care consists of the use of specialists and hospitals for the treatment of problems requiring special equipment or skills not possessed by primary care physicians. Tertiary care is the use of specialists and hospitals for health problems requiring skills and equipment existing in only a small number of health centers in the nation, mostly at medical schools.[77]

Primary care medicine is fundamentally different from secondary and tertiary care medicine. Because patients are not screened before their visits, primary care physicians are confronted with an extraordinary variety of disorders, ranging from the trivial to the life-threatening. Many of the disorders, such as upper respiratory infections, are self-limited or unmodifiable by medical treatment. Patients are seen early in the course of their disorders, when identifying symptoms are often ambiguous or absent and misleading symptoms are often present. Many disorders involve physical, social, and psychological factors operating simultaneously.

The diagnostic algorithm used by the primary care physician differs from that used by the specialist. The specialist uses standardized procedures designed to correlate the patient's symptoms with some underlying pathology relevant to the specialty. If the specialist eliminates all possible pathologies in the specialty as causes of the patient's problems, he dismisses the patient as not being his concern. The primary care physician can neither use the same procedures on all patients nor dismiss patients who do not fall within his domain. Instead, he uses an entirely different algorithm, starting with the differentiation between serious and nonserious illness. To do so, he must have a good knowledge of both the patient's personal history and the diseases prevalent in the community. Once the initial distinction has been made, the primary care physician makes additional dichotomous distinctions (e.g., urgent or not urgent, bacterial or viral) until a satisfactory diagnosis has been made. A satisfactory diagnosis often does not include the identification of some underlying pathology if it is unnecessary for the care of the patient.[78]

Specialists are seldom able to use the primary care physician's algorithm effectively. They lack a good understanding of the range of disorders prevalent in the community. They are trained to use elaborate tests and technical procedures appropriate for a small range of disorders, not the extremely broad range of complaints confronting the primary care physician. The diagnostic algorithm of specialty medicine deals with advanced pathology rather than the many mild and self-limited disorders confronting the primary care physician. The specialist's concern with advanced pathology also leads to an effort to obtain total confirmation of the diagnosis, while the primary care physician must be able to act in the face of much lower levels of certainty.[79]

The treatments used by the primary care physician differ from those of the specialist. The former is more likely to treat well-understood conditions. According to Chase, "these manageable disorders cut across many of the traditional and newly planned specialty areas. Common to all is the fact that there is a well established therapeutic strategy that may competently be directed by a broadly educated physician without the highly specialized education and experience that superspecialty certification implies."[80] As new therapeutic procedures become routinized, the role of primary care physicians has expanded to include greater responsibility for their use.

Given the need for distinctive professional skills in primary care, the American Academy of General Practice was organized in 1947 and residencies in general practice were established in 1948. However, neither provided recognition comparable to board certification in the specialties. In the early 1960s, fewer than 900 residency positions were offered in general practice and only about one-half of them were filled, mostly by foreign medical graduates.[81]

Interest gradually developed in a specialty board in family practice. Specialists had high prestige, charged high fees, and had more hospital privileges. If general practitioners were to be their equals, they needed a specialty board and specialty certification. However, many general practitioners and specialists opposed a specialty board in primary care. The American Academy of General Practice feared that the board might exclude surgery, which many general practitioners considered to be an important part of general practice. On the other hand, the AMA and the American Board of Medical Specialties opposed a specialty board for primary care physicians that included surgery. Many general practitioners also considered residencies for primary care to be unnecessary.[82]

In 1959 the American Board of General Practice was incorporated. It languished until it was approved by the American Academy of General Practice in 1967 and the Liaison Committee for Specialty Boards in 1969. Both the board and the academy later changed their names from "general" practice to "family" practice. The board proved to be an immediate success. Between 1974 and 1983, it granted 15.4 percent of all general certificates awarded by specialty boards, second only to the 25.5 percent awarded by the American Board of Internal Medicine and about twice as many as any other board.[83]

The major criticism of the board and the academy has been their support for the performance of surgery by family physicians. A 1970 study of four regions in the United States found that general and family practitioners performed 13.5 percent of all surgical procedures, but only 8.7 percent of all surgical procedures weighted by the California Relative Value scale. The general or family practitioners who performed any surgery did so with a median frequency of less than one per month (excluding assisting at vaginal deliveries). The study recommended that "there is no need to have surgical operations performed by both nonsurgeons and well trained surgeons." It added, however, "if nonsurgeons are to be induced to cease doing surgical operations, specialist surgeons must, at a minimum, cease giving general medical care.[84]

Primary care physicians provide a disproportionate amount of office care. One study in the 1970s found that general and family physicians, who comprised 16 percent of all physicians, provided 40 percent of all office visits to office-based physicians. Thirty-five percent of their patients were being treated for chronic conditions, second only to the 57 percent being treated for chronic conditions by specialists in internal medicine.[85]

Specialists and the Delivery of Primary Care

The shortage of primary care physicians has led to the suggestion that primary care be provided by qualified specialists, especially general internists and pediatricians. However, those two specialties differ from general and family practice in many respects. The Mendenhall study found that only 4.9 percent of the patients of internists were under 20 years of age, compared with over 20 percent of the patients of general and family practitioners and 98.1 percent of the patients of pediatricians. At the other extreme, 71.2 percent of the patients of internists were 45 years of age or older, compared to about 45 percent of the patients of general and family practitioners.[86]

The widely different age distributions of patients in the three specialties affected the way that they practiced medicine. The study found that 25.9 percent of the ambulatory patient encounters of pediatricians involved well patients, compared to about 13 percent of those of general and family practitioners and only 6.6 percent of those of general internists. Diagnostic tests were ordered in only 34.9 percent of ambulatory patient encounters of pediatricians, compared to about 40 percent of those of general and family practitioners and 59.0 percent of those of general internists. Furthermore, 35.7 percent of all patient encounters of general internists occurred in the hospital, compared to about 20 percent of those of general and family practitioners and 16.3 percent of those of pediatricians.[87]

General internists differed from the other two groups in the sources of their patients and their fees. The Mendenhall study found that only 68.3 percent of the ambulatory and hospital encounters of general internists were self-referred, compared to about 93 percent of those of primary and family practitioners and 87.2 percent of those of pediatricians. General internists had 10.1 percent of their ambulatory and hospital encounters referred by another physician for consultation, compared to almost none of those of general and family practitioners and pediatricians. With regard to fees, one study found that in 1973 and in 1982 internists charged about twice as much as the other two specialties for initial office visits, and 50 percent more for office visits of established patients.[88]

Internists have been more likely than the other two groups to become subspecialists during their careers. One survey obtained data on the 1971 and 1976 self-designated specialties of 10 percent of the physicians who graduated from medical school in 1960 and 1964. Of those in internal medicine in 1971, 24.7 percent of the 1960 cohort and 22.2 percent of the 1964 cohort had moved to a subspecialty of internal medicine in 1976. Of those in general and family practice in 1971, 7.5 percent of the 1960 cohort and 10.5 percent of the 1964 cohort had moved to a specialty in 1976, primarily to subspecialties in internal medicine. Among pediatricians, 9.3 percent of the 1960 cohort and 8.5 percent of the 1964 cohort moved to other specialties between 1971 and 1976.[89] These findings demonstrate that general internists and pediatricians cannot be substituted for family physicians.

Regardless of the fact that most physicians prefer specialty medicine, the major demand of the public is for primary care medicine. If primary care physicians are not available, patients will seek primary care from specialists, especially when the illnesses are minor and the treatments are standardized. Specialists can resist this pressure only if they are in very short supply and have enough patients in their practices. More often, however, specialists must provide some primary care to keep their patients satisfied, especially when the patients have difficulty finding primary care physicians. Thus, as a larger proportion of physicians have specialized in nonprimary care fields, they have had to provide more primary care. When everyone is a specialist, no one is a specialist.

Specialists practice primary care by treating unrelated medical problems of their regular patients. A gynecologist will care for a regular patient's infection or a cardiologist will treat a heart patient's diabetes rather than refer them to an internist or family physician.[90] This enables specialists to satisfy their patients without jeopardizing their specialty status.

Internists are the major specialists who provide primary care. One survey of 107 internists in Milwaukee, Wisconsin, about 1966 found that 56 percent of them reported that they were spending at least three-fourths of their time acting as family physicians. A 1972 survey of 783 physicians who served residences in internal medicine at the Mayo Clinic between 1935 and 1970 found that 73 percent of them reported that more than one-half of their practice constituted primary care, defined in the study as "that care rendered by a physician to whom the patient regularly turns first for any complaint or advice." A mail survey that produced 334 responses by internists in direct patient care in Massachusetts found that 65.6 percent of them provided some primary care and 31.4 percent spent at least one-half of their time on primary care.[91]

Subspecialists in internal medicine also provide much primary care. One study of cardiologists in noninstitutional settings found that only 58.7 percent of their office patients and 61.2 percent of their hospital patients were "primary cardiac" patients. The "primary non-cardiac" patients had problems that were "predominantly non-specialty in character so far as diagnosis and treatment is concerned," although many of them also had some cardiac conditions. The Mendenhall study found that, depending on the specialty, between 40 and 70 percent of the patient encounters of most nonsurgical subspecialists were "principal care encounters," defined as comprehensive care for regular patients (the exceptions were specialists in infectious diseases, allergy, and dermatology). Less than one-third of the encounters were consultations referred by other physicians (except for specialists in infectious diseases), and less than one-sixth were specialized care encounters to regular patients (except for allergists and dermatologists). Thus, most nonsurgical specialists do not spend most of their time on activities for which they were trained.[92]

Surgical specialists have also had to extend the range of their work activities. The slack workload of many surgeons has led them to broaden the range of the operations that they perform. Both neurosurgeons and orthopedic surgeons perform disc and spinal cord surgery and general surgeons do much colon and rectal surgery. Surgeons have also turned to nonsurgical patient care. The Mendenhall study found that, depending on the surgical specialty, between 20 and 40 percent of the patient encounters of surgeons were for comprehensive care for regular patients, except in obstetrics-gynecology, where the proportion was 65 percent. Less than one-third of all their patient encounters were for consultations referred by other physicians and less than 30 percent were for specialized care encounters with regular patients.[93] Clearly, surgeons are providing a significant amount of nonsurgical medical care for their patients.

Given the fact that only about one-sixth of all physicians are in general practice and family medicine, these findings indicate that much primary care is being provided by specialists. The major question raised by this finding is whether specialists are trained to provide primary care of acceptable quality. This will be a major theme in the analysis of medical schools to follow.

Medicine has changed in many ways since mid-century. Older persons and lower income persons receive much more care. More cases of chronic and degenerative diseases require treatment. The larger amount of hospital and office care has led to a greater use of instruments in medical care but has also reduced the physicians' understanding of social and family factors in illness. Specialization has narrowed the focus of physicians and greater wealth may have affected their values. The enormous growth in treatments of all kinds has increased the need for careful judgment because of the greater possibilities of error, excessive use, and harmful side effects. A new kind of medical education is needed to prepare physicians for contemporary medical practice.

10

Hospitals and Health Care

The use of hospitals for medical care became more varied after 1950. More patients were admitted for a wide variety of conditions and more different types of treatments were provided. Many new technologies were adopted that have raised costs considerably. Hospitals employed more residents, foreign medical graduates, and nurses.

Increases in Hospital Activities and Staffing

Between 1946 and 1983, hospitals grew both in size and importance in the health care system. The number of short-term nonfederal hospitals increased by only one-third, but the number of beds and the average daily census doubled and the number of admissions increased 2.6 times (Table 10.1), while the U.S. population grew by only two-thirds. Much of the additional use was for nonsurgical care. During the 1928–1943 period, 74 percent of all hospital admissions were surgical. This declined to 60 percent between 1956 and 1968 and to 50 percent between 1975 and 1981. Outpatient care grew even more rapidly than inpatient care, with the number of hospital outpatients doubling between 1965 and 1983.[1]

The hospital system has become dominated by large hospitals, practically all of which have affiliated with medical schools. In 1983, the 18 percent of nonfederal short-term hospitals that had 300 or more beds admitted 50 percent of the patients, carried out 59 percent of the surgery, and had 55 percent of the outpatient visits and 61 percent of the births. They employed 72 percent of all physicians and dentists employed in hospitals and 90 percent of all medical and dental residents. At least 60 percent of them had nurseries for premature infants, hemodialysis units, radiation therapy or isotope facilities, computerized tomograhy (CT) scanners, and cardiac catheterization facilities, and almost one-half had open-heart surgery facilities. Most also offered types of care not traditionally associated with hospitals. Practically all of them provided social work services and physical therapy, at least 75 percent provided occupational and speech therapy, and 40 percent provided outpatient psychiatric care. On the other hand, fewer than one-third provided family planning, home care, or hospice services, or partial hospitalization for psychiatric patients.[2]

The expanding services of nonfederal short-term general hospitals has led to the employment of larger numbers of workers. The number of full-time equivalent workers increased at a rate double that of patient admissions: from .5 million in

TABLE 10.1. Nonfederal Short-Term General Hospitals, 1946–1983[a]

Year	Hospitals	Beds	Admissions	Average Daily Census	Outpatient Visits	FTE[b] Personnel	U.S. Population
1946	4,444	473	13,655	341	n.a.	505	141,900
1950	5,031	505	16,663	372	n.a.	662	152,300
1960	5,407	639	22,970	477	92,631[c]	1,080	180,700
1970	5,859	848	29,252	662	133,545	1,929	205,100
1983	5,843	1,021	36,201	750	213,995	3,102	234,200

[a]Includes some special hospitals. All figures are in thousands, except the number of hospitals, which are as stated.
[b]Full Time Equivalent.
[c]1965.

Sources: American Hospital Association, *Hospital Statistics: 1984 Edition* (Chicago: American Hospital Association, 1984), p. 5; U.S. Bureau of the Census, *Statistical Abstract of the United States, 1984*, (Washington, D.C.: U.S. G.P.O., 1983), p. 6.

1946 (compared to 13.7 million admissions), to 1.4 million to 1965 (compared to 26.5 million admissions), and to 3.1 million in 1983 (compared to 36.2 million admissions). In 1977, 11.3 percent of all physicians with patient care as their major professional activity were full-time staff members of hospitals. Three of the fastest growing medical specialties—radiology, pathology, and anesthesiology—have been hospital based. Other rapidly growing occupations that have been primarily hospital-based include active registered nurses, who increased from 375,000 in 1950 to 1,415,000 in 1982; therapists, up from 148,000 in 1972 to 252,000 in 1980; health administrators, up from 118,000 to 228,000 over the same period; and health technologists and technicians, up from 315,000 to 657,000.[3]

Community physicians have found hospital staff privileges to be increasingly important to their practices. As late as 1951, about 17 percent of the physicians in New York City had no hospital appointments and another 12 percent could not admit their private patients to hospitals. A national survey of physicians in 1982 found that 91.4 percent had hospital admitting privileges, including 90.5 percent of general and family physicians and 97.0 percent of medical and surgical specialists.[4]

Hospital Costs and Hospital Insurance

For many years hospital costs have been the most rapidly rising component of health-care costs. Between 1950 and 1982 daily hospital room charges increased more than 18-fold, 3 times the overall increase in the medical care component of the Consumer Price Index. Hospital-care expenditures have grown from 30.4 to 42.0 percent of all expenditures for health services and supplies over the same period.[5]

The rising costs of hospital care have been concentrated in a small proportion of patients. A 1976 study of 2,238 patient records in six hospitals found that 13.3 percent of all patients in the sample accounted for one-half of the total billings for all patients. Forty percent of the 20 percent of the patients with the highest costs were 65 years of age or older (compared to 15 percent of the other patients), and about 35 percent of them experienced complications during treatment (five times the number experienced by the other patients). About 20 percent of the high-cost patients died in the hospital, as opposed to less than 4 percent of the other patients. In contrast to the long hospital stays of the nineteenth century, fewer than 25 percent of the high-cost patients had single prolonged or cost-intensive hospitalizations. Two-thirds of them had repeated hospitalizations during the year.[6]

The growth in hospital care has been financed by public and private hospital reimbursement plans. In 1982, 53.1 percent of all personal expenditures for hospital care were supported by government payments, including Medicare and Medicaid, and 33.2 percent were supported by private insurance plans, especially Blue Cross. Private insurors were particularly important in short-term private hospitals.[7]

Blue Cross plans and private hospitals began their close association with the development of the first plans during the depression of the 1930s by hospital administrators and physicians who sought to increase hospital utilization. The plans spread throughout the nation and have insured over 40 percent of the total number of persons with private hospital insurance coverage since 1960. In 1979, an estimated 85.4 million persons were covered by Blue Cross plans, compared to 109.8 million persons covered by all other private hospital insurance plans combined. Blue Cross plans have also been used by the federal government as the primary contractor for hospital services under Medicare and by over 80 percent of all hospitals as their local fiscal intermediaries for Medicare payments. They have been used less often for Medicaid payment. Until 1972, the American Hospital Association maintained interlocking directorates with the national Blue Cross Association and owned the name "Blue Cross" and Blue Cross insignia. In 1970, 42 percent of the members of all Blue Cross boards represented hospitals and another 14 percent represented the medical profession.[8]

Blue Cross plans have adopted reimbursement systems favorable to hospitals. Instead of reimbursing insured individuals for hospital stays, like other private insurors, Blue Cross has reimbursed hospitals directly for reasonable costs incurred. Under these cost-plus plans, Blue Cross has not used any criteria of reasonableness or prudence in determining "allowable costs," such as by comparing hospitals in a community. As a result, according to Law, hospitals suppliers, pathologists, radiologists, and others have received inflated prices for goods and services relative to those available outside of hospitals. Law has observed that "hospitals are paid in advance for whatever they claim. Books are audited, often years later, by commercial auditors with no particular expertise in health services and no capacity to judge whether or not a cost is reasonable."[9] In recent years, many Blue Cross plans have added new types of coverage that make greater efforts to control costs.

Other private health insurors have not insured enough people to be able to reduce reimbursements to health-care providers, even though some have tried to do so. When a large private insurance company began to monitor physician claims in the early 1970s, physicians threatened to refuse to deal with it directly, which forced the company to abandon its program. This kind of threat has been very effective in limiting the power of private insurors.[10]

The federal government, through Medicare and Medicaid, has had little impact on hospital expenses until the 1980s. The Social Security Administration and its successor, the Health Care Financing Administration, accepted most aspects of existing reimbursement systems as a basis for compensation at the inception of Medicare and Medicaid in 1965.[11] Pressure from Congress led to the creation of prospective reimbursement systems after 1983. These have provided a fixed payment to hospitals for the treatment of all patients in the same diagnosis related group (DRG), thereby offering financial incentives to hospitals to reduce the cost of the patient's care. The long-term effectiveness of prospective payment systems and their ability to resist modifications favorable to hospitals have yet to be determined.

Private insurors and the federal government have shown limited concern with standards of hospital quality. Since 1951, hospitals have been accredited by the Joint Committee on Accreditation of Hospitals (JCAH), composed of representatives of the American Hospital Association, the American Medical Association, and several other organizations. Its accreditation automatically made a hospital eligible to be a Medicare provider in 1965, although the policy was altered some time later. JCAH accreditation standards generally paid more attention to the hospital's physical plant, medical records, and formal professional staff qualifications than to factors affecting the quality of care, such as the number of professional staff caring for patients or the findings of tissue review committees. In 1979, new accreditation standards provided for greater documentation of hospital performance.[12]

The Expansion of Hospital Technology

Hospital care has been revolutionized by many new technologies. One of the first was the manufacture of disposable products by hospital supply firms. Until the 1940s hospitals made their own bandages, prepared their own intravenous solutions, and reused equipment for blood transfusions and similar procedures. Incomplete sterilization of the equipment often produced unfavorable reactions in patients. Manufactured products have safeguarded patients and employees through assured sterility and the immediate disposal of contaminated items.[13]

Another major innovation was the autoanalyzer, which automatically performed many blood, urine, and similar tests at a lower cost per test and more quickly than could laboratory technicians. It became so popular that a battery of tests has been commonly performed on all patients at admission, often unrelated to their conditions and unsolicited by their physicians. A study at one large general hospital found that the number of laboratory tests per patient-day increased from 3.56 in 1971 to 6.86 in 1979, and that the proportion of total hospital costs expended on laboratory tests increased from 7.1 percent to 9.0 percent over the same period.[14]

Laboratory tests have been administered routinely because they were covered by the patient's insurance and were inexpensive compared to other aspects of hospital care. Physicians have also relied heavily on laboratory tests to make clinical decisions. Under cost-based reimbursement systems, hospitals have tended to encourage the use of tests that produce substantial revenues and need not be priced competitively with tests in nonhospital laboratories. One 1970 study found that, among clinical laboratories performing over 100,000 tests per year, hospital laboratories averaged a price of $3.17 per test compared to $1.82 per test in independent laboratories unconnected with hospitals. Smaller independent and hospital laboratories had nearly identical average prices of about $3.50 per test.[15]

The high level of utilization of clinical laboratory, X-ray, and similar tests has led many observers to conclude that they have contributed more to raising aggregate hospital costs than technologies that were more expensive to purchase and operate. Efforts to control them have been difficult because of the large number of physicians who must be monitored.[16] This suggests that physicians should acquire a proper understanding of the uses and limitations of clinical tests in their medical education.

Many new technologies have involved high purchase, operating, and patient-care costs. These have included general intensive care units, coronary care units, burn units, inhalation therapy units, units using radioactive elements for diagnosis and therapy, renal dialysis units, open-heart surgery units, CT scanners, and facilities for organ transplants and artificial organ implants. An intensive care unit has generally employed more than twice as many workers per bed as regular facilities in a short-term general hospital and costs three times as much per bed to operate. The Surgery Study Group recommended in 1971 that "optimal resources" for a 6-bed cardiac surgical intensive care unit included 16 registered nurses, 10 licensed practical nurses and technicians, 5 aides, 5 secretaries, plus the necessary residents and physicians. Hospital technologies have often become more expensive to operate overtime, unlike most other innovations. For example, the department of inhalation therapy at the Massachusetts General Hospital grew from a budget of $32,000 and 4 employees in 1959 to a budget of $884,000 and 70 employees in 1976.[17]

New technologies have had high rates of obsolescence. In the 1950s more than 90 percent of all hospitals with 200 or more beds had orthovoltage X-ray units for radiation therapy. X-ray therapy was replaced in the 1960s by radium therapy, which in turn was replaced by cobalt therapy, which was replaced in the 1970s by linear accelerators. Each of these replacement technologies was more expensive than its predecessor. Because many hospitals have not been able to afford the newer technologies, X-ray and radium therapy units have remained the most prevalent types of radiation therapy units.[18]

New hospital technologies, such as the CT scanner, have tended to supplement rather than replace existing technologies. A study at one medical school hospital found that three years after its installation, a CT scanner performed almost 4,000 CT scans. Yet the number of electroencephalographs and conventional radionuclide brain scans did not decrease over that period. The CT Scanner was therefore responsible for almost $1 million in additional revenue to the hospital.[19]

A major issue in new technologies has been their effectiveness. Unlike pharmaceuticals, medical technologies have not had to provide rigorous evidence of efficacy or usefulness prior to their introduction. Most have not been systematically compared to other means of diagnosis or treatment using a full range of relevant criteria. Perry observed in 1978 that "within the research community there is no structured mechanism for identifying optimum clinical procedures . . . flowing from research or for interventions already in practice. . . . [W]hen there is controversy over the optimal intervention for prevention, diagnosis, or treatment of a disease, there is no formal process in place to resolve conflicting claims."[20]

The problems of evaluation have varied by type of technology. Diagnostic technologies have been difficult to evaluate because of the tendency to expand the conditions in which they were used, thereby reducing the proportion of tests with positive results. One study found that the proportion of positive findings in CT head scans declined over a period of time from about two-thirds to about one-half. This pattern has raised costs and led to the purchase of additional units, while the total number of positive findings from the technology may have shown little change. Therapeutic technologies, which have been more restricted in their use, have been difficult to evaluate because most of them have not cured disease, but rather improved the condition of a sick patient, maintained the life of a terminally ill one, or relieved symptoms. It has rarely been possible to measure how much improvement occurred or how much meaningful time was added to the patient's life.[21]

Hospitals have invested heavily in new technologies because of outside pressures and their internal decision-making structures. The public and community physicians have wanted new technologies to be available in most community hospitals. Hospital administrators have been motivated by cost-based reimbursement systems to expand hospital facilities. If an operating year surplus was used to purchase a new technology, any increase in the hospital's costs would usually lead to higher levels of reimbursements in future years. The specific technologies adopted have been chosen by individual physicians or specialty units, whose primary interest was to enhance the services that they provided. Few of them were concerned with overall hospital operations, the availability of facilities in nearby hospitals, or the most cost-effective way to provide care.[22]

The manner of selecting new technologies has often resulted in their underutilization. The Surgery Study Group found that about 1970 "many facilities performing cardiac surgery are underutilized to a degree that raises serious questions about their value" and the ability of their staffs to maintain their professional skills. The committee suggested a minimum of four to six cardiac operations with extracorporeal circulation weekly, a level reached by fewer than 30 percent of the hospitals with such facilities.[23]

There has been little interest in new technologies that can integrate or limit hospital care. Hospital physicians have rarely used computers to take patient histories and write patient records, even though many records are so voluminous that much information in them has been inaccessible. They have also seldom used computerized decision-making aids, which have been essential to the effective use of many technologies. Few technologies that reduced or prevented hospital stays have been introduced or studied, despite the estimate that 20 percent of hospital care has been unnecessary.[24]

Hospital illnesses resulting from new technologies have received little attention, although iatrogenic illnesses in hospitals have been quite common. One survey in the early 1960s found that 18.5 percent of 1,014 patients in a large hospital suffered one or more medical complications in the hospital. They averaged 28.7 days of hospitalization, compared to 11.4 days for the rest of the sample. Deaths related to treatment occurred in 8.1 percent of those experiencing medical complications. Another study in 1979 of 815 patients admitted to the medical wards of a university teaching hospital found that 36 percent had "one or more iatrogenic illnesses with a total of 497 such occurrences." Seventy-six patients had "major complications," which produced an average length of stay of 19.3 days, 11.5 of them after the first major complication. The complications were believed to have "contributed to the death of" 15 patients. Of the 497 complications, 41.9 percent were drug related and 35.2 percent were caused by diagnostic and therapeutic procedures. Neither study included complications that occurred after the patients were released from the hospital.[25]

It is evident that the use of hospital technologies needs to be improved if hospitals are to provide beneficial and cost-effective patient care. Appropriate education of physicians is essential to that end.

Hospital Outpatient Care

Hospitals have offered three basic kinds of outpatient care. The emergency care service has become a general clinic for the routine and emergency medical problems of the nearby population. Specialty outpatient clinics, of which there may be dozens in a large teaching hospital, have provided care in individual medical specialties or illnesses. The newest type of outpatient care has been the use of hospital diagnostic and therapeutic facilities on an outpatient basis.[26]

Hospital outpatient care has increased much faster than has inpatient care. Between 1956 and 1983, the total number of outpatient visits to all hospitals increased over 4 times, from 66.0 million to 273.2 million, while the total number of inpatient admissions increased only 2.5 times, from 15.6 million to 38.9 million. Between 1965 and 1983 in short-term nonfederal hospitals, the number of outpatient visits more than doubled, from 92.6 million to 214.0 million, while the number of inpatient admissions increased about one-third, from 26.5 million to 36.2 million. Hospital outpatient visits accounted for 13.7 percent of all ambulatory visits by patients to physicians' offices, clinics, hospitals in 1964, and 15.1 percent of the visits in 1981.[27]

Many users of outpatient clinics have relied on them for much of their medical care. One 1960 study examined 644 outpatients of an urban hospital clinic for the medically indigent over a three-month period. It found that one-half of the patients used the clinic as their "central source of medical care" and another one-sixth had no particular central source of care. A 1976 survey of 1,803 outpatients at 17 Veterans Administration (VA) hospitals found that 67 percent of the respondents considered the VA hospital to be their "usual" source of outpatient care."[28]

The quality of care in hospital outpatient departments has continued to be a major problem. A common pattern in large hospitals has been for patients to be treated for different disorders in different specialty clinics, with no clinic assuming responsibility for their overall care. Outpatient medical care has also been adversely affected by changes in staffing. The young physicians who used to staff outpatient departments to increase their private practices and obtain appointments to the inpatient staff have not done so for years because of the shortage of physicians. Hospitals have replaced them with residents and part-time salaried physicians, who have often been less motivated to provide high quality care.[29]

Outpatient departments have lacked administrative and professional leadership and resources. Power in hospitals has been vested primarily in the staff physicians in the inpatient services. They have been most interested in the quality of care given to inpatients, especially their private patients. Many inpatients have also had a choice of hospitals, so that competition has tended to keep up the quality of inpatient care. Those who have used the outpatient facilities often lacked access to other sources of care. Hospitals thus have maintained a level of outpatient services sufficient to avoid adverse publicity in the community and to satisfy the practice needs of the residents and physicians who have staffed them.

Public Hospitals

State and local short-term general hospitals, which have been widely used in medical education, have provided a decreasing amount of care relative to not-for-profit and profit short-term hospitals. In 1946, public hospitals had 28.1 percent of all beds and 24.7 percent of the average daily census in the three types of hospitals. In 1983 they had only 20.5 percent and 19.5 percent, respectively. In 1965 they cared for 32.3 percent of short-term hospital outpatients, but this declined to 24.4 percent in 1983. They did retain their share of short-term hospital admissions: 19.7 percent in 1946 and 19.5 percent in 1983. Their expenses per inpatient-day were $70.56 in 1946, compared to $74.94 in not-for-profit hospitals and $71.40 in profit hospitals. In 1983 the corresponding figures were $341.30, $373.62, and $385.42.[30]

Public hospitals have become more similar to private hospitals. Their average length of stay declined from 11.4 days in 1946 to 7.6 days in 1983, compared to a decline from 8.8 to 7.7 days in not-for-profit hospitals and from 6.6 to 6.5 days in profit hospitals. Public hospitals had only 13.3 percent of the births in the three types of hospitals in 1946, but 22.8 percent of them in 1983. Public hospitals have become as likely as not-for-profit hospitals of the same size to have major hospital technologies and social and rehabilitation services for their patients.[31]

Many public hospitals have affiliated with medical schools, which have staffed them with residents and faculty members in return for funding and the use of patients in teaching and research. Close to 75 percent of medical schools in 1940 and in 1965 reported affiliation with a public community hospital. In 1982, 40 nonfederal public hospitals had common ownership with medical schools and 22 were closely affiliated with them, compared to only 24 and 27 private hospitals, respectively. Twenty-three other public hospitals were also affiliated with medical schools, suggesting that at least two-thirds of all medical schools were affiliated with public hospitals in 1982. In 1983, state and local hospitals had 33.2 percent of all medical and dental residents in community hospitals affiliated with medical schools, even though they accounted for only 17.4 percent of all inpatient- and outpatient-days in affiliated hospitals.[32]

Hospital Residents and Interns

The shortage of physicians has forced hospitals to rely increasingly on interns and residents to care for patients. In the 1970s, the rotating internships that provided postgraduate training in general medicine for one or two years were replaced by residencies that provided training in a medical specialty over three or more years. The number of house officers in hospitals and some other institutions has increased from 19,453 in 1950 to 72,397 in 1983.[33]

Hospitals have offered internships and residencies because house officers have been readily available and have received low salaries. In 1958–1959, interns in hospitals affiliated with medical schools received average stipends of $1,860 and those in unaffiliated hospitals received $2,376. In 1968–1969, interns in affiliated hospitals earned $6,011 and those in unaffiliated hospitals earned $6,851. The median stipend of first-year residents reached $14,775 in 1979–1980 and $20,800 in 1984, which was still far below the salaries of comparable professionals. Hospitals also received partial reimbursement for stipends to house officers under Medicare and Medicaid as educational costs.[34]

Hospitals unaffiliated with medical schools have had more difficulty attracting house officers than affiliated hospitals. In order to attract more house officers, many unaffiliated hospitals have affiliated with medical schools in recent years, although the closeness of the relationship has varied widely. A study of surgical residencies found that in 1961–1962, hospitals affiliated with medical schools had 49.5 percent of the 2,584 surgical residency programs and 57.4 percent of the 12,824 surgical residents. In 1974–1975, affiliated hospitals had 91.2 percent of the 1,675 programs and 93.8 percent of the 18,159 residents.[35]

Residencies have been designed to provide education through supervised patient care and other activities, supplemented by more formal training. In practice, residency programs have been established more to meet the hospital's need for manpower than the community and nation's need for physicians in the specialty. Residents have often spent most of their time providing patient care with little supervision. They have received insufficient guidance and evaluation from the hospital staff and obtained most of their training from more experienced residents. Residents have normally been the only physicians present on the wards during much of the day, which has given them major responsibility for much patient care. While this can result in a fresh approach to the patient's problems, it can also place his care in the hands of an inexperienced tyro.[36]

In dealing with ward patients without personal physicians, house officers have been given a great deal of discretion. This has seldom benefited the patient. Because house officers rotate among the hospital services, the residents who care for individual patients change regularly. Responsibility for the patient's care in hospitals affiliated with medical schools has been vested in a "team" or "committee," which Duff and Hollingshead described as follows:

> Committee sponsorship . . . was provided by medical students, interns and residents—all physicians in training; the patient had a committee of student physicians instead of a single, responsible physician. Members of the committee were, for the most part, interested in the . . . patient to the extent that his disease advanced their learning or their research opportunities. . . .
>
> The patients represented diseases, not persons, to the members of the committee. They believed any inconvenience their learning might cause was amply repaid in the services the patients received.

On the wards suspicion, distrust, and confusion were extreme and common. The performance of the physician tended to keep alive this distrust. The patient hoped for the best care and an explanation of what was being done. Although he may have been given optimal treatment, if he did not get an explanation of what was being done he often felt that he was being used as a "guinea pig." He thought that the physician did not "talk my language." In fact physicians often misinformed the patient concerning his illness and the intended treatment.[37]

Some physicians have proposed that hospitals reduce their use of residents for patient care and employ more full-time salaried hospital physicians. Residents have been relatively unskilled providers of patient care, have spent only a fraction of their time on it, have used their patient care activities primarily for self-education, and have become more expensive. Careers in hospital medicine have become common in health maintenance and other organizations that employ salaried physicians. Full-time hospital practice has also been the prevailing mode of specialty practice in most European countries. With the increasing supply of physicians in the United States, it should become more attractive to physicians here.

Foreign Medical Graduates in Hospitals

The shortage of physicians after mid-century forced many hospitals to offer residencies to foreign medical graduates (FMGs), physicians of foreign birth who received their medical education in a country other than the United States or Canada. Many FMGs have shown evidence of training inferior to that provided in American medical schools. Since 1957, FMGs seeking entrance to U.S. training programs have been examined by the Educational Council for Foreign Medical Graduates (ECFMG), using questions from examinations of the National Board of Medical Examinations given to U.S. medical students. Often as many as 40 percent of the FMGs taking the examinations have been repeating them. Up to 1972, the proportion passing the examination varied from 31 to 46 percent.[38]

The number of FMGs has grown rapidly, at first due to exchange programs begun in 1949 and the Fulbright-Hays Act of 1961, and later to the 1965 government ruling that the shortage of physicians exempted FMGs from the need to provide proof of employment or educational opportunity. The proportion of all newly licensed physicians who were FMGs increased from 5.1 percent in 1950 to 17.7 percent in 1960, 27.3 percent in 1970, and 35.4 percent in 1975. The proportion of FMGs graduating from European medical schools declined from a majority of all FMGs in the 1950s to only 17.2 percent of 3,935 FMGs taking examinations for admission to graduate training in 1973, at which time 57.4 percent were graduates of Asian medical schools. In 1976 Congress enacted legislation that made it more difficult for FMGs to immigrate to the United States or to remain in the United States for an indefinite period. In 1981, 16.6 percent of all newly licensed physicians were FMGs.[39]

The number of FMGs serving as house officers increased from 2,072 in 1950 to a high of over 18,000 annually in the early 1970s, and then declined to 13,221 in 1983. As a proportion of all house officers, they increased from 9.6 percent in 1950 to 26.5 percent in 1960, exceeded 30 percent in the early 1970s, and declined to

18.4 percent in 1983. One 1973–1974 survey found that 44 percent of FMGs had practiced medicine for one to four years before coming to the United States and another 19 percent had practiced for five or more years. Seventy-six percent reported that they came to the United States to learn a specialty, 66 percent mentioned the high salaries in the United States, and 50 percent referred to the lack of opportunities in their home countries. The respondents were about evenly split between those who wanted to return to their countries of origin and those who wanted to remain in the United States.[40]

The survey found that FMGs usually accepted positions in less attractive residency programs. The great majority of them were hired sight unseen. Twenty-nine percent took residencies in hospitals unaffiliated with medical schools, compared to 8 percent of the graduates of U.S. medical schools. Forty-one percent entered hospitals that had fewer than five residency programs, compared to 7 percent of U.S. medical school graduates. FMG house officers had hours of work, salaries, and service expectations that were comparable to those of U.S. medical school graduates.[41]

FMGs have had difficulty obtaining licenses to practice and certification by specialty boards. Between 1964 and 1972, the failure rate of FMGs in state licensing examinations was 36 percent, compared to 6 percent among American graduates. In 1972, the failure rate of FMGs in all specialty board examinations was 63 percent, compared to 27 percent among American medical school graduates. Many FMGs obtained temporary licenses and have been employed in institutions like state mental hospitals that have been unable to attract U.S. medical graduates.[42]

A much smaller number of FMGs have come to the United States as practicing physicians or were United States citizens who were educated in foreign medical schools (USFMGs). The number of physicians admitted as immigrants increased from 1,900 in 1950 to 3,200 in 1970, reached a high of 7,100 in 1977, and then declined to 3,000 in 1979 as a result of changes in the immigration laws. The number of USFMGs in internships and residencies in U.S. hospitals grew rapidly in the 1970s and reached 6,990 in 1983. This number, which includes residents in up to four years of service, may be compared to the 16,000 graduates of U.S. medical schools in 1983.[43]

Thousands of FMGs have entered the United States neither fully licensed nor in approved graduate training programs, and therefore not legally physicians. Many of them have failed to become physicians or enter training programs. One study of 3,935 FMGs taking the ECFMG examination in the United States in 1973 (70 percent of whom were permanent U.S. residents) found that only 18 percent were taking the examination for the first time and that 36 percent were taking it for at least the fourth time. About 60 percent were employed in health-care occupations, two-thirds of them in hospitals. Over 70 percent of those in the health field provided direct patient care, sometimes without supervision. The study concluded that "a large number of FMGs are functioning in a medical underground delivering patient care in an unsupervised and unregulated fashion."[44]

FMG physicians have provided much health care to the American public. In 1959, only 8.6 percent of all physicians in the United States were FMGs. Between 1962 and 1971, 75,639 FMGs entered the U.S. compared to 77,867 graduates of

American medical schools. In every year between 1975 and 1981, 19 percent of all physicians in active practice have been graduates of foreign medical schools. In 1977, FMGs constituted 20.1 percent of all physicians engaged in patient care, 17.0 percent of all office-based physicians engaged in patient care, 37.1 percent of all full-time hospital staff, and 19.5 percent of all those in full-time medical school teaching.[45]

Whatever the problems of foreign medical graduates, the American health-care system would have deteriorated significantly in the last two decades without them. They have provided a substantial amount of care both in and outside of hospitals. They have worked where American physicians did not want to work and did not have to work because of the extreme shortage of graduates of American medical schools. The increasing supply of American-trained physicians will diminish the role of FMGs in the future, but the gap that they filled demonstrates the need to examine the role of American medical schools in meeting the nation's demand for physicians.

Nursing

The growth in hospital patient care after mid-century led to an increase in the number of active registered nurses from 375,000 in 1950 to 1,273,000 in 1980, or from 249 to 506 nurses per 100,000 population. Hospitals and nursing homes employed 48.5 percent of registered nurses in 1949 and 73.7 percent of them in 1980. Nurses employed in private duty work decreased from 21.6 percent of all nurses in 1949 to 1.6 percent in 1980.[46]

The increased complexity of hospital care has stratified nursing occupations. In 1950, 46.8 percent of all hospital nurses were registered nurses, 8.3 percent were practical nurses (which usually required 12 months of training), and 45.0 percent were nursing aides. By 1972, only 36.6 percent were registered nurses, 20.0 percent were practical nurses, and 43.7 percent were nursing aides. Registered nurses have assumed greater administrative responsibilities as a result of the increase in hospital practical nurses and nursing aides. In 1980, 19.4 percent of registered nurses in hospitals were full-time administrators, head nurses, or instructors, and many others had some administrative responsibilities.[47]

Nursing education has moved from hospital diploma schools to collegiate schools of nursing. In 1953, 91.7 percent of the 29,255 graduates of nursing programs were graduates of hospital diploma schools, 7.4 percent were graduates of bachelor's degree programs, and 0.9 percent were graduates of community college programs. In 1976, 25.6 percent of the 77,633 graduates were graduates of hospital diploma schools, 29.2 percent were graduates of bachelor's degree programs, and 45.2 percent were graduates of community college programs. Academic programs have become more popular because the expanded intellectual content of nursing education could not be provided in hospital schools. Hospitals have also found that the costs of diploma nursing schools exceeded their benefits.[48]

Collegiate schools of nursing have had several problems. Classroom training has often been poorly integrated with hospital training and the emphasis on the former has given students insufficient clinical experience. Internships and other programs to provide clinical training have often suffered from the exploitation of student labor. Four-year nursing schools have also found it difficult to differentiate the nursing functions of their graduates from those of the graduates of two-year programs, with resulting dissatisfaction for the better educated nurses.[49]

Nursing has developed new specialized patient-care roles such as nurse practitioners, midwives, clinical specialists, and anesthetists, most of which have required education beyond the baccalaureate level. In 1980 only 5 percent of 1.2 million registered nurses were employed in those capacities, primarily in hospitals, physicians' offices, or public health agencies.[50]

Thus nursing has become increasingly restricted to the hospital. Within the hospital, the registered nurse's role in patient care has become circumscribed by physicians, who make most treatment decisions, by practical nurses, who provide most of the routine patient care, and by new kinds of therapists and technicians. Most registered nurses, according to Aiken, "remain hospital management's representatives at the ward level." She observed that nursing's problem has been that, despite their administrative role, "nurses' professional legitimacy derives from what their clinical expertise can bring to patient care—not their administrative skills."[51]

If there is to be an independent professional role for nurses in the hospital, it can only be that proposed by Florence Nightingale—the delineation of specific aspects of patient care for which nurses assume responsibility. In contemporary hospital medicine, the great need at the patient's level has been for coordination of the care provided by many different specialists. Instead of assuming this coordinating function, nursing has moved toward greater specialization of its own, often in unsuccessful competition with physicians.

Thus hospitals have expanded many of their traditional functions and assumed many new ones, including a closer relationship with medical schools. These new functions do not appear to have brought about major improvements in their training of residents or nurses. The effect of medical school affiliation on hospitals will be examined in more detail in a subsequent chapter.

11

The Organization of
Medical Schools After 1950

Between 1950 and 1980, state and federal funding made higher education a major component of American society in terms of the number of institutions, students, and faculty members; the range of academic and professional programs; and the capital investment and expenditures. Medical schools also grew from small, narrowly based institutions that educated undergraduate medical students to large academic medical centers that provided a wide range of educational, research, and patient-care activities. The schools changed their internal structures by replacing part-time faculty members with full-time faculty and restricting clinicians' private practices to the medical school. Their independent sources of funding and autonomy affected relations with their parent universities, affiliated health schools, and the community.

General Higher Education After 1950

The most distinctive feature of higher education after mid-century has been its greater accessibility to students. The number of degree-credit enrolled college students increased from 2.7 million in 1949 to 5.9 million in 1965, 11.2 million in 1975, and 12.4 million in 1982. Between 1950 and 1982, the proportion of the 25- to 29-year-old population who had completed four or more years of college rose from 7.7 percent to 21.7 percent, even though the number of persons in that age group increased by two-thirds. The most rapid growth in higher education occurred from the late 1950s to the mid-1970s, when total degree-credit enrollment tripled. From 1975 to the early 1980s, three-fourths of the growth has been due to part-time students.[1]

The greater accessibility of higher education has especially benefited those groups of students who had low rates of college attendance at mid-century. The number of women students increased from 0.8 million in 1949 to 6.4 million in 1981, while the number of men increased from 1.9 million to 6.0 million. Between 1950 and 1982, the proportion of blacks 25 to 29 years of age who had completed four or more years of college increased from 2.8 percent to 15.8 percent. In 1979, blacks accounted for 10.5 percent of high school graduates and 10.0 percent of college enrollees. In the same year, hispanics accounted for 4.3 percent of high school graduates and 4.2 percent of college enrollees.[2]

Changes have occurred in the academic status of many students. Part-time students increased from 2.0 million in 1966 to 5.2 million in 1982, while full-time students increased from 4.4 million to 7.2 million. Graduate students have increased more rapidly than undergraduate students. Between 1949–1950 and 1980–1981, the number of bachelors' and first professional degrees awarded increased 2.3 times from 432,058 to 1,007,096, the number of masters' degrees increased 5.1 times from 58,183 to 295,739, and the number of doctorates increased 5.1 times from 6,420 to 32,958. The number of first professional degrees considered separately more than doubled from 31,236 in 1965–1966 to 71,956 in 1980–1981.[3]

Institutions of higher education have grown both in numbers and size. The total number increased from 1,851 in 1949 to 3,280 in 1982, with public institutions increasing from 821 to 1,493, and private ones from 1,409 to 1,787. The former now dominate enrollments: between 1949 and 1982, the 1.4 million students in public institutions increased sevenfold to 9.7 million, while the 1.3 million students in private institutions doubled to 2.7 million. In 1980, the 11 percent of all institutions of higher education with at least 10,000 students (89 percent of which were public institutions) enrolled one-half of all students. Many colleges and universities organized branch campuses, which comprised 5 percent of all institutions of higher education in 1982.[4]

Academic institutions that offered a limited curriculum in 1950 have undergone the most significant changes. Many private liberal arts colleges, technical institutes, and agricultural colleges have developed a full range of undergraduate and graduate programs. Two-year colleges, mostly public community colleges, increased from 518 in 1950, with 217,000 degree-credit students, to 1,274 in 1981, with 4.7 million students. State teachers' colleges became state colleges or regional state universities with a wide variety of undergraduate and graduate programs. In 1980, two-year colleges enrolled about 25 percent of all college students and state colleges and regional state universities another 25 percent.[5]

Students have shown preferences for a wide variety of undergraduate degree programs in the last three decades. Vocational programs have been chosen by about 60 percent of all students who received undergraduate degrees in every year since 1950. The most popular vocational programs, business and education, together produced one-third or more of all undergraduate degrees annually. Education was the more popular during the 1950s and 1960s, but then declined to under 13 percent of all undergraduate degrees awarded in 1980 due to the reduced demand for teachers. Degrees in business steadily increased to about 20 percent of undergraduate degrees awarded in 1980. Another one-eighth to one-sixth of undergraduate degrees in most of these years were granted in the natural sciences, mathematics, and engineering. Enrollments in the less vocational disciplines have fluctuated widely from year to year. The proportion of undergraduate degrees awarded in the social and behavioral sciences, arts, foreign languages, English, philosophy, and comparable fields rose during the 1960s and fell after the mid-1970s.[6]

Sex differences in undergraduate degrees awarded, which were important during the 1950s and 1960s, declined in the 1970s. Over the three-decade period, about one-fourth of all men received degrees in business and another one-fourth received degrees in the basic or applied sciences. During the 1950s and 1960s, over two-thirds of the women received degrees in education, arts, humanities, and social sciences, but this proportion declined to less than one-half by 1980. The proportion of women who received undergraduate degrees in business and the basic and applied sciences increased from under 10 percent in the 1950s and 1960s to over 20 percent in 1980. The proportion with degrees in the health professions increased from under 5 percent in the 1950s and 1960s to over 11 percent in 1980, partly due to the growth of academic nursing programs.

Undergraduate academic disciplines have shown a trend toward subspecialization. In 1980, the National Center for Educational Statistics listed 25 undergraduate fields of study in engineering, over 40 in education, 21 in the health professions, 20 in the physical sciences, and 18 in business, to cite only a few.[7]

The number of master's degrees awarded annually has increased fivefold between 1950 and 1980, and has exceeded the rate of growth of comparable undergraduate degrees in many fields. Master's degrees have become professional as well as an academic degrees. From 1950 to 1980, one-third to one-half of all masters' degrees awarded annually have been in education. The proportion awarded over the period in business increased from about 7 percent to 20 percent and in the health professions from 1 percent to over 5 percent.

Doctoral degrees have shown a fivefold growth in the last 30 years. The most significant changes have been a halving of the proportion of doctoral degrees in the physical sciences from about 20 percent to 10 percent, and an increase in the proportion of doctoral degrees in education up to about one-fourth of the total. The proportion of doctoral degrees in biology has doubled to over 10 percent, but this was counterbalanced by an almost equal decline in degrees in agriculture.

Trends in first professional degrees have varied widely by field. Between 1955–1956 and 1980–1981, the number of degrees granted in law increased 4.4 times from 8,262 to 36,331, those in medicine increased 2.3 times from 6,810 to 15,505, and those in dentistry increased 1.8 times from 2,975 to 5,460. These rates of growth can be compared to the 3.7-fold increase in the number of nonprofessional doctorates awarded from about 9,000 to 32,958.[8]

The proportion of degrees awarded to women has greatly increased, especially at the doctoral level. They received about one-third of bachelors' and masters' degrees annually in the 1950s and 1960s, and about one-half of them in 1980. They received about 10 percent of nonprofessional doctoral degrees awarded annually before 1970 and 30 percent of those awarded in 1980, which involved a tenfold increase in the number of women doctorates. Women received fewer than 5 percent of the degrees in law, medicine, and dentistry in the 1950s. By 1970, the proportions were unchanged in law and dentistry, and up slightly in medicine. In 1980–1981, women received 32 percent of the degrees in law, 25 percent of those in medicine, and 14 percent of those in dentistry. Over the three-decade period, the number of law degrees awarded to women increased 41 times while those awarded to men tripled, and the number of medical degrees awarded to women increased 12 times while those awarded to men doubled.[9]

The growth in black enrollments in institutions of higher education has not been matched by comparable growth in degrees awarded. In 1978–1979 blacks received 6.6 percent of all bachelors' degrees, 6.5 percent of all masters' degrees, 3.9 percent of all doctoral degrees, and 4.1 percent of all first professional degrees. For hispanics, the proportions were 2.2 percent, 1.8 percent, 1.3 percent, and 1.9, percent, respectively.[10]

The expansion of higher education has led to an increase in the number of faculty members. Between 1960 and 1980, the total instructional staff increased from 276,000 to 865,000, and the full-time faculty at or above the level of instructor tripled from 154,000 to 475,000. Average faculty salaries in four-year colleges and universities increased from $6,015 in 1958 to $25,449 in 1981, a rate of increase comparable to that of civilian employees of the federal government. Full professors, whose average salaries increased from $8,072 to about $33,437 over the period, have earned about 1.5 times as much as assistant professors throughout the entire period. Salaries of university administrators have generally increased in direct proportion to those of faculty members, with college presidents earning just about twice the average for all faculty members during the two-decade period.[11]

Total expenditures for all institutions of higher education increased from $2.2 billion in 1949–1950 to $64.1 billion in 1980–1981. This 29-fold increase was almost three times greater than the increase in the overall gross national product and twice as great as the increase in the GNP for the government sector. The total value of the physical plant and assets of institutions of higher education grew from $7.4 billion in 1949–1950 to $109.7 billion in 1980–1981, and the proportion of the amount in endowment decreased from 36 percent to 19 percent. State and local governments were the source of at least 40 percent of all funds expended by public institutions from the early 1960s to about 1980, but they have contributed little to private institutions. The federal government was the source of about 18 percent of the funds expended by public institutions in the 1960s and early 1970s, but declined to about 13 percent in 1980. It was also the source of about 25 percent of the funds expended by private institutions from the early 1960s to the mid-1970s, but declined to about 19 percent in 1980. In 1980–1981 federal funds for higher education amounted to $9.7 billion and state and local funds amounted to $19.3 billion.[12]

Instruction has received one-third of all expenditures annually between 1949–1950 and 1980–1981. Separately budgeted research rose from 4 percent of all expenditures in 1939–1940 to 10 percent in 1949–1950 and 18 percent in 1959–1960, at which level it remained for several years. It declined to about 9 percent throughout the 1970s, although the dollar amount grew to $5.7 billion in 1980–1981. In 1980–1981 public institutions expended more of their budgets on instruction than private institutions (35.1 percent to 27.0 percent) and less on student aid (2.5 percent to 6.6 percent). Differences in other types of expenditures were small.[13]

Research expenditures have been funded primarily by the federal government. Federal grants for research, research facilities, and training fellowships and traineeships increased from $566 million in 1960 to $4.0 billion in 1980. In 1980, institutions of higher education received 37.3 percent of all federal funds expended for basic and applied research. In 1976–1977, 10 of 3,046 institutions accounted for 20.2 percent of all federal research expenditures in institutions of higher education, and another 20 institutions accounted for an additional 23.1 percent.[14]

Student academic expenses have risen steadily. In 1957–1958, yearly tuition and fees were $187 in four-year public institutions and $661 in four-year private

TABLE 11.1. Approved Medical Schools, 1949–1983

Year	Schools Providing Clinical Training			Basic Science Schools		
	All	Public	Private	All	Public	Private
1949–50	72	32	40	7	6	1
1959–60	81	37	44	4	3	1
1969–70	87	44	43	6	4	2
1983–84	126	76	50	1	1	0

Sources: "Medical Education in the United States," *JAMA* 144 (1950): 118, 130; 174 (1960): 170–71; 214 (1970): 1488–89; 252 (1984): 1590–94.

institutions. By 1967–1968 the costs had increased to $313 in public institutions and $1,350 in private ones. In 1983–1984, the comparable figures were $3,160 for public institutions and $7,540 for private institutions. Dormitory room rates have increased sixfold and board rates more than threefold between 1957 and 1983.[15]

Financial aid to students has also increased, especially that provided by the federal government. Scholarship and fellowship awards by institutions of higher education reached $2.5 billion in 1980–1981. Federal aid has become so important that in 1979–1980, about three-fourths of all college sophomores and juniors received some kind of federal aid in the form of grants, loans, or work-study.[16]

The rising costs of higher education have meant that college students have continued to come disproportionately from upper income families. In 1979, 28.0 percent of all families with the head of household present and with family members 18–24 years of age had family incomes of $25,000 or more, but they produced 41.6 percent of all college students. On the other hand, 22.0 percent of the same type of families had family incomes of less than $10,000, but they produced only 11.7 percent of all college students. This pattern was characteristic of white, black, and hispanic families.[17]

Changes in the Structure of Medical Schools

Before the 1950s, many states considered medical schools to be neither a public responsibility nor an essential health facility. In 1949–1950, there were 72 four-year medical schools and 7 two-year basic science schools (Table 11.1). Of the four-year medical schools, 32 were public institutions and 43 were private. The schools were located in only 32 states and the District of Columbia, although most of the populous states had medical schools. Between 1930 and 1949, only 3 new four-year medical schools had been established, and a fourth was expanded from a two-year to a four-year school.[18]

Many more medical schools were established after mid-century, especially by state governments. The number of four-year schools in operation increased to 81 in 1959–1960, 87 in 1969–1970, and 126 in 1983 (Table 11.1). Of the schools established after 1949, 44 were public and 10 were private. In 1983–1984, 44

TABLE 11.2. Undergraduate Enrollments in Medical Schools, 1950–1979

Year	Schools	Students	Students per School	First-Year Students in Public Schools	Students per 10,000 Population
1950–51	79	26,186	331	47.3%	1.7
1960–61	86	30,288	352	50.0	1.7
1970–71	103	40,487	393	54.9	2.0
1975–76	114	55,818	490	57.8	2.6
1980–81	126	65,497	520	61.4	2.9
1983–84	127	67,443	531	60.7	2.9

Sources: "Datagram," *Journal of Medical Education* 51 (1976): 1027; "Medical Education in the United States," *JAMA* 243 (1980): 853; 252 (1984): 1528; Carl M. Stevens, "Medical Schools and the Market for Physicians' Services," in *Higher Education and the Labor Market*, ed. Margaret S. Gordon (New York: McGraw-Hill, 1974), p. 515; U.S. Bureau of the Census, *Statistical Abstract: 1984* (Washington D.C.: U.S. G.P.O., 1983), p. 6.

states, the District of Columbia, and Puerto Rico had medical schools, and 28 of them had two or more medical schools. Many private medical schools became public responsibilities. In 1978–1979, 35 private medical schools received $79 million from the 16 states in which they were located.[19]

Undergraduate medical student enrollments increased 2.6 times between 1950–1951 and 1983–1984, from 1.7 to 2.9 students per 10,000 population (Table 11.2). The increase was due to growth both in the average class size per school and in the number of medical schools. The proportion of first-year medical students who were enrolled in public medical schools increased from 47.3 percent in 1950 to 60.7 percent in 1983–1984.

The average number of full-time faculty members per school increased fifteenfold from 1951 to 1983 (Table 11.3). The number of full-time faculty members in the clinical fields increased far more rapidly than those in the basic sciences and grew from 44 percent of the full-time faculty in a sample of medical schools in 1940 to 76 percent of all faculty in 1983. Unpaid volunteer faculty have practically replaced paid part-time faculty. In 1951, medical schools used 3,933 full-time, 5,930 part-time, and 5,700 volunteer faculty, with 95.4 percent of the part-time and volunteer faculty having M.D. degrees. In 1983–1984, medical schools reported 56,564 full-time faculty (76.2 percent in the clinical disciplines), 9,864 part-time faculty (90.7 percent in the clinical disciplines), and 104,240 volunteer faculty (94.3 percent in the clinical disciplines).[20]

Academic Health Centers

Many medical schools have shared a site with schools for other health occupations. This has led to the formation of academic health centers that have consisted of a medical school, a hospital, and at least one other health profession school. In 1983, there were 123 academic health centers, 72 of them public institutions. Seventy-nine had one or more allied health schools, 75 had nursing schools, and 59 had

TABLE 11.3. Full-Time Medical School Faculty, 1940–1982

Year	All Faculty	Basic Science	Clinical Science	Average per School
1951[a]	3,575	1,506	2,069	50.4
1960	11,111	4,003	7,108	129.2
1970	26,504	8,053	18,451	257.3
1976	39,330	10,728	28,602	339.1
1983	56,564	13,488	43,076	445.4

[a]71 of 72 medical schools.

Sources: Lee Powers, Joseph F. Whiting, and K. C. Opperman, "Trends in Medical School Faculties," *Journal of Medical Education* 37 (1962): 1070; Hilliard Jason and Jane Westberg, *Teachers and Teaching in U.S. Medical Schools* (Norwalk, Conn.: Appleton-Century-Crofts, 1982), pp. 10–11; Anne E. Crowley, Sylvia I. Etzel, and Edward S. Petersen, "Undergraduate Medical Education," *JAMA* 252 (1984): 1526–28.

dental schools. Sixty-nine had university hospitals. Public academic health centers were more likely to have each of these arrangements than private academic centers. Although practically all medical schools have been part of academic health centers, this has not been the case for schools of nursing and allied health professions. Only about 10 percent of their graduates in recent years have received degrees from schools located in academic health centers.[21]

Academic health centers have varied in their relationship to the parent university and in their organizational structure. A study of 87 centers in 1980 by the Association of Academic Health Centers (AAHC) found that 59 percent of the centers were proximate to the parent university and organizationally related to it, 17 percent were geographically distant from the parent university, and 24 percent were not related to a parent university. Administratively, 84 percent of the academic health centers had a chief administrative officer placed above the deans of the schools. The chief administrative officers have assumed a growing amount of line authority and responsibility for the policies of the centers.[22]

Academic health centers have been dominated by their medical schools. Of the 182 chief administrative officers of health centers appointed between 1960 and 1976, 153 were M.D.s and 12 were Ph.D.s in the basic medical sciences. The AAHC study included a survey of the chief administrative officers and deans of all health center schools that found that the dean of the medical school was considered to be the "second most influential person in the academic health center" after the chief administrative officer. The administrators also perceived the medical schools to be "dominant in the development of policy" in the center.[23]

Medical schools have had great influence in academic health centers. Their faculty members have regularly taught many students in the other schools. In 1956, medical schools taught 29,130 medical students, 2,417 graduate students in the basic medical sciences, and provided some instruction to 29,681 students in dentistry, nursing, pharmacy, and other health fields. In 1983–1984, they taught 67,443 medical students, 18,204 graduate students in the basic medical sciences, and provided some instruction to 53,167 students in other health fields as well as 24,302 other students. Medical schools have been the major recipients of external funds in health centers, undertaken most of the scholarly research, provided the leadership for the center hospital, and attracted patients to it. Morris has observed that "no academic center can be stronger than its school of medicine. Medicine plays a sustaining role in the health sciences education similar to the role of the college of arts and sciences in the remainder of the university."[24]

The imbalance among schools in academic health centers has created a number of problems. In 1980, one-half of the centers used the medical school's basic science department to teach all basic science courses, one-fourth had separate basic science departments within each school, and the remainder had health center departments or university departments. When medical schools have taught the basic medical sciences, according to the AAHC study, "students in the schools other than medicine insist they get second class instruction, frequently from junior or less experienced and less qualified faculty." A separate school for the basic science departments was strongly favored (a rating of 6 or 7 on a 7-point scale) by 90 percent of the nursing deans and allied health deans and by 73 percent of the pharmacy deans and the chief administrative officers, but by only 59 percent of the medical school deans and dentistry deans.[25]

Another problem has involved innovations in teaching. Some health profession schools other than medicine want the teaching hospital to sponsor more ambulatory and home care, but the AAHC study found that the medical school faculty was "often oriented and heavily committed to the in-patient service." A similar lack of agreement among the schools occurred with regard to interdisciplinary health sciences education. The AAHC study found that over 87 percent of the deans of pharmacy, nursing, and allied health programs favored more interdisciplinary education, compared to only 48 percent of the medical school deans. Morris has observed that opposition by medical schools has made "efforts to translate this attractive and sensible idea into programs of action . . . generally unimpressive."[26]

Financial factors have been largely responsible for the lack of joint activities in academic health centers. Budgets have usually been distributed to individual schools rather than to programs. Medical schools have also obtained much of their revenue from sources outside the university that have not been under the center's control. Academic health centers have thus remained an aggregation of individual schools. Evans has concluded: "Very few academic health centers have been able to develop an overriding sense of purpose and commitment to the objectives of the center as a whole. . . . The objectives of the academic health center are usually ill-defined and they tend to be subordinated to the aspirations of individuals and to the goals of administrative subunits."[27]

The Medical School and the University

The autonomy of medical schools has also been evident in their relations with their parent universities. Some medical schools have been physically separated from their affiliated universities due to their independent origin or a need to be located close to a large population center and its hospitals. In 1983, 26 of 108 medical schools affiliated with universities were located in different cities, and many of those in the same cities had separate campuses. Medical schools have had considerable organizational autonomy because much of their funding has come from third-party health insurors and federal research agencies rather than from the University. University hospitals have also relied on outside sources for funding, and their budgets have often equalled those of the rest of the total university budget.

The autonomy of medical schools has troubled both university administrators and medical educators. Babbidge has observed:

> Medical schools are, if you will pardon the expression, somewhat eccentric parts of their universities. They differ from other segments of the university—and even from other professional schools—in a number of respects. They seem to me to be more independent, if you will, of the parent institution, less comfortable in the harness of central institutional purposes, more under the direct influence of their nonacademic professional colleagues than that of their faculty colleagues, and more inclined to "go it alone" when it comes to matters of educational or financial policy.[28]

Medical educators have also been concerned about the relationship. One former medical school dean wrote that "the universities have never fully accepted medical education as their financial responsibility; medical schools have been tolerated as long as they paid their own way and did not disturb community relations." Medical school and university faculty members have never had the mutually beneficial relationship that was supposed to result from university affiliation, according to Chapman:

> Education for medicine has not become a pan-university responsibility and interest, and its various elements stoutly resist any move in this direction. . . . [S]uspicion, and even hostility, . . . have grown up between the faculties of arts and sciences and those of the medical school. . . . [T]he medical school's basic scientists and the scientists in other divisions of the university hold largely to their separate ways, each understanding well enough that bioscience itself moves at its own accelerating pace, but each claiming that separate obligations are so special that neither has much to contribute to the other.[29]

The Medical School and the Community

Many medical schools have had difficulty establishing good relations with the local community and its physicians. In the late 1970s, 61 of 120 medical schools were located in the 40 largest cities and 32 were in inner city neighborhoods. The hospitals of the urban medical schools have often been the only sources of medical care available to nearby residents. Because major teaching hospitals have become tertiary care centers, they have been ill equipped to meet the residents' primary care and other medical needs. Their urban locations have also discouraged suburban residents from seeking care there.[30]

Medical schools have been unwilling to cooperate in efforts to regionalize community medical facilities to prevent unnecessary duplication, especially when such measures have involved cost control. Clinical faculty members have been heavily oriented to specialty care and have resisted any measures that would reduce their ability to provide it. Medical schools that have received federal grants for research on specialized care have been concerned that they would lose the grants if they lacked suitable facilities in their own hospitals.[31]

Relations between medical schools and community physicians have also been a problem. Before mid-century, the many part-time faculty members helped maintain amicable relations between local practitioners and the medical school. The new full-time faculty members usually come from other communities, have been aloof from the local profession, and have competed with local physicians when they see private patients at the medical school. Medical schools have claimed that clinical practice by full-time faculty members has been essential to increase their earnings and the medical school's income, to maintain and improve faculty skills, and to provide patients for medical students. Community practitioners have felt that the faculty members have been subsidized by the medical school and benefited unfairly from the school's prestige and publicity. They have also been disturbed by the faculty's control over beds in community hospitals affiliated with the medical school. Lewis and Sheps have observed that the " 'town and gown' conflict rarely disappears completely and can be quite severe. . . . [T]he prevailing pattern is more one of a truce in which both sides attempt to avoid open antagonism or rupture."[32]

New Medical Schools

One consequence of the poor relations between medical schools and their communities has been the establishment of public medical schools intended to be unlike traditional medical schools. These new medical schools have often been opposed by the existing medical schools. A notable example was the medical school for the armed forces (the Uniformed Services University of the Health Sciences) in Bethesda, Maryland. It was established by Congress in the mid-1970s despite the objections of the Association of American Medical Colleges and the willingness of three local medical schools to assume that function.[33]

The most important new medical schools have been community-based medical schools and clinical campuses of medical schools. Community-based medical schools have been designed to train additional physicians at a moderate cost, to make a medical education available to more students, and to improve the medical facilities in communities. They have used the basic science programs of a local liberal arts university and taught the clinical courses in community hospitals, using local practitioners as part-time faculty members. At least 10 community-based medical schools have been established since 1960, and some of the same principles have been used in other new medical schools. Five similar medical schools were established as a result of 1972 federal legislation that aided new public medical schools created in affiliation with Veterans Administration hospitals. Clinical campuses have been satellite campuses of public medical schools that provided only the clinical part of medical education in affiliated community hospitals. Nine were in operation in 1985, mostly in medical schools with insufficient nearby clinical facilities.[34]

Community-based medical schools were designed to be as antithetical as possible to existing medical schools. Instead of the expense of a university hospital and a full-time clinical faculty, they used community hospitals and local practition-ers. Instead of the specialty and research orientation of existing medical schools, they were designed to prepare physicians for primary care. Lacking the traditional departmental structure, they were better able to experiment.[35]

Community-based medical schools have experienced resistance from existing medical schools. According to Lewis and Sheps, the idea "received little support or encouragement from most of the current leaders in medical education. Negative attitudes were expressed not only in private but also in the accreditation process" which focused on traditional criteria like ownership of a university hospital, a research faculty, and the teaching of the basic medical sciences.[36]

No new community-based medical schools have been established since the mid-1970s, largely because of the growing supply of physicians. Nevertheless, their popularity among state governments has indicated significant public dissatisfaction with the structure and operation of traditional medical schools. Most medical schools have failed to recognize or deal with the sources of dissatisfaction.

Medical School Administration

Medical schools have adopted a highly decentralized organizational structure. The dean and associate deans have been at the top of the hierarchy. Below them have been the chairmen of academic departments, which are composed of faculty members. The largest departments have been subdivided into divisions. The director of the hospital has reported either to the dean, or, in most academic health centers, to the chief administrative officer of the center.

The administrative role of the dean has diminished in recent years because of his reduced control over the medical school budget. Most research grants and contracts have been awarded as a result of applications submitted by individual faculty members, who have had effective control over the disbursement of the funds. Income from faculty clinical activities has been constrained in a similar way. The large university hospital budget has been allocated to meet operating expenses. The discretionary funds available to the dean have often been quite small.[37]

The dean's influence has been examined in several research studies. One survey in the mid-1970s asked 870 professionals in nine medical schools and their teaching hospitals to rank the degree of influence of several groups from 1 to 5, with 5 defined as "maximum influence." The dean's office was ranked below department chairmen as a source of influence in educational, patient care, and research policies, and also below individual faculty members in patient care and research policies (Table 11.4). A later study that used a similar method of ranking the influence of individuals and groups in medical schools on several types of decisions found that department heads were rated first in more areas than deans.[38]

The limited authority of the dean has removed him from participation in many important medical school decisions. According to Lewis and Sheps, "What is sorely lacking is greater certainty about who is in charge. Greater unity is needed in institutional decision making as to specific purposes and priorities, the content of activities, and the size, effectiveness, and fiscal implications of all programs." It

TABLE 11.4. Ranking of Influence of Groups on Medical School Educational Policies

Policy[a]	Dean's Office	Department Chairmen	Individual Faculty	Medical Students
Educational policy	3.84	3.94	2.99	2.63
Patient-care policy	2.51	3.85	2.04	1.59
Research policy	2.57	3.55	3.23	1.28

[a]Average for 9 centers.

Source: Marvin R. Weisbord, Paul R. Lawrence, and Martin P. Charns, "Three Dilemmas of Academic Medical Centers," *Journal of Applied Behavioral Science* 14 (1978): 286–87, 294.

has also affected the dean's survival in office. Wilson and McLaughlin found that recent deans, whose mean age at appointment was 48 years, have averaged slightly over 5 years in office. They estimated that 30 percent of all terminations were involuntary.[39]

Much power has been delegated to the rapidly growing medical school departments. A 1957 survey of departments of medicine, usually the largest departments in medical schools, found an average of 15 faculty members per department. By 1980, many departments of medicine had 100 or more faculty members. Even in a specialized field like pediatrics, a survey of 77 medical schools around 1980 found an average of about 35 full-time faculty members per department. The budgets of departments of medicine grew from an average of $54,000 for 25 departments surveyed in 1940 to $210,000 for 36 departments surveyed in 1950. In 1979, the department of medicine of the University of Washington, which had about 150 faculty members, had a budget of $33 million. Large departments have been closer to full-fledged organizations than units of organizations.[40]

Academic departments have grown for several reasons. Their teaching responsibilities have expanded to include not only a larger number of undergraduate medical students, but also more graduate students in the basic science departments and more interns, residents, and clinical fellows in the clinical departments. Funding to employ more faculty members has come from sponsored research and, in clinical departments, from hospital and outpatient care reimbursements by third parties. The survey of 77 pediatrics departments, 45 of which had budgets for faculty of over $2 million, found that only 45 of them received one-half or more of faculty salary income from their universities. The $33 million dollar budget of the University of Washington department of medicine in 1979 was obtained largely from outside sources, with 77 percent coming from the National Institutes of Health (NIH) and the Veterans Administration. Departments have viewed these funds, according to Lewis and Sheps, "which they have 'generated,' as 'belonging' to solely to them and not available for other school programs."[41]

Department chairmen have accumulated sufficient power that they have been considered as or more influential than deans (Table 11.4). Even within the larger academic health centers, according to the AAHC study, the chairmen of the clinical departments were "extremely important power brokers in the administrative hierarchy and in the organization and governance" of the centers.[42]

Clinical department chairmen have had great authority because, as chiefs of their services in the teaching hospital, they have controlled beds and patients needed for teaching and research. This dual role has placed an enormous administrative burden on them. It has also created a serious conflict of interest. The chairmen have been responsible both for the education of medical students and residents and the cost-effective staffing of their hospital services. The educational needs have created pressure to admit patients based on their teaching or research value rather than their need to be hospitalized. Administrative needs have led to the use of low-cost student labor for routine chores instead of educationally useful activities. Conflict has also existed between the bureaucratic routines needed in the hospital and the scheduling of educational activities for students.[43]

Because clinical department chairmen have spent most of their time administering research grants and hospital services rather than providing clinical leadership, their backgrounds have changed. Fewer chairmen have been experienced clinicians and more have been researchers with little clinical experience. This has not only weakened the clinical skills of the department, but it has also placed educational leadership in the hands of persons unskilled in the activities that are the basis of a medical education.[44]

Decentralization has also occurred within clinical departments in the form of divisions based on clinical subspecialties. While divisions have grouped faculty members with common interests and facilitated patient care and the assignment of responsibility, they have also balkanized departments into groups that have perceived themselves as having little in common with each other.[45]

Substantial power has also accrued to those faculty members who have attracted outside funding. Some have been responsible for long-running research projects that employed many workers and provided substantial income to the medical school. Others have had lucrative private practices that have filled teaching hospital beds and been important sources of hospital revenue. External funding has redirected the allegiance of such faculty members from the medical school to the sources of funding. For faculty members with research grants, according to Fein and Weber, "the overall goals of the school may well be slighted as key faculty members view their principal responsibility as that of ensuring a financial base for their own empires." Faculty members with large private practices, according to Evans, have achieved a degree of independence that "imposes serious constraints on the pursuit of goals which can only be achieved if there is a broadly based cooperative effort."[46] Both types of faculty members have used graduate students, residents, and fellows to assist them in their research and patient-care activities. Here also the students' educations may be subordinated to the professional needs of faculty members.

The delegation of power to departments in medical schools has permitted flexibility among departments, enabled them to respond quickly to changes in the environment, and taken maximum advantage of the skills of the faculty. It has also led to the absence of a coherent set of medical school objectives, policies, and priorities. Dominated as medical schools have been, according to Lewis and Sheps, by "multiple sources of funds, multiple centers of power, multiple focuses of leadership, and academic traditions that extol the virtues of faculty decision making and strongly inhibit administrative decision making,'' they have been unable to minimize these negative consequences of decentralization.[47]

Medical School Finances

As medical schools have increased their patient care and research activities, their budgets have grown correspondingly. The operating expenses of American medical schools have become the largest of any medical schools in the world, more than twice as large as those in many other countries.[48] Because their affiliated universities have been unwilling to assume responsibility for these expenses, medical schools have been forced to look elsewhere for financial support.

Before mid-century, medical schools relied heavily on tuition and part-time and volunteer faculty members. Deitrick and Berson found that in 1940, tuition provided 20 percent of the income in 22 public medical schools and 35 percent of the income in 37 private ones. They also found that as late as 1950 the volunteer faculty carried out a ''large portion of the teaching of medical students [and] the training of interns and residents,'' and that ''few medical schools could operate their present programs without'' them.[49]

After mid-century, new sources of income enabled medical school expenditures to increase at an almost explosive rate. Total expenditures were $69.5 million in 1947, $884 million in 1965, and $8.2 billion in 1982 (Table 11.5), a 117-fold increase in 35 years. This is almost four times greater than the 30-fold increase in expenditures of all institutions of higher education, which grew from $2.2 billion in 1949–1950 to $64.1 billion in 1980–1981. These medical school expenditures have not included those of their major teaching hospitals. The hospital budgets averaged $45 million in 1977, with individual hospitals varying from $4 million to $219 million.[50]

The major new sources of medical school income have been research, state and federal aid for educating physicians, and patient care. Income from sponsored research and indirect cost recovery (research overhead), primarily from the federal government, reached 54.6 percent of the income for expenditures of private medical schools and 42.7 percent of that of public medical schools in 1965. That proportion declined in the late 1960s, although the dollar amounts continued to rise. State and federal funds at that time emphasized training programs, which accounted for 30.1 percent of the income of private and 22.2 percent of that of public medical schools in 1970. During the 1970s, patient-care income assumed greater importance as Medicare and Medicaid began to feed large sums into medical schools. By 1982, 35.8 percent of the income of private medical schools and 24.5 percent of that of public schools came from professional fees and hospital reimbursements.

These data demonstrate how nonteaching activities have come to dominate the medical school budget. In 1982–1983, income from professional fees, sponsored research, indirect cost recovery, and reimbursements from the hospital accounted for 66.2 percent of the total income of private medical schools and 46.0 percent of the total income of public medical schools. In a very real sense, medical schools have become the locus of entrepreneurial efforts by faculty members to obtain income for a variety of professional activities, many of which have been only marginally related to each other and to the educational functions of medical schools.

TABLE 11.5. Medical School Expenditures by Sources of Income, 1947–1982

Income Source	Private Schools					Public Schools				
	1947	*1960*	*1965*	*1970*	*1982*	*1947*	*1960*	*1965*	*1970*	*1982*
All sources[a]	$42.7	247	478	881	3,647	26.8	192	406	818	4,531
Tuition/fees	19.4%	8.1	6.0	5.1	9.2	13.6	4.3	3.0	2.1	3.2
State appropriations	1.4	3.5	2.4	3.6	3.0	62.2	31.3	26.6	30.2	33.0
Indirect cost recovery	b	4.7	7.4	7.5	9.0	b	3.6	5.8	4.3	4.5
Professional fee income	b	2.7	2.5	5.4	22.6	b	3.2	3.3	8.2	17.0
Hospital reimbursement	b	b	b	b	13.2	b	b	b	b	7.5
Sponsored research	26.0	43.1	47.2	32.8	21.4	16.5	31.8	36.9	22.4	17.0
Sponsored training and multipurpose	b	13.3	16.8	30.1	10.8	b	11.3	14.8	22.2	8.6
Other operating income	53.2	24.6	17.6	15.5	10.8	7.7	14.4	9.6	10.5	9.2
Total	100	100	99.9	100	100	100	99.9	100	99.9	100

[a]Income in millions of dollars.
[b]None or not broken out separately.
Sources: U.S. Surgeon General's Committee on Medical School Grants and Finances, *Part II: Financial Status and Needs of Medical Schools* (Washington, D.C.: U.S. G.P.O., 1951), pp. 34–35; John A. Cooper, "Undergraduate Medical Education," in *Advances in American Medicine*, ed. John Z. Bowers and Elizabeth F. Purcell (New York: Josiah Macy, Jr., Foundation, 1976), 1:296–97; H. Paul Jolly et al., "US Medical School Finances," *JAMA* 252 (1984): 1539.

Because of the importance and extent of their functions, medical schools have achieved a major role in medicine and the medical profession. This was perhaps most clearly expressed when the AMA reorganized in the late 1970s and authorized voting delegates from medical schools as well as medical societies.[51] It has also been evident in the contribution of medical schools to basic science and clinical research, patient care, and the operations of the growing number of affiliated hospitals. Medical schools have become a major part of the American health-care system.

At the same time, other institutions have assumed some of the functions previously monopolized by medical schools. Science departments of colleges and universities have undertaken much research in the basic biological sciences. Hospitals have carried out clinical research, trained residents, and provided tertiary patient care. Some community physicians have developed specialized skills equal to those of clinical faculty members. The education of undergraduate medical students has remained the one unique function of medical schools. Thus it is useful to examine how the initiatives provided by the funding programs described above have affected medical schools. Each major group of programs will be examined individually and chronologically.

12

Medical School Research

Research in medical schools developed after World War I with specific projects funded by foundations, firms, and industries. After World War II, medical schools greatly expanded their research activities with funding from the federal government. Medical school researchers became the most important performers of research funded by the National Institutes of Health, which delegated most of its responsibility for setting research policy to academic medical researchers. Both basic science and clinical research in medical schools has been directed toward an understanding of biological processes rather than the prevention and treatment of disease. Medical school research has become a specialized activity separate from other medical school activities.

Medical School Research before 1950

Research in medical schools began in earnest after 1900 with the employment of full-time faculty members. The quantity of research was limited and the quality did not meet European standards. Erwin Chargaff reminisced that when he came to the United States in 1928, "I found a scientifically underdeveloped country dominated by an unhurried, good-natured, second-rateness. European scientists who visited the country at that time were attracted by the feeling of freedom generated by the wide open spaces and even more by the then very pleasant aroma of the dollar."[1]

Research was at first funded from medical school endowments and grants from a few major foundations, such as the Rockefeller Foundation and the Carnegie Foundation. By the mid-1930s, about 20 private foundations had a major interest in health and spent a total of about $7 million annually for medical research and medical education. About this time also, the American Foundation for Mental Hygiene, the American Cancer Society, the National Foundation for Infantile Paralysis, and other health-related associations began to fund research related to their interests. Private firms also sponsored research with direct commercial applications. In return, they used the names of the medical schools in advertisements as providing "scientific" data to support their claims.[2]

By 1940, research had become a measurable factor in medical school budgets. In that year Deitrick and Berson found that 59 of the 77 medical schools spent $3.2 million on research: 22 public medical schools spent 8.9 percent of their combined budgets of $9.5 million on research, and 37 private medical schools spent 13.0 percent of their budgets of $17.8 million on research. By comparison, total U.S.

medical research expenditures were estimated at $45 million in 1941: $3 million sponsored by the federal government; $25 million sponsored by industry; and $17 million sponsored by national and local foundations, health-related associations, and other organizations. A few medical schools carried out most of the separately funded research. Deitrick and Berson studied 32 four-year medical schools and found that 2 of them spent 31 percent of all restricted funds for research.[3]

World War II increased the amount of medical research and its sponsorship by the federal government. Penicillin, gamma globulin, and cortisone were all developed by joint efforts of the federal government, private industry, medical schools, and other organizations. In medical schools, according to the 1947 Steelman report, "fundamental research practically ceased in favor of applied research and development; investigation was concentrated exclusively upon diseases and conditions of military importance." These included "shock and infection in injuries, burns, and traumatic surgery; malaria, venereal infections, and other parasitic diseases; aviation medicine; and nutrition," as well as drugs and medical supplies and equipment. The total amount spent on medical research by the Office of Scientific Research and Development during the war was less than $25 million.[4]

Immediately after World War II, medical research returned to the sponsorship of commercial firms and health-related associations. In 1947, $88 million was expended for medical research in all types of laboratories. Industry provided $35 million of the funds, government $28 million, and the remaining $25 million was provided by foundations, associations, and other sources. Some of the research carried out in medical schools concerned major health problems, such as research on heart and vascular diseases funded by the life insurance industry and research on infantile paralysis, cancer, tuberculosis, and other diseases supported by health-related associations. Much of it was commercial, such as that sponsored by the sugar industry, vitamin firms, bird and fox breeding firms, food manufacturers, and canning firms.[5]

The Federal Government and Medical Research

Federal medical research began formally in 1887 with the establishment of a Hygienic Laboratory in New York, which was moved to Washington in 1891 and placed under the Public Health Service in 1902. It was redesignated the National Institute of Health (NIH) in 1930. In 1937, Congress created the National Cancer Institute within the Public Health Service to carry out research on cancer and provide fellowships and other support for research training. Although practically all federal medical research before World War II was carried out in government laboratories, the cancer institute could award grants to outside investigators upon the recommendation of an advisory group of eight scientists. The grants paid neither salaries to the researchers nor defrayed any indirect costs to their institutions.[6]

Major changes in federally funded medical research occurred during World War II. The federal government administered a large and successful war-related medical research program in nongovernment laboratories, which demonstrated the viability of external research. The Public Health Service Act of 1944 made the National

Cancer Institute a division of the National Institute of Health, thereby creating an organizational structure that could encompass other institutes. It also gave the surgeon general of the Public Health Service broad powers to award external grants and fellowships for research on diseases and disabilities of man.[7]

After the war, the National Institute of Health added new categorical institutes, which led to a change of title in 1948 to the National Institutes of Health. By 1983, the NIH had national institutes in the following areas: cancer; heart, lung, and blood; arthritis, diabetes, and digestive and kidney diseases; aging; allergy and infectious diseases; child health and human development; dental research; environmental health sciences; eye; general medical sciences; and neurological and communicative disorders and stroke.[8] The unsystematic and overlapping way in which individual institutes were established was particularly advantageous to researchers, who could resubmit proposals rejected by one agency to others.

Federal funding for medical research increased substantially after the war. By 1952, the federal government had become the largest sponsor of medical research, providing $73 million, compared to $60 million from industry, and $40 million from other sources. At that time, federal medical research was almost equally divided between intramural research carried out in government laboratories and extramural research carried out in nonprofit institutions and institutions of higher education (with 1.4 percent carried out in industrial laboratories).[9]

Many medical schools benefited from the increase in research funding. While 10 medical schools had 72 percent of all separately budgeted research funds in 1941, they had only one-half of the funds in 1948. The number of medical schools with no separate research budgets declined from at least 13 in 1940 to 5 in 1948. A survey of deans in 1951 found that research grants increased the amount of laboratory space and facilities, led to the establishment of new clinics, and permitted more clinics to be used in teaching. The deans reported that research raised the level of faculty competence, improved the quality of teaching, and "has not interfered in any way with teaching responsibilities."[10]

Impetus for providing greater federal funding for medical research and the training of medical researchers was provided by the Steelman report of 1947, the Surgeon General's Committee on Medical School Grants and Finances of 1951, and the President's Commission on the Health Needs of the Nation of 1953. Support was also generated by the leaders of health-related voluntary associations, especially the American Cancer Society. Political leadership was provided by Congressman John Fogarty and Senator Lister Hill, each of whom, according to Greenberg, "was determined to pour a fortune into medical research, regardless of the wishes of the Eisenhower administration and the fears of many of the conservatives who ruled the nation's medical schools."[11]

As a result of these efforts, federal funding for biomedical research and research training grew rapidly, from $139 million in 1955 to $1.2 billion in 1965 and $6.1 billion in 1984 (Table 12.1). The NIH became the major agency funding federal biomedical research and increased its proportion of all funds disbursed from about 40 percent in the early 1950s to close to 70 percent after 1975.

Although federal aid for medical research was viewed favorably by the public, Congress began to question the NIH's administration of the funding in the early

TABLE 12.1. Federal Support of Biomedical Research, 1947–1984
(in 000,000s)

Agency	1947	1950	1955	1960	1965	1970	1975	1984
All federal government	$27	73	139	448	1,174	1,667	2,832	6,087
Department of Health, Education, and Welfare	12	36	70	311	826	1,177	—	—
National Institutes of Health	8	27	60	281	715	873	1,880	4,257

Sources: James A. Shannon, *Federal Support of Biomedical Sciences* (Washington, D.C.: Association of American Medical Colleges, 1976), pp. 85, 87; National Institutes of Health, *NIH Data Book 1985* (Washington, D.C.: U.S. G.P.O., 1985), p. 2.

1960s. A Congressional inquiry at that time produced a requirement that the NIH tighten up its funding policies and be more critical of the dollar amounts in grant proposals.[12] Since the late 1960s, the rate of growth of federal funding for biomedical research has declined, but it has maintained its proportion of the gross national product and has grown significantly faster than inflation.

Nongovernmental organizations have also increased their support for medical research. In 1972, total expenditures for biomedical research and development exceeded $3.5 billion, with the federal government spending 60.7 percent, private industry 26.4 percent, private nonprofit organizations 6.4 percent, and state and local governments 6.4 percent. In 1984, total expenditures reached $11.5 billion, with the federal government spending 52.8 percent and industry 38.9 percent.[13]

Federal Medical Research Funding and Medical Schools

During the late 1940s and early 1950s, when federal medical research was carried out primarily in government laboratories, government commissions and nongovernmental groups proposed that most medical research be transferred to medical schools. The Public Health Service would continue to operate a few laboratories for intramural research, but its primary research role would be to dispense and oversee extramural grants and contracts. This not only represented a major shift of U.S. policy, but it also differed from medical research policy in Europe, where government medical research institutes had a long and distinguished history. The general issue of intramural versus extramural research was controversial enough that President Truman vetoed a bill creating the National Science Foundation in 1947 because it gave too much power to scientists outside the federal government.[14]

Several reasons were advanced why most medical research should be transferred to medical schools. The 1951 report of the Surgeon General's Committee on Medical School Grants and Finances claimed that research in medical schools would permit "large numbers of scientific specialists" to work together on large-scale research projects and that "good teaching depends heavily on close contact with

TABLE 12.2. Medical School Research Expenditures by Source, 1960–1981 (in 000,000s)

Source of Expenditure	1960–1961	1965–1966	1970–1971	1975–1976	1982–1983
Sponsored research					
Federal	$119	307	358	659	1,203
State and local	5	12	16	a	20
Nongovernmental	44	56	98	167	330
Sponsored training					
Federal	44	112	192	291	200
Other	6	10	29	82	191

[a]Included with nongovernmental

Note: Table does not show sponsored expenditures for multipurpose, public service, and other programs.

Sources: John A. D. Cooper, "Undergraduate Medical Education," in *Advances in American Medicine*, ed. John Z. Bowers and Elizabeth F. Purcell (New York: Josiah Macy, Jr., Foundation, 1976), 1:296–97; H. Paul Jolly et al., "US Medical School Finances," *JAMA* 252 (1984): 1535–37.

research." Medical schools could train the needed researchers. The committee also believed that "the strongest medical research structure for the Nation is a dispersed structure" in medical schools throughout the country rather than one concentrated in "relatively few centers."[15]

NIH budgets began to emphasize extramural research in 1957. From 1950 to 1956 over 40 percent of its funds, which increased from $28 to $73 million over the period, were used for intramural research by a staff of employees that reached 6,334 in 1956. In 1957, the intramural proportion of all research dropped abruptly to 32 percent and then declined steadily to 17 percent in 1963, when the total research budget reached $570 million. In 1984, 12 percent of a research budget of $4.4 billion was spent on intramural research by a staff of 10,634 employees.[16]

Medical schools benefited greatly from increased extramural research. Their expenditures for research and research training increased from $218 million in 1960–1961 to $693 million in 1970–1971 and $1.94 billion in 1982–1983 (Table 12.2). The federal government accounted for more than three-fourths of the combined research and training expenditures in medical schools during the period. Industry and philanthropic organizations funded 21 percent of the research in 1982–1983.

Basic and Applied Medical Research

Early federal legislation creating medical research institutes in the Public Health Service stressed practical medical concerns. The National Cancer Institute was established in 1937 "to promote research in the cause, prevention, and methods of diagnosis and treatment of cancer." The National Heart Institute of 1948 had a similar mission, and was instructed to "provide training . . . , including refresher courses for physicians" and to "assist States and other agencies in use of, the most effective methods of prevention, diagnosis, and treatment of heart diseases." The

National Institute of Mental Health of 1949 was also designed to assist state programs. The two early institutes directed toward basic research (the Experimental Biology and Medicine Institute of 1947 and the National Microbiological Institute of 1948) were created by administrative order, not legislation. The former became the National Institute of Allergy and Infectious Diseases by administrative order in 1955. The latter was merged into the National Institute of Arthritis and Metabolic Diseases, which was created by Congress in 1950 with a mission practically identical to that of the National Cancer Institute.[17]

A practical approach appealed to the scientific leaders of World War II. They had seen the remarkable achievements of short-term concentrated research in the war and believed that research could produce meaningful results in a reasonable period of time. For example, the 1951 report of the Surgeon General's committee dismissed any distinction between basic and applied research: "We are inclined to think that classifications of research as 'basic' or 'applied' have very limited usefulness as designations for specific research undertakings. Our concern is with the substantive characteristics of the studies and not with the semantics of classification."[18]

By the mid-1950s, medical research had failed to produce major findings with direct practical applications. At this point a new generation of academic scientists proposed another approach. They sought increased funding for the study of basic biological life processes and other open-ended research questions that offered no immediate solutions but strived for fundamental discoveries in the years to come. They claimed that this kind of research was best carried out by letting groups of scientists in each field decide what research should be funded through the peer review process.[19]

The new NIH leadership was sympathetic to this approach, although it was clearly at variance with the legislative mandates described above. James Shannon, director of the NIH from 1955 to 1968, justified the change in this way: "The simply stated goal of the NIH has always been to develop a scientific base for the formulation and solution of medical problems." He conceded that the NIH was also expected to have a "reasonable balance of fundamental and applied activities," although that was rarely evident in its funding policies.[20]

The NIH therefore embarked upon a program that emphasized basic research. The Wooldridge report to President Lyndon Johnson in 1965 noted that "a newcomer would infer, from a quick reading of the legislation and a glance at the organization chart, that NIH is engaged primarily in tightly targeted attacks on a finite list of human diseases, with the intention of annihilating these, one after another." In fact, the report said, the "NIH devotes its principal efforts to a broad program of investigation of life processes, rather than to a search for direct cure or prevention of disease. It employs this approach for a simple and valid reason: life science is so complex, and what is known about fundamental biological processes is so little, that the 'head on' attack is today frequently the slowest and most expensive path to the cure and prevention of disease." The report provided no evidence, historical or contemporary, to support the last assertion.[21]

Medical schools have been the major beneficiaries of the NIH's emphasis on basic research. In every year from 1975 to 1984, they received one-half of all NIH awards and two-thirds of all awards going to institutions of higher education. Medical schools were also affiliated with practically all of the hospitals that received 7 percent of all awards and had ties to many of the nonprofit research institutes that received 9 percent of all awards.[22]

The Medical Research Policy of the NIH

In its emphasis on basic research, the NIH has spent billions of dollars on what McDermott has called a "gigantic experiment in . . . the laissez-faire or investigator-chosen system for obtaining our biomedical research." The mechanism for doing this has been the peer review system, in which experienced researchers in a discipline have evaluated the proposals for research funding made by others in the same discipline. Peer review panels have been given great influence in the selection of projects to fund. The advocates of peer review, who are the researchers themselves, have claimed that it has assured that the research has measured up to the highest standards of professional competence.[23]

The peer review process has been subjected to considerable criticism. It has been alleged that reviewers have been chosen from a small group of scientists in a few elite academic institutions and have recommended research projects on the basis of personal relationships with the researchers. It has also been alleged that most NIH awards have been given to a few large research-oriented medical schools. In testimony before the House of Representatives in 1961, Shannon said that to be rated highly an applicant "must be known to be a productive research worker, to have resources available to him, and to be contained within the scientific environment that is conducive to research." He conceded that these standards limited the number of institutions that received awards and made it difficult to create a dispersed structure of many schools with active research programs. The latter had been a major rationale for extramural research.[24]

Studies of the members of peer review panels and those who have received awards in all types of academic institutions have found a concentration of researchers with certain personal characteristics and from certain institutions. However, the studies also found that the institutions trained most of the Ph.D.s and carried out much of the research. The selection of panels and awarding of grants thus has been representative of the major research institutions. No evidence was provided as to whether this structure has fostered or hindered an increase in the number of research institutions.[25]

Another criticism of the peer review process has been that funding choices have been based on the characteristics of the researchers rather than the quality of the projects, and that researchers have been given great flexibility in pursuing their assigned projects, which has made it difficult for the NIH to establish research goals. These practices have been based on a set of beliefs about the research process shared by most scientists. Shannon described them in his 1961 testimony:

> The basic premise on which all NIH programs have from their inception been based is that its grantees . . . must be allowed the greatest possible freedom of action in determining the nature, the direction, and the conduct of their research. . . .

> Generally speaking, . . . new knowledge of a revolutionary sort—commonly
> called a scientific breakthrough—cannot be engineered, cannot be predicted and
> consequently will not yield to science-direction however brilliant. In the future, as in
> the past, it will arise from an unexpected quarter. . . . Advances will come most
> quickly if competent investigators are encouraged to deploy themselves where their
> hunches take them and are allowed to proceed in a manner that seems to them most
> effective.[26]

The belief of scientists that most research breakthroughs are based on unanticipated findings by individual researchers has not been supported by the history of
scientific achievements. The unique discovery made by a single researcher has been
the exception in the annals of science. Most seminal research areas have been
sufficiently well publicized that they have attracted many researchers, with the
result that independent similar or functionally equivalent discoveries have occurred
at close intervals. Furthermore, individual findings have never been as important as
scientists think they are. A sequence of major discoveries, almost invariably made
by different researchers, has been necessary to convert findings into useful
contributions. Dowling has written about the discoveror of the sulfa drugs:

> Should it be Gelmo who synthesized the parent compound, Eisenbergy who showed
> its effectiveness in the test tube, Domagk who demonstrated this in animals, the
> group at the Pasteur Institute who identified the basic drug, the industrial chemists
> who modified the molecule to produce sulfapyridine, Whitby who showed its
> effectiveness in animals, or the clinicians who treated the first patients with
> pneumonia? The fallacy of honoring a single individual for the discovery of a new
> drug is nowhere better shown.[27]

The support of individual researchers has also become less justifiable since
teams of investigators have begun to make the major research decisions. The
proportion of single-authored articles in the *New England Journal of Medicine*
declined from 91 percent in 1916 to 49 percent in 1946, 29 percent in 1951, and 4
percent in 1976 and 1977. Other journals have shown the same trends.[28] Research
has become a collective process as amenable to goal setting and the measurement
of achievements as other organizational activities.

Another issue in the peer review process has been the definition of peers, who
can conceivably be scientists in the field involved, scientists in all fields interested
in the topic, or users of the findings of the research. The NIH has assigned first-level
reviews of research proposals to study sections composed largely of academic
scientists in the field involved or closely related fields. Their recommendations have
been reversed by second-level councils in less than 2 percent of all cases, according
to the NIH in 1984. Rettig has observed that study section "review came to be a
powerful device by which the external scientific community determined which
research proposals submitted to it by NIH should be considered acceptable for
funding." This review process has not been used by most other federal research
agencies. Some have had functional or problem-oriented study sections and one has
even had a study section designed to deal with "advanced concepts." Many have

had detailed administrative reviews to ensure that the research has addressed the mission of the agency.[29]

Peer reviews by those in the same discipline have tended to be intellectually conservative. Experienced researchers, according to Blissett, have a "large investment of time and memory in a particular research tradition" and have preferred to award grants "to those who are continuing well-established lines of research." Scientists who have headed large research teams with many graduate students and researchers have been under pressure to obtain continuing funding and therefore have followed traditional paths. Blissett observed that young scientists "must cast about for problems that are sufficiently 'consensible' to insure respect and that utilize techniques whose results are rather clearly defined. An approach that does not fit well-established models of research or an experiment that involves the manipulation of rather novel techniques may prove professionally disastrous."[30]

The policy of letting disciplines select research questions in isolation from other disciplines has contributed little to the advancement of science or clinical medicine. Research chosen by disciplines has emphasized refinements in existing techniques and the development of theoretical paradigms distinguished more by their internal consistency than their ability to explain important natural phenomena. As John von Neumann has observed about similar developments in mathematics, "there is a grave danger that the subject will develop along the line of least resistance, . . . and that the discipline will become a disorganized mass of details and complexities." Weinberg has concluded that "the most valid criteria for assessing scientific fields come from without rather than from within the scientific discipline that is being rated. . . . [W]e must given the highest priority to those scientific endeavours that have the most bearing on the rest of science." The peer review process has done the opposite.[31]

The NIH's emphasis on basic research, the internal development of disciplines, and conservative funding policies were noted in two major evaluations of the agency, one in 1965 by the NIH Study Committee of the Office of Science and Technology (the Wooldridge report) and the other in 1976 by the President's Biomedical Research Panel. The Wooldridge report found that the NIH's extramural research was "typically of high quality" and that it was steadily improving, despite a tenfold increase in funding in eight years. The research funded consisted "very largely of basic research [and training] in biomedical sciences and related disciplines." The report found that funding policies had encouraged scientists to migrate into and graduate students to select the better supported fields, but that the NIH had done little to deal with the problem of program balance.[32]

Statements in the Wooldridge report by representatives of some scientific disciplines raised a number of specific issues. The microbiology panel report noted that interest in molecular biology had led to insufficient research on such issues as allergy, parasitology, host-parasite relationships involving bacteria, and mycobacteria generally. The physiology report complained about "an undesirable tendency to follow scientific fashions, perhaps resulting in part from our method of supporting research projects, since applications utilizing established techniques and ideas may be more likely to receive approval than those with unusual or unique features." It also observed that the emphasis on basic research had led "towards reductionist type of research and a minimum of synthesis. This follows naturally as the organs and their systems are dissected into even smaller components for study and as cellular biology receives greater emphasis today."[33]

The disciplinary clusters of the 1976 President's Biomedical Research Panel repeated many of the criticisms of the Wooldridge report. The Immunology and Microbiology Cluster reiterated the concern about the lack of research in the mechanisms by which bacteria cause disease, in antibiotic-resistant bacteria, and in host-bacteria relationships. Another cluster criticized the neglect of the biochemistry of the reproductive system due to preferences of physiology and biochemistry departments for the cardiovascular, renal, and central nervous systems. Parasitology continued to be a neglected field, despite its massive global importance. The absence of basic research on the effect of external etiological agents such as cigarette smoke on the lung was noted, although the agents have been found to be important causes of many diseases. Clusters in new fields like nutrition and communicative sciences complained that the peer review process tended to be "conservative and to reinforce research trends."[34]

Even clusters from well-funded areas conceded the slowness with which progress was being made in providing practical medical knowledge. The Biochemistry, Molecular Genetics, and Cell Biology Cluster observed about developments in cellular biology: "Yet, for all its ferment and excitement, this period has not generated the kind of critical knowledge required for the solution of the major health problems of our day." The report observed that the past 25 years had been spent in "analysis of the components of the cell," and that "only now does the body of available information begin to approach the level at which" some successful applications can be anticipated.[35]

The belief that scientific progress occurs through discoveries in basic science that are then applied to human needs has found little support in the history of science. Far more frequently, productive research has begun with a direct response to human needs, which, if successful, has led to basic research to understand the processes involved. The development of almost all drugs has begun with practical discoveries about the action of the drugs, followed by findings about the underlying biological processes, which in turn were used to improve the drugs. The development of bacteriology and the understanding of illnesses like hypertension and diabetes followed the same route. Most improvements in the prevention and treatment of cancer have come from practical rather than basic science research. The flow of findings back and forth between applied and basic research has produced a much greater record of achievement than the approach in which basic research has preceded its applications.[36]

A last issue to be discussed here has been the unwillingness of the NIH to establish research programs to achieve specific goals. Medical researchers have shown that they can function equally well under programmed as well as self-directed research. Many medical school research activities have been funded by nongovernmental organizations and federal contracts, which do not give researchers the latitude permitted by NIH grants. Yet these programs have attracted large numbers of researchers who have pursued the research as diligently as those working under NIII-funded grants. Furthermore, directed research has been repeatedly found to be as productive as investigator-chosen research in providing meaningful findings.[37]

Some observers have claimed that the NIH's refusal to establish goals and priorities for research has reduced the value of the research that it has funded. Richard Trumbull, Executive Director of the American Institute of Biological Sciences, observed that research agencies must justify research expenditures to the public and that this could best be done through research programs. If federal agencies established research programs, science would not be constrained but rather improved:

> Programming can . . . provide maximum honing for the cutting edge of a science. It can achieve interaction of disciplines to assure development of their interfaces. Further, it can improve apportionment of funding across research entities and thereby enhance better understanding of a function, organic system, physical system or disease. . . .
>
> [I]t *is* possible to structure and manage research programs incorporating the work of many basic research tasks without imposing any [inhibitions] upon the investigators involved.[38]

Trumbull maintained that programming would also increase cooperation among scientists and disciplines. He stated:

> Despite the magnanimity and service orientation attributed to scientists, there is a need for a greater feeling of "teamwork," coordinated search for solutions, cooperative development of education and training programs, and recognition and appreciation of contributions of others. This need extends within and across disciplines. In short, there is an individualization, a competitiveness that is counterproductive and inhibits achievement of societal goals. . . . [T]he full potential of science will not be realized in this environment and . . . governmental programs constitute unique vehicles for their development by elimination of management mechanisms which encourage their continuance.[39]

Since the mid-1970s, according to a 1984 report of the Institute of Medicine, the NIH has been "repeatedly confronted by those who seek more research results that will have practical implications." Congressmen have tried to add new categorical institutes or to change the mission and authority of the NIH. In response, the NIH has adopted a new internal structure for most categorical institutes based on research programs (e.g., diseases) rather than research mechanisms (e.g., grants), and it has taken a more active role in setting research priorities by consulting with researchers. However, it has not adopted adequate formal mechanisms to involve the ultimate users of the findings in the determination of fundable research. Furthermore, individual institutes have gained power through decentralization and an appeal to their own constituencies.[40] The overall impact of the change has thus been limited.

The NIH's problems have been intensified by the mismatch between its organizational structure and the structure of medical schools. The NIH has been organized into institutes based on research programs, such as illnesses or organs that are susceptible to serious disease. Medical schools have been organized into disciplines with distinctive bodies of academic knowledge. Each structure has been useful for internal purposes, but it has not been possible for the two to mesh when brought together. Instead, the NIH's peer review process has superimposed the disciplinary structure of medical schools on its own programmatic structure. This adaptation has weakened the NIH's own structure and has reduced its ability to mobilize efforts toward its legislative mission.

If the NIH is to improve its functioning, it will need to alter the hitherto sacrosanct peer review process. Academic disciplines should be required continually to justify their contribution to the commonweal before feeding at the common funding table. This can be done only by giving greater responsibility for awarding funding to users in other disciplines, especially the ultimate users in clinical medicine and public health.

The Impact of Medical Research on Medical Schools

Funded research has become a major source of income for medical schools. The proportion of all medical school expenditures that were supported by sponsored research and research training increased from about one-fifth in the late 1940s to over one-third in the early 1960s. Support for research continued to increase thereafter, but its proportion of total medical school income declined to one-fourth during most of the 1970s and the early 1980s due to greater increases in other sources of income. In 1982–1983, medical schools received $1.9 billion for research and research training, $1.4 billion of it from the federal government. In the same year, research and research training accounted for 21.5 percent of the expenditures of public medical schools and 27.3 percent of the expenditures of private schools. Expenditures for research varied from $96,000 to $65 million among medical schools, with a median amount of $7.7 million.[41]

Research has become the primary determinant of the status of medical schools within the academic medical community. A 1971 ranking of the quality of medical school faculties based on a survey of full-time medical school faculty members found that the research productivity and funding of the schools provided the best explanation of the ratings.[42]

Faculty members have reported that medical schools have placed great emphasis on research. One study asked them to rank (from a low of 1 to a high of 5) the degree to which six activities provided the following rewards: (a) professional and academic rewards; (b) personal satisfaction from the work itself; and (c) financial rewards. The six activities included undergraduate medical education, graduate medical education, house staff medical education, patient care, research, and administration. A ranking of the average scores for each activity showed that professional and academic rewards were provided most often by research (3.54), patient care (2.70), and house staff education (2.69). Personal satisfaction was provided most often by patient care (4.34), research (4.10), and house staff education (4.05). Financial rewards were provided most frequently by patient care (3.16), administration (2.48), and research (2.24). Another survey in the late 1970s found that 76 percent of about 2,000 faculty respondents said that research "strongly contributes" to the "system of rewards (e.g., promotions, raises) for faculty members" at their medical school. No other factor (patient care, teaching, school service, or community service) was rated as strongly contributing by more than 19 percent of the faculty.[43]

The pressure on faculty members to be productive researchers has raised questions about ethical issues in their research on human subjects. Since 1966, all institutions funded by the Public Health Service have been required to have special committees approve all research on human subjects in order to protect the rights of the subjects. One study examined a number of measures of the organization, operation, and effectiveness of juries that reviewed research on human subjects in medical schools, teaching hospitals, mental hospitals, community hospitals, and research institutes. Medical schools had the least satisfactory performance in every item measured "by a notable margin." McDermott has observed that "these juries are senior men. They got to be senior by cutting and slashing their way through the ethics of clinical investigation. They are then supposed to tell young men that they cannot do the same thing. . . . Medical juries . . . are a superficial, veneer-like approach." Gray found that researchers placed pressure on juries to approve their research and that research was rarely monitored once approved. He concluded that juries have had little effect on researchers.[44]

Federal Funding of Medical School Research

Two major strategies have been proposed for the allocation of federal research funds among medical schools. In 1951 the Surgeon General's Committee on Medical School Grants and Finances stated that one strategy was to "distribute grants so that the investigators and projects financed will produce, so far as can be judged in advance, the most significant research findings." This option involved "seeking out well-established investigators, or those of outstanding promise, and backing them quite heavily." It favored medical schools with strong research programs, extensive facilities, and many skillful researchers. The other strategy was to distribute funds among many medical schools so that "the research potential of the Nation will be maximized in the future, even though the immediate returns on funds currently distributed may not be the maximum possible." The Committee believed "that the strongest medical research structure for the Nation is a dispersed structure," although funds should be given to those able to deliver results promptly when necessary.[45]

The NIH, like most federal research funding agencies, chose to concentrate federal research funds in the wealthiest schools. About 1960, the 10 wealthiest medical schools received over 12 times as much funding from federal research grants as the 10 poorest medical schools. In 1965, President Lyndon Johnson tried to alter this pattern by directing funding agencies to administer their programs "not only with a view to producing specific results but also with a view to strengthening institutions and increasing the number of institutions capable of performing research of high quality." This executive order had little impact on the NIH or other federal agencies. Two years after the policy was disseminated, the top 14 medical schools received 41 percent of NIH awards and in 1973 they received 44 percent.[46]

Federal research funds have continued to favor a small proportion of medical schools. A study found that in 1978–1979 the top 20 medical schools in terms of research funding spent 50 percent of the $887 million in federal research funds received by 120 medical schools. The second highest group of 20 spent 24 percent. The bottom 20 spent 1 percent. The top medical schools differed from the others primarily in their ability to have their NIH grants funded. Using a sample of 5 schools from each of the top 40, middle 40, and lowest 40 groups of schools in terms of funding, the study found that the schools in each group had similar numbers of grant applications per full-time faculty member and applications approved per faculty member. However, 43 percent of the applications of the 5 schools in the top group were funded, compared to 38 percent of those of the 5 schools in the middle 40, and only 26 percent of those of the 5 schools in the bottom 40. The greater success of the top group of schools was explained by the growing need of high-level research for multidisciplinary teams of researchers, elaborate facilities, and complex equipment. The leading schools also had more resources with which to prepare grant applications, partly due to funds from previous grants.[47]

NIH funding has also favored the major research schools through its emphasis on large multiyear grants rather than small grants of short duration. Few small schools have had the resources needed to undertake long-term grants that require extensive facilities. In 1975, 79.4 percent of the $1.1 billion awarded as research grants was for continuation grants; in 1984, this rose to 84.6 percent of the $3.1 billion awarded.[48]

External research funding has altered relations between medical schools and their faculty members. Many faculty members have depended on grants for part of their salaries. In 1961–1962, approximately one-third of the basic science faculty and one-fourth of the clinical faculty received all or part of their salaries from federal sources. In 1970–1971, these proportions increased to about one-half of the total faculty.[49]

In some schools, a few faculty members have obtained a large proportion of the NIH research grants and contracts. This funding has paid overhead costs to medical schools and supported faculty members, graduate students, and other employees. The faculty members involved have had great influence and been freed from involvement in normal medical school activities. In one school with 241 research grants in fiscal 1976 and 12 research contracts totalling $33 million in 1975, 2 grantees were responsible for 23 percent of the total amount. Altogether, 15 grants accounted for 43 percent of the total NIH research grant funding in that institution, and 15 grants accounted for 48 percent of the comparable funding in another institution with similar levels of support.[50]

Research funding by the NIH, according to James Shannon, built "tight, rather exciting bonds between the scientist and the NIH. These necessarily bypassed their own institutional arrangements and incidentally produced a new set of loyalties." This new set of loyalties has been the bane of medical school administrators. One dean observed that "many individual investigators regarded the medical school as a sort of way station along the road in their career objectives, settling in one for a time, then moving bag and baggage to another, and feeling put upon if the medical school suggested that it too might have a stake in their research and the equipment used in it."[51]

One way for the NIH to strengthen ties between faculty members and their medical schools has been by awarding institutional grants to medical schools for disbursement to faculty members with the advice of the faculty. In 1960, federal legislation authorized the NIH to give up to 15 percent of total research and training funds as institutional grants. However, no more than 8 percent was ever awarded in any year and in 1980 the proportion was less than 2 percent. Shannon has written that institutional grants "could have been an extraordinary instrument of institutional stability and self-determination." They were funded at low levels because of "the disinclination of the university to administer research and training funds with imagination, the lack of university faculty support of the program, and the coolness of [Congress] to fluid funds with no demonstrated programmatic responsibility." The NIH funded institutional grants for some years as a proportion of the school's total grant support in the previous year. This enriched the wealthy schools and made it more difficult for the schools with less funding to use them to develop a research base.[52]

Another mechanism for strengthening faculty and medical school ties has involved equipment purchased with NIH grant funds, which was then owned by the medical school. If the NIH had required faculty members to share the equipment, the school's role would have been strengthened and the equipment would have been better utilized. Instead, as Stetten has remarked about the heyday of medical school research, "each scientist who required a complex piece of equpiment had little hesitancy in selecting from the top of the line the most costly version available. If his neighbor down the corridor had need of a similar instrument, he would in general be provided with one of his own, even though both instruments lay fallow for much of the day."[53]

Research Training Programs

A major mission of the NIH has been to provide training funds to ensure an adequate supply of researchers. NIH clinical fellowships and traineeships have been awarded for research training or full-time research to graduate students, postdoctoral students, and special students. The sponsoring unit within the medical school or hospital has also received grants for faculty salaries and other expenses involved in operating the programs. In 1960, $91.6 million was awarded for fellowships and traineeships, which increased to $157.6 million in 1972.[54]

While many researchers were trained with these grants, a large number of the clinical fellows and trainees entered private practice instead of research and teaching. For this reason, the program was eliminated for several years and revived in 1975 with a requirement that recipients who did not engage in research or teaching repay the stipend or provide care for underserved populations. This accelerated an ongoing decline in the number of M.D.s obtaining postdoctoral traineeships. From 1968 to 1976, the number of M.D. recipients dropped from about 3,000 to 1,500, while the number of Ph.D. recipients increased from about 500 to 1,500. Postdoctoral research fellowships showed similar trends. Consequently, NIH training funds have been increasingly used to train Ph.D.s, who would enter research careers anyway, rather than to encourage nonresearchers to become researchers.[55]

Training programs have been especially beneficial to medical schools and their faculties. For many years, according to Stetten, "the custom developed of providing a fellowship to almost every recent Ph.D. in the biomedical sciences. It was not unusual to find a distinguished professor surrounded by a cloud of postdoctoral fellows who were actually conducting most of the experiments described in the professor's grant application."[56] Clearly, fellowship programs were intended neither to benefit every Ph.D. in the biomedical sciences nor to provide inexpensive labor for medical school professors. Even more important, the practice of awarding fellowships to almost every Ph.D. did not encourage students to enter fields with a shortage of researchers and to avoid those with a surplus.

These questionable uses of training grant funds have led to a reduction in their proportion of NIH funding. In 1972, training grants comprised 12.6 percent of the $1.25 billion that NIH awarded. In 1984, only 4.7 percent of total NIH awards of $3.6 billion went for research training.[57]

The Impact of Medical Research on Basic Science Departments

The research impetus provided by NIH funding transformed the basic medical sciences from small departments that taught undergraduate medical students and serviced the teaching hospital into large departments oriented toward research and graduate training. Most medical school basic science departments were poorly prepared for this change. In order to improve their research skills, they hired more faculty members with Ph.D. degrees. In 1951, 46 percent of full-time basic science faculty members had Ph.D. degrees (without M.D. degrees). This increased to 56 percent in 1960 and 80 percent in 1978 (excluding pathologists).[58]

Research in the basic medical sciences has emphasized a reductionism made possible by the electron microscope, which permitted researchers to study genes, proteins, and cellular and subcellular structures generally. Reductionism has adversely affected the medical aspects of the basic sciences. For example, according to the microbiology panel of the Wooldridge report, the "glamour and scientific status" of molecular biology as a research field led to the appointment of molecular biologists as heads of many microbiology departments. According to the panel: "For the most part, these molecular biologists are concerned with micro-organisms only as tools for their genetic or biochemical research. . . . [D]epartments centered around such studies frequently fail to deal adequately with the teaching of the medical aspects of microbiology."[59]

As basic science departments became less competent to teach the medical aspects of their subjects, the clinical disciplines have assumed that responsibility. King observed in 1965 that "it is a rare medical school today where the most competent gastrointestinal physiologist in the school is in a basic science department rather than a clinical department. . . . Few anatomists can match the knowledge of muscles and joints particularly in the functional sense, of the well trained orthopedic surgeon."[60]

Basic science departments increasingly emphasized the training of graduate students, who brought income to the departments through training grants, provided low-cost labor as research assistants, and promoted a research emphasis. Basic science departments have become major educators of biological scientists. In 1968, 30 percent of all Ph.D.s awarded in the biological sciences were given to students trained in medical schools. In 1982–1983, basic science departments had 3,708 master's degree students, 10,728 Ph.D. degree students, and 3,828 postdoctoral students, compared to 66,886 undergraduate medical students enrolled in medical schools. In 1980–1981, they awarded 21.3 percent of all master's degrees and 42.0 percent of all doctoral degrees in the biological sciences.[61]

Life science departments in arts and sciences colleges have become increasingly similar to medical school basic science departments as both have obtained research funding from the same federal agencies. For example, biochemistry, once predominantly a medical school discipline, has become a major department in many arts and sciences colleges. Some new medical schools have used arts and sciences life science departments to teach their basic science courses.[62]

Clinical Departments and Medical Research

Clinical departments have responded to large-scale research funding by developing academic research orientations similar to those of the basic science departments. In the era before federal research funding, clinical faculty members, who were practicing physicians, carried out a limited amount of research on the natural history of disease and its treatment in living patients. The new full-time clinical faculty members have emphasized laboratory research, the study of specific organs or components of organs, and other biological phenomena.

This change has been documented in several studies of clinical research. One study examined a single article in each issue of three influential weekly medical journals, the *New England Journal of Medicine, JAMA,* and *Lancet,* in 1946, 1956, 1966, and 1976. Over the three-decade period, the proportion of articles concerned with treatment declined from 44 percent to 30 percent, the proportion concerned with disease manifestations declined from 35 percent to about 22 percent, and the proportion concerned with causation increased from 10 percent to 25 percent. The proportion of articles that reported symptoms in the patients declined from 88 percent to 63 percent, and the proportion that reported clinical signs decreased from 90 percent to 68 percent. The authors concluded that "medical research increasingly has been defined as basic biomedical laboratory research, which emphasizes pathogenic mechanisms of disease and treatments." The authors attributed these changes to the increased number of clinical researchers who have not been regularly engaged in patient care.[63]

Despite the superior technical skills of the new researchers, the study found a decline in the methodological quality of the research. The proportion of studies that examined a cohort of patients over a period of time, a methodologically superior approach, declined from 60 percent to about 35 percent, while studies that examined a cross-section of patients, a less satisfactory method, increased from 25 percent to 45 percent. In addition, neither the number of subjects in the studies nor the duration of patient follow-ups had increased. These changes may have been due to greater pressure to publish research results promptly.[64]

Another study examined research papers from the 1953 to the 1967 meetings of two clinical research societies composed primarily of academic physicians. The proportion of papers and abstracts which the authors categorized as concerning disease in humans or animals declined from about 80 percent to about 60 percent. The proportion of abstracts dealing with human beings or human substances in whole or part declined from about 90 percent to about 60 percent. The proportion categorized as using data obtained in history taking and physical examinations rather than from laboratory tests alone declined from about 40 percent to about 15 percent. The proportion with no disease or human aspects whatsoever increased from about 5 percent to 30 percent.[65]

Some scientists have felt that this kind of laboratory research has not been the most suitable basic research for clinical medicine. Seldin has observed about basic research:

> Basic to what? . . . neither tools nor techniques by themselves confer upon scientific activity any special claim to fundamental status. . . . [T]he term "basic" must be defined in terms of the frame of reference from which the problems emerge. In this light, what is "basic" for biochemistry may be crude or even irrelevant when the problems are posed by issues arising from a clinical context. . . .
>
> [A]n excessive reductionist emphasis may be doomed to failure because it is by no means certain that physiologic laws can, even in principle, be uniformly reduced to a more fundamental level. . . . [I]t may always be necessary to retain concepts and assert relations within and among organ systems that are neither defined in nor derived from basic biochemistry.[66]

Basic laboratory research has led to the appointment of clinical faculty members whose skills have been primarily in laboratory techniques. In this environment, according to Seldin, "basic research becomes prized for the sophisticated tools and techniques utilized rather than for the penetration of questions raised or the insights provided by the answers found." The new laboratory researchers and the practicing clinicians, according to Feinstein, have comprised "two cultures" in clinical departments. The contact of laboratory researchers with patients has often been limited to a laboratory analysis of the patient's "excreta, fluids, cells, tissues, films, or graphic tracings." The patient, whom the researcher rarely saw, was treated more "as a diseased organism than . . . a sick person." Feinstein observed that "the hiatus between these two cultures has steadily increased at most medical centers."[67]

The Usefulness of Clinical Research for Patient Care

Evaluations of the enormous amount of clinical research undertaken in medical schools have questioned its contribution to the quality or cost-effectiveness of patient care. One major research emphasis has been on new medical technologies, such as new surgical procedures. In the *New England Journal of Medicine* in 1976, 31 percent of the 196 original articles and 17 percent of the 172 special articles dealt with new technologies, and 89 percent of the senior authors of the new technology articles were medical school faculty members. Many of the new technologies were

TABLE 12.3. Research Literature Cited by Expert Teams, Textbooks, and *MEDLARS* Data Base, by Disorder

Disorder	Total Citations	Cited by All Three	Cited by Two Only	Cited by One Only
Bipolar disorder	2,623	4	63	2,556
Malignant melanoma	1,195	3	47	1,145
Rheumatic heart disease	1,436	2	68	1,366

Source: John W. Williamson, Peter G. Goldschmidt, and Irene A. Jillson, "Medical Practice Information Demonstration Project: Final Report," mimeographed (Baltimore, 1979), p. 124.

introduced without systematic comparisons with existing technologies, adequate safeguards, or careful follow-up evaluations.[68]

The methodological soundness of much clinical research has also been questioned. One study located 28 review articles that assessed the quality of medical literature in a specific field. The authors of the review articles reported that a median of only 20 percent of the 4,200 original research articles reviewed met their often limited criteria (e.g., use of statistical tests) of scientific adequacy. Many of the methodologically poor studies were overly optimistic. Eight of the review articles found that nearly 80 percent of 449 articles judged methodologically inadequate reported positive findings, compared with 25 percent of 305 studies judged methodologically adequate.[69]

Probably the most basic issue is whether clinical research has built a solid core of clinical medical knowledge. One study assessed the degree to which physicians agreed about the state of medical knowledge in three areas: bipolar disorder (manic-depressive psychosis), malignant melanoma, and rheumatic heart disease. The researchers obtained independent lists of the most important research articles from three sources: (1) teams of experts in each field, (2) references in three leading textbooks in each field, and (3) citations in *MEDLARS*, a computerized data base. The three sources exhibited almost total disagreement as to the articles in their fields worth citing (Table 12.3). Even among the three textbooks chosen as the best in each of the three fields, the researchers found that fewer than 1 percent of the references cited in any one textbook were also cited in the other two.[70]

One reason for the lack of agreement was that most of the research was not directly applicable to medical practice. The study sampled 365 articles in the three disorders cited in *MEDLARS*, which were then assessed by specialists for applicability. Only 37 percent of the articles were considered applicable to medical practice, and 4 percent contained information considered "ready for use in practice."[71]

One effort to improve the methodological quality of clinical research has been the use of researchers with both M.D. and Ph.D. degrees. These researchers have been able to ask questions that physicians consider important and carry out research using methodological tools considered suitable by Ph.D.s. Combined degree programs have been offered for many years and were available in 87 of 116 medical schools in 1976. However, among basic science faculty members in 1977–1978, only 6.8 percent had both M.D. and Ph.D. degrees. Among the clinical faculty, only 4.1 percent had both M.D. and Ph.D. degrees. Furthermore, the number of faculty members with both degrees grew more slowly from 1967–1968 to 1977–1978 than did the number with only one degree.[72]

Medical Research and the Social Sciences

The NIH has defined basic research almost completely in biological and biomedical terms.[73] This emphasis has greatly limited the amount of social science research and has affected the NIH's ability to contribute to national health goals and priorities. Medicare, Medicaid, programs to train more physicians, and other activities of the federal government have established a national commitment to provide health care to all citizens in a cost-effective manner. Most of the nation's greatest health-care problems in recent years have involved the delivery and financing of health care, which can be understood only through social science research. Although the NIH has been the major federal agency funding medical research, it has failed to incorporate these federal health goals into its mission. As a result, medical schools have not emphasized social science research in their activities.

Recent Changes in Federal Research Funding

After the mid-1960s, Congress reduced the rate of increase of biomedical research funding, partly to underwrite programs to expand medical school enrollments. Congress also became dissatisfied with the failure of basic research to produce the expected results. Hearings in the Senate in 1976, according to a reporter, focused on a single theme: "Why don't you people in the NIH and the medical schools spend less time 'understanding' disease and more time preventing or curing it?" A House of Representatives subcommittee reported in 1977 that while it favored basic research on diabetes, it "is certainly not convinced that all progress must wait on a complete understanding" of the disease.[74]

The NIH altered its mix of research funding for some years to meet these criticisms. In the 1950s and 1960s, practically all research funds were awarded as grants, which have broad guidelines about the research to be carried out and have been strongly preferred by scientists and the NIH. Grants have been used for basic research and have been awarded on the recommendations of disciplinary study sections. In response to criticisms about the lack of useful results from grants, the NIH funded more research in the 1970s in the form of contracts, where the funding agency has expected specific results using techniques, a timetable, and often personnel determined prior to the award. Contracts have been used for "targeted" research and have given more power to NIH administrators. By 1975 contracts accounted for 25.4 percent of the $1.5 billion awarded for research and development. The trend was reversed when congressional interests turned elsewhere, and in 1984 contracts accounted for only 11.1 percent of the $3.5 billion awarded.[75]

Medical research has continued to prosper in recent years. Congress has maintained a high level of federal funding for both medical research and the NIH. Between 1975 and 1984, NIH funding increased by 12.6 percent, adjusted for inflation, to $4.3 billion. Both the NIH and the medical schools have maintained their dominant roles as research funders and performers. In 1975, 66.4 percent of the $2.8 billion federal health research and development budget was spent by NIH; in 1984, this proportion reached 69.9 percent of a $6.1 billion budget. The proportion of NIH funding awarded to medical schools was 50.5 percent in 1975 and 51.9 percent in 1984, and a significant part of the remainder was awarded to organizations affiliated with medical schools.[76]

As biomedical research projects have become larger and more elaborate, a fundamental change has occurred in the nature of medical school research. Originally, research was part of the normal academic responsibilities of faculty members, and grants were designed to defray unusual or large expenses that were needed for the research. In recent years, medical school research has become a specialized activity of teams of investigators funded by large grants. In 1984 the average NIH continuation grant received $155,000 and the average new grant $106,000.[77] The weaker medical schools have received little funding, and the richer schools have developed distinct research structures with full-time researchers. Medical research in medical schools, which was originally justified because of the benefits that would accrue to medical education, has become widely separated from it.

Thus, although research has transformed medical schools, it has had few of the effects predicted for it after World War II. It has not spread research funding among most medical schools and created a dispersed structure for medical research. Instead, it has increased the disparity between the wealthy and the poor medical schools. It has not served to integrate research and medical education. Instead, new kinds of students have been admitted to medical schools to learn research techniques, while medical students have become increasingly dissatisfied with the research orientation of faculty members, as will be shown below. It has been an inefficient and costly mechanism to increase medical knowledge, in that only a small proportion of the total resources invested has been used to improve the state of medicine. It has turned medical schools from professional schools that trained physicians into large and complex organizations with many disparate goals, some of which have detracted from the training of physicians.

Even as research organizations, medical schools have had major deficiencies. Large-scale biological and biochemical research in recent years has required the participation of chemists, physicists, mathematicians, and computer scientists, all of whom have been located in colleges and universities rather than medical schools. Because medical school faculty members have had so little contact with their academic colleagues in science departments, they have been unable to draw upon these resources. Medical schools have thus been caught in a dilemma created by their efforts to expand beyond their professional functions and their inability to duplicate resources found elsewhere in universities. This dilemma suggests the need for the reallocation of medical school functions in order to retain the professional functions in the medical school and place nonprofessional ones in the university.

13

The Medical School Clinical Faculty

Large-scale federal funding of research in the 1950s and 1960s enabled medical schools to hire many full-time clinical faculty members who differed from their part-time colleagues in their orientation toward research and patient care. When research funding leveled off in the late 1960s, medical schools turned to patient-care revenues from Medicare and Medicaid to pay faculty salaries. Faculty earnings from research and clinical activities have led to inbalances in the attention given to patient care, teaching, and research.

Research and the Expansion of the Full-Time Faculty

Until well past mid-century, most clinical faculty members were part-time teachers with extensive private practices. In 1951, part-time faculty members comprised 32 percent of the non-M.D. faculty and 80 percent of the M.D. faculty, and they provided 40 percent of the total faculty time spent on all activities. The use of part-time faculty members in the clinical fields was considered advantageous because they retained their clinical skills and were paid lower salaries.[1]

When the federal government began large-scale funding of research in medical schools, full-time clinical faculty positions became more feasible because the government compensated faculty members for their research time. Some faculty members carried out federally funded research during the summer months to supplement their academic-year salaries. Many others carried out funded research during the academic year, with the medical schools receiving compensation on a prorated basis for the time lost from teaching and other academic obligations. Medical schools were also reimbursed by all grants for research overhead expenses. By 1970, 49 percent of all medical school faculty members received partial or full support for their research activities.[2]

Because research detracted from the private practices of clinical faculty members, few of them would have made the necessary financial sacrifices to undertake research and live on normal academic salaries. Medical schools and the NIH therefore used several devices to create nominal faculty salaries for purposes of grant funding that were much higher than the actual faculty salaries paid by medical schools. One method was for the medical school to pay only a part, such as one-third, of a faculty member's salary, while the total salary was used in grant applications. If the grant called for one-half of the time of the faculty member, the granting agency paid one-half of the nominal salary, rather than one-half of what the

TABLE 13.1. Full-Time and Part-Time Faculty Members in Medical Schools, 1951–1984

Faculty Status	1951	1960	1967	1975	1984
Basic science					
Full time	1,656	3,753	5,932	10,728	13,783
Part time and volunteer	1,051	1,388	3,025	5,208	6,974
Clinical					
Full time	2,277	6,948	13,490	28,602	44,984
Part time and volunteer	10,579	23,261	37,258	73,072	116,028

Sources: "Medical School Staffing Patterns," *Journal of Medical Education* 43 (1968): 943; "Undergraduate Medical Education," *JAMA* 236 (1976): 2957–59; Anne E. Crowley, Sylvia I. Etzel, and Edward S. Petersen, "Undergraduate Medical Education," *JAMA* 254 (1985): 1566.

medical school was actually paying the faculty member. This made it possible for many more clinical faculty members to engage in research. The same practice was carried over with less justification to medical school faculty members in other disciplines.

NIH grants led to the appointment of large numbers of full-time researchers in medical schools. Many of them were given faculty appointments and participated in teaching, thereby enabling the medical schools to obtain additional faculty members at no cost as long as the research funds were available. If the research funding (called "soft money") were discontinued, the medical school either had to dismiss the researchers or pay them out of its own funds (called "hard money"). The effect of research support on faculty size was shown in a regression analysis of basic science departments and departments of medicine in 1973. Research funding was found to be the most consistent predictor of differences among departments in the number of their faculty members.[3]

Because of research funding, full-time faculty members have come to dominate medical school faculties. Between 1951 and 1967, the number of full-time basic science faculty members increased over 3.5 times and the number of full-time clinical faculty members increased almost 6 times (Table 13.1). Between 1967 and 1984, the full-time basic science faculty doubled and the full-time clinical faculty tripled. The number of part-time and volunteer faculty members increased by a greater amount, but the proportion who received a salary decreased from 51 percent in 1951 to 8 percent in 1984. In 1984, full-time faculty members accounted for 94.0 percent of all paid basic science faculty and 82.9 percent of all paid clinical faculty.[4]

Medical school faculties have grown significantly faster than the number of medical, allied health, nursing, and other kinds of students that they have taught. These data are customarily measured in terms of full-time equivalents (FTE), in which, as an example, 2 half-time students (or faculty members) are defined as equal to 1 FTE student (or faculty member). Between 1951 and 1960, the number of FTE faculty members per 100 FTE students increased from 15 to 23. Using other data, between 1963–1964 and 1970–1971, the number of FTE faculty increased by 83.2 percent, from 14,468 to 26,504, while the number of FTE students of all kinds increased by only 40.2 percent, from 69,929 to 98,012.[5]

Clinical Faculty Members and Clinical Practice

During the heyday of federal research funding, medical schools hired many clinicians on a strict full-time, or straight salary, basis because that was the most suitable way to prorate federal research funding. The strict full-time plan adversely affected the medical school, the clinical faculty, the educational program, and patient care. Probably the most damaging effect was financial. Strict full-time clinicians were paid salaries competitive with private practitioners, which created budgetary problems in all medical schools and drove at least one to virtual bankruptcy.[6]

Strict full-time clinicians usually limited their patient-care activities to supervising the patients of their interns, residents, and fellows. As a result, according to Petersdorf, they did "not lay on hands themselves. This . . . has detracted from the clinical competence of many faculty who spend more time in delegating responsibility for care to others than in dispensing it themselves." The patients often received less satisfactory care because the faculty members did not believe that they were personally responsible for providing patient care.[7]

Strict full-time clinical faculty members had little interest in paying patients. They were often casual about collecting fees and did not encourage the patients to obtain their health care in the teaching hospital. Prepaid health-care plans established in a few medical schools foundered because of lack of faculty interest and motivation. Community physicians stopped referring patients to university hospitals because no faculty member took direct responsibility for the care of their patients. University hospitals experienced severe financial problems.[8]

In order to assess the impact of the strict full-time plan on patient-care activities, Maloney interviewed 94 strict and geographic full-time faculty members (the latter were compensated for the care of private patients), which he grouped into surgeons and nonsurgeons. The geographic full-time surgeons and nonsurgeons each had more hospitalized patients under their personal care than their strict full-time counterparts. Geographic full-time surgeons performed more operations and geographic full-time nonsurgeons performed more complete examinations than their strict full-time counterparts. In order to "measure of the quality of [the physician's] personal relationship with the patient and the patient's family," the faculty members were asked whether they personally asked families for permission to perform an autopsy or left it to others. Strict full-time faculty members were much less likely than geographic full-time faculty members to request autopsies personally. Using these and other measures, Maloney concluded: "Without economic incentive, clinical faculty of medical schools will not accept personal involvement in the care of the sick if they have any reasonable alternative which permits them to maintain their self-respect."[9]

The strict full-time system produced major problems in the teaching hospital. Strict full-time clinicians spent their time in the laboratory rather than in clinical activities, which made them less effective clinical instructors and curtailed their time with students. Because they admitted few paying patients to teaching hospitals, medical students were unable to see patients from a variety of social classes. Strict full-time faculty members were also ineffective in managing the teaching hospital. Lepore has observed:

> [T]he best way [for a clinician] to test the performance of his hospital is by having under his personal care a limited number of private patients whose treatment and management are . . . by the physician himself. [He] finds out very quickly how well his orders are being followed, how the laboratory and radiology divisions are functioning, whether nursing care is good or bad, and if the performance of his aides is up to snuff or disaster prone.[10]

The strict full-time plan was strongly opposed by the local population, especially in smaller communities, because paying patients were denied the services of faculty specialists. Community physicians, on the other hand, were quite comfortable with it. They had always objected to private practice in the medical school by faculty members. They claimed that the medical school subsidized clinical faculty members by providing them with office space and personnel and that faculty members benefited unfairly from the school's reputation and publicity.[11]

By the late 1960s, most medical schools were disillusioned with the strict full-time plan. The additional research produced was weighed against the greater financial, patient-care, and teaching burdens and found wanting. Consequently, medical schools once again required faculty members to practice medicine if they wanted their earnings to equal those of private practitioners.

The Geographic Full-Time System

The geographic full-time system, which permitted faculty members to practice medicine for personal gain only inside the medical school, first developed on a large scale in the 1950s. In 1956, 31 of 34 public medical schools surveyed by the AMA employed some faculty members on a geographic full-time basis and 22 employed some on a strict full-time basis. Of 37 private medical schools, 31 had some geographic full-time faculty members and 33 had some strict full-time faculty members. All the medical schools employed many part-time clinical faculty members. Practically all of the 63 deans replying to the survey reported that geographic full-time plans were necessary to attract and retain faculty members by enabling them to supplement their salaries with earnings from patient care.[12]

The early geographic full-time plans were administered with an astonishing casualness. A 1958 analysis found that many medical schools did not know how many hours faculty members devoted to private patients, how much money they received, or what happened to the money. A study of 19 plans found that only 10 ever handled patient revenues and only 3 had "vague references" to compulsory participation. As late as 1970, 20 percent of the deans in a survey did not know the total practice income of the faculty in all of their departments. Medical schools thus gave geographic full-time faculty members the benefits of a full-time position, absorbed some of the costs of their patient-care activities (as community physicians correctly complained), but did not know what the faculty members were doing. In many medical schools, a geographic full-time appointment was actually a part-time job with a full-time salary.[13]

Such a system was ripe for abuses. Many clinical faculty members obtained large incomes from their practices by taking advantage of the teaching hospital, the medical school facilities, and the free labor of medical students and house officers. Deitrick and Berson cited instances about 1950 of faculty members with salaries of $3,000 to $5,000 who earned over $25,000 from their clinical activities. A less common occurrence was pressure from medical schools to have faculty members spend their time on patient care to the exclusion of other activities.[14]

The geographic full-time system did not compensate faculty members for the care of the indigent, who were widely used by medical schools used for teaching and research. Faculty members cared for these patients as part of their normal academic responsibilities. Teaching hospitals received some reimbursement for the care of the indigent from welfare agencies, but the agencies could hardly be expected to pay for the full educational and patient-care costs of teaching hospitals. The substantial hospital deficits were made up by some combination of endowment, general university funds, and increased charges to paying patients.[15]

The care of the indigent in medical schools was revolutionized by the enactment of Medicare and Medicaid in 1965. The two programs paid for the hospital care and physicians' fees of many indigent patients in the same way that private insurance paid for paying patients. Medical school faculty members became the personal physicians of Medicare and Medicaid patients and were reimbursed for their patient-care activities. Problems arose when Congress discovered that too many faculty members were "double billing" for services actually rendered by house officers and also included as part of the hospital's bill. In 1969 and 1972, regulations were enacted that required faculty members to deliver "personal and identifiable" services to patients in order to be compensated.[16]

Medicare and Medicaid were remarkably effective sources of practice income to medical schools and faculty members. Had medical schools tried to increase their practice income from paying patients, they would have had to undertake expensive programs to upgrade their facilities and staff in order to attract paying patients away from community physicians. Educational activities and relations with community physicians would have suffered. Instead, Medicare and Medicaid converted the medical school's major existing source of patients—the indigent—from subsidized to full-pay patients with all payments made directly by the federal or state government. Medical schools did not even experience competition from private physicians for the care of these patients because of the shortage of physicians and the lack of other sources of medical care near many teaching hospitals. Medicare added a bonus by giving medical schools extra payments to cover the educational costs involved in providing care.[17]

The enactment of Medicare and Medicaid, coupled with the simultaneous leveling off of research funding, led medical schools to turn to patient care as a major source of income. They formalized their medical practice plans to ensure that they received a fair proportion of faculty earnings from patient care. A study of faculty practice plans in 1977 found that 70 percent of them had been implemented since 1960 and that 90 percent of the public and 75 percent of the private plans had been revised since 1970. The new or newly revised plans replaced the casual oversight and desultory reporting of the old ones with elaborate legal contracts.

Hilles and Fagan reported in 1977: "Seldom are any patient related income generating activities by participants . . . excluded from the plan. Several mechanisms for monitoring faculty practice activities are in effect [simultaneously] at most medical schools, including employment agreements, required financial statements and central billing and fee collection procedures." Most of the plans required participation in the plan as a condition of employment, banned any outside practice by the faculty member, and covered all the faculty member's patient-care activities, no matter where provided.[18]

The plans also replaced the once simple distinction between strict full-time and geographic full-time faculty with a myriad of subtle shadings. Most strict full-time plans used patient-care income to help pay salaries and made it clear to faculty members that unless they generated a certain amount of patient-care income, salaries would be reduced or faculty positions would be eliminated. Strict full-time faculty members sometimes received bonuses if practice earnings exceeded a certain amount, which was completely antithetical to the purpose of that kind of appointment. Geographic full-time plans placed restrictions on the faculty member's patient-care activities and often gave all practice income above a specified ceiling to the medical school. Both strict and geographic full-time faculty members found that their incomes were now closely tied to their patient-care activities through individual and group incentive systems. Petersdorf observed: "The bottom line is that if the faculty wants to eat, the faculty has to practice. And if it wants to eat well it has to provide excellent service."[19]

Practice plans became a major source of medical school revenue. In 1956–1957, fewer than 25 percent of the schools supplying financial information to the Association of American Medical Colleges identified any income from practice plans. In 1974–1975, over 70 percent reported income from practice plans. In 1956–1957, the proportion of unrestricted income (which included everything except the direct costs of sponsored research and training and several other items) derived from practice plans was 2.6 percent. This proportion rose to 7.1 percent in 1971–1972 and 16.5 percent in 1983. The proportion of all medical school revenues obtained from the provision of medical services of all kinds increased from 12.2 percent in 1970 to 29.7 percent in 1981. This may be compared with revenues from research, which declined from 25.6 percent in 1970 to 21.9 in 1981.[20]

Clinical Activities of Faculty Members

Dependence on patient-care income has led to an increase in the number of full-time clinical faculty members who provide patient care. In the same way that research funds led to the employment of full-time researchers in medical schools, patient-care funds have led to the employment of clinicians with major time commitments as health-care providers.[21]

Patient care has significantly affected the work activities of clinical faculty members. This was shown in Maloney's study of geographic and strict full-time faculty, which was carried out when strict full-time faculty salaries did not depend on patient-care activities. Geographic and strict full-time surgeons and nonsurgeons did not differ in their teaching time, with all four groups averaging about 12 hours a week. With regard to research, strict full-time surgeons and nonsurgeons averaged about 16 hours a week on research, compared to only 8 hours for their geographic full-time counterparts. On the other hand, grants obtained by the geographic full-time surgeons and nonsurgeons were somewhat larger than those of their strict full-time counterparts. Maloney developed a "visibility index" of publications and found that the indices of the geographic full-time faculty rated slightly higher than those of the strict full-time faculty.[22]

With regard to patient care, Maloney's study showed that geographic and strict full-time surgeons and geographic full-time nonsurgeons all spent between 15 and 20 hours per week in patient-care activities, but that strict full-time nonsurgeons spent less than 4 hours per week in patient care. In the years since the study, all clinical faculty members have spent more time on patient care because of the federal requirement that they provide "personal and identifiable" services to Medicare patients to receive fees. According to Cluff this has created problems for medical education:

> [I]t is as inappropriate for faculty to abrogate responsibility for care of indigent patients as it is for them to usurp responsibility in the care of private patients. The turmoil experienced by medical faculty in justifying, demonstrating, and document- ing their responsibility for patient care in teaching settings in order to be reimbursed for their services has often resulted in an excessive effort to treat patient records and has diverted attention from the care of the patient and training of students, which after all are most important.[23]

Practice plans have had the effect of improving faculty satisfaction with their earnings. Maloney found that 88 percent of the geographic full-time surgeons and 72 percent of the geographic full-time nonsurgeons were satisfied with their earnings, compared to only 38 percent of the strict full-time surgeons and 24 percent of the strict full-time nonsurgeons.[24]

The Allocation of Practice Income

Disputes over the allocation of clinical practice income among groups in the medical school, as one study observed, "have unseated medical school deans and university presidents, caused serious confrontations between deans and clinical faculty, and precipitated great debate about which mission—education or patient care—should be predominant in the medical school."[25] Two issues have been especially controversial: (1) how much money should go to the faculty and how much to the medical school; and (2) how the income going to the medical school should be distributed within the school.

A substantial part of the patient-care income of medical schools has been used for faculty salaries. One study of seven medical schools in 1974 found that, on the average, 57.3 percent of professional fee revenues were used for clinical faculty compensation. In the five public schools in the study, professional fees, sponsored funds, and state and general funds each provided one-third of the total of $52.4 million used to compensate faculty members. The use of professional fees for faculty salaries has produced efforts toward self-enrichment that have distorted the functions and goals of the medical school. Chapman has remarked about the

> full-time faculty who cannot effectively discharge their academic obligations, including research, because they are engaged in what amounts to a major commitment to private medical care. There seems to be great reluctance to acknowledge that, in some of our medical schools, that commitment is indeed major, for the insidious reason that it generates mammoth personal incomes. This particular feature, and the distorting and limiting effects that inevitably flow from it, . . . more than any other, is likely to return us to the pre-Flexerian era, if allowed to run unchecked.[26]

In order to gain more control over the disbursement of practice income, medical schools have specified that the first claim on plan revenues has been the cost of plan operations. Participating faculty members have then received a specified amount, and the remainder has been given to the departments and/or the dean. The funds given to the departments have usually been used to compensate other faculty members or pay for travel and equipment. The amount allocated to individual departments has been strongly affected by their ability to generate practice income. Surgical specialties have had great income-generating ability, while pediatrics, public health, basic sciences, and some others have had little or none. The higher income-generating departments have usually received the lion's share of the professional fee income, which has not only exacerbated the differences between rich and poor departments, but has also decentralized power within the medical school.[27]

Large clinical practice incomes have led some to suggest that medical schools should appoint faculty members with different values in order to strengthen their educational programs. Cluff has observed:

> There are large rewards for faculty who can leisurely discuss patient problems at length with students and residents . . . , who can watch budding doctors emerge into good physicians . . . , who have the time to pursue scholarly interests . . . working in an environment where learning is the essential ingredient. . . . These rewards should not substitute for the financial requirements to meet personal and family needs, but all these rewards must be taken into account if medical schools are to thrive and are to have the faculty who serve their own and societal purposes as well.[28]

Changes in the Characteristics of Clinical Faculty Members

Full-time clinical faculty members have changed in many ways in recent years. They have had less clinical experience prior to their medical school appointments. As late as 1968, only 19.5 percent of clinical faculty members received their first faculty appointment within five years of receiving the M.D. degree. By 1978, 52.7 percent of the faculty received their first academic appointment within that period.[29] Because most faculty members in recent years have spent the first five years after receiving the M.D. degree in residency training and a subsequent fellowship, many of them have never worked professionally outside a medical school or an affiliated hospital.

Another trend since mid-century has been a decrease in faculty experience in private practice, due to the expansion of the full-time system. In 1967–1968, only 15.2 percent of all full-time clinical faculty members had experience in private practice, and in 1977–1978 only 13.2 percent did. The decline over the decade was from 11.1 to 8.6 percent in departments of internal medicine, from 16.3 to 13.6 percent in departments of surgery, and from 21.0 to 15.1 percent in departments of pediatrics. Lippard has written of this development: "I . . . wonder whether the medical school is not becoming the haven for the man who would avoid the rigorous competition of independent practice yet wishes to continue to operate in a narrow technical field, rather than the man of broad background and wide interest who has the capability to kindle in his students the desire to join in an exciting life venture."[30]

Many clinical faculty members have shown little interest in the normal measures of clinical competence, because in 1976–1977 32 percent of them were not board certified.[31] Faculty members have not needed board certification because they obtained most of their patients and their hospital appointments as a result of their affiliation with the medical school, not their personal skills and reputations. Many clinical faculty members without board certification have never been carefully evaluated as clinicians, because their appointments were based primarily on their research skills.

In recent years, the number of full-time medical school faculty members has exceeded the size of the faculty in most liberal arts colleges. The median number of full-time basic science faculty members was 78 in 1974–1975 and 94 in 1984–1985. The median number of full-time clinical faculty members was 195 in 1974–1975 and 300 in 1984–1985. Between 1965–1966 and 1980–1981, the average number of faculty members in 5 basic science departments in 86 established medical schools increased from 9.4 to 14.8. In clinical fields, the growth was from an average of 11.8 faculty members in 14 fields in 1965–1966 to 20.1 in 16 fields in 1980–1981. The average number of full-time faculty members increased from 36 to 93 in departments of medicine, from 23 to 45 in departments of psychiatry, from 16 to 43 in departments of pediatrics, and from 17 to 32 in departments of surgery. Close contact between students and faculty members and collegial relations among the faculty have been unlikely to develop under these conditions.[32]

One major difference between faculty members in medical schools and those in arts and sciences departments has been their salaries. Since 1950, according to Rogers, "using our new public dollars, we made [medical school] faculty members the most highly paid educational professionals anywhere in the world."[33] This can be seen in an analysis of faculty salaries in 1940–1949 (Table 13.2) and 1970–1981 (Table 13.3). Those data in Table 13.2 that show average maximum salaries for all full-time basic science and clinical faculty members were based on 13 public and 21 private medical schools. The data showing salaries of anatomists were obtained from a survey of 57 of 76 anatomy department chairmen. An examination of the table shows that the salaries listed for full-time basic science faculty members were about 20 percent higher than those listed for anatomists. This probably reflected the greater wealth of the medical schools that employed most full-time faculty members. The wide range of salaries among anatomists was more indicative of the variations that actually existed among medical schools.

TABLE 13.2. Medical School Faculty Salaries, 1940–1949

	Instructor		Assistant Professor		Associate Professor		Professor	
	1940	1949	1940	1949	1940	1949	1940	1949
Average maximum full-time salary								
Basic sciences	$2,526	4,133	3,606	5,974	4,579	7,037	7,578	10,702
Clinical fields	2,918	5,527	4,274	7,372	6,378	8,862	9,580	14,069
Anatomy salaries								
Average minimum	—	2,855	—	3,995	—	4,889	—	6,633
Average maximum	—	4,053	—	4,950	—	5,929	—	8,303
Lowest minimum	—	1,500	—	2,500	—	4,000	—	4,000
Highest minimum	—	4,200	—	5,400	—	6,200	—	10,000
Lowest maximum	—	2,300	—	3,600	—	4,900	—	5,500
Highest maximum	—	5,000	—	6,200	—	10,000	—	15,000

Sources: John E. Deitrick and Robert C. Berson, *Medical Schools in the United States at Mid-Century* (New York: McGraw-Hill, 1953), p. 197; "Report of the Committee on Survey of Economic Status and Professional Opportunities of Anatomists," *Anatomical Record* 105 (1949): 150.

The salaries of medical school faculty members in 1940 and 1949 can be compared to the salaries of all college faculty members and the incomes of private practitioners. Direct comparisons were not possible because of the use of maximum rather than average salaries for medical school faculty members and the lack of information about the number of faculty members in each rank. In 1940, the average salary of all college teachers was $2,906 and the average nonsalaried physician earned $4,441.[34] In the same year, the average basic science medical school faculty member, who was then an M.D., probably earned as much as the average nonsalaried general practitioner. The average full-time clinical faculty member, who was a specialist, probably earned over $6,000, which would have been close to the incomes of many specialists in private practice. Many M.D. faculty members supplemented their salaries with earnings from private patients.

By 1949, salaries of faculty members declined substantially relative to incomes of nonsalaried physicians but maintained their advantage over college teachers. In that year, basic science faculty members probably earned about $6,000 and clinical faculty members about $8,000, plus any income from private patients. In 1949, college teachers earned an average of $4,234 and nonsalaried physicians $11,744.[35]

In 1970, the salaries of basic science faculty, who were now more likely to be Ph.D.s than M.D.s, varied from $15,000 to $22,900 depending on rank, and were about 40 percent higher than the median annual salaries of faculty members of all institutions of higher education (Table 13.3). The salaries of clinical faculty members varied from about $22,000 to about $37,000, depending on rank and specialty, and were more than twice the median annual salaries of faculty members generally. The salaries of clinical assistant professors were compared with those of younger practicing physicians, and those of clinical full professors with older practicing physicians for three specialties shown in the table. The earnings of

TABLE 13.3. Salaries of Faculty Members and Practicing Physicians, 1970–1981

Median Salaries of Faculty Members	Assistant Professors		Associate Professors		Full Professors	
	1970	1981	1970	1981	1970	1981
Medical school clinical department						
Medicine	$22.0	50.0	26.4	64.0	32.5	77.0
Surgery	25.0	64.0	31.0	84.0	37.0	103.0
Obstetrics/gynecology	24.0	57.0	28.8	70.0	33.1	83.0
All medical school basic science departments	15.0	28.9	18.0	35.9	22.9	48.6
All institutions of higher education	10.7	21.2[a]	13.0	25.7[a]	16.8	33.7[a]

[a]Public institutions only.

Practice Income of Practicing Physicians[b]	Years of Age			
	Under 35 1970	Under 36 1982	51—60 1970	46–65[c] 1982
Internal medicine	$27.2	55.0	47.6	91.0
Surgery[c]	34.0	75.0	60.2	115.8
Obstetrics/gynecology	37.2	70.0	51.5	115.5

[b]Incomes in 1970 are "averages;" in 1982, medians.
[c]Average of ages 45–55 and 56–65.

Sources: "Datagrams: Faculty Salaries," *Journal of Medical Education* 46 (1971): 377–78; William C. Smith, *Report on Medical School Faculty Salaries 1981–1982* (Washington, D.C.: Association of American Medical Colleges, 1982), pp. 15–17; U.S. Bureau of the Census, *Statistical Abstract of the United States: 1980* (Washington, D.C.: U.S. G.P.O., 1980), p. 171; U.S. Bureau of the Census, *Statistical Abstract of the United States: 1982–83* (Washington, D.C.: U.S. G.P.O., 1982), p. 165; Judith Warner and Phil Aherne, *Profile of Medical Practice, 1974 Edition* (Chicago: American Medical Association, 1974), p. 197; Roger A. Reynolds and Jonathan B. Abram, eds., *Socioeconomic Characteristics of Medical Practice 1983* (Chicago: American Medical Association, 1983), p. 120.

practicing physicians exceeded the salaries of faculty members by less than 50 percent at younger ages and by more than 50 percent at older ages.

Between 1970 and 1981, clinical faculty salaries showed a much greater rate of increase than basic science faculty salaries, due to increased earnings from professional fees. Basic science faculty salaries just about doubled, as did those of faculty members at all institutions of higher education. Clinical faculty salaries increased about 2.5 times from 1970 to 1981, making them close to the earnings of practicing physicians in 1982. In medicine and surgery, both assistant and full professors approached parity with their counterparts in private practice. Earnings in obstetrics/gynecology, as well as those in other highly specialized fields, continued to be higher for practicing physicians, although by smaller amounts than in 1970.

These comparisons between clinical faculty members and private practitioners have not included the many indirect economic benefits of an academic position. Faculty members have had an easier time attracting patients because the reputation of the medical school has made their personal skills and reputation unimportant. They have not had to set up and manage an office, with its attendant problems. They have benefited from the assistance of other faculty members and house staff in caring for their patients. They have enjoyed the economic security and fringe benefits of a medical school appointment. Overall, the benefits of a clinical faculty position have reached a level where they equal or surpass those of many private practitioners.

The Decline in the Part-Time Clinical Faculty

The employment of many full-time faculty members in medical schools has led some to question the need to continue using local private practitioners as part-time clinical faculty members. It is claimed that medicine has progressed too rapidly for part-time faculty members to keep up with the latest developments and that academic medicine now requires skills in research methodology and the biomedical sciences that they do not possess. It has also been suggested that students should be exposed to a research environment in medical school because they will be in more practical environments during their careers. The learning of practical clinical skills can be delayed until the student's residency.[36]

Ratings of faculty members by 266 medical students in 1964 supported some aspects of this position. Full-time faculty members were rated more highly than part-time faculty members for their emphasis on basic pathophysiological processes, knowledge of their subspecialty, and demands for outside readings. The two groups were rated equally in aspects of their relations with students and patients.[37]

The supporters of part-time faculty members have had different views. Janeway has observed that most full-time faculty members have been "highly trained specialists, who know a great deal about a relatively narrow field, who are very competent in the laboratory with a certain set of basic science techniques, and in the clinic with a particular group of patients, but who are increasingly far-removed from the realities of the daily practice of medicine in the community." The part-time faculty member, according to Sheps et al., "can demonstrate to a student, in a manner that would be difficult for a full-time faculty member, how to take continuing, complete responsibility for the personal care of patients. He can more easily have thorough knowledge of his patients, their families, and their circumstances." A 1984 survey found that 89 percent of medical students and 79 percent of residents "supported increasing the involvement of practicing physicians in defining essential knowledge and skills and educating medical students." This view was shared by only 53 percent of basic science and clinical faculty members and deans.[38]

Part-time faculty members have also provided important benefits to medical schools. They have served as additional instructors at low cost, which has made it possible to reduce class size. They have provided patient care in the clinics and teaching hospitals, and have hospitalized many patients, which has increased the hospital's income and provided more patients for teaching. Part-time faculty members have had ties to the community that have been useful in raising funds and dealing with governments. They have also provided continuity, in contrast to the often highly mobile full-time faculty members.

It seems evident that full- and part-time faculty have had complementary rather than conflicting roles and that both have been of benefit to medical schools. Nevertheless, relations between the two groups have been strained. Full-time and part-time faculty members have competed for the use of hospital beds, operating rooms, and other facilities, as well as for referral patients. Many full-time faculty members have been disturbed by the part-time faculty member who "heavily uses beds, hospital facilities, house staff, and the prestigious name of the institution—and contributes nothing."[39]

The part-time faculty members have had their own grievances. They have been displaced as teachers by inexperienced faculty members and residents. Few have received even a nominal salary while full-time faculty members with lucrative private practices have been paid high salaries. Part-time faculty members have been discriminated against in many ways by the medical school, even though they have contributed an important perspective unavailable from the full-time faculty. Lepore has observed: "Promotions, academic rank, and responsibility were begrudgingly given to the clinical teaching staff, especially those contaminated by their commitment to practice. . . . The . . . attitude was that practically anyone can teach clinical medicine or practice and only quasi-geniuses can do laboratory research."[40]

It is unlikely that the traditional part-time faculty members will ever regain the position they had before 1950, when they participated heavily in teaching, patient care, and policy making. Despite the preferences expressed by medical students and residents for more participation by part-time faculty members, control over medical education has irrevocably passed into the hands of the full-time faculty.

Conclusion

Since mid-century, medical school clinical faculty members have become isolated from the outside community in many ways. They have lost contact with the practicing medical profession, despite their patient-care activities and equal earnings. This separation has occurred because individual faculty members have not had to cultivate relations with practicing physicians for referral patients. Most of their patients either have had no personal physicians or have been referred to a particular unit in the academic medical center, not to an individual faculty member. Thus, faculty members have had little incentive to attend local medical society meetings or participate in other activities of the local medical community.

Medical school faculty members have become isolated from ordinary patient care. Instead of treating patients typical of community practice, they have cared for the exceptionally poor, those requiring highly specialized care, and those who have used medical school clinics because they had no regular physicians. It has not been possible to understand or teach the modern practice of medicine with these kinds of patients. Modern medical practice requires involvement in the long-term care of patients with chronic as well as acute conditions and the recognition of the effect of social and psychological factors in illness.

Full-time clinical medical school faculty members have become estranged from their academic colleagues. Their patient-care activities have required work schedules and activities different from those of other academicians. Their research activities have strengthened their ties to funding agencies and weakened their ties to their institutions. For all these reasons, the academic physician has become a different kind of medical practitioner and a different kind of professional educator.

14

Hospitals Affiliated with Medical Schools

After mid-century, university hospitals became more involved in research and the care of patients with very serious illnesses. This new orientation has created financial, teaching, and patient-care problems. In order to obtain access to more patients and patients with ordinary illnesses, medical schools affiliated with veterans' and community hospitals. Many of these hospitals have become similar to university hospitals as a result.

Types of Hospital Affiliations

Medical schools experienced a serious shortage of facilities in their customary teaching hospitals after 1950. Many university hospitals had few beds or set aside many of their beds for the private patients of the faculty. Patients admitted for research purposes had serious or life-threatening diseases instead of the commonplace disorders needed for training medical students. The public hospitals affiliated with medical schools had heavy patient-care obligations that reduced their teaching and research activities.[1]

To obtain the use of more beds, medical schools affiliated with more community and public hospitals. The closeness of the affiliation has varied as a function of the ability of the medical school to appoint the hospital staff, the number of patients who could be used in teaching, and the type of students—residents and/or undergraduate medical students—who could be taught there. In 1962, 85 medical schools had 269 close or major affiliations and 180 limited affiliations with hospitals. Fifty-one of the hospitals with major affiliations were university hospitals and 100 others gave medical schools the exclusive right to appoint the hospital staffs.[2]

Dependence on university hospitals has continued to decline so that in 1975, only 60 of 107 medical schools owned 1 or more teaching hospitals, with an average of 600 total beds. All of the medical schools averaged 5.5 major affiliated hospitals, which provided an average of 2,800 beds per school. Public medical schools were more likely to own hospitals than private schools (39 of 62 public schools compared to 21 of 45 private schools), but they averaged fewer affiliated hospitals (5.1 compared to 6.0).[3]

In 1982, 419 hospitals were members of the Council of Teaching Hospitals (COTH), of which only 64 were university hospitals. Members of COTH included

270

84 state or municipal hospitals, 71 Veterans Administration and 3 other federal hospitals, and 261 voluntary or other nonpublic hospitals. In 1976–1977, undergraduate medical students served a required clerkship in at least one major clinical department in 276 of the 405 COTH hospitals. The remaining hospitals offered medical students electives or specialty clerkships, or provided only residency training.[4]

COTH hospitals have been major providers of health care. In 1982, the 337 COTH short-term nonfederal hospitals comprised only 5.7 percent of all such hospitals, but they had 18.8 percent of all inpatient beds, 18.4 percent of all admissions, 18.1 percent of all emergency visits, and 26.2 percent of all ambulatory visits. Their expenses constituted 27.4 percent of the total expenses of all short-term nonfederal hospitals, and they employed 55.9 percent of all full-time equivalent (FTE) physicians and dentists and 75.5 percent of all FTE residents. COTH hospitals also had higher costs than nonteaching hospitals. In 1973 their cost per admission was $1,293, 30 percent greater than that in all U.S. hospitals. In 1977, it reached $2,383, 58 percent greater than that in all U.S. hospitals.[5]

COTH hospitals have included most of the large short-term general hospitals but few of the small ones. In 1982, 56 percent of the 333 short-term nonfederal hospitals with 500 or more beds were teaching hospitals, as were 24 percent of the 276 with 400 to 499 beds. Less than 1 percent of the 4,165 hospitals with fewer than 200 beds were affiliated with medical schools.[6]

University Hospitals

University hospitals designed for research and teaching have always been financial burdens to their medical schools. Before World War II, the deficits were usually small enough to be absorbed into the medical school's overall budget. By 1950, the growing deficits forced medical schools to place their hospitals on a separate financial basis, although the change did little to alter the situation. By the mid-1960s, according to Knowles, many university hospitals had "selective admission policies, shabby patient facilities, and deteriorating physical plant, wards full of special 'research' patients, failure (or refusal) to accept alcoholic patients or expand emergency facilities, a two-class system of care . . . and disregard for the outpatient department," all of which led "to a demoralized and spiritless institution." Their elaborate equipment and the skilled labor needed for teaching and research made them more expensive to operate than other hospitals and aggravated their financial problems.[7]

Many university hospitals lost their positions as leading hospitals during the 1960s and 1970s. New suburban hospitals had much of the equipment used in university hospitals, provided more amenities for patients, and were more accessible. Their medical staffs had most of the specialized skills found in university hospitals and accepted local physicians. With these advantages, community hospitals were able to attract many patients away from university hospitals. As an example, in 1948, 70 percent of the patients at the Johns Hopkins Hospital were referred from outside of the Baltimore area. By the mid-1970s, 80 percent came from a 10-mile radius around the hospital.[8]

During the 1970s and 1980s, third-party reimbursements induced university hospitals to improve their patient care. In 1982, Blue Cross and commercial insurors provided 29.1 percent of the income of a sample of the 43 university hospitals that received state appropriations and 38.0 percent of the income of a sample of the 23 other university hospitals. Medicare and Medicaid provided another 35.0 of the income of the state-funded hospitals and 43.9 percent of the income of the other hospitals. Net patient revenues averaged $81 million in the former hospitals and $88 million in the latter. To facilitate patient care, the medical school and hospital roles of faculty members have been differentiated, sometimes to the extent of separate salaries. University hospitals have also employed their own physicians with their own practice plans.[9]

In 1983, Medicare began to base reimbursements to hospitals on prospective payment systems rather than actual costs incurred. Payment was determined by the patient's placement in one of 467 diagnosis-related groups (DRGs), as well as his age, complications, and other factors. Some analyses have shown that teaching hospitals, which have had patients with more serious illnesses, also have had patients within DRGs who were more seriously ill. Because differences within DRGs have not been compensated, teaching hospitals may have been adversely affected by prospective payment systems. However, differences within DRGs have accounted for only a small proportion of the higher costs of teaching hospitals. Much more important have been the DRG case mix, direct educational costs, the number of residents, and hospital wage differentials, most of which have been directly or indirectly reimbursed by Medicare.[10]

Another financial problem in university hospitals has been the provision of free care to the uninsured poor. This problem has been caused primarily by the public ownership of many teaching hospitals. A 1982 comparison of major teaching hospitals (including university hospitals) and a large number of nonteaching hospitals in the 100 largest cities found that public teaching hospitals provided 11 percent of the total volume of care and 31 percent of the total uncompensated care, and that private teaching hospitals provided 32 percent of the total volume of care but only 21 percent of the uncompensated care.[11]

University hospitals and medical schools have been divided by many different interests. This has been most clearly manifested in their administrative structures. The chiefs of hospital services have been medical school department chairmen, who have appointed the medical staffs of their services and have been responsible for patient care. They have given higher priority to education and research than to patient care. This has conflicted with the hospital's need for effective cost-control mechanisms, efficient scheduling, allocation of resources, and integration of the various services.[12]

Faculty research and patient-care activities have posed significant financial burdens for university hospitals. The hospitals have acquired the most advanced equipment available and have become referral centers for organ transplants, open-heart surgery, brain surgery, and the treatment of severe burns. Equipment and patient-care costs have been high. The methods of practice of the procedure-oriented specialists have raised costs even higher, and the use of teams of specialists to treat practically all patients has added even more to the costs.

University hospitals have also had to pay for educational costs like the supervision of students; student use of space, equipment, and supplies; tests and other procedures performed for educational purposes; and the salaries and benefits of residents. Some of these costs have been offset by services performed by students and residents that would otherwise have to be performed by other workers.[13]

Few efforts have been made to reduce research and educational costs in university hospitals by holding faculty members directly responsible for them, largely because of faculty opposition. In the few cases where responsibility has been assigned, costs have been reduced. Thus it is not clear how much of the extra costs of university hospitals now attributed to education and research have actually been due to poor management, faculty domination, and budgetary policies.[14]

University Hospital Patients

University hospitals were found to vary widely in their patient mix in a 1976 study of 81 major teaching hospitals, which included some that were not university owned. Twenty of the hospitals, all but one publicly owned and most located in inner cities, had nonprivate patients only. Twenty-three, all privately owned, had over 95 percent private patients, who were generally admitted by their personal physicians. Most of these were in small towns or suburban areas. The remaining 38 had both private and nonprivate patients and drew them from a large geographic area.[15]

Patients in university hospitals have been treated in a highly fragmented manner by a variety of faculty specialists and house officers. Folkman has observed:

> The idea that for each patient one doctor should have constant responsibility seems self-evident. Yet, its actual practice is confounded by almost every tradition established in our modern medical centers: residents rotate; visits visit; attendings attend (usually for one month of the year); consultings consult. . . . The patient's family doctor who referred him to the medical center usually cannot take care of him there. Even if the referring doctor is a member of the hospital's full-time staff, he often finds himself in conflict with interns and residents when he wants to write orders on his own patients. The residents feel he is usurping their prerogatives.[16]

Duff and Hollingshead found that this lack of responsibility was a major issue dividing faculty members and hospital administrators:

> Often, both the patient and the hospital have difficulty identifying the physician who is actually responsible for a particular individual's care. This is a source of concern to the hospital administrators, who worry about legal action if patients are not properly cared for. . . . They look askance at the university faculty who exercise vast authority in the hospital. . . . They view the uncontrolled and loosely supervised coming and going of the young, disease-oriented, experimental-minded student physicians as possessing authority far beyond what is justified by their experience and training. Because the hospital administrators have overall responsibility for patient care but little authority over the provision of that care, this is a matter of much concern for them.[17]

Patients admitted to teaching hospital without private physicians have been assigned a staff physician to care for them. Because the physician will not care for them later as private patients, he has had little incentive to give them personalized attention. Furthermore, faculty members and house staff have tended to be research and disease oriented. Duff and Hollingshead quoted a university hospital administrator as saying:

> All of the interest is essentially in the disease rather than in the patient who has the disease. They get all excited about the focal pathology of the patient, for example, who has pneumonia and they forget about how the patient got the disease, what his precise diagnosis and prognosis are, and what kind of management and prophylaxis he will receive. This is a very narrow focus and is the result of the atmosphere created by the individuals who control it—the faculty. . . . These young doctors treat the patients . . . as part of the teaching equipment of the place.[18]

The wide social class differences between staff physicians and the patients without private physicians have created serious problems of communication. Duff and Hollingshead reported: "On the wards, suspicion, distrust, and confusion were extreme and common. The performance of physicians tended to keep alive this distrust." Patients were rarely told their problems in language that they could understand and they in turn withheld information from staff physicians for fear it might be misunderstand or misused. Staff physicians felt little need to create a relationship of mutual trust or to concern themselves with problems unrelated to the immediate diagnosis, such as the patient's personal and family life and its effect on the patient's condition.[19]

Outpatient Services of University Hospitals

University hospital outpatient services have consisted of as many as 100 or more specialty and subspecialty clinics for the care of ambulatory patients, plus an emergency room for emergency care. Faculty members have established specialty clinics because patients with particular conditions can be treated during a few hours of each week and used efficiently for research and teaching. The clinics have been much less satisfactory for the patients. Patients with ordinary problems have had no clinics that would take them. Patients with appropriate diseases who lack "interesting" complications have been given low priority. Patients with multiple disorders have been placed in several clinics, often attending different clinics on different days, with no clinic assuming responsibility for their overall care. Patients have often seen different physicians on each visit, and, if hospitalized, have been given no continuity of care between inpatient and outpatient services. Many times patients have attended inappropriate specialty clinics at their own initiative. Care provided by house officers has usually been inadequately supervised.[20]

Medical schools have claimed that outpatient services have had low priority because they constituted a significant financial burden. Many outpatients have not had health insurance or were not adequately covered for outpatient services by Medicare, Medicaid, or private insurors. When outpatients have been used for educational purposes, the cost of their care has risen because house officers have been slow and inefficient.

At the same time, the costs of outpatient clinics have been inflated by university hospital budgetary and management policies. The proration of costs among all hospital services has forced outpatient departments, which have been open 8 hours daily and have usually used simple technologies, to absorb some of the costs of inpatient services that have been open 24 hours a day and used expensive technologies. Clinical department chairmen have assumed responsibility for individual outpatient clinics, allocated resources to them, and specified support services. Yet, according to Berman and Moloney, "[H]ospitals have not traditionally held these same chairmen responsible for the financial consequences of their decisions. Few chairmen even consider the financial viability of the outpatient department within their scope of concern or are even aware of the financial statements which report clinic losses." Until cost-effective management practices are employed in university hospital outpatient departments, their financial viability will remain an open question.[21]

Some teaching hospitals have developed well-organized outpatient clinics that have successfully attracted patients and provided them with satisfactory care. These clinics have not solved all of the problems enumerated above, but they have demonstrated that the customary situation can be improved. In most medical schools, however, the outpatient services have changed little from the situation described by Weinerman and Steiger in 1964: "Resources have been inadequate, staffing uncertain and unstable, services fragmentary and impersonal, and status at the bottom of the medical school pecking order."[22]

The House Officer in the University Hospital

Residents have become a major source of professional manpower in university hospitals, as shown by their rising salaries in recent years. In 1960–1961, first-year residents in all hospitals earned about $2,700. In 1970–1971, the median salary of first-year residents in COTH hospitals was $8,115 and in 1984–1985 it was $20,808. In 1983–1984, residents' salaries constituted 3.5 percent of the operating budgets of COTH hospitals. Patient revenues and general operating appropriations provided 81 percent of the income for the salaries.[23]

House officers have been responsible for a significant amount of patient care, according to a 1976 Institute of Medicine study of 81 teaching hospitals. They usually initiated the treatment of all patients without private physicians, but did not do so for patients with private physicians. They carried out the daily management of patients within an approved treatment plan for patients with and without private physicians. House officers also wrote the discharge summaries for both kinds of patients, although they signed them only in the case of patients without their own physicians.[24]

Because of their inexperience, house officers have been responsible to other professionals involved in the patient's care. These have included staff specialists, an attending physician, more senior members of the house staff, and nonphysicians such as social workers. Each professional has often had poorly defined responsibility for some aspect of the patient's care. As a result, house officers have carried out many of their duties with little direct supervision. The Institute of Medicine study found that in inpatient and outpatient duty, house officers acted in the presence of a senior house officer or attending physician about 40 percent of the time, acted independently with an expectation of future review about 40 percent of the time, and acted independently without expectation of review about 10 percent of the time. The proportion of time that house officers acted independently was not affected by whether the hospital was primarily for private or nonprivate patients, or whether the house officers were in their first, second, or third year. When supervision occurred, house officers with more years of training were supervised more often by attending physicians and less often by senior house officers.[25]

Medical schools have claimed that giving house officers autonomy and letting them make mistakes has been, according to Millman, "a natural part of the training process. Although residents and interns may be reprimanded for mistakes, they are also seen as working with a 'beginner's license' that grants them some pardon from responsibility."[26] The finding of the Institute of Medicine study that residents' autonomy did not increase from their first to their third year of residency indicates a failure to recognize that the amount of autonomy should vary with the extent of the resident's experience.

House officers have viewed their service responsibilities as part of their professional training. They have been more interested in treating patients whom they believed would further their education than in providing excellent patient care. Many studies have reported that house officers who served as hospital admitting officers preferred to admit cases on the basis of their educational value rather than the patient's need for hospitalization.[27]

The Future of the University Hospital

In recent decades both community and university hospitals have changed in ways that have affected the university hospital's role. Major community hospitals have become more like traditional university hospitals. They have taught students, carried out research, and provided highly specialized care. They have performed some major educational functions better than have university hospitals. Lippard observed that one great educational value of hospital-based medical education has been that "the patients that one sees in the outpatient clinics and hospital wards are suffering from diseases that are prevalent today."[28] This situation has existed in recent years only in community hospitals, which have attracted patients with many different backgrounds and illnesses. University hospitals have become tertiary care and research centers with highly atypical patients.

Even as research institutions, university hospitals have been only partially successful. Their research has been concerned with disease processes in sick patients, the development of new methods of diagnosis and cure, and clinical trials of new medical procedures. They have not carried out research on the effective utilization and operation of hospitals, the relationship between hospital care and ambulatory and nursing home care, and new types of payment systems. One way to do this would have been for medical schools to sponsor health maintenance organizations (HMOs), and to use the HMO's population for research on the delivery of health services. Yet HMOs established at medical schools have often failed, primarily because of lack of commitment by the faculty. Medical schools could also have undertaken research and pilot projects on the regionalization of health facilities because of their multiple hospital affiliations. Instead, they have viewed hospital affiliations as a source of "clinical material."[29]

Many observers have been concerned over the narrowly defined functions of university hospitals. Westerman has written:

> At best the [university] hospital is perceived as an academic support unit which often ends up being a costly service operation, providing a fertile field for faculty private-practice income squabbles and a rich source of public misunderstandings. Even the laudable care to the indigent is tempered by the resources drained from the higher priority, purely academic university functions. . . .
>
> [T]he buildings are costly, require constant renovations and additions, and are lavishly equipped according to the newest and most expensive of unproved medical technology. In fact, the university hospital is so technology-oriented that there is question whether the "clinical laboratory" serves anyone's needs but those of the most advanced graduate students.[30]

It has frequently been proposed that university hospitals and medical schools should be financially and administratively independent organizations. Movement in this direction has occurred since the 1970s. As it does, university hospitals will become similar to community hospitals. Faculty domination will be replaced by a larger role for hospital administrators. The right of the faculty to admit patients solely because of their research value and to purchase expensive and rarely used equipment will be curtailed. The decades of emphasis of many university hospitals on research and clinical specialization at the expense of teaching and patient care will be replaced by greater balance among their functions.

Medical Schools and Veterans Administration Hospitals

The first hospitals for veterans were constructed by the federal government after World War I. Their activities increased significantly after 1924 when they were permitted to admit veterans with non-service-connected disabilities, with those unable to pay given first preference. The 86 veterans' hospitals in 1940 had 56,596 beds, and 78 percent of all patients had non-service-connected problems.[31]

The status of veterans' hospitals before World War II has been the subject of some controversy. On the one hand, their approval by the American College of Surgeons in 1927 placed them among the better hospitals in the nation. On the other hand, few of their physicians were certified by specialty boards, low levels of funding made it difficult to obtain able physicians and necessary equipment, and bureaucratic procedures prevailed. Veterans' hospitals were generally isolated from the leading elements of American medicine.[32]

After World War II, in order to obtain additional staff to deal with the expected rise in the amount of hospital care, the Veterans Administration (VA) affiliated many of its hospitals with medical schools and agreed to construct future VA hospitals near medical schools. In 1945, in Policy Memorandum No. 2, the VA permitted medical schools, acting through a dean's committee of senior faculty, to nominate a part-time attending staff of faculty members and residents, and to train residents in VA hospitals under the supervision of the faculty. The chiefs of the hospital services were nominated by the medical school or, in the case of full-time employees of the VA, were to be acceptable to the medical school. Faculty members and residents were responsible both to the VA hospital director and the medical school.[33]

An alternative to the affiliation of VA hospitals with medical schools was for the VA to hospitalize veterans in community hospitals and reimburse the hospitals for their expenses. The AMA and others favored this alternative because it would strengthen community hospitals and raise the quality of hospital care for the whole community, especially in rural areas. Sarason has suggested that the VA chose to affiliate with medical schools because of the recommendations of medical school faculty consultants then in the armed forces. He observed that "their sincerity was as unquestioned as their ability to dispassionately consider alternatives was lacking," given the "self-serving" nature of the decision.[34]

In 1948, 58 medical schools operated residency programs in 68 VA hospitals, and many also provided undergraduate instruction in them. In 1965, all 46 VA hospitals within 5 miles of a medical school and 44 of the 125 others were affiliated with medical schools. Affiliated VA hospitals had 59 percent of the VA general hospital beds and were affiliated with a total of 77 medical schools. In 1976, 74 of 138 VA hospitals were members of the Council of Teaching Hospitals. They had 70 percent or more of all VA hospital beds, admissions, inpatient days, and outpatient visits.[35]

VA hospitals have played a major role in the establishment of new medical schools. Of 11 medical schools established between 1940 and 1965, 9 used VA hospitals for undergraduate teaching, with 6 of them having no university hospital in 1965. Of 7 medical schools that were converted from two-year to four-year schools over the same period, 4 used VA hospitals in their undergraduate teaching. Federal legislation enacted in 1972 led to the establishment of 5 other public medical schools with the assistance of the VA and the use of VA hospitals.[36]

Medical school faculty members have provided a significant amount of care in VA hospitals. In 1965, about 44 percent of all VA staff had academic appointments. A 1976 study of 81 VA hospitals by the National Academy of Sciences (NAS) found that medical school faculties provided two-thirds or more of the FTE physicians in 65 of the VA hospitals in surgery, in 47 of the VA hospitals in medicine, and in 32 of the VA hospitals in psychiatry. Medical school residents provided one-third or more of the care in 68 of 81 medical services and 76 of 81 surgical services. Medical school staffs have been primarily part time. The study found that 84 percent of the full-time VA hospital physicians and 79 percent of the clinical service chiefs considered themselves primarily VA physicians, while 63 percent of the part-time physicians considered themselves primarily medical school faculty members.[37]

Medical schools have used VA hospitals for much residency and undergraduate training. VA hospitals provided 12 percent of all residency positions in 1948 and 10 percent of them in 1964. In 1965, the VA permitted residents on VA salaries to receive training in university hospitals in gynecology, pediatrics, and other fields not available in VA hospitals. This was an important financial benefit to the medical schools. In 1974–1975, VA hospitals provided 38 percent of all residencies in internal medicine, 16 percent of those in surgery, and 14 percent of those in psychiatry. With regard to undergraduate training, in 1964, 27 percent of American medical students spent some time in VA hospitals. As many or more have done so since.[38]

The quality of patient care in VA hospitals has been a subject of dispute. The 1976 NAS study found that VA hospital outpatients were more than twice as likely to be admitted as inpatients as patients who made office visits to physicians generally, that the average length of stay in VA hospitals was more than twice as long as in nonfederal private and public general hospitals, and that VA hospital patients were somewhat more likely to need minimal nursing care than patients in nonfederal private and public general hospitals. VA hospitals have also been accused of keeping beds filled in order to receive appropriations. On the other hand, government regulations have made it easier to admit VA patients as inpatients than to treat them as outpatients, many VA outpatient departments have lacked adequate facilities, and alternative sources of ambulatory and nursing home care have often not been available for the many elderly patients.[39]

The NAS studied 14 VA hospitals to examine the impact of medical school affiliation on VA hospital care. Of the 3 hospitals without medical school affiliations, 2 were given an overall rating by the NAS of "inadequate" and 1 of "adequate." Of the 11 with medical school affiliations, 2 were rated "outstanding" and 9 were rated "adequate." The study found that residents in affiliated hospitals performed 88 percent of all surgical operations. In 69 percent of the operations performed by residents, "the operation was not supervised by a member of the VA full-time or part-time staff service as first assistant surgeon." VA hospital residents also expressed concern with the lack of supervision in their responses to a questionnaire. Twenty-five percent of the respondents felt that they were not adequately supervised, and 41 percent felt that the quality of education was lower in VA hospitals than in non-VA settings.[40]

The NAS study also found that many VA hospitals failed to meet the standards of the Joint Commission on Accreditation of Hospitals (JCAH) concerning the performance of a minimum number of certain types of operations. For example, of 25 VA hospitals performing kidney transplants, only 3 exceeded the minimum number recommended by the JCAH. The NAS study concluded: "The VA has installed many expensive specialized medical facilities that, in many hospitals, are used at rates far below their capacity" and duplicate underutilized facilities in community hospitals. Most of the facilities were constructed in VA hospitals affiliated with medical schools. Many were unnecessary because VA hospitals have been permitted since 1966 to contract with other hospitals to perform services for them. In 1975, 92 percent of the contracts were with university hospitals, a policy which has provided substantial financial and other benefits to medical schools.[41]

VA hospitals have also often been deficient in their outpatient services. The NAS studied 24 VA hospital outpatient services, most in hospitals affiliated with medical schools, and rated none as outstanding, 11 as adequate, and 13 as inadequate. It also found that VA hospital outpatient services had "serious problems regarding continuity and comprehensiveness of care." Medical schools have thus neglected VA hospital outpatient departments in the same way that they have neglected their university hospital outpatient departments. This is particularly unfortunate because a survey found that two-thirds of VA outpatients considered the VA hospital as their "usual source of outpatient care." VA outpatient facilities could therefore have provided excellent primary care training if medical schools had chosen to use them for that purpose.[42]

Medical schools have also been accused of altering VA hospital admission and patient-care policies to suit their interests. The Executive Director of the National Association of VA Physicians testified before Congress in 1980 that medical school faculty members "admit veteran patients not on the basis of need but according to their value as 'teaching material,'" and that rehabilitation services and facilities have been neglected to provide more facilities for surgery for teaching purposes.[43]

These findings indicate that medical schools have imposed a university hospital framework on VA hospitals, despite the different patient-care responsibilities involved. Sarason has observed: "Health policy for veterans . . . sought to interrelate two organizational cultures—the university medical center and a large, complex federal bureaucracy. Neither of the organizations had experience with such a formal interrelationship, and neither attempted to understand the other's culture."[44]

Medical Schools and Community Hospitals

The great majority of hospitals affiliated with medical schools have been private and public community hospitals. Medical schools have added these affiliations because of the growing number of students and residents who need clinical experience, the paucity of patients with typical problems in university hospitals, and the establishment of new medical schools without university hospitals.[45]

Private community hospitals have affiliated with medical schools for several reasons. Medical school affiliation has enabled them to improve their residency programs in order to attract residents and obtain accreditation. Affiliation has provided the community physicians on their staffs with the services of residents and medical school faculty specialists. It has also enhanced the reputation of the hospitals.[46]

Public hospitals have affiliated with medical schools because of staffing problems. Community physicians have been unwilling to serve on their staffs because the hospitals have not admitted their private patients. In order to obtain a medical staff, municipal hospitals, like VA hospitals, have affiliated with medical schools to use faculty members and residents as staff physicians. As was also the case with VA hospitals, the decisions to affiliate were controversial and provided little evidence that affiliation was the best solution to the hospitals' problems.[47]

The education and supervision of residents in private affiliated hospitals have been the responsibility of the community physicians who have served on their staffs. However, the physicians have not been educators and their primary obligations have been to their private patients. They have provided less instruction than have faculty members and have delegated residents less authority over their private patients than the residents desired. Residents in turn have felt isolated and neglected by the medical school. Many community hospitals have hired full-time directors of education to improve their training programs. Because the directors have had no authority over the hospital's community physicians or the medical schools, their positions have been tenuous ones.[48]

In order to improve teaching in affiliated hospitals, some medical schools have assigned faculty members to them. Although this has been a major benefit to the hospitals, it has required the medical school to duplicate resources. The faculty members have often felt isolated and have had little time for research, so that a core of faculty members has been needed in each hospital to create an academic environment. Even then, it has often been difficult to carry out traditional academic research in many community hospitals.[49]

Although medical schools have affiliated with community hospitals in order to teach primary and secondary care, they have tended to remake the hospitals in the mold of university hospitals. Several New York City medical schools assumed responsibility for staffing the city's municipal hospitals in the early 1960s. They introduced highly specialized inpatient care facilities and created dozens of specialty outpatient clinics characteristic of university hospitals. They de-emphasized the home-care programs that had been carried on by municipal hospitals since the 1940s. Two decades later, in 1982, an evaluation by New York City criticized many aspects of medical school management and noted that they had failed to provide the "effective and efficient high quality ambulatory care" specified in the affiliation agreements.[50]

Medical school research programs have led to the de-emphasis of primary care in affiliated community hospitals. Research in affiliated New York City hospitals was rarely concerned with the health problems of the populations involved, but instead concentrated on diseases or therapeutic techniques more appropriate to university hospitals. The medical schools made large expenditures for specialized equipment of marginal value to the hospitals, and reorganized hospital facilities to create more space for their research projects. They also tried to change the patient populations to admit more patients of research interest.[51]

In general, medical schools have failed to use community hospitals to broaden the educational or research experiences of their faculty or students. Burlage observed of the experience in New York City: "The zeal of these private institutions was not to become generally responsible for community health needs. . . . Instead, what these institutions sought was 'access' to certain patients of these expanded patient populations."[52]

This examination of VA, municipal, and private hospital affiliations has shown that medical schools have disregarded the original purpose of using community hospitals—to provide medical students and residents with the opportunity to care for typical patients in a typical hospital environment. In both these hospitals and university hospitals, the emphasis has been on the subspecialty and biomedical research interests of full-time clinical faculty members. As a result, medical schools have failed to provide medical students with adequate training in the care of patients typical of community practice.[53]

15

Medical School Enrollments and Admissions Policies

After shortages of physicians developed in the 1950s and 1960s, federal and state governments undertook programs to increase the number of medical students. Government funding led to the creation of many new medical schools and to substantial enrollment increases in existing schools. Medical schools admitted larger numbers of women, minority, and low-income students. The impact of medical schools on the career choices of students has been limited.

Early Federal Aid to Medical Education

Federal funding for medical research immediately after World War II was designed to avoid politically controversial issues like federal aid for medical education and health care. The 1947 Steelman report on medical research noted that it did not examine "equally important" problems, such as financial assistance for medical education, equal access to health care, continuing medical education for physicians, or "the mass application of science to the prevention of many communicable diseases."[1]

The same restraints prevailed with regard to early federal aid for the construction of medical school research facilities. Some medical school research facilities were built with the help of federal funds during and after World War II, but the first federal legislation specifically designed to fund construction of medical school research facilities was the Health Research Facilities Act of 1956. It provided matching grants equal to 50 percent of the cost of research facilities and equipment, and benefited practically all medical schools. In 1960, medical schools received $13.8 million to construct research facilities. This may be compared to $106.4 million for research grants and $41.5 million for research training grants in the same year.[2]

Federal grants for research and research training were often used for other activities. As early as 1951, the Surgeon General's Committee on Medical School Grants and Finances reported that "Public Health Service grants have undoubtedly improved some aspects of undergraduate instruction in every medical school," with most of the improvements resulting from training rather than research grants. By the early 1970s, according to Freymann, of $1.3 billion given to medical schools for research, "about $800 million was 'redeployed' into institutional and departmental support. . . . The distinction between research and education became as fluid as the imagination of the individual grantees wished it to be.'' Research funds became so important in financing medical education that in 1963 the AMA Council on Medical Education expressed concern over the "financial dependence of the schools on research funds to help conduct their general educational programs.''[3]

Federal funding had its greatest educational impact on graduate education in the basic sciences and postdoctoral clinical education. Students in those fields received stipends from federal research training grants and worked in laboratories and research facilities built with federal research construction grants. Between 1958 and 1967, research training grants increased from $12.7 million to $107.5 million. This produced a 64 percent increase in graduate and postdoctoral students between 1964 and 1967, but only a 6 percent increase in the number of undergraduate medical students.[4]

Federal Efforts to Increase Medical School Enrollments

During the 1950s, health insurance coverage and a rising standard of living enabled many more persons to enjoy the benefits of medical care. However, the 233,000 physicians in 1950 increased to only 275,000 in 1960, which reduced the number per 100,000 persons from 149 to 148. The decline would have been greater except for the immigration of physicians. The proportion of newly licensed physicians who graduated from foreign medical schools (excluding Canadian schools) increased from 5.1 percent in 1950 to 17.7 percent in 1960.[5]

Despite the failure of medical schools to train enough physicians to meet the nation's needs, some medical educators joined the leaders of organized medicine in opposing federal programs to increase the supply of physicians. During the 1950s, a number of medical school deans opposed federal aid, and the AMA supported only one-time matching grants to medical schools for the construction and renovation of physical facilities. In 1956, Congress considered adding grants for the construction of educational facilities to the Health Research Facilities Act. The proposal failed because it was opposed by the AMA, many research-oriented medical school faculty members, and leaders of health voluntary associations. The AMA feared government control over medical education, and the other groups believed that it would dilute the nation's medical research effort. Medical educators began to change their attitudes soon thereafter, and in 1963 the AMA also called for more medical school graduates, although it did not formally support federal aid for the operational costs of medical schools until 1968.[6]

The shortage of physicians continued to be a major problem in the early 1960s. The number of physicians per 100,000 population increased only slightly from 148 in 1960 to 153 in 1965, due once again to the immigration of foreign-educated physicians, who accounted for 16.7 percent of all newly licensed physicians in 1965. Between 1959–1960 and 1964–1965, the number of newly licensed graduates of medical schools rose by only 4.6 percent, from 7,081 to 7,409 (Table 15.1). This was due partly to the establishment of seven new medical schools between 1954–1955 and 1964–1965.[7]

Direct aid to medical schools for medical education was first provided in the Health Professions Educational Assistance Act of 1963. One impetus for the

TABLE 15.1. U.S. Medical Schools and Medical School Graduates, 1949–1984

Year	Medical Schools	Degrees Conferred	Degrees Conferred per School
1949–1950	79	5,533	70.0
1954–1955	81	6,977	86.1
1959–1960	85	7,081	83.3
1964–1965	88	7,409	84.2
1969–1970	101	8,367	82.8
1974–1975	114	12,714	111.5
1979–1980	126	15,135	120.1
1983–1984	127	16,327	128.6

Sources: J. R. Schofield, *New and Expanded Medical Schools, Mid-Century to the 1980s* (San Francisco: Jossey-Bass, 1984), pp. 10, 32; Anne. E. Crowley, Sylvia I. Etzel, and Edward S. Petersen, "Undergraduate Medical Education," *JAMA* 254 (1985): 1568.

legislation was the shortage of physicians in rural areas, which was mentioned by many congressmen during testimony on the legislation. Another was the high cost of medical education and the availability of federal financial aid to students in scientific fields. Between 1956–1957 and 1960–1961, the number of applicants to medical schools decreased by 10 percent, and the proportion that was admitted increased from 50.3 to 57.6 percent. A representative of the Association of American Medical Colleges (AAMC) reported to a congressional committee in 1962 that some medical schools "have had to scrape the bottom of the barrel of applicants to fill their classes." He noted that federal aid to students in the GI bill had "resulted in not only a bumper crop of fine applicants for the study of medicine," but also the admission of "an extremely satisfactory group of students" who could not otherwise afford a medical education. Both the AAMC and the AMA supported construction and renovation grants; the AAMC supported scholarships for students and the AMA did not oppose them; neither organization called for grants to cover medical school operating expenses.[8]

The 1963 legislation provided federal funding for one-half of the construction costs of educational facilities in existing schools and two-thirds of the costs in new schools or for major expansions of existing schools. Medical schools that received construction grants for the expansion of enrollment capacities were required to increase their entering classes by 5 percent or 5 students, whichever was greater, and to maintain the increase for 10 years. Funding was given for loans of up to $2,000 per student per year, but not for scholarships. In 1965, the federal government gave medical schools a total of $503.9 million, which included $59.1 million for the construction of teaching facilities, $32.3 million for the construction of research facilities, $6.6 million for student loans, $107.2 million for research training, and $298.7 million for research. Thus 87 percent of all federal funds for medical schools went for research, and 94 percent of all federal aid for students went for research training.[9]

Not only was the legislation to assist medical education funded at a much lower level than that for research, it was also tied more closely to specific social goals. Educational funding provided scholarships only to low-income students; research training grants were not restricted to needy students. Basic educational improvement and some construction grants were tied to specific enrollment increases; federal research grants were not related to usable results. The basic educational improvement grants provided identical levels of funding to high-cost and low-cost schools; research grants were based on policies that favored the richer schools. Funds for operating expenses were disbursed through the medical school administration; research grants were under the de facto control of the faculty, even though they were nominally awarded to the school.

In 1965 Congress amended the act to award basic improvement grants of $12,500 per school plus $250 per full-time student in 1966 and $25,000 per school plus $500 per student in 1967–1969 to medical schools that would undertake a one-time expansion of their enrollments by the greater of 2.5 percent or 5 students. The legislation also increased funding for the loan program and provided grants to schools for scholarships of up to $2,500 per student per year for students from low-income families. The Health Manpower Act of 1968 continued and broadened the above programs. Special projects grants were provided for a variety of purposes, including assistance to schools in financial distress.[10]

Between 1965 and 1971, the federal government poured $5.1 billion in direct funding into medical schools. Medical education received less than 18 percent of the funds, which included $564.9 million to construct teaching facilities, $225.1 million for capitation and special projects grants, and $105.0 million for scholarships and loans. Medical research received the remaining 82 percent, which included $122.8 million for research facilities, $2.6 billion for research, and $1.1 billion for research training grants. Once again, over 90 percent of the federal aid to students went for training researchers and less than 10 percent went for scholarships and loans to needy medical students, despite the serious shortage of physicians.[11]

State governments increased their aid to medical schools at this time, partly because federal legislation required medical schools to maintain certain levels of nonfederal spending. In 1960–1961, 87 medical schools reported receiving $81 million from state and local governments and $181 million from the federal government. In 1965–1966, they received $143 million in state and local funds and $481 million in federal funds. In 1970–1971, 92 medical schools reported receiving $385 million from state and local governments and $779 million from the federal government.[12]

The requirement in the federal legislation that funding depended on enrollment increases mobilized medical schools into action. Between 1960–1961 and 1970–1971, the 86 medical schools established before 1960 increased their total entering class from 8,298 to 10,539 students and their average entering class size from 96 to 122. In 1970–1971, the 17 medical schools established after 1960 enrolled 809 students in their entering classes, an average of 48 students per school.[13]

The funding principles of the 1960s were expanded in the Comprehensive Health Manpower Training Act of 1971. The federal share of construction funding now reached a maximum of 80 percent and private medical schools were given construction loan guarantees and interest subsidies. Capitation funding authorized

$2,500 per student and $4,000 per graduate in exchange for one-time enrollment increases of the greater of 10 students or 5 percent of the first-year class in schools with entering classes of 100 or more students, and a straight 10 percent in smaller schools. Additional aid was provided for new schools, schools in financial distress, and schools undertaking specified projects. Loans and scholarships were continued. Between 1972 and 1976, medical schools received $5.8 billion in direct federal funding, which included $655 million for capitation and special projects, $109 million for loans and scholarships, and $234 million to construct teaching facilities. Once again, 82 percent of the funds went to research, with $3.5 billion awarded for research grants and contracts, and $770 million for research training. Research training received 88 percent of all student aid.[14]

The Health Professions Educational Assistance Act of 1976 extended these programs through 1980. Construction grants were retained, and loans and scholarships were significantly modified. Capitation grant authorization was reduced to about $2,000 annually, but medical schools were required only to maintain enrollments and expenditures of nonfederal funds. The reduction, according to a House of Representatives committee in 1980, was intended "to serve notice to schools that capitation assistance, in perpetuity, should not be considered a foregone conclusion and that schools should assume more responsibility for seeking alternative sources of funding for their core medical education financial support."[15]

By this time, the physician manpower problem had become one of obtaining more primary-care physicians rather than more physicians generally. The 1971 legislation had recognized this need by funding hospital residency programs and residents in family medicine. The 1976 legislation carried this further by tying medical school capitation funds to the proportion of residents in primary care specialties. The proportion was required to increase by steps to a minimum of 50 percent of all residencies by 1980. Medical schools could not disaffiliate other residency programs to reach the proportion.[16]

Medical schools received substantial aid from the 1976 legislation and they continued to expand their enrollments. Between 1977 and 1980, they received a total of over $6.9 billion in federal aid, 78 percent of which went for research. About $1.5 billion went for educational or other programs, $5.4 billion went for research grants and research training, and $79 million went for construction. The total entering class of the 86 medical schools that existed in 1960 grew from 10,559 in 1970 to 13,753 in 1980, from an average of 122 to 159 medical students per school. The number and enrollments of schools established after 1960 reached 17 in 1970 with 789 students, and 40 in 1980 with 3,567 students.[17]

The 1976 legislation began a new era in relations between the federal government and medical schools. Medical schools had requested an unconditional basic grant for each school and bonuses for special projects, such as increasing the number of primary care physicians. The House of Representatives committee rejected this proposal on the grounds "that Federal support on such a substantial level should only be extended to those schools which agree to fulfill nationally perceived needs." In other words, medical schools believed they had an irrevocable claim on the federal treasury, while the House of Representatives held that federal "support has always been tied to specific requirements."[18]

In 1980 the House and Senate committees proposed many new federal requirements for medical schools as a condition of future funding, which signified their continuing belief in the need for rigid funding formulas to induce medical schools to meet national goals. The proposed legislation was not enacted because of the election of Ronald Reagan as president. Instead, existing funding was continued for family medicine and some other programs, but capitation grants were eliminated after 1980. Between 1981 and 1983, medical schools received $5.7 billion from federal funds, $5.1 billion of which went for research and research training. Other federal aid was reduced to one-half of its previous annual level.[19]

Another reason for the change in federal policy was the recognition that the states had assumed major responsibility for medical education. In 1970–1971 state and local government funding and federal nonresearch funding each provided 19 percent of the income for the operations of medical schools. In 1980–1981, state and local governments provided 23 percent, but federal nonresearch funding provided only 6 percent. State governments also established most of the new medical schools. Of the 37 four-year medical schools established in the 50 states after 1960, 29 were state owned, 6 were private schools that received state support, 1 was federally owned, and only 1 was strictly private. These 37 schools plus 2 private schools in Puerto Rico accounted for 39 percent of the total increase in medical school enrollments between 1959–1960 and 1979–1980.[20]

Despite public concern over the shortage of physicians, federal aid to medical schools had consistently emphasized research rather than education. Between 1965 and 1983, medical schools received $23.5 billion in direct payments from the federal government, over 75 percent of which went for research, research facilities construction, and research training. The most striking disparity was that between funding to train researchers and scholarships and loans for medical students. Financial aid to train researchers, regardless of need, amounted to $1.9 billion between 1965 and 1976, while scholarships and loans to needy medical students totalled only $214 million.

Federal and state funding enabled medical schools to attain an unparalleled level of educational affluence. The schools received research funding on a scale that defense contractors envied. Their affiliations with VA hospitals provided many direct and indirect financial benefits. Their patient-care revenues, buttressed by extra federal payments to cover educational costs, exceeded those of other types of hospitals. Their basic science faculties earned salaries far beyond those of other academicians and their clinical faculties earned almost as much as private practitioners. Medical students were the crown princes of higher education, enjoying unique student-faculty ratios and academic support services. The campuses of medical schools were more abundantly equipped and staffed than those of any other institutions of higher education anywhere in the world.

Medical School Undergraduate Enrollments

Since mid-century, medical school undergraduate enrollments have varied considerably relative to the total population and the pool of available students (Table

TABLE 15.2. Medical School Undergraduate Enrollments, 1950–1982

Year	Total	Per 10,000 U.S. Population	First-Year Class	
			Number	As Percent of All Bachelor's Degrees
1950	26,191	1.72	7,182	1.66
1955	28,639	1.73	7,686	2.69
1960	30,288	1.68	8,298	2.12
1965	32,835	1.69	8,759	1.75
1970	40,487	1.97	11,348	1.43
1975	56,244	2.60	11,695	1.27
1980	65,497	2.88	17,204	1.85
1982	66,886	2.88	17,230	1.81
1983	67,443	2.88	17,175	n.a.
1984	67,090	2.84	16,992	n.a.

Source: Davis G. Johnson, *U.S. Medical Students 1950–2000* (Washington, D.C.: Association of American Medical Colleges, 1983), pp. 66–67; U.S. Bureau of the Census, *Statistical Abstract, 1985* (Washington, D.C.: U.S. G.P.O., 1982), pp. 6, 149.

15.2). Enrollments grew more slowly than the U.S. population from 1950 to 1960, grew slightly faster than the population through the 1960s, increased rapidly during the period of capitation funding in the 1970s, and then leveled off in the 1980s. The ratio of medical students to all bachelor's degree recipients rose in the late 1950s, declined steadily until about 1975, and rose thereafter.

The number of students who have applied to medical school (Table 15.3) has varied with the number of college graduates and the proportion who applied to medical school, the number of students who reapplied to medical school after having been rejected, and the number of available places in medical school freshman classes. These factors have interacted with each other to produce significant short-term variations in applications. For example, in the early 1970s a larger proportion of a growing number of college graduates applied to medical school at the same time that the number of students who reapplied to medical school after having been rejected rose to about one-fourth of the total number of applicants.[21] This substantially decreased the proportion of applicants who were accepted.

Medical School Admission Policies

Since mid-century, medical school admissions committees have increased their emphasis on preparation in the sciences and mathematics. Between 1952 and 1977, the mean quantitative test scores of accepted medical students on the Medical College Admission Test (MCAT) rose from 526 to 633, and the mean science test scores from 525 to 639, but the mean verbal test scores only rose from 522 to 580, and the mean general information test scores from 519 to 559.[22] Medical students have also taken more science and mathematics courses in college.

The emphasis of admissions committees on science preparation has not been justified by research on the performance of medical students. Many studies have

TABLE 15.3. Medical School Applicants, 1950–1982

Year	Applicants	Percent of Applicants Accepted	Applicants as Percent of all Bachelor's Degrees
1950	22,300	33	5.2
1955	14,900	53	5.2
1960	14,400	60	3.7
1965	18,700	48	3.7
1970	25,000	46	3.2
1975	42,300	38	4.6
1980	36,100	48	3.9
1982	35,700	48	3.7
1983	35,200	49	n.a.
1984	35,944	48	n.a.

Sources: Davis G. Johnson, *U.S. Medical Students 1950–2000* (Washington, D.C.: Association of American Medical Colleges, 1983), pp. 34, 40–41; Anne E. Crowley, Sylvia I. Etzel, and Edward S. Petersen, "Undergraduate Medical Education," *JAMA* 254 (1985): 1568; U.S. Bureau of the Census, *Statistical Abstract, 1985* (Washington, D.C.: U.S. G.P.O., 1985), p. 149.

found that the scores of students on both the old and the new MCAT tests have had only low to moderate correlations with performance in medical school basic science courses and practically no correlation with performance in clinical and other nonscience courses. A study of 96 students who graduated from one medical school between 1977 and 1979 compared the achievements of those with undergraduate majors in the sciences to those with undergraduate majors in nonscience disciplines. Both groups of students had similar scores on the science parts of the MCAT admission tests. Performance in medical school was measured by grades and scores on Parts I and II of the test of the National Board of Medical Examiners. The study found that the two groups of students had similar levels of performance in both the basic sciences and the clinical subjects.[23]

Despite these findings, admissions committees have continued to emphasize the sciences because of their own interests and values. According to the 1984 report, *General Professional Education of the Physician,* this has encouraged college students who seek admission to medical school "to focus their studies on biology, chemistry, and physics" to the exclusion of other subjects equally important in the education of a physician.[24]

The number of low-income students in medical schools has grown in recent years due to federal financial aid. In 1956–1957, the median family income of enrolled medical students was $8,420, 83 percent higher than the median family income of $4,599 for married couple families in 1955. In 1974–1975, the median family income of enrolled medical students was $20,249, 36 percent higher than the median family income for married couple families of $14,867 in 1975. In 1957–1958, before the enactment of legislation providing federal loans and scholarips, only 11 percent of medical students received financial aid. In 1967–1968, shortly after its enactment, 15 percent of all students received loans or scholarships. In 1977–1978, 41 percent of all medical students were given aid. The

TABLE 15.4. Women in Medical Schools, 1950–1983

Year	Percent of Medical Students Who Were Women	Percent of Applicants Accepted	
		Men	Women
1950–1952	5.9	33	31
1955–1956	5.5	54	50
1960–1961	5.8	60	63
1965–1966	7.9	48	48
1970–1971	9.6	46	47
1975–1976	20.5	36	38
1980–1981	26.5	48	46
1982–1983	29.3	49	47

Source: Davis G. Johnson, *U.S. Medical Students 1950–2000* (Washington, D.C.: Association of American Medical Colleges, 1983), pp. 40, 66–67.

number of students having some debt increased from 46 percent in 1956–1957 to 83 percent in 1981–1982. The average size of the debt increased from $2,334 to $21,051, which in constant dollars amounted to a 2.7-fold increase.[25]

Income has continued to be a major factor limiting medical school attendance. In 1981, 43 percent of those accepted to medical school came from families with incomes of $30,000 or more and only 13 percent came from families with incomes of under $15,000. In 1982–1983, tuition and expenses at private medical schools averaged $18,000 per year. While some student loan programs have permitted repayment at relatively low interest rates, others have required students to repay many times the amount borrowed in times of high interest rates. Most medical schools have failed to help students by expanding internal scholarship programs funded by contributions from graduates and others. There has also been a need for more federal programs that enable medical students to repay financial aid through service obligations, such as in medically underserved areas or the Armed Forces.[26]

The increase in the number of women attending medical school has been one of the most fundamental changes in the characteristics of medical students. From 1950 to 1970, the proportion of medical students who were women rose gradually from 6 to 10 percent (Table 15.4). Women applicants to medical school were accepted in the same proportion as men applicants, which indicated an absence of overt sex discrimination. Since that time, many more women have entered medical school (as well as other professional schools), so that the proportion of medical students who were women reached 29.3 percent in 1982.

Medical school treatment of applicants from minority backgrounds has long been a source of criticism. Until after mid-century, blacks were excluded from all medical schools in the South, where the majority of the black population lived. Two medical schools, Howard in Washington, D.C., and Meharry in Nashville, Tennessee, provided medical education for black students from those states. Northern medical schools, although not completely closed to blacks, made little effort to find or attract qualified black students. The problem was exacerbated by the paucity of approved hospitals that provided internships to black medical graduates.[27]

Desegregation of medical schools and teaching hospitals was brought about after World War II by federal legislation and court decisions. Southern medical schools began to desegregate after 1950, and by the 1960s all of them were open to black students. Northern medical schools began to recruit black students actively in the late 1960s. Additional internships and residencies also became available to blacks at that time. The proportion of black first-year medical students in predominantly white medical schools rose from less than 1 percent between 1948 and 1967 to between 5 and 6 percent from 1971–1972 to 1983–1984. These proportions have been far below stated goals and have shown virtually no growth since 1970. One problem has been that black students admitted to medical schools have averaged significantly lower MCAT scores than white students.[28]

For many years medical schools also discriminated against other minority groups, especially Jews, Catholics, and those with physical disabilities. For example, studies in the 1950s found that Jews in New York State were not admitted to medical schools in the same proportion as other winners of regents' scholarships and were subject to other forms of discrimination. Action by state officials was required to eliminate the bias.[29] Students with some kinds of physical disabilities or chronic diseases have been discriminated against by medical schools on the unproven assumption that their conditions adversely affected their ability to practice medicine. Federal legislation enacted in the 1970s banned such practices generally.

The Impact of Medical Education on Medical Students

Medical students, according to medical educators, should receive an education in more than the scientific and technical aspects of medicine. They should develop an understanding of the physician's role in the community and the health-care system and some insight into how they will personally function in that role. Students should learn about the social and personal consequences of medical decisions, which will enable them to use their knowledge with discretion and judgment. They should learn how to establish meaningful relations with patients and their families and how to anticipate and deal with the many problems that arise in such relationships.

Studies have produced little evidence of this kind of learning. A longitudinal study of a class in one medical school in the late 1950s by Becker et al. found that the demands of coursework and examinations made it difficult for students to be concerned with problems they would confront in the years after medical school. Eichna entered medical school in 1975 after retiring as chairman of a department of medicine and spent four years as a student taking all courses and passing all examinations. He found that the focus of students was on the short-term accumulation of information. Eichna believed that this was due to the pedagogical methods used in medical schools.[30]

Leserman administered questionnaires to medical students in three medical schools in their first year in 1975 and in their senior year in 1978, obtaining 341 responses. She compared the political, social, and economic values of medical students towards issues such as the nature of the health care system and the role of the medical profession. Over the four-year period, all students tended to become more conservative, with men having more conservative beliefs as both freshmen and seniors than women. Leserman concluded that the "medical school is a conservative environment that tends to reinforce conservative values on political and economic issues in medicine."[31]

In a 1974 review of the literature on the subject, Rezler found evidence of few long-lasting specific attitude changes that occurred over the four years of medical school. She concluded that the selection of medical students was a more important factor in determining the values of physicians than the content of medical education.[32] Thus the bias of medical school admissions committees toward students with strong interests in the sciences has had a major impact on the values of physicians.

The Effect of the Medical School on the Specialty Choice of Students

For many years medical students have changed their career preferences during medical school from primary care to other medical specialties. One study in the mid-1950s found that the proportion of students in three medical schools who planned to go into general practice declined from one-half in the first year to one-fourth in the fourth year. The Leserman study in the late 1970s found that 50 percent of the first-year students chose family practice, compared to only 16 percent of the fourth-year students.[33]

One apparent reason for this change has been that faculty members have encouraged medical students to enter specialty practice. Leserman asked the fourth-year medical students whether certain fields were discouraged or encouraged in their medical schools. Thirty-five percent of the respondents said that family practice was discouraged, 22 percent said that primary care was discouraged, but only 5 percent said that specialty practice was discouraged. While faculty members have favored specialty practice, evidence has suggested that their preferences have had little impact on students. The leading research-oriented medical schools have claimed for decades that they have prepared their students for careers in research and teaching, but the great majority of their graduates have entered practice instead. A 1953 study found that no more than 10 percent of the graduates of any medical school from 1925 to 1949 held full-time faculty positions in 1951. A study of medical schools in the early 1970s found that no more than 17 percent of the graduates of any medical school chose academic careers, despite the vast increase in the number of academic positions over the period.[34]

Other studies have tried to predict specialty choice through multiple regression techniques. A statistical discriminant analysis found that the "background charac-teristics of physicians, especially rank in medical school class," were the major factors associated with the choice among broad groups of specialties. The research orientation of the faculty, as measured by the amount of research funding of the medical school, was related to specialty choice only "to a slight degree." Research has failed to find any significant relationships between specialty choice and characteristics of the specialties, such as earnings.[35]

Employment opportunities were found to play a major role in specialty choice in a comparison of students in British and American medical schools, both of which have been specialty and hospital oriented. On entering medical school, only 16 percent of British students were interested in general practice, compared to 22 percent of American students. At graduation, the proportion of British students interested in general practice increased to 29 percent, while the proportion of American students with similar interests decreased to fewer than 10 percent. The study explained the changes by the fact that British physicians had fewer opportunities to enter specialty practice than American physicians. British medical students became aware of that fact during their medical education and changed their career preferences accordingly.[36]

Thus, employment opportunities and the structure of medical practice appear to be major factors determining specialty choice. When physicians have been in very short supply, medical students have been able to select any specialty they preferred and earn a handsome livelihood. When most career opportunities have been in primary care, physicians have entered those fields. Thus effort to modify students' career choices should be directed toward structuring the professional opportunities available to them rather than influencing the values of students or faculty members.[37]

This chapter has shown that medical schools have undertaken few voluntary efforts to redress social problems involving medical students. The increase in the number of medical school graduates in the 1960s and 1970s was obtained largely by rigid requirements attached to federal and state funding. The admission of more low-income, minority, and handicapped students resulted from federal student aid, court decisions, legislation, and public pressure. Discrimination in favor of students with extensive training in the natural sciences has continued, despite the lack of evidence that it has been either necessary or beneficial. Although medical schools have become quasi-public institutions, they have often failed to recognize their resulting public obligations.

16

Undergraduate Medical Education

Undergraduate medical education has changed markedly in the decades after mid-century. The basic medical sciences have been de-emphasized; clinical training in the specialties has replaced that in general medicine; and both types of training have been compressed to permit much of the fourth year to be used for electives. The patients used for teaching in the major teaching hospitals have become less typical of those found in community practice. Innovations in medical education have been successful only when they have been compatible with other interests of the faculty.

The Goals of Undergraduate Medical Education

As medicine and medical schools have changed, major differences of opinion have developed over the goals of undergraduate medical education. Practicing physicians have continued to believe that the fundamentals of clinical medicine should be emphasized. A survey in the 1970s of 903 physicians found that over 97 percent of them believed that each of the following was "a proper goal of medical school training:" "knowing enough medical facts;" "being skillful in medical diagnosis;" "making good treatment plans;" "understanding the doctor-patient relationship;" "understanding the extent to which emotional factors can affect physical illness;" "being able to keep up with new developments in medicine;" and being able to use and evaluate sources of medical information. Only 52 percent felt that "being able to carry out research" was a proper goal of medical school training.[1]

Medical students have also believed that undergraduate medical education should emphasize clinical training. Bloom asked students at one medical school in the early 1960s whether they would prefer to "work at some interesting research problem that does not involve any contact with patients," or to "work directly with patients, even though tasks are relatively routine." About 25 percent of the students in all four classes chose research, while 58 percent of the freshmen and 70 percent of the juniors and seniors chose patient care. The same study also asked students their criteria for ranking classmates "as medical students." Clinical skills were the predominant criteria used by students, with "ability to carry out research" ranking far down on the list.[2]

Faculty members, on the other hand, have emphasized the basic and preliminary nature of undergraduate medical education. Many of them have believed that it should emphasize the biomedical sciences and the pathophysiological processes involved in disease and prepare students for specialty training during the residency. Becker et al. found that faculty members could not "understand why students make such a fuss over being allowed to 'do things.' . . . What, the faculty asks, is the hurry? They see the educational process extending, ideally, through all the years of . . . practice. There will be plenty of time . . . to learn things."[3]

A major factor influencing the content of undergraduate medical education has been the tests of the National Board of Medical Examiners (NBME), which have been designed for use as state licensing examinations. The NBME has used a three-part examination since 1922. Part I has tested students on the basic medical sciences after their first two years of medical school. Part II has tested them on the clinical subjects in their senior year of medical school. Part III has tested patient-management skills and has been administered during the first year of graduate training. Over the years, Parts I and II have changed from essay to multiple-choice examinations, and Part III from an actual bedside examination to a paper and pencil test.[4]

Most medical schools have used NBME tests for internal evaluations of medical students. In 1983–1984, 62 medical schools required a passing grade on Part I for graduation, 35 required that it be taken but did not require a passing grade for graduation, and 29 made the examination optional. A passing grade on Part II was required for graduation at 48 schools and was optional at only 36 schools. As a result, many medical schools have emphasized the content of the examinations in their curricula. A 1965 study found a high correlation ($r = .71$) between the scores of 232 students on the National Board Part II test in clinical medicine and their cumulative medical school grade. The correlation between the students' scores on the Part II test and their grades for the senior year clerkship in medicine was moderate ($r = .45$).[5]

Many observers have claimed that the NBME examinations have been deficient as measures of what medical students should learn in medical school. The multiple-choice questions, according to Eichna, "glorify facts, many of which are detailed and some . . . necessary only for an expert in the field. Only minimal thinking is needed. Problem-solving is virtually absent." The separation of the examinations into three parts administered at different times has reduced the need for students to integrate what they have learned. A 1984 report for the Association of American Medical Colleges, *Physicians for the Twenty-First Century*, concluded: "the National Board's multiple-choice examinations evaluate only a limited range of the qualities that medical school graduates should have, but because faculties rely on them so heavily, the evaluation of important skills that students should acquire during medical school is relatively neglected." A 1982 report by the Council on Medical Education of the American Medical Association, "Future Directions for Medical Education," urged that "scores on extramural examinations should be used by faculties with caution."[6]

The Teaching of the Basic Medical Sciences

Before mid-century, basic science departments in medical schools differed significantly from their counterparts in liberal arts colleges. While science departments in liberal arts colleges taught both their own graduate and undergraduate students and students from other fields, the basic science departments in medical schools taught few graduate students in their own fields. Most basic medical scientists were content to teach medical students because of their interest in the medical applications of their subjects.[7]

After mid-century, the great majority of basic medical scientists were trained as Ph.D.s rather than M.D.s and pursued research unrelated to medicine in their own disciplines. Anatomists became cellular biologists, bacteriologists became micro-biologists, and they and the biochemists, physiologists, and pharmacologists did research on cellular and molecular processes that had little direct relevance for clinical medicine.[8] Basic science faculty members became both unqualified to teach the medical applications of their subjects and uninterested in doing so.

Large-scale federal funding for research beginning in the 1950s gave the basic science departments research grants to increase their research activities and training grants to establish or expand their own graduate programs. Flushed by this infusion of ready cash and the presence of their own graduate students, the basic medical sciences declared their independence, or at least quasi-independence, from their self-perceived colonial status in the medical school. No longer, they declared, would they condescend to teach the basic sciences as mere service courses for medical students. No longer would they emphasize the medical applications of their subjects (which they did not understand anyway) at the expense of pure science.[9]

To a substantial degree, this has occurred. Anatomy, which had traditionally been the foremost subject in the first year of medical school, abandoned this pedagogical role. Dissection was de-emphasized, to the consternation of the surgeons, and replaced by molecular and cellular biology, to the dismay of the students. Pharmacology moved away from clinical applications toward the mechanisms of drug actions. Applied areas of growing importance like genetics, epidemiology, nutrition, human sexuality, and geriatrics were either slighted or shunted off to overburdened departments of preventive medicine. The basic science departments did not abandon their service roles completely because they still had to teach medical students the older as well as the newer aspects of the biomedical sciences. Consequently, basic medical science departments, according to Wagner, have been doing "high powered research and teaching watered-down premedicine."[10]

Medical students have reacted to the teaching of basic science material unrelated to medicine with unalloyed hostility. They have been dismayed to find that their basic science courses were, according to studies in the 1970s, "college revisited." Coombs and Boyle reported that the "courses judged as the worst ones were those in which professors 'try to make academic graduate students out of us' by teaching 'straight hard-core science' without providing clinical applications. . . . [T]hey resent the fact that so little effort appears to be spent in making the material relevant for their own future role as physicians."[11]

Basic science teaching has changed in other ways as well. Responsibility for each basic science course has been divided among subspecialists in each department. One 1982 survey found that an average of nine faculty members shared responsibility for medical student biochemistry courses and seven others provided occasional lectures. One consequence has been that basic science faculty members have spent little time with medical students. Magraw et al. have estimated that many of them have spent two-thirds of their time on research and teaching their departmental graduate students and only one-third teaching students in medicine and other health fields.[12]

Several major innovations have been introduced to try to improve basic science teaching. One widely adopted innovation has been for clinical faculty members to participate in the teaching of basic science courses in order to explain the clinical applications of the material. These clinical correlations have often been confusing to the first- and second-year students, who have not had enough clinical training to understand them. The opposite arrangement, the participation of basic science faculty members in clinical courses, has seldom occurred because of the inability of basic medical scientists to relate their research to clinical problems. Thus the overall effect has been to reduce the amount of curriculum time devoted to the biomedical sciences.[13]

Another major innovation, advocated primarily by clinicians, was to teach the basic science courses in terms of organ systems rather than disciplines. Under this approach, all basic science departments jointly taught students about the nervous system, the cardiovascular system, and so on. During the analysis of each system, clinicians presented material showing clinical correlations of the basic science material. This approach was pioneered at Western Reserve University medical school, which integrated the lecture and the laboratory aspects of its basic science curriculum in the early 1950s with financial support from a private foundation.[14]

While the organ systems approach was adopted in varying degrees by about one-fourth of the medical schools, it soon declined in popularity, even at Western Reserve University. In 1983–1984, 91 percent of medical schools used a disciplinary-based basic science curriculum, often with an added course correlating the basic sciences and disease manifestations, and only 9 percent used an organ systems approach. One reason for the demise of the new approach was the inability of basic medical scientists to synthesize their knowledge about individual organ systems, despite their claim that integration among the sciences has increased. Furthermore, few basic medical scientists supported the changes, partly because they created major problems of logistics and coordination.[15]

The most long-lasting innovations in basic science teaching have resulted from the elective system, which was a reaction to the crowded curriculum that had developed about mid-century. For example, at Duke University medical school in 1930, only 54 percent of the student's teaching hours were spent in required courses, with the remainder devoted to elective courses and free time. In 1950 and 1955, 97 percent of all teaching hours were spent in required courses. The solution proposed by clinicians was to increase the total number of years of training by adding a required multiyear residency and to make the fourth year of medical school an elective year. To free the fourth year for electives, the required basic science and clinical courses were each reduced from four semesters to three. Clinical courses were also placed earlier in the curriculum to prepare students for the earlier clerkships. In 1983–1984, 71 of 143 U.S. and Canadian medical schools had introductory clinical courses in the first year, and the remainder had similar courses in the second year.[16]

The reduced teaching time in the basic sciences has led to the use of more lectures and less laboratory work. In 1983–1984, medical schools averaged close to 1,000 lecture hours in the preclinical sciences. Lectures occupied an average of 54 percent of all time devoted to preclinical subjects while laboratories averaged only 25 percent. Most of the laboratory time was in anatomy and pathology, with some of the other sciences having little or none. For example, only 45 medical schools had any laboratory work in biochemistry. The report, *Physicians for the Twenty-First Century,* expressed concern over the dependence of basic science teaching on lectures and called for "major reductions in this passive form of learning."[17]

The use of the fourth year for electives also forced medical schools to eliminate or reduce some basic science courses. In 1983–1984, more than 50 schools did not require courses in genetics and more than 32 did not require courses in preventive medicine or epidemiology. In the remainder, an average of 27 hours was devoted to genetics and 51 to preventive medicine. Medical schools have claimed that students could take these and other basic science courses as electives. However, the great majority of students have taken their elective courses in clinical subjects rather than the basic sciences. Furthermore, some basic science departments have not offered elective courses, preferring to teach their own graduate students. Large research-oriented schools have been less likely than other medical schools to offer elective courses in social aspects of medicine.[18]

Visscher has observed that "it is ironic that at a time when the competent practice of medicine has become very much more dependent upon science, and more successful because of it, . . . there should be a nearly uniform trend in medical schools . . . to deemphasize science in the education of physicians." Yet basic medical science departments themselves discarded or neglected the medical applications of their subjects. They did so because federal funding for basic science research and graduate student training reduced their dependence on medical school support and enabled them to focus on their own research and graduate programs.[19]

The emphasis of basic science departments on research and graduate training has not received widespread support from medical schools. Not only has their participation in the education of medical students been reduced, but in 1979–1980 their budgets accounted for only 15 percent of total medical school budgets, compared to 53 percent spent by clinical departments.[20] If federal funds for basic science research and graduate training were reduced, few medical schools would replace them. The reorientation of the basic medical sciences was brought about and has survived because of federal research funding, not the educational policies of medical schools.

Undergraduate Clinical Education

Clinical education has differed from basic science education because of the craftlike nature of many aspects of clinical medicine. While basic science education has emphasized scientific features like the study of formal research techniques and empirical generalizations induced from research studies, much clinical education has used the kind of practical training that characterized the apprenticeship.

Students have been taught to base their patient-care decisions as much on their personal clinical experiences as on textbook generalizations or findings in the basic sciences. One detailed 1964 study of 82 teaching sessions in 9 medical schools found little reference to basic science material in clinical teaching on rounds and in the outpatient department, and only moderate reference to it in lectures and seminars.[21]

Because of the high degree of medical school faculty specialization, the clinical curriculum has been fragmented into courses in the individual medical and surgical specialties and subspecialties. Creditor has observed that general "'physicianship' is nowhere taught in most medical schools. There is no course in 'how to be a doctor,' although there are many in 'how to be an internist,' 'how to be a surgeon,' etc." Each course has been subdivided into units taught by different faculty subspecialists, so that students have seen individual faculty members for only short periods of time. A working group for the report, *Physicians for the Twenty-First Century,* observed that the fragmentation of teaching has made it "almost impossible to control the degree of detail the subspecialists teach and to ensure that students learn essential principles and concepts. . . . This multifaculty approach to teaching medical students is so pervasive and so obstructive to the rational delineation of essential knowledge that it is the primary problem that must be solved if medical school is to provide students with a well integrated general professional education."[22]

Faculty specialization has also led to a poorly balanced curriculum. Lewis and Sheps have observed that "the diverse research and clinical interests of the faculty provide an intellectual smorgasbord that does not reflect many health problems that play a significant role in the lives of the public. The curriculum designed by such faculty is warped and uneven, with important elements entirely missing or referred to hastily and inadequately." Complicated diseases of interest to specialists have often been emphasized at the expense of the more common ailments seen in daily practice.[23]

The undergraduate clinical curriculum has had three major components: classroom teaching, practical training in the care of hospitalized patients in teaching hospitals, and practical training in the care of ambulatory patients in teaching hospital outpatient clinics. While both students and clinical faculty members have strongly preferred the latter two forms of teaching, the foundations of clinical medicine have been taught in classroom courses.

The most fundamental clinical courses have taught the student to diagnose the patient's illness through history taking, a physical examination, and the use of laboratory tests. History taking has required the student to develop skills in obtaining the cooperation of the patient and eliciting meaningful information; the study of physical examinations has involved the enhancement of the senses of sight, touch, and hearing that can be mastered only through frequent and prolonged repetition; and laboratory testing has required students to interpret tests under a wide variety of conditions to evaluate their appropriateness and accuracy. None of these skills can be acquired easily or quickly, and a thorough undergraduate medical education should devote continuous attention to them from the first clinical courses taken by medical students to graduation.

In practice, diagnostic skills have been taught to medical students in a superficial and haphazard manner. A working group for the report, *Physicians for the Twenty-First Century,* concluded that "although basic clinical skills have the central role in modern medicine, there is evidence that graduating physicians fall considerably short of mastering these skills. Deficiencies in history taking, physical examination, and diagnostic skills have been observed by a number of investigators. . . . Interpersonal communication skills were found to be underdeveloped in medical students, and no improvement was noted as the students progressed through medical school."[24]

Several factors have contributed to the poor teaching of diagnostic skills. One has been the use of inexperienced faculty members, residents, and even third- and fourth-year medical students to teach the skills to first- and second-year medical students. Another has been inadequate time for teaching diagnostic skills because of the elective system. Learning to establish rapport with patients and to structure interviews to obtain useful responses is a time-consuming process. Learning the psychomotor skills involved in the physical examination requires frequent practice of the techniques while being monitored closely by instructors to prevent the development of faulty habits. None of this has been possible in the abbreviated curriculum. Poor pedagogy has also been a problem, such as the separation of the teaching of interviewing from the teaching of history taking, so that students have not been required to demonstrate their proficiency in both skills simultaneously.[25]

Many clinical educators have believed that diagnostic skills do not need to be taught thoroughly because they will improve with experience. However, one review of 73 studies of the teaching of history taking concluded: "Longitudinal studies indicate that medical students do not uniformly improve their interviewing skills simply by means of practice in clinical settings, and that on certain measures their skills actually decline from the first year to the fourth." Another study of the performance of physical examinations by 72 medical students and first-, second-, and third-year residents found improvements in some aspects of the examination among the second- and third-year residents, but not in all aspects or even in the most important ones.[26]

One major cause of the lack of improvement in diagnostic skills of medical students and residents has been the failure of faculty members to monitor their performance. The study of 82 clinical teaching sessions referred to above found that "in an overwhelming majority of our observations on rounds and in [outpatient department] sessions, the instructor did not ask students to do any part of the physical examination under his supervision or to interview the patient briefly. Thus, we encountered only rarely a teacher's direct evaluation of the student's technique." Engel reported that over a two-decade period he "encountered few who can report having been monitored in the interview and physical examination of more than one or two patients. . . . Often students are merely asked to report on their findings. . . . And only rarely is further attention given to checking clinical skills beyond the prescribed exercises in the first or second year."[27]

The teaching of laboratory testing has been equally deficient. Because of the elective system, many courses on laboratory medicine have eliminated laboratory exercises, so that students have acquired only a textbook understanding of the tests.

Few medical schools have had required courses in the clinical use of laboratory test data during the last two years of medical school when the student is involved in patient care. The only instruction has consisted of informal discussions between students and the physicians who oversee their work. Once again the prevailing philosophy has been that students will learn all they need to know through personal experience. Students have been told to emphasize thoroughness in their patient work-ups, which has generally meant that they may order as many laboratory tests as they want, regardless of cost, necessity, or patient discomfort. This has led to a slipshod and inefficient use of laboratory tests. Studies have found that students and house officers have used only a small proportion of the tests that they ordered. Indeed, they often did not remember whether they ordered the tests or not.[28]

Poor teaching of laboratory testing has encouraged excessive testing and raised the costs of patient care, while good teaching has been shown to produce the opposite result. Studies have found that medical students and residents usually had little knowledge of the costs of laboratory tests and rarely considered costs in their decisions to order them. Appropriate educational programs have led to the use of more discretion and better judgment. In one study, the test-ordering practices of a number of first-year residents were monitored and made the subject of personal meetings with instructors. The residents showed a steady decline in the number of tests they ordered both during and after the experiment, while a control group showed no change.[29]

Another deficiency in clinical medical education has involved the teaching of the appropriate use and side effects of the growing number of drugs. Dowling has observed that "when students graduate from medical schools, their training in the use of drugs . . . is spotty and often scanty. During the subsequent internship and residency training systematic study of drugs is rare. . . . [M]any house officers find that while the sum of what they have learned about drugs may be large, the facts are always scattered, often ill-assorted, and sometimes discordant."[30]

A new development in medicine has been the use of computers to assist physicians in diagnosis, patient management, and the retrieval of medical information. American medical schools have shown little interest in teaching students the medical information sciences and have lagged behind some of their European counterparts in this regard.[31]

Perhaps the most fundamental deficiency in the teaching of diagnostic skills has been the lack of concern with clinical reasoning. This problem was noted in 1964 by the study of 82 clinical teaching sessions referred to above, which found that "clinical reasoning and the solving of clinical problems often are taught implicitly, but rarely explicitly. [Students] were not taught how to weigh the importance and relevance of the data before them, or how to proceed logically and economically with further investigations." It was also reported by several working groups for the 1984 report, *Physicians for the Twenty-First Century,* one of which observed that "students are not prepared as critical and quantitative thinkers and clinical problem solvers . . . when they graduate from medical school." The groups urged faculty members to be more concerned with teaching students how to gather and evaluate clinical data, how to apply the scientific method to the study of patients, and how to systematically evaluate claims promoting the use of specific diagnostic procedures and therapies.[32]

There have been several reasons for all of these pedagogical failures. Primary among them has been specialization within the faculty, so that no single locus of responsibility has existed for undergraduate clinical training. Under divided responsibility, skills which have been partially taught to students in one course have not been refined in later courses. Another problem has been faculty belief in the pedagogical value of unsupervised practical experience for students. This has too often served as a rationalization for the neglect of students by the faculty.

Clinical Training and Clerkships

Medical schools have believed that students should have maximum contact with sick patients and that hospital patients have been superior to ambulatory patients for this purpose. Hospitalized patients are available to students at all times and their records can be carefully maintained. They are more seriously ill than ambulatory patients and therefore display more distinctive characteristics of their illnesses. The progress of their illnesses and their reactions to therapy are apt to be more rapid. Medical students working in the hospital can call upon the large hospital medical staff and its many diagnostic and therapeutic services to help them.[33]

Patients in teaching hospitals, although valuable for the teaching of specialized care, have been unsuitable for the teaching of primary and routine hospital care, preventive medicine, rehabilitation, and minor emotional disorders. These patients have been admitted by faculty members because they were of research interest or had problems that required the faculty's highly specialized skills. Such patients have tended to be very seriously ill with acute disorders or acute episodes of chronic disorders, or to have multiple disorders. They have rarely suffered from the more common illnesses found among patients in community practice. The treatment of such patients has emphasized the technical aspects of patient management. Eichna has written that "patients are looked on not as ill people, but almost as impersonal beings that exist for the student's own development. Faculty confirm this attitude in their teaching."[34]

Students have also had strong preferences about the kinds of patients they wish to treat. Coombs found in a survey at one medical school that 82 percent of senior medical students preferred acutely ill patients to chronically ill ones, and 93 percent preferred organically ill patients to emotionally ill ones. He observed:

> Being young and action oriented, as well as ambitious to succeed as doctors, most students naturally prefer working with patients who respond rapidly to treatment. Visible positive results provide immediate gratification for the fledgling doctor and help build self-confidence. . . . Most students find it depressing to deal with chronically ill patients [because] progress and recovery are seldom experienced with these patients.[35]

While students and faculty members may have preferred patients with significant organic illnesses, such patients have not been the most appropriate ones for training community physicians, who will treat many minor illnesses, emotional problems, and chronic disorders. Eichna has observed that the goal of medical education is not to satisfy faculty or student interests, but to prepare students for the practice of medicine as it exists in the community. The unfortunate confluence of student and faculty interests in certain atypical kinds of patients has altered this goal.[36]

The standard method of clinical teaching has been to have students observe faculty members or residents while they care for patients. Such teaching has rarely been systematic. The study of 82 teaching session referred to above found that "too often, especially on rounds and in the [outpatient department], teaching was haphazard and mediocre. . . . Many staff members teach by practicing their profession and thinking out loud from time to time."[37]

Medical school faculty members have not had the skills to teach general medical care to students. Most of them have never been private practitioners or worked outside of academic medical centers and many have been primarily researchers. Even faculty clinicians with large practices have seldom assumed personal responsibility for the long-term overall care of patients. Because of their isolation from community medical practice, all faculty members have lacked an understanding of community medicine to impart to students. Furthermore, clinical teaching has been so subdivided among faculty members that, according to the report, *Physicians for the Twenty-First Century,* "students complain that they see many faculty members, each for short periods only, and that they neither know or are known by the faculty. This anonymous relationship between students and faculties is inconsistent with a general professional education directed toward the personal development of each student."[38]

Hospital inpatient teaching has taken several forms. One major type of bedside instruction has occurred on ward rounds, where a senior faculty member has visited the patients on his service accompanied by students. Each student, who has been assigned a number of patients, has reported on the patient's condition based on a previous history and physical examination, laboratory test results, and sometimes library research into the patient's illness. The senior physician and others have then analyzed the student's report either in the patient's presence or in a conference room. As students have listened to the critiques of their presentations, they have learned the techniques of clinical reasoning as practiced by a senior physician.[39]

Ward rounds have lost some of their educational value in recent years. A veritable crowd has developed around the bedside as the students receiving instruction have included residents, postgraduate fellows, and sometimes other trainees and allied health students. Senior faculty members have usually given most of their attention to residents, who have been the closest to completing their education. This has been to the detriment of undergraduate medical students, who have needed a much more elementary level of training. The teaching has also tended to be narrowly focused. A study of about 100 ward rounds at four hospitals found that most of the teaching time was spent on physical factors involved in the patient's illness to the neglect of any emotional and interpersonal factors. Other influences weakening the quality of bedside teaching have included the shorter stays of patients and pressures for faculty members to care for more patients under current reimbursement systems.[40]

A second type of clinical teaching has involved grand rounds, formal presentations attended by students and the medical staff. These were once major events where previously treated patients were displayed and their cases described by faculty members and residents who had treated them. In recent years, patients have receded from view in grand rounds. A study of responses by 101 chief medical residents found that patients were rarely present or interviewed. The presentations consisted largely of lectures reviewing the diagnosis, treatment, and basic pathophysiological processes involved with little mention of the psychosocial and economic aspects of the patient's illness. Some presentations were simply lectures with only a brief mention of the patient.[41]

Other teaching devices have included clinicopathological conferences, in which the clinician has described a case and made a diagnosis, which was then verified or refuted by the pathologist. These once highly popular conferences have come to emphasize exotic problems and have rarely been used in teaching in recent years. Mortality conferences have analyzed hospital-related deaths. Millman reported that most of the cases described at one teaching hospital "conveniently seem to involve an illness that would have ended in the patient's death in any case, even if the correct diagnosis had been made immediately. There is a strange absence of cases reviewed in these meetings in which the patient clearly would have lived had it not been for the medical mismanagement." She attributed this to the desire of the staff members to maintain harmony.[42]

The major form of clinical education has been the clerkship, in which students have participated in hospital patient-care activities in order to learn the tasks and responsibilities of the physician. In 1983–1984 clerkships were required in the third or fourth year in all medical schools in departments of medicine (for an average of 12 weeks), surgery (for an average of 11 weeks), pediatrics (for an average of 8 weeks), obstetrics/gynecology (for an average of 7 weeks), and psychiatry (for an average of 6 weeks). Some schools have also required clerkships in other fields. Under the elective system, practically all medical students have either returned to some of the services in their elective part of their senior year or taken similar courses in other specialties.[43]

Most of the direct supervision and instruction of clinical clerks has been provided by residents, who are on the wards more often than faculty members. They have given classroom lectures to students, supervised their clinical activities, answered their questions, and interrogated them about medical problems. Residents have had no academic authority over students, so students have interacted with them more freely than with faculty members. A 1974 study of nine medical schools found that "house officers provide 40 percent of the contact medical students have with their teachers, including full-time and part-time faculty."[44]

Residents have lacked the skills needed to be effective teachers. Jonas has observed that they have been "the least experienced teachers, not trained to teach, not paid to teach, not hired to teach, and have as their major responsibility patient care, at the same time they are supposed to be learning themselves." Studies have found that residents provided lower quality teaching than faculty members and attending physicians and that they considered their teaching responsibilities to be less important than their own education and their patient-care responsibilities. A survey of over 450 medical school departments found that the great majority of them did not even evaluate residents on their teaching performance.[45]

The changing nature of teaching hospitals in recent decades has adversely affected the clinical clerkship. The many seriously ill patients have needed the specialized care of faculty members, residents, and postgraduate fellows, so that unskilled medical students have been unable to treat them. Faculty members and residents have often been so busy with their own patient-care activities that, according to *Physicians for the Twenty-First Century*, "they are unable to devote sufficient time and effort to the general professional education of clinical clerks." Other problems noted by the report were the failure to give students "clearly stated goals for the experience" and to "develop procedures and adopt explicit criteria for the systematic evaluation of students' clinical performance."[46]

Several studies have found that less than one-third of the clerkship time of medical students was spent in educationally productive activities, such as caring for patients and interacting with the hospital staff. Most of their time was spent in performing routine laboratory tests, running errands, filling out forms, and performing other chores that could be assigned to hospital workers. Because clerks have been unskilled and their labor has been free, hospitals have tended to use them as inexpensive labor.[47]

Although clinical clerks have worked with members of other health occupations in providing patient care, medical students have rarely been trained in teamwork between physicians and other health professionals. One 1982 study found that only 16 of 105 U.S. and Canadian medical schools surveyed taught a required undergraduate course in the team approach to health-care delivery.[48]

In recent years, the appropriateness of some required clerkship rotations, especially surgery, has come under question. Aspiring surgeons have been taught the necessary skills more thoroughly and systematically in their residencies, and other physicians have not been allowed to operate in most hospitals. Surgeons have justified a required clerkship by observing that students should understand pre- and post-operative care and learn about medical problems that require surgery, subjects which have rarely been taught elsewhere in the curriculum. However, even surgeons have conceded that surgical teaching has manifested, as one observed, an "over-compulsive focus on the operation itself."[49]

Undergraduate Training in Ambulatory Care

Ambulatory patients have provided several important teaching benefits not available from hospitalized patients: their illnesses have been more representative of those seen in office practice; they have been seen at an earlier stage of their illnesses and displayed the early symptoms of disease; and they have been seen under typical office conditions that have enabled students to receive training in problems like the long-term management of chronic illnesses and noncompliance with a medical regimen. Medical students have also been given more responsibility in the care of ambulatory patients because of the less serious nature of their illnesses.[50]

Most medical student training in ambulatory care has occurred in teaching hospital outpatient departments, which have usually had major deficiencies because of the strong preferences of medical schools for inpatient care. Physical facilities have often been unattractive to patients and have not met all the needs of the physicians and students. Resources have been inadequate, staffing has lacked continuity, medical care has been episodic, patient records have been fragmentary, and the numerous specialty clinics have been poorly coordinated. In addition, the patients attending teaching hospital outpatient clinics frequently have had serious social and emotional disorders.[51]

Student training in ambulatory care reached a nadir in the 1950s and 1960s when faculty subspecialization and research funding led to an almost total emphasis on inpatient care. Although some improvement has occurred subsequently, ambulatory care training has continued to receive minor consideration. In 1973, only 72 percent of medical schools surveyed required a defined ambulatory care experience, which increased to 82 percent of those surveyed in 1976. The duration of the experience was two months or less in 57 percent of the medical schools requiring it in 1973. The teaching of ambulatory care has also been fragmented by departments. Only 27 percent of the schools surveyed in both 1973 and 1976 "had identified a single locus for coordinating institution-wide ambulatory care education efforts."[52]

Beginning in the 1970s, ambulatory care clerkships have been organized in community hospitals and nonhospital settings like satellite medical centers and community clinics. In 1976, 60 percent of 94 medical schools surveyed reported that one-half or more of their medical students had nonhospital ambulatory care experiences. A major reason for this development was the insufficient number of patients available in teaching hospital clinics due to the increased size of medical school classes and the larger number of medical schools.[53]

Health maintenance organizations (HMOs), which have provided preventive, primary, and hospital care for a prepaid group of patients, have been an obvious site for ambulatory care training. The advantages of HMOs to medical schools have included: the stability of their populations, which has enabled students to deal with the same patients over a period of time; the large amount of primary and preventive care; the balanced mix of patients from different social classes; and the assured flow of income. However, largely because of faculty opposition, in 1976 only 16 percent of medical schools surveyed had affiliations with HMOs. Faculty members have not been interested in HMO patients, who have not needed their subspecialized, cost-intensive inpatient care. Faculty research had also seldom been concerned with primary or preventive care, so that HMOs have had little research value.[54]

Medical schools have provided most of their training in primary care in the general medical clinics in their teaching hospitals. The patients who have used these clinics have been poorly suited for teaching primary care. A study of 287 patients at one university hospital clinic in 1975 (excluding those with obvious specialty problems) found that 31 percent had hypertension, 20 percent had diabetes, and 18 percent had ischemic heart disease. Another 1975 study of 349 patients at a general medical clinic at a different university hospital found a similar mix of serious diseases, with 47 percent of the sample having undergone hospitalization during the previous two-year period. Only 55 percent of the patients kept at least three-fourths of their scheduled visits. The patients had a mean age of 50 years, often had "complex functional, psycho-social" problems, and 70 percent lived within five miles of the hospital.[55]

Many teachers in the outpatient clinics have been volunteer faculty members who have taken the positions to obtain admitting privileges for their patients in the teaching hospital. A 1959 study found that medical students in university hospital outpatient departments were supervised by part-time or volunteer faculty in 43 percent of the cases, by full-time faculty in 33 percent of the cases, and by residents in 14 percent of the cases. In recent years, full-time faculty members have assumed greater responsibility for the teaching of ambulatory care. However, few of them have had any experience in private practice or in the delivery of primary care.[56]

The quality of teaching in the outpatient departments has been generally inferior to ward teaching. One survey of over 1,000 interns in 1960 found that 47 percent agreed that during their senior year in medical school, "the best clinical teachers in our school did little teaching in the out-patient clinics." The poor quality of the teaching has also been indicated by studies in the early 1970s of the care received by patients being treated for nonemergency conditions in university hospital emergency rooms. Two studies of 132 and 166 patients, respectively, found that only one-fourth of them were judged to have received adequate care. Physical examinations were inadequate, obviously necessary tests were omitted, referrals were made to other physicians without the patient's record being available to the second physician, and numerous other failures of good medical care occurred.[57]

Although there have been many reasons for the poor teaching of ambulatory care, the most fundamental one has been faculty indifference. Cluff observed in 1981:

> Medical schools have far to go to imbue ambulatory medical settings with the emphasis upon discipline, responsibility, and accountability that has in the past typified hospital inpatient programs. Such training and education must be characterized by both faculty and trainees accepting and assuming continuing, ongoing, long-term responsibility for the care of each patient if students and residents are to become good physicians.[58]

Innovations in Clinical Medical Education

The Preceptorship

One of the earliest innovations in clinical education was the preceptorship, where a senior medical student spent a month or two in the office of a practicing physician, usually in a community distant from the medical school. The preceptors were given formal appointments at the medical school and had regular contact with medical school administrators about their duties. The first preceptorships were offered in the 1920s to provide training in ambulatory care and to encourage students to practice in rural communities. By 1955, 1,400 students were involved in preceptorships in 27 medical schools. More recently some public medical schools have offered preceptorships in urban medically underserved areas to encourage students to enter primary care in those areas. Overall, however, preceptorships have not been widely used by medical schools.[59]

Preceptorship programs have been criticized by medical educators for several reasons: the preceptors have not been experienced teachers; the activities and responsibilities of medical students have varied widely in content and quality; and it has not been possible to monitor students and preceptors effectively because of their infrequent contact with the medical school.[60]

Rising has suggested that these criticisms have misunderstood the goals of the preceptorship. The preceptorship has provided an opportunity for students to learn something about the practice of medicine in the community. Students have seen patients from many different backgrounds, learned about medical economics and office management, acquired an understanding of the professional and civic role of the physician, and observed how physicians have related to hospitals, pharmacists, nurses, and other health workers. The preceptorship has functioned as "a type of retreat for medical students, during which they can develop some mature ideas concerning their own values and goals." Rising has observed that its greatest value has been for those students who have not entered primary care: "[F]or the physician going directly into a specialty, it will likely be his sole opportunity to become familiar with the family physician's problems; for the teacher and investigator, it may well be their only direct contact with the private practice of medicine."[61]

Rising's survey of almost 800 graduates of the University of Kansas medical school who took preceptorships between 1951 and 1960 found that 85 percent preferred it to other courses that they might have taken instead, and 64 percent thought it should be retained as a required course. The respondents in specialty practice had the same attitudes as those in family practice. More recent studies have also found widespread student support for preceptorships.[62] Nevertheless, it has remained a rarely used form of clinical training.

Comprehensive Care Programs

In the 1950s, some medical educators became concerned with the poor quality of ambulatory care training in a period of growing emphasis on hospitalized patients and specialty medicine. Medical students in outpatient departments rarely saw the same patients more than once, they saw patients only for one particular condition, and they did not participate in the team care of patients with physicians, other health workers, and social workers.[63]

This concern led to the development of undergraduate programs in clinical training for comprehensive care. Comprehensive care programs sought to increase the responsibility of students for the care of patients, to teach them about the personal and social factors involved in illness, and to train them to integrate the skills of different providers of patient care. In most cases, a medical student was given some responsibility for the primary and preventive care of a family or individual patient over a period of time and was expected to establish a personal relationship with the family by visiting their home. In caring for the patient, the student consulted with a team consisting of physicians, health workers, and social workers.

In the early and mid-1950s, three medical schools established extensive comprehensive care programs that were heavily subsidized by private foundations. At Cornell University and the University of Colorado medical schools, students spent over five months in a comprehensive care clerkship, and at Western Reserve University medical school, over a year in a community clinic. A 1965 survey found that five medical schools had at some time developed comprehensive care programs as part of the medical school curriculum, and about a dozen others had programs "closely related in objectives."[64]

The major problem that confronted all comprehensive care programs was the difficulty of finding families suitable for training medical students. The most satisfactory families were stable geographically and as a family unit, conscientious in attending the clinics, and had no serious illnesses or social or emotional problems beyond the expertise of the students. The families available to most medical schools and used in the programs usually had low incomes, multiple complex disorders, and significant social and economic problems.[65] Little effort was made to use or develop health maintenance organizations, which had populations that were well suited for teaching comprehensive care.

Student reactions to the programs were generally favorable, although not overwhelmingly so. Surveys of some of the classes at Cornell University showed that about one-fourth of the students were "very satisfied" with the program and another half were "reasonably satisfied." Many students reported that they had more personal responsibility for diagnosis and treatment in the comprehensive care clinics than in the traditional clinics. On the other hand, students disliked the limited range of organic illnesses of the comprehensive care patients compared to patients in more traditional clinics and the larger number of emotional disorders. Students were often discouraged by the severe and chronic problems of some of the families, about which they could do little.[66]

Studies were made of the educational impact of two of the programs. At the University of Colorado it was found that a control group of students developed increasingly negative attitudes toward comprehensive care during their medical school training, while students involved in the program showed no change in their attitudes. At Cornell the program led students to attach greater importance to social and emotional factors in illness. Neither program found any effect, positive or negative, on medical knowledge or skill. No studies were undertaken to test for the persistence of the attitude changes.[67]

Comprehensive care programs survived for less than a decade, although a 1974 survey found that many medical schools later adopted somewhat similar programs in family or community medicine. The reasons for the discontinuation of the programs included their costs, which often relied on outside funding, the substantial amount of faculty time and effort required, and the difficulty of finding suitable patients. The programs were also often ill-defined, reflecting, as White observed, "a sort of 'be kind to patients' movement . . . unrelated to any adequate understanding of medical practice in the real world." Bloom observed "that the momentum of specialization dies hard, and . . . the effort to turn medical education away from its concentration on the hospitalized patient foundered against surprisingly unyielding barriers."[68]

Community-Based Medical Schools

In the 1960s and early 1970s, public pressure to increase the supply of physicians led some state governments to establish low-cost community-based medical schools to train primary care physicians. Community-based medical schools economized by providing basic science education either at the main university or, in the case of clinical campuses, at a designated campus of the medical school. Most clinical faculty members were local practitioners who served on a part-time or volunteer basis. Hospital teaching was carried out in a nearby community hospital. Although no standard definition of a community-based medical school has been developed, between 15 and 20 medical schools with these characteristics were established in the 1960s and 1970s, none in large metropolitan areas.[69]

Community-based medical schools have been the descendants of nineteenth-century medical schools in their emphasis on community medical problems and practices. They have had the advantage over their forebearers of more stable sources of funding and closer ties to universities. They have shared the problems of affiliated hospitals with little interest in teaching. They have had more difficulty recruiting qualified faculty members because of their locations in small communities with few outstanding physicians. Furthermore, the great improvements in medical knowledge in this century have made much teaching by practitioners, as Aronson and Murray have observed, "pragmatic, superficial and symptom-oriented without appropriate correlation with the basic sciences."[70]

Community-based medical schools have adopted an untraditional curriculum that has not been favorably received. They have replaced some basic science courses with social science and humanities courses. This has adversely affected the scores of their students on Part I of the NBME examinations, which tests for knowledge of the basic medical sciences. They have emphasized primary care and have lacked departments in some of the clinical specialties. This has led to criticisms by medical educators and accreditation committees. As a result, some community-based medical schools have reverted to more conservative educational programs.[71]

Despite their problems, community-based medical schools have performed creditably compared to their more traditional counterparts. They have recruited able students and their graduates have compared favorably with those of other medical schools.[72] It remains to be seen whether they can continue to innovate in an environment as conservative as that of medical education.

The Elective System

The innovation that has had the greatest impact on medical education has been the conversion of most of the fourth year of medical school to electives. The elective system was a reaction to a curriculum dilemma that developed during the 1950s and 1960s. Medical schools created so many new departments and divisions in the clinical specialties that all of them could not be given a clerkship rotation or lecture time. One obvious solution was to remove all specialties from the undergraduate curriculum and place them in the residency, and to limit undergraduate training to general medicine and primary care, the only aspects of medicine used by all clinicians. However, the specialty departments jealously guarded their prerogatives, and internal medicine, which taught general medicine and was powerful enough to have influenced the decision, had itself become fragmented into subspecialties uninterested in general medical education.

In the 1960s, the clinical departments resolved the problem by permitting students to choose their own specialty courses. This was done by reducing the required curriculum to three years and converting most of the fourth year to elective courses.[73] Little effort was made to make the elective program an educationally meaningful experience. Departments have been left free to select the courses that they wished to offer, or not to offer courses at all. Medical schools have rarely coordinated the offerings of the various departments to ensure that students had a meaningful range of elective courses. Students have been allowed great latitude in their choices with few constraints to ensure that they selected an appropriate balance of courses.

The elective system has been adopted in varying degrees by practically all medical schools. In 1983–1984, a survey of 120 medical schools found that the proportion of the senior year used for electives was 80 percent or more in 33.3 percent of the schools, between 60 and 79 percent in 31.7 percent of the schools, between 20 and 59 percent in 33.3 percent of the schools, and none at all in 2 schools. Over 80 percent of the schools permitted off-campus electives in physicians' offices, community hospitals unaffiliated with medical schools, and public agencies. A 1983–1984 analysis of elective courses taken by 10,279 graduating medical students found that the great majority of them were in the clinical specialties. Very few students took courses in public health and preventive medicine, and only a small number took courses in the basic medical sciences.[74]

The elective system has been widely criticized as contributing little toward the general professional education of medical students. Eichna has observed that "instead of a culminating year of high learning, it is a year of drift, lax evaluation, and passive absorption." The report of the AAMC, *Physicians for the Twenty-First Century*, and that of the AMA Council on Medical Education, "Future Directions for Medical Education," criticized the manner in which students chose electives, the lack of faculty oversight, and the failure of the faculty to apply appropriate standards of evaluation to student performance in elective courses.[75]

The major problem has been the use of electives by students to prepare for their residencies. Medical students have taken many of their elective courses in their future specialties, thereby duplicating the content of their residency programs and narrowing their professional training. Many have taken electives in hospitals in which they would like to receive residency appointments in order to make a good impression on the staff. When students have taken electives off-campus, medical schools have had little knowledge of the quality of training or the student's performance. A 1983 survey of 278 medical students and residents found that 42 percent of them felt that pressure "on students to use their senior year to pursue career goals to the exclusion of their general professional education [was a] problem deserving of special attention."[76]

The elective system has reduced the amount of training of medical students in general medicine. This was the goal of many medical educators. Some used the establishment of elective programs that would enable students to specialize in their senior year as a justification for the elimination of comprehensive care programs. Both "Future Directions for Medical Education" and *Physicians for the Twenty-First Century* criticized this premature specialization. They called for medical school faculties to ensure that elective programs were used for the advancement of the general professional education of medical students, not their specialty training.[77]

The impact of the elective system on the training of medical students in general medicine can be seen in a comparison of clinical medical education in 1950 and in the 1980s. In 1950, students spent the last two years of medical school receiving clinical and clerkship training in general medicine. Three decades later, clerkship training in general medicine was moved to the third year and much of the fourth year was given over to specialty training or to shopping around for residency positions. No discernable decline has occurred in the need of physicians for training in general medicine since 1950.

Thus, innovations in medical education have fallen afoul of the internal power structure of medical schools. Clinical departments have supported those innovations that have enabled them to teach their specialties to medical students and treat patients with illnesses requiring their specialized skills. The elective year has prospered because it has met these objectives, despite extensive evidence that it has been of little educational benefit. Preceptorships have not been widely adopted, allegedly because of the lack of medical school control over preceptors. However, the elective system has enabled students to take off-campus electives that have been under less faculty control than preceptorships. Comprehensive care programs were discontinued allegedly because of the lack of suitable patients. However, the clinical specialties have steadily opposed affiliations with health maintenance organizations that would have provided the kinds of patients needed to make comprehensive care teaching successful. All too often, the medical school curriculum has been a by-product of faculty interests rather than a program to educate medical students.

Conclusion

The problems of undergraduate medical education have been most clearly manifested in the lack of agreement concerning its content. The 1984 report for the Association of American Medical Colleges, *Physicians for the Twenty-First Century,* stated: "Highly specialized medical faculty members all too often do not clearly specify the knowledge, skills, values, and attitudes that students should acquire during their clinical education. Faculty members . . . rarely achieve consensus on what students should accomplish . . . in terms specific enough to provide direction to students or permit adequate evaluation of their accomplishments."[78]

Lack of agreement about the goals of undergraduate medical education has resulted from the growth of other medical school activities of equal or greater importance to faculty members. *Physicians for the Twenty-First Century* concluded that "despite frequent assertions that the general professional education of medical students is the basic mission of medical schools, it often occupies last place in the competition for faculty time and attention. Graduate students, residents, research, and patient care are accorded higher priorities." Both that report and the 1982 AMA report, "Future Directions for Medical Education," agreed that faculty specialization in particular had adversely affected the education of medical students. The latter observed that specialization has led to "aggregates of semiautonomous units that . . . often become further and further separated from the educational philosophy of the parent discipline. Technological skills may be emphasized at the expense of the broad education needed by graduates to select a specialty knowledgeably and to provide general medical care."[79]

Some have argued that many traditional aspects of undergraduate medical education have become obsolete because specialization has eliminated the common core of knowledge once considered essential for all physicians. Both the AAMC and the AMA reports vigorously rejected that position. The AAMC report observed that "all physicians, regardless of specialty, require a common foundation of knowledge, skills, values, and attitudes." Both reports stated that the undergraduate years of medical education were the most suitable time for physicians to acquire a broad perspective of medicine. Contemporary medical schools, which have been structured around academic departments rather than educational programs, have not provided that kind of training.[80]

17

Graduate Medical Education

Graduate medical education has become as important as attendance at medical school in the training of physicians. Up to 1970, most graduates of medical schools first took an internship in general medicine and then a residency in a specialty. After 1970, practically all medical school graduates entered residency training in a specialty immediately after graduation. Residency programs have been located in hospitals affiliated with medical schools and have been accredited by specialty boards, which have been controlled by medical school faculty members. This situation has led to insufficient breadth of training and lax regulation of the programs.

The Internship

The internship, which followed graduation from medical school until its elimination after 1970, consisted of one or two years of hospital training, usually unconnected with any medical specialty. It was designed to provide gradually increasing responsibility for patient care, supplemented by formal teaching in rounds and seminars. In practice, as George Miller observed in 1963, it was "virtually impossible to find an internship [program with] a graded and sequential course of study leading to relatively well-defined goals." This was also the finding of several surveys of interns and physicians. A 1959 survey of 2,616 interns found that the two most frequently cited deficiencies of internships were lack of "sufficient review and criticism of your work with patients," cited by 47 percent, and "adequate instruction in the application of scientific knowledge to patient care," cited by 34 percent. A 1952 survey of 6,662 graduates of the medical school classes of 1937 and 1947 and a later survey of over 3,000 interns and residents produced similar findings.[1]

Formal instruction during the internship was usually casual and unsystematic. Stephen Miller's study of one university hospital found that interns spent only a few hours per week in formal lectures and conferences and on rounds. In teaching on rounds, "the visiting physician does not prepare a lecture or other teaching material. He simply walks onto the ward and responds to patients and their problems with opinions and examples from his own clinical experience." The educational value of rounds therefore depended on the illnesses of the patients and the relevant skills of the physicians.[2]

Interns had few educationally meaningful relationships with staff members and residents. One survey of 1,165 interns in 1958–1959 found that 53 percent "were dissatisfied with their opportunity to work closely with the senior staff." Only one-half reported that residents, who provided most of their instruction, "tended to work as a team" with them. Interns learned little about other hospital employees. The survey found that "less than one-third of the interns felt that they had learned anything concerning the role of the hospital administrator, the business side of running a hospital, or the relationship of the medical staff to administration and the board of trustees."[3]

The tasks performed in the hospital wards by interns included many of little educational value. Their stipends were low, and hospitals had little incentive to use their skills efficiently. Time studies of the work activities of interns have found that they spent much of their time carrying out laboratory tests on patients, running errands, and taking histories. They did not spend much time caring for patients. The studies found that they saw patients for only a small proportion of their total work time.[4]

Interns also worked in the outpatient clinics, where they carried out physical examinations, performed laboratory tests, and helped care for patients needing immediate attention. Although this provided more training in patient care than did inpatient work, much of it involved treating minor illnesses and injuries in the emergency room. Interns rarely saw ambulatory patients more than once and never saw well patients, who comprise a large proportion of the patients seen by many physicians.[5]

Internships were available in both community and teaching hospitals. Community hospitals provided training in the care of patients with typical illnesses and social and economic backgrounds, but their staff members were busy private practitioners who had little interest in medical education and often restricted the intern's opportunity to care for private patients. Teaching hospitals had a more pronounced educational atmosphere, but their patients were primarily poor and seriously ill, and most teaching was done by residents with little clinical experience. Residents were most skilled in new forms of therapy and diagnosis and in exotic diseases, which biased the teaching hospital internship in that direction.[6]

A survey of interns in one community hospital and one university hospital found that their attitudes were affected by their different environments. Three-fourths of the interns in the community hospital attached "great importance" to their "ability to establish rapport with patients" compared to none of the interns in the university hospital. Community hospital interns were also less interested in exotic diseases than their university hospital counterparts.[7]

Internships were divided into three major types: straight, rotating, and mixed. Straight internships involved training in one specialty, usually internal medicine or surgery, and were attached to residency programs. Rotating internships provided training in a number of different specialties. Mixed internships, which were not widely used, provided training in medicine, surgery, and perhaps one other specialty. Rotating and mixed internships emphasized general medical training and were often similar in practice. Both were unconnected with residency programs.

Most practitioners considered the rotating internship to be educationally superior to the straight internship because of its greater breadth of training. In 1953, a committee of the Council on Medical Education of the AMA expressed a unanimous preference for the rotating internship. In support of its position, the committee cited a survey of 6,662 medical school graduates of the classes of 1937 and 1947. Over 90 percent of those in both classes who took rotating internships said they would do so again, while of those who took straight internships, 43 percent of the 1937 class and 36 percent of the 1947 class said that they now preferred rotating internships. The committee acknowledged the problem in rotating internships of "circuit riding" students through too many specialties too quickly.[8]

Medical students were more likely to choose rotating than straight internships. Between 1953 and 1963, the number of interns in rotating or mixed internships in all types of hospitals remained at about 10,000, while the number in straight internships increased only from 990 to 2,044. In 1970, about 10,000 interns enrolled in rotating or mixed internships, while the number in straight internships rose to about 6,000.[9] Most of the increase in straight internships was due to the unavailability of additional rotating internships.

Straight internships were most common in university hospitals, although even there they were taken by only 31 percent of the interns in 1959–1960. The 1953 AMA committee observed that "particularly in university hospitals, straight services are often retained because of the attitude of the chiefs who consider relatively short-term rotating internships more of a nuisance than an asset and who further wish more prolonged contact with their men in order to forge a strong intradepartmental chain of command. Some chiefs are far more concerned with the efficient conduct of their own service than with the value of the internship as a preparation for the practice of medicine." Between 1953 and 1963 the proportion of university hospitals offering rotating internships declined from 74 percent to 44 percent. In 1961 the Association of American Medical Colleges recommended the elimination of the one-year rotating internship and its replacement by a multiple year program.[10]

Most medical school faculty members did not support straight internships or the specialization that they encouraged. A 1970 survey gave 994 full-time medical school faculty members a set of 57 medical school objectives with which they were asked to agree or disagree. Only 44 percent agreed with the objective, to "abolish interns and integrate into residencies," and 31 percent agreed with the objective, to "encourage students to enter specialty practice." Over 80 percent of the respondents agreed with the objective, to "induce students to enter careers in family and community medicine."[11]

Despite the strong support for rotating internships among practicing physicians, medical students, and faculty members, the AMA effectively eliminated them in 1970 when it changed internship accreditation policies. Prior to 1970, most internship programs were free-standing, that is, not connected with residency programs, even though an internship was a requirement for entering a residency. The AMA decided that after 1971, all newly accredited internship programs had to be part of residency programs accredited by specialty boards, and that after 1975, all free-standing internship programs lost accreditation. The 1970 decision permitted specialty boards to approve residency programs in which the student took no internship but began training in the specialty immediately, and within a year, all of them did so. Students shunned internships unaffiliated with residency programs for fear that they would not gain later admission to residency programs. The new policy thus effectively eliminated rotating and mixed internships.[12]

The AMA's action was basically a reaction to accusations that it was doing nothing to relieve the widely publicized shortage of physicians. It announced that the new policy enabled medical students to complete their residencies and enter practice a year earlier, thereby increasing the supply of physicians in the short run.[13] However, the change did not increase medical school enrollments, which kept the long-run supply of physicians unchanged.

The AMA would not have taken so radical a step without the support of groups closely related to residency training. Engel has suggested that the movement was "sponsored primarily by the specialty boards" that approved residency programs and have been composed largely of medical school faculty members, as will be shown below. Medical school clinical departments had been having difficulty recruiting residents because of the shortage of physicians. They realized that it was much easier to recruit their own medical students to their residency programs while the students were still in medical school than after they graduated and left for an internship elsewhere.[14]

The elimination of the rotating internship has created serious problems for medical students. A rotating internship enabled them to have a year of practical experience after graduation, usually outside the medical school, where they could mature as physicians, gain some breadth of perspective, and choose a specialty. It also provided a badly needed year of general medical education. Its elimination has required them to choose a specialty early in their senior year, when many have been unprepared to do so.[15]

The elimination of the rotating internship adversely affected the skills of residents. A study analyzed the scores of students on Part II of the NBME examinations, which is taken in the senior year of medical school and measures clinical knowledge, and Part III, which is taken near the end of the first year of the residency and "measures essential diagnostic and therapeutic skills that the medical profession and society expect all physicians to have." Using 1,514 graduates of one medical school from 1970 to 1979, the study compared the test scores of students whose first year of graduate training was in a narrow specialty (surgery, pediatrics, obstetrics/gynecology, psychiatry, or pathology) with the test scores of students whose first year was comparable to a rotating or mixed internship (family medicine, internal medicine, flexible programs). The students with a narrow first-year training showed significant declines from their Part II scores to their Part III scores while those with a broad first-year training showed no changes.[16]

The elimination of the rotating internship has created problems for some residency programs and medical specialties. Residency programs in some specialties had recruited most of their residents from interns who had rotated through their specialties and become interested in the fields. Other specialties, like psychiatry, used rotating internships to educate interns about the importance of their fields. Still others wanted their residents to obtain a broad first graduate year experience that was not possible within their own highly specialized residency programs.[17]

In response to these criticisms, a "flexible" year option was provided in what was now called PGY-1, or postgraduate year one, for medical students undecided on their choice of specialty. Students recognized that this placed them at a serious disadvantage in applying for residency programs, and only 7 percent of graduating students entered flexible programs in the late 1970s and early 1980s. Even so, there has been a shortage of positions in flexible option programs, so that students undecided on a specialty, according to a 1978 report of the American Board of Medical Specialties, have had to resort to "devious maneuvers . . . to find a good general first postgraduate year experience." In 1982, the flexible year was redesignated a "transitional year" and placed under the control of residency programs, which further weakened it.[18]

Some residency programs have required residents to take their first postgraduate year in a program broader than their own, usually family medicine, internal medicine, or surgery. This has not operated satisfactorily for either the residents or the programs in which they spent their first year. The residents have received an inadequate education because they left the broader three-year programs in midstream. The broader programs have naturally emphasized the training of their own residents and have had difficulty developing suitable training for the other residents.[19]

The elimination of the rotating internship has further reduced the amount of training in general medicine that students have received. Until the 1960s most students spent a total of three years in clinical training in general medicine—the last two years of medical school plus the internship. Since then, a large part of the last year of medical school has been converted to specialty training because of the elective system, and the internship has been replaced by the first year of the residency. Only the third year of medical school has remained as a year of clinical training in general medicine. The effects of these changes have been so unsatisfactory that the AMA Council on Medical Education, in a repudiation of the 1970 AMA policy, recommended in 1982 that the "first year of postdoctoral medical education for all graduates should consist of a broad year of general training."[20]

The Residency

Over the last several decades, residency programs have been increasingly restricted to teaching hospitals. This has been due to the preferences of residents and the boards that certify specialists. In 1962–1963, only 24.5 percent of the 1,464 hospitals with approved graduate programs were affiliated with medical schools. They trained 49.1 percent of the 12,024 interns and 61.9 percent of the 36,162 residents. In 1974–1975, 67.5 percent of the 1,683 hospitals with approved residency programs were affiliated with medical schools, and they trained 92.9 percent of the 33,509 residents. A few large teaching hospitals have come to dominate residency training: in 1984, 46 percent of all residents were trained in 100 hospitals. Some residency programs have grown so large that they have affiliated with several hospitals and other clinical sites in order to provide training for their residents in all of the subspecialties.[21]

Teaching hospital residency programs have been the responsibility of individual clinical departments in the medical school, not the medical school itself. In university-owned or major affiliated hospitals, medical school departments have operated the residency programs and financed them from their patient-care and other revenues. In other affiliated hospitals, they have appointed a training director to operate the educational program or provided educational exercises in the hospital. Such ties have often been weak and have seldom included the participation of other clinical and basic science departments in the medical school. The training received by residents in these hospitals has been uneven and limited.[22]

Residency programs have been tied to the patient-care activities of hospitals in several ways. Income from patient care covered an estimated 85 percent of the costs of residency programs in 1985. The major sources of income have been Medicare and Blue Cross, which have provided reimbursements for both the costs of patient care and direct educational costs. Patient-care activities have also been responsible for the creation of many residency programs. A 1978 survey asked 225 directors of graduate training programs at nine medical schools to identify the most important reasons for establishing the programs. Sixty-two percent cited "available funding for graduate medical education costs" (primarily from patient care), and 61 percent cited "patient care needs of teaching hospital." Only 15 percent cited the need for more specialists and 14 percent the quality of the medical education they were able to provide.[23]

Reliance on patient-care revenues to support residency programs has led hospitals to treat residents as employees rather than students receiving an education. Studies in the late 1970s showed that residents spent an average of 62 percent of their time in patient-care activities and 15 percent in patient care associated with teaching medical students and others. Another 10 percent was spent in learning, and the remainder in research and administration. As residents moved from their first to their third year, they spent less time in patient care and more in all of the other activities. In their patient-care and teaching activities, second- and third year-residents assumed some of the duties of faculty members.[24]

The granting of so much independent responsibility for patient care to residents has been a source of dispute. Many faculty members have believed that residents must assume responsibility to learn to be physicians. On the other hand, the proficiency of residents still in training has remained legally and professionally suspect until their competence has been demonstrated by board certification. As evidence of the problems involved, a 1983 study of 209 patients examined by 12 residents found errors in the examinations of about 60 percent of the patients, despite the fact that the house officers knew they were being evaluated. The authors reported that "the errors were not minor and that their correction frequently led to major changes in differential diagnosis and therapy."[25]

The training of residents has suffered from most of the problems found in the training of interns. Programs have not provided for systematic evaluations of residents or a gradual increase in their patient-care responsibilities with the improvement of their skills. The programs have disregarded the teaching of basic medical skills, especially those not needed in the specialty. Many residents have not received training in all of the subspecialties in their programs because they were rotated only among those subspecialty services that needed their labor. Residency programs have provided insufficient training in ambulatory care. A 1976 survey of

410 residency training directors in internal medicine, a specialty that has provided much ambulatory care, found that residents spent an average of 16 percent or less of their time in ambulatory care in each of the three years of the programs. A 1980 survey of 221 alumni of one internal medicine residency program before 1976 found that only 31 percent of the alumni were satisfied with their ambulatory training, compared to 85 percent who were satisfied with their inpatient training.[26]

The use of teaching hospitals for residency programs has led to an overemphasis on highly specialized care and on the treatment of patients with very severe illnesses. The report, *Prescription for Change,* observed that new technologies "threaten to turn teaching hospitals into overlarge intensive care units, offering excellent experience in care of the very sickest patients, but unbalancing the education of the resident, who is deprived of experience with more customary diagnostic and therapeutic procedures."[27]

Fellowships

In the 1970s, about one-third of all residents extended their graduate training to include a fellowship of one or two years beyond the third year of residency, primarily to obtain a subspecialty certificate from a specialty board. In order to encourage fellows to enter research and teaching, in 1975–1976, 37 percent of funding for fellows came from the federal government and 10 percent from private foundations, with only 44 percent coming from patient revenues. In contrast, 87 percent of the funding for residents came from patient revenues.[28]

Instead of receiving training for research and teaching, fellows have spent most of their time in clinical activities, because, according to Peterson, they "provide the cheapest form of labor available." They have had the skills necessary to perform expensive diagnostic and therapeutic procedures and carry out much of the teaching of medical students, while their stipends have been only slightly higher than those of residents. Hospitals therefore have sought out clinical fellows even more eagerly than residents. After their training, most fellows have entered clinical practice rather than research and teaching. *Prescription for Change* recommended that funding for graduate medical education should not extend beyond the number of years (usually three) required for eligibility for a general certificate in a specialty.[29]

Specialty Boards and Residency Training

Because residency training has been a requirement for certification in a specialty, it has come under the control of the specialty boards. Each specialty board has formally accredited residency programs and required all applicants for certificates to have completed an accredited program. Accreditation committees have preferred residency programs affiliated with medical school departments, so that practically all programs have established such affiliations to ensure their accreditation.

The membership of the specialty boards has been dominated by the same medical school faculty members who have operated the residency programs, thus

TABLE 17.1. Percentage of Faculty Members on Member Boards of the American Board of Medical Specialties, 1980

Percentage of Faculty Members	Specialty Boards	
	Number	*Percentage*
0–19	1	4.3
20–39	7	30.4
40–59	8	34.8
60–79	7	30.4
80–100	0	0.0

Sources: American Board of Medical Specialties, *Annual Report and Reference Handbook—1980* (Evanston, Ill.: 1980); *National Faculty Directory 1981* (Detroit: Gale Research Co., 1980), 2 vols.

enabling them to establish the standards used to accredit their own programs. An analysis was made of the number of medical school faculty members listed in the 1981 *National Faculty Directory* who served as members of the 23 specialty boards listed in the 1980 *Annual Report* of the American Board of Medical Specialties (Table 17.1). Overall, 46.4 percent of the 352 board members listed were faculty members. Faculty members comprised at least 40 percent of the members of 15 of the 23 boards.

Under these circumstances, accreditation standards have left much to be desired. Specialty boards have seldom kept their accreditation policies abreast of existing needs. Their standards have changed little over the years and have lagged behind developments in medical knowledge and technology. As an example, most specialty boards have added subspecialty certificates to their general certificates. Although subspecialty training has been clearly differentiated from general specialty training and has become quite popular, most specialty boards have not accredited sub-specialty training programs.[30]

Most specialty boards have limited their membership to physicians in the specialties involved and have excluded representatives from related or broader specialties. The committees that review residency programs have had a similar membership plus representatives of the AMA. This has led to a disregard for broader issues in medical manpower and specialty training. When questioned by the U.S. comptroller general's office about shortages or oversupplies of certain kinds of specialists, "the specialty boards, residency review committees, and [the council that coordinates medical education] all stated it was their concern but not their role to see that the number of physicians trained is consistent with the approximate number needed." The specialty boards said that they were "primarily responsible for determining the competence in the fields of candidates who appear voluntarily for examinations and for certifying as diplomates those who are qualified." This answer minimized the role of the boards in accrediting residency programs, which has been by far their most important function.[31]

Specialty boards have adopted self-centered policies for accrediting new residency programs, despite the dependence of their programs on other activities of the hospital involved. A 1979 review of their procedures found that practically none of them examined in detail the other residency programs in the applicant program's hospital. They did not inquire about the names of the other specialty residency programs, their accreditation status, and the faculty members who taught in them. Few asked about the overall operations of the hospital and the facilities not directly related to the program, such as ambulatory care services, emergency rooms, or intensive care units.[32]

Because specialty boards have been controlled by medical school faculty members who operate the residency programs, their accreditation procedures have often shown as much concern for the service needs of the programs as the quality of their training. Site visits have been casual and superficial. Until the mid-1970s, residency programs were often placed on probation and left there for years without public notification of their status or subsequent termination. Approval and disapproval of program requests has been inconsistent and sometimes contradicted the written evidence, which strongly suggests preferential treatment. In the 1980s, some efforts have been made to strengthen residency program approval and review procedures. However, so long as the programs are approved and regulated by boards composed largely of the specialists who operate the programs, loose practices will remain the norm.[33]

The parochialism and lack of accountability of residency programs have long been subjects of debate. In order to broaden the programs and encourage cooperation among them, in 1971 the Association of American Medical Colleges (AAMC) called for corporate academic medical center responsibility for graduate medical education. According to Holden, medical school clinical department chairmen and faculty members voiced "the strongest reluctance to shift the authority [for graduate medical education] to schools of medicine. . . . For decades they had functioned as independent proprietors of their residencies, and they had rarely been questioned about their programs, even by their colleagues." Teaching hospitals were also unwilling to accept responsibility for their residency programs. Holden reported that "they expressed a considerable degree of anxiety" about assuming control and much preferred the existing situation that relieved them of any responsibility.[34]

According to a 1980 report for the AAMC, "the attainment of acceptable university quality in graduate medical education . . . has been hampered by the perpetuation of the philosophy that each program in every specialty is independent from all other programs." This philosophy has been diametrically opposed to that of undergraduate medical education, where all departments have accepted the overall authority of the medical school. It has also become obsolete, because all residency programs have relied on support specialties like radiology, pathology, and psychiatry, and many programs have rotated their residents through other specialties. The report observed that if "all students are to be prepared to be proficient practitioners of their specialties, graduate medical faculties must assume greater responsibility for the quality of their programs and develop internal standards and criteria as well as rely upon the external accreditation and certification systems. . . . The quality of all programs in an institution should be the concern of the entire institution."[35]

Instead of medical school responsibility for graduate medical education, the specialty boards have relied on a coordinating council of appropriate organizations. The council has included representatives of the American Board of Medical Specialties (composed of the specialty boards), the Council of Medical Specialty Societies, the American Hospital Association, the American Medical Association, and the Association of American Medical Colleges. The inability of these councils to achieve useful results has been most evident in their periodic reorganizations.[36]

As more physicians have sought board certification, the specialty boards have simplified their testing procedures. Originally, the tests included direct observation of physical examinations by candidates and even patient records from candidates' hospitals. In recent years boards have replaced these measures with written and oral examinations. This has de-emphasized those aspects of any specialty that have been difficult to measure in tests and produced a lockstep approach to certification. Some observers have also questioned whether the most important characteristics of a good specialist, such as clinical skills, have actually been measured.[37]

Specialty boards have been unwilling to cooperate to improve their testing. A joint "basic surgical examination" was administered by five surgical boards from 1972 to 1977, but then was abandoned (four other surgical boards refused to participate at all). Holden observed that the surgical boards conceded that they shared the same skills and knowledge regarding the nonoperative forms of surgical therapy and many complications of surgery, such as shock, hemorrhage, and sepsis. Yet they refused to agree on an examination that would have both simplified matters for all concerned and been of much higher quality because of the greater time and attention that could have been devoted to improving it.[38]

Another issue has been the reduction in certification requirements by all specialty boards. An example is the American Board of Internal Medicine, by far the largest specialty board. Before 1970, the board required more than six years' work after medical school for certification: four years of training in general internal medicine, and two years of either practice or training in a subspecialty, followed by a written examination and a later oral examination. About 1970, the oral examination was eliminated and the requirements for certification in general internal medicine were reduced to three years of general internal medicine, or two years of general internal medicine and one of subspecialty internal medicine before the written examination.[39]

The American Society of Internal Medicine called this reduction in requirements a "misdirection in . . . professional leadership" and claimed that specialists certified under the new requirements were inferior to those previously certified "with respect to total knowledge accumulated, maturity, judgment or well-established habit patterns of practice." Although the halving of the total training period was allegedly designed to produce more general internists, more internists took subspecialty training instead. Later, the board, in what Petersdorf called a "gesture of mea culpa," increased the requirements in general internal medicine from two to three years, but the end result was a significant reduction in requirements for certification.[40]

The number of approved residency programs has declined in recent years due to the closing of programs unaffiliated with medical schools. The 5,686 residency programs in 1959 have been reduced to 4,811 in 1984, a decrease in the median number of programs per specialty from 120 to 94 (Table 17.2). Because the number

TABLE 17.2. Trends in Residency Programs, 1959–1984

	1959	1984
Number of specialties	30	41
Number of programs offered	5,686	4,811
Median number of programs/specialty	120	94
Number of residents in programs	27,509	75,125
Median number of residents/specialty	322	522

	Number of Specialties	
Average Number of Residents/Program	*1959*	*1984*
Up to 4.99	23	18
5.00–9.99	7	9
10.00–14.99	0	3
15.00–19.99	0	6
20.00–24.99	0	2
25.00 or more	0	3

Sources: JAMA 174 (1960): 576; *JAMA* 254 (1985): 1587–89.

of residents increased from 27,509 to 75,125, the median number of residents per specialty grew from 322 to 522.

Because specialty boards have been dominated by the operators of specialty programs, they have shown little concern over the small size of many programs. Although the average number of residents per program has increased significantly since 1959, many residency programs remained very small in 1984 (Table 17.2). Boards in 18 specialties averaged fewer than 5 residents per program and 9 others averaged between 5 and 10. The specialties with larger per program averages have also accredited many small programs. Because residents have been further subdivided according to their year of training, the small programs have not been pedagogically viable. They have not had enough faculty members to provide adequate training, have had too few residents to organize seminars or classes, and have provided residents with an insufficient range of patient disorders. Petersdorf has observed that many of them are primarily designed "to provide cheap labor for hospitals, to keep the attending staff happy, or as a prestige item to attract patients."[41]

As the education provided in medical school has become more preliminary in nature, residency training has become a major part of the general medical education of the physician. Yet most residency prorgams have continued to provide practical training in a narrow specialty. This has been due to the dependence of the programs on the patient-care activities of residents and the perception of faculty members that residency programs have been the responsibility of individual departments rather than the medical school. Reducing the patient-care activities of residents will require replacing their labor with that of salaried physicians, which has already occurred in prepayment plans.[42] Making medical schools directly responsible for all residency programs in their teaching hospitals will reduce the parochialism that has pervaded the programs. As currently structured, residency training has become an anachronism in medical education.

18

Training in Primary Care

Training in primary care has received limited attention in medical schools despite state and federal funding to increase its emphasis. Departments of internal medicine, which have been responsible for most training in primary care, have shifted their interests to the medical subspecialties. Departments of family practice, which have been established by most medical schools in response to government pressure, have had a limited role in the undergraduate curriculum. Residency programs in family practice have become widespread and popular with medical students.

Primary Care Medicine and Medical Schools

Primary care has been defined as that type of medicine practiced by the first physician whom the patient contacts. Most primary care has involved well-patient care, the treatment of a wide variety of functional, acute, self-limited, chronic, and emotional disorders in ambulatory patients, and routine hospital care. Primary care physicians have provided continuing care and coordinated the treatment of their patients by specialists. The major specialties providing primary care have been family practice, general internal medicine, and pediatrics.[1]

General and family physicians in particular have been major providers of ambulatory care. This was shown in a study of diaries kept in 1977–1978 by office-based physicians in a number of specialties. General and family physicians treated 33 percent or more of the patients in every age group from childhood to old age. They delivered at least 50 percent of the care for 6 of the 15 most common diagnostic clusters and over 20 percent of the care for the remainder. The 15 clusters, which accounted for 50 percent of all outpatient visits to office-based physicians, included activities related to many specialties, including pre- and postnatal care, ischemic heart disease, depression/anxiety, dermatitis/eczema, and fractures and dislocations.[2]

According to the study, ambulatory primary care was also provided by many specialists who have not been considered providers of primary care. A substantial part of the total ambulatory workload of general surgeons involved general medical examinations, upper respiratory ailments, and hypertension. Obstetricians/gynecologists performed many general medical examinations. The work activities of these and other specialists have demonstrated that training in primary care has been essential for every physician who provides patient care, not just those who plan to become family physicians, general internists, or pediatricians.[3]

Primary care physicians have assumed responsibility for many treatments once considered the province of specialists. The need for specialty care has been reduced by better drugs and diagnostic techniques and the nonsurgical management of conditions that previously required surgery. The routinization of the treatment of diseases like diabetes, hypertension, and ischemic heart disease has put the care of those patients within the capabilities of many primary care physicians. The diary study referred to above found that in 1977–1978, general and family physicians provided 52, 57, and 41 percent of the ambulatory care given to patients with those three illnesses, respectively. As other medical innovations become standardized, they too will become part of the normal work activities of primary care physicians. In addition, many new medical problems, such as genetics and nutrition, have fallen within the purview of primary care.[4]

Despite the importance of primary care, medical schools and major teaching hospitals have become poor places to learn the appropriate skills. Faculty members have emphasized the specialties in their teaching, research, and patient care, and have been leaders of the specialty boards and societies. According to the Millis report, "medical schools provide excellent models of the scientist-research scholar and the hospital-based specialist, but rarely if ever do they provide models of comprehensive health care or of physicians who are successful and highly regarded for providing that kind of medical service." Teaching hospitals have cared for patients who have had serious and multiple problems and have not received continuing care. Bogdonoff has observed that, for the student trained in a major teaching hospital, "most of the patients he sees in community practice turn out to have the wrong diseases."[5]

Medical schools have also not provided sufficient training in the nonclinical aspects of medicine that have been important in primary care. In 1983–1984, 133 U.S. and Canadian medical schools provided an average of 91 required hours in the behavioral sciences and 10 provided none; 111 schools provided an average of 51 required hours in preventive medicine and epidemiology and 32 provided none.[6]

Many medical school faculty members have claimed that a physician who has been properly trained in the various specialties will be well qualified to provide primary care. However, the two types of medicine have required different skills that can be neither interchanged nor learned in the same clinical situations. The student in a specialty must learn to master a small number of diagnostic tests and therapeutic procedures by using them on carefully screened patients. The student in primary care must learn to diagnose and treat a wide range of disorders using many different kinds of tests and procedures on unscreened patients.[7]

The major impetus for better training in primary care has come from state and federal governments. Between 1968 and 1980, 41 states funded education for family practice by aiding medical schools or medical students planning to enter primary care specialties. Some states established community-based medical schools with the specific objective of training primary care physicians.[8]

The federal government first aided primary care training in 1971 by providing grants, fellowships, and traineeships to teaching hospitals to train medical students, interns, and residents in programs in family medicine. In 1976 the aid was expanded to include medical schools and programs in general internal medicine and general pediatrics, and to provide fellowships for students in those fields. Fellowships were also awarded to physicians who were being trained to teach family medicine. Grants were provided to new medical schools that emphasized primary care and to assist in the construction of ambulatory primary care teaching facilities in medical schools and hospitals.[9]

The 1976 legislation also tied the capitation grants that went to all medical schools to their primary care activities. In order to receive the grants, medical schools had to place a certain proportion of the first-year residents in all of their affiliated hospitals into three primary care programs—general internal medicine, family medicine, and general pediatrics. The required proportions rose from 35 percent for fiscal 1978 grants, to 40 percent for fiscal 1979 grants, and to 50 percent for fiscal year 1980 grants and those thereafter. While medical schools could have welcomed this funding as an opportunity to redress a major weakness in their curriculum, instead they regarded the quid pro quo as an imposition. In 1980, a report for the Association of American Medical Colleges stated:

> [T]he relationship between the academic medical centers and the [federal] government has moved from one of harmony with mutual understanding and support to one of coercion. Laws, regulations, and agency policies have been based on the thesis that the academic medical centers are unwilling to become involved in modifying the distribution of specialists. Rather than providing incentives to change and then allowing the centers to initiate programs best suited to their missions and resources over a reasonable time period, the government has attempted to coerce all institutions by threatening to withhold support and has expected responses to occur in an unrealistically short time.[10]

The central role accorded to internal medicine in training for primary care made it the medical school department most affected by this legislation. However, departments of internal medicine have moved away from primary care. Subspecialists have comprised the great majority of their faculties, set the intellectual tone of the departments, treated most of the patients, and generated most of the income. Subspecialization has also played a growing role in residency programs in internal medicine. Between 1974 and 1983 the American Board of Internal Medicine awarded 41,272 certificates in general internal medicine and 21,793 special certificates in nine subspecialties of internal medicine.[11]

Most departments of internal medicine have undertaken primary care training on a very limited scale. In 1979, small divisions of general internal medicine were located within departments of medicine in 95 of 123 primary medical school teaching hospitals. A survey of 82 of them found that all but 5 were organized after 1970, usually to train residents in primary care. Clinical activities provided an average of 46 percent of the divisions' revenues and federal grants 14 percent. The divisions employed only 6 percent of all full-time faculty members in departments of internal medicine, and 78 percent of the faculty were instructors or assistant professors. Their teaching and patient-care responsibilities were quite heavy and detracted from their research activities. The programs provided significantly more training in primary care than traditional residencies in internal medicine.[12]

Most residents in internal medicine have not received adequate training in ambulatory care, except for the small number in primary care tracks. A 1981–1982 study of ambulatory care training in internal medicine residencies in hospitals affiliated with medical schools compared 30 programs with both primary care and traditional tracks and 66 programs with traditional tracks only. In hospitals with both kinds of tracks, one-fourth of the residents were in the primary care tracks. About one-half of the primary care tracks provided at least four months of block time when second- and third-year residents spent at least 80 percent of their time in ambulatory care. Only 1 percent of the traditional tracks had comparable ambulatory care training and about one-half of them had no block time in ambulatory care during the entire residency. The study found that in those schools with both kinds of tracks the primary care tracks retained the traditional specialty focus on patient care and management and had little effect on the traditional tracks.[13]

These findings have raised questions about the commitment of departments of internal medicine to general internal medicine. Many divisions of general internal medicine were organized to obtain federal funding and provide care for the growing number of patients in the general medical clinics, not to alter the focus of the departments. They have been given fewer resources than the more specialized divisions and have had little influence on the teaching activities of the departments.

Departments of internal medicine have also provided first-year residency training for many residents in other specialties. Fifteen percent of the 4,140 first-year residents in internal medicine in 1976 changed to another specialty in their second year, almost one-half of all first-year residents changing from one specialty to another. Forty-seven percent of those changing went to another medical specialty, such as dermatology or psychiatry, and 35 percent went to a "support specialty," such as radiology or physical medicine. Although the residents from other specialties have needed training in general internal medicine, departments of internal medicine have given few resources to that type of training.[14]

Departments of Family Practice

Before the 1970s, the few departments of family practice were little more than refurbished departments of preventive medicine with limited resources and few students. The impetus for change occurred in the late 1960s and 1970s when many states enacted legislation that either created departments of family medicine or encouraged medical schools to do so. Federal legislation enacted in 1976 increased this pressure by providing project grants to medical schools to establish departments of family medicine. The departments were required to be comparable to other clinical departments in status, faculty, and curriculum, and to control a three-year family practice residency that could enroll at least 12 residents per year.[15]

As a result of these external pressures, in 1973 47 percent of medical schools surveyed had departments of family practice, with a mean of 5.8 full-time faculty members. By 1976, 67 percent of 106 medical schools studied had family practice departments, with a mean of 7.5 faculty. In 1984, 75 percent of medical schools had departments of family practice and another 9 percent had divisions of family practice within other departments. Public medical schools have devoted more resources to family practice than have private ones. In 1976, only 11 of 62 public medical schools had no full-time faculty members in family practice, compared to 28 of 44 private medical schools.[16]

Because of the newness of the field, faculty members in departments of family practice have differed from those in other clinical departments. A 1976–1977 study found that only about one-half of their faculty members had family practice as their primary specialty, while 70 to 80 percent of clinicians in other specialties had their own fields as their primary specialty. Furthermore, 60 percent of faculty members in departments of family practice had experience in private practice, compared to 11 percent of all faculty members, which suggests that many of the former were recruited from the community.[17]

Departments of family practice have had difficulty achieving full acceptance in medical schools. In 1983–1984, only 56 of 139 U.S. and Canadian medical schools required clerkships in family practice, with an average duration of five weeks. Elective courses in family practice were taken by about one-fourth of all medical students. Many family practice programs have had limited patient-care facilities for use in training students. In 1976, only 62 percent of family practice departments had line responsibility for outpatient clinics and 53 percent had line responsibility for inpatient beds.[18]

Several reasons have been suggested for the low status of family practice in medical schools. Family practice relies heavily on other specialties, especially internal medicine, and lacks their distinctive diagnostic and therapeutic techniques. It treats many illnesses that are poorly understood and seldom life threatening. It lacks the research base of other specialties because it does not study particular organs, disease pathologies, or procedures. Family practice has not generated much research or patient-care income. Its research is not the biomedical kind favored by the NIH and its patient-care activities do not involve the high technology specialty practice which brings in so much revenue.[19]

Residencies in Family Practice

The number of residency programs in family practice has increased significantly since the establishment of its specialty board in 1969. Before that time, the few primary care residency programs did not lead to specialty certification and therefore enrolled few residents. The number of approved programs has grown from 151 in 1972 to 386 in 1984–1985 and the number of residents from 1,035 to 7,588. Residents in family practice comprised about 10 percent of all residents during the early 1980s, which made family practice the third largest residency program after internal medicine (which had about 24 percent of all residents) and general surgery (which had about 11 percent). Until the late 1970s, a shortage of residency positions prevented even more students from entering residency programs in family practice. The shortage was alleviated largely by the state and federal legislation described above.[20]

Most residency programs in family practice have been affiliated with medical schools but not directly administered by them. Of the 384 approved residencies in family practice in 1984, only 16 percent were based in medical schools, 15 percent were in community hospitals and administered by medical schools, 54 percent were in community hospitals and affiliated with medical schools, and 15 percent were unaffiliated. One reason for the use of community hospitals has been their emphasis on primary and secondary care rather than the tertiary care characteristic of most university hospitals.[21]

Residency programs in family practice have varied widely in quality. This has been due both in their rapid development and the wide variety of hospitals in which the programs have been located. Some programs have also devoted excessive time to surgery at the expense of other fields more appropriate to primary care. Residency training in primary care has relied on rotations through other specialties, which has created a problem in providing adequate training in continuity of patient care.[22]

Despite their problems, residency programs in family practice have become very popular among medical students. This occurred despite the reluctance of medical schools to teach family practice, the indifference or hostility of medical school faculty members to family practice, and the limited contact of medical students with family practice during medical school. It occured despite the failure of the family practice specialty board and society to exclude surgery and other fields better left to other specialties, to exert proper oversight over residency programs, or to develop a satisfactory schedule of residency training. Although family practice has had a significant appeal to many medical students, its acceptance by medical schools has been due to direct but sporadic pressure from government. If family practice were allowed to develop in a more sympathetic medical school environment and to mature under the more disciplined leadership of departments of family practice, it might well become the largest of the medical specialties.

19

Epilogue

The expansion of the functions of medical schools since mid-century has had many unanticipated and adverse consequences for medical education. As a result, medical schools have lost some of their societal support.

In the years since 1900, medical schools have made major changes in their structure in order to solve specific educational problems. University hospitals were built to provide clinical training in hospitals that emphasized education and research rather than patient care. Full-time clinical faculty members were employed in order to professionalize a role previously occupied by part-time practitioner-educators. Biomedical research was undertaken to enable faculty members to advance medical knowledge and enhance their skills as educators. Internships and residencies became restricted to hospitals affiliated with medical schools to replace the poorly supervised practical experience provided in community hospitals with a more structured education administered by professional educators.

Each of these changes assumed that medical schools could be removed from the hurly-burly of professional life and made to fit the model of the liberal arts college. This assumption failed to recognize the fundamental differences between the two types of institutions. In liberal arts education, the body of knowledge taught to students need not be suitable for practical application in the community. In many fields, like most of the humanities, it has rarely been used outside of institutions of higher education. In others, like the social sciences, the knowledge has been sufficiently tentative that its direct application has been problematic. In still others, like most natural sciences, the knowledge has been so highly specialized that it could not provide a basis for viable careers. As a result, most faculty members in the liberal arts and sciences have spent their careers in teaching and research without the option of nonacademic employment in their disciplines.

Medical schools, on the other hand, have continually influenced and been influenced by the practice of medicine in the community. The knowledge taught in medical schools has affected the way that physicians have practiced medicine, but it has also been tested by practitioners and fed back to the faculty for modification and refinement. The practical aspects of medical education have sought to provide models of the best way to practice medicine, but they have been based on the modes of practice in the community. Clinical faculty members have spent part of their time as academicians and part as practicing physicians and have had the option of leaving academic employment for professional careers.

The failure of medical schools to recognize the differences between liberal arts and professional training has affected each of the institutional changes described above. University hospitals, which were designed to emphasize teaching and research, failed to recognize the primacy of patient care in all hospitals. This confusion over goals created a conflict between faculty members and hospital administrators that has never abated. Medical schools that established university hospitals also underestimated the number of patients and the variety of disorders required for teaching and research and the inability of any one hospital to satisfy the need. As a result, university hospitals have become less important in medical education.

The greatest problem of university hospitals has involved their high cost of operation. In order to remain financially solvent, they have emphasized reimbursable patient care at the expense of medical education. Many of them have attracted paying patients by not using them for teaching. All have reduced costs by using the inexpensive labor of medical students, interns, and residents to carry out activities of little educational value. They have increased their reimbursements from third-party insurors like Medicare and Medicaid by affiliating with other hospitals and employing physicians largely to practice medicine. The effects of these changes have only confirmed the view that medical education and patient care could never be coequal functions of hospitals.

Full-time clinical faculty members were appointed to be educators and researchers uncontaminated by contact with commercial activities. This new role failed to recognize the ease with which academic physicians could enter private practice. In order to attract and retain full-time clinical faculty members, medical schools have had to make their incomes competitive with those of private practitioners. Because the necessary funding has not been available from normal educational resources, faculty members have supplemented their salaries with outside earnings. During the 1950s and 1960s, when federal research grants were a major source of faculty income, full-time faculty members spent much of their time carrying out funded research. Subsequently, the availability of patient-care income has led faculty members to spend much of their time in that activity. In both situations, the distinction between the old part-time faculty member and the new full-time one has become blurred.

Full-time clinical faculty members were also appointed to increase the emphasis on teaching. This failed to recognize that the content of any faculty member's teaching has depended on the kind of medicine that he practiced. Part-time faculty members taught the type of medicine that they practiced in the community. Full-time faculty members have taught a type of medicine that has been viable in major teaching hospitals, but impractical or inappropriate in the community. They have emphasized highly specialized and expensive methods of patient care and have disregarded ambulatory care, continuing care, well-patient care, and social and psychological aspects of illness.

Research by medical school faculty members was designed to enable them to contribute to and teach the latest in usable medical knowledge. Little attention was paid to the impact of the research on faculty skills and the content of medical education. Faculty members in the basic sciences became Ph.D.s rather than M.D.s. Their research has emphasized scientific issues unrelated to medicine, which in turn has oriented their teaching toward pure science and away from its medical applications. Faculty members in the clinical fields have become hospital-oriented specialists. This has led to an emphasis in both research and teaching on the clinical specialties at the expense of general medical care, cost-effective medical care, and preventive medicine.

The availability of income specifically for research and patient care has created cadres of professional researchers in medical schools and large staffs of practicing physicians in teaching hospitals. Most of these workers have had little contact with or interest in the education of medical students. Their presence has redirected medical schools away from their primary function of medical education and created significant confusion over goals and priorities.

The movement of internships and residencies to hospitals affiliated with medical schools was intended to strengthen their educational content and reduce the amount of routine patient care that house officers provided. This change failed to recognize the highly specialized activities of teaching hospitals and the economic imperatives of patient care in any hospital. Residency training in major teaching hospitals has emphasized the treatment of atypical patients with serious and multiple disorders. Residents have continued to provide large amounts of routine and unsupervised care.

As research and patient care have become more important in shaping the content of medical education, the role of medical students has diminished. During the nineteenth century, medical schools had no major activities besides medical education and depended on tuition and fees for income. Students thus became active participants in choosing the curriculum. Since the middle of this century, government funding to medical schools and faculty members for education, research, and patient care has constituted the major source of support. This has made medical students passive recipients of a curriculum chosen by the faculty. While the new curriculum has increased the emphasis on the fundamentals of medicine, it has shown less concern with training community practitioners. A curriculum influenced by medical students would have given greater emphasis to primary care. It would have placed less emphasis on those aspects of the basic sciences unrelated to clinical medicine. Requirements for admission would have been more closely related to achievement in medical school.

Two problems have been conspicuous in contemporary medical schools. The first has been the extent to which patient-care activities have overwhelmed the educational functions of major teaching hospitals. Freymann has observed:

> I believe that the answer to why so little has been done to change the direction of medical education lies less in the past rigidity of the medical curriculum than in the rigid heart of medicine's educational environment—the wards of the teaching hospital. . . . It is impossible to teach a balanced curriculum in an educational environment whose core is preempted by inpatient services.''[1]

It has been suggested that medical schools give greater autonomy to major teaching hospitals by decreasing the staffing role of medical school faculty members, removing the clinical department chairmen as chiefs of service, and separating patient-care and educational functions more distinctly. Faculty members have resisted these proposals They have had extraordinary control over the admission and care of hospital patients for use in teaching and research. They have increased their earnings by caring for patients who have come to the teaching hospital because of its renown or location, not their personal reputations.

The second problem has been the inconsistent policies of state and federal governments. On the one hand, governments have been responsible for every significant innovation in medical education since mid-century: opportunities for more students to attend medical school through financial aid programs and equal opportunity statutes; the many new medical schools and the new facilities and larger enrollments in older ones; education for the new specialty of family practice; research support for faculty members and students; and funding to support residency and fellowship training. On the other hand, government funding policies have emphasized basic research unrelated to medicine, created training programs to prepare physicians for excessively specialized fields, and been responsible for the research and patient-care ventures of medical schools that have detracted from medical education.

Government policies have been inconsistent because each problem has been addressed as though it were unrelated to all other problems. Funding for research, for education, and for patient care have disregarded the fact that all three have been interrelated. Each has been considered independently largely because of pressure from interest groups in or related to medical schools, which have stressed the uniqueness of each problem and shown little concern with its impact on medical education.

Medical schools have made no attempt to coordinate their multiple activities by creating organizational structures to separate them and protect the integrity of their educational programs. Each clinical department has continued to be responsible for a large number of heterogeneous educational, patient-care, and research programs. Teaching hospitals have had to juggle a growing number and variety of students, research programs, and patient-care activities. The need for administrators directly below the medical school dean with specific line responsiblity and separate budgets for undergraduate medical education, graduate medical education, research, and patient care has long been recognized. However, so long as most medical school income is channeled to individual faculty members and departments, it will not be possible to implement any structure that is based on programs rather than administrative units.

In recent years, medical schools have been set adrift from their traditional sources of support—their affiliated universities, community hospitals and physicians, and government. Affiliated universities have shunned their escalating budgets and entrepreneurial ventures. Community hospitals and physicians have viewed them as competitors rather than partners in the medical enterprise. Governments have been reluctant to commit further resources to organizations that have not used previous ones to meet societal needs. Many medical schools have recognized their waning local constituencies and tried to replace them with national ones, but very few medical schools can achieve national stature and none can survive as national institutions alone.

Medical schools can increase their societal support only by strengthing their unique contributions to their local and regional constituencies—by recognizing the primacy of medical education, by teaching primary care medicine to all of their students and training more primary care physicians, by matching their patient-care activities to the prevailing illnesses in their communities, and by carrying out research that will help solve community medical and public health problems. The history of medical schools has shown that those schools which have addressed community needs have enjoyed public confidence, respect, and support.

Notes

Chapter 1

1. Richard M. Magraw, *Ferment in Medicine* (Philadelphia: Saunders, 1966), pp. 30–35.

2. William A. Pusey, "The Importance of Being Historically Minded," *Journal of the American Medical Association* 89 (1927): 2082.

3. Donald W. Seldin, "Some Reflections on the Role of Basic Research and Service in Clinical Departments," *Journal of Clinical Investigation* 45 (1966): 978.

4. This analysis is based on the following works by Alvan R. Feinstein: *Clinical Judgment* (Baltimore: Williams and Wilkins, 1967); "What Kind of Basic Science for Clinical Medicine?" *New England Journal of Medicine* 283 (1970): 847–52; "Scientific Methodology in Clinical Medicine," *Annals of Internal Medicine* 61 (1964): 564–79. See also Seldin, "Some Reflections on the Role of Basic Research and Service in Clinical Departments."

5. Alvan R. Feinstein, "The Basic Elements of Clinical Science," *Journal of Chronic Diseases* 16 (1963): 1125–33; and Feinstein, *Clinical Judgment*, pp. 72–127.

6. Harry F. Dowling, *Fighting Infection* (Cambridge: Harvard University Press, 1977), p. 247; Seldin, "Some Reflections on the Role of Basic Research and Service in Clinical Departments," p. 977; Marlan Blissett, *Politics in Science* (Boston: Little, Brown, 1972), p. 63; Judith P. Swazey and Karen Reeds, *Today's Medicine, Tomorrow's Science* (Washington, D.C.: National Institutes of Health, 1978), pp. 4–5.

7. One theory of organizational decision making which will not be examined here views organizations as basing decisions on the desire to attain certain organization goals. Georgiou has concluded that "almost invariably, studies demonstrate the fruitlessness of understanding organizations as goal attaining devices." Cohen and March have observed in their study of college presidents that universities are "organizational systems without clear objectives. . . . [F]or many purposes the ambiguity of purpose is produced by our insistence on treating purpose as a necessary property of a good university." Petro Georgiou, "The Goal Paradigm and Notes Toward a Counter Paradigm," *Administrative Science Quarterly* 18 (1973): 292; Michael D. Cohen and James G. March, *Leadership and Ambiguity: The American College President* (New York: McGraw-Hill, 1974), pp. 196–97.

8. Ibid., pp. 112–14, 104, 107.

9. David A. Garvin, *The Economics of University Behavior* (New York: Academic Press, 1980), pp. 2–5.

10. Lawrence B. Mohr, *Explaining Organizational Behavior* (San Francisco: Jossey-Bass, 1982), p. 103.

11. Charles Perrow, "The Analysis of Goals in Complex Organizations," *American Sociological Review* 26 (1961): 854–66; Georgiou, "The Goal Paradigm and Notes Toward a Counter Paradigm;" Howard E. Aldrich and Jeffrey Pfeffer, "Environments of Organizations," *Annual Review of Sociology* 2 (1976): 79–105.

12. Vernon W. Lippard, *A Half-Century of American Medical Education: 1920–1970* (New York: Josiah Macy, Jr., Foundation, 1974), pp. 52–53; Rosemary Stevens, *American Medicine and the Public Interest* (New Haven: Yale University Press, 1971), pp. 360–61; Cohen and March, *Leadership and Ambiguity: The American College President,* pp. 102, 107–8.

13. Ray E. Brown, "Financing Medical Education," in William G. Anlyan et al., *The Future of Medical Education* (Durham, N.C.: Duke University Press, 1973), p. 178.

14. Cf. Cohen and March, *Leadership and Ambiguity: The American College President,* pp. 100–2.

15. Howard S. Becker et al., *Boys in White* (1961; reprint ed., New Brunswick, N.J.: Transaction Books, 1977), pp. 270–71, 343–45; Robert H. Coombs and Blake P. Boyle, "The Transition to Medical School: Expectations versus Reality," in *Psychosocial Aspects of Medical Training,* ed. Robert H. Coombs and Clark E. Vincent (Springfield, Ill.: Thomas, 1971), pp. 96–98; John L. Caughey, "Clinical Experience and Clinical Responsibility: The Attitudes of Students," *Journal of Medical Education* 39 (1964): 434–35.

16. Becker et al., *Boys in White,* pp. 342–45.

17. Thomas H. Ham, "Educational Environment as Related to the Development of the Individual Student," in *The Ecology of the Medical Student,* ed. Helen Hofer Gee and Robert J. Glaser (Evanston, Ill.: Association of American Medical Colleges, 1958), pp. 74–75. The mean rankings for the 10 items varied from 2.5 to 8.4.

18. Robert H. Coombs, *Mastering Medicine* (New York: Free Press, 1978), pp. 42–47; Samuel W. Bloom, *Power and Dissent in the Medical School* (New York: Free Press, 1973), pp. 111, 122.

19. Hilliard Jason and Jane Westberg, *Teachers and Teaching in U.S. Medical Schools* (Norwalk, Conn.: Appleton-Century-Crofts, 1982), pp. 25, 36, 123–24; Jonathan R. Cole and James A. Lipton, "The Reputations of American Medical Schools," *Social Forces* 55 (1977): 662–84.

20. Ham, "Educational Environment as Related to the Development of the Individual Student," pp. 74–75; Bloom, *Power and Dissent in the Medical School,* pp. 7–8; Patricia L. Kendall, "The Relationship Between Medical Educators and Medical Practitioners," *Journal of Medical Education* 40, Part 2 (1965): 240.

21. Ibid.

22. Stephen P. Strickland, *Politics, Science, and Dread Disease* (Cambridge: Harvard University Press, 1972), p. 155.

23. Cf. William R. Willard, *Manpower and Educational Needs in Selected Professional Fields: Medicine* (n.p.: Southern Regional Education Board, 1973).

24. Jack Hadley, ed., *Medical Education Financing* (New York: Prodist, 1980); H. Hugh Fudenberg and Vijaya L. Melnick, eds., *Biomedical Scientists and Public Policy* (New York: Plenum Press, 1978).

25. Richard A. Rettig, *Cancer Crusade* (Princeton, N.J.: Princeton University Press, 1977).

Chapter 2

1. The first part of this chapter is based on William G. Rothstein, *American Physicians in the Nineteenth Century* (Baltimore: Johns Hopkins University Press, 1972), pp. 26–62.

2. Luther Hill, quoted in Iago Galdston, "Diagnosis in Historical Perspective," *Bulletin of the History of Medicine* 9 (1941): 379.

3. J. Worth Estes, "Therapeutic Practice in Colonial New England," in *Medicine in Colonial Massachusetts, 1620–1820,* ed. Philip Cash, Eric H. Christianson, and J. Worth Estes (Boston: Colonial Society of Massachusetts, 1980), pp. 293–96, 341.

4. Ibid., pp. 316–29.

5. Ibid., pp. 314, 316–29.

6. Ibid., pp. 341–42.

7. Ibid., pp. 299–304.

8. Ibid.

9. Ibid., pp. 300–5.

10. John Shrady, ed., *The College of Physicians and Surgeons, New York* (New York: n.d.) 1:73–76; Howard A. Kelly and Walter L. Burrage, *American Medical Biographies* (Baltimore: 1920), pp. 760–61; Emily A. Smith, *The Life and Letters of Nathan Smith* (New Haven: Yale University Press, 1913), pp. 65–66, 77.

11. Estes, "Therapeutic Practice in Colonial New England," pp. 308–10, 352.

12. Madge E. Pickard and R. Carlyle Buley, *The Midwest Pioneer* (New York: Schuman, 1946); Estes, "Therapeutic Practice in Colonial New England," p. 301.

13. Eric H. Christianson, "The Medical Practitioners of Massachusetts, 1630–1800," in *Medicine in Colonial Massachusetts, 1620–1820,* p. 54; Philip Cash, "The Professionalization of Boston Medicine, 1760–1803," in ibid., p. 90; Leo J. O'Hara, "An Emerging Profession: Philadelphia Medicine 1860–1900" (Ph.D. diss., University of Pennsylvania, 1976), pp. 20–22.

14. Estes, "Therapeutic Practice in Colonial New England," p. 295.

15. James J. Tyler, "Dr. Luther Spelman, Early Physician of the Western Reserve," *Ohio State Medical Journal* 34 (1938): 420–23.

16. Douglas L. Jones, "Charity, Medical Charity, and Dependency in Eighteenth-Century Essex County, Massachusetts," in *Medicine in Colonial Massachusetts, 1620–1820,* pp. 209–12; Estes, "Therapeutic Practice in Colonial New England," p. 295.

17. Albert Deutsch, "The Sick Poor in Colonial Times," *American Historical Review* 46 (1941): 560–79; David J. Rothman, *The Discovery of the Asylum* (Boston: Little, Brown, 1971), pp. 33–35; Jones, "Charity, Medical Charity, and Dependency in Eighteenth-Century Essex County, Massachusetts," pp. 199–213.

18. Leland V. Bell, *Treating the Mentally Ill: From Colonial Times to the Present* (New York: Praeger, 1980), p. 4; Rothman, *The Discovery of the Asylum,* pp. 33–41.

19. Rothman, *The Discovery of the Asylum,* p. 40; Benjamin J. Klebaner, "Public Poor Relief in America, 1790–1860," (Ph.D. diss., Columbia University, 1952), pp. 224–31; Robert J. Hunter, *The Origin of the Philadelphia General Hospital: Blockley Division* (Philadelphia, 1955), pp. 12–15; Robert J. Carlisle, ed., *An Account of Bellevue Hospital* (New York, 1893), pp. 27–28.

20. Gerald Grob, *Mental Institutions in America* (New York: Free Press, 1973), pp. 14–16.

21. Commission on Hospital Care, *Hospital Care in the United States* (Cambridge: Harvard University Press, 1957), pp. 434–35.

22. Deutsch, "The Sick Poor in Colonial Times," pp. 575–76; Hunter, *The Origin of the Philadelphia General Hospital: Blockley Division,* p. 15.

23. N. I. Bowditch, *A History of the Massachusetts General Hospital* (Boston, 1851), pp. 4–8.

24. Benjamin Franklin, *Some Account of the Pennsylvania Hospital* (Baltimore: Johns Hopkins Press, 1954), pp. 18–22.

25. Ibid., p. 4 (spelling modernized).

26. Ibid.

27. Ibid., pp. 5, 37; William H. Williams, *America's First Hospital: The Pennsylvania Hospital, 1751–1841* (Wayne, Pa.: Haverford House, 1976), pp. 10–14.

28. Thomas G. Morton, *The History of the Pennsylvania Hospital: 1751–1895* (Philadelphia, 1895), pp. 208–9; Eric Larrabee, *The Benevolent and Necessary Institution* (Garden City, N.Y.: Doubleday, 1971), pp. 107–8.

29. Grob, *Mental Institutions in America*, pp. 22, 48, 54.

30. Larrabee, *The Benevolent and Necessary Institution*, p. 108; William L. Russell, *The New York Hospital: A History of the Psychiatric Service 1771–1936* (New York: Columbia University Press, 1945), p. 43; Morton, *The History of the Pennsylvania Hospital: 1751–1895*, p. 210.

31. Robert W. Downie, "Pennsylvania Hospital Admissions, 1751–1850: A Survey," *Transactions and Studies of the College of Physicians of Philadelphia* 32 (1964): 27, 30, 34; Bowditch, *A History of the Massachusetts General Hospital*, pp. 385–86.

32. Morton, *The History of the Pennsylvania Hospital: 1751–1895*, p. 210; Larrabee, *The Benevolent and Necessary Institution*, p. 108.

33. Williams, *America's First Hospital: The Pennsylvania Hospital, 1751–1841*, pp. 59, 81–82, 151; Russell, *New York Hospital: A History of the Psychiatric Service 1771–1936*, pp. 73–75.

34. Benjamin J. Lewis, *VA Medical Programs in Relation to Medical Schools* (Washington, D.C.: U.S. G.P.O., 1970), pp. 24–26; Leonard K. Eaton, *New England Hospitals: 1790–1833* (Ann Arbor: University of Michigan Press, 1957), p. 24.

35. Williams, *America's First Hospital: The Pennsylvania Hospital, 1751–1841*, pp. 130; Downie, "Pennsylvania Hospital Admissions, 1751–1850: A Survey," pp. 24–25; Russell, *New York Hospital: A History of the Psychiatric Service 1771–1936*, p. 66; Larrabee, *The Benevolent and Necessary Institution*, p. 205.

36. Williams, *America's First Hospital: The Pennsylvania Hospital, 1751–1841*, pp. 14–15; Eaton, *New England Hospitals: 1790–1833*, pp. 105–10.

37. Klebaner, "Public Poor Relief in America, 1790–1860," pp. 254–482.

38. Charles E. Rosenberg, "Social Class and Medical Care in Nineteenth-Century America: The Rise and Fall of the Dispensary," *Journal of the History of Medicine* 29 (1974): 33; Charles C. Savage, "Dispensaries Historically and Locally Considered," in *Hospitals, Dispensaries and Nursing*, ed. John S. Billings and Henry M. Hurd (Baltimore: Johns Hopkins Press, 1894), pp. 633–35; Francis W. Sinkler, "The Philadelphia Dispensary," in *Founder's Week Memorial Volume*, ed. Frederick P. Henry (Philadelphia, 1909), p. 745.

39. C. Herbert Baxley, ed., *A History of the Baltimore General Dispensary* (Baltimore, 1963), pp. 16–20, 22, 46.

40. John Duffy, *A History of Public Health in New York City, 1625–1866* (New York: Russell Sage Foundation, 1968), pp. 245–47, 507; Sinkler, "The Philadelphia Dispensary," p. 749; Baxley, *A History of the Baltimore General Dispensary*, p. 97.

41. C. Helen Brock, "The Influence of Europe on Colonial Massachusetts Medicine," in *Medicine in Colonial Massachusetts 1620–1820*, pp. 107–9; Martin Kaufman, *American Medical Education: The Formative Years, 1765–1910* (Westport, Conn.: Greenwood Press, 1976), pp. 9–10.

42. Christianson, "The Medical Practitioners of Massachusetts, 1630–1800," pp. 56–58.

43. Ibid., p. 61.

44. Ibid., pp. 57, 61; Philip Cash, "The Professionalization of Boston Medicine, 1760–1803," pp. 70, 90.

45. Rothstein, *American Physicians in the Nineteenth Century*, pp. 85–87; Kaufman,

American Medical Education: The Formative Years, 1765–1910, pp. 6–8. The discussion below is based on a number of autobiographies of physicians trained in the late eighteenth and early nineteenth centuries.

46. Louis L. Tucker, *Puritan Protagonist: President Thomas Clap of Yale College* (Chapel Hill: University of North Carolina Press, 1962), p. 27; Charles M. Haar, ed., *The Golden Age of American Law* (New York: Braziller, 1965), p. 84; Paul M. Hamlin, *Legal Education in Colonial New York* (New York, 1939), pp. 42–45.

47. Cash, "The Professionalization of Boston Medicine, 1760–1803," p. 76.

48. See the following studies by Robert F. Seybolt: *The Evening School in Colonial America* (Urbana, Ill.: University of Illinois Press, 1925); *The Evening Schools of Colonial New York City* (Albany, N.Y., 1921); *The Private Schools of Colonial Boston* (Cambridge: Harvard University Press, 1935); *Source Studies in American Colonial Education: The Private School* (Urbana: University of Illinois, 1925).

49. John B. Blake, "The Development of American Anatomy Acts," *Journal of Medical Education* 30 (1955): 432.

50. Edward C. Atwater, "The Protracted Labor and Brief Life of a Country Medical School," *Journal of the History of Medicine* 34 (1979): 352.

51. William Norwood, *Medical Education in the United States Before the Civil War* (Philadelphia: University of Pennsylvania Press, 1944).

52. Ibid., pp. 174, 187, 225–26.

53. Richard Hofstadter and Walter P. Metzger, *The Development of Academic Freedom in the United States* (New York: Columbia University Press, 1955), pp. 115–19; Gerard W. Gawalt, *The Promise of Power: The Emergence of the Legal Profession in Massachusetts 1760–1840* (Westport, Conn.: Greenwood Press, 1979), pp. 141–43.

54. Theodore Hornberger, *Scientific Thought in the American Colleges 1638–1800* (1946; reprint ed., New York: Octagon Books, 1968), pp. 18–21, 27–28, 48–57, 65, 72; Hofstadter and Metzger, *The Development of Academic Freedom in the United States*, pp. 195–96.

55. Walter C. Eells, *Baccalaureate Degrees Conferred by American Colleges in the 17th and 18th Centuries* (Washington, D.C.: U.S. Department of Health, Education and Welfare, 1958), pp. 4–10.

56. Leon B. Richardson, *History of Dartmouth* (Hanover, N.H.: Dartmouth College Publications, 1932), 1:246–49; Alexander Cowie, *Educational Problems at Yale College in the Eighteenth Century* (New Haven: Yale University Press, 1936), p. 26; Charles F. Thwing, *The American College in American Life* (New York: Putnam, 1897), p. 14.

57. Rothstein, *American Physicians in the Nineteenth Century*, pp. 93, 98.

58. Frederick C. Waite, *The First Medical College in Vermont: Castleton, 1818–1862* (Montpelier: Vermont Historical Society, 1949), pp. 51–53, 93–94; Martin Kaufman, *The University of Vermont College of Medicine* (Hanover, N.H., 1979).

59. Waite, *The First Medical College in Vermont: Castleton, 1818–1862*, p. 107; David F. Allmendinger, Jr., *Paupers and Scholars* (New York: St. Martin's Press, 1975).

60. Norwood, *Medical Education in the United States Before the Civil War*, pp. 403–4.

61. Ibid., p. 404.

62. Waite, *The First Medical College in Vermont: Castleton, 1818–1862*, pp. 67, 109–11.

63. Ibid., pp. 77, 98.

64. Ibid., p. 99.

65. Cf. D. Hayes Agnew, "The Medical History of the Philadelphia Almshouse," in *History of Blockley*, ed. John W. Croskey (Philadelphia: Davis, 1929), pp. 33–40.

66. See Shrady, *The College of Physicians and Surgeons, New York*, pp. 362–64.

67. John B. Blake, "Anatomy," in *The Education of American Physicians,* ed. Ronald L. Numbers (Berkeley and Los Angeles: University of California Press, 1980), pp. 29–47; Audrey B. Davis, *Medicine and Its Technology* (Westport, Conn.: Greenwood Press, 1981), pp. 31–32.

68. Henry B. Shafer, *The American Medical Profession: 1783 to 1850* (New York: Columbia University Press, 1936), p. 65; Charles B. Johnson, "Getting My Anatomy in the Sixties," *Bulletin of the Society of Medical History of Chicago* 3 (1923): 109–10.

69. James Whorton, "Chemistry," in *The Education of American Physicians,* pp. 78–82; John H. Warner, "Physiology," in *The Education of American Physicians,* pp. 50–54.

70. David L. Cowen, "Materia Medica and Pharmacology," in *The Education of American Physicians,* pp. 97–105.

71. Shafer, *The American Medical Profession: 1783 to 1850,* pp. 69–72; Davis, *Medicine and Its Technology,* pp. 32–33.

72. Edward C. Atwater, "Financial Subsidies for American Medical Education Before 1940" (Masters degree essay, Johns Hopkins University, 1974).

Chapter 3

1. This account is drawn from William G. Rothstein, *American Physicians in the Nineteenth Century* (Baltimore: Johns Hopkins University Press, 1972).

2. Stanley J. Reiser, *Medicine and the Reign of Technology* (Cambridge, England: Cambridge University Press, 1978), pp. 31–4; Audrey B. Davis, *Medicine and Its Technology* (Westport, Conn.: Greenwood Press, 1981), pp. 87–92.

3. Harry F. Dowling, "The Impact of New Discoveries on Medical Practice," in *Mainstreams of Medicine,* ed. Lester S. King (Austin: University of Texas Press, 1971), pp. 108–9; William H. Hubbard, Jr., "The Origins of Medicinals," in *Advances in American Medicine,* ed. John Z. Bowers and Elizabeth F. Purcell (New York: Josiah Macy, Jr., Foundation, 1976), 2:692.

4. Heber Chase, *The Medical Student's Guide* (Philadelphia, 1842), p. 35.

5. John H. Hollister, *Memories of Eighty Years* (Chicago, 1912), p. 60.

6. Samuel D. Gross, *Autobiography* (Philadelphia: Barrie, 1887), 1:152–53.

7. Quoted in Rothstein, *American Physicians in the Nineteenth Century,* p. 62; John S. Haller, Jr., *American Medicine in Transition: 1840–1910* (Urbana: University of Illinois Press, 1981).

8. Gross, *Autobiography,* p. 56.

9. Ibid., p. 58. See John Duffy, *Sword of Pestilence: The New Orleans Yellow Fever Epidemic of 1853* (Baton Rouge: Louisiana State University Press, 1966); Charles E. Rosenberg, *The Cholera Years* (Chicago: University of Chicago Press, 1962).

10. C. W. Townsend and A. Coolidge, Jr., "The Mortality of Acute Lobar Pneumonia," *Transactions of the American Climatological Association* 6 (1889): 41–43; Katherine A. Harvey, "Practicing Medicine at the Baltimore Almshouse, 1828–1850," *Maryland Historical Magazine* 74 (1979): 226–28.

11. U.S. Bureau of the Census, *Historical Statistics of the United States* (Washington, D.C.: U.S. G.P.O. 1975), 1:76; Barnes Riznik, "The Professional Lives of Early Nineteenth-Century New England Doctors," *Journal of the History of Medicine* 19 (1964): 7n; Edward C. Atwater, "The Medical Profession in a New Society, Rochester, New York (1811–60)," *Bulletin of the History of Medicine* 47 (1973): 229.

12. Gross, *Autobiography,* pp. 152–53; Leo J. O'Hara, "An Emerging Profession: Philadelphia Medicine 1860–1900," (Ph.D. diss., University of Pennsylvania, 1976), p. 33.

13. Riznik, "The Professional Lives of Early Nineteenth-Century New England Doctors," pp. 14–15; O'Hara, "An Emerging Profession: Philadelphia Medicine 1860–1900," pp. 36–38.

14. James H. Cassedy, "The Flourishing and Character of Early American Medical Journalism, 1797–1860," *Journal of the History of Medicine* 38 (1983): 135–50.

15. Charles F. Bolduan, "Public Health in New York City," *Bulletin of the New York Academy of Medicine* 19 (1943): 423–40.

16. Howard P. Chudacoff, *The Evolution of American Urban Society* (Englewood Cliffs, N.J.: Prentice-Hall, 1975), p. 56.

17. Oscar Handlin, *Boston's Immigrants,* rev. ed. (1959; reprint ed., New York: Atheneum, 1968), pp. 101–14; Betsy Blackmar, "Re-Walking the 'Walking City': Housing and Property Relations in New York City, 1780–1840," *Radical History Review* 21 (1979): 131–48; John H. Griscom, *The Sanitary Condition of the Laboring Population of New York* (1845; reprint ed., New York: Arno Press, 1970), pp. 6–10.

18. Handlin, *Boston's Immigrants,* pp. 114–16, 330; Thomas E. Cone, Jr., *History of American Pediatrics* (Boston: Little, Brown, 1979), pp. 73–74.

19. Handlin, *Boston's Immigrants,* p. 240; Priscilla F. Clement, *Welfare and the Poor in the Nineteenth-Century City* (Cranbury N.J.: Associated Universities Presses, 1985), pp. 174–76; Robert Ernst, *Immigrant Life in New York City, 1825–1863* (1949; reprint ed., Port Washington, N.Y.: Friedman, 1965), p. 201.

20. John Duffy, *A History of Public Health in New York City, 1625–1866* (New York: Russell Sage Foundation, 1968), pp. 247, 506–11.

21. Michael M. Davis, Jr., and Andrew R. Warner, *Dispensaries: Their Management and Development* (New York: Macmillan, 1918), p. 8; Duffy, *A History of Public Health in New York City, 1625–1866,* pp. 507, 509.

22. Edward C. Atwater, "Financial Subsidies for American Medical Education Before 1940" (Masters degree essay, Johns Hopkins University, 1974), pp. 44–47.

23. Eric Larrabee, *The Benevolent and Necessary Institution* (Garden City, N.Y.: Doubleday, 1971), p. 211; Harry F. Dowling, *City Hospitals* (Cambridge: Harvard University Press, 1982), pp. 13–14; William H. Williams, *America's First Hospital: The Pennsylvania Hospital, 1751–1841* (Wayne, Pa.: Haverford House, 1976), p. 144; Ernst, *Immigrant Life in New York City, 1825–1863,* p. 200; Handlin, *Boston's Immigrants,* pp. 118–19.

24. Harvey, "Practicing Medicine at the Baltimore Almshouse, 1828–1850," pp. 225–26; Robert W. Downie, "Pennsylvania Hospital Admissions, 1751–1850," *Transactions and Studies of the College of Physicians of Philadelphia* 4th series, 32 (1964): 22, 26; Charles Lawrence, *History of the Philadelphia Almshouse and Hospitals* (n.p.: 1905), pp. 151–53.

25. Harvey, "Practicing Medicine at the Baltimore Almshouse, 1828–1850," pp. 229–30; Downie, "Pennsylvania Hospital Admissions, 1751–1850," pp. 28–29; Thomas G. Morton, *The History of the Pennsylvania Hospital, 1751–1895* (Philadelphia, 1895), p. 201.

26. Harvey, "Practicing Medicine at the Baltimore Almshouse, 1828–1850," pp. 230–31; Downie, "Pennsylvania Hospital Admissions, 1751–1850," p. 34.

27. Ibid., pp. 22–23; Gerald N. Grob, *Mental Institutions in America* (New York: Free Press, 1973), pp. 69–74, 84–85; Lawrence, *History of the Philadelphia Almshouse and Hospitals,* pp. 151–52.

28. David B. Lovejoy, Jr., "The Hospital and Society: the Growth of Hospitals in Rochester, New York," *Bulletin of the History of Medicine* 49 (1975): 537–40; William M. Welch, "The Municipal Hospital for Contagious and Infectious Diseases," in *Founders Week Memorial Volume,* ed. Frederick P. Henry (Philadelphia, 1909), pp. 521–26.

29. Dowling, *City Hospitals,* p. 17; D. B. St. John Roosa, "The Old New York Hospital," *Post-Graduate* 15 (Jan, 1900): 19.

30. Toba S. Kerson, "Almshouse to Municipal Hospital," *Bulletin of the History of Medicine* 55 (1981): 208; Harvey, "Practicing Medicine at the Baltimore Almshouse, 1828–1850," p. 224; D. Hayes Agnew, "The Medical History of the Philadelphia Almshouse," in *History of Blockley,* ed. John W. Croskey (Philadelphia:, Davis, 1929), p. 51.

31. Larrabee, *The Benevolent and Necessary Institution,* pp. 121–22; Agnew, "The Medical History of the Philadelphia Almshouse," pp. 49–50; James C. White, *Sketches from My Life, 1833–1913* (Cambridge, Mass.: Riverside Press, 1914), p. 72.

32. Lawrence, *History of the Philadelphia Almshouse and Hospitals,* pp. 156–57.

33. Harvey, "Practicing Medicine at the Baltimore Almshouse, 1828–1850," p. 232; Lawrence, *History of the Philadelphia Almshouse and Hospitals,* pp. 158–59.

34. Thomas A. Emmet, *Incidents of My Life* (New York: Putnam, 1911), p. 331.

35. Dowling, *City Hospitals,* pp. 15–16; J. Collins Warren, *To Work in the Vineyard of Surgery,* ed. Edward D. Churchill (Cambridge: Harvard University Press, 1958), p. 51.

36. Duffy, *A History of Public Health in New York City, 1625–1866,* pp. 253–54, 488; Ernest Caulfield, "The General State of American Pediatrics in 1855 with Particular Reference to Philadelphia," *Pediatrics* 19 (1957): 458; Leonard K. Eaton, *New England Hospitals: 1790–1833* (Ann Arbor: University of Michigan Press, 1957), pp. 222–25.

37. Lovejoy, "The Hospital and Society: the Growth of Hospitals in Rochester, New York," p. 544; Duffy, *A History of Public Health in New York, 1625–1866,* p. 502; George Rosen, *The Specialization of Medicine* (1944; reprint ed., New York: Arno Press, 1972), p. 34; Eaton, *New England Hospitals: 1790–1833,* p. 226.

38. Larrabee, *The Benevolent and Necessary Institution,* pp. 210–11.

39. Francis R. Packard, "The Pennsylvania Hospital," in *Founders' Week Memorial Volume,* p. 601; Agnew, "The Medical History of the Philadelphia Almshouse," p. 39.

40. Rothstein, *American Physicians in the Nineteenth Century,* p. 93.

41. David B. Potts, "American Colleges in the Nineteenth Century," *History of Education Quarterly* 11 (1971): 367; M. L. North, "A Glance at Medicine in Philadelphia— No. II," *Boston Medical and Surgical Journal* 26 (1842): 27.

42. Atwater, "Financial Subsidies for American Medical Education Before 1940," p. 33.

43. Robert P. Hudson, "Patterns of Medical Education in Nineteenth Century America" (Masters degree essay, Johns Hopkins University, 1966), p. 53; O'Hara, "An Emerging Profession: Philadelphia Medicine, 1860–1900," pp. 97, 113; Frederick C. Waite, "The Professional Education of Pioneer Ohio Physicians," *Ohio State Archaeological and Historical Quarterly* 48 (1939): 190.

44. Frederick C. Waite, *The First Medical College in Vermont: Castleton, 1818–1862* (Montpelier: Vermont Historical Society, 1949), pp. 100–6; Frederick C. Waite, *The Story of a Country Medical College* (Montpelier, Vt.: Vermont Historical Society, 1945), pp. 122–24; Hudson, "Patterns of Medical Education in Nineteenth Century America," p. 29.

45. Rothstein, *American Physicians in the Nineteenth Century,* p. 129; Colin B. Burke, *American Collegiate Populations* (New York: New York University Press, 1982), pp. 132–33, 187–88.

46. Thomas F. Harrington, *The Harvard Medical School* (New York: Lewis, 1905), 2:491–92; Joseph Carson, *A History of the Medical Department of the University of Pennsylvania* (Philadelphia: Lindsay and Blakiston, 1869), pp. 219–20; Waite, *The First Medical College in Vermont: Castleton, 1818–1862,* pp. 104–13.

47. Charles B. Johnson, *Sixty Years in Medical Harness* (New York: Medical Life Press, 1926), pp. 13–14; John Shrady, ed., *The College of Physicians and Surgeons, New York* (New York: Lewis, n.d.), p. 89.

48. Harrington, *The Harvard Medical School* 2:473; N. S. Davis, *History of Medical Education and Institutions in the United States* (Chicago: Griggs, 1851), p. 167.

49. William F. Norwood, *Medical Education in the United States Before the Civil War* (1944; reprint ed., New York: Arno Press, 1971), pp. 392–95.

50. Stanley M. Guralnick, *Science and the Ante-Bellum College* (Philadelphia: American Philosophical Society, 1975), pp. 98–100; James H. Cassedy, "The Microscope in American Medical Science, 1840–1860," *Isis* 67 (1976): 81–82.

51. George H. Daniels, *American Science in the Age of Jackson* (New York: Columbia University Press, 1968), pp. 4–5, 234–35; The main sources of biographical information were Norwood, *Medical Education in the United States Before the Civil War;* Martin Kaufman, Stuart Galishoff, and Todd L. Savitt, eds., *Dictionary of American Medical Biography* (Westport, Conn.: Greenwood Press, 1984); Howard A. Kelly and Walter L. Burrage, *American Medical Biographies* (Baltimore, 1920).

52. Samuel C. Busey, *Personal Reminiscences and Recollections* (Washington, D.C., 1895), p. 41.

53. Waite, *The First Medical College in Vermont: Castleton, 1818–1862*, pp. 53–54; Guralnick, *Science and the Ante-Bellum College*, pp. 98–99, 114; Clark A. Elliott, "The American Scientist in Antebellum Society," *Social Studies of Science* 5 (1975): 93–108; Sally G. Kohlstedt, *The Formation of the American Scientific Community* (Urbana: University of Illinois Press, 1976), pp. 192, 210–11, 219.

54. Guralnick, *Science and the Ante-Bellum American College*, p. ix.

55. Thomas R. Lounsbury, "The Sheffield Scientific School," in *Yale College*, ed. William L. Kinglsey (New York: Holt, 1879), 2:105–11; Russell H. Chittenden, *History of the Sheffield Scientific School* (New Haven: Yale University Press, 1928); Charles L. Jackson and Gregory P. Baxter, "Chemistry: 1865–1929," in *The Development of Harvard University 1869–1919*, ed. Samuel E. Morison (Cambridge: Harvard University Press, 1930), p. 259; Hector J. Hughes, "Engineering," in Ibid., pp. 414–15; Leon B. Richardson, *History of Dartmouth College* (Hanover, N.H.: Dartmouth College Publications, 1932), 1:422–27.

56. R. Freeman Butts, *The College Charts its Course* (New York: McGraw-Hill, 1939), pp. 129–31; [Charles W. Eliot], "The New Education" *Atlantic Monthly* 23 (1869): 203–20, 358–67.

57. Bruce Sinclair, "The Promise of the Future: Technical Education," in *Nineteenth-Century American Science*, ed. George H. Daniels (Evanston, Ill.: Northwestern University Press, 1972), pp. 268–69.

58. A. E. Fossier, "History of Medicine in New Orleans from Its Birth to the Civil War," *Annals of Medical History* n.s. 6 (1934): 341–42.

59. White, *Sketches from My Life, 1833–1913*, pp. 54, 152.

60. J. S. Billings, "Literature and Institutions," in Edward H. Clarke et al., *A Century of American Medicine 1776–1876* (1876; reprint ed., Brinklow, Md., 1962), pp. 298–327.

61. Davis, *Medicine and Its Technology*, pp. 32–33; Eugene F. Cordell, *Historical Sketch of the University of Maryland School of Medicine* (Baltimore, 1891), p. 125.

62. Norwood, *Medical Education in the United States Before the Civil War*, p. 401.

63. Cordell, *Historical Sketch of the University of Maryland School of Medicine*, pp. 45–46, 83–84.

64. John Ware, Jacob Bigelow, and O. W. Holmes, "The Views of the Medical Faculty of Harvard University, Relative to the Extension of the Lecture Term," *Transactions of the American Medical Association* 2 (1849): 354.

65. Ibid., pp. 357–58.

66. George W. Corner, *Two Centuries of Medicine: A History of the School of Medicine, University of Pennsylvania* (Philadelphia: Lippincott, 1965), p. 90; *43d Annual Circular of the Medical Department of the University of Maryland, Session 1850–51* (Baltimore, 1850).

67. Busey, *Personal Reminiscences and Recollections*, pp. 31–37.

68. Gross, *Autobiography*, pp. 197–98.

69. Edward Parrish, *Summer Medical Teaching in Philadelphia: An Introductory Lecture* (Philadelphia, 1857), p. 4.

70. Dale C. Smith, "The Emergence of Organized Clinical Instruction in the Nineteenth Century American Cities of Boston, New York, and Philadelphia," (Ph.D. diss., University of Minnesota, 1979), pp. 127–45.

71. Harrington, *The Harvard Medical School*, 2:496–501; White, *Sketches from Mr. Life, 1833–1913*, pp. 54–72; Smith, "The Emergence of Organized Clinical Instruction in the Nineteenth Century American Cities of Boston, New York, and Philadelphia," pp. 189–210.

72. Harrington, *The Harvard Medical School*, 2:497–500.

73. Chase, *The Medical Student's Guide*, pp. 27–28.

74. Simon Baatz, "'A Very Diffused Disposition:' Dissecting Schools in Philadelphia, 1823–25," *Pennsylvania Magazine of History and Biography* 108 (1984): 203–15; Smith, "The Emergence of Organized Clinical Instruction in the Nineteenth Century American Cities of Boston, New York, and Philadelphia," pp. 68–72; 113–19; Parrish, *Summer Medical Teaching in Philadelphia: An Introductory Lecture*, pp. 7–9; Harold J. Abrahams, *Extinct Medical Schools of Nineteenth-Century Philadelphia* (Philadelphia: University of Pennsylvania Press, 1966), pp. 111–12.

75. Smith, "The Emergence of Organized Clinical Instruction in the Nineteenth Century American Cities of Boston, New York, and Philadelphia," pp. 124–26; Parrish, *Summer Medical Teaching in Philadelphia: An Introductory Lecture*, p. 13.

76. "Some Account of the Schools of Medicine . . . , " *Medical and Surgical Reporter* n.s. 3 (Oct., 1859): 18–20; Parrish, *Summer Medical Teaching in Philadelphia: An Introductory Lecture*, pp. 9–13.

77. Ibid., p. 4.

78. Smith, "The Emergence of Organized Clinical Instruction in the Nineteenth Century American Cities of Boston, New York, and Philadelphia," pp. 172–74; Martin Kaufman, *The University of Vermont College of Medicine* (Hanover, N.H., 1979), pp. 56–57.

79. Parrish, *Summer Medical Teaching in Philadelphia: An Introductory Lecture*, p. 19.

80. See Smith, "The Emergence of Organized Clinical Instruction in the Nineteenth Century American Cities of Boston, New York, and Philadelphia;" Agnew, "The Medical History of the Philadelphia Almshouse," pp. 33–51.

81. White, *Sketches from My Life, 1833–1913*, pp. 56–57.

82. M. L. North, "A Glance at Medicine in Philadelphia—No. III," *Boston Medical and Surgical Journal* 26 (1842): 42–43; St. John Roosa, "The Old New York Hospital," p. 15.

83. Virginia G. Drachman, "The Loomis Trial: Social Mores and Obstetrics in the Mid-Nineteenth Century," in *Health Care in America*, ed. Susan Reverby and David Rosner (Philadelphia: Temple University Press, 1979), pp. 67–83.

84. Lawrence, *History of the Philadelphia Almshouse and Hospitals*, p. 98; White, *Sketches from My Life, 1833–1913*, p. 60.

85. Larrabee, *The Benevolent and Necessary Institution*, pp. 217–18.

86. Lawrence, *History of the Philadelphia Almshouse and Hospitals*, pp. 98–99.

87. W. W. Gerhard, "Remarks on Clinical Education," *American Journal of the Medical Sciences* 18 (1836): 388.

88. Hudson, "Patterns of Medical Education in Nineteenth Century America," p. 108.

89. Waite, *The Story of a Country Medical College*, p. 26. See E. C. Dudley, *The Medicine Man* (New York: Sears, 1927), pp. 150, 210–11.

90. Victor C. Vaughn, *A Doctor's Memories* (Indianapolis: Bobbs-Merrill, 1926), pp. 193–94; Dudley, *Medicine Man*, p. 160. See also Charles B. Johnson, "Getting my Anatomy in the Sixties," *Bulletin of the Society of Medical History of Chicago* 3 (1923): 111–14.

91. Otto Juettner, *Daniel Drake and His Followers* (Cincinnati: Harvey, 1909), p. 42; Gross, *Autobiography,* 1:154–59.

92. O'Hara, "An Emerging Profession: Philadelphia Medicine 1860–1900," pp. 74–75: George H. Calcott, *A History of the University of Maryland* (Baltimore: Maryland Historical Society, 1966), p. 129; Frederick C. Waite, *Western Reserve University Centennial History of the School of Medicine* (Cleveland: Western Reserve University Press, 1946), p. 133; Waite, *The Story of a Country Medical College*, p. 119; Waite, *The First Medical College in Vermont: Castleton, 1818–1862*, p. 97.

93. See Rothstein, *American Physicians in the Nineteenth Century.*

Chapter 4

1. U.S. Bureau of the Census, *Historical Statistics of the United States* (Washington, D.C.: U.S. G.P.O., 1975), 1: 76.

2. Francis A. Long, *A Prairie Doctor of the Eighties* (Norfolk, Nebr., 1937), pp. 129, 165–66; Arthur E. Hertzler, *The Horse and Buggy Doctor* (Garden City, N.Y.: Blue Ribbon Books, 1941), pp. 61–94; William N. Macartney, *Fifty Years a Country Doctor* (New York: Dutton, 1938), pp. 104–5.

3. Charles B. Johnson, *Sixty Years in Medical Harness* (New York: Medical Life Press, 1926), pp. 93–94; J. M. T. Finney, *A Surgeon's Life* (New York: Putnam, 1940), pp. 62–63.

4. Hertzler, *The Horse and Buggy Doctor*, pp. 51–53.

5. Ibid., pp. 78, 99, 96.

6. Arpad G. Gerster, *Recollections of a New York Surgeon* (New York: Hoeber, 1917), p. 211; Norman Walker, "The Medical Profession in the United States," *Edinburgh Medical Journal* 37 (1891): 245.

7. Gerster, *Recollections of a New York Surgeon,* pp. 162–63.

8. Hertzler, *The Horse and Buggy Doctor,* pp. 110–11; John Duffy, *A History of Public Health in New York City, 1866–1966* (New York: Russell Sage Foundation, 1974), pp. 159–162; U.S. Bureau of the Census, *Historical Statistics of the United States,* 1: 63.

9. Long, *A Prairie Doctor of the Eighties,* p. 116.

10. Johnson, *Sixty Years in Medical Harness,* pp. 100–1.

11. U.S. Bureau of the Census. *Historical Statistics of the United States,* 1:63; Isaac A. Abt, *Baby Doctor* (New York: McGraw-Hill, 1944), pp. 89–91; Thomas E. Cone, Jr., *History of American Pediatrics* (Boston: Little, Brown, 1979), pp. 105–24.

12. William G. Rothstein, *American Physicians in the Nineteenth Century* (Baltimore: Johns Hopkins University Press, 1972), pp. 181–97.

13. Abt, *Baby Doctor,* pp. 17–18.

14. Long, *A Prairie Doctor of the Eighties,* p. 122.

15. Stanley J. Reiser, *Medicine and the Reign of Technology* (Cambridge, England: Cambridge University Press, 1978), pp. 45–121; Audrey B. Davis, *Medicine and its Technology* (Westport, Conn.: Greenwood Press, 1981).

16. Ibid., pp. 149–50, 236.

17. Ibid., pp. 185–86.

18. Audrey B. Davis, "Life Insurance and the Physical Examination," *Bulletin of the History of Medicine* 55 (1981): 397–403.

19. Davis, *Medicine and its Technology*, pp. 181–82; William G. Rothstein, "Pathology: The Evolution of a Specialty in American Medicine," *Medicine Care* 17 1979): 979–80.

20. Davis, *Medicine and its Technology*, p. 147; Rothstein, *American Physicians in the Nineteenth Century*, pp. 272, 324–25.

21. *Ibid.*, pp. 265–81.

22. Davis, *Medicine and Its Technology*, p. 240.

23. Rosemary Stevens, *American Medicine and the Public Interest* (New Haven, Conn.: Yale University Press, 1971); Rothstein, *American Physicians in the Nineteenth Century*, p. 213.

24. Ibid., pp. 207–12; James C. White, *Sketches from My Life, 1833–1913* (Cambridge, Mass.: Riverside Press, 1914), pp. 270–71.

25. Gerster, *Recollections of a New York Surgeon*, p. 191; Robert T. Morris, *Fifty Years a Surgeon* (New York: Dutton, 1935), pp. 108–20; Cone, Jr., *History of American Pediatrics*, p. 125; J. L. Bubis, *Women Are My Problem* (New York: Comet Press, 1953), pp. 11–12.

26. Rothstein, *American Physicians in the Nineteenth Century*, pp. 211–12.

27. Robert P. Hudson, "Patterns of Medical Education in Nineteenth Century America" (Masters degree essay: Johns Hopkins University, 1966), p. 124; Rothstein, *American Physicians in the Nineteenth Century*, pp. 211–12; Edward C. Atwater, "The Physicians of Rochester, New York: 1860–1910," *Bulletin of the History of Medicine* 51 (1977): 105.

28. Rothstein, *American Physicians in the Nineteenth Century*, pp. 250–53.

29. Robert F. Weir, "Personal Reminiscences of the New York Hospital," *General Bulletin of the Society of the New York Hospital* 1 (1917): 23–25.

30. J. Collins Warren, *To Work in the Vineyard of Surgery*, ed. Edward D. Churchill (Cambridge: Harvard University Press, 1958), pp. 75–77.

31. Franklin H. Martin, *The Joy of Living* (Garden City, N.Y.: Doubleday Doran, 1933), 1:254, 210; Joseph C. Aub and Ruth K. Hapgood, *Pioneer in Modern Medicine: David Linn Edsall of Harvard* (Boston, 1970), p. 15.

32. Macartney, *Fifty Years a Country Doctor*, p. 65–72.

33. Finney, *A Surgeon's Life*, pp. 88–91.

34. B. A. Watson, "Lister's System of Aseptic Wound Treatment," *Transactions of the American Surgical Association* 1 (1883): 219–23.

35. Warren, *To Work in the Vineyard of Surgery*, pp. 167–68; Frederic A. Washburn, *The Massachusetts General Hospital* (Boston: Houghton Mifflin, 1939), p. 73.

36. Finney, *A Surgeon's Life*, pp. 81, 112–18; Macartney, *Fifty Years a Country Doctor*, pp. 77–78; John B. Wheeler, *Memoirs of a Small-Town Surgeon* (New York: Stokes, 1935), pp. 217–38; Long, *A Prairie Doctor of the Eighties*, pp. 82–94; Urling C. Coe, *Frontier Doctor* (New York: Macmillan, 1940), pp. 12–13; Morris, *Fifty Years a Surgeon*.

37. Ibid., pp. 126, 84.

38. E. C. Dudley, *The Medicine Man* (New York: Sears, 1927), p. 243. See also Victor C. Vaughn, *A Doctor's Life* (Indianapolis: Bobbs-Merrill, 1926).

39. Hertzler, *The Horse and Buggy Doctor*, pp. 214–18; Almroth E. Wright, "A Lecture on the Treatment of War Wounds," *Lancet* 1 (1917): 943–45.

40. Thomas A. Emmet, *Incidents of My Life* (New York: Putnam, 1911), p. 334; Martin, *The Joy of Living*, 1:386; Hertzler, *The Horse and Buggy Doctor*, pp. 224, 247.

41. Macartney, *Fifty Years a Country Doctor*, pp. 164–65.

42. Charles C. Savage, "Dispensaries Historically and Locally Considered," in *Hospi-*

tals, Dispensaries, and Nursing, ed. John S. Billings and Henry M. Hurd (Baltimore: Johns Hopkins Press, 1894), pp. 639–42; Alexander Lambert, "Report of the Committee on Social Insurance," *Journal of the American Medical Association* 68 (1917): 1752; Morris J. Vogel, *The Invention of the Modern Hospital* (Chicago: University of Chicago Press, 1980), p. 90; C. Herbert Baxley, ed., *A History of the Baltimore General Dispensary* (Baltimore, Md., 1963), p. 97; Leo. J. O'Hara, "An Emerging Profession: Philadelphia Medicine, 1860–1900," (Ph.D. diss., University of Pennsylvania, 1976), pp. 215–16.

43. David B. Delavan, *Early Days of the Presbyterian Hospital* (n.p.: 1926), p. 167; Savage, "Dispensaries Historically and Locally Considered," p. 647.

44. Michael M. Davis, Jr. and Andrew R. Warner, *Dispensaries: Their Management and Development* (New York: Macmillan, 1918), pp. 353–54; Lambert, "Report of the Committee on Social Insurance," p. 1752.

45. Savage, "Dispensaries Historically and Locally Considered," p. 649; Lambert, "Report of the Committee on Social Insurance," p. 1752; Charles E. Rosenberg, "Social Class and Medical Care in Nineteenth-Century America," *Journal of the History of Medicine* 29 (1974): 40–41.

46. Joseph Hirsh and Beka Doherty, *The First Hundred Years of the Mount Sinai Hospital of New York* (New York: Random House, 1952), pp. 60–62; Savage, "Dispensaries Historically and Locally Considered," p. 639n; George H. M. Rowe, "Historical Description of the Buildings and Grounds of the Boston City Hospital," in *A History of the Boston City Hospital,* ed. David W. Cheever et al. (Boston, 1906), p. 67; John B. Blake, "The Municipal History of the Boston City Hospital," in ibid., p. 125.

47. Savage, "Dispensaries Historically and Locally Considered," p. 638; Hirsh and Doherty, *The First Hundred Years of the Mount Sinai Hospital of New York,* pp. 62–63; Vogel, *The Invention of the Modern Hospital,* pp. 50–51, 89–91.

48. Michael M. Davis, Jr., "Present Status and Problems of Out-Patient Work," *Transactions of the American Hospital Association* 15 (1913): 318–19, 330.

49. Davis and Warner, *Dispensaries: Their Management and Development,* p. 244.

50. Vogel, *The Invention of the Modern Hospital,* pp. 8–12; Abt, *Baby Doctor,* pp. 39, 129, 134–36.

51. Philip Shoemaker and Mary Van Hulle Jones, "From Infirmaries to Intensive Care: Hospitals in Wisconsin," in *Wisconsin Medicine,* ed. Ronald L. Numbers and Judith W. Leavitt (Madison: University of Wisconsin Press, 1981), p. 108; Thomas G. Morton, *The History of the Pennsylvania Hospital, 1751–1895* (Philadelphia, 1895), p. 242; Thomas G. Morton and William Hunt, *Surgery in the Pennsylvania Hospital* (Philadelphia: Lippincott, 1880), p. 349.

52. Vogel, *Invention of the Modern Hospital,* pp. 73–74; Shoemaker and Jones, "From Infirmaries to Intensive Care: Hospitals in Wisconsin," p. 108; David Rosner, *A Once Charitable Enterprise* (Cambridge, England: Cambridge University Press, 1982), p. 44.

53. Jon M. Kingsdale, "The Growth of Hospitals," (Ph.D. diss., University of Michigan, 1981), p. 92.

54. For the same development in colleges, see David B. Potts, "American Colleges in the Nineteenth Century," *History of Education Quarterly* 11 (1971): 363–80.

55. Anthony King, "Hospital Planning: Revised Thoughts on the Origin of the Pavilion Principle in England," *Medical History* 10 (1966): 360–73; George W. Adams, *Doctors in Blue* (New York: Schuman, 1952), pp. 127, 151, 168.

56. Harry F. Dowling, *City Hospitals* (Cambridge: Harvard University Press, 1982), pp. 68–69; William Rideing, "Hospital Life in New York," *Harper's* 57 (1878): 178–79.

57. Vogel, *Invention of the Modern Hospital,* p. 10; Delavan, *Early Days of the Presbyterian Hospital,* p. 51.

58. Ibid., p. 87; Rideing, "Hospital Life in New York," p. 178.

59. Joan E. Lynaugh, "The Community Hospitals of Kansas City, Missouri, 1870 to 1915" (Ph.D. diss., University of Kansas, 1982), pp. 34, 59; Rosemary Stevens, "Sweet Charity: State Aid to Hospitals in Pennsylvania, 1870–1910," *Bulletin of the History of Medicine* 58 (1984): 301–7.

60. Rosner, *A Once Charitable Enterprise,* pp. 40–41; Kingsdale, "The Growth of Hospitals," p. 49; Morton, *The History of the Pennsylvania Hospital, 1751–1895,* p. 241.

61. Rosemary Stevens, "'A Poor Sort of Memory': Voluntary Hospitals and Government before the Depression," *Milbank Memorial Fund Quarterly* 60 (1982): 558–68.

62. Kingsdale, "The Growth of Hospitals," pp. 117–8, 121–39; Rosner, *A Once Charitable Enterprise,* pp. 51–52.

63. Gerster, *Recollections of a New York Surgeon,* p. 161; Campbell Douglas, "Notes on American Hospitals," *Glasgow Medical Journal* 61 (1904): 100–4.

64. Dowling, *City Hospitals,* pp. 45–51; O'Hara, "An Emerging Profession: Philadelphia Medicine 1860–1900," p. 330.

65. Rosner, *A Once Charitable Enterprise,* p. 103; Stephen A. Welch, "Some of the Conditions Affecting the Practice of Medicine in the City of Providence," *Providence Medical Journal* 16 (1915): 194.

66. Dowling, *City Hospitals,* p. 57.

67. Kingsdale, "The Growth of Hospitals," p. 221; William H. Bennett, "St. Christopher's Hospital for Children," in *Founders' Week Memorial Volume,* ed. Frederick P. Henry (Philadelphia, 1909), pp. 808, 819; Charles Sinkler, "The Philadelphia Orthopedic Hospital and Infirmary for Nervous Diseases," in ibid., p. 795; James V. Ingham, "The Maternity Hospital," in ibid., pp. 803–4.

68. Lynaugh, "The Community Hospitals of Kansas City, Missouri, 1870–1915," pp. 22–24, 38, 60; Vogel, *The Invention of the Modern Hospital,* pp. 103–4.

69. Hertzler, *The Horse and Buggy Doctor,* pp. 248–77; John M. Dodd, *Autobiography of a Surgeon* (New York: Neale, 1928), pp. 85–90; Kingsdale, "The Growth of Hospitals," pp. 51–52.

70. John G. Blake and A. Lawrence Mason, "The Medical Department," in *A History of Boston City Hospital,* p. 216; George W. Gay, "Reminiscences of the Boston City Hospital," in ibid., pp. 239–40.

71. Henry M. Hurd, "The Medical Service of a Hospital," in *Hospital Management,* ed. Charlotte A. Aiken (Philadelphia: Saunders, 1911), pp. 100–1; Charles P. Emerson, "The American Hospital Field," in ibid., pp. 68–69.

72. David W. Cheever, "Teaching and Appointments," in *A History of Boston City Hospital,* p. 279; Charles F. Withington, "Medical Education in the Hospital—The House Officers," in ibid., pp. 288–89; Robert J. Carlisle, ed., *An Account of Bellevue Hospital* (New York, 1893), p. 100.

73. Arthur A. Bliss, *Blockley Days* (n.p.: 1916), p. 24.

74. Warren, *To Work in the Vineyards of Surgery,* p. 30n; Martin, *The Joy of Living,* p. 357.

75. Weir, "Personal Reminiscences of the New York Hospital," p. 36.

76. Ibid., pp. 35–36; Cheever, "Teaching and Appointments," p. 279.

77. Abt, *Baby Doctor,* pp. 158–59.

78. Hudson, "Patterns of Medical Education in Nineteenth Century America," p. 108.

79. Washburn, *The Massachusetts General Hospital,* pp. 158–66; J. Chalmers DaCosta, *The Trials and Triumphs of the Surgeon* (Philadelphia: Dorrance, 1944), pp. 368–72.

80. Dudley, *The Medicine Man,* pp. 202–3.

81. Ibid., pp. 233–34; Gay, "Reminiscences of the Boston City Hospital," pp. 240–43.

82. Bliss, *Blockley Days,* p. 14; Macartney, *Fifty Years a Country Doctor,* p. 44.

83. Finney, *A Surgeon's Life,* p. 70.

84. Hurd, "The Medical Service of a Hospital," pp. 101–2; Dowling, *City Hospitals,* pp. 51–54.

85. Nancy Tomes, "'Little World of Our Own:' The Pennsylvania Hospital Training School for Nurses, 1895–1907," *Journal of the History of Medicine* 33 (1978): 508–9.

86. Cook has observed: "The popular imagination pictures Florence Nightingale . . . as the 'ministering angel.' And such . . . she was. But the deeper significance of her work . . . lies elsewhere. It was as Administrator and Reformer, more than as Angel, that she showed her peculiar powers." Edward Cook, *The Life of Florence Nightingale* (London: Macmillan, 1913), 1:xxv–xxvi, 208–9: Henry K. Beecher, "The Relief of Suffering," in *The Hospital in Contemporary Life,* ed. Nathaniel W. Faxon (Cambridge: Harvard University Press, 1949), pp. 90–91.

87. Lucy R. Seymer, comp., *Selected Writings of Florence Nightingale* (New York: Macmillan, 1954), pp. 266–67, 290–91; Abby H. Woolsley, *A Century of Nursing* (1916; reprint ed., New York: State Charities Aid Association, 1950), p. 182.

88. Seymer, *Selected Writings of Florence Nightingale,* pp. 291, 223.

89. Dorothy Giles, *A Candle in Her Hand: A Story of the Nursing Schools of Bellevue Hospital* (New York: Putnam, 1949); Jane E. Mottus, *New York Nightingales* (Ann Arbor, Mich.: UMI Research Press, 1981).

90. Janet M. Hooks, *Women's Occupations Through Seven Decades,* Women's Bureau Bulletin No. 218 (Washington, D.C.: U.S. G.P.O., 1947), p. 34; Giles, *A Candle in Her Hand: A Story of the Nursing Schools of Bellevue Hospital,* p. 162. Mottus, *New York Nightingales,* pp. 93, 95, 131, 49; Tomes, "'Little World of Our Own:' The Pennsylvania Hospital Training School for Nurses, 1895–1907," pp. 518–21; Woolsley, *A Century of Nursing,* pp. 158–59.

91. May A. Burgess, *Nurses, Patients, and Pocketbooks* (New York, 1928), p. 35; Hooks, *Women's Occupations Through Seven Decades,* p. 162.

92. Mottus, *New York Nightingales,* pp. 58–61; Isabel M. Stewart, *The Education of Nurses* (New York: Macmillan, 1943), p. 118.

93. M. Adelaide Nutting, *Educational Status of Nursing* (Washington, D.C.: U.S. G.P.O., 1912), pp. 16–17, 23–24.

94. Stewart, *The Education of Nurses,* pp. 100–3, 165; Mary A. Nutting, *A Sound Economic Basis for Schools of Nursing* (New York: Putnam, 1926), pp. 11–14, 31, 315, 339–41.

95. Stewart, *The Education of Nurses,* pp. 105–6.

96. Nutting, *Educational Status of Nursing,* pp. 29, 32–35.

97. Ethel Johns and Blanch Pfefferkorn, *The Johns Hopkins Hospital School of Nursing, 1889–1949* (Baltimore: Johns Hopkins Press, 1954), pp. 42, 63; Jo Ann Ashley, *Hospitals, Paternalism, and the Role of the Nurse* (New York: Teachers College Press, 1976), pp. 25–26, 54–55; Nutting, *Educational Status of Nursing,* p. 21.

98. Mottus, *New York Nightingales,* pp. 168–71; George H. M. Rowe, "Historical Sketch of the Boston City Hospital Training School for Nurses," in *A History of Boston City Hospital,* p. 389.

99. Philip A. Kalisch and Beatrice J. Kalisch, *The Advance of American Nursing* (Boston: Little, Brown, 1978), pp. 365, 229, 241.

100. Stewart, *The Education of Nurses,* p. 95; A. McGehee Harvey and Victor A. McKusick, eds., *Osler's Textbook Revisited* (New York: Appleton-Century-Crofts, 1967), pp. 59, 101.

101. Tomes, "'Little World of Our Own:' The Pennsylvania Hospital Training School for Nurses, 1895–1907," pp. 507–30; Delavan, *Early Days of the Presbyterian Hospital,* p. 104.

Chapter 5

1. Colin B. Burke, "The Expansion of American Higher Education," in *The Transformation of Higher Learning: 1860–1930,* ed. Konrad H. Jarausch (Stuttgart, Germany: Klett-Cotta, 1982), pp. 111–12.

2. W. Scott Thomas, "Changes in the Age of College Graduation," *Popular Science Monthly* 63 (1903): 159–71.

3. Edwin C. Broome, *A Historical and Critical Discussion of College Admission Requirements* (New York: 1903), pp. 53, 66–67; Theodore R. Sizer, *Secondary Schools at the Turn of the Century* (New Haven: Yale University Press, 1964), p. 37; Allan Nevins, *The State Universities and Democracy* (Urbana: University of Illinois Press, 1962), p. 76; William C. Collar, "The Action of the Colleges upon the Schools," *Educational Review* 1 (1891): 422–41.

4. Charles F. Adams, *Three Phi Beta Kappa Addresses* (Boston: Houghton Mifflin, 1907), p. 11; Broome, *A Historical and Critical Discussion of College Admission Requirements,* pp. 73–87; Charles W. Eliot, "President's Report for 1897–98," *Annual Reports of the President and Treasurer of Harvard College, 1897–98* (Cambridge, 1898) pp. 18–21; F. A. P. Bernard, *Annual Report of the President of Columbia College* (New York: Van Nostrand, 1871), pp. 25–30.

5. Henry S. Canby, *Alma Mater* (New York: Farrar and Rinehart, 1936), pp. 62–64.

6. Robert N. Corwin, *The Plain Unpolished Tale of the Workaday Doings of Modest Folk* (New Haven, 1946), pp. 93–94.

7. Quoted in Russell H. Chittenden, *History of the Sheffield Scientific School* (New Haven: Yale University Press, 1928), 1:138; Andrew S. Draper, "Educational Organization and Administration," in *Monographs on Education in the United States,* ed. Nicholas M. Butler (Albany, N.Y., 1900), 1:31; Stanley M. Guralnick, "The American Scientist in Higher Education, 1820–1910," in *The Sciences in the American Context,* ed. Nathan Reingold (Washington, D.C.: Smithsonian Institution Press, 1979), p. 129.

8. Robert A. McCaughey, "The Transformation of American Academic Life: Harvard University 1821–1892," *Perspectives in American History* 8 (1974): 276, 332.

9. Ibid.

10. Barnard, *Annual Report of the President of Columbia College,* pp. 39–43; William R. Harper, *The Trend in Higher Education* (Chicago: University of Chicago Press, 1905), p. 363; George E. MacLean, *Present Standards of Higher Education in the United States* (Washington, D.C.: U.S. G.P.O., 1913), pp. 27, 60.

11. William G. Rothstein, *American Physicians in the Nineteenth Century* (Baltimore: Johns Hopkins University Press, 1972), pp. 98, 287.

12. James B. Herrick, *Memories of Eighty Years* (Chicago: University of Chicago Press, 1949), p. 40.

13. John Shrady, ed., *The College of Physicians and Surgeons, New York* (New York: Lewis, n.d.), 1:226; Illinois State Board of Health, *Medical Education, Medical Colleges, and the Regulation and Practice of Medicine in the United States and Canada, 1765–1891* (Springfield, Ill., 1891), p. xvii.

14. Richard G. Boone, *Education in the United States* (New York: Appleton, 1890), pp. 211–220; Shrady, ed., *The College of Physicians and Surgeons, New York,* pp. 241–43; Thomas F. Harrington, *The Harvard Medical School* (New York: Lewis, 1905), 3:1305.

15. John C. Dalton, *History of the College of Physicians and Surgeons in the City of New York* (New York, 1888), pp. 192–93; Frederic H. Gerrish, "Report of the Committee on the Requirements for Preliminary Education . . . , " *Bulletin of the American Academy of Medicine* 1 (1894): 435–39.

16. Leslie B. Arey, *Northwestern University Medical School: 1859–1959* (Evanston, Ill.: Northwestern University, 1959), p. 104.

17. Franklin H. Martin, *The Joy of Living* (New York: Doubleday, Doran, 1933), 1:130–32.

18. Ibid., 1:137–39.

19. Herrick, *Memories of Eighty Years,* p. 48; Arpad G. Gerster, *Recollections of a New York Surgeon* (New York: Hoeber, 1917), p. 248; Norman Walker, "The Medical Profession in the United States," *Edinburgh Medical Journal* 37 (1891): 243–44.

20. E. C. Dudley, *The Medicine Man* (New York: Sears, 1927), p. 250; Joseph C. Aub and Ruth K. Hapgood, *Pioneer in Modern Medicine: David Linn Edsall of Harvard* (Boston, 1970), p. 16.

21. Shrady, ed., *The College of Physicians and Surgeons, New York,* 1:301–2; Herrick, *Memories of Eighty Years,* p. 43.

22. The following sources were used: Harold J. Abrahams, *The Extinct Medical Schools of Baltimore, Maryland* (Baltimore: Maryland Historical Society, 1969); Margaret B. Ballard, *A University is Born* (Union, W. Va., 1965); George H. Calcott, *A History of the University of Maryland* (Baltimore: Maryland Historical Society, 1966); Abraham Flexner, *Medical Education in the United States and Canada* (1910, reprint ed.: New York: Arno Press, 1972), pp. 234–39. Data for the Maryland Medical College and the Baltimore University were obtained from every fourth name in a listing of all matriculants in Abrahams, *The Extinct Medical Colleges of Baltimore, Maryland.* Data for the other schools, except Johns Hopkins University, were obtained from the lists of matriculants and graduates in the annual catalogues from 1876 to 1900. Data were not available for all schools for all analyses.

23. James C. White, *Sketches from My Life, 1833–1913* (Cambridge, Mass.: Riverside Press, 1914), p. 194; Arey, *Northwestern University Medical School: 1859–1959,* pp. 36, 267; Leo J. O'Hara, "An Emerging Profession: Philadelphia Medicine 1860–1900," (Ph.D. diss., University of Pennsylvania, 1976), pp. 153–54; Martin Kaufman, *The University of Vermont College of Medicine* (Hanover, N.H., 1979), p. 76.

24. E. Fletcher Ingals, "The Necessities of a Modern Medical College," *Bulletin of the American Academy of Medicine* 2 (1895): 238–39; Shrady, ed., *The College of Physicians and Surgeons, New York,* 1:299–300.

25. Alan M. Chesney, *The Johns Hopkins Hospital and the Johns Hopkins University School of Medicine* (Baltimore: Johns Hopkins Press, 1943), 1:158; J. M. T. Finney, *A Surgeon's Life* (New York: Putnam, 1940), p. 107.

26. Frederick C. Waite, *Western Reserve University Centennial History of the School of Medicine* (Cleveland: Western Reserve University Press, 1946), pp. 367, 401–2; Arey, *Northwestern University Medical School: 1859–1959,* pp. 201–2.

27. Calcott, *A History of the University of Maryland,* pp. 209, 256; George W. Corner, *Two Centuries of Medicine: A History of the School of Medicine, University of Pennsylvania* (Philadelphia: Lippincott, 1965), p. 187.

28. Edward P. Cheyney, "The University of Pennsylvania," in *Founders' Week Memorial Volume,* ed. Frederick P. Henry (Philadelphia, 1909), p. 244.

29. George M. Gould, *The Jefferson Medical College of Philadelphia* (New York: Lewis, 1904), 1:195–96.

30. Dalton, *History of the College of Physicians and Surgeons in the City of New York,* pp. 74–76; Gould, *Jefferson Medical College of Philadelphia,* 1:196.

31. Charles B. Johnson, *Sixty Years in Medical Harness* (New York: Medical Life Press, 1926), pp. 56, 61–65.

32. Augustus Maverick, "'Vienna Caustic,'" *New York Medical Journal* 97 (1913): 694; Henry Hun, *A Guide to American Medical Students in Europe* (New York: Wood, 1883).

33. Thomas N. Bonner, *American Doctors and German Universities* (Lincoln: University of Nebraska Press, 1963), pp. 24, 39; Hun, *A Guide to American Medical Students in Europe,* p. 3; Robert P. Hudson, "Patterns of Medical Education in Nineteenth Century America," (Masters degree essay, Johns Hopkins University, 1966), p. 88.

34. Maverick, "'Vienna Caustic,'" p. 695.

35. Bonner, *American Doctors and German Universities,* pp. 69, 74–75, 80–81; Maverick, "'Vienna Caustic,'" p. 694.

36. Hun, *A Guide to American Medical Students in Europe,* p. 2; Maverick, "'Vienna Caustic,'" p. 696.

37. Ibid.

38. Bonner, *American Doctors and German Universities,* pp. 51–52, 89–103.

39. H. C. Wood, Jr., "Medical Education in the United States," *Lippincott's Magazine* 16 (1875): 707.

40. Corner, *Two Centuries of Medicine: A History of the School of Medicine, University of Pennsylvania,* pp. 138–40.

41. Albert R. Baker, "Evolution of the American Medical College," *Bulletin of the American Academy of Medicine* 5 (1901): 500; J. Whitridge Williams, "Medical Education and the Midwife Problem in the United States," *Journal of the American Medical Association* 58 (1912): 1–3.

42. Kaufman, *The University of Vermont College of Medicine,* pp. 64, 141.

43. Dudley S. Reynolds, "Specialism in Regular Course," *Bulletin of the American Academy of Medicine* 1 (1893): 392–94.

44. Ibid., p. 393.

45. Robert P. Hudson, "Abraham Flexner in Perspective," *Bulletin of the History of Medicine* 46 (1972): 551; Shrady, *The College of Physicians and Surgeons, New York* 1:126–27; Dalton, *History of the College of Physicians and Surgeons in the City of New York,* pp. 195–96.

46. Norman Bridge, *The Marching Years* (New York: Duffield 1920), p. 87; Frederick C. Waite, "Changes in the Medical Educational Program in Ohio from 1890 to 1910," *Ohio State Medical Journal* 45 (1949): 1086; Waite, *Western Reserve University Centennial History of the School of Medicine,* p. 185; Eugene F. Cordell, *Historical Sketch of the University of Maryland School of Medicine* (Baltimore, 1891), p. 153.

47. Frederick C. Waite, "Advent of the Graded Curriculum in American Medical Colleges," *Journal of the Association of American Medical Colleges* 25 (1950): 318–20; White, *Sketches from My Life, 1833–1913,* p. 188.

48. Rothstein, *American Physicians in the Nineteenth Century,* pp. 286–88.

49. Dean F. Smiley, "History of the Association of American Medical Colleges," *Journal of Medical Education* 32 (1957): 516–17. Walker, "The Medical Profession in the United States," p. 241; Corner, *Two Centuries of Medicine: A History of the School of Medicine, University of Pennsylvania,* p. 193; White, *Sketches from My Life, 1833–1913,* pp. 158–59.

50. Charles E. McClelland, *State, Society and University in Germany: 1700–1914* (Cambridge, England: Cambridge University Press, 1980), pp. 174–76, 204–5, 212–13, 279–87.

51. Joseph Ben-David, "Roles and Innovations in Medicine," *American Journal of Sociology* 65 (1960): 559–64.

52. Joseph Ben-David and Awraham Zloczower, "Universities and Academic Systems in Modern Societies," *European Journal of Sociology* 3 (1962): 45–84.

53. Bonner, *American Doctors and German Universities,* pp. 107–8.

54. Walker, "The Medical Profession in the United States," p. 241.

55. Arthur E. Hertzler, *The Horse and Buggy Doctor* (Garden City, N.Y.: Blue Ribbon Books, 1941), p. 43.

56. John H. Warner, "Physiology," in *The Education of American Physicians,* ed. Ronald L. Numbers (Berkeley and Los Angeles: University of California Press, 1980), pp. 64–67; James Whorton, "Chemistry," in ibid., pp. 72–73, 83–86; Robert E. Kohler, *From Medical Chemistry to Biochemistry* (Cambridge, England: Cambridge University Press, 1982), pp. 10, 114–16.

57. Lewellys F. Barker, "Medicine and the Universities," *American Medicine* 4 (1902): 143; H. W. Conn, "Bacteriology in Our Schools," *Science* 11 (1888): 123–25.

58. Waite, "Changes in the Medical Education Program in Ohio from 1890 to 1910," pp. 1085–86.

59. Hertzler, *The Horse and Buggy Doctor,* pp. 193–94.

60. Corner, *Two Centuries of Medicine: A History of the School of Medicine, University of Pennsylvania,* pp. 187–88; Hertzler, *The Horse and Buggy Doctor,* p. 193.

61. Kohler, *From Medical Chemistry to Biochemistry,* pp. 133–38.

62. White, *Sketches from My Life, 1833–1913,* p. 304; James H. Means, *The Association of American Physicians* (New York: McGraw-Hill, 1961), p. 49.

63. Five of those traced were both members of the AAP and presidents of the AMA; 18 were both members of the ASA and presidents of the AMA. One physician was a member of both the AAP and the ASA. Physicians were listed in all appropriate organizations. For a history of the AAP, see Means, *The Association of American Physicians.* Gerster said of the ASA: "Unquestionably this body was composed of what was then the best in the surgical calling of the United States;" Gerster, *Recollections of a New York Surgeon,* p. 239.

64. Herrick, *Memories of Eighty Years,* pp. 186–87; William Osler, "On the Need for a Radical Reform in our Methods of Teaching Senior Students," *Medical News* 82 (1903): 49–50.

65. William Osler, "After Twenty-Five Years," *Montreal Medical Journal* 28 (1899): 830; A. McGehee Harvey and Victor A. McKusick, *Osler's Textbook Revisited* (New York: Appleton-Century-Crofts, 1967), pp. 1–7.

66. W. Gilman Thompson, "The Instruction of Senior Students in Medicine," *Medical News* 82 (1903): 53.

67. Ibid.

68. Ibid., pp. 53–54; Herrick, *Memories of Eighty Years,* pp. 189–90.

69. Ibid., p. 188; William Osler, "The Natural Method of Teaching the Subject of Medicine," *Journal of the American Medical Association* 36 (1901): 1677.

70. Thompson, "The Instruction of Senior Students in Medicine," p. 54.

71. Gould, *The Jefferson Medical College of Philadelphia,* 1:52, 115, 163, 323–34; J. Collins Warren, *To Work in the Vineyard of Surgery,* ed. Edward D. Churchill (Cambridge: Harvard University Press, 1958), pp. 50–51.

72. Michael M. Davis, *Clinics, Hospitals and Health Centers* (New York: Harper, 1927), p. 32–34.

73. Isaac Abt, *Baby Doctor* (New York: McGraw-Hill, 1944), pp. 25–26.

74. Ibid.; Dalton, *History of the College of Physicians and Surgeons in the City of New York,* pp. 125, 146–48.

75. Earnst E. Irons, *The Story of Rush Medical College* (Chicago, 1953), p. 23.

76. Dalton, *History of the College of Physicians and Surgeons in the City of New York,* pp. 156, 162–64, 181; Shrady, *The College of Physicians and Surgeons, New York,* 1:158, 192–93, 219, 248; William A. Pusey, "The Importance of Being Historically Minded," *Journal of the American Medical Association* 89 (1927): 2080.

77. Dalton, *History of the College of Physicians and Surgeons in the City of New York,* pp. 183–84.

78. Osler, "The Natural Method of Teaching the Subject of Medicine," p. 1674; Osler, "On the Need for a Radical Reform in our Methods of Teaching Senior Students," p. 50.

79. Osler, "The Natural Method of Teaching the Subject of Medicine," p. 1675.

80. Walker, "The Medical Profession in the United States," p. 141.

81. Arey, *Northwestern University Medical School: 1859–1959*, p. 156.

82. Gerster, *Recollections of a New York Surgeon*, pp. 210–11.

83. Frederic A. Washburn, *The Massachusetts General Hospital* (Boston: Houghton Mifflin, 1939), p. 99.

84. Gordon Atkins, *Health, Housing and Poverty in New York City: 1865–1898* (Ann Arbor, Mich., 1947), pp. 237–38; Shrady, *The College of Physicians and Surgeons, New York*, 1:280.

85. Harry F. Dowling, *City Hospitals* (Cambridge: Harvard University Press, 1982), p. 62; Arey, *Northwestern University Medical School: 1859–1959*, p. 275; Washburn, *The Massachusetts General Hospital*, p. 149; John M. Dodd, *Autobiography of a Surgeon* (New York: Neale, 1928), p. 73; D. B. St. John Roosa, "The Old New York Hospital," *Post Graduate* 15 (Jan., 1900): 16.

86. Rosemary Stevens, "Sweet Charity: State Aid to Hospitals in Pennsylvania, 1870–1910," *Bulletin of the History of Medicine* 58 (1984): 299–300, 489; Joan E. Lynaugh, "The Community Hospitals of Kansas City, Missouri, 1870 to 1915" (Ph.D. diss., University of Kansas, 1982), pp. 38–40.

87. Dale C. Smith, "The Emergence of Organized Clinical Instruction in the Nineteenth Century American Cities of Boston, New York, and Philadelphia" (Ph.D. diss., University of Minnesota, 1979), pp. 263–67.

88. John B. Wheeler, *Memoirs of a Small-Town Surgeon* (New York: Stokes, 1935), pp. 43–44; Francis A. Long, *A Prairie Doctor of the Eighties* (Norfolk, Nebr., 1937), p. 23.

89. W. J. Herdman, "Clinical Instruction at the University of Michigan," *Bulletin of the American Academy of Medicine* 2 (1895): 96–98.

90. Wheeler, *Memoirs of a Small-Town Surgeon*, pp. 46–47; Martin, *The Joy of Living*, 1:178.

91. Osler, "The Natural Method of Teaching the Subject of Medicine," p. 1676; Osler, "On the Need for a Radical Reform in our Methods of Teaching Senior Students," p. 52.

92. Osler, "The Natural Method of Teaching the Subject of Medicine," p. 1676.

93. David W. Cheever, "Teaching and Appointments," in *A History of the Boston City Hospital*, ed. David W. Cheever et al. (Boston, 1906), p. 281.

94. Abrahams, *The Extinct Medical Schools of Baltimore, Maryland*, p. 71; Aub and Hapgood, *Pioneer in Modern Medicine: David Linn Edsall of Harvard*, p. 251n; Arey, *Northwestern University Medical School: 1859–1959*, p. 215.

95. Steven J. Peitzman, "'Thoroughly Practical': America's Polyclinic Medical Schools," *Bulletin of the History of Medicine* 54 (1980): 166–87; Gould, *The Jefferson Medical College of Philadelphia*, pp. 234–35; James A. Harrar, *The Story of the Lying-In Hospital of the City of New York* (New York, 1938), pp. 68, 70.

96. Peitzman, "'Thoroughly Practical': America's Polyclinic Medical Schools," pp. 176–84.

Chapter 6

1. Lewis Mayers and Leonard V. Harrison, *The Distribution of Physicians in the United States* (New York: General Education Board, 1924), pp. 47, 175.

2. Michael L. Berger, "The Influence of the Automobile on Rural Health Care, 1900–29," *Journal of the History of Medicine* 28 (1973): 319–35; Mayers and Harrison, *The Distribution of Physicians in the United States*, pp. 3–39.

3. Milton Terris and Mary Monk, "Changes in Physicians' Careers," *JAMA* 160 (1956): 653–54; Willard C. Rappleye, *Graduate Medical Education* (Chicago: University of Chicago Press, 1940), p. 261; U.S. Bureau of the Census, *Historical Statistics of the United States* (Washington, D.C.: U.S. G.P.O. 1975), 1:76.

4. Rappleye, *Graduate Medical Education*, p. 267.

5. Lewellys F. Barker, *The Young Man and Medicine* (New York: Macmillan, 1928), p. 129.

6. James C. White, *Sketches from My Life, 1833–1913* (Cambridge, Mass.: Riverside Press, 1914), pp. 268–69.

7. George Rosen, *The Structure of American Medical Practice, 1875–1941* (Philadelphia: University of Pennsylvania Press, 1983), pp. 98–101; Daniel M. Fox, "Social Policy and City Politics," *Bulletin of the History of Medicine* 49 (1975): 186, 192.

8. Rosen, *The Structure of American Medical Practice, 1875–1941*, pp. 59–60.

9. U.S. Bureau of the Census, *Historical Statistics of the United States*, 1:57, 63.

10. Ibid., 1:58; William G. Rothstein, *American Physicians in the Nineteenth Century* (Baltimore: Johns Hopkins University Press, 1972), pp. 277–78.

11. U.S. Bureau of the Census, *Historical Statistics of the United States*, 1:63; U.S. President's Commission on the Health Needs of the Nation, *Building America's Health* (Washington, D.C.: U.S. G.P.O., 1953), 3:30.

12. U.S. Bureau of the Census, *Historical Statistics of the United States*, 1:58.

13. W. C. Rappleye, "Survey of Medical Education," *Journal of the American Medical Association* 88 (1927): 843; U.S. President's Commission on the Health Needs of the Nation, *Building America's Health*, 2: 269.

14. Paul B. Beeson, "Changes in Medical Therapy During the Past Half Century," *Medicine* 59 (1980): 79–99.

15. William N. Hubbard, Jr., "The Origins of Medicinals," in *Advances in American Medicine*, ed. John Z. Bowers and Elizabeth F. Purcell (New York: Josiah Macy, Jr., Foundation: 1976), 2:706; Harry Dowling, *Fighting Infection* (Cambridge: Harvard University Press, 1977), pp. 105–7.

16. Hubbard, "The Origins of Medicinals," pp. 704, 706, 709.

17. Ronald Hare, *The Birth of Penicillin* (London: George Allen and Unwin, 1970), pp. 142–44.

18. Dowling, *Fighting Infection*, p. 124.

19. Mitchell H. Charap, "The Periodic Health Examination: Genesis of a Myth," *Annals of Internal Medicine* 95 (1981): 733–35; Stanley J. Reiser, *Medicine and the Reign of Technology* (Cambridge, England: Cambridge University Press, 1978), pp. 216–17.

20. Charap, "The Periodic Health Examination: Genesis of a Myth," pp. 734–35.

21. Francis D. Moore, "Surgery," in *Advances in American Medicine*, 2:639–42; Edward H. Richardson, *A Doctor Remembers* (New York: Vantage Press, 1959), p. 177.

22. Campbell Douglas, "Notes on American Hospitals," *Glasgow Medical Journal* 61 (1904): 103–4; Robert T. Morris, *Fifty Years a Surgeon* (New York: Dutton, 1935), p. 173.

23. Moore, "Surgery," 2:639–42; Hare, *The Birth of Penicillin*, pp. 174–75.

24. Benjamin A. Barnes, "Discarded Operations," in *Costs, Risks and Benefits of Surgery*, ed. John P. Bunker, Benjamin A. Barnes, and Frederick Mosteller (New York: Oxford University Press, 1977), pp. 109–23; Beeson, "Changes in Medical Therapy During the Past Half Century," p. 82.

25. Rappleye, *Graduate Medical Education*, p. 261.

26. Feather D. Hair, "Hospital Accreditation" (Ph.D. diss., Vanderbilt University, 1972), pp. 78–79; Rappleye, "Survey of Medical Education," p. 843.

27. Rosemary Stevens, *American Medicine and the Public Interest* (New Haven: Yale University Press, 1971), pp. 542–43.

28. Rappleye, "Survey of Medical Education," p. 844. Michael M. Davis and C. Rufus Rorem, *The Crisis in Hospital Finance* (Chicago: University of Chicago Press, 1932), p. 165.

29. Michael M. Davis et al., "The Growth of Dispensary Work," *Transactions of the American Hospital Association* 18 (1916): 102–3; David Rosner, *A Once Charitable Enterprise* (Cambridge, England: Cambridge University Press, 1982), pp. 146–63; Charles Rosenberg, "Social Class and Medical Care in Nineteenth-Century America: The Rise and Fall of the Dispensary," *Journal of the History of Medicine* 29 (1974): 49–51.

30. Michael M. Davis, "The Functions of a Dispensary or Out-patient Department," *Boston Medical and Surgical Journal* 171 (1914): 336–39; Hair, "Hospital Accreditation," pp. 65–67.

31. Jay Stoeckle and Lawrence A. May, eds., *Richard Cabot on Practice, Training and the Doctor-Patient Relationship* (Oceanside, N.Y.: Dabor Science Publications, 1977), p. 24.

32. Ibid., p. ix.

33. Ibid., p. 40.

34. Albert R. Lamb, *The Presbyterian Hospital and the Columbia-Presbyterian Medical Center, 1868–1943* (New York: Columbia University Press, 1955), pp. 97–98.

35. Philip Shoemaker and Mary V. H. Jones, "From Infirmaries to Intensive Care: Hospitals in Wisconsin," in *Wisconsin Medicine,* ed. Ronald L. Numbers and Judith W. Leavitt (Madison: University of Wisconsin Press, 1981), p. 125.

36. Monroe Lerner and Odin W. Anderson, *Health Progress in the United States 1900–1960* (Chicago: University of Chicago Press, 1963), pp. 256, 267; Richard W. Wertz and Dorothy C. Wertz, *Lying-In: A History of Childbirth in America* (New York: Free Press, 1977), p. 133.

37. S. S. Goldwater, *On Hospitals* (New York: Macmillan, 1951), pp. 206–7; Jon M. Kingsdale, "The Growth of Hospitals" (Ph.D. diss., University of Michigan, 1981), p. 406.

38. Harry F. Dowling, *City Hospitals* (Cambridge: Harvard University Press, 1982), pp. 137–50.

39. Ibid., pp. 132–35.

40. Kingsdale, "The Growth of Hospitals," p. 344.

41. Davis and Rorem, *The Crisis in Hospital Finance,* p. 84; Kingsdale, "The Growth of Hospitals," pp. 80–81.

42. Cecil K. Austin, "Medical Impressions of America," *Boston Medical and Surgical Journal* 166 (1912): 801.

43. Joseph C. Doane, "A Brief History of the Philadelphia General Hospital from 1908 to 1928," in *History of Blockley,* comp., John W. Croskey (Philadelphia: Davis, 1929), p. 119; Frederic A. Washburn, *The Massachusetts General Hospital* (Boston: Houghton Mifflin, 1939), pp. 376–77; Michael M. Davis, *Clinics, Hospitals, and Health Centers* (New York: Harper, 1927), pp. 6–7.

44. Robert E. Kohler, *From Medical Chemistry to Biochemistry* (Cambridge, England: Cambridge University Press, 1982), pp. 227–32.

45. David Rosner, "Business at the Bedside: Health Care in Brooklyn, 1890–1915," in *Health Care in America,* ed. Susan Reverby and David Rosner (Philadelphia: Temple University Press, 1979), p. 120; E. H. L. Corwin, *The American Hospital* (New York: Commonwealth Fund, 1946), pp. 51–52; U.S. Bureau of the Census, *Historical Statistics of the United States,* 1:210–11.

46. David Rosner, "Gaining Control: Reform, Reimbursement and Politics in New

York's Community Hospitals, 1890–1915,'' *American Journal of Public Health* 70 (1980): 535–37; Rosemary Stevens, '''A Poor Sort of Memory': Voluntary Hospitals and Government before the Depression,'' *Milbank Memorial Fund Quarterly* 60 (1982): 568–74.

47. Joan E. Lynaugh, "The Community Hospitals of Kansas City, Missouri, 1870 to 1915,'' (Ph.D. diss., University of Kansas, 1982), pp. 74–76; Morris J. Vogel, *The Invention of the Hospital* (Chicago: University of Chicago Press, 1980), pp. 63–64; Niles Carpenter, *Hospital Service for Patients of Moderate Means* (Washington, D.C.: Committee on the Cost of Medical Care, 1930), p. 23; Rosner, *A Once Charitable Enterprise*, p. 66.

48. Ibid., pp. 44, 50, 83–87.

49. Carpenter, *Hospital Service for Patients of Moderate Means*, pp. 9–12.

50. Washburn, *The Massachusetts General Hospital*, pp. 249–52.

51. Carpenter, *Hospital Service for Patients of Moderate Means*, p. 66; Joseph Hirsh and Beka Doherty, *The First Hundred Years of the Mount Sinai Hospital of New York: 1852–1952* (New York: Random House, 1952), pp. 216–18; Kingsdale, "The Growth of Hospitals,'' pp. 376–77.

52. Washburn, *The Massachusetts General Hospital*, p. 528; Corwin, *The American Hospital*, p. 60.

53. Kingsdale, "The Growth of Hospitals,'' pp. 276, 343–44, 413.

54. Ibid., pp. 275–76, 405, 410.

55. Washburn, *The Massachusetts General Hospital*, pp. 259–62; Richard C. Cabot, "Group Practice: Diagnostic and Pay Clinics,'' *Journal of the American Medical Association* 77 (1921): 1911.

56. E. H. Lewinski-Corwin, *The Hospital Situation in Greater New York* (New York: Putnam, 1924), pp. 233–79; Hair, "Hospital Accreditation,'' pp. 45–47, 72–73, 77–80.

57. Washburn, *The Massachusetts General Hospital*, pp. 67–68, 165, 168, 446–47.

58. Hirsh and Doherty, *The First Hundred Years of the Mount Sinai Hospital of New York: 1852–1952*, pp. 156–57.

59. Henry J. Bigelow, "Fees in Hospitals,'' *Boston Medical and Surgical Journal* 120 (1889): 377.

60. Ibid., pp. 377–78.

61. Rosner, *A Once Charitable Enterprise*, pp. 108–11; Charles E. Rosenberg, "Inward Vision and Outward Glance: The Shaping of the American Hospital, 1880–1914,'' *Bulletin of the History of Medicine* 53 (1979): 367–68.

62. Morris, *Fifty Years a Surgeon*, p. 88.

63. Lewinski-Corwin, *The Hospital Situation in Greater New York*, pp. 176–77; Hair, "Hospital Accreditation,'' pp. 270–308.

64. J. L. Bubis, *Women are My Problem* (New York: Comet Press, 1953), p. 103; Kingsdale, "The Growth of Hospitals,'' pp. 211, 220.

65. Ibid., p. 233; Goldwater, *On Hospitals*, pp. 112–13.

66. Rosner, *A Once Charitable Enterprise*, pp. 52–54; Hair, "Hospital Accreditation,'' pp. 42–43, 57.

67. Jean A. Curran, *Internships and Residencies in New York City, 1934–1937* (New York: Commonwealth Fund, 1938), pp. 39–40; G. Canby Robinson, *Adventures in Medical Education* (Cambridge: Harvard University Press, 1957), p. 64.

68. Eric Larrabee, *The Benevolent and Necessary Institution* (Garden City, N.Y.: Doubleday, 1971), p. 297; Robinson, *Adventures in Medical Education*, p. 73.

69. Stevens, *American Medicine and the Public Interest*, pp. 117–18; Corwin, *The American Hospital*, p. 120.

70. J. A. Curran, "Surgical Internships over the Past Fifty Years,'' *American Journal of*

Surgery n.s. 51 (1941): 36–38; W. H. Smith, "Adequate Medical Service for a Community," *Journal of the American Medical Association* 76 (1921): 1059.

71. Stevens, *American Medicine and the Public Interest*, pp. 118–20.

72. Ibid., pp. 118, 129; Corwin, *The American Hospital*, p. 120.

73. Curran, "Surgical Internships over the Past Fifty Years," pp. 37–38; Rappleye, *Graduate Medical Education*, p. 253.

74. Rappleye, "Survey of Medical Education," p. 844; Curran, *Internships and Residencies in New York City, 1934–37*, p. 315; Rappleye, *Graduate Medical Education*, pp. 39, 53, 57, 59, 7–8.

75. Paul Reznikoff, "The Education of a Physician," *Journal of the Association of American Medical Colleges* 14 (1939): 298.

76. Curran, *Internships and Residencies in New York City, 1934–37*, pp. 41–44; Stevens, *American Medicine and the Public Interest*, pp. 120–21.

77. Ray L. Wilbur, "Progress in Graduate Medical Education," *Journal of the American Medical Association* 114 (1940): 1143; Rappleye, *Graduate Medical Education*, p. 101.

78. Ibid., pp. 120–22, 133–35.

79. Ibid., p. 104.

80. Loyal Davis, *Fellowship of Surgeons* (Springfield, Ill.: Thomas, 1960), pp. 243–44.

81. U.S. President's Commission on the Health Needs of the Nation, *Building America's Health*, 3:185, 205.

82. Nathaniel W. Faxon, *The Massachusetts General Hospital: 1935–1955* (Cambridge: Harvard University Press, 1959), p. 329.

83. Committee for the Study of Nursing Education, *Nursing and Nursing Education in the United States* (New York: Macmillan, 1923), pp. 331–33, 342–59; May A. Burgess, *Nurses, Patients, and Pocketbooks* (New York, 1928), p. 438.

84. Ibid., pp. 439–40; Isabel M. Stewart, *The Education of Nurses* (New York: Macmillan, 1943), p. 209.

85. Burgess, *Nurses, Patients, and Pocketbooks*, p. 434.

86. Committee on the Grading of Nursing Schools, *Nursing Schools Today and Tomorrow* (New York, 1934), p. 89; Committee for the Study of Nursing Education, *Nursing and Nursing Education in the United States*, pp. 165–67.

87. Burgess, *Nurses, Patients, and Pocketbooks*, p. 124.

88. Vern and Bonnie Bullough, *The Care of the Sick* (New York: Prodist, 1978), pp. 165, 167; Burgess, *Nurses, Patients, and Pocketbooks*, pp. 97–98.

Chapter 7

1. U.S. Bureau of the Census, *Historical Statistics of the United States* (Washington, D.C.: U.S. G.P.O., 1975), 1:76, 379, 383, 386. A major study of medical education during this period that was published too late for inclusion in this study is: Kenneth M. Ludmerer, *Learning to Heal: The Development of American Medical Education* (New York: Basic Books, 1985).

2. Ibid., p. 386.

3. Laurence R. Veysey, *The Emergence of the American University* (Chicago: University of Chicago Press, 1965), pp. 320–24; Joseph Ben-David, *The Scientist's Role in Society* (Englewood Cliffs, N.J.: Prentice-Hall, 1971), pp. 154–55.

4. Robert A. McCaughey, "The Transformation of American Academic Life: Harvard University 1821–1892," *Perspectives in American History* 8 (1974): 292–314; Ernest Earnest, *Academic Procession* (Indianapolis: Bobbs-Merrill, 1953), pp. 284–85.

5. Edward D. Eddy, Jr. *Colleges for Our Land and Time* (New York: Harper, 1957), p. 210; McCaughey, "The Transformation of American Academic Life: Harvard University 1821–1892," pp. 287–90.

6. Allan Nevins, *The State Universities and Democracy* (Urbana: University of Illinois Press, 1962), pp. 86–88; Eddy, *Colleges for Our Land and Time*, pp. 56–59, 119–22, 216–19.

7. R. L. Duffus, *Democracy Enters College* (New York: Scribner's 1936), pp. 50–51, 65, 126, 143.

8. Gerald E. Markowitz and David K. Rosner, "Doctors in Crisis: A Study of the Use of Medical Education Reform to Establish Modern Professional Elitism in Medicine," *American Quarterly* 25 (1973): 89–91; Samuel L. Baker, "Physician Licensure Laws in the United States, 1865–1915" *Journal of the History of Medicine* 39 (1984): 192–94.

9. Victor Johnson, "The Council on Medical Education and Hospitals," in Morris Fishbein, *A History of the American Medical Association 1847 to 1947* (Philadelphia: Saunders, 1947), pp. 895–97.

10. Commission on Medical Education, *Final Report* (New York, 1932), Table 90.

11. E. Richard Brown, *Rockefeller Medicine Men* (Berkeley and Los Angeles: University of California Press, 1979), p. 176; Lewellys F. Barker, "Medicine and the Universities," *American Medicine* 4 (1902): 143–44; "Nebraska College of Medicine Closes Voluntarily," *Journal of the American Medical Association* 52 (1909): 1862.

12. William G. Rothstein, *American Physicians in the Nineteenth Century* (Baltimore: Johns Hopkins University Press, 1972), p. 294.

13. Brown, *Rockefeller Medical Men*, pp. 142–51; Michael J. Lepore, *Death of the Clinician* (Springfield, Ill.: Thomas, 1982), p. 29. A recent analysis of the Flexner report and the role of foundations can be found in: Howard S. Berliner, *A System of Scientific Medicine: Philanthropic Foundations in the Flexner Era* (New York: Travistock, 1985).

14. John M. Dodson, "Report of the Council on Medical Education," *Journal of the American Medical Association* 72 (1919): 1752; Brown, *Rockefeller Medical Men*, p. 151.

15. Willis G. Tucker, "Albany Medical College," in *History of Medicine in New York*, ed. James J. Walsh (New York, 1919), 2:643–44.

16. "The Proprietary Medical School," *New York Medical Journal* 91 (1910): 1343–44; "The Report of the Carnegie Foundation on Medical Education," *Medical Record* 77 (1910): 1097; "The Carnegie Foundation Report on Medical Education," *Journal of the American Medical Association* 44 (1910): 1948–49.

17. Abraham Flexner, *Medical Education in the United States and Canada* (New York: Carnegie Foundation for the Advancement of Teaching, 1910), pp. 53–61, 92, 96–101.

18. Ibid., pp. 10–11; Robert P. Hudson, "Abraham Flexner in Perspective," *Bulletin of the History of Medicine* 46 (1972): 545–61.

19. Flexner, *Medical Education in the United States and Canada*, p. 11.

20. Ibid., pp. 15, 19; H. D. Arnold, "Report of the Reference Committee on Medical Education," *Journal of the American Medical Association* 54 (1910): 2061–62.

21. Harold Perkin, "The Historical Perspective," in *Perspectives on Higher Education*, ed. Burton R. Clark (Berkeley and Los Angeles: University of California Press, 1984), p. 38; Flexner, *Medical Education in the United States and Canada*, pp. 146, 151.

22. Dodson, "Report of the Council on Medical Education," p. 1753; *Future Directions for Medical Education* (Chicago: American Medical Association, 1982), pp. 61, 73; Johnson, "The Council on Medical Education and Hospitals," pp. 914–15.

23. Ibid., pp. 909–10.

24. Ibid., pp. 910–12; Commission on Medical Education, *Final Report;* Herman G.

Weiskotten et al., *Medical Education in the United States: 1934–1939* (Chicago: American Medical Association, 1940), pp. 5–6.

25. Irving J. Lewis and Cecil G. Sheps, *The Sick Citadel: The American Academic Medical Center and the Public Interest* (Cambridge, Mass.: Oelgeschlager, Gunn and Hain, 1983), p. 123; George F. Zook and M. E. Haggerty, *The Evaluation of Higher Institutions I: Principles of Accrediting Higher Institutions* (Chicago: University of Chicago Press, 1936), p. 124.

26. Elton Rayack, *Professional Power and American Medicine* (Cleveland: World, 1967), pp. 72–78.

27. Arthur D. Bevan, "Cooperation in Medical Education and Medical Service," *Journal of the American Medical Association* 90 (1928): 1176; Commission on Medical Education, *Final Report*, Table 89; U.S. Bureau of the Census, *Historical Statistics of the United States*, 1:76; Rayack, *Professional Power and American Medicine*, p. 72.

28. Robert C. Derbyshire, *Medical Licensure and Discipline in the United States* (Baltimore: Johns Hopkins Press 1969), pp. 63–65, 68.

29. George M. Gould, *The Jefferson Medical College of Philadelphia* (New York: Lewis, 1904), 1:260–65; George H. Callcott, *A History of the University of Maryland* (Baltimore: Maryland Historical Society, 1966), pp. 265, 279–80.

30. William H. Welch, *Papers and Addresses* (Baltimore: Johns Hopkins Press, 1932), 3:27–40, 92–103.

31. Weiskotten et al., *Medical Education in the United States: 1934–1939*, pp. 16, 20; Saul Jarcho, "Medical Education in the United States—1910–1956," *Journal of the Mount Sinai Hospital* 26 (1959): 356, 368.

32. Weiskotten et al., *Medical Education in the United States: 1934–1939*, pp. 25, 114.

33. Joseph C. Aub and Ruth K. Hapgood, *Pioneer in Modern Medicine: David Linn Edsall of Harvard* (Boston, Mass., 1970), p. 221; Weiskotten et al., *Medical Education in the United States: 1934–1939*, p. 5; Burton D. Myers, "Twenty Years' Progress in Buildings, Physical Equipment, Finances, Faculty and Enrollment," *Proceedings of the Annual Congress on Medical Education, Medical Licensure, Public Health and Hospitals* (1925): 3; Esther L. Brown, *Physicians and Medical Care* (New York: Russell Sage Foundation, 1937), pp. 88, 91.

34. Commission on Medical Education, *Final Report*, p. 283; Weiskotten et al., *Medical Education in the United States: 1934–1939*, pp. 104–8.

35. Commission on Medical Education, *Final Report*, p. 283; Ward Darley, "The Financial Status of Medical Education," in *Medical Education Today*, ed. Dean F. Smiley (Chicago: Association of American Medical Colleges, 1953), pp. 53–54; Irving S. Cutter, "The School of Medicine," in *Higher Education in America*, ed. Raymond A. Kent (Boston: Ginn, 1930), p. 328; Aub and Hapgood, *Pioneer in Modern Medicine: David Linn Edsall of Harvard*, p. 320.

36. Weiskotten et al., *Medical Education in the United States: 1934–1939*, pp. 106–7, 112.

37. Ibid., p. 40; Vernon W. Lippard, *A Half-Century of American Medical Education: 1920–1970* (New York: Josiah Macy, Jr., Foundation, 1974), p. 52.

38. Eugene J. Dubois, "The Development of Clinical Subjects as Contributing to University Work," *Science* 82 (1935): 474.

39. Francis W. Peabody, "The Soul of the Clinic," *Journal of the American Medical Association* 90 (1928): 1193–95.

40. Commission on Medical Education, *Final Report*, p. 11; Weiskotten et al., *Medical Education in the United States: 1934–1939*, p. 67.

41. James G. Burrow, *AMA: Voice of American Medicine,* (Baltimore: Johns Hopkins Press, 1963), p. 319.

42. Brown, *Physicians and Medical Care,* p. 90; Lewis and Sheps, *The Sick Citadel,* p. 120.

43. Ibid., pp. 122–23.

44. Frederick C. Zapffe, "The Curriculum," *Proceedings of the Association of American Medical Colleges,* 35th meeting (1925): 145–47; Martin Kaufman, "American Medical Education," in *The Education of American Physicians,* ed. Ronald Numbers (Berkeley and Los Angeles: University of California Press, 1980), pp. 24–25.

45. William W. Graves, "Some Factors Tending Toward Adequate Instruction in Nervous and Mental Diseases," *Journal of the American Medical Association* 63 (1914): 1708.

46. Ibid., pp. 1709–10; Franklin G. Ebaugh and Charles A. Rymer, *Psychiatry in Medical Education* (New York: Commonwealth Fund, 1942), pp. 5, 108, 110, 491–92.

47. Jean A. Curran and Eleanor Cockerill, *Widening Horizons in Medical Education* (New York: Commonwealth Fund, 1948), pp. 21–24.

48. Judith W. Leavitt, "Public Health and Preventive Medicine," in *The Education of American Physicians,* pp. 258–67; Weiskotten et al., *Medical Education in the United States: 1934–1939,* p. 207.

49. Aub and Hapgood, *Pioneer in Modern Medicine: David Linn Edsall of Harvard,* pp. 182–86, 259; John G. Freymann, *The American Health Care System* (New York: Medcom, 1974), p. 46.

50. Weiskotten et al., *Medical Education in the United States: 1934–1939,* pp. 119, 129, 137, 146, 155, 161.

51. N. P. Colwell, "Present Needs of Medical Education," *Journal of the American Medical Association* 82 (1924): 838; Weiskotten et al., *Medical Education in the United States: 1934–1939,* pp. 121, 130, 138, 148, 156, 161.

52. Alan M. Chesney, *The Johns Hopkins Hospital and the Johns Hopkins University School of Medicine: 1867–1893* (Baltimore: Johns Hopkins University Press, 1943), 1:235; Robert E. Kohler, *From Medical Chemistry to Biochemistry* (Cambridge, England: Cambridge University Press, 1982), pp. 115–16.

53. W. C. Rappleye, "Survey of Medical Education," *Journal of the American Medical Association* 88 (1927): 844; Commission on Medical Education, *Final Report,* pp. 174–75, 181–82; Weiskotten et al., *Medical Education in the United States: 1934–1939,* p. 85.

54. Welch, *Papers and Addresses,* 3:57–58.

55. Kohler, *From Medical Chemistry to Biochemistry,* pp. 156–57; Lippard, *A Half-Century of American Medical Education: 1920–1970,* pp. 8–10.

56. Chesney, *The Johns Hopkins Hospital and the Johns Hopkins University School of Medicine: 1867–1893,* 1:236.

57. Weiskotten et al., *Medical Education in the United States: 1934–1939,* pp. 126, 135, 143, 152, 158, 165; Joseph Ben-David, "Scientific Productivity and Academic Organization in Nineteenth Century Medicine," *American Sociological Review* 25 (1960): 828–43.

58. C. M. Jackson, "Progress in Anatomy Since 1900," *Proceedings of the Annual Congress on Medical Education, Medical Licensure, Public Health and Hospitals* (March, 1925), pp. 7–8; John B. Blake, "Anatomy," in *The Education of American Physicians,* ed. Ronald L. Numbers, pp. 41–43.

59. Ibid., pp. 44–45; Weiskotten et al., *Medical Education in the United States: 1934–1939,* p. 121.

60. American Physiological Society, *History of the American Physiological Society,*

Semicentennial 1887–1937 (Baltimore, 1938), pp. 4, 71; Weiskotten et al., *Medical Education in the United States: 1934–1939*, pp. 136–44.

61. Kohler, *From Medical Chemistry to Biochemistry*, pp. 160–62.

62. Ibid., pp. 192, 195–98, 207; Weiskotten et al., *Medical Education in the United States: 1934–1939*, p. 130.

63. Kohler, *From Medical Chemistry to Biochemistry*, pp. 215–16, 227–29; Albert P. Mathews, "Twenty Years of Growth and Development of Biochemistry," *Proceedings of the Annual Congress on Medical Education, Medical Licensure, Public Health, and Hospitals* (March, 1925), p. 12.

64. Kohler, *From Medical Chemistry to Biochemistry*, pp. 232–33, 284–85; Weiskotten et al., *Medical Education in the United States: 1934–1939*, pp. 134–35.

65. William G. Rothstein, "Pathology: The Evolution of a Specialty in American Medicine," *Medical Care* 17 (1979): 978–81; Richard H. Shryock, *American Medical Research Past and Present* (New York: Commonwealth Fund, 1947), p. 90.

66. James Ewing, "Twenty Years' Progress in American Teaching of Pathology," *Proceedings of the Annual Congress on Medical Education, Medical Licensure, Public Health and Hospitals* (March, 1925), p. 23.

67. Rothstein, "Pathology: The Evolution of a Specialty in American Medicine," pp. 979–80; Weiskotten et al., *Medical Education in the United States: 1934–1939*, pp. 161–62.

68. David L. Cowen, "Materia Medica and Pharmacology," in *The Education of American Physicians*, pp. 100, 105, 108–11; Weiskotten et al., *Medical Education in the United States: 1934–1939*, pp. 145–53.

69. Ewing, "Twenty Years' Progress in American Teaching of Pathology," p. 24; Weiskotten et al., *Medical Education in the United States: 1934–1939*, pp. 154–59.

70. American Physiological Society, *History of the American Physiological Society, Semicentennial 1887–1937*, pp. 76–77, 92–94, 120.

71. Ibid., pp. 83–85; Harvey Cushing, "The Binding Influence of a Library on a Subdividing Profession," *Bulletin of the Johns Hopkins Hospital* 46 (1930): 35.

Chapter 8

1. Michael J. Lepore, *Death of the Clinician* (Springfield, Ill.: Thomas, 1962), pp. 20–22; Welch, *Papers and Addresses*, 3:98.

2. Joseph Ben-David, "The Universities and the Growth of Science in Germany and the United States," *Minerva* 7 (1968–69): 2–5, 7, 10–11; Charles E. McClelland, *State, Society, and University in Germany: 1700–1914* (Cambridge, England: Cambridge University Press, 1980), pp. 280–81.

3. Ibid., pp. 260–64; M. G. Seelig, "Some Fallacies in the Argument against Full-Time Clinical Instruction," *Proceedings of the Association of American Medical Colleges*, 25th meeting (1915): 37–38; Alexander Busch, "The Vicissitudes of the Privatdozent," *Minerva* 1 (1963): 328–30.

4. Fritz K. Ringer, *The Decline of the German Mandarins: The German Academic Community, 1890–1933* (Cambridge: Harvard University Press, 1969), pp. 37, 55–56; James B. Herrick, *Memories of Eighty Years* (Chicago: University of Chicago Press, 1949), p. 123.

5. McClelland, *State, Society and University in Germany: 1700–1914*, pp. 234–45; Ringer, *The Decline of the German Mandarins: The German Academic Community, 1890–1933*, p. 39.

6. Ben-David, "The Universities and the Growth of Science in Germany and the United States," pp. 7–8.

7. Abraham Flexner, *Medical Education in the United States and Canada* (1910; reprint ed., New York: Arno Press, 1972), pp. 102, 142, 151.

8. E. Richard Brown, *Rockefeller Medical Men* (Berkeley and Los Angeles: University of California Press, 1979), pp. 100–1; J. Collins Warren, *To Work in the Vineyard of Surgery,* ed. Edward D. Churchill (Cambridge: Harvard University Press, 1958), p. 192.

9. Ibid., pp. 211–12; George W. Corner, *A History of the Rockefeller Institute: 1901–1953* (New York: Rockefeller Institute Press, 1964), pp. 45, 51–52, 94; Richard H. Shryock, *American Medical Research Past and Present* (New York: Commonwealth Fund, 1947), pp. 94–95.

10. Frederick S. Lee, W. B. Cannon, and R. M. Pearce, "Medical Research in its Relation to Medical Schools," *Proceedings of the Association of American Medical Colleges,* 27th meeting (1917): 21–22; Thomas B. Turner, *Heritage of Excellence: The Johns Hopkins Medical Institutions: 1914–1947* (Baltimore: Johns Hopkins University Press, 1974), pp. 95–96; Rosemary Stevens, *American Medicine and the Public Interest* (New Haven: Yale University Press, 1971), p. 69.

11. Ibid.; Brown, *Rockefeller Medical Men,* pp. 183–86.

12. Daniel M. Fox, "Abraham Flexner's Unpublished Report," *Bulletin of the History of Medicine* 54 (1980): 477; Waldemar A. Nielson, *The Big Foundations* (New York: Columbia University Press, 1972), pp. 55–56; William A. Pusey, "The Importance of Being Historically Minded," *Journal of the American Medical Association* 89 (1927): 2081–82.

13. Raymond B. Fosdick, *Adventure in Giving* (New York: Harper and Row, 1962), pp. 167, 172; Carleton B. Chapman, "The Flexner Report," *Deadalus* 103 (1974): 106; Ernest V. Hollis, *Philanthropic Foundations and Higher Education* (New York: Columbia University Press, 1938), pp. 212–13.

14. Donald Fleming, *William H. Welch and the Rise of Scientific Medicine* (Boston: Little, Brown, 1954), pp. 131, 156, 175–77.

15. William Osler, "The Inner History of the Johns Hopkins Hospital," *Johns Hopkins Medical Journal* 125 (1969): 189–91.

16. Lepore, *Death of the Clinician,* pp. 37–38; Edward H. Richardson, *A Doctor Remembers* (New York: Vantage Press, 1959), p. 192.

17. Lepore, *Death of the Clinician,* pp. 53–64; Lewellys F. Barker, *Time and the Physician* (New York: Putnam, 1942), pp. 106, 147–52.

18. Alan M. Chesney, *The Johns Hopkins Hospital and the Johns Hopkins University School of Medicine: 1905–1914* (Baltimore: Johns Hopkins Press, 1963), 3:287, 295–96, 299–300.

19. Fleming, *William H. Welch and the Rise of Scientific Medicine,* p. 179; Lewellys F. Barker, *The Young Man and Medicine* (New York: Macmillan, 1928), pp. 74–75.

20. Richardson, *A Doctor Remembers,* pp. 188–89.

21. Barker, *Time and the Physician,* pp. 190, 192, 205; G. Canby Robinson, *Adventures in Medical Education* (Cambridge: Harvard University Press, 1957), pp. 162–66; J. M. T. Finney, *A Surgeon's Life* (New York: Putnam, 1940), p. 229; Richardson, *A Doctor Remembers,* p. 200.

22. Ibid., p. 197; Turner, *Heritage of Excellence: The Johns Hopkins Medical Institutions: 1914–1947,* pp. 225–26, 535.

23. Ibid., pp. 226–228.

24. Jon M. Kingsdale, "The Growth of Hospitals," (Ph.D. diss., University of Michigan, 1981), pp. 346, 353–59, 363.

25. C. R. Bardeen, "Aims, Methods, and Results in Medical Education," *Proceedings of the Association of American Medical Colleges,* 26th meeting (1916): 7–9.

26. Brown, *Rockefeller Medical Men,* p. 165; Fosdick, *Adventure in Giving,* pp. 159–61, 164; Lepore, *Death of the Clinician,* pp. 188–205; Ilza Veith and Franklin C. McLean, *The University of Chicago Clinics and Clinical Departments, 1927–1952* (Chicago: University of Chicago Press, 1952), p. 23; Robinson, *Adventures in Medical Education,* pp. 158–59, 176.

27. Lepore, *Death of the Clinician,* pp. 88–89, 142–44, 149–51; Albert R. Lamb, *The Presbyterian Hospital and the Columbia-Presbyterian Medical Center, 1868–1943* (New York: Columbia University Press, 1955).

28. Lepore, *Death of the Clinician,* pp. 98–127.

29. Ibid., pp. 160–62; Arthur D. Bevan, "Supplement to the Report of the Council on Medical Education and Hopsitals," *Journal of the American Medical Association* 76 (1921): 1765–66; Fosdick, *Adventure in Giving,* p. 160.

30. William H. Welch, "Discussion," *American Medical Association Bulletin* 10 (1915): 259; Reginald Fitz, "The Teaching of Medicine from the Standpoint of a Half-Time Teacher," *Proceedings of the Annual Congress on Medical Education, Medical Licensure and Hospitals* (1930): 49–51.

31. Arthur D. Dunn, "The Full-Time System of Teaching from the Standpoint of a Practitioner and Teacher," *Proceedings of the Annual Congress on Medical Education, Medical Licensure and Hospitals* (1930): 53; Theodore C. Janeway, "Outside Professional Engagements by Members of Professional Faculties," *Journal of the American Medical Association* 90 (1928): 1315.

32. Lepore, *Death of the Clinician,* p. 93.

33. David L. Edsall, "The Product of Medical Education," *Boston Medical and Surgical Journal* 191 (1924): 291–92; Fitz, "The Teaching of Medicine from the Standpoint of a Half-Time Teacher," p. 50.

34. Arthur D. Bevan, "Cooperation in Medical Education and Medical Service," *Journal of the American Medical Association* 90 (1928): 1176–77; Lepore, *Death of the Clinician,* pp. 48–50.

35. Arthur D. Bevan, "Discussion," *Proceedings of the Association of American Medical Colleges,* 25th meeting (1915): 41.

36. Frederic A. Washburn, *The Massachusetts General Hospital* (Boston: Houghton Mifflin, 1939), pp. 241–43; Lamb, *The Presbyterian Hospital and the Columbia-Presbyterian Medical Center, 1868–1943,* pp. 198–99.

37. Fosdick, *Adventure in Giving,* pp. 162, 165, 167–68; Ellen C. Cangi, "Abraham Flexner's Philanthropy," *Bulletin of the History of Medicine* 56 (1982): 166–68, 173–74; Joseph C. Aub and Ruth K. Hapgood, *Pioneer in Modern Medicine: David Linn Edsall of Harvard* (Boston, 1970), pp. 278–80; Lamb, *The Presbyterian Hospital and the Columbia-Presbyterian Medical Center, 1868–1943,* pp. 222–24, 445–48.

38. Weiskotten et al., *Medical Education in the United States: 1934–1939,* pp. 171, 180, 189, 197, 202–6; Turner, *Heritage of Excellence: The Johns Hopkins Medical Institutions: 1914–1947,* pp. 413, 459.

39. Edward D. Churchill, "The Development of the Hospital," in *The Hospital in Contemporary Life,* ed. Nathan W. Faxon (Cambridge: Harvard University Press, 1949), pp. 40–41; Walter L. Niles, "The Cornell Pay Clinic," *Journal of the American Medical Association* 77 (1921): 1755; Veith and McClean, *The University of Chicago Clinics and Clinical Departments, 1927–1952,* pp. 23–24, 28–29.

40. Abraham Flexner, *Medical Education: A Comparative Study* (New York: Macmillan, 1925), pp. 324–25.

41. Vernon W. Lippard, *A Half Century of American Medical Education: 1920–1970*

(New York: Josiah Macy, Jr., Foundation, 1974), p. 54; Harvey Cushing, "The Binding Influence of a Library on a Subdividing Profession," *Bulletin of the Johns Hopkins Hospital* 46 (1930): 37.

42. Weiskotten et al., *Medical Education in the United States: 1934–1939*, pp. 177, 185, 194, 201; Eugene J. DuBois, "The Development of Clinical Subjects as Contributing to University Work," *Science* 82 (1935): 473; Aub and Hapgood, *Pioneer in Modern Medicine: David Linn Edsall of Harvard*, p. 302.

43. Elliott C. Cutler, "Undergraduate Teaching of Surgery," *Annals of Surgery* 102 (1935): 498–504; Martin Kaufman, *The University of Vermont College of Medicine* (Hanover, N.H., 1979), p. 157; Henry A. Christian, James H. Means, and Francis W. Peabody, "Teaching of Medicine at Harvard Medical School," *Methods and Problems of Medical Education*, 8th series (New York: Rockefeller Foundation, 1927), p. 75; Turner, *Heritage of Excellence: The Johns Hopkins Medical Institutions, 1914–1947*, p. 249.

44. Samuel W. Lambert, "Twenty Years' Progress in the Teaching of Internal Medicine and the Medical Specialties," *Proceedings of the Annual Congress on Medical Education, Medical Licensure, Public Health and Hospitals* (1925): 27; Weiskotten et al., *Medical Education in the United States: 1934–1939*, pp. 86–87, 173–75; Cutler, "Undergraduate Teaching of Surgery," p. 500.

45. Edward C. Atwater, "'Making Fewer Mistakes': A History of Students and Patients," *Bulletin of the History of Medicine* 57 (1983): 180–81.

46. Richard C. Cabot, "Medical Ethics in the Hospital," *Nosokomeion* 2 (1931): 151–59.

47. Jean A. Curran, *Internships and Residencies in New York City, 1934–1937* (New York: Commonwealth Fund, 1938), pp. 126–28; Stevens, *American Medicine and the Public Interest*, pp. 260–61.

48. Francis W. Peabody, "The Care of the Patient," *Journal of the American Medical Association* 88 (1927): 877–78; Edsall, "The Product of Medical Education," pp. 288–89.

49. Ibid., p. 289; Commission on Medical Education, *Final Report* (New York, 1932), p. 209; W. McKim Marriott, "Use of the Outpatient Department in Medical Education," *Proceedings of the Annual Congress on Medical Education, Medical Licensure and Hospitals* (1936): 54; Irving S. Cutter, "The Use of the Outpatient Department in Medical Teaching," *Proceedings of the Annual Congress on Medical Education, Medical Licensure and Hospitals* (1928): 45.

50. George Shambaugh, "The Outpatient Clinic and the Problem of Instruction in Clinical Medicine," *Journal of the American Medical Association* 88 (1927): 844; Alan M. Chesney, *The Johns Hopkins Hospital and the Johns Hopkins University School of Medicine: 1893–1905* (Baltimore: Johns Hopkins Press, 1958), 2:260–61, 485; Margaret S. Brogden, "The Johns Hopkins Hospital Department of Social Service, 1907–31," *Social Service Review* 38 (1964): 90.

51. Alan M. Chesney, *The Hospitals of Baltimore and the Indigent Sick* (Baltimore, 1932), pp. 7, 9–10.

52. Turner, *Heritage of Excellence: The Johns Hopkins Medical Institutions, 1914–1947*, pp. 18–19, 151, 286, 293, 401.

53. Ibid., p. 566; Edsall, "The Product of Medical Education," p. 289.

54. Paul F. Clark, *The University of Wisconsin Medical School* (Madison: University of Wisconsin Press, 1967), pp. 33–34; W. H. Goodrich and V. P. Sydenstricker, "Attendance on City's Poor as Part of Clinical Instruction at the Medical Department, University of Georgia," *Methods and Problems of Medical Education*, 6th series (New York: Rockefeller Foundation, 1927), pp. 247–49.

55. Commission on Medical Education, *Final Report*, p. 173.

56. Horace D. Arnold, "Report of the Sub-Committee on Curriculum for the Clinical

Years," *Proceedings of the Association of American Medical Colleges,* 20th meeting (1910): 138.

57. Lippard, *A Half-Century of American Medical Education: 1920–1970,* pp. 13, 54.

58. Weiskotten et al., *Medical Education in the United States: 1934–1939,* p. 87; Commission on Medical Education, *Final Report,* pp. 201–2; Franklin G. Ebaugh and Charles A. Rymer, *Psychiatry in Medical Education* (New York: Commonwealth Fund, 1942), p. 64.

59. Commission on Medical Education, *Final Report,* pp. 198, 255.

60. DuBois, "The Development of Clinical Subjects as Contributing to University Work," p. 476.

61. N. P. Colwell, "The Hospital's Function in Medical Education," *Journal of the American Medical Association* 88 (1927): 781–82.

62. Ibid.; Weiskotten et al., *Medical Education in the United States: 1934–1939,* p. 101; C. Rufus Rorem, *The Public's Investment in Hospitals* (Chicago: University of Chicago Press, 1930), pp. 102–104.

63. Weiskotten et al., *Medical Education in the United States: 1934–1939,* p. 112.

64. Harry F. Dowling, *City Hospitals* (Cambridge: Harvard University Press, 1982), pp. 109–111, 124; Weiskotten et al., *Medical Education in the United States: 1934–1939,* p. 97.

65. Kingsdale, "The Growth of Hospitals," pp. 310, 358, 403, 429–31.

66. Lamb, *The Presbyterian Hospital and the Columbia-Presbyterian Medical Center, 1868–1943,* pp. 161–64, 225–35, 357; Robinson, *Adventures in Medical Education,* pp. 189–90.

67. Lepore, *Death of the Clinician,* pp. 236–37.

68. Willard C. Rappleye, *The Current Era of the Faculty of Medicine Columbia University, 1910–1958* (New York: Columbia University Press, 1958), p. 19; S. S. Goldwater, *On Hospitals* (New York: Macmillian, 1951), pp. 119–21.

69. E. H. Lewinski-Corwin, *The Hospital Situation in Greater New York* (New York: Putnam, 1924), p. 172.

70. Weiskotten et al., *Medical Education in the United States: 1934–1939,* pp. 96–97; James C. White, *Sketches from My Life, 1833–1913* (Cambridge, Mass.: Riverside Press, 1914), pp. 180–81.

71. Chesney, *The Hospitals of Baltimore and the Indigent Sick,* pp. 5, 12.

72. Rosemary Stevens, "Sweet Charity: State Aid to Hospitals in Pennsylvania, 1870–1910," *Bulletin of the History of Medicine* 58 (1984): 489, 491; Chesney, *The Hospitals of Baltimore and the Indigent Sick,* p. 13; Turner, *Heritage of Excellence: The Johns Hopkins Medical Institutions, 1914–1947,* pp. 312, 562; Kingsdale, "The Growth of Hospitals," pp. 313, 352–53.

73. Weiskotten et al., *Medical Education in the United States: 1934–1939,* pp. 96–97; Turner, *Heritage of Excellence: The Johns Hopkins Medical Institutions, 1914–1947,* pp. 304–5.

74. Henry K. Beecher and Mark D. Altschule, *Medicine at Harvard* (Hanover, N.H.: University Press of New England, 1977), p. 201; Aub and Hapgood, *Pioneer in Modern Medicine: David Linn Edsall of Harvard,* p. 229.

Chapter 9

1. U.S. Bureau of the Census, *Statistical Abstract of the United States: 1980* (Washington, D.C.: U.S. G.P.O., 1980), p. 30; U.S. Bureau of the Census, *Statistical Abstract of the United States: 1984* (Washington, D.C.: U.S. G.P.O., 1983), p. 31.

2. National Center for Health Statistics, *Health, United States, 1983* (Washington, D.C.: U.S. G.P.O., 1983), pp. 97, 99.

3. National Center for Health Statistics, *Health, United States, 1981* (Washington, D.C.: U.S. G.P.O., 1981), p. 117; National Center for Health Statistics, *Health, United States, 1983*, p. 105.

4. U.S. Bureau of the Census, *Statistical Abstract of the United States: 1984*, p. 123.

5. National Center for Health Statistics, *Health, United States, 1983*, pp. 107–13.

6. U.S. Bureau of the Census, *Statistical Abstract of the United States: 1984*, pp. 121–23.

7. National Center for Health Statistics, *Health, United States, 1983*, p. 137; Thomas W. Bice, Robert L. Eichhorn, and Peter D. Fox, "Socioeconomic Status and Use of Physician Services," *Medical Care* 10 (1972): 261–71.

8. Karen Davis, "Public-Policy Implications," in *Ambulatory Care: Problems of Cost and Access*, ed. Stuart A. Altman, Joanna Lion, and Judith L. Williams (Lexington, Mass.: Lexington Books, 1983), pp. 13–25.

9. National Center for Health Statistics, *Health, United States, 1983*, p. 137.

10. U.S. Bureau of the Census, *Statistical Abstract of the United States: 1984*, pp. 113–17; National Center for Health Statistics, *Health, United States, 1976–1977* (Washington, D.C.: U.S. G.P.O., 1977), pp. 290–91; National Center for Health Statistics, *Health, United States, 1983*, p. 149.

11. U.S. Bureau of the Census, *Statistical Abstract of the United States: 1980*, p. 119; U.S. Bureau of the Census, *Statistical Abstract of the United States: 1984*, p. 118.

12. American Hospital Association, *Hospital Statistics: 1984* (Chicago, 1984), pp. xxiii, 208.

13. National Center for Health Statistics, *Health, United States, 1983*, pp. 177, 187.

14. National Center for Health Statistics, *Health, United States, 1982* (Washington, D.C.: U.S. G.P.O., 1982), pp. 151–52; Marshall W. Raffel, *The U.S. Health Care System* (New York: Wiley, 1980), p. 371.

15. National Center for Health Statistics, *Health, United States, 1983*, pp. 184, 186.

16. Ibid., p. 186; U.S. Bureau of the Census, *Historical Statistics of the United States* (Washington, D.C.: U.S. G.P.O., 1975), 1:82; U.S. Bureau of the Census, *Statistical Abstract of the United States: 1984*, p. 107.

17. National Center for Health Statistics, *Health, United States, 1983*, pp. 198–99; Health Care Financing Administration, *HCFA Statistics* (n.p.: U.S. Department of Health and Human Services, Sept., 1984), pp. 16, 20–21.

18. National Center for Health Statistics, *Health, United States, 1980* (Washington, D.C.: U.S. G.P.O., 1980), p. 101.

19. Ibid., pp. 104–106; National Center for Health Statistics, *Health, United States, 1983*, pp. 171, 178, 182.

20. Ibid., pp. 102–4.

21. Benson B. Roe, "The UCR Boondoggle," *New England Journal of Medicine* 305 (1981): 41–45; Thomas L. Delbanco, Katharine C. Meyers, and Elliot A. Segal, "Paying the Physician's Fee," *New England Journal of Medicine* 301 (1979): 1316–17.

22. Ibid., p. 1318.

23. National Center for Health Statistics, *Health, United States, 1980*, pp. 52, 107–8; U.S. Bureau of the Census, *Statistical Abstract of the United States: 1984*, p. 117.

24. National Center for Health Statistics, *Health, United States, 1980*, pp. 106–7.

25. National Center for Health Statistics, *Health, United States, 1983*, pp. 161–62.

26. Ibid., p. 163; National Center for Health Statistics, *Health, United States, 1976–1977*, p. 308.

27. William B. Schwartz et al., "The Changing Geographic Distribution of Board-Certified Physicians," *New England Journal of Medicine* 303 (1980): 1032–36.

28. William G. Rothstein, "Pathology: The Evolution of a Specialty in American Medicine," *Medical Care* 17 (1979): 975–88; Paul B. Beeson, "The Natural History of Medical Subspecialties," *Annals of Internal Medicine* 93 (1980): 624–26.

29. Rosemary Stevens, *American Medicine and the Public Interest* (New Haven: Yale University Press, 1971), pp. 181, 245, 542–43.

30. Ibid., pp. 298–99: Morton C. Creditor and Una K. Creditor, "Residency: The Fallacy of Need," *New England Journal of Medicine* 293 (1975): 1202.

31. American Board of Medical Specialties, *Annual Report and Reference Handbook—1984* (Evanston, Ill., 1984), pp. 7–31, 53–54.

32. Ibid., pp. 55–56; Stevens, *American Medicine and the Public Interest,* p. 320.

33. Edithe J. Levit and William D. Holden, "Specialty Board Certification Rates," *JAMA* 239 (1978): 411.

34. John G. Freymann, *The American Health Care System* (New York: Medcom, 1974), pp. 67–68; Raffel, *The U.S. Health Care System,* p. 129; Roger A. Reynolds and Jonathan B. Abram, eds., *Socioeconomic Characteristics of Medical Practice 1983* (Chicago: American Medical Association, 1983), pp. 54–64.

35. Avedis Donabedian, Solomon J. Axelrod, and Leon Wysewianski, *Medical Care ChartBook,* 7th ed. (Washington, D.C.: AUPHA Press, 1980), pp. 166, 169.

36. Maryland Y. Pennell and Marion E. Altenderfer, *Health Manpower Source Book* (Washington, D.C.: U.S. G.P.O., 1952), 1:48–51; U.S. Bureau of the Census, *Historical Statistics of the United States,* 1:166.

37. Reynolds and Abram, eds., *Socioeconomic Characteristics of Medical Practice 1983,* p. 46.

38. National Center for Health Statistics, *Health, United States, 1976–1977,* pp. 259, 262–63.

39. Ibid., p. 263–64.

40. National Center for Health Statistics, *Health, United States, 1980,* p. 53. See also Eugene G. McCarthy and Madelon L. Finkel, "Surgical Utilization in the U.S.A.," *Medical Care* 18 (1980): 883–91.

41. Paul B. Beeson, "Changes in Medical Therapy During the Past Half Century," *Medicine* 59 (1980): 81.

42. U.S. Bureau of the Census, *Statistical Abstract of the United States: 1980,* pp. 487, 828.

43. Harry F. Dowling, *Medicines for Man* (New York: Knopf, 1970), pp. 288–89.

44. Henry E. Simmons and Paul D. Stolley, "This is Medical Progress?" *JAMA* 227 (1974): 1024, 1026, 1028.

45. John E. McGowan, Jr., and Maxwell Finland, "Usage of Antibiotics in a General Hospital," *Journal of Infectious Diseases* 130 (1974): 165–68.

46. Ingrid Waldron, "Increased Prescribing of Valium, Librium, and Other Drugs," *International Journal of Health Services* 7 (1977): 38; Hugh J. Parry et al., "National Patterns of Psychotherapeutic Drug Use," *Archives of General Psychiatry* 28 (1973): 770.

47. Dianne Fejer and Reginald Smart, "The Use of Psychoactive Drugs by Adults," *Canadian Psychiatric Association Journal* 18 (1973): 314; Waldron, "Increased Prescribing of Valium, Librium, and Other Drugs," p. 39.

48. Ibid., pp. 37–62; Parry et al., "National Patterns of Psychotherapeutic Drug Use," pp. 769–83.

49. "Another Side of the Coin," *JAMA* 227 (1974): 1049.

50. Abraham Chaiton et al., "Patterns of Medical Drug Use—A Community Focus," CMA Journal 10 (1976): 33–37; George J. Warheit, Sandra A. Arey, and Edith Swanson, "Patterns of Drug Use: An Epidemiologic Overview," *Journal of Drug Issues* 6 (1976): 223–27.

51. Calvin M. Kunin, "In Comment," *JAMA* 227 (1974): 1031; Elina Hemminki, "Review of Literature on the Factors Affecting Drug Prescribing," *Social Science and Medicine* 9 (1975): 111–16.

52. Marshall H. Becker et al., "Correlates of Physicians' Prescribing Behavior," *Inquiry* 9 (Sept., 1972): 32–34; Paul D. Stolley et al., "The Relationship Between Physician Characteristics and Prescribing Appropriateness," *Medical Care* 10 (1972): 17–28.

53. Steven A. Schroeder et al., "Use of Laboratory Tests and Pharmaceuticals," *JAMA* 225 (1973): 969–73.

54. Ira M. Rutkow and George D. Zuidema, "'Unnecessary Surgery': An Update," *Surgery* 84 (1978): 672.

55. Rita J. Nickerson et al., "Doctors Who Perform Operations," *New England Journal of Medicine* 295 (1976): 921–26, 982–89.

56. Ibid., pp. 985–86; *Medical Practice in the United States* (Princeton, N.J.: Robert Wood Johnson Foundation, 1981), p. 69; Walter W. Hauck, Jr., et al., "Surgeons in the United States," *JAMA* 236 (1976): 1871.

57. Ira M. Rutkow, Alan M. Gittelsohn, and George D. Zuidema, "Surgical Decision Making," *Annals of Surgery* 190 (1979): 409–19.

58. Paul M. Gertman et al., "Second Opinions for Elective Surgery," *New England Journal of Medicine* 302 (1980): 1169.

59. James P. LoGerfo, "Variations in Surgical Rates: Fact vs. Fantasy," *New England Journal of Medicine* 297 (1977): 387–89; John P. Bunker, Benjamin A. Barnes, and Frederick Mosteller, eds., *Costs, Risks, and Benefits of Surgery* (New York: Oxford University Press, 1977).

60. Heather Stockwell and Eugene Vayda, "Variations in Surgery in Ontario," *Medical Care* 17 (1979): 390; Noralou P. Roos, Leslie L. Roos, Jr., and Paul D. Henteleff, "Elective Surgical Rates—Do High Rates Mean Lower Standards?" *New England Journal of Medicine* 297 (1977): 360–65.

61. James P. LoGerfo et al., "Rates of Surgical Care in Prepaid Group Practices and the Independent Setting," *Medical Care* 17 (1979): 1–9; Eugene Vayda, "A Comparison of Surgical Rates in Canada and in England and Wales," *New England Journal of Medicine* 289 (1973): 1224–29; Harold S. Luft, "How Do Health-Maintenance Organizations Achieve their 'Savings'?" *New England Journal of Medicine* 298 (1978): 1336–43.

62. John E. Wennberg et al., "Changes in Tonsillectomy Rates Associated with Feedback and Review," *Pediatrics* 59 (1977): 921–26; Frank J. Dyck et al., "Effect of Surveillance on the Number of Hysterectomies in the Province of Saskatchewan," *New England Journal of Medicine* 296 (1977): 1326–28.

63. Eugene G. McCarthy and Madelon L. Finkel, "Second Opinion Elective Surgery Programs," *Medical Care* 16 (1978): 984–94; John P. Bunker and Byron W. Brown, Jr., "The Physician-Patient as an Informed Consumer of Surgical Services," *New England Journal of Medicine* 290 (1974): 1051–55.

64. Cf. Bunker, Barnes, and Mosteller, eds., *Costs, Risks, and Benefits of Surgery*.

65. Herman M. Somers, "The Malpractice Controversy and the Quality of Patient Care," *Milbank Memorial Fund Quarterly* 55 (1977): 201; Leon S. Pocincki, Stuart J. Dogger, and Barbara P. Schwartz, "The Incidence of Iatrogenic Injuries," in U.S. Secretary's Commission on Medical Malpractice, *Appendix Report of the Secretary's*

Commission on Medical Malpractice (Washington, D.C.: U.S. Department of Health, Education, and Welfare, 1973), pp. 54–56; Mary Knudson, "33% of Hospital Infections are Preventable, Study Finds," *Baltimore Sun*, 31 July, 1983, p. A12.

66. Pocincki, Dogger, and Schwartz, "The Incidence of Iatrogenic Injuries," p. 62; Somers, "The Malpractice Controversy and the Quality of Patient Care," pp. 201–2.

67. Reynolds and Abram, *Socioeconomic Characteristics of Medical Practice 1983*, pp. 19–20.

68. James L. Peterson, "Consumers' Knowledge of and Attitudes Toward Medical Malpractice," in *Appendix Report of the Secretary's Commission on Medical Malpractice*, p. 665; Edmund G. Doherty and Carl O. Haven, "Medical Malpractice and Negligence," *JAMA* 238 (1977): 1656–58; Somers, "The Malpractice Controversy and the Quality of Patient Care," p. 202.

69. Ibid., pp. 202–4.

70. E. Kathleen Adams and Stephen Zuckerman, "Variations in the Growth and Incidence of Medical Malpractice Suits," *Journal of Health Politics, Policy, and Law* 9 (1984): 484–85; Somers, "The Malpractice Controversy and the Quality of Patient Care," p. 204; William B. Schwartz and Neil K. Komesar, "Doctors, Damages and Deterrence," *New England Journal of Medicine* 298 (1978): 1287.

71. Richard W. Magraw, *Ferment in Medicine* (Philadelphia: Saunders, 1966), pp. 79, 81.

72. Schwartz and Komesar, "Doctors, Damages and Deterrence," pp. 1282, 1287; Melvin H. Rudov, Thomas I. Myers, and Angelo Mirabella, "Medical Malpractice Insurance Claim Files Closed in 1970," in *Appendix Report of the Secretary's Commission on Medical Malpractice*, pp. 9–10.

73. Robert C. Derbyshire, *Medical Licensure and Discipline in the United States* (Baltimore: Johns Hopkins Press, 1969), pp. 77–79, 87–88.

74. E. Cheraskin and W. M. Ringsdorf, Jr., *Predictive Medicine* (Mountain View, Calif.: Pacific Press, 1973), pp. 25–27; Nedra B. Belloc, "Relationship of Health Practices and Mortality," *Preventive Medicine* 2 (1973): 67–81: Milton Terris, "Epidemiology as a Guide to Health Policy," *Annual Review of Public Health* 1 (1980): 323–44.

75. Reynolds and Abram, eds., *Socioeconomic Characteristics of Medical Practice 1983*, pp. 120–21.

76. *Medical Practice in the United States*, pp. 22–25.

77. Spyros Andreopoulos, ed., *Primary Care: Where Medicine Fails* (New York: Wiley, 1974), pp. 1–2; Institute of Medicine, *A Manpower Policy for Primary Health Care* (Washington, D.C.: National Academy of Sciences, 1978), pp. 16–20.

78. I. R. McWinney, "Problem-Solving and Decision-Making in Primary Medical Practice," *Proceedings of the Royal Society of Medicine* 65 (1972): 934–38.

79. Daniel M. Barr, "Primary and Specialized Care," *Journal of Medical Education* 53 (1978): 176–85.

80. Robert A. Chase, "Proliferation of Certification in Medical Specialties," *New England Journal of Medicine* 294 (1976): 497.

81. *Family Practice: Creation of a Specialty* (Kansas City, Mo.: American Academy of Family Physicians, 1980), pp. 25, 28–29; Phillip R. Canfield, "Family Medicine: An Historical Perspective," *Journal of Medical Education* 51 (1976): 907.

82. George A. Silver, "Family Practice: Resuscitation or Reform," *JAMA* 185 (1963): 188–91; *Family Practice: Creation of a Specialty*, pp. 20, 29, 42.

83. Ibid., pp. 55, 58–59; American Board of Medical Specialties, *Annual Report and Reference Handbook—1984*, p. 55.

84. Nickerson et al., "Doctors Who Perform Operations," pp. 921–25, 988.

85. Institute of Medicine, *A Manpower Policy for Primary Health Care,* pp. 30–31.

86. *Medical Practice in the United States,* p. 20.

87. Ibid., pp. 22, 50.

88. Ibid., p. 26; U.S. Health Resources Administration, *A Report to the President and Congress on the Status of Health Professions Personnel in the United States,* Second Report (Washington, D.C.: U.S. G.P.O., 1980), p. I-36; Reynolds and Abram, *Socioeconomic Characteristics of Medical Practice 1983,* pp. 98, 102.

89. William D. Holden and Edithe J. Levit, "Migration of Physicians from One Specialty to Another," *JAMA* 239 (1978): 206–7.

90. Charlotte L. Rosenberg, "How Much General Practice by Specialists?" *Medical Economics* (1975): 130–35.

91. William W. Engstrom, "Are Internists Functioning as Family Physicians?" *Annals of Internal Medicine* 66 (1967): 613–16; Richard J. Reitmeier et al., "Participation by Internists in Primary Care," *Archives of Internal Medicine* 135 (1975): 255–57; Henry Wechsler, Joseph L. Dorsey, and Joanne D. Bovey, "A Follow-Up Study of Residents in Internal Medicine, Pediatrics, and Obstetrics-Gynecology Training Programs in Massachusetts," *New England Journal of Medicine* 298 (1978): 16, 19.

92. Robert C. Mendenhall, "The Advisory Committee's Data Base," in Forrest H. Adams and Robert C. Mendenhall, *Evaluation of Cardiology Training and Manpower Requirements* (Washington, D.C.: U.S. G.P.O., 1974), pp. 267–69; *Medical Practice in the United States,* pp. 78–79.

93. Ibid.; Guy Odom, "Neurological Surgery in Our Changing Times," *Journal of Neurosurgery* 37 (1972): 266; Herbert J. Lerner, *Manpower Issues and Voluntary Regulation in the Medical Specialty System* (New York: Prodist, 1974), pp. 27, 46.

Chapter 10

1. Monroe Lerner and Odin W. Anderson, *Health Progress in the United States 1900–1960* (Chicago: University of Chicago Press, 1963), pp. 256, 267; U.S. Bureau of the Census, *Statistical Abstract of the United States: 1984* (Washington, D.C.: U.S. G.P.O., 1983), p. 117.

2. American Hospital Association, *Hospital Statistics: 1984 Edition,* (Chicago: American Hospital Association, 1984), pp. 12, 23, 193–98.

3. Ibid., p. 5; John C. Gaffney and Gerald L. Glandon, eds., *Profile of Medical Practice 1979* (Chicago: American Medical Association, 1979), p. 157; U.S. Bureau of the Census, *Statistical Abstract of the United States: 1978* (Washington, D.C.: U.S. G.P.O., 1978), p. 104; U.S. Bureau of the Census, *Statistical Abstract of the United States: 1984,* p. 109.

4. Hospital Council of Greater New York, *Hospital Staff Appointments of Physicians in New York City* (New York: Macmillan, 1951), pp. 8, 13–15; Roger A. Reynolds and Jonathan B. Abram, *Socioeconomic Characteristics of Medical Practice 1983* (Chicago: American Medical Association, 1983), p. 32.

5. National Center for Health Statistics, *Health United States, 1983* (Washington, D.C.: U.S. G.P.O., 1983), pp. 182, 187.

6. Christopher J. Zook and Francis D. Moore, "High-Cost Users of Medical Care," *New England Journal of Medicine* 302 (1980): 996–1002.

7. U.S. Bureau of the Census, *Statistical Abstract of the United States: 1984,* p. 104.

8. Ibid., p. 108; Sylvia A. Law, *Blue Cross: What Went Wrong?* (New Haven: Yale University Press, 1974), pp. 6–9, 19, 26, 41–42, 46.

9. Ibid., pp. 11, 93–97.

10. Ibid., pp. 97; Lawrence G. Goldberg and Warren Greenberg, "The Effect of Physician-Controlled Health Insurance," *Journal of Health Politics, Policy and Law* 2 (1977): 62–65.

11. Judith M. Feder, *Medicare: The Politics of Federal Hospital Insurance* (Lexington, Mass.: Lexington Books, 1977), pp. 9–25.

12. Feather D. Hair, "Hospital Accreditation: A Developmental Study of the Social Control of Institutions," (Ph.D. diss., Vanderbilt University, 1972), pp. 109–17, 187–92; William Worthington and Laurens H. Silver, "Regulation of Quality of Care in Hospitals," in *Medicine, Law and Public Policy,* ed. Nicholas N. Kittrie, Harold L. Hirsh, and Glen Wegner (New York: AMS Press, 1975), pp. 56–57; P. J. Sanzaro, "Quality Assessment and Quality Assurance in Medical Care," *Annual Review of Public Health* 1 (1980): 59.

13. American Medical Association, *Report of the Commission on the Cost of Medical Care: Vol. III. Significant Medical Advances* (Chicago: American Medical Association, 1964), 3:72–87.

14. Harvey V. Fineberg, "Clinical Chemistries," in *Medical Technology: The Culprit Behind Health Care Costs?,* ed. Stuart H. Altman and Robert Blendon (Washington, D.C.: Health Resources Administration, 1979), pp. 151–52; David F. Hardwick et al., "Laboratory Costs and Utilization," *Journal of Medical Education* 56 (1981): 308–9.

15. Fineberg, "Clinical Chemistries," pp. 147–48; David I. Kosowsky, "The Expanding Role of Private Industry in Health Care Through Technology," in *Technology and the Quality of Health Care,* ed. Richard H. Egdahl and Paul M. Gertman (Germantown, Md.: Aspen Systems, 1978), pp. 36–37.

16. Thomas W. Moloney and David E. Rogers, "Medical Technology—A Different View of the Contentious Debate over Costs," *New England Journal of Medicine* 301 (1979): 1413–19.

17. J. Gordon Scannell et al., "Optimal Resources for Cardiac Surgery," *Circulation* 44 (1971): A-228; Charles A. Sanders, "Technology and the Hospital," in *Medical Technology: The Culprit Behind Health Care Costs?,* p. 58.

18. Louise B. Russell, "The Diffusion of New Hospital Technologies in the United States," *International Journal of Health Services* 6 (1976): 565–67, 573–76.

19. Steven A. Schroeder and Jonathan A. Showstack, "The Dynamics of Medical Technology Use," in *Medical Technology: The Culprit Behind Health Care Costs?,* p. 191.

20. Seymour Perry, "The Role of NIH in Health Technology—Development, Assessment and Transfer," in *Technology and the Quality of Health Care,* p. 26.

21. Steven A. Schroeder, "Medical Technology and Academic Medicine," *Journal of Medical Education* 56 (1981): 635; Clifton R. Gaus, "Biomedical Research and Health Care Costs," in *Report of the President's Biomedical Research Panel* (Washington, D.C.: U.S. Department of Health, Education, and Welfare, 1976), Supplement 3, pp. 277–82.

22. Feder, *Medicare: The Politics of Federal Hospital Insurance,* pp. 1, 81; Sanders, "Technology and the Hospital," pp. 61–62.

23. Scannell et al., "Optimal Resources for Cardiac Surgery," pp. A–221–23.

24. C. A. Caceres, "Current Problems in the Clinical Introduction of New Technology and their Solutions," in *Technology and the Quality of Health Care,* pp. 3–17; David E. Berman and Paul E. Gertman, "Variations in Hospital Use, Inappropriate Use, and Public-Policy Consequences," in *Regional Variations in Hospital Use,* ed. David L. Rothberg (Lexington, Mass.: Lexington Books, 1982), pp. 242–43.

25. Elihu M. Schimmel, "The Hazards of Hospitalization," *Annals of Internal Medicine* 60 (1964): 100–9; Knight Steel et al., "Iatrogenic Illness on a General Medical Service at a University Hospital," *New England Journal of Medicine* 304 (1981): 638–42.

26. Herman M. Somers and Ann. R. Somers, *Medicare and the Hospitals* (Washington, D.C.: Brookings Institution, 1967), pp. 72–73.

27. David E. Rogers, *American Medicine: Challenges for the 1980s* (Cambridge, Mass.: Ballinger, 1978), p. 72; American Hospital Association, *Hospital Statistics: 1984 Edition*, pp. 4–5; National Center for Health Statistics, *Health United States, 1983*, p. 137.

28. Jerry A. Solon, Cecil G. Sheps, and Sidney S. Lee, "Patterns of Medical Care: A Hospital's Outpatients," *American Journal of Public Health* 50 (1960): 1906–8; National Academy of Sciences, *Study of Health Care for American Veterans* (Washington, D.C.: U.S. G.P.O., 1977), p. 118.

29. John G. Freymann, *The American Health Care System* (New York: Medcom, 1974), pp. 200, 255; Marcia Millman, *The Unkindest Cut: Life in the Backrooms of Medicine* (New York: Morrow, 1977), p. 65.

30. American Hospital Association, *Hospital Statistics, 1984 Edition*, p. 6.

31. Ibid., pp. 6, 193–98.

32. Herbert E. Klarman, *Hospital Care in New York City* (New York: Columbia University Press, 1963), pp. 156–57; Harry F. Dowling, *City Hospitals* (Cambridge: Harvard University Press, 1982), p. 124; Report of the Task Force on Academic Health Centers, *Prescription for Change* (New York: Commonwealth Fund, 1985), p. II/56; American Hospital Association, *Hospital Statistics: 1984 Edition*, pp. 180–81.

33. Association of American Medical Colleges, *Graduate Medical Education: Proposals for the Eighties* (Washington, D.C.: Association of American Medical Colleges, 1980), p. 163; Anne E. Crowley, "Summary Statistics on Graduate Medical Education in the United States," *JAMA* 252 (1984): 1548.

34. Paul Wing, "Clinical Costs of Medical Education," *Inquiry* 9 (Dec., 1972): 42; Association of American Medical Colleges, *Graduate Medical Education: Proposals for the Eighties*, p. 167; Task Force on Academic Health Centers, *Prescription for Change* (New York: Commonwealth Fund, 1985), p. I/11.

35. James N. Haug, "Misconceptions on Surgical Residency Positions," *Bulletin of the American College of Surgeons* 61 (Sept., 1976): 7.

36. Alexander Leaf, "Health Manpower Needs," *New England Journal of Medicine* 298 (1978): 1255; Raymond S. Duff and August B. Hollingshead, *Sickness and Society* (New York: Harper and Row, 1968), pp. 57–63, 375–76.

37. Ibid., pp. 127, 371, 133.

38. Marshall W. Raffel, *The U.S. Health Care System* (New York: Wiley, 1980), pp. 95–96.

39. Frank D. Campion, *The AMA and U.S. Health Policy Since 1940* (Chicago: Chicago Review Press, 1984), pp. 460–64; U.S. Bureau of the Census, *Statistical Abstract of the United States: 1984*, p. 109; Raffel, *The U.S. Health Care System*, p. 106; Robert J. Weiss et al., "Foreign Medical Graduates and the Medical Underground," *New England Journal of Medicine* 290 (1974): 1409.

40. Association of American Medical Colleges, *Graduate Medical Education: Proposals for the Eighties*, p. 163; Crowley, "Summary Statistics on Graduate Medical Education in the United States," p. 1550; Rosemary Stevens, Louis W. Goodman, and Stephen S. Mick, *The Alien Doctors* (New York: Wiley, 1978), pp. 28, 42–43, 226.

41. Ibid., pp. 88, 115, 125, 182.

42. Robert J. Weiss et al., "The Effect of Importing Physicians," *New England Journal of Medicine* 290 (1974): 1455.

43. U.S. Bureau of the Census, *Statistical Abstract of the United States: 1984*, p. 109; Crowley, "Summary Statistics on Graduate Medical Education in the United States," p. 1551.

44. Weiss et al., "Foreign Medical Graduates and the Medical Underground," pp. 1408–12.

45. Herbert J. Lerner, *Manpower Issues and Voluntary Regulation in the Medical Specialty System* (New York: Prodist, 1974), pp. 127–28; U.S. Bureau of the Census, *Statistical Abstract of the United States: 1984,* p. 109; Gaffney and Glandon, eds., *Profile of Medical Practice 1979,* pp. 157, 170.

46. U.S. Bureau of the Census, *Statistical Abstract of the United States: 1984,* p. 109; Kathleen Cannings and William Lazonick, "The Development of the Nursing Labor Force in the United States," *International Journal of Health Services* 5 (1975): 206; Eugene Levine and Evelyn B. Moses, "Registered Nurses Today," in *Nursing in the 1980s,* ed. Linda H. Aiken (Philadelphia: Lippincott, 1982), p. 487.

47. Cannings and Lazonick, "The Development of the Nursing Labor Force in the United States," pp. 187, 202; Levine and Moses, "Registered Nurses Today," pp. 490–91.

48. Philip A. Kalisch and Beatrice J. Kalisch, *The Advance of American Nursing* (Boston: Little, Brown, 1978), p. 652; Raffel, *The U.S. Health Care System,* pp. 164–65; Paul J. Feldstein, *Health Associations and the Demand for Legislation* (Cambridge, Mass.: Ballinger, 1977), p. 153.

49. Vern and Bonnie Bullough, *The Care of the Sick: The Emergence of Modern Nursing* (New York: Prodist, 1978), pp. 194–98.

50. Levine and Moses, "Registered Nurses Today," pp. 490–91.

51. Linda Aiken, "Nurses," in *Handbook of Health, Health Care, and the Health Professions,* ed. David Mechanic (New York: Free Press, 1983), pp. 416, 426.

Chapter 11

1. National Center for Educational Statistics: *Digest of Educational Statistics: 1983–84* (Washington, D.C.: U.S. G.P.O., 1983), pp. 13, 93, 101.

2. Ibid., pp. 13, 91, 101; Nancy B. Dearman and Valena W. Plisko, *The Condition of Education, 1981 Edition* (Washington, D.C.: U.S. G.P.O., 1981), p. 148.

3. National Center for Educational Statistics, *Digest of Educational Statistics: 1983–84,* pp. 93, 101, 132.

4. Ibid., pp. 8, 93, 101, 104, 110.

5. Ibid., p. 104; U.S. Bureau of the Census, *Historical Statistics of the United States, Colonial Times to 1970* (Washington, D.C.: U.S. G.P.O., 1975), 1:382; Lewis B. Mayhew, *The Carnegie Commission on Higher Education* (San Francisco: Jossey-Bass, 1974), pp. 149–54, 172–76.

6. Undergraduate vocational programs include agriculture, architecture, biology, business, communications, computer science, education, engineering, health professions, mathematics, and the physical sciences. These findings are drawn from tables of earned degrees conferred in editions of U.S. Bureau of the Census, *Statistical Abstract,* and National Center for Educational Statistics, *Digest of Educational Statistics.*

7. National Center for Educational Statistics, *Digest of Educational Statistics: 1983–84,* pp. 113–17.

8. Ibid., pp. 101, 128.

9. Ibid.

10. Dearman and Plisko, *The Condition of Education, 1981 Edition,* pp. 154, 156.

11. National Center for Educational Statistics, *Digest of Educational Statistics: 1983–84,* pp. 101, 103; U.S. Bureau of the Census, *Statistical Abstract of the United States: 1970* (Washington, D.C.: U.S. G.P.O., 1970), p. 128; U.S. Bureau of the Census, *Statistical Abstract of the United States: 1984* (Washington, D.C.: U.S. G.P.O., 1983), p. 335.

12. National Center for Educational Statistics, *Digest of Educational Statistics: 1967* (Washington, D.C.: U.S. G.P.O., 1967), p. 17; National Center for Educational Statistics, *Digest of Educational Statistics: 1983–84,* p. 101; U.S. Bureau of the Census, *Statistical Abstract of the United States: 1984,* p. 448.

13. National Center for Educational Statistics, *Digest of Educational Statistics: 1983–84,* pp. 143–45.

14. National Center for Educational Statistics, *Digest of Educational Statistics: 1980,* pp. 153, 184–85, 187.

15. National Center for Educational Statistics, *Digest of Educational Statistics: 1967,* p. 92; National Center for Educational Statistics, *Digest of Educational Statistics: 1983–84,* p. 141.

16. Ibid., pp. 143; Dearman and Plisko, *The Condition of Education, 1981 Edition,* p. 140.

17. Ibid., p. 152.

18. Maryland Y. Pennell and Marion E. Altenderfer, *Health Manpower Source Book I. Physicians* (Washington, D.C.: U.S. G.P.O., 1952), p. 35; U.S. Congress, House, Committee on Interstate and Foreign Commerce, *Medical School Inquiry* (Washington, D.C.: U.S. G.P.O., 1957), p. 198.

19. "Medical Schools in the United States," *JAMA* 252 (1984): 1590–94; Irving J. Lewis and Cecil G. Sheps, *The Sick Citadel: The American Academic Medical Center and the Public Interest* (Cambridge: Oelgeschlager, Gunn and Hain, 1983), p. 59.

20. Harold S. Diehl, Margaret D. West, and Robert W. Barclay, "Medical School Faculties in the National Emergency," in *Medical Education Today,* ed. Dean F. Smiley (Chicago: Association of American Medical Colleges, 1953), pp. 24, 26; Anne E. Crowley, Sylvia I. Etzel, and Edward S. Petersen, "Undergraduate Medical Education," *JAMA* 252 (1984): 1526.

21. Robert H. Ebert and Sarah S. Brown, "Academic Health Centers," *New England Journal of Medicine* 308 (1983): 1200–2.

22. Association of Academic Health Centers, *The Organization and Governance of Academic Health Centers* (Washington D.C.: Association of Academic Health Centers, 1980), 2:32–34, 36, 129, 132; John R. Hogness and Gwynn C. Akin, "Administration of Education Programs in Academic Health Centers," *New England Journal of Medicine* 296 (1977): 659.

23. Marjorie P. Wilson and Curtis P. McLaughlin, *Leadership and Management in Academic Medicine,* (San Francisco: Jossey-Bass, 1984), p. 67; Association of Academic Health Centers, *The Organization and Governance of Academic Health Centers,* 2:104, 206.

24. American Medical Association, *Money and Medical Schools* (Chicago: American Medical Association, 1963), p. 28; Crowley, Etzel, and Petersen, "Undergraduate Medical Education," p. 1526; President's Biomedical Research Panel, *Report Supplement 2: Impact of Federal Health-Related Research Expenditures upon Institutions of Higher Education* (Washington, D.C.: U.S. G.P.O., 1976), pp. 4–12; Alvin L. Morris, "Inter-School Relationships in Academic Health Centers," in Association of Academic Health Centers, *The Organization and Governance of Academic Health Centers,* 3:156, 160.

25. Association of Academic Health Centers, *The Organization and Governance of Academic Health Centers,* 2:92, 136, 302; Hogness and Akin, "Administration of Education Programs in Academic Health Centers," pp. 662–63.

26. Association of Academic Health Centers, *The Organization and Governance of Academic Health Centers,* 2:96, 98; Morris, "Inter-School Relationships in Academic Health Centers," p. 163.

27. John R. Evans, "Organizational Patterns for New Responsibilities," *Journal of Medical Education* 45 (1970): 992.

28. Homer D. Babbidge, "Financing Universities and Medical Schools," *JAMA* 180 (1962): 725.

29. Vernon W. Lippard, *A Half-Century of American Medical Education: 1920–1970* (New York: Josiah Macy, Jr., Foundation, 1974), p. 124; Carleton B. Chapman, "Education for Medicine in the University," in *Beyond Tomorrow: Trends and Prospects in Medical Science* (New York, 1977), pp. 49–50.

30. David E. Rogers and Robert J. Blendon, "The Academic Medical Center: A Stressed American Institution," *New England Journal of Medicine* 298 (1978): 941–42.

31. Lewis and Sheps, *The Sick Citadel: The American Academic Medical Center and the Public Interest*, p. 88.

32. Patricia L. Kendall, "The Relationship between Medical Educators and Medical Practitioners," *Journal of Medical Education* 40, Part 2 (1965): 137–245; Lewis and Sheps, *The Sick Citadel: The American Academic Medical Center and the Public Interest*, p. 197.

33. William R. Willard, *Manpower and Educational Needs in Selected Professional Fields: Medicine* (n.p.: Southern Regional Educational Board, 1973), p. 1; Victor Cohen, "Area School for Military MDs Gains," *Washington Post*, 24 September 1972, pp. C1, C5.

34. R. M. Magraw et al., "Perspectives from New Schools—the Costs and Financing of Medical Education," *New England Journal of Medicine* 289 (1973): 558–62; Ebert and Brown, "Academic Health Centers," p. 1202.

35. Joseph G. Pittman and Daniel M. Barr, "Undergraduate Education in Primary Care: the Rockford Experience," *Journal of Medical Education* 52 (1977): 982–83. See also Robert L. Evans, Joseph G. Pittman, and Richard C. Peters, "The Community Based Medical School," *New England Journal of Medicine* 288 (1973): 713–19.

36. Lewis and Sheps, *The Sick Citadel: The American Academic Medical Center and the Public Interest*, pp. 149–51. Cf. Andrew D. Hunt and Lewis E. Weeks, eds., *Medical Education since 1960* (n.p.: Michigan State University Foundation, 1977), pp. 369–73, 386–88.

37. Robert J. Glaser, "The Medical Deanship: Its Half-Life and Hard Times," *Journal of Medical Education* 44 (1969): 1119–21.

38. Wilson and McLaughlin, *Leadership and Management in Academic Medicine*, p. 124.

39. Lewis and Sheps, *The Sick Citadel: The American Academic Medical Center and the Public Interest*, p. 214; Wilson and McLaughlin, *Leadership and Management in Academic Medicine*, pp. 43, 53.

40. Robert G. Petersdorf, "The Evolution of Departments of Medicine," *New England Journal of Medicine* 303 (1980): 491–93; Lewis and Sheps, *The Sick Citadel: The American Academic Medical Center and the Public Interest*, p. 207; Robert J. Haggerty, "Private Foundations and the Future of Academic Pediatrics," in *The Current Status and Future of Academic Pediatrics*, ed. Elizabeth F. Purcell (New York: Josiah Macy Jr. Foundation, 1981), p. 50; John E. Deitrick and Robert C. Berson, *Medical Schools in the United States at Mid-Century* (New York: McGraw-Hill, 1953), p. 365.

41. Petersdorf, "The Evolution of Departments of Medicine," pp. 491–93; Haggerty, "Private Foundations and the Future of Academic Pediatrics," pp. 49, 51; Lewis and Sheps, *The Sick Citadel: The American Academic Medical Center and the Public Interest*, p. 207.

42. Association of Academic Health Centers, *The Organization and Governance of Academic Health Centers*, 2:91.

43. Raymond S. Duff and August B. Hollingshead, *Sickness and Society* (New York:

Harper and Row, 1968), pp. 45–47; Council of Teaching Hospitals, *Toward a More Contemporary Understanding of the Teaching Hospital* (n.p.: 1979), pp. 17–19.

44. Lawrence S. Kubie, "The Half-Failure of the Full-Time System as an Instrument of Medical Education," *Pharos* 34 (1971): 64–66; Michael J. Lepore, *Death of the Clinician* (Springfield, Ill.: Thomas, 1982), p. 323.

45. Petersdorf, "The Evolution of Departments of Medicine," p. 490.

46. Rashi Fein and Gerald I. Weber, *Financing Medical Education* (New York: McGraw-Hill, 1971), p. 42; Evans, "Organizational Patterns for New Responsibilities," p. 992.

47. Lewis and Sheps, *The Sick Citadel: The American Academic Medical Center and the Public Interest,* p. 191.

48. Ronald V. Christie, *Medical Education and the States: The Changing Pattern in Ten Countries* (Washington, D.C.: U.S. G.P.O., 1976), p. 45.

49. Deitrick and Berson, *Medical Schools in the United States at Mid-Century,* pp. 91, 95, 26.

50. National Center for Educational Statistics, *Digest of Educational Statistics: 1983–84,* pp. 143–44; Lewis and Sheps, *The Sick Citadel: The American Academic Medical Center and the Public Interest,* p. 164.

51. Frank D. Campion, *The AMA and U.S. Health Policy Since 1940* (Chicago: Chicago Review Press, 1984), pp. 87–88.

Chapter 12

1. Erwin Chargaff, "In Praise of Smallness—How Can We Return to Small Science?" *Perspectives in Biology and Medicine* 23 (1980): 374.

2. John E. Deitrick and Robert C. Berson, *Medical Schools in the United States at Mid-Century,* (New York: McGraw-Hill, 1953), pp. 33–34; U.S. President's Commission on the Health Needs of the Nation, *Building America's Health* (Washington, D.C.: U.S. G.P.O., 1953), 2:235–36; Esther E. Lape, *Medical Research: A Midcentury Survey* (Boston: Little, Brown, 1955), 1:292, Ernest V. Hollis, *Philanthropic Foundations and Higher Education* (New York: Columbia University Press, 1938), pp. 214–16.

3. Irving Ladimer, "Trends in Support and Expenditures for Medical Research, 1941–52" *Public Health Reports* 69 (1954): 114; Deitrick and Berson, *Medical Schools in the United States at Mid-Century,* pp. 87–90.

4. Stephen P. Strickland, *Research and the Health of Americans* (Lexington, Mass.: Lexington Books, 1978), p. 1; John R. Steelman, *The Nation's Medical Research* (Washington, D.C.: U.S. G.P.O., 1947), pp. 4–5.

5. Lape, *Medical Research: A Midcentury Survey,* pp. 295–96; Ladimer, "Trends in Support and Expenditures for Medical Research, 1941–52," p. 114.

6. National Institutes of Health, *The National Institutes of Health Almanac* (Washington, D.C.: U.S. G.P.O., 1965), pp. 1–3; G. Burroughs Mider, "The Federal Impact on Biomedical Research," in *Advances in American Medicine,* ed. John Z. Bowers and Elizabeth F. Purcell (New York: Josiah Macy, Jr., Foundation, 1976), 2:833–34.

7. Ibid., pp. 838–40.

8. National Institutes of Health, *NIH Data Book: 1983* (Washington, D.C.: U.S. G.P.O., 1983), pp. i, 59.

9. Ladimer, "Trends in Support and Expenditures for Medical Research, 1941–52," pp. 114, 116.

10. U.S. Surgeon General's Committee on Medical School Grants and Finances, *Medical School Grants and Finances Part I: Conclusions and Recommendations* (Washington, D.C.: U.S. G.P.O., 1951), pp. 13, 36–38.

11. Steelman, *The Nation's Medical Research;* U.S. Surgeon General's Committee on Medical School Grants and Finances, *Medical School Grants and Finances;* U.S. President's Commission on the Health Needs of the Nation, *Building America's Health,* 2:239; Daniel S. Greenberg, *The Politics of Pure Science* (New York: World, 1967), p. 130.

12. Ibid., pp. 283–84.

13. National Institutes of Health, *NIH Data Book: 1983,* p. 2; National Institutes of Health, *NIH Data Book: 1985* (Washington, D.C.: U.S. G.P.O., 1985), p. 2.

14. Mider, "The Federal Impact on Biomedical Research," p. 847.

15. U.S. Surgeon General's Committee on Medical School Grants and Finances, *Medical School Grants and Finances,* p. 12.

16. Dean E. Wooldridge, *Biomedical Science and Its Administration* (Washington, D.C.: U.S. G.P.O., 1965), p. 60; National Institutes of Health, *The National Institutes of Health Almanac,* pp. 13, 80; National Institutes of Health, *NIH Data Book: 1985,* pp. 8, 55.

17. National Institutes of Health, *The National Institutes of Health Almanac,* pp. 20–43.

18. U.S. Surgeon General's Committee on Medical School Grants and Finances, *Medical School Grants and Finances,* p. 7n.

19. Joseph S. Murtaugh, "Biomedical Sciences," in *Science and the Evolution of Public Policy,* ed. James A. Shannon (New York: Rockefeller University Press, 1973), p. 163.

20. James A. Shannon, "Federal Support of Biomedical Sciences," *Journal of Medical Education* 51, Part 2 (July, 1976): 11, 15.

21. Wooldridge, *Biomedical Science and its Administration,* pp. 95, 2.

22. Ibid., p. 23.

23. Walsh McDermott, "The University as an Agent of Change," in *Community Medicine,* ed. Willoughby Lathem and Anne Newbery (New York: Appleton-Century-Crofts, 1970), p. 13.

24. U.S. Congress, House, Committee on Government Operations. *Health Research and Training Hearings August 1–2, 1961,* pp. 56–57.

25. Thane Gustafson, "The Controversy over Peer Review," *Science* 190 (1975): 1061–63; U.S. President's Biomedical Research Panel, *Report Appendix D: Selected Staff Papers* (Washington, D.C.: U.S. G.P.O., 1976), pp. 70–74.

26. U.S. Congress, House, Committee on Government Operations. *Health Research and Training Hearings August 1–2, 1961* (Washington, D.C.: U.S. G.P.O., 1961), p. 13.

27. Robert K. Merton, "Singletons and Multiples in Scientific Discovery," *Proceedings of the American Philosophical Society* 105 (1961): 470–86; Robert K. Merton, "Priorities in Scientific Discover," *American Sociological Review* 22 (1957): 635–59; S. G. Gilfillan, *The Sociology of Invention* (1935; reprint ed., Cambridge: M.I.T. Press, 1970); Harry F. Dowling, "The Impact of New Discoveries on Medical Practice," in *Mainstreams of Medicine,* ed Lester S. King (Austin: University of Texas Press, 1971), p. 110.

28. David T. Durack, "The Weight of Medical Knowledge," *New England Journal of Medicine* 298 (1978): 774.

29. Institute of Medicine, *Responding to Health Needs and Scientific Opportunity* (Washington, D.C.: National Academy Press, 1984), pp. 35–36; Richard A. Rettig, *Cancer Crusade* (Princeton: Princeton University Press, 1977), p. 53; Strickland, *Research and the Health of Americans,* pp. 61–74; Gustafson, "The Controversy over Peer Review," pp. 1060, 1064.

30. Marlan Blissett, *Politics in Science* (Boston: Little, Brown, 1972), pp. 97–98.

31. Alvin M. Weinberg, "Criteria for Scientific Choice," in *Criteria for Scientific Development*, ed. Edward Shils (Cambridge, Mass.: MIT Press, 1968), pp. 27, 32.

32. Wooldridge, *Biomedical Science and its Administration*, pp. 3–4, 12–13, 95.

33. Ibid., pp. 154–57, 185.

34. U.S. President's Biomedical Research Panel, *Report Appendix A: The Place of Biomedical Sciences in Medicine and the State of the Science*, pp. 66–67, 171, 205; *Report Supplement 3: Written Statements Supplementing Verbal Testimonies of Witnesses*, p. 158; *Report Supplement 4: Statements of Professional, Scientific, and Voluntary Health Organizations*, pp. 330, 335–36 (Washington, D.C.: U.S. G.P.O., 1976).

35. U.S. President's Biomedical Research Panel, *Report Appendix A: The Place of the Biomedical Sciences in Medicine and the State of the Science*, p. 28.

36. Roberts, "Influences on Innovation," pp. 55–56; Harry F. Dowling, *Fighting Infection* (Cambridge: Harvard University Press, 1977), pp. 247–48.

37. Edward B. Roberts, "Influences on Innovation: Extrapolations to Biomedical Technology," in *Biomedical Innovation*, ed. Edward B. Roberts et al. (Cambridge: MIT Press, 1981), pp. 55–57.

38. U.S. President's Biomedical Research Panel, *Report Supplement 3: Written Statements Supplementing Verbal Testimonies of Witnesses*, pp. 13–15.

39. Ibid., p. 17.

40. Institute of Medicine, *Responding to Health Needs and Scientific Opportunity*, pp. 8–9, 16–17, 30.

41. Table 11.5; H. Paul Jolly et al., "US Medical School Finances," *JAMA* 252 (1984): 1535–36.

42. Jonathan R. Cole and James A. Lipton, "The Reputations of American Medical Schools," *Social Forces* 55 (1977): 662–84.

43. Marvin R. Weisbord, Paul R. Lawrence, and Martin P. Charns, "Three Dilemmas of Academic Medical Centers," *Journal of Applied Behavioral Science* 14 (1978): 300; Hilliard Jason and Jane Westberg, *Teachers and Teaching in U.S. Medical Schools* (Norwalk, Conn.: Appleton-Century-Crofts, 1982), pp. 25, 36, 123–24.

44. Bernard Barber et al., *Research on Human Subjects* (New York: Russell Sage Foundation: 1973), pp. 12, 171, 177; Bradford H. Gray, *Human Subjects in Medical Experimentation* (New York: Wiley, 1975), pp. 50, 53, 249, 253.

45. U.S. Surgeon General's Committee on Medical School Grants and Financies, *Medical School Grants and Finances*, p. 12.

46. American Medical Association, *Money and Medical Schools* (Chicago: American Medical Association, 1963), p. 44; Murtaugh, "Biomedical Sciences," pp. 167–68; Grace M. Carter et al., *Federal Manpower Legislation and the Academic Health Centers* (Santa Monica, Calif.: Rand, 1974), p. 73.

47. David Perry, David R. Challoner, and Robert J. Oberst, "Research Advances and Resource Constraints," *New England Journal of Medicine* 305 (1981): 320–23.

48. National Institutes of Health, *NIH Data Book: 1985*, p. 37.

49. "Medical School Faculties," *JAMA* 218 (1971): 1215.

50. Chargaff, "In Praise of Smallness—How Can We Return to Small Science?" p. 378.

51. Shannon, "Federal Support of Biomedical Sciences," p. 18; Thomas B. Turner, *Accounting of a Stewardship: The Johns Hopkins Medical School 1957–1968* (n.d.), p. 34.

52. Donald S. Frederickson, "Is There a Federal Philosophy about Academic Medicine?" *Bulletin of the New York Academy of Medicine* 57 (1981): 459; Shannon, "Federal Support of Biomedical Sciences," pp. 47–8; Julius B. Richmond, *Currents in American Medicine* (Cambridge: Harvard University Press, 1969), p. 34.

53. De Witt Stetten, Jr., "Research in a No-Growth Economy—Can Excellence be Preserved?" *Prespectives in Biology and Medicine* 23 (1980): 359, 364–65.

54. Alice M. Rivlin, *The Role of the Federal Government in Financing Higher Education* (Washington, D.C.: Brookings Institution, 1961), pp. 87, 89; National Institutes of Health, *NIH Data Book: 1983,* p. 21.

55. James B. Wyngaarden, "The Clinical Investigator as an Endangered Species," *New England Journal of Medicine* 301 (1979): 1254–56.

56. Stetten, Jr., "Research in a No-Growth Economy—Can Excellence be Preserved?" pp. 359, 367.

57. National Institutes of Health, *NIH Data Book: 1983,* p. 21; National Institutes of Health, *NIH Data Book: 1985,* p. 17.

58. Lee Powers, Joseph F. Whiting, and K. C. Oppermann, "Trends in Medical School Faculties," *Journal of Medical Education* 37 (1962): 1082; Elizabeth J. Higgins, *Comparison of Characteristics of U.S. Medical School Salaried Faculty in the Past Decade 1968–1978* (Washington, D.C.: Association of American Medical Colleges, 1979), p. 23.

59. Wooldridge, *Biomedical Science and its Administration,* p. 156.

60. Thomas C. King, "Influences for Change in Medical Education," *Annals of the New York Academy of Sciences* 128 (1965): 547–48.

61. William G. Van der Kloot, "The Education of Biomedical Scientists," in William G. Anlyan et al., *The Future of Medical Education* (Durham, N.C.: Duke University Press, 1973), pp. 95, 97; National Center for Educational Statistics, *Digest of Educational Statistics: 1983–84* (Washington, D.C.: U.S. G.P.O., 1983) p. 113; Anne E. Crowly, Sylvia I. Etzel, and Edward S. Petersen, "Undergraduate Medical Education," *JAMA* 250 (1983): pp. 1509–11.

62. Bruce L. R. Smith and Joseph J. Karlesky, *The State of Academic Science* (New York: Change Magazine Press, 1977), pp. 140–41.

63. Suzanne W. Fletcher, Robert H. Fletcher, and M. Andrew Greganti, "Clinical Research Trends in General Medical Journals. 1946–76" in *Biomedical Innovation,* ed. Edward B. Roberts et al. (Cambridge: MIT Press, 1981), pp. 284–300.

64. Ibid., pp. 293–96.

65. Alvan R. Feinstein, Neal Koss, and John H. Austin, "The Changing Emphasis in Clinical Research," *Annals of Internal Medicine* 66 (1967): 396–408; Alvan R. Feinstein and Neal Koss, "The Changing Emphasis in Clinical Research," *Archives of Internal Medicine* 125 (1970): 885–91.

66. Donald W. Seldin, "Some Reflections on the Role of Basic Research and Service in Clinical Departments," *Journal of Clinical Investigation* 45 (1966): 977.

67. Ibid., p. 977; Alvan R. Feinstein, "Scientific Methodology in Clinical Medicine," *Annals of Internal Medicine* 61 (1964): 564–66.

68. Steven A. Schroeder and Jonathan A. Showstack, "The Dynamics of Medical Technology Use," in *Medical Technology: The Culprit Behind Health Care Costs?,* ed. Stuart A. Altman and Robert Blendon (Washington, D.C.: U.S. G.P.O., 1979), pp. 192–95; J. P. Bunker, D. Hinkley, and W. V. McDermott, "Surgical Innovation and Its Evaluation," *Science* 200 (1978): 937–41.

69. John W. Williamson, Peter G. Goldschmidt, and Theodore Colton, "The Quality of Medical Literature: Analysis of Validity Assessments," mimeographed (Baltimore, 1983), pp. 1–11, see also Rebecca DerSimonian et al., "Reporting on Methods in Clinical Trials," *New England Journal of Medicine* 306 (1982): 1332–37.

70. John W. Williamson, Peter G. Goldschmidt, and Irene A. Jillson, "Medical Practice Information Demonstration Project: Final Report," mimeographed (Baltimore: 1979), pp. 124–25.

71. Ibid., pp. 113–17.

72. Association of American Medical Colleges, *Institutional Characteristics of U.S. Medical Schools 1975–1976* (Washington, D.C.: U.S. G.P.O., 1978), p. 36; Higgins, *Comparisons of Characteristics of U.S. Medical School Salaried Faculty in the Past Decade 1968–1978*, pp. 22–25.

73. David Tilson, Jonathan W. Reader and Robert S. Morison, "The Federal Interest," in *The Diffusion of Medical Technology,* ed. Gerald Gordon and G. Lawrence Fisher (Cambridge, Mass.: Ballinger, 1975), p. 19.

74. Barbara J. Culliton, "Kennedy Hearings: Year-Long Probe of Biomedical Research Begins," *Science* 193 (1976): 33; Daniel C. Maldonado, "Beyond the Warring Elements," in *Biomedical Scientists and Public Policy,* ed. H. Hugh Fudenberg and Vijava L. Melnick (New York: Plenum Press, 1978), p. 155.

75. Irving J. Lewis and Cecil G. Sheps, *The Sick Citadel: The American Academic Medical Center and the Public Interest* (Cambridge: Oelgeschlager, Gunn and Hain, 1983), pp. 201–2; National Institutes of Health, *National Institutes of Health Almanac,* pp. 65, 75; National Institutes of Health, *NIH Data Book: 1985,* p. 17.

76. Ibid., pp. 5, 9, 23.

77. Ibid., p. 37.

Chapter 13

1. Harold S. Diehl, Margaret D. West, and Robert W. Barclay, "Medical School Faculties in the National Emergency," in *Medical Education Today,* ed. Dean F. Smiley (Chicago: Association of American Medical Colleges, 1953), pp. 24, 27.

2. "Medical School Faculties," *JAMA* 218 (1971): 1215.

3. A. P. Williams et al., "The Effect of Federal Biomedical Research Programs on Academic Medical Centers," in President's Biomedical Research Panel, *Report Supplement 2: Impact of Federal Health-Related Research Expenditures upon Institutions of Higher Education* (Washington, D.C.: U.S. G.P.O., 1976), Part IV, p. 46.

4. Diehl, West, and Barclay, "Medical School Faculties in the National Emergency," p. 26; Anne E. Crowley, Sylvia I. Etzel, and Edward S. Petersen, "Undergraduate Medical Education," *JAMA* 254 (1985): 1566.

5. Lee Powers, Joseph F. Whiting, and K. C. Oppermann, "Trends in Medical School Faculties," *Journal of Medical Education* 37 (1962): 1079; "Medical School Faculties," p. 1213.

6. Bernard Siegel, "Medical Service Plans in Academic Medical Centers," *Journal of Medical Education* 53 (1978): 794–95.

7. Robert G. Petersdorf, "Faculty Practice Income—Implications for Faculty Morale and Performance," *Clinical Research* 21 (1973): 914; R. M. Magraw et al., "Perspectives from the New Schools—the Costs and Financing of Medical Education," *New England Journal of Medicine* 289 (1973): 561.

8. Petersdorf, "Faculty Practice Income—Implications for Faculty Morale and Performance," pp. 914–15.

9. James V. Maloney Jr., "A Report on the Role of Economic Motivation in the Performance of Medical School Faculty," *Surgery* 68 (1970): 1–15.

10. Michael J. Lepore, *Death of the Clinician* (Springfield, Ill.: Thomas, 1982), p. 214; Patricia L. Kendall, "The Relationship between Medical Educators and Medical Practitioners," *Journal of Medical Education* 40, Part 2 (1965): pp. 146–50.

11. Ibid., pp. 149–59.

12. Joseph D. McCarthy, "Report of the Council on Medical Service," *Minutes Of the House of Delegates Chicago Session 1956* (Chicago: American Medical Association, 1956), pp. 38, 40.

13. Augustus J. Carroll, *A Study of Medical College Costs* (Evanston, Ill.: Association of American Medical Colleges, 1958), p. 92; Siegel, "Medical Service Plans in Academic Medical Centers," p. 794.

14. John E. Deitrick and Robert C. Berson, *Medical Schools in the United States at Midcentury* (New York: McGraw-Hill, 1953), pp. 108–10.

15. American Medical Association, *Money and Medical Schools* (Chicago: American Medical Association, 1963), pp. 69–71: Raymond S. Duff and August B. Hollingshead, *Sickness and Society* (New York: Harper and Row, 1969), pp. 40–42.

16. Institute of Medicine, *Medicare-Medicaid Reimbursement Policies* (Washington, D.C.: U.S. G.P.O., 1976), pp. 14–18.

17. Ibid., p. 14.

18. William C. Hilles and Sharon K. Fagan, *Medical Practice Plans at U.S. Medical Schools* (Washington, D.C.: U.S. G.P.O., 1977), 1:13–15, 39–40.

19. Robert G. Petersdorf, "Impact of Health Care Services on Medical Education in the United States," *Danish Medical Bulletin* 27, suppl. 1 (1980): 55; Institute of Medicine, *Medicare-Medicaid Reimbursement Policies,* pp. 108–31.

20. Hilles and Fagan, *Medical Practice Plans at U.S. Medical Schools,* 1:36; H. Paul Jolly et al., "US Medical School Finances," *JAMA* 250 (1983): 1527; H. Paul Jolly et al., "US Medical School Finances," *JAMA* 254 (1985): 1576.

21. President's Biomedical Research Panel, *Report Supplement 2: Impact of Federal Health-Related Research Expenditures upon Institutions of Higher Education,* p. 51.

22. Maloney, "A Report on the Role of Economic Motivation in the Performance of Medical School Faculty," pp. 9–10.

23. Ibid., pp. 8–9; Leighton E. Cluff, "Responsibility, Accountability, Self-Discipline: Changing Emphases in Medical Education," *Pharos* 44 (Winter, 1981): 5.

24. Maloney, "A Report on the Role of Economic Motivation in the Performance of Medical School Faculty," p. 12.

25. Association of Academic Health Centers, *The Organization and Governance of Academic Health Centers* (Washington, D.C.: Association of Academic Health Centers, 1980), 2:93.

26. Institute of Medicine, *Medicare-Medicaid Reimbursement Policies,* pp. 115, 118; Carleton B. Chapman, "Education for Medicine in the University," in *Beyond Tomorrow: Trends and Prospects in Medical Science* (New York, 1977), p. 47.

27. Institute of Medicine, *Medicare-Medicaid Reimbursement Policies,* pp. 121–23; Vernon W. Lippard, *A Half Century of American Medical Education: 1920–1970* (New York: Josiah Macy, Jr., Foundation, 1974), p. 58.

28. Cluff, "Responsibility, Accountability, Self-Discipline: Changing Emphases in Medical Education," p. 5.

29. H. Paul Jolly, Elizabeth J. Higgins, and Maryn P. Goodson, *Trends in Medical School Faculty Characteristics* (Washington, D.C.: Association of American Medical Colleges, 1980), p. 47.

30. Elizabeth F. Higgins, *Comparison of Characteristics of U.S. Medical School Salaried Faculty in the Past Decade 1968–1978* (Washington, D.C.: Association of American Medical Colleges, 1979), p. 93; Vernon Lippard, "The Medical School—Janus of the University," *Journal of Medical Education* 30 (1955): 703.

31. Pamela J. Griffith and Coralie Farlee, *Description of Salaried Medical School Faculty, 1971–72 and 1976–77* (Washington, D.C.: U.S. G.P.O., 1977), p. 58.

32. Michael G. McShane, *Medical Schools in the United States: A Descriptive Study* (Washington, D.C.: Association of American Medical Colleges, 1977), p. 79; J. R. Schofield, *New and Expanded Medical Schools, Mid-Century to the 1980s* (San Francisco: Jossey-Bass, 1984), p. 153. Data for 1984–1985 provided by the Association of American Medical Colleges.

33. David E. Rogers, "Medical Academe and the Problems of Primary Care," *Journal of Medical Education* 50, Part 2 (1975): 174–75.

34. U.S. Bureau of the Census, *Historical Statistics of the United States* (Washington, D.C.: U.S. G.P.O., 1975), 1:176.

35. Ibid.

36. "Debates: With Increasing Growth of Full-Time Clinical Faculties, Practicing Physicians Should Play a Decreasing Role in Instruction of Students," *JAMA* 176 (1961): 846–849.

37. Harry F. Dowling and Nicholas J. Cotsonas, Jr., "The Training of the Physician," *New England Journal of Medicine* 271 (1964): 716–18.

38. Charles A. Janeway, "The Decline of Primary Medical Care," *Pharos* 37 (1974): 75; Cecil G. Sheps et al., "Medical Schools and Hospitals: Interdependence for Education and Service," *Journal of Medical Education* 40, Part 2 (Sept., 1965): 49; "Report of the Louis Harris and Associates Survey on the Status of Medical Education," *Journal of Medical Education* 59, Part 2 (Nov., 1984): 196.

39. Eugene Bricker, "The Private Surgeon in a University Hospital," *Surgery* 74 (1973): 496–97; Walter F. Ballinger and John A. Collins, "Integration of Full-Time and Voluntary Surgeons in a University Hospital," *Surgery* 74 (1973): 490–91.

40. David E. Rogers, *American Medicine: Challenge for the 1980s* (Cambridge: Ballinger, 1978), p. 78; Lepore, *Death of the Clinician,* pp. 236, 242–43.

Chapter 14

1. John E. Deitrick and Robert C. Berson, *Medical Schools in the United States at Mid-Century* (New York: McGraw-Hill, 1953), p. 144; John C. Nunemaker, "Responsibility of the Medical School-Teaching Hospital for Affiliated Intern and Residency Programs in Community Hospitals," *Journal of Medical Education* 37 (1962): 291.

2. Ibid., pp. 289–90; Irving J. Lewis and Cecil G. Sheps, *The Sick Citadel: The American Academic Medical Center and the Public Interest* (Cambridge: Oelgeschlager, Gunn and Hain, 1983), pp. 62–63.

3. Association of American Medical Colleges, *Institutional Characteristics of U.S. Medical Schools 1975–1976* (Washington, D.C.: U.S. G.P.O., 1978), pp. 155–56, 160–61.

4. Data for 1982 provided by the Association of American Medical Colleges; Council of Teaching Hospitals, *Toward a More Contemporary Public Understanding of the Teaching Hospital* (n.p., 1979), pp. 39–42.

5. Ibid., pp. 41–44.

6. Data provided by Association of American Medical Colleges.

7. John H. Knowles, "Medical School, Teaching Hospital, and Social Responsibility," in *The Teaching Hospital: Evolution and Contemporary Issues,* ed. John H. Knowles (Cambridge: Harvard University Press, 1966), p. 98–99; Cecil Sheps et al., *Medical Schools and Hospitals* (Evanston, Ill.: Association of American Medical Colleges, 1965), p. 31.

8. David E. Rogers and Robert J. Blendon, "The Academic Medical Center," *New England Journal of Medicine* 298 (1978): 941–42, 946.

9. "Net Patient Revenue at University-Owned Teaching Hospitals, 1982," *Journal of Medical Education* 60 (1985): 656–57; Institute of Medicine, *Medicare-Medicaid Reimbursement Policies* (Washington, D.C.: U.S. G.P.O., 1976), pp. 108–11.

10. Task Force on Academic Health Centers, *Prescriptions for Change* (New York: Commonwealth Fund, 1985), pp. III:6–7; Susan D. Horn et al., "Interhospital Differences in Severity of Illness," *New England Journal of Medicine* 313 (1985): 20–24.

11. Task Force on Academic Health Centers, *Prescription for Change,* p. II:15.

12. Council of Teaching Hospitals, *Toward a More Contemporary Public Understanding of the Teaching Hospital,* pp. 17–19.

13. Ibid., p. 24.

14. Lewis and Sheps, *The Sick Citadel: The American Academic Medical Center and the Public Interest,* pp. 134–35, 177; Robert Heyssel, "The Role of the Clinical Department Chairman in Hospital Management," in Association of Academic Health Centers, *The Organization and Governance of Academic Health Centers* (Washington, D.C.: Association of Academic Health Centers, 1980), 3:207–14.

15. Institute of Medicine, *Medicare-Medicaid Reimbursement Policies,* pp. 135–39.

16. Judah Folkman, "Is There a Doctor in the House?" *Harvard Medical Alumni Bulletin* 54 (1980): 38.

17. Raymond S. Duff and August B. Hollingshead, *Sickness and Society* (New York: Harper, 1968), p. 47.

18. Ibid., pp. 48–49.

19. Ibid., pp. 127, 132–33, 367–70; Emily Mumford, *Interns: From Students to Physicians* (Cambridge: Harvard University Press, 1970), pp. 113–14; Cecilia M. Roberts, *Doctor and Patient in the Teaching Hospital* (Lexington, Mass.: Lexington Books, 1977), pp. 56–57.

20. Steven Jonas et al., *Health Care Delivery in the United States* (New York: Springer, 1977), p. 129; Thomas L. Delbanco and John N. Parker, "Primary Care at a Teaching Hospital," *Mount Sinai Journal of Medicine* 45 (1978): 628–29.

21. Richard A. Berman and Thomas W. Moloney, "Are Outpatient Departments Responsible for the Fiscal Crisis Facing Teaching Hospitals?" *Journal of Ambulatory Care Management* 1 (1978): 39–41, 51–53.

22. Delbanco and Parker, "Primary Care at a Teaching Hospital," pp. 628–45; E. Richard Weinerman and William A. Steiger, "Ambulatory Service in the Teaching Hospital," *Journal of Medical Education* 39 (1964): 1020.

23. Paul Wing, "Clinical Costs of Medical Education," *Inquiry* 9 (1972): 42; "House Staff Expenditures and Funding in COTH Member Hospitals," *Journal of Medical Education* 60 (1985): 422–24.

24. Institute of Medicine, *Medicare-Medicaid Reimbursement Policies,* pp. 139–43.

25. Council of Teaching Hospitals, *Toward a More Contemporary Public Understanding of the Teaching Hospital,* pp. 19–20; Institute of Medicine, *Medicare-Medicaid Reimbursement Policies,* pp. 142–47.

26. Marcia Millman, *The Unkindest Cut: Life in the Backrooms of Medicine* (New York: Morrow, 1977), pp. 93–94.

27. Duff and Hollingshead, *Sickness and Society,* p. 114; Roberts, *Doctor and Patient in the Teaching Hospital,* pp. 28–29; Mumford, *Interns: From Students to Physicians,* pp. 179–80.

28. David E. Rogers, *American Medicine; Challenge for the 1980s* (Cambridge, Mass.: Ballinger, 1978), pp. 85–87; Vernon W. Lippard, *A Half-Century of American Medical Education: 1920–1970* (New York: Josiah Macy, Jr., Foundation, 1974), p. 11.

29. Robert H. Ebert, "Medical Education in the United States," in *Doing Better and Feeling Worse,* ed. John H. Knowles (New York: Norton, 1977), p. 183; Bernard W.

Nelson, "HMOs and Academic Medical Centers," in *Health Maintenance Organizations and Academic Medical Centers,* ed. James I. Hudson and Madeline M. Nevins (Menlo Park, Calif.: 1981), pp. 11–17; John H. Knowles, "Medical School, Teaching Hospital, and Social Responsibility," p. 100.

30. John H. Westerman, "A Requiem for the University Hospital?" *Health Care Management Review* 5 (1980): 23.

31. Benjamin J. Lewis, *VA Medical Programs in Relation to Medical Schools* (Washington, D.C.: U.S. G.P.O., 1970), pp. 64–66, 69.

32. Ibid., pp. 11, 70–79, 99–100.

33. Ibid., pp. 103–4, 123–25, 149.

34. Ibid., p. 30; Seymour B. Sarason, "An Asocial Psychology and a Misdirected Clinical Psychology," *American Psychologist* 36 (1981): 829.

35. Lewis, *VA Medical Programs in Relation to Medical Schools,* pp. 128, 145–47, 178; Council of Teaching Hospitals, *Toward a More Contemporary Public Understanding of the Teaching Hospital,* p. 52.

36. Lewis, *VA Medical Programs in Relation to Medical Schools,* p. 258; Robert H. Ebert and Sarah S. Brown, "Academic Health Centers," *New England Journal of Medicine* 308 (1983): 1202.

37. Lewis, *VA Medical Programs in Relation to Medical Schools,* p. 240; National Academy of Sciences, *Study of Health Care for American Veterans* (Washington, D.C.: U.S. G.P.O., 1977), pp. 65, 245–47.

38. Lewis, *VA Medical Programs in Relation to Medical Schools,* pp. 1–2, 132, 239; National Academy of Sciences, *Study of Health Care for American Veterans,* pp. 247–49.

39. Ibid., pp. 119, 82, 78, 115–16, 144, 147.

40. Ibid., pp. 134, 166–67.

41. Ibid., pp. 164, 271–72, 256–57, 262.

42. Ibid., pp. 118–19.

43. Vernon A. Guidry, Jr., "Probe Questions Propriety of VA Doctors' Outside Incomes," *Baltimore Sunday Sun,* 19 September 1982, p. A12.

44. Sarason, "An Asocial Psychology and a Misdirected Clinical Psychology," p. 829.

45. Joseph A. Keyes, Perry D. Cohen, and George R. DeMuth, *Medical School— Clinical Affiliation Study* (Washington, D.C.: Association of American Medical Colleges, 1977), pp. 61–62.

46. Ibid., pp. 64–66.

47. Robb K. Burlage, *New York City's Municipal Hospitals* (Washington, D.C.: Institute for Policy Studies, 1967), pp. 31–33; Harry F. Dowling, *City Hospitals* (Cambridge: Harvard University Press, 1982), pp. 178–81; Robert R. Alford, *Health Care Politics* (Chicago: University of Chicago Press, 1975), pp. 41–42. Cf. Russell A. Nelson, *The Governance of Voluntary Teaching Hospitals in New York City* (New York: Josiah Macy, Jr., Foundation 1974); Mariana Robinson and Corinne Silverman, *The Reorganization of Philadelphia General Hospital* (Indianapolis: Bobbs Merrill, 1959).

48. Robert G. Petersdorf, "Impact of Health Care Services on Medical Education in the United States," *Danish Medical Bulletin* 27, suppl. 1 (1980): 56; James H. Foster, "The Full-Time Surgeon in a Private Hospital and the Town-Gown Conflict," *Surgery* 74 (1973): 499–500.

49. Robert G. Petersdorf, "The Evolution of Departments of Medicine," *New England Journal of Medicine* 303 (1980): 492–93; John W. Collotron, "Competition: The Threat to Teaching Hospitals," in *Financing Health Care,* ed. Duncan Yaggy and William G. Anlyan (Cambridge, Mass.: Ballinger, 1982), p. 161; Keyes, Cohen, and DeMuth, *Medical School—Clinical Affiliation Study,* pp. 67–69.

50. Dowling, *City Hospitals,* pp. 182–83; Ronald Sullivan, "City Seeking Hospital Pacts That Improve Basic Services," *New York Times,* 2 August 1982, p. B1.

51. Burlage, *New York City's Municipal Hopsitals,* pp. 218, 221, 265–68, 325–26.

52. Ibid., p. 277.

53. Thomas W. Moloney and David E. Rogers, "Medical Technology—A Different View of the Contentious Debate over Costs," *New England Journal of Medicine* 301 (1979): 1417.

Chapter 15

1. John R. Steelman, *The Nation's Medical Research* (Washington, D.C.: U.S. G.P.O., 1947), pp. xi–xii, 33.

2. Alice Rivlin, *The Role of the Federal Government in Financing Higher Education* (Washington, D.C.: Brookings Institution, 1961), pp. 44–45; Vernon W. Lippard, *A Half-Century of American Medical Education: 1920–1970* (New York: Josiah Macy, Jr., Foundation, 1974), p. 75; John A. Cooper, "Undergraduate Medical Education," in *Advances in American Medicine,* ed. John Z. Bowers and Elizabeth F. Purcell (New York: Josiah Macy, Jr., Foundation, 1976), 1:277.

3. U.S. Surgeon General's Committee on Medical School Grants and Finances, *Medical School Grants and Finances Part I: Conclusions and Recommendations* (Washington, D.C.: U.S. G.P.O., 1951), p. 35; Paul J. Feldstein, *Health Associations and the Demand for Legislation* (Cambridge: Ballinger, 1977), pp. 220–21; John G. Freymann, *The American Health Care System* (New York: Medcom, 1974), p. 88; American Medical Association, *Money and Medical Schools* (Chicago: American Medical Association, 1963), p. 40.

4. Freymann, *The American Health Care System,* p. 88.

5. U.S. Bureau of the Census, *Statistical Abstract of the United States: 1982–83* (Washington, D.C.: U.S. G.P.O., 1982), p. 107.

6. J. R. Schofield, *New and Expanded Medical Schools, Mid-Century to the 1980s* (San Francisco: Jossey-Bass, 1984), p. 17; James A. Shannon, "Federal Support of Biomedical Sciences," *Journal of Medical Education* 51, Part 2 (July, 1976): 44–45; Frank D. Campion, *The AMA and U.S. Health Policy Since 1940* (Chicago: Chicago Review Press, 1984), pp. 179–80, 240–43; Feldstein, *Health Associations and the Demand for Legislation,* pp. 63–66.

7. U.S. Bureau of the Census, *Statistical Abstract of the United States: 1982–83,* p. 107.

8. U.S. Congress. House. Committee on Interstate and Foreign Commerce, *Training of Physicians, Dentists and Professional Public Health Personnel,* Hearings on H.R. 4999, H.R. 8774, and H.R. 8833. 87th Cong., 2d sess. (Washington, D.C.: U.S. G.P.O., 1962), pp. 112, 117, 133; U.S. Congress. House. Committee on Interstate and Foreign Commerce, *Health Professions Educational Assistance,* Hearings on H.R. 12, H.R. 180, H.R. 2527, H.R. 3182, and H.R. 3180. 88th Cong., 1st sess. (Washington, D.C.: U.S. G.P.O., 1963), pp. 40–44, 58, 269–70.

9. *Chronology Health Professions Legislation: 1956–79* (Washington, D.C.: U.S. G.P.O., 1980), pp. HP:5–6; Cooper, "Undergraduate Medical Education," p. 277.

10. *Chronology Health Professions Legislation: 1956–79,* pp. HP:8–15.

11. Cooper, "Undergraduate Medical Education," p. 277.

12. *Chronology Health Professions Legislation: 1956–79,* pp. HP:8, HP:13; *Medical Education: Institutions, Characteristics and Programs* (Washington, D.C.: Association of American Medical Colleges, 1979), p. 20.

13. Schofield, *New and Expanded Medical Schools, Mid-Century to the 1980s*, pp. 32, 45.

14. *Chronology Health Professions Legislation: 1956–79*, pp. HP:20–28; Mary A. Fruen, "An Overview of the Medical Education System," in *Medical Education Financing*, ed. Jack Hadley (New York: Prodist, 1980), p. 44.

15. *Chronology Health Professions Legislation: 1956–79*, pp. HP:42–61; *Health Professions Educational Assistance and Nurse Training Amendments of 1980*, Hearings on H.R. 7206, U.S. House Committee on Interstate and Foreign Commerce, 96th Cong., 2d sess. (Washington, D.C.: U.S. G.P.O., 1980), p. 54.

16. Ibid., p. 83; *Chronology Health Professions Legislation: 1956–79*, pp. HP: 26, HP:44.

17. Data provided by the Association of American Medical Colleges; Schofield, *New and Expanded Medicals Schools, Mid-Century to the 1980s*, pp. 32, 45.

18. *Health Professions Educational Assistance and Nurse Training Amendments of 1980*, p. 53.

19. Ibid., passim; *Health Professions Training and Distribution Act of 1980*, Hearings on S. 2375, U.S. Senate Committee on Labor and Human Resources, 96th Cong., 2d sess. (Washington, D.C.: U.S. G.P.O., 1980). Data provided by the Association of American Medical Colleges.

20. H. Paul Jolly et al., "US Medical School Finances," *JAMA* 250 (1983): 1527; Schofield, *New and Expanded Medical Schools, Mid-Century to the 1980s*, pp. 48–50.

21. Davis G. Johnson, *Physicians in the Making* (San Francisco: Jossey-Bass, 1983), p. 55.

22. Davis G. Johnson, *U.S. Medical Students 1950–2000* (Washington, D.C.: Association of American Medical Colleges, 1983), p. 46.

23. Agnes G. Rezler and Joseph A. Flaherty, *The Interpersonal Dimension in Medical Education* (New York: Springer, 1985), pp. 1–8; Robert L. Dickman et al., "Medical Students from Natural Science and Nonscience Undergraduate Backgrounds," *JAMA* 243 (1980): 2506–9.

24. *Physicians for the Twenty-First Century* (Washington, D.C.: Association of American Medical Colleges, 1984), pp. 4–8.

25. Johnson, *U.S. Medical Students 1950–2000*, pp. 74; U.S. Bureau of the Census, *Statistical Abstract of the United States: 1982–83*, p. 434; Johnson, *Physicians in the Making*, pp. 168, 172.

26. "Parental Income of 1981 First-Year Medical School Applicants and Accepted Students," *Journal of Medical Education* 58 (1983): 829–31; John I. Sandson, "A Crisis in Medical Education," *New England Journal of Medicine* 308 (1983): 1286–89.

27. Steven Shea and Mindy T. Fullilove, "Entry of Black and Other Minority Students into U.S. Medical Schools," *New England Journal of Medicine* 313 (1985): 934.

28. Ibid., pp. 935–38.

29. Johnson, *Physicians in the Making*, pp. 82, 85.

30. Howard S. Becker et al., *Boys in White* (1961; reprint ed., New Brunswick, N.J.: Transaction Books, 1977), pp. 423–24; Ludwig W. Eichna, "Medical-School Education, 1975–79," *New England Journal of Medicine* 303 (1980): 727–34.

31. Jane Leserman, *Men and Women in Medical School* (New York: Praeger, 1981), pp. 51–55, 94–96, 138, 142, 146–47.

32. Agnes Z. Rezler, "Attitude Change During Medical School: A Review of the Literature," *Journal of Medical Education* 49 (1974): 1023–30.

33. Patricia L. Kendall and Hanan C. Selvin, "Tendencies Toward Specialization in Medical Training" in *The Student-Physician*, ed. Robert K. Merton, George G. Reader and

Patricia L. Kendall (Cambridge: Harvard University Press, 1957), p. 156; Leserman, *Men and Women in Medical School,* pp. 102–3.

34. Ibid.; Harold S. Diehl, Margaret D. West, and Robert W. Barclay, "Staffing Patterns at Four-Year Medical Schools," in *Medical Education Today,* ed. Dean F. Smiley (Chicago: Association of American Medical Colleges, 1953), p. 39; Greer Williams, *Western Reserve's Experiment in Medical Education and its Outcome* (New York: Oxford University Press, 1980), pp. 380, 392.

35. A. P. Williams et al., "The Effect of Federal Biomedical Research Programs on Academic Medical Centers," in U.S. President's Biomedical Research Panel, *Report of the President's Biomedical Research Panel, Supplement 2: Impact of Federal Health-Related Research Expenditures upon Institutions of Higher Education* (Washington, D.C.: U.S. G.P.O., 1976), pp. 35–39; Jack Hadley, "Physician Supply and Distribution," in *National Health Insurance,* ed. Judith Feder, John Holahan, and Theodore Marmor (Washington, D.C.: Urban Institute, 1980), p. 196.

36. Joel J. Alpert and Evan Charney, *The Education of Physicians for Primary Care* (Washington, D.C.: Health Resources Administration, 1973), p. 7.

37. Cf. William G. Rothstein, "The Significance of Occupations in Work Careers," *Journal of Vocational Behavior* 17 (1980): 328–43.

Chapter 16

1. Harrison G. Gough and Wallace B. Hall, "Physicians' Retrospective Evaluations of their Medical Education," *Research in Higher Education* 7 (1977): 29–34.

2. Samuel W. Bloom, *Power and Dissent in the Medical School* (New York: Free Press, 1973), pp. 81, 188, 242, 270–71, 343–44.

3. Howard S. Becker et al., *Boys in White* (1961; reprint ed., New Brunswick, N.J.: Transaction Books, 1977), pp. 345–47.

4. Bryce Templeton, "The National Board of Medical Examiners and Independent Assessment Agencies," in *Evaluation in Medical Education Past, Present, Future,* ed. Thomas Stamph and Bryce Templeton (Cambridge, Mass.: Ballinger, 1979), pp. 126–32.

5. August G. Swanson, "Medical Education in the United States and Canada," *Journal of Medical Education* 59, Part 2 (Nov., 1984): 54; John B. Hickam, William P. Deiss, and Regina Frayser, "Intramural Use of Extramural Examinations," *JAMA* 192 (1965): 828–31.

6. Ludwig W. Eichna, "Medical-School Education, 1975–79," *New England Journal of Medicine* 303 (1980): 732; *Physicians for the Twenty-First Century* (Washington, D.C.: Association of American Medical Colleges, 1984), p. 29; "Future Directions for Medical Education," *JAMA* 248 (1982): 3230.

7. Vernon W. Lippard, *A Half-Century of American Medical Education: 1920–1970* (New York: Josiah Macy, Jr., Foundation, 1974), p. 47.

8. Ibid., pp. 47–48.

9. Robert R. Wagner, "The Basic Medical Sciences, the Revolution in Biology and the Future of Medical Education," *Yale Journal of Biology and Medicine* 35 (1962): 1–4.

10. Ronald L. Numbers, ed. *The Education of American Physicians* (Berkeley and Los Angeles: University of California Press, 1980); Wagner, "The Basic Medical Sciences, the Revolution in Biology and the Future of Medical Education," pp. 1–7; Max Pepper, "Association of Teachers of Preventive Medicine," in *Summaries of Reports to the Panel by U.S. and Canadian Medical Schools* (Washington, D.C.: Association of American Medical Colleges, 1983), p. 229.

11. Robert H. Coombs and Blake P. Boyle, "The Transition to Medical School," in

Psychosocial Aspects of Medical Training, ed. Robert H. Coombs and Clark E. Vincent (Springfield, Ill.: Thomas, 1971), pp. 96–100; Marcel A. Fredericks and Paul Mundy, *The Making of a Physician* (Chicago: Loyola University Press, 1976), pp. 31, 34.

12. "Report of the Working Group on Essential Knowledge," *Journal of Medical Education* 59, Part 2 (Nov., 1984): 114; R. M. Magraw et al., "Perspectives from the New Schools—The Costs and Financing of Medical Education," *New England Journal of Medicine* 289 (1973): 561.

13. Greer Williams, *Western Reserve's Experiment in Medical Education and Its Outcome* (New York: Oxford University Press, 1980), pp. 110.

14. Ibid., p. 56 and passim.

15. Steven Jonas, *Medical Mystery* (New York: Norton, 1978), pp. 255, 278–79; Williams, *Western Reserve's Experiment in Medical Education and Its Outcome,* pp. 470–73; Swanson, "Medical Education in the United States and Canada," pp. 37–38.

16. Philip Handler and Eugene A. Stead, "Historical Background," in *Undergraduate Medical Education and the Elective System: Experience with the Duke Curriculum, 1966–75,* ed. James F. Gifford Jr. (Durham, N.C.: Duke University Press, 1978), p. 4; Swanson, "Medical Education in the United States and Canada," p. 39.

17. Ibid., pp. 38, 50; *Physicians for the Twenty-First Century,* p. 11.

18. Swanson, "Medical Education in the United States and Canada," p. 51; Association of American Medical Colleges, *Study of Medical Education: Interrelationships between Component Variables* (Washington, D.C.: U.S. G.P.O., 1975), p. 53.

19. Maurice B. Visscher, "The Decline in Emphasis on Basic Medical Sciences in Medical School Curricula," *Physiologist* 16 (1973): 53.

20. J.R. Schofield, *New and Expanded Medical Schools, Mid-Century to the 1980s* (San Francisco: Jossey-Bass, 1984), p. 137.

21. Becker et al., *Boys in White,* pp. 231–35; Charles L. Bosk, *Forgive and Remember: Managing Medical Failure* (Chicago: University of Chicago Press, 1979), pp. 84–94; Franz Reichsman, Francis E. Browning, and J. Raymond Hinshaw, "Observations of Undergraduate Clinical Teaching in Action," *Journal of Medical Education* 39 (1964): 149, 152.

22. Quoted in Jonas, *Medical Mystery,* p. 284; "Report of the Working Group on Essential Knowledge," p. 115.

23. Irving J. Lewis and Cecil G. Sheps, *The Sick Citadel: The American Academic Medical Center and the Public Interest* (Cambridge, Mass.: Oelgeschlager, Gunn and Hain, 1983), pp. 138–40.

24. "Subgroup Report on Clinical Skills," *Journal of Medical Education* 59, Part 2 (Nov., 1984): 139.

25. Stanley Wiener and Morton Nathanson, "Physical Examination: Frequently Observed Errors," *JAMA* 236 (1976): 854; Agnes G. Rezler and Joseph A. Flaherty, *The Interpersonal Dimension in Medical Education* (New York: Springer, 1985), p. 135.

26. J. Gregory Carroll and Judy Monroe, "Teaching Medical Interviewing," *Journal of Medical Education* 54 (1979): 498; John F. Aloia and Ernesto Jonas, "Skills in History-Taking and Physical Examination," *Journal of Medical Education* 51 (1976): 410–15.

27. Reichsman, Browning, and Hinshaw, "Observations of Undergraduate Clinical Teaching in Action," p. 151; George L. Engel, "Are Medical Schools Neglecting Clinical Skills," *JAMA* 236 (1976): 861.

28. Paul F. Griner and Robert J. Glaser, "Misuse of Laboratory Tests and Diagnostic Procedures," *New England Journal of Medicine* 307 (1982): 1338; Patrick C. Ward et al., "Systematic Instruction in Interpretive Aspects of Laboratory Medicine," *Journal of Medical Education* 51 (1976): 648–49; Richard H. Dixon and John Laszlo, "Utilization of Clinical Chemistry Services by Medical House Staff," *Archives of Internal Medicine* 134

(1974): 1064–67; Paul F. Griner and Benjamin Liptzin, "Use of the Laboratory in a Teaching Hospital," *Annals of Internal Medicine* 75 (1971): 157–63.

29. Louis P. Myers and Steven A. Schroeder, "Physician Use of Services for the Hospitalized Patient," *Milbank Memorial Fund Quarterly* 59 (1981): 481–507; Albert R. Martin et al., "A Trial of Two Strategies to Modify the Test-Ordering Behavior of Medical Residents," *New England Journal of Medicine* 303 (1980): 1330–36.

30. Harry F. Dowling, *Medicines for Man* (New York: Knopf, 1970), pp. 272, 294.

31. Nina Matheson and Donald A. Lindberg, "Subgroup Report on Medical Information Science Skills," *Journal of Medical Education* 59, Part 2 (Nov., 1984): 155–59.

32. Reichsman, Browning, and Hinshaw, "Observations of Undergraduate Clinical Teaching in Action," p. 158; "Report of the Working Group on Fundamental Skills," *Journal of Medical Education* 59, Part 2 (Nov., 1984): 125–28.

33. Joseph A. Keyes, Perry D. Cohen, and George R. DeMuth, *Medical School— Clinical Affiliation Study* (Washington, D.C.: Association of American Medical Colleges, 1977), pp. 111–13.

34. Eichna, "Medical-School Education, 1975–79," p. 734.

35. Robert H. Coombs, *Mastering Medicine: Professional Socialization in Medical School* (New York: Free Press, 1978), pp. 157–60; Becker et al., *Boys in White*, pp. 327–31.

36. Eichna, "Medical-School Education, 1975–79," p. 728.

37. Reichsman, Browning and Hinshaw, "Observations of Undergraduate Clinical Teaching in Action," pp. 159–60.

38. Richard M. Magraw, *Ferment in Medicine* (Philadelphia: Saunders, 1966), p. 151; *Physicians for the Twenty-First Century*, p. 22.

39. Henry E. Payson and Jack D. Barchas, "A Time Study of Medical Teaching Rounds," *New England Journal of Medicine* 273 (1965): 1468–71.

40. Edward C. Atwater, "Internal Medicine," in *The Education of American Physicians*, pp. 171–72; Charles G. Child III, "Surgical Clerkship," *JAMA* 202 (1967): 128; Payson and Barchas, "A Time Study of Medical Teaching Rounds," pp. 1469–70; "Subgroup Report on Clinical Skills," p. 143.

41. Morton D. Bogdonoff, "A Brief Look at Medical Grand Rounds," *Pharos* 45 (1982): 16–18.

42. Alvan R. Feinstein and Jennifer R. Niebyl, "Changes in the Diagnostic Process During 40 Years of Clinico–Pathological Conferences," *Archives of Internal Medicine* 128 (1971): 774–80; Schofield, *New and Expanded Medical Schools, Mid-Century to the 1980s*, p. 294; Marcia Millman, *The Unkindest Cut: Life in the Backrooms of Medicine* (New York: Morrow, 1977), pp. 96–99.

43. Swanson, "Medical Education in the United States and Canada," pp. 39–40, 52.

44. Becker et al., *Boys in White*, pp. 351–54; Institute of Medicine, *Costs of Education in the Health Professions*, Parts I and II (Washington, D.C.: U.S. G.P.O., 1974), p. 63.

45. Jonas, *Medical Mystery*, pp. 293–94; Klaus Roghmann et al., "The Pediatric Internship as a Teaching Technique," *Pediatrics* 56 (1975): 241–42; Xenia Tonesk, "The House Officer as a Teacher: What Students Expect and Measure," *Journal of Medical Education* 54 (1979): 613–16.

46. John L. Caughey, "Clinical Experience and Clinical Responsibility," *Journal of Medical Education* 39 (1964): 430; *Physicians for the Twenty-First Century*, p. 17.

47. Dale N. Schumacher, "An Analysis of Student Clinical Activities," *Journal of Medical Education* 43 (1968): 383–87; Lawrence R. LaPalio, "Time Study of Students and House Staff on a University Medical Service," *Journal of Medical Education* 56 (1981): 61–64.

48. Cheryl McPherson and Larry A. Sachs, "Health Care Team Training in U.S. and Canadian Medical Schools," *Journal of Medical Education* 57 (1982): 282–87.

49. Williams, *Western Reserve's Experiment in Medical Education and Its Outcome*, pp. 85–86; Francis D. Moore, "Surgical Teaching in the Development of Clinical Competence," *JAMA* 202 (1967): 122–23.

50. "Report of the Working Group on Essential Knowledge," p. 120.

51. E. Richard Weinerman, "Innovation in Ambulatory Services," *Journal of Medical Education* 41 (1966): 712–21; John E. Deitrick, "Organization of Outpatient Departments," *Journal of Medical Education* 41 (1966): 710–11; David E. Rogers and Robert J. Blendon, "The Academic Medical Center," *New England Journal of Medicine* 298 (1978): 945–47.

52. Steven A. Schroeder, Stephen M. Werner, and Thomas E. Piemme, "Primary Care in the Academic Medical Centers," *Journal of Medical Education* 49 (1974): 824; Joseph J. Giacalone and James I. Hudson, "Primary Care Education Trends in U.S. Medical Schools and Teaching Hospitals," *Journal of Medical Education* 52 (1977): 972–73.

53. Ibid., p. 973; Keyes, Cohen, and DeMuth, *Medical School—Clinical Affiliation Study*, p. 121.

54. Giacalone and Hudson, "Primary Care Education Trends in U.S. Medical Schools and Teaching Hospitals," pp. 973–74; James I. Hudson and Madeline M. Nevins, eds., *Health Maintenance Organizations and Academic Medical Centers* (Menlo Park, Calif.: 1981).

55. Arthur A. Berarducci, Thomas L. Delbanco, and Mitchell T. Rabkin, "The Teaching Hospital and Primary Care," *New England Journal of Medicine* 292 (1975): 615–20; Suzanne W. Fletcher et al., "A Teaching Hospital Medical Clinic," *Journal of Medical Education* 54 (1979): 384–91; Peter Rudd et al., "A General Medical Clinic,"*Journal of Medical Education* 54 (1979): 766–74.

56. "Supplementary Tables," *Journal of Medical Education* 34, Part 2 (1959): 215.

57. Richard H. Saunders, Jr., "The University Hospital Internship in 1960," *Journal of Medical Education* 36 (1961): 635–36; Robert H. Brook and Robert L. Stevenson, Jr., "Effectiveness of Patient Care in an Emergency Room," *New England Journal of Medicine* 283 (1970): 904–7; Robert H. Brook, Morris H. Berg, and Phillip A. Schechter, "Effectiveness of Nonemergency Care Via an Emergency Room," *Annals of Internal Medicine* 78 (1973): 333–39.

58. Leighton E. Cluff, "Responsibility, Accountability, Self-Discipline," *Pharos* 44 (Winter, 1981): 2.

59. Charles E. Lewis, Rashi Fein, and David Mechanic, *A Right to Health* (New York: Wiley, 1976), pp. 61–63.

60. Michael J. Gordon, Ralph R. Hadac, and C. Kent Smith, "Evaluation of Clinical Training in the Community," *Journal of Medical Education* 52 (1977): 888–89.

61. Jesse D. Rising, "The Rural Preceptorship," *Journal of the Kansas Medical Society* 63 (1962): 81, 84.

62. Ibid., pp. 83–84; Frank A. Hale et al., "The Impact of a Required Preceptorship on Senior Medical Students," *Journal of Medical Education* 54 (1979): 396–401.

63. A list of studies of comprehensive care programs can be found in George G. Reader and Rosemary Soave, "Comprehensive Care Revisited," *Milbank Memorial Fund Quarterly* 54 (1976): 412–14. See also Williams, *Western Reserve's Experiment in Medical Education and Its Outcome*.

64. Joel J. Alpert and Evan Charney, *The Education of Physicians for Primary Care* (Washington, D.C.: U.S. G.P.O., 1973), pp. 27–30; Peter V. Lee, *Medical Schools and the Changing Times* (Evanston, Ill.: Association of American Medical Colleges, 1962),

pp. 30–31, 37, 74–75; Parnie S. Snoke and E. Richard Weinerman, "Comprehensive Care Programs in University Medical Centers," *Journal of Medical Education* 40 (1965): 627–31.

65. Ibid., p. 646.

66. Patricia Kendall, "Student Evaluation of the Cornell Comprehensive Care and Teaching Program," in *Comprehensive Medical Care and Teaching* ed. George G. Reader and Mary E. Goss (Ithaca, N.Y.: Cornell University Press, 1967), pp. 59, 312–34; Kenneth R. Hammond and Fred Kern, Jr., *Teaching Comprehensive Medical Care* (Cambridge: Harvard University Press, 1959), pp. 324–25.

67. Ibid., pp. 132–33; Patricia Kendall and James A. Jones, "General Patient Care: Learning Aspects," in *Comprehensive Medical Care and Teaching,* pp. 73–120.

68. Reader and Soave, "Comprehensive Care Revisited," pp. 401–3; Kerr L. White, "General Practice in the United States," *Journal of Medical Education* 39 (1964): 341; Samuel W. Bloom, "The Process of Becoming a Physician and the Context of Medical Education," in *Medical Education and Primary Health Care,* ed. Horst Noack (Baltimore: University Park Press, 1980), p. 152.

69. Magraw et al., "Perspectives from the New Schools—the Costs and Financing of Medical Education," pp. 558–62; Lewis and Sheps, *The Sick Citadel: The American Academic Medical Center and the Public Interest,* pp. 149–50.

70. Lawrence D. Aronson and Raymond H. Murray, "Internal Medicine Clerkship Experience in Community Hospitals," in *Medical Education Since 1960,* ed. Andrew D. Hunt and Lewis E. Weeks (n.p.: Michigan State University Foundation, 1977), pp. 236–38.

71. Hunt and Weeks, *Medical Education Since 1960,* pp. 370–73, 386–88; Lewis and Sheps, *The Sick Citadel: The American Academic Medical Center and the Public Interest,* pp. 151–53.

72. Ibid., p. 153.

73. *Graduate Medical Education: Proposals for the Eighties* (Washington, D.C.: Association of American Medical Colleges, 1980), pp. 38–39.

74. Data provided by Association of American Medical Colleges; *1984–85 AAMC Curriculum Directory* (Washington, D.C.: Association of American Medical Colleges, 1984), p. 309; Swanson, "Medical Education in the United States and Canada," pp. 51, 53.

75. Eichna, "Medical-School Education, 1975–79," p. 731; *Physicians for the Twenty-First Century,* pp. 18–19; "Future Directions for Medical Education," p. 3231.

76. Ibid.; "Report of the Louis Harris and Associates Survey on the Status of Medical Education," *Journal of Medical Education* 59, Part 2 (Nov., 1984): 194, 196.

77. Reader and Soave, "Comprehensive Care Revisited," p. 397; "Future Directions for Medical Education," p. 3231; *Physicians for the Twenty-First Century,* pp. 18–19.

78. *Physicians for the Twenty-First Century,* p. 15.

79. Ibid., p. 20; "Future Directions for Medical Education," p. 3225.

80. *Physicians for the Twenty-First Century,* p. xi; "Future Directions for Medical Education," p. 3225.

Chapter 17

1. George E. Miller, "Medical Education and the Rise of Hospitals," *JAMA* 186 (1963): 1077; Helen H. Gee and Charles F. Schumacher, "Internship: Fact and Opinion," *Journal of Medical Education* 36, Part 2 (1961) 34, 52; Patricia L. Kendall, "The Learning Environment of Hospitals," in *The Hospital in Modern Society,* ed. Eliot Freidson, (Glencoe, Ill.: Free Press, 1963), pp. 198, 202–3; "Report of the Advisory Committee on Internships . . . , " *JAMA* 151 (1953): 501–5.

2. Stephen J. Miller, *Prescription for Leadership: Training for the Medical Elite* (Chicago: Aldine, 1970), pp. 106–7, 113–14.

3. Richard H. Saunders, Jr., "The University Hospital Internship in 1960," *Journal of Medical Education* 36 (1961): 576, 595, 597–98.

4. Miller, *Prescription for Leadership: Training for the Medical Elite,* p. 91; William Gillanders and Michael Heiman, "Time Study Comparisons of 3 Intern Programs," *Journal of Medical Education* 46 (1971): 142–49; Henry E. Payson, Eugene C. Gaenslen, Jr., and Fred L. Stargardter, "Time Study of an Internship on a University Medical Service," *New England Journal of Medicine* 264 (1961): 439–43.

5. Miller, *Prescription for Leadership: Training for the Medical Elite,* pp. 99–106; Melvin D. Levine, Leon S. Robertson, and Joel J. Alpert, "A Descriptive Study of a Pediatric Internship," *Pediatrics* 44 (1969): 986–90.

6. Emily Mumford, *Interns: From Students to Physicians* (Cambridge: Harvard University Press, 1970), pp. 98–109; 184–85, 203–7.

7. Ibid., pp. 184, 204–5.

8. "Report of the Advisory Committee on Internships . . . , " pp. 502–3.

9. Charles G. Child, III, "Assets and Liabilities of the University Hospital Internship," *JAMA* 189 (1964): 294–95.

10. "Report of the Advisory Committee on Internships . . . , " p. 503; Saunders, "The University Hospital Internship in 1960," p. 571; Child, "Assets and Liabilities of the University Hospital Internship," p. 296.

11. Howard W. Houser, *Objectives in American Medical Education: A National Survey of Medical Faculty Opinion* (Iowa City: University of Iowa, 1971), pp. 102, 112 13, 124.

12. Herbert J. Lerner, *Manpower Issues and Voluntary Regulation in the Medical Specialty System* (New York: Prodist, 1974), pp. 9–10.

13. Richard D. Lyons, "A.M.A.'s Head Asks for More Doctors," *New York Times,* 25 June 1970, p. 36.

14. George L. Engel, "Must We Precipitate a Crisis in Medical Education to Solve the Crisis in Health Care?" *Annals of Internal Medicine* 76 (1972): 488–89.

15. Lerner, *Manpower Issues and Voluntary Regulation in the Medical Specialty System,* pp. 136–37; John S. Graettinger, "A Tracking Study of U.S. Medical School Graduates from the First to the Second Postdoctoral Year," *Journal of Medical Education* 55 (1980): 647–55.

16. Joseph S. Gonnella and J. Jon Veloski, "The Impact of Early Specialization on the Clinical Competence of Residents," *New England Journal of Medicine* 306 (1982): 275–77.

17. Warren H. Pearse, "The American College of Obstetricians and Gynecologists," in *The Current Status and Future of Academic Obstetrics,* ed. John Z. Bowers and Elizabeth F. Purcell (New York: Josiah Macy, Jr., Foundation, 1980), pp. 102–3; John Romano, "The Elimination of the Internship—An Act of Regression," *American Journal of Psychiatry* 126 (1970): 1565.

18. Graettinger, "A Tracking Study of U.S. Medical School Graduates From the First to the Second Postdoctoral Year," p. 649; "Report of the Task Force on the Clinical Base Year Experience," *American Board of Medical Specialties Proceedings* (March 16 and 17, 1978), p. 17; Anne E. Crowley, "Summary Statistics on Graduate Medical Education in the United States," *JAMA* 252 (1984): 1553.

19. Lerner, *Manpower Issues and Voluntary Regulation in the Medical Specialty System,* pp. 136–37.

20. "Future Directions for Medical Education," *JAMA* 248 (1982): 3232.

21. *Graduate Medical Education Present and Prospective* (New York: Josiah Macy, Jr., Foundation, 1980), pp. 29–30; Rosemary Stevens, *American Medicine and the Public*

Interest (New Haven: Yale University Press, 1971), p. 393; *Prescription for Change* (New York: Commonwealth Fund, 1985), p. I:6; *Graduate Medical Education: Proposals for the Eighties* (Washington, D.C.: Association of American Medical Colleges, 1980), p. 20.

22. Irving J. Lewis and Cecil G. Sheps, *The Sick Citadel: The American Academic Medical Center and the Public Interest* (Cambridge, Mass.: Oelgeschlager, Gunn and Hain, 1983), p. 112; *Graduate Medical Education Present and Prospective*, p. 7.

23. *Prescription for Change*, pp. I:12–14; U.S. Comptroller General, *Are Enough Physicians of the Right Types Trained in the United States?* (Washington, D.C.: U.S. G.P.O., 1978), pp. 40–42.

24. *Graduate Medical Education Present and Prospective*, pp. 116–18; Institute of Medicine, *Medicare-Medicaid Reimbursement Policies* (Washington, D.C.: 1976), p. 162; Lewis and Sheps, *The Sick Citadel: The American Academic Medical Center and the Public Interest*, p. 185.

25. Rue Bucher and Joan G. Stelling, *Becoming Professional* (Beverly Hills, Calif.: Sage, 1977), pp. 126–27; Nelda P. Wray and Joan A. Friedland, "Detection and Correction of House Staff Errors in Physical Diagnosis," *JAMA* 249 (1983): 1035–37.

26. *Graduate Medical Education: Proposals for the Eighties*, pp. 30–32; Bucher and Stelling, *Becoming Professional*, pp. 86–87; *Prescription for Change*, p. I:22; Alvin R. Tarlov et al., "National Study of Internal Medicine Manpower: I. Residency Training 1976–1977," *Annals of Internal Medicine* 88 (1978): 414, 419; Seth M. Kantor and Paul F. Griner, "Educational Needs in General Internal Medicine as Perceived by Prior Residents," *Journal of Medical Education* 56 (1981): 749–52.

27. *Prescription for Change*, pp. I:21–22.

28. Jack Hadley, ed., *Medical Education Financing* (New York: Prodist, 1980), p. 27; Graduate Medical Education National Advisory Committee, Volume 5: *Educational Environment Technical Panel* (Washington, D.C.: U.S. G.P.O., 1981), p. 36.

29. Robert G. Petersdorf, "The Doctors' Dilemma," *New England Journal of Medicine* 299 (1978): 629–30; *Prescription for Change*, p. I:29.

30. *Graduate Medical Education: Proposals for the Eighties*, pp. 80, 82, 105–6.

31. Ibid., pp. 60–61, 69; U.S. Comptroller General, *Are Enough Physicians of the Right Types Trained in the United States?*, p. 56.

32. *Graduate Medical Education: Proposals for the Eighties*, pp. 69–70, 177–83.

33. Ibid., pp. 66–67, 77–81.

34. Lerner, *Manpower Issues and Voluntary Regulation in the Medical Specialty System*, pp. 160–61; William D. Holden, "Developments in Graduate Medical Education," in *Recent Trends in Medical Education* (New York: Josiah Macy, Jr., Foundation, 1976), p. 263.

35. *Graduate Medical Education: Proposals for the Eighties*, pp. 22–24, 28.

36. Frank D. Campion, *The AMA and U.S. Health Policy Since 1940* (Chicago: Chicago Review Press, 1984), pp. 443–47.

37. Frederic D. Burg and F. Howell Wright, "Evaluation of Pediatric Residents and Their Training Programs," *Journal of Pediatrics* 80 (1972): 183–89; Robert L. Taylor and E. Fuller Torrey, "The Pseudo-Regulation of American Psychiatry," and Shervert H. Frazier, "A Commentary on the 'Pseudo-Regulation of American Psychiatry,'" *American Journal of Psychiatry* 129 (1972): 658–68.

38. William D. Holden, "The American Medical Specialty Boards," in *Evaluation in Medical Education Past, Present, Future*, ed. Thomas Samph and Bruce Templeton (Cambridge, Mass.: Ballinger, 1979), pp. 176–77.

39. Petersdorf, "The Doctors' Dilemma," p. 631.

40. Lerner, *Manpower Issues and Voluntary Regulation in the Medical Specialty System*, p. 177n; Petersdorf, "The Doctors' Dilemma," p. 632. See also Richard J. Reitmeir and

John A. Benson, Jr., "As the Board Sees It," *New England Journal of Medicine* 299 (1978): 1308–9.

41. Robert G. Petersdorf, "Is the Establishment Defensible?" *New England Journal of Medicine* 309 (1983): 1055.

42. *Graduate Medical Education: Proposals for the Eighties,* pp. 122–25; Robert G. Petersdorf, "Health Manpower: Numbers, Distribution, Quality," *Annals of Internal Medicine* 82 (1975): 698.

Chapter 18

1. John P. Geyman, *Family Practice,* 2d ed. (Norwalk, Conn.: Appleton-Century-Crofts, 1985), pp. 67–72.

2. Roger A. Rosenblatt et al., "The Content of Ambulatory Medical Care in the United States," *New England Journal of Medicine* 309 (1983): 892–94.

3. Ibid., pp. 892–95.

4. Paul B. Beeson, "The Natural History of Medical Subspecialties," *Annals of Internal Medicine* 93 (1980): 624–26; Rosenblatt et al., "The Content of Ambulatory Medical Care in the United States," p. 893.

5. John S. Millis et al., *The Graduate Education of Physicians* (Chicago: American Medical Association, 1966), pp. 42–43; Morton D. Bogdonoff, "A Change in the Training Model for the Practicing Internist," *Archives of Internal Medicine* 126 (1970): 697.

6. August G. Swanson, "Medical Education in the United States and Canada," *Journal of Medical Education* 59, Part 2 (Nov., 1984): 51.

7. Daniel M. Barr, "Primary and Specialized Care," *Journal of Medical Education* 53 (1978): 176–85.

8. Charles E. Lewis, Rashi Fein, and David Mechanic, *A Right to Health* (New York: Wiley, 1976), pp. 80–82; *State Legislation and Funding for Family Practice Programs* (Kansas City, Mo.: American Academy of Family Physicians, 1980), pp. 5–6.

9. *Chronology Health Professions Legislation 1956–79* (Washington, D.C.: U.S. Public Health Service, 1980), pp. HP–28, 42–56.

10. Ibid., p. HP–44; *Graduate Medical Education: Proposals for the Eighties* (Washington, D.C.: Association of American Medical Colleges, 1980), p. 113.

11. Alvin R. Tarlov, "Academic General Internal Medicine," *Annals of Internal Medicine* 96 (1982): 239–40; American Board of Medical Specialties, *Annual Report and Reference Handbook—1984* (Evanston, Ill., 1984), pp. 55–56.

12. Robert H. Friedman et al., "General Internal Medicine Units in Academic Medical Centers," *Annals of Internal Medicine* 96 (1982): 233–38; Tarlov, "Academic General Internal Medicine," pp. 239–40; John M. Eisenberg, "Curricula and Organization of Primary Care Residencies in Internal Medicine" *Journal of Medical Education* 55 (1980): 345–53.

13. Jennifer Daley and John T. Harrington, "The Characteristics of Training in Ambulatory Medicine in U.S. Residencies," *Journal of Medical Education* 60 (1985): 355–66.

14. John S. Graettinger, "A Tracking Study of U.S. Medical School Graduates From the First to the Second Postdoctoral Year," *Journal of Medical Education* 55 (1980): 649–50.

15. *State Legislation and Funding for Family Practice Programs,* pp. 1–4; *Chronology Health Professions Legislation 1956–1979,* p. HP–52.

16. Joseph J. Giacalone and James I. Hudson, "Primary Care Education Trends in U.S. Medical Schools and Teaching Hospitals," *Journal of Medical Education* 52 (1977): 977; Geyman, *Family Practice,* p. 262; Association of American Medical Colleges, *Institutional*

Characteristics of U.S. Medical Schools 1975–1976 (Washington, D.C.: U.S. G.P.O., 1978), p. 105.

17. Pamela J. Griffith and Coralie Farlee, *Description of Salaried Medical School Faculty, 1971–72 and 1976–77: Final Report* (Washington, D.C.: U.S. G.P.O., 1977), pp. 24, 49.

18. Swanson, "Medical Education in the United States and Canada," pp. 52–53; Giacalone and Hudson, "Primary Care Education Trends in U.S. Medical Schools and Teaching Hospitals," pp. 976–77.

19. Colin Baker, "The Discipline of Family Medicine," *Marriage and Family Review* 4 (1981): 159; John P. Geyman, "Family Practice in Evolution," *New England Journal of Medicine* 298 (1978): 597; William G. Anlyan, "How Do We Meet the Needs?" in *The Current Status and Future of Academic Obstetrics,* ed. John Z. Bowers and Elizabeth F. Purcell (New York: Josiah Macy, Jr., Foundation, 1980), pp. 168–70.

20. *Family Practice: Creation of a Specialty* (Kansas City, Mo.: American Academy of Family Physicians, 1980), pp. 28–30; Lynn Paringer and Richard M. Scheffler, "Major Trends in Graduate Medical Education," in *Graduate Medical Education Present and Prospective* (New York, N.Y.: Josiah Macy, Jr., Foundation, 1980), pp. 40–42; Anne E. Crowley, "Graduate Medical Education in the United States, 1984–1985," *JAMA* 254 (1985): 1587–89; Robert A. Derzon, "The Marriage of Medical Schools and Teaching Hospitals," *Journal of Medical Education* 53 (1978): 22; *Chronology Health Professions Legislation, 1956–1979,* p. HP–44.

21. Geyman, *Family Practice,* pp. 100–4, 135.

22. Gerald T. Perkoff, "General Internal Medicine, Family Practice or Something Better?" *New England Journal of Medicine* 299 (1978): 656.

Chapter 19

1. John G. Freymann, *The American Health Care System* (New York: Medcom, 1974), pp. 197–99.

Index